HISTORY OF
CUMBERLAND COUNTY

JOSEPH WILLIAM WELLS

HISTORY OF CUMBERLAND COUNTY

By J. W. WELLS

Educator

Judge of Cumberland County

1934-1937

Southern Historical Press, Inc.
Greenville, South Carolina

This volume was reproduced from
An 1947 edition located in the
Publisher's private Library

All rights reserved. No part of this publication may be reproduced,
stored in a retrieval system, transmitted in any form, posted
on to the web in any form or by any means without
the prior written permission of the publisher.

Please direct all correspondence and orders to:

www.southernhistoricalpress.com
or
SOUTHERN HISTORICAL PRESS, Inc.
PO Box 1267
375 West Broad Street
Greenville, SC   29601
southernhistoricalpress@gmail.com

Originally published: Louisville, KY. 1947
Copyright 1947 by J. W. Wells
ISBN #0-89308-890-0
All rights Reserved.
Printed in the United States of America

*Dedicated
to the
Children of
Cumberland County*

CUMBERLAND COUNTY, MY NATIVE HOME

O Cumberland, most sacred spot,
To hear thy name brings thrills untold,
And I would mean and meager be
If from thee good things I should hold.

'Tis thou that feedest me each day,
Much gratitude to thee I owe;
'Tis not in my weak power to give
A mite of what thou dost bestow.

Upon thy breast at eventide
I prostrate for a sweet repose,
A dream of peace and joy within
My mind with fullest measure flows.

Adorned with flow'rs, in spring thou art,
Delicious fruits thy summers yield,
With golden grain thy autumn's crowned;
Then winter snows around thee steal.

Among thy towering vine-clad hills,
Year in, year out, the song birds sing;
Thy crystal water doth appease
My thirst none else on earth can bring.

I know God's favors smile on thee—
Kentucky's child of fairest face—
For in thy sunny clime there dwell
The choicest ones of Adam's race.

Thanks to my Maker's holy will
'T has been my lot in years gone by
To be thy child, Fair Cumberland,
And 'tis my wish until I die.

And may my love for thee not wane
But stronger grow each day I live,
For distant lands are naught to me
For thou, my home on earth didst give.

And when my life with thee is done
And dawns the hour of friendship's gloom,
Wilt thou in thy unselfish arms
Embrace me in thy silent tomb?

And build above my lifeless form
A grassy mound with roses free
That look to God, and hear Him say:
"My Cumberland, I'm proud of thee."

PREFACE

Cumberland County is one of the oldest and best counties of Kentucky. Two reasons account for its early exploration:

First, when the people of the eastern states turned their attention westward, seeking new experiences and new wilds, they came upon a passway through the Appalachian Mountains that led them into a hunter's paradise, with countless numbers of buffaloes, deer, elk, turkeys, and fur-bearing animals, together with clusters of wild fruits and natural curiosities, surrounded with scenic beauty untold.

Second, traveling was done mainly by water, and Cumberland River was the first stream of size that met the eyes of the early adventurers, and its banks and fertile valleys being clothed with impenetrable canebrakes rising from that deep alluvial soil, created intense excitement that echoed even beyond the seas. Ambitious pioneers resolved to gratify their desires by visiting and laying claims to this Cumberland "land of promise" that embraces the territory of which Cumberland County is now a part.

The writing of this history should have taken place many years ago, before the historic fire of 1933 sent up in flames the records of much of the ancient history of this good old county, when collecting of its data would have been an easier task, but I wish to extend my thanks to the ones who have assisted me in this work. First of all do I thank my tireless collaborator, Mrs. Nora Dixon McGee, for her contributions of early Cumberland history. Then I want to thank The Filson Club, the Extension Library, Mrs. Emma Guy Cromwell and Mrs. Cantrill, librarians, Superintendent E. E. Garrison, Senator Farmer, J. H. Morgan, J. E. Morgan, State Superintendent J. W. Brooker, and the many individuals who helped chronologize the family trees herein.

The collection of poems found in the back of this volume, some of which date from the teen-years of the author, were placed there by the request of many of the writer's students to commemorate the happy days of their childhood when they recited them to the listening public. For I wrote them primarily for children, all of whom have a deep abiding place in my heart.

Very sincerely,

J. W. WELLS.

CONTENTS

		Page
1.	EARLY EXPLORERS IN KENTUCKY	1
2.	EARLY HISTORY OF CUMBERLAND COUNTY	11
3.	EARLY LAWS OF KENTUCKY	14
4.	RELIGION	59
5.	EDUCATION	82
6.	COUNTY OFFICERS	110
7.	PROFESSIONAL MEN, BANKS, AND BANKERS	121
8.	NEWSPAPERS AND PRINTING	126
9.	TRANSPORTATION	129
10.	WEATHER	146
11.	CREEKS	149
12.	WILD LIFE	158
13.	AGRICULTURE	162
14.	TOWNS	178
15.	POSTOFFICES AND POSTAGE RATES	181
16.	SILENT CITIES	189
17.	WEAPONS OF WAR	196
18.	OUR FLAG	204
19.	CUMBERLAND COUNTY AT WAR	205
20.	WORLD WAR I	226
21.	WORLD WAR II	236
22.	OUTSTANDING CHARACTERS	280
23.	THE 120 COUNTIES OF KENTUCKY	287
24.	MISCELLANY	303
	Rubber	303
	Electricity	305
	Automobiles	306
	Fences	307
	Superstitions	308
	Our Months	310

Contents

MISCELLANY—Continued

	Page
Origin of Days of Note	311
What Is Home?	313
Governors of Kentucky	314
48 States and Number of Counties	315
Counties of England	317
Potpourri	318

25. ORIGIN OF NAMES 321
26. PIONEER GENEALOGIES 342

HISTORY OF CUMBERLAND COUNTY

Three types of people constituted the tide of immigrants that broke the solitude of Kentucky's dawning days.

First, the hunters, whose mission was to view the water courses, mountains, valleys, apply names to them, and make reports on wild game.

Second, the hardy homeseekers, most of whom were of small means whose intentions were to cultivate the new rich lands, clear the timber, and lay foundations of homes, towns, and churches.

Third, then came the surveyors to mark the boundaries of individual possessions and urban corporations.

The second class of immigrant here referred to poured into Kentucky from Virginia in search of the rich lands for homes. Some of them purchased farms from those companies and some of them would select a site for settlement, blaze the trees around it, erect a cabin, clear a garden, and dream of fortunes for their children in years to come.

The loose laws of the State of Virginia allowed this kind of work to go on for years, overlooking the necessity of having the farms first surveyed and recorded before settlement as the National Government advised, but too late did Virginia wake up to find herself entangled in a myriad of controversies in land titles which was in most cases a total loss to the innocent occupants. Daniel Boone was a fair specimen of these, as you will note later.

No limit was fixed as to the number of warrants that might be sold to any one man in the early days of this state, so a wide speculation in lands of the absentee owners resulted.

The first and greatest leader of the first class referred to here was Thomas Walker, who brought with him five companions. They left Virginia, March 6, 1750, to explore the "western waters." They traveled in a westerly direction toward Kentucky until they came in front of a great mass of earth towering some 3,000 feet into the air. Walker named it Cumberland Mountains (some say he called it Steep Ridge at the time), and a little farther south he spied a pass through the mountains which he named Cumberland Gap. Marks on the trees and crosses found here in the Gap gave evidence that white men had been there previous to this time. Pushing on west, he came upon the banks of a beautiful stream of water, on Tuesday, March 17, 1750. He gave the name Cumberland River to that stream, which name it has borne ever since, and its identity has never been disputed. All were named in honor of the Duke of Cumberland, Prime Minister of England at that time. The Indians called the mountains "Wasioto" and the river, "Shawnee."

Walker thus left the State of Virginia with "Cumberland" on his lips applying it to many of Kentucky's ancient landmarks. He made his exit through the Gap on his way back home, June 20, 1750, and ten years later made a second trip over much of Kentucky.

Early Explorers

The year of 1754 finds the French and English in war for the domination of the New World. This war was known as the "French and Indian War," which closed in 1763 and resulted in an English victory, leaving France without any territory on continental America. During this period of war little was done toward exploring Kentucky.

In 1763, the same year in which England drove France from the continent, King George III issued his proclamation which provided that all British possessions south of Canada and west of the Allegheny Mountains should be kept for the Indians and should be exempt from white settlement.

Whether this was for the love he had for the Indians or because of the growing power of the colonies we are unable to determine, but we shall see the fortune that blessed Kentucky as a result of the King's survey of this territory.

Sir William Johnson was selected by the King to survey the Northern District, but through mistake from some cause or other he made the Ohio River the southern boundary to the mouth of the Tennessee River, and followed the Tennessee River to its source as the eastern boundary of the Indian Reservation. You see, through this error all of Kentucky east of the Tennessee River, which was all of the present state except the eight counties included in the Jackson Purchase, was thrown open to settlers.

As a result of the error made by Johnson, Kentucky became the pioneer state of the West.

To keep on friendly terms with the Indians, who laid claim to this part of Kentucky which Johnson threw open to settlement, referred to above, a treaty was signed at Fort Stanwix, 1768, between the Iroquois Indians and the agents of the British Crown, by which the Iroquois yielded their claim to all lands south of the Ohio River, for which they received "satisfactory pay."

In 1770 another agreement was reached between Virginians and the other Indian tribes who had claims to this territory, for which they were recompensed. In 1775 Richard Henderson purchased Kentucky land from Cherokees for 10,000 pounds. Later this was made void.

Thus, you can see that the early hunters, explorers, and settlers were not encroaching on the lands of another, but you will see from the atrocious deeds of the Indians when the explorers first went upon this land, that they regarded the treaty as a mere "scrap of paper."

The tribes that occupied or laid claim to southern and central Kentucky as their hunting paradise were the Cherokees, Chickasaws, and Catawbas. The tribes that claimed northern Kentucky were the Shawnees, Wyandots, and Delawares.

Following these treaties with the Indians, we shall here make mention of a few of the most important hunters, explorers, surveyors, and settlers of the state, as our aim is not to write a history of Kentucky but only one of her counties, yet, the connection must be shown at this time.

The year 1769 finds Daniel Boone, with his trusty rifle and five companions, in Kentucky for the first time, viewing the gigantic forests, discovering new streams of water, treading fertile valleys, seeing untold numbers of buffaloes, deer, elk, bears, turkeys, and various small game.

Boone was captured by the Indians that year, but after seven days made his escape to find his camp deserted, leaving him alone in the wilderness. Returning to Virginia, he did not try it alone again, but brought his family together with five other families. They trudged along until they came to Cumberland Gap where they were attacked by a band of Indians. Six of the party were killed, one of them being Boone's son. A party of 40 people had joined them just before they reached the Gap. After the fight was over, the whole of them turned their pack horses, hogs, and cattle and went back home. Returning to Kentucky Boone built a fort at Boonesborough, 1774, which was attacked by the Indians more than once with loss of life.

Boone continued his fearless work of exploring eastern, central, and southern Kentucky, meeting with many hardships, until the year of 1790, when he lost all his real estate in the state through defective titles. Then he moved back to Virginia.

In the year 1797 an exploring party in Kentucky saw Daniel and his family on their way to Missouri, seeking newer, deeper wilds.

He remained in Missouri until his death in 1820, and he and his wife were buried there. Upon the establishment of a new rural cemetery at Frankfort, Kentucky, in 1845, the people of the state planned to consecrate it by removing the remains of Boone and his wife to it. This was done on August 20, 1845. His daughters, Jemima, Susannah, Lavina, and Rebecca were buried in Kentucky. His sons who did not get killed in this state were buried in Missouri. Daniel Boone lived to be 86.

The next band of explorers which we shall consider will be the Long Hunters of 1770. There were 40 of them gathered from the Holston, Clinch, and New River settlements, headed by Col. James Knox. They came and wended their way to the banks of Cumberland River in what is now Wayne County, Kentucky. Here they established a central camp, where they would store their meat, furs, and other products. The crew separated into four different groups which went in different directions with the understanding that they should meet back at the central camp in Wayne County every five weeks to deposit their labor's reward. Colonel Knox with nine of the best hunters of this crew made his way through Clinton, Barren, Cumberland, Monroe, Green, and Hart counties. About two years were spent by Knox and his men in and around the counties referred to. One authority says they hunted and explored all the region on the border of Tennessee and Kentucky on Cumberland River. Their absence of two years from Virginia gave rise to the title, Long Hunters.

Governor Dunmore of Virginia sent out two men to locate and survey lands for the soldiers who had fought in the Indian wars and also the French and Indian War which closed in 1763. Thomas

Bullitt and James Harrod led the parties. Bullitt went along the Ohio River, and Harrod, swinging farther south, founded Harrodsburg, 1774, the oldest town in Kentucky. Military lands were surveyed and marked off for the soldiers. Hence, Military Lines.

Scarcely had Harrod built his fort when the news came to him through Boone and Michael Stoner—who had come 800 miles to warn them—of a great Indian attack which was expected to be perpetrated by all the Indian tribes under their leader, Cornstalk. This was known as Dunmore's War in West Virginia, out from the border of Kentucky. The battle was called Point Pleasant, in which 17 officers and 75 soldiers were killed. The Indians finally gave up and withdrew, and once more promised to give Kentucky to the whites.

John Finley, Simon Kenton, Richard Henderson, Levi Todd, William Preston, Hancock Taylor, McAfees, and George Rogers Clark were a few of the outstanding pioneers of Kentucky, but whether or not any of them ever trod Cumberland County is not known; except Clark, which we shall show later.

Many bloody battles and skirmishes with the Indians stain the pages of early Kentucky history. It is only through blood that victory is won.

During the Revolutionary War, 1775-1783, little aid was given the state by Virginia. At the close of the war the population had increased to nearly 30,000 souls. First census of the state in 1790 gave 73,677. You see that the population of Kentucky was greatly increased following the Revolution. One reason was the cry for land for soldiers; another, the Scotch-Irish were pouring into the country from Ireland in search of land, having left Ireland on account of religious persecution.

On December 31, 1776, Kentucky was organized by the Virginia Legislature as Kentucky County of Virginia. It remained so until 1780, when it was divided into three counties, Jefferson, Fayette, and Lincoln. To these three, six others were added prior to its admission as a state, June 1, 1792, making nine when Kentucky became a state. (See Counties of Kentucky.)

Green County was organized in 1792 from sections of Lincoln and Nelson. At that time Green embraced Cumberland, Adair, Taylor, and parts of Barren, Metcalfe, and Pulaski counties.

EXPLORERS IN CUMBERLAND COUNTY

Cumberland County, of which we shall now speak, was organized in 1798 as the thirty-second county of the State of Kentucky. At the time of its organization it was a very large county, including parts of Metcalfe, Monroe, Russell, Wayne, and Clinton counties. It received its name from Cumberland River which flows through it from one end to the other. As has been stated the river got its name from Cumberland Gap which got its name from Cumberland Mountains that Dr. Walker, 1750, named in honor of the Duke of Cumberland, Prime Minister of England.

The word "Cumberland" is rich with antiquity. It can be traced to Japheth, the second son of Noah. Japheth's son, Gomer, produced descendants called Cimmerins in west Asia, Cymries of Europe, Cumbrians of the British Isles, the Duke of which was called the Duke of Cumberland (William Augustus, 1727-60).

He was Prime Minister of England at the time Walker discovered the river that bears his title—Cumberland.

The word Cumberland has been applied to hundreds of other divisions of land, streams, institutions, colleges, churches, organizations, roads, and towns.

Nine states, all of which are east of the Mississippi River, have counties named Cumberland. They are Kentucky, Tennessee, Virginia, North Carolina, Illinois, Indiana, Maine, New Jersey, and Pennsylvania.

Fort Cumberland, Maryland, was erected in 1755, and from it the noted Cumberland Road was made, over which many pioneers came to the states west of the Cumberland Mountains. The road was begun in 1806 at the fort and ran west 800 miles to Vandalia, Illinois, and was known as The National Pike. So named was the first pike in America, which cost over six million dollars and took 34 years to complete.

The Cumberland was the first ship ever sunk by an *Iron* ship, in 1862.

Like the Mother State of Kentucky it is almost a futile task to try to name the first white man that set foot on, or saw, what originally was what now is Cumberland County.

A Virginia record tells us that in the year 1769 Col. James Smith, Uriah Stone, Joshua Horton, William Baker, and a mulatto slave passed through the Cumberland Gap to southern Kentucky, which they explored, and then embarking on the Cumberland River from Kentucky, passed down its entire length to the Ohio, and after almost a year of wandering returned to Virginia to join the Long Hunters in the following year, 1770. If they followed the river, they must have passed through the entire width of this county.

In 1770 the Long Hunters, 40 in number, played a very important part in the history of Cumberland and adjoining counties. The names of those I have been able to secure are: James Knox, Richard Knox, William Allen, Josiah Drake, Obadiah Terrell, John Rains, Uriah Stone, Henry Smith, Edward Cowan, Christopher Stoph, Humphrey Hogan, Cassius Brooks, Robert Crocket, James Graham, John Montgomery, Abraham Bledsoe, Richard and Henry Skaggs, David Linch, Kasper Mansco, Billy Russell, Joshua Horton, William Baker, and two Hughs.

Not all of the Long Hunters came to Cumberland County, but Abraham Bledsoe, Kasper Mansco, and eight or nine others drifted down Cumberland River as far as the present town of Creelsboro and on down to the Rock House where they explored the river bottoms on both sides of the river and made a stay in the bottom to which the Bledsoes came a little later and made a permanent settlement. After their stop at the Rock House for a few days they continued their journey down the river, hunting and exploring for several miles through the dismal brakes and thickets. After their five weeks had about expired, Bledsoe turned his face towards what he thought was their "agreed camp." On reaching it he found to his chagrin that the Indians had plundered the camp, stolen every pot, pan, kettle, and all the skins which had been deposited there. He carved upon a large sycamore tree close to the camp the gist of his plight seasoned with a little profanity, thus: "2300 deerskins lost; ruination, by ——." A. B.

One Kentucky historian says a number of the Long Hunters constructed rafts on the Cumberland River, loaded them with meat and pelts and drifted down the Cumberland, Ohio, and Mississippi to New Orleans, which had been a flourishing market since it was founded by the French in 1718. Just what became of them is a myth. But we do know that Cumberland County was filled with people that bore the names, Baker, Allen, Montgomery, Graham, Hugh, Stone, Smith, Cowan, Bledsoe, et cetera.

Trees and rocks have preserved much of the ancient history of Cumberland County, and as time will weather away rocks, and trees decay and perish, unless someone takes note of these data, they pass into oblivion.

Many inscriptions have been found both on trees and rocks in and around Cumberland County. Some of them have been recorded and some of them have been allowed to fade beyond recognition, to be perpetuated from one generation to another only as traditional.

On a tree near Tompkinsville (now Monroe County) was found the following writing which remained there for three-quarters of a century and was recorded before it faded away:

D. BOON 1777

On two other beech trees not far apart standing on the bank of Cumberland River, this county (now Monroe), were carved the names of two surveyors that read thus:

DANIEL SMITH   DR. THOS. WALKER
FEB. 25, 1780   FEB. 25, 1780

Hannah Boone came to Kentucky with her brother Daniel in 1769. She had previously married John Stewart, who in 1770 came to the territory that afterwards became Cumberland and Monroe counties. John was killed by some Indians while on his way from Mill Creek Church to McMillin's Landing, and his body was placed in a sycamore tree. Daniel afterwards found his body. Hannah then married Richard Pennington and lived the balance of her time with her son, Daniel Boone Pennington, near the Old Mill Creek Church. She died there in 1828 and was buried on a point near the Old Church. Afterwards her remains were removed to the State Park Cemetery of Old Mulkey, nearby.

Daniel Boone tells us in his own writing that he and his brother left the old fort in the latter part of July, 1770, and "proceeded to Cumberland River and reconnoitered all that part of the country until March 1771." Along with this description Daniel tells us that he "gave names to the different streams and other waters."

What one knew in pioneer days everybody knew, because one crew of hunters returning with the glowing accounts of the new country would inspire others that sat and listened to the stories. Referring again to the Long Hunters who came to Cumberland County in 1770, we must remember that Boone conversed with them and met them several times. Boone's sphere was not limited. His delight was in covering as much new territory as it lay in the power of one human being to cover. No forest was too dark or dismal for him. When one region was sought out and explored thoroughly, he lingered not but moved on to the "happy unknown." Having familiarized himself with most of Kentucky, with the hope of finding greater wilds he pushed on into Missouri.

While the deep bottoms were inhabited by savage red men Boone used caution not to fall into their hands if possible. On the trail of the Long Hunters he made a trip to the northern part of Cumberland County in 1771. The Indians occupied the valley of Cumberland River at that time, and he traversed the woodland stretching from the Cumberland Gap to near the present site of Tompkinsville, Kentucky. In the northern part of the present territory of Cumberland County, on Buck Branch, now owned by L. C. Allen, near a small sulphur spring, he carved his name and date on a slate rock, to wit.:

D. BOON 1771

This work is nearly as plain as it was the day it was carved. Octogenarians tell us it looks just like it did before the Civil War. Others say their grandparents saw it there when small boys. The oily, sulphur water together with the sediment that has kept it covered these many years have prevented erosion.

Another initial and date is carved on the same rock; the date is plain, which reads "1797."

A number of names have been cut since the discovery of the spring by Boone, some date 1879, others are crumbled away.

Daniel Boone spelled his own name on the trees and rocks with the final "e" omitted. North Carolina and Tennessee verify this statement. So that is the way he has written it on this slate rock. With the name and date as it is now, protected by the soft sulphur water and shielded from the sun and air, it will be there centuries yet.

Buck Branch is a small stream on the north side of Cumberland River about a mile in length, flowing between two towering hills covered with unbroken forest and connecting with a long stretch of woods, yet the largest body of timber in this county. This woodland was one of the last deer resorts in Cumberland County. Tradition tells us that this ridge was a portion of Boone's trail down Cumberland River, used when he visited his relatives southwest of Burkesville and around the Old Mill Creek settlement, not far from the town of Tompkinsville, Kentucky.

INDIANS

The first title that ever affected the land that is embraced in the present limits of Cumberland County was that referred to as given by the Iroquois Indians and signed at Ft. Stanwix, New York, 1768, by which they yielded all claims to the white settlers.

The second was that signed by the chief of the Cherokee Indians on March 17, 1775, to Col. Richard Henderson of North Carolina, at Sycamore Shoals, by which that part of Cumberland County that lies north of the Cumberland River was purchased from them for a "satisfactory consideration of merchandise" and turned over to Henderson and his company who took immediate steps to explore and settle the territory.

The Iroquois, so far as we know, never occupied Cumberland County. Their principal territory was in the State of New York, but they laid claims to the lands that included this county.

The Cherokees made their headquarters in the western part of North Carolina, but did most of their hunting in the Cumberland Valley. Bands of them would come to this county and camp for months and perhaps years at a time, the signs of which we may still see on the creeks and river bottoms. A permanent camping site was located on Indian Creek which is now in Clinton County. Much flint was available for their arrowheads on this creek; besides, on the west prong of this creek was one of the most important salt licks where the wild game, especially buffalo and deer, which were abundant for a long time after the white settlers made their first appearance, would congregate by the thousands to lick the salty water that exudes from the rock wall. The last deer in that neighborhood was killed by A. B. Thomas in 1892.

On the banks of Cumberland River where nothing but pure sand makes up the soil and subsoil for more than fifty feet deep, one can see signs of Indian camps where, from fifty to two hundred feet in extent, will be seen Indian relics such as arrowheads, Indian axes, shells, crude masonry, rock bowls, and myriads of flint scraps which go to prove their habitation. These old camp sites when stirred by a turning plow show a black appearance mingled with streaks of white decayed shells, which, through all these years, have retained their fertility.

In 1927 George Guffy discovered three burial grounds of Indians in the northern part of the county, one just across the river in Russell County, near the Rock House; one in Irish Bottom under the Dripping

Spring cliff; and one on the Lawson Bottom side of the river, under the Five Pillars, which are five huge rocks left standing on the highest summit of a hill overlooking Irish and Shoestring bottoms.

He obtained from these mounds many beads and relics which brought him, all told, about $45.00. A skeleton was found in the Dripping Spring cliff. All this goes to show that at one time this part of Cumberland Valley with its gigantic forests, natural shelters, and dismal cane thickets was the Red Man's Paradise.

While building a new W.P.A. road through the lands of Leon Turner near W. E. Davis's place on Marrowbone Creek, in 1936, a group of Indian graves were dug into. They were walled up with smooth flat rocks. Beads and relics were found. The road builders readjusted all they could, and left them undisturbed.

Many places in the county like this are to be seen.

The greatest Indian battle of which we have any record that was fought on the present soil of Cumberland County, was that of Little Renox Creek in the year of 1790, near the Falls about three miles north of Burkesville. The battle came about in this manner: Thirty-three miles north of Burkesville, or three miles from the present town of Columbia, Adair County, the early white settlers had built a stockade in an Indian-infested portion of this country. The settlers had for their minister a Rev. John Tucker, who was the first Methodist minister of southern Kentucky. The Indians made a raid on his home in which he was slain. Then, banding themselves together, the marauding crew attacked the stockade, overpowered the whites and fled with much booty to their camp at Little Renox Falls. Along with their booty they had captured a small white girl and carried her with them to their camp.

The news of her seizure was noised abroad at once by her folks and the other settlers. Colonel William Casey was at the head of another group of settlers not far from the place of her capture. He hastily gathered his group together and armed them with swords and flintlock rifles and followed the trail of the marauders, but did not contact them until they had reached their camp at the Renox Falls. As the white men approached the wigwam, a dog owned by the Indians began to bark, upon which the Indian chief came to the tent door and shouted: "Wolf! Wolf!" The chief was shot by the white pursuers, and a hasty skirmish followed, in which all the Indians who took part in the fight were slain. No whites were lost in the battle, and they succeeded in rescuing the small white girl unharmed, and delivered her to her parents. The dead Indians were buried by their people near the scene of the battle. The graves still mark the place. They are square graves, as all Indian graves were in this part of the wilderness, telling their mode of burial—standing.

CHAPTER 2

EARLY HISTORY OF CUMBERLAND COUNTY

At the close of the French and Indian War, 1763, the State of Virginia enacted the Military Bounty Warrant Law, which allowed soldiers tracts of new land for their services in war. While there were no ways to grant them pensions after the war was over, this act induced many families to move farther west to their new possessions. Within the period from 1763 to 1778, common citizens could also obtain possession of some of this land under the "Settlement Right" or the "Improvement Right" laws of Virginia. All that was necessary under this law to come in possession of land was to visit or have someone go onto a certain body of land, mark it off by trees, cut initials of the claimant at each corner of the tract, and construct a rude cabin thereon. It was not required that the claimant live on it at first, just so he paid into the State Treasury his purchase price of $2.25 per 100 acres.

This is the dim period of Cumberland's history. Very few records are obtainable to relate or describe the movements of this part of the county's life. Nevertheless, we know from what little evidence we have that people came and went in groups all over Cumberland County. Were it possible for the writer of this volume to establish the facts connected with this obscure period and pass them down to the reading public of today, he feels they would meet with interest beyond compare. But we are left only to guess and to judge from what few facts we have as to what transpired during this foggy period of the county's life.

In the year of 1778 the Virginia Assembly passed what it called the "pre-emption" law. This gave the settler the right, if he wished, to add to his original plot of land another 1,000 acres adjoining thereto at the cost of 40 cents per acre. Cumberland County had several of these large tracts granted.

The initial-marking of corners met with many disappointments. Overlapping of claims gave trouble. Sometimes at a later date usurpers would hack off the letters from the trees and lay claim to the lands of another. Then the first claimant would have to appear in court and establish his claim with proper evidence. Shrewd attorneys from the Mother State saw a future for them to get rich so they had Virginia to appoint a Commission with the power to hold sessions all over Kentucky to adjust those disputed claims. Over 3,000 controversies were settled in 1779. The two Commissioners who worked with Cumberland County and adjoining territory in 1782 were Nathan Montgomery and William Casey.

An example of those claims is here given, which was copied from a very old record:

"In June 1776 as I was going from Harrodsburg down to Cumberland along with Moses Kirkpatrick, William Stewart, John Clark, Walter Brisco, John Peters and John Robinson we stopped at a big spring on Pittman Creek and built a cabin on 1000 acre tract for John Morgan.

"Sworn to in court.
"Daniel Brown."

The above Pittman Creek likely was the one by that name west of Columbia that goes into the Green River, and not ours by the same name; but as most of those parties named had large grants in Cumberland County, we gather that this County was well known to them at that time.

Another Provision of the Act of 1778 by the Virginia Legislature declared: "That all the region between the Ohio, Green, and Tennessee rivers and the Cumberland Mountains be reserved for Military Claims." This included Cumberland County, and we learn from old papers of the county that most of the territory fell under this list and there is scarcely a neighborhood within the county which does not have a farm calling for the old "Military Line." Bear in mind this was the year of the Revolution when hope of freedom seemed lost forever, and every inducement had to be brought out to keep courage in the soldiers. They were enduring the hardships of war brought upon them from many different angles. The bitterest of winter weather had to be met with scant clothing. A pair of shoes cost $200 in currency and other things that could be had at all, cost in proportion to shoes. The bare earth with leaves or straw made the bedding, and medicine was rarely to be seen in camp life. The "Continental Currency" with which the soldiers were paid gave rise to the saying, "not worth a continental."

To add to the burdens of that year, General Gates, feeling a bit egotistic over the conquering of Burgoyne's Army the previous year, tried to arouse a feeling of indignation among the soldiers against General Washington, which feeling was carried to Congress and inflated by the friends of Gates for the purpose of trying to overthrow Washington as commander in chief of all the forces, and to have appointed in his stead Gates himself. The scheme did not work, but through the untiring effort and daily prayers of Washington the soldier remained faithful to his belief and looked forward to the dawn of peace when the shackles of tyranny would be broken forever and the clank of arms be heard no more, whereupon he could be reunited with loved ones and hie to the new lands of promise to enjoy freedom in its fullest measure and become monarch of the little kingdom that he could call his own. Thus casting aside the memory of hardships, he set out to obtain a title to some of the new territory which the Government had set aside to recompense him for his noble services. So Cumberland County became the depository of hundreds of new families after the war closed.

Some think the "Scotch-Irish" were so named from intermarriage —this is not true. In 1611 King James of England induced a number of thrifty Scotchmen to move into Ireland. They did this, and by the beginning of 1700 their commercial business antagonized that of England, upon which England passed stringent laws against them, both from a religious and commercial standpoint. They could not endure the persecutions. Hence, one-third of the population of America by 1775 was Scotch-Irish, and much of Cumberland County was populated by these thrifty immigrants.

Chapter 3

EARLY LAWS OF KENTUCKY

In 1795 the first law passed by the Kentucky Legislature respecting lands provided that any man over the age of 21 might be granted not over 200 acres of land in the state at the rate of $30 per hundred acres, to be given title when paid for.

In 1797 another law was passed which provided that if any person over the age of 21 would settle on a new land in the state before July 1, 1798, clear, fence, and cultivate as much as two acres he would be granted as much as 200 acres of land by the state at the rate of $60.00 per hundred acres for first-class and $40.00 per hundred acres for second-class lands, with one year's credit on the same.

This sudden rise in the price of land slowed the tide of immigrants and caused another law to be enacted in 1798 which allowed a settler 200 acres at $40.00 for first-class and $30.00 for second-class and allowed nine years to pay for it.

There being two main ways of entrance into the State of Kentucky—one by the Ohio River, which was hazarded by Indian attacks, and the other by the Wilderness Trail through the Cumberland Gap—this county commenced to be populated fast on the passing of the above laws.

The first census of the State in 1790 showed the population to be a few over 73,000, with 12,000 blacks. There is no way to ascertain the population of Cumberland County at that time, but we know it was sparse. There was a period between 1770 and 1790 that Cumberland County was seen mostly by hunters and viewers. Of course the territory that embraces Cumberland County, in 1790 was Lincoln County.

Land grants were made by the State of Virginia to soldiers and officers, and as a result of the above laws immigrants swarmed into the county. These grants were made by the Kentucky Legislature after Kentucky became a state. The following is a list of some of the many bodies of lands and the ones that took advantage of the sales.

The State dealt this land out until 1835, when the Legislature of Kentucky turned over to each county its portion of unappropriated lands.

In order to induce settlers to emigrate to Kentucky the Legislature passed an act in 1795 that called for the following: "A wagon road 30 feet wide from Crab Orchard to Cumberland Gap." It also appropriated 500 pounds in 1797 to arrange the toll gates along this road.

Mrs. Julia Drake of Athens College, Alabama, furnishes me with a little data to show the expenses of those travels as per her great-uncle's diary.

John Orndorff left Virginia April 22, 1805; arrived at Burkesville June 5, 1805, distance 634 miles.

Horse feed	21-10-10	Toll gate	1- 7- 9
Family	6-10-10	Blacksmith	1- 4- 6
Ferry	2- 1-10	Total	32-15- 9

LAND GRANTS

As Copied from the Old Records of Cumberland County

For J. E. King, 200 acres on Renox Creek, Aug. 1798
Andrew Hamilton, 200 A. on Bear Creek, Aug. 11, 1799
David Acree, 200 A. on lower end of bottom opposite Renox Cr.
John Silvertooth, 200 A. in Stockton Valley, Aug. 23, 1799
Ben. Rice, 200 A. on Marrowbone Creek, May 13, 1799
Solomon Brents, 200 A. head waters of Indian Creek, 10-10-1799 (Green)
William Cross, 200 A. on Spring Creek in Stockton V., Oct. 1799
William Cross, 200 A. south side of Poplar Mts., in October, 1799
David Haggard, 200 A. on Little Renox Creek, Aug. 24, 1799
Frances Lawson, 200 A. joining Robinson 1000 A., 1798 (Lawson BO)
John Reneau Assn. of Wm. Reneau, 200 A. on Wolf R. below a branch called Lick Branch, Aug. 28, 1798
William Wood, on east fork of Lick Br. on Obey R., 200 A., 1798
Isaac Denton, 200 A. north side of Wolf R., Aug. 30, 1798
David Evans, 200 A. on Willis Creek, Aug. 24, 1798
John Emmerson assn. of Elijah King, 200 A. on Sulphur Cr., '99
John Emmerson assn. of John Bass, 200 A. north side of Goose Cr., '99
Edward Adkins, 200 A. head of Willis Cr., Oct. 1799
Chas. Burks, 200 A. adjoining the Lexington Seminary, 1000 A. survey on waters of Illwill Cr.
Robert Allen, joins Robt. Pottinger, Elijah Kirkpatrick, and John Engart on Mashack Creek, 1798, 73 A.
John Davis, 200 A. on Indian Creek, 1798
Trustees of Bourbon Academy, about 5,000 A. scattered over the county on Mud Camp, Meshack, Potter, Sulphur Lick, and Beaver Creek, in 1799
David Acree, 200 on Slate Fork of Bear Creek joins Bond's, 1800
Solomon Brents, 200 A. on and between Bear and Raft creek, 1799
John Emmerson, 200 A. on Bear Creek, 1800
Daniel Clift, 200 A. lower end of Elliott's Bottom (now Wells), Aug. 1801

History of Cumberland County

David Wells, 100 A. upper end of Elliott Bottom (Wells), May 1802
John Lee, 200 A. on Indian Cr., July 1800
William Beard, 200 A. in first bottom above Wells B., 1800
William Beard, 200 A. in what's called Salt Lick Bottom, 1800
Thomas Johnson, 200 A. ¾ miles below Beaver Cr. and ½ mile of Wild Goose Shoals, July 1800
Hannaiah Lincoln, 200 A. north Cumb. joining J. Bland, Aug. 1800
Nancy Collins, 200 A. head of Indian Cr. joining Alexander McFarland's survey, 1799
David Sexton, 34 A. two hundred poles above mouth of Crocus C., 1800
Allen Wilson, 50 A. forty yards below Buffalo Lick on west fork of Indian Creek, May 25, 1804
Moses Kirkpatrick, 100 A. north Cumb., Feb. 1801
Geo Francisco, 1798, 200 A. on Marrowbone Cr.
David Haggard, 200 A. on Little Renox Creek, 1798
Athens Seminary, several thousand A. in Cumb. for New Sem., 1803
Daniel Sexton, 200 A. on Sexton Creek of Illwill, in 1800
Michael Craft, 400 A. on Illwill Cr., June 1801 (Ridge)
Mary Ann Spear, 497 A. on ridge between Kettle and Sulphur, 1802
Woodford Academy, survey on Bear, Indian and Illwill C., 1805
John Emmerson, 200 A. on Bear Cr., 1800
James Fergus, 200 A. on Little Willis Creek, Mar. 1805
Elisha Moore, west fork of Willis Cr., 50 A., 1802
Geo. Athens, 100 A. on Upper Whetstone Cr., June 1805
Wm. Whiticer, 75 A. on 3 forks of Willis Cr., 1800
Henry Yakey, 100 A. in Swan Pond Bottom, 1800
James McClure, 325 A. in Swan Pond B., 1800
Henry Davis, 300 A. head of Kettle Cr., 1805
Joseph Ray, 61 A. on Marrowbone Cr., 1803
John Berry, 100 A. middle fork of Judio Cr., 1805
James Cain, 75 A. on head waters of Kettle Cr., 1805
Moses Blakeman, 100 A. July, 1803 Caseys Fork Marrowbone
Isaac Garmon, 200 A., Apr. 1802, Caseys Fork Marrowbone Cr.
Fredrick Fudge, 106 A., June 1801, branch of Marrowbone where Samson Allen's mill now is.
Henry Miller, 43½ A. on Mud Camp Cr., Mar. 1802
Austin Sims, 72 A. left fork of Judio Cr.
Jeramiah & Wm. Smith, Marrowbone Cr., 1805
Joseph Cincaid and John Berry, 171 A. on Judio Cr., 1803
Jesse Bow, 87 A. on Bear Cr., 1805
Samuel Burks, 100 A. on Oil Fork of Bear Cr.
William Roberts, on Slate Fork of Bear Cr., 1805
John Thurman, 100 A. on Cedar Cr., 1801
Thomas Lewis, 138 A. on creek called Lewis' Run, June 1801
Olive Hill, 100 A. on Lewis Run Creek, 1806
Lewis Ellison, 55 A. on Lewis Run Cr., June 1801
John Wisdom, on Caseys Fork Marrowbone, 100 A., Oct. 1805

Chas. Chamberland, 81 A. on Mar. Cr., Oct. 1803 on Military line
John Bedford, 200 A. on head of Kettle Cr., Oct. 1801
Christopher Myers, 400 A. on Lick Branch of Wolf River, Mar. 1801
Daniel Liester, 200 A., June 1801, on Creek ½ mile below Rock House at the first forks of the creek north Cumb. R.
Morgan Morgan, 98 A. on Crocus at mouth of Sand Lick cr., July 1801
James Carty, 40 A. at upper end of Steel Bottom joining Wm. Carty, Wm. Crogan, and Wm. Ferrell, Oct. 1803
Wm. Stapp, 100 A. on west fork of Black Fish Creek, 1802
Jacob Buchannan, 200 A. Sand Lick Cr., July 1801
Wm. Wells, 200 A. on ridge between Illwill and Indian Crks., 1803
Adam Garmon, 200 A. on Casey Fork of Marrowbone Cr., July 1802, joining William Spearman
John Reneau, 400 A., Mar. 1801, on Wolf River
William Ritchey, 666 A. on branch of Marrowbone Cr., June 1801
Isaac Taylor, 400 A. on Marrowbone Cr., June 1801
Ogilsberry Higginbotham, 200 A. on waters of Miller Creek near a large Cave Spring, July 1805
Alex Conner, 300 A. on middle Forks of Indian Creek, Mar. 1802
David Wells, 100 A. in bottom opposite Rock House, May 1802
Sam Elliott, 146 A. on Crocus Creek, Aug. 1804
Andrew Cowan, 50 A., Mar. 1801, Smith Creek
John Cape, 250 A. joining John Logan and Crow's Improvement on south side of river (Irish Bottom), Mar. 1801
Joel Crow, 150 A. joining John Cape, Mar. 1801 (Crow Creek)
Redman Crews, south side of Marrowbone Cr., 118 A., Mar. 1803
James Carty, 50 A. in Lawsons Bottom joining Crogan's surv., 1807
John Carty, 120 A. in Lawsons Bottom on Crogan line, Nov. 1806
Frances Barrett, 130 A. on Brush Creek, Mar. 1807
Benjamine Ferguson, 200 A. on Smith Creek, Nov. 1802
Isaac Walker, 100 A. on wolf-pen creek, of Goose Creek, Mar. 1801
Spencer Fletcher, on ridge between Crocus and Renox, 60 A., July 1807
Geo. Heath, 73 A., Jan. 1806, on Clover Creek
John Journey, 71 A. on Clover Creek joining Lowery, July 1807
Thos. Lincoln, 98 A., Aug. 1804, north Cumb. joining Gee and Thos. Ray
Thos. Lincoln, 200 A., June 1801, on road from Kirkpatricks to the Marrowbone Springs
Francis Emmerson, 172 A., June 1801, on Goose Creek
Absolum Scott, 11 A. Apr. 1804, south corner to Renolds 730 A.
For Justices of Cumb. Co., 1150 A. for Seminary, Sept. 1807, on ridge between Bear Creek and Whetstone
On Branch of Marrowbone Creek, 400 A. for Sem., Oct. 10, 1807
For Adair County Seminary, 700 A. near Poplar Mts., May 1807
Robert and James Galoway, lands on Galoway cr., 1801
Geor. Robinson, 153 A. joining Robert Johnsons 1000 A., June 1801
Richard Renolds, 50 A. in Lawsons Bottom joining Wm. Montgomery, May 1801

J. E. King, 3500 A., 1801
John Baker, 50 A. Big Renox, July 1805
Joseph Bledsoe, 47½ A. in Rock house Bottom, Apr. 1803
Rockcastle and Casey Counties had many surveys for seminaries in Cumberland County, 1807
William Ray, 200 A. on Mud Camp waters for settlement, Sept. 1798
Elizabeth Craft, 177 A. on Illwill Cr., June 1801
Mill Site condemned from Edward Cheatham for Peter Zimmerman on Lewis Creek, 1817
Mill Site condemned one Acre for Geo. Sexton, on north west side of Big Renox creek between the junction of the two creeks and the river, Feb. 22, 1817
Ballenger Wade, 200 A. on Marrowbone Creek, Jan. 1815, K.L.W.
Walter Nunn, 300 A. on Caseys Fork, 1815 by K.L.W.
Arthur Hopkins, great amount of land at Junction of West Fork and Crocus Creeks, 1815-16 by K.L.W.
Peter Stalcup, 40 A. on river adjoining Wilson Cary, Robt. Allen, Oct. 1817 by K.L.W.
Ephriam Easter, 50 A. on upper Whetstone Cr., May 18, 1818, K.L.W.
Jesse Simpson assn. of William Winfree, 50 A., June 1818, Tear Coat creek on both sides, K.L.W.
Daniel C. Myers, 50 A., July 1818, Spring Cr., K.L.W.
John Gabbart, 100 A. in Lawsons Bottom, Oct. 30, 1818, K.L.W.
John Ferrell, 50 A. east fork of lower Whetstone cr. assn. of James Murphy, K.L.W.
Joseph Bledsoe, 100 A. on Cumberland River from John Cape's survey on south to Wells Bottom crossing Tear Coat Creek
Joshua Grider, 50 A. on River below mouth of Indian Cr., 1819
William Goggins, 150 A. north side of river from John Cape's to William Ferrell (Goggin's Ferry), Nov. 6, 1818
John Bailey, assignee of John M. Alexander, on Allen's Creek 50 A. Sept. 1820

MILITARY GRANTS BY VIRGINIA

Wm. Croghan, 10 Military grants in Cumb. C. several 1000 acres, 1782-8
Abraham Chaplain, 400 A., 1780, on Cumberland Trace, 2000 in 1785
Henry, John, Ben, and Robert Lawson, several thousand in 1783
Wright Wescott, 4000 A., 1783, for three years service
John Willis, 1000 A., 1783, on Willis Creek
William Wood, 700 A., 1783, head of Clear Fork Cr.
Wm. Reynolds, 1000 A., 1791, on W. F. Crocus Cr.
John Robertson, 1000 A., Dec. 20, 1784, on Cumberland River
Joseph Phelps, 1400 A. on Otter Creek, 1783
Chas. Ewell, 1000 A., 1786, Cumb. R.
Adam Craig, 300 A., 1796
Alex Humphrey, 430 A., 1798, Crocus Cr.

Robt. Jones, 1400 A., 1792, on M-Bone Cr.
James Kennedy, 165 A., 1791, on Marrowbone Cr.
Morris Lloyd, 1000 A., 1792, Crocus Cr., and 400 A. on E. F. Cro. C.
Robt. Means, 1666 A. Cumb R.—200 on Pitman Cr. 1787—666 A. 1791
    —M.B. Cr.—1000 A. 1797 on Cumb. R.
James McDonald, 1000 A., 1791 on Crocus Cr.
Geo. Pickett, 1000 A., 1791, on M.B., 900 A., 1785, Cumb. R.
Abraham Price, 400 A., 1787, on Cumb. R.
Andrew Renolds, 3426 A. Cumb. R., 1792-3
Henry Renicks, 1474 A., 1798, Cumb. R.; 970 on Russell Cr.; 212
    Butler Cr.
Geo. Rice, 1200 A. Cumb. R., 1797
Wm. Roberts, 1480 A., 1792, on Cumb. R.; 372 on M-Bone, 1792
Goulston Stapp, 1200 A. C. R., 1792
Wm. Smith, 666 A. Cumb. R., 1784
Patrick Simpson, 730 A. M-bone, 1791; 400 Cumb. R., 1792
John Scott, 87 A., 1794, on Cumb. Trace
Thomas Todd, 1000 A. 1785, on Russell Cr.
David Walker, 1000 A. Cumb. R., 1798
John Maston, 3 surveys on Pitman Creek, 1784
John and Geo. Walden, 400 A., 1786, on Cumb. R.
James Young, 200 A. M-bone, 1791; 292 on Cumb. R., 1797
Thomas Young, 1800 A., 1797, on Cumb. R.
Cary Wyatt, 1000 A., 1784, on Crocus Cr.

GRANTS BY KENTUCKY

James W. Taylor, 1347 A., 1807-10, Cumb. R.
Samson Allen, 200 A., 1798, on M-Bone
Robt. Allen, 200 A., and John Allen, 200 A. both on M-Bone
Zachariah Anderson, 200 A., 1805, on Ray Fork of Mud Camp
Reubin Alexander, 118 A., 1807, on M-Bone
Lewis M. Arnold, 200 A., 1806, on Cumb. R.
Jacob Antle, 100 A., 1806, on W. F. Black Cr.
John Adkind, 200 A., 1799, on Cumb. R.
M. Archer, 200 A., 1799, on Goose Cr.
Aaron Anderson, 100 A., 1800, on Cumb. R.
William Asbery, 14 A., 1806, on Illwill Cr.
Geo. Allison, 100 A., 1805, on Upper Whetstone
Eli Barbee, 234 A., 1799, on Cumb. R.
Absolum Ballew, 47 A., 1806, on Salt Lick Cr.
Thomas Barton, 139 A., 1806, on M-Bone
Jerry Black, 373 A., 1807, on Cumb. R.
Joseph Black Heirs, 45 A. on Black Cr. 1801
John Bland, 200 A., 1806, on Meshack Cr.
Sam Blair, 38 A., 1806, on Clear Fork Cr.
William Brake, 200 A., 1813, on Illwill Cr.
Alex Beaty, 200 A., 1799, on Lick Cr.; Martin B., 200 A. Beaver cr.
John Beard, 50 A., 1807, south of Poplar Mts.

Moses Beck, 32 A., 1803, on Indian Cr.
Edward Beck, 160 A., 1807, on Ind. Cr.
Sam Brents, 200 A., 1804, on Cumb. R.
Peter and James Brents, 400 A., 1799, on Ind. Cr. and Ridge
John Breeding, 200 A., 1799, on Sulphur Cr.
Stephen Bedford, 187 A., 1798, on Cumb. R.
Tom Bentley, 200 A., 1799, on Cumb. R.
James Breeding, 157 A., 1799, on Harrods Fork of Cro. Cr.
Sam Biggerstaff, 4 tracts of 1000 A., 1798, Cumb. R.
David Binns, 100 A., 1806, on Cro. Cr.
Martin Bridgefarmer, 150 A., 1806, on Ind. Cr.
Jesse D. Brown, 200 A., 1806, on Illwill and Ind. Crks.
Joseph Brown, 178 A., 1806, on Illwill Cr.
Granville Bowman, 270 A., 1799, on Clover Cr.; 300 on Cumb. R.
Ben Bowman, 50 A., 1808, on Mud Camp
Wm. Bowman, 87 A., 1808, on Beaver Cr.
Henry Bow, 45 A., 1807, on Otter Cr.
Jesse Bow, 88 A., 1806, on Bear Cr.
Wm. Butler, 200 A., 1798, on Crocus Cr.
Israel Bunch, 228 A., 1807, on Clover Cr.
Geo. Beshong, 200 A., 1799, on Anderson Cr.
Wm. Byers, 400 A., 1807, Illwill
Reubin Bryson, 144 A., 1806, on Illwill Cr.; 200 A. 1799, on Illwill
Ben Campbell, 200 A., 1799, on Smith Cr.
David Campbell, 200 A., 1799, on Harrods F.
John Carter, 200 A., 1805, on Illwill, and 150 A. on Spring Cr.
Friend Carter, 100 A., 1806, on Lick Cr.
Josiah Carter, 114 A., 1800, on Cumb. R.
Sam Carter, 106 A., 1805, M-Bone Cr.
Asa Chapman, 66 A., 1806, Cumb. R.
Henry and Geo. Clark, 800 A., 1799, on Illwill and Ind. Crks.
John Crawford, 200 A., 1799, on Cumb. R.
Abraham Crabtree, 200 A. Cumb. R., 1797
Wm. and Ben Cain, 200 A., 1805, on Bear Cr.
Tom Chandler, 200 A. M-B, 1800
Wm. and Chas. Chamberlain, 535 A., 1799 M.B. Cr.
John Cape, Sr., 575 A., 1798-1805, on Cumb. R.; John, Jr., 200, 1799, Cumb.
Henry Cary, 200 A., 1799, on Cumb. R.
Shadrach Claywell, 175 A., 1806, on Illwill
John Christian, 224 A., 1805, on Illwill
Moses Cook, 100 A., 1805, Illwill
Thomas Cox, 82 A., 1811, on Lick Branch
Sam Cole, 200 A., 1815, on Wolf R.
Robt. Cross, 400 A., 1800, on Clear Fork
James Cowan, 200 A., 1800, on Spring Cr.
Wm. Cowen, 200 A., 1807, on Smith Cr.
Andrew Cowen, 150 A., 1807, on Smith Cr.
Joseph Conn, 200 A., 1805, on M-B.

Early Laws of Kentucky 21

Elijah Crouch, 200 A., 1797, on Spring Cr.
James Crouch, 200 A., 1799, on Clear Fork
Lawrence Conner, 200 A., 1806, on M. F. Ind. Cr.
John Cruze, 45 A., 1805, on Ray Branch
Chas. Davis, 100 A. Sulphur Cr., 200 in 1800 on Cumb. R.
Moses Davis, 175 A., 1799, on Kettle Cr.
Peter Davis, 200 A., 1806, on Illwill
James Davis, 32 A., 1813, Ind. Cr.
Wyatte Daniel, 100 A., 1805, Cumb. R.
Jesse Deweese, 200 A., 1799, E. F. Lick Cr.
Epharim Dicken, 550 A., 1799-00, Cumb. R. and Sulphur Cr.
Abner Dooley, 200 A., 1798, M-B.
Matthew Ewing, 100 A., 1807, W. F. Crocus Cr.
Francis Emmerson, 425 A., 1798, Cumb. R.
John Emmerson, 800 A., 1799, Cumb. R.
Christopher Ellis, 900 A., 1799-05, Sulphur Cr.
John and Jesse Ellis, 230 A., 1805, on Ind. Cr.
Sam Elliott, 230 A., Crocus cr.; Tom Elliott, 340 A., 1799, Spr. Cr.
Lewis Ellison, 55 A., 1805, on Lewis Cr.
John Franklin, 200 A., 1799, on Obey R.
Wm. Ferrell, 200 A., 1798, Cumb. R.
Sam Farris, 15 A., 1807, Bear Cr.
Champ Ferguson, 200 A., 1799, Spr. Cr.
John Fletcher, 150 A., 1798, on Crocus cr.
Thomas Fletcher, 110 A., 1807, W. F. Cro. cr.
Spencer Fletcher, Heira, 50 A., W. F. Cro. Cr.
Arthur Frogg, 200 A., 1799, Ind. cr.; Wm. Sr., 35 A. Wolf cr.
James Firkin, 183 A., 1806, Renox cr.
John Fudge, 300 A., 1806, on Groves Cr.
Thomas Garrett, 160 A., 1806, on Bear Cr.
Geo. Greer, 300 A., 1798, on Oil F. Bear Cr.
Jesse Gee, 200 A., 1798, on Meshack Cr.
Joseph Grider, 97 A., 1812, on Butler Cr.
James Gibbons, 200 A., 1799, Spr. Cr.
Geo. Groves, 166 A., 1805, M-Bone Cr.
Wm. Goodson, 1100 A., 1799, Ind. cr.
James Guthrie, 50 A., 1805, Illwill Cr.
Adam Guthrie, 1805, 200 A., Illwill
Mark Hardin, 200 A., 1799, Crocus Cr.
Joseph Hall, 400 A., 1798, Cumb. R.
Wm. Hall, 170 A., 1805, Cumb. R.
John Hargrove, 200 A., 1799, Illwill Cr.
Robt. Harvey, 200 A., 1798, Harrods F. Crocus
John Hay, 200 A., 1799, E. F. Big Barren R.
David Haggard, 100 A., 1799, Lit. Renox
Arthur Hopkins, 1000 A., 1799, Crocus C.
John Holland, 24 A. W. F. Cro. Cr.
Henry Hoots, 34 A., 1810, Hendricks Cr.

Ed Hunter, 150 A., 1799, Cumb. R.
Wm. Hunter, 300 A., 1806, M. F. Ind. Cr.
Sam Hunter, 200 A., 1799, Beaver Cr.
John Hurt, 111 A., 1805, Casey F.
Wm. Huff, 200 A., 1799, Clear F.
Moses Hull, 200 A., 1807, Spr. Cr.
Wm. Irvin, 200 A., 1800, Spr. Cr.
Elijah Jackman, 200 A., 1800, Cumb. R.
Thomas Jackman, 200 A., 1800, Cumb. R.
Wm. Gentle, 36 A., 1806, Oil F. B. C.
David Jones, 400 A., 1799, Cumb. R. and Spr. C.
Mike Johnson, 200 A., 1799, Bear C.
Tom Johnson, 100 A., 1805, Casey F.; and, 1799, 200 on Bear C.
John Journey, 200 A., 1799, Clover C.
John Keen, 300 A., 1799, on Sulphur C.
John E. King, 600 A., 1797-9, Renox C.
Moses Kirkpatrick, 407 A., 1796-1806, Cumb. R. & Meshack C.
Elihu K—, 200 A., 1799, Meshack C.
Philip Lawson, 200 A., 1799, Sulphur C.
Reubin Lawlace, 270 A., 1806 Greasy C.
John Lewis, 200 A., 1805, Mud Camp
Thos. Lewis, 138 A., 1805, Lewis C.
Daniel Lester, 200 A., 1800, Cumb. R.
James Logan, 350 A., 1799, M. F. Kettle Cr.
Solomon Long, 200 A., 1799, Spr. C.
Jacob Lollar, 230 A., 1799, Cumb. R.
Reuben Lollar, 400 A., 1805, M. F. Kettle C.
Wm. Mays, 200 A., 1800, M.B.C.
Caleb Maxey, 159 A., 1806, Brush C.
David McGill, 400 A., 1799, Willis C.
John McGill, 200 A., 1800, Cumb. R.
Jacob Miller, 200 A., 1798, Crocus C.
Jno. K. Miller, 179 A., 1799, Mud C., and 200 on Crocus C.
Wm. Montgomery, 600 A., 1796, W. F. Crocus C.
John Montfort, 400 A., 1799, Spr. & Illw.
Dan Myers, 200 A., 1799, Clear F.
James McColgan, 200 A., 1799, Mud Camp
James McGlasson, 75 A., 1807, Sand Lk.
Wm. McMurtery, 200 A., 1799, Skeggs
David McNeeley, 100 A., 1799, Cumb. R.
James Nance, 100 A., 1805, Mud Cp.
Francis Ogden, 500 A., 1798, Mud Cp. and Cumb. R.
John Page, 300 A., 1798, Mashes C.
Anderson Page, 46 A., 1815, Mud Cp. C.
Francis Petty, 200 A., 1806, Oil F. Bear C.
Francis Pierce, 200 A., 1807, no stream
John Peery, 200 A., 1799, Ill. W. C.
James Pierce, 325 A., 1805, Swan Pond B.

Wm. Reed, 200 A., 1799, Cumb. R. & Ind. C.
Ben Rice, 200 A., 1799, M-Bone
Isaac Rutledge, 1798, Harrods F. Cro.
John C. Sconce, 150 A., 1806, Kettle C.
James Saufley, 200 A., 1806, Cro. C.
Thomas Stewart, 48 A., 1807, Casey F.
Wm. Spears, 170 A., 1805, Kettle C.
Joseph Spears, 172 A., 1806, Mitchel F.
Benjamin Spears, 100 A., 1806, Ket. Cr.
Wm. Spearman, 500 A., 1805, Potters and Casey F.
John W. Semple, 600 A., 1799, Ind. and Clover Cks.
Wm. Sconce, 50 A., 1806, Kettle C.
Wm. Smith, 110 A., 1805, M.B.C.
Jno. Smith, 75 A., 1805, Kettle C.
Samuel Smith, 151 A., 1806, Illwill
Britain Smith, 400 A., 1806, Illwill
Jonathan Smith, 200 A., 1799, Willis C.
Absalom Scott, 283 A., 1807, Goose C., and 100 on Wolf Pen C.
Allen C. Scott, 400 A., 1806, Sulphur C.
Joseph and Alexander Sprowles, 800 A., 1799, Ind. C.
Eli Shugart, 200 A., 1800, Slate F. Bear C.
Vince Tayloy, 100 A., 1807, Potter C.
Ashford Skipworth, 400 A., Potter & Galoway, 1850
Wm. Taylor, 200 A., 1799, Crocus C.
Wm. H. Talbot, 200 A., 1799, Clear F.
Henry H. Trice, 200 A., 1798, Cumb. R.
Waddy Thompson, 200 A., 1798, Spr. C.
Chas. Thomas, 50 A., 1806, Rock House
Wm. Tooley, 150 A., 1819, Mashes C.
John Trotter, 200 A., 1799, N. F. Willis C.
John Thurman, 12 grants in Cumb. Co.
Thomas Thurman, 600 A., 1799, Illwill & Bear Cks.
Axum L. Vaughn, 91 A., 1805, Illwill
Allen Vincent, 380 A., 1806, Bear & Illwill
Hardin Williams, 200 A., 1799, Ind. C.
Thomas Wms., 200 A., 1799, Cumb. R.
Richard Wms., 200 A., 1799, Sulphur
Epharim Wms., 35 A., 1806, Mud Camp
Stephen White, 100 A., 1798, Cumb. R.
John Wisdom, 75 A., Casey F., 1798
Francis Wisdom, 200 A., M.F.M-Bone, 1798
Wm. & Jno. Wood, 300 A., 1799, Spr. C.
Robt. Young, 162 A., 1805, E. F. Renox C.
Matthew Young, 400 A., 1798, Illwill
Andrew Young, 200 A., 1802, Cumb. R.
Tom Young, 200 A., 1803, Renox C.
Andrew Cummings, 300 A., 1818, F. M-Bone
John & James Davis, 150 A., 1816, W. F. Ind. C.

Wm. Gray, 100 A., 1818, Casey C.
Benjamin Lewis, 100 A., 1822, E. F. Whetstone C.
Nathan Norris, 50 A., 1823, Bear C.
Wm. Noris, 100 A., 1836, W. F. Cro.
Wm. Nunn, 6 grants M.B. & meshacks Cks.
Walter Nunn, 6 grants M.B. & Meshacks, 1816
James and Wm. Obanion, 450 A., 1819, Mud Camp
Langston Pace, 50 A., 1819, M.B.
Absalom Pharis, 227 A., 1819, Bear C.
James W. Radford, 172 A., 1819, Willis C., Cumb. R.
John Reneau, 555 A., 1824, Wolf R.
Robt. Reid, 350 A., 1817, Willis C.
Joe & James Riddle, 60 A., 1823, Sulf. C.
James Riddle, 100 A., 1824, Willis C.
John Rush, 50 A., 1823, Sulphur C.
Tom Spencer, 150 A., 1818, Lester C.
Robt. and Guy Self, 370 A., 1818, N. Cumb. R.
Sam Stockton, 150 A., 1816, Renox C.
Beverly and Joe Vawter, 87 A., 1818, Mud Camp
Ballenger Wade, 300 A., 1816, M-Bone
Matthew Walkup, 300 A., 1816, Crocus C.
Richard Wade, 150 A., 1820, M.B.
John Willis, 100 A., 1822, Sulphur C.
Barrett White, 100 A., 1822, Potter C.
Wm. Winfrey, 100 A., 1819, Cumb. R.
Frank Winfrey, 352 A., 1832, Cumb. R.
Wm. Wood, 1300 A., 1816, Spr. C.
James Young, Jr., 200 A., 1816, Renox

BY THE COUNTY (After 1835)

Chas. Back, 150 A., 1850, L. F. Lester C.
Jacob Brake, 40 A., 1861, Fanny Cr.
Wm. Brake, 145 A., 1889, Bear C.
John H., G. W., & T. W. M. Bledsoe, 333 A., 1850, Lester C.
John A. Bowman, 600 A., 1837, Whetstone C.
Jesse Bow, 325 A., 1851, Bear C.
William Carver, 790 A., 1839-53, Bear & Illwill
N. J. Cash, 130 A., 1860, Bear
Moses & Bennett Capps, 500 A., 1855-60, Kettle C.
Richard & Edward Cheatham, 470 A., 1865, Crocus
R. G. Cole, 290 A., 1865, Cro.
Cornelius Conner, 4000 A., 1836-56, Ind. C.
Humphrey Coofey, 370 A., 1847, Lester C.
Jess & John Coe, 1500 A., 1836-50, Kettle C.
James A. Dixon, 200 A., 1886, Goose C.
M. C. Dillon, 350, 1866, Big Renox
Jordan & Ephraim Easter, 150 A., 1856, Whetstone

Robt. Elliott, 1400 A., 1840-59, Crocus and Cumb. R.
Thos. Ellison, 500 A., 1851, Clover and Potter Cks.
Thos. M. Emmerson, 300 A., 1830, Renox
William Farmer, 100 A., 1850, Fannys F.
H. J. Garmon, 700 A., 1860, M-Bone
Jacob, David, James, Adam, Jr., Jno. T., John M., & Wm. Gorman, 1800 A., Casey Cr.
Henry Graham, 50 A., 1847, bet. Sulphur and Illwill
Zebulon Norris, 300 A., 1850, Bear C.
Jas. T., — 800 A., 1865, Cro.
Sam Thrasher, 150 A., 1847, Sexton F.
Davidson J. Thrasher, 300 A., 1850-90, Illwill
Fred Appleby, 50 A., 1841, Willis C.
Wm. Appleby, 80 A., 1853, Willis C.

Another absentee speculator was William Thompson of Virginia, who got patent on 1,000 acres on "Marrowbone or Crocus Creek," 1792, who sold his to John Winbush who sold to Robert Campbell who in turn sold to James Breckinridge, all before the first resident purchaser settled to stay, in the person of William Ritchey, in 1800.

In the early 90's Robert Wadkins of Virginia had a large survey run off which passed to James Brown and Andrew Renolds who sold the patent on 1,840 acres to William Smith and Nathan Thurman for 400 Pounds, who moved to it to live. This was in 1796, and the description shows the vague ideas of locations: "in the first big bottom above the mouth of Marrowbone Creek supposed to be in Logan County." Many such wild locations are on record like this and the one above.

September 8, 1791, 900 acres taken up by George Pickett of Virginia, who sold to Nathaniel Savage on "Marrowbone or Crocaus," being a part of the military lands set aside for the soldiers of the Virginia Line in 1778. This was purchased by the Alexanders, 1805.

Brown & Renolds of Richmond, Virginia, had a Military Grant of 638 acres south of Renox, 1796, a part of which went to T. T. Lowery the following year.

In 1801 William Goggins, 200 acres on Indian Creek in Cumberland and Wayne counties, to William Hunter 1812 for 200 Pounds, to Micajah in 1830 (son of William).

August 1797, John McEllany of Richmond, Virginia, patented most of Wash Bottom and sold to Thomas Wash later.

Military Warrant by the County of Kentucky, February 24, 1788, to Robert Johnson, assignee of Charles Ewell for 1,000 acres of land. This was in Irish Bottom.

In 1791 John Maston patented 1,000 acres on Big Renox Creek. Maston sold to Henry Banks and Banks to Robert Means.

In 1791 Robert Means had grant of 666 2/3 acres on branch of Marrowbone Creek. Here Means was assn. of Banks and Banks of John Maston.

May 9, 1792, William Thomas had grant on Marrowbone Creek of 1,000 acres.

Ishmel Tipton grant on West Fork of Crocus Creek, 1,474 acres.
James Lynn, 1,100 acres on Big Renox. Military Grant.
David Rice, 1799, Military Grant.
George Rice had a Military Grant on Cumberland River, 1799, of 1,564 acres.
Wright Wescott, 1,000 acres on north side of Marrowbone Creek.
Golson Stapp, 620 acres first big bottom above Rock House.
Garrard Williams, 1,000 acres north Cumberland.
Brown and Renolds —— acres, January 1, 1796, at mouth of Renox and adjoining Garrard Williams.
William Croghan, 700 acres in Lawson Bottom, November 29, 1794.
John Bailey, 1784, 1,000 acres, part of Howards Bottom, Steels Bottom up to Big Willis Creek.
Vorheer and Weisenger, 1,000 acres on Brush Creek and Ridges.
About 1789 John Wright patented north half of Irish Bottom, which he sold to Joseph McCormick who sold to John Crawford whose 11 heirs sold to Micajah Hunter in 1832.
John Rice of Hendricks County, Virginia, had Military Grant to his four sons, Ed, Geo., James, and John, 381 A. in Potters Bottom, 1792.
What became Whetstone Precinct later was called, "Kingdom of the Nine Johns." John Steel, John Bailey, John Carty, John Willis, John Robertson, John Cape, John Wright, John Crawford, John Self, first settlers.

CUMBERLAND RIVER BOTTOMS

The slices from Cumberland County that helped to form Russell and Clinton counties included four big bottoms which were original Cumberland County lands, Swan Pond, which was settled by the McClures in 1800 and named for the pond therein;

Salt Lick Bottom which was taken up by the Beards in 1800 and named for the lick on the creek where the wild animals congregated for salt;

Wells Bottom which was first called the "Bottom opposite the Rock House"; then it assumed the name of Elliotts Bottom for Sam Elliott who had grants there; in 1802 David Wells had several hundred acres granted by the General Assembly together with what he purchased, becoming the greatest landowner in 1802, the Bottom assumed his name (see Land Grants);

Jackman Bottom which got its name from the first great landowners in that Bottom—Thomas being the first; Elijah next with 400 acres in 1800; and

Rock House Bottom, one of the oldest bottoms on Cumberland River which is described in different chapters of this writing.

Irish Bottom, the first bottom now in the county, is another old bottom. Charles Ewell patented the lower half, 1786, sold to Robert

Johnson and Johnson to John Robertson, 1800. In 1789 John Wright was granted the north half and he sold to Joseph McCormick who sold to John Crawford, leaving a strip in the center which was taken up by John Cape, 1798. Robertson paid $1,000 for 1,000 acres. Named from Scotch-Irish settlers.

Shoestring Bottom is a small bottom opposite Irish Bottom. It was a part of John Cape's grant and was called Bunch Bottom until the first 90's when the steamboat men gave it the name it now bears, on account of its shape, like a shoestring.

Lawson Bottom included several grants, found elsewhere. It is below Shoestring Bottom, lying in the first big bend of the river going down. Like the other bottoms, much of the land was included in Military Grants. Philip, Lewis, and Francis Lawson, the last of which had large grants in the bottom, lived here. The bottom got its name from Frances Lawson as checked in 1790. Henry, John, Benjamin, and Robert Lawson were there in 1783.

Steel Bottom is another small rich bottom opposite Lawson and was included in John Baily's Military Grant of 1784 and was named for John Steel.

Howards Bottom is the next big bottom on the south side of the river. James Brown and Andrew Renolds (Ronalds in Virginia), two attorneys of Henrico County, Virginia, obtained 666 2/3 acres of land in 1793-4 in "Big Bottom opposite mouth of Crocus Creek." Ronalds died in 1798 leaving a will to Catherine, his wife, and six children, and the residue of his property to friends—Buchannan, Graham, and Wiseham. Wiseham was made executor, but died in 1804. Before his death he and Brown had drawn up an agreement with James Howard of Henry County, Virginia, that Howard should have the 666-plus acres of land for twelve shillings per acre, paid in specie, one third paid down 1805, one third in 1806, and the other in 1807. William Renolds had gotten this same land several years before the attorneys had as a Military Grant.

James Howard moved to his new farm to live a few years after his last payment and the bottom began to be called by its present name.

Clay Lick Bottom is the next big bottom on the north side of the river. It received its name from the Buffalo lick near the town of Bakerton, due to the presence of so much clay dirt made bare by the stamping of the buffaloes.

Scotts Bottom follows on the south side of the river. First settlers were located by being in the big "Bottom opposite the mouth of Rennicks Creek." Andrew Renolds had a grant of 730 acres in this bottom, 1792, and north of Goose Creek. In 1804 Absolum Scott established a ferry across Cumberland River at the mouth of Goose Creek and became the owner of 394 acres of land adjoining the ferry. The bottom soon took on the name of the ferry which it bears today.

Burkesville Bottom is better described in other places within this writing. Samuel Burkes' Headright land furnished the location for the town (Deed Book B, p. 334).

Herrifords Bend is the name of the next big bottom down the river on the north side. It was distinguished by being the "First big Bottom above the mouth of Marrowbone Creek." It was surveyed for Robert Wadkins for service, in 1791, and sold to Andrew Ronalds and James Brown who in turn sold 1,840 acres to William Smith and Nathan Thurman in 1796. They came to it to live. It was still without a name until the Herrifords became owners of much of it and it assumed the name.

Whites Bottom is the next big bottom on the south side of the river. John and Lewis Potter had large grants in the south end of the bottom in the 80's. Following them was John Rice of Hendricks County, Virginia, who had a Military Grant for his four sons—Ed, George, James, and John, of 381 acres in 1792. George Rice had also 1,200 acres the same year, all of which was in Potters Bottom. The bottom went by this name until the turn of the 1800's when Barret White and other Whites moved in and gave it the present name.

Wash Bottom is the next big bottom on the north side of the river. It was a Military Grant for George Picket in 1785, for services in the Revolutionary War. Then John McEllany's heirs patented the bottom in 1797 and sold out to Thomas Wash several years later, from whom it received its present name. It, like Irish Bottom, previous to this date was designated as "On Cumberland River."

Salt Lick Bend is the next big bottom on the south side of Cumberland River. It is in the largest loop of Cumberland River which lies within the county. The river bends around the bottom about eighteen miles while across the neck is little more than a stone's cast. The salt lick where wild animals made their haunt gave it its name.

Judio Bottom (now Cary Bottom) is a very old place of settlement. Abraham Price had a Military Grant in the bottom, 1787, of 400 acres. This is the last bottom in the county.

SEMINARY LANDS OF CUMBERLAND COUNTY

To the Trustees of the Bourbon Academy of Bourbon County, Ky., granted by the Commonwealth of Kentucky, October 24, 1799, 500 acres of land on the head waters of Moone Shine Creek.

To the Bourbon Academy Trustees, October 25, 1799, 500 acres of land on the head waters of Skaggs Beaver Creek, adjoining John Piper and Samuel Parkers lines.

To the Trustees of the Bourbon Academy, October 31, 1799, 1,000 acres of land on Parkers Branch adjoining Robert Burnsides tract.

To the Trustees of the Bourbon Academy, by the Commonwealth of Kentucky, October 10, 1799, 500 acres of land in Cumberland County, on the Ridge between Mud Camp and Skaggs Creeks.

To the Trustees of the Bourbon Academy, by the Commonwealth of Kentucky, ——, 1799, 400 acres of land in Cumberland County, on Meshacks Creek.

To the Trustees of the Bourbon Academy, by the Commonwealth of Kentucky, November 30, 1799, 500 acres of land in Cumberland County, on the Sulphur Lick Creek.

To the Trustees of the Bourbon Academy, November 30, 1799, 200 acres of land by the Commonwealth of Kentucky, said land lying on Potters Creek.

To the Trustees of the Bourbon Academy, May, 1799, 400 acres of land on Sulphur Lick Creek, adjoining William Byrd's survey.

To the Trustees of the Bourbon Academy, by the Commonwealth of Kentucky, May 20, 1800, 550 acres of land on Sulphur Lick Creek.

To the Trustees of the Bourbon Academy, by the Commonwealth of Kentucky, 585 acres of land on the waters of Sulphur Lick Creek, 5-20-1800.

To the Trustees of the Bourbon Academy, by the Commonwealth of Kentucky, February 14, 1800, 365 acres of land on waters of Sulphur Lick Creek, adjoining Christopher Ellis and John Reaves lands.

To the Trustees of the Bourbon Academy, by the Commonwealth of Kentucky, January 9, 1800, 365 acres of land lying on Sulphur Creek.

To the Trustees of the Woodford Academy of Woodford County, by the Commonwealth of Kentucky, 350 acres of land, August 25, 1805, on the south side of Cumberland River adjoining John McFarland on the Ridge between Illwill and Indian Creeks.

To the Trustees of Woodford Academy, by Commonwealth of Kentucky, 400 acres August 26, 1805, on Bear Creek, on Robert Galoway's line.

To the Trustees of the Woodford Academy, 1805, by the Commonwealth of Kentucky, 1,450 acres on the west side of Indian Creek, Cumberland County, corner to Joe Criner's pre-emption and with John Criner's pre-emption line.

To the Trustees of the New Athens Seminary, August 21, 1807, 25 acres, on right fork of Island Branch, adjoining Ilijah Lettier.

To the New Athens Seminary, October 10, 1807, 93 acres of land on the right fork of Sulphur Creek, adjoining Richard Williams survey and John Spears survey.

To the New Athens Seminary, September 18, 1807, 200 acres of land granted by the Commonwealth of Kentucky.

CUMBERLAND COUNTY

To the Trustees of the Cumberland Seminary, Cumberland County, October 8, 1807, 400 acres of a branch of Marrowbone, on the line of John Marston, now (1807) John Ritchey's 666 2/3 acres.

To the Trustees of Cumberland Seminary, November 18, 1807, 750 acres of land on the head waters of Sulphur Creek.

To the Trustees of Cumberland Seminary, by the Commonwealth of Kentucky, November 17, 1807, 150 acres of land on the head waters of Indian Creek adjoining Alexander McFarlands.

To the Trustees of the Cumberland Seminary, by the Commonwealth of Kentucky, November 16, 1807, 200 acres of land on Cumberland River above the mouth of Marrowbone Creek, on Haggard's Branch.

To the Trustees of the Cumberland Seminary, November 14, 1807, 100 acres of land on north side of Cumberland River, adjoining John King and Samuel Studdard.

To the Trustees of Cumberland Seminary, November 13, 1807, 25 acres of land on the river above Marrowbone Creek and joining Reynold's survey.

To the Trustees of the Cumberland Seminary, October 12, 1807, 564 acres of land on head waters of Illwill Creek, joining John Philips, Sr., and John, Jr., and McClains.

To the Trustees of the Cumberland Seminary, September 28, 1807, 1,150 acres of land between the waters of Bear Creek and Whetstone Creek.

To the Trustees of the Cumberland Seminary, April 3, 1809, 8 acres of land on the waters of Willis Creek, about one mile south of a saltpeter cave now occupied by James Taylor & Company.

To the Trustees of Cumberland Seminary, January 13, 1810, 8½ acres of land on the waters of Obeys River, below Reynold's improvement and below his mill, crossing Reynold's Branch below the mill and including the Big Falls.

ADAIR COUNTY

To the Trustees of Adair County Seminary, October 16, 1807, 700 acres of land on the north side of Poplar Mountains, adjoining Peter Brents, Thomas Brents and Goodson's lines.

To the Trustees of Adair Seminary, February 11, 1812, 1½ acre of land on the main fork of Crocus Creek, joining Josiah Carmens.

CASEY COUNTY

To the Trustees of Liberty Academy, June 1, 1812, 100 acres of land north side of River on Miller's Creek, and adjoining Garland Akin.

To the Casey Academy, January 1, 1812, 23 acres of land on Miller's Creek, adjoining Akins and Dillingham.

To the Trustees of the Casey Academy, January 1, 1812, 35 acres of land on east side of Crocus Creek.

LEWIS COUNTY

To the Trustees of the Lewis Academy of Lewis County, March 19, 1812, 28 acres of land on Miller's Creek adjoining Oglesberry Higginbothams.

ROBERTSON COUNTY

To the Trustees of Robertson County Academy, March 23, 1817, 100 acres of land, on Smiths Creek adjoining Sam Dicksons, Jacob Meeks, and David Cowen.

To the Trustees of Robertson Academy, May 25, 1818, 100 acres of land adjoining William Hudson and Croghan.

BATH COUNTY

To the Trustees of the Seminary of Bath County, January 22, 1821, 112½ acres of land on the Ridge between Mud Camp and Meshacks creeks and adjoining Samuel Brents.

ROCKCASTLE COUNTY

To the Trustees of Rockcastle Seminary, April 27, 1811, 4 acres of land on Fannys Fork on Illwill Creek, adjoining Michael Craft.

To the Trustees of Rockcastle Seminary, August 12, 1811, 2 acres and 28 poles on Big Renox Creek, ¼ mile above Gearheart's improvement, including the noted Sulphur Springs.

To the Trustees of the Rockcastle Seminary, September 23, 1801, 18½ acres of land on Raft Creek, corner to William Thurman.

To the Trustees of Rockcastle Seminary, 11½ acres of land, September 3, 1811, on north side of Raft Creek.

To the Trustees of Rockcastle Seminary, September 23, 1811, 59 acres of land adjoining Nathan Thurman and Henry Cary.

To the Trustees of Rockcastle Seminary, September 30, 1811, one acre of land on southwest side of Poplar Mountains, adjoining Francis Pierce.

To the Trustees of Rockcastle Seminary, September 30, 1811, two one-acre tracts on west side of Poplar Mountains near a large cave.

To the Trustees of Rockcastle Seminary, June 22, 1812, 10 acres of land on a branch of Bear Creek, joining Samuel Pharris.

To the Trustees of Rockcastle Seminary, February 21, 1814, 100 acres of land on Renox Creek, adjoining James Young and Joe Akin.

To the Trustees of Rockcastle Seminary, September 12, 1814, 100 acres of land on Mud Camp Creek, adjoining McColgan, John Smith, and Francis Ogden.

To the Trustees of Rockcastle Seminary, September 14, 1814, 100 acres of land on Spring Creek, on east side of Coperas Pond Mountains.

To the Trustees of Rockcastle Seminary, July 8, 1815, 100 acres of land on Beech Branch of Crocus Creek, adjoining Arthur Hopkins.

To the Trustees of Rockcastle Seminary, September 6, 1811, 13 acres of land on Raft Creek, joining Wm. Thurman.

To the Trustees of Rockcastle Seminary, June 5, 1820, 100 acres of land on northeast branch of Marrowbone Creek, adjoining James Carter.

FIRST TAX LIST OF CUMBERLAND COUNTY, MAY 1, 1799

Below is given the list of the taxable property, including lands, horses, and cattle, and slaves as shown by the first list taken and signed by John Lasley who was Tax Commissioner for the district including all the lands in original Cumberland County and lying on the south side of Cumberland River. Much of this territory was taken to form Clinton and Wayne counties later.

Due to illiteracy and carelessness of officers many names are misspelled; as Brents which they spelled Brunts, and Grider as Griner, or Crider, Criner.

Names of Persons over 21	Blacks	Horses and Cattle	Acres	Streams
William Adams		3	200	Beaver Creek
Joseph Alexander		5	200	Beaver Creek
James Allcorn		1	200	Sinking Cr.
Wyatt Atkins		3		
Nicholas Alexander		4	200	Cumb. River
Jeremiah Allen		2		
Archibald Alexander		2	200	Cumb. River
James Bates				
Solomon Brunts		1	600	Indian Creek
Zachariah Burnett	1	3		
Joseph Bird		3		
Cage Burnet		1		
Francis Bird		2		
Spencer Bevins		1	200	Sinking Creek
Edward Beck				
Moses Beck		5		
Daniel Barren		3	200	
Bond Burnet		4	100	Beaver Creek
Andrew Baker			200	Elk Spring Cr.
John Balch		2		
Elisha Blevins		2		
Joseph Bunch		1		
Drury Bunch		2		
Joseph Beard	1	2	1,621	Elk Spring Cr.
James Bevins	1	2	200	Sinking Creek
William Beard	7	1	400	Elk Spring Cr.
George Bruton		1	200	Beaver Creek
Henry Biggs		2	200	Beaver Creek
Thomas Bodkins		1	200	Beaver Creek
James Barnet		5		
William Bartleson		3		
Zachariah Bartleson		6	200	Beaver Creek
David Burris		2	200	Cumb. River
Levy Brasheare				

Names of Persons over 21	Blacks	Horses and Cattle	Acres	Streams
Samuel Boyd			200	Cumb. River
Henderson Bates			100	Spring Creek
James Bates		3	100	Spring Creek
William Bond	1	2	100	Bear Creek
Peter Brunts		3	400	Spring Creek
Isaac Burris				
James Brunts		5	200	Spring Cr.
Julius Burton		1		
Samuel Blair		2	200	Spring Cr.
James Barnes				
Nathaniel Bartlett		3	200	Smith Creek
Daniel Bridgeman		1		
Joshua Bartlet				
Samuel Black		9		
Allen Burton		5		
Joseph Bond		1	200	
William Beaty		2	200	Lick Creek
James Beaty		2	200	Lick Creek
Robert Cross	1	1		
John Criner		2	200	Indian Creek
James Coffey		1		
Francis China		2		
John Coffey		3	150	Otter Creek
Elijah Camron		1		
John Crawford		4	200	
Rolly Clack		2	200	Sinking Creek
David Cowan		3	150	Kennedy Creek
Edward Cullum		1	200	Beaver Cr.
David Cox		1		
John Cape, Sr.		4	200	Cumb. River
George Chrystal		1		
Richard Chrystal		2	200	Beaver Cr.
John Caperton		4	200	Beaver Cr.
Thomas Cloyd				
Nicholas Koger	1	1	150	Kennedy Creek
Samuel Cox		1		
James Cowan, Jr.				
James Cowan		4	200	Spring Creek
Joseph Carter		2	200	Illwill Cr.
William Cross		1	200	Spring Creek
James Collins		1		
Michael Crawford		3		
Hugh Campbell		8	200	Spring Cr.
Benjamin Campbell		5	200	Spring Cr.
John Cowan		1		
George Criner		5	200	Indian Creek

Names of Persons over 21	Blacks	Horses and Cattle	Acres	Streams
Byran Combs		2	200	Indian Creek
Isaac Crabtree	2			
James Clarke		3		
Friend Carter			200	Illwill Cr.
Jeremiah Denton		5	200	Spring Creek
Samuel Denny		9		
Nancy Dabney		1		
John Davis		3		
John Denny		4		
Michael Doan			250	
George Duncan		3	111½	Sinking Creek
Thomas Dotson			250	Silver Cr. (Madison)
Jesse Dotson				
Robert Dysart		1		
Mose Davis	2	3	200	Kettle Creek
Joshua Davis		1	200	Kettle Creek
David Davis			160	Kettle Creek
Morris Davis			150	Kettle Creek
Henry Dorheaty		2		
Charles Debril	1	2	460	Cumb. River
William Dewberry		1		
Isaac Denton		7	200	Spring Creek
William Evans		3		
James Evans		4	200	Beaver Creek
Joseph Evans			200	Beaver Creek
Andrus Evans	1	3		
Samuel Eldridge		1		
Nathaniel Evans		2	200	Spring Creek
David Evans		2	400	Willis Creek
Thomas Elliott	8	6	200	Spring Creek
William Franklin	2	3	300	Elk Spring Cr.
David Frame		2		
Samuel Forbes		3	200	Beaver Creek
Thomas Farris		2	200	Spring Creek
Dudley Farris			200	Smith Creek
Champion Ferguson		1	200	Spring Creek
James French	1	4		
Samuel Francis		3		
John Francis	4	6	200	Beaver Creek
Henry Guffey		1	200	Otter Creek
Ephraim Guffey		2		
Henry Garner		3	200	Beaver Cr.
James Green				
James Gooding		1	100	Beaver Creek
Richard Gooding		2	200	Sinking Cr.
Conrad Good				

Names of Persons over 21	Blacks	Horses and Cattle	Acres	Streams
Stewart Gilkey		1		
Robert Galloway		4	200	Bear Creek
Samuel Gibson		8		
Samuel Green		1		
John Gross			100	Smith Cr.
James Gibbons		4	300	Spring Cr.
James Galloway		2		
Richard Gording		1		
Jacob Huffacre		1	200	Beaver Creek
Malachi Hicks	1	8		
John Hancock		1		
William Hancock		3		
Benjamin Hancock, Jr.		1		
Benjamin Hancock, Sr.		1	200	Otter Creek
Joseph Hinde		2	100	
Robert Henderson	3	21	1,300	Beav. & Otter Cks.
Edward Hunter		6	200	Beaver Cr.
Henry Hereford		4		
Joseph Hall		1	200	Cumb. River
Jesse Harold			100	Spring Cr.
John Hinds		1	200	
Philip Huff		2		
Daniel Huff		2	200	Spring Cr.
William Huff		2	100	Spring Cr.
James Hillis	1		100	Spring Cr.
Andrew Hamilton		3	200	Cumb. River
William Hall		2	192	Cumb. R.
James Ingram		5	200	Beaver Cr.
John Irvin		5	200	Cumb. R.
Abraham Irvin		2	200	Cumb. R.
James Irvin	5	4	200	Cumb. R.
Godfrey Isbell		4	200	Beaver Cr.
John Irvin	1	1	200	Spring Cr.
William Irvin			200	Spring Cr.
Robert Irvine				
William Jones		4		
Thomas Jarvis				
Edward Jenkins				
William Jones				
Elliott Jones		4	200	Beaver Cr.
Martha Jones	1	1		
Jonathan Jones, Sr.		1		
Jonathan Jones, Jr.		3	200	Spring Cr.
David Jones		1	200	Spring Cr.
Peter Jump		2	146	Cumb. R.
William Jones		4	200	Elk Spring Cr.
Benjamin James		3		

Names of Persons over 21	Blacks	Horses and Cattle	Acres	Streams
Thomas Johnson	1	8	200	Otter Cr.
James Jones			200	
John January	1	4	100	Cumb. R.
Joshua Jones		2	200	Cumb. R.
John Jones				
John Johnson		3	200	Cumb. R.
John Jones		2		
Enoch James		1	200	Cumb. R.
William Jones		3	200	Green River
James Jones		2		
Baker King		8	200	Cumb. R.
James Kincaid			100	Bear Cr.
William Lee		4	300	Smith Creek
William Lane				
Jonathan Lane		1		
John Lynn		1		
Matthew Looper				
Joel Long			200	Spring Creek
John Long		1	200	Spring Creek
Hugh Lamb		5		
John Lee		3		
William Looper				
Alexander McFarland		3	400	Indian Creek
Charles Matney		2		
Brooks Matney		1	2,500	
Walter Matney		1	200	
Vardery Magby		4		
William Mullins		6	600	Otter Creek
Daniel McFarland			200	Indian Creek
John McFarland		1	200	Indian Creek
Andrew McFarland		2	200	Beaver Creek
William McCluskey		1		
Thomas McCullom		2	200	
Hugh McDurmid		4		
James McWhorter		2		
Benjamin Martin		2	200	Kennedy Creek
William McHenry		4	200	
William McMurry		1		
Samuel Monday		7	200	
John McCaney		5	200	
Banister Malone		1	100	Cumb. R.
Elisha Moore		1	100	Willis Creek
Joseph McComery		3		
Joseph Meighs		1		
John Mounts		3		

Names of Persons over 21	Blacks	Horses and Cattle	Acres	Streams
Isaac Meadows		4		
John Mitchel		3	100	Cumb. R.
Tobias Morodoc		2		
John Miller		5	200	Cumb. R.
John Mason		2		
Andrew Mason		1		
Oliver Matthews		1	100	Cumb. R.
Jacob Meek		4		
Jacob Meek Jr.				
Jeremiah Meek		1	200	Smith Creek
Edward Mattok				
Pearson Miller		2	100	Spring Creek
Thomas Norman		2	200	Cumb. R.
Joshua Nickles		4		
John Owen		3		
Nathan Potts		3	200	Otter Creek
John Potts		3		
William Preast		2	200	Beaver & Otter Cr.
Philip Payne	2	6	400	Cumberland R.
Abraham Price		9	150	Fishing Creek
Ezekiel Parris				
Samuel Pickens		1		
Joseph Patton		2	200	Spring Cr.
John Philips Sr.	1	3	200	Illwill Cr.
John Philips Jr.		1	200	Illwill Cr.
Lewis Potter			200	Cumb. R.
John Potter		2	100	Cumb. R.
William Quay				
David Robinson			200	Spring Cr.
John Ridgeway		2		
William Ray		1	200	
William Robinson		1		
John Ridgeway		3		
Geo. Robinson		3	300	Cumb. R.
John Robinson	1	4	700	Cumb. R.
John Robinson		1	200	Spring Cr.
James Robinson		2		
Stephenson Robinson		2	200	Spring Cr.
Moses Robinson		1	200	Spring Cr.
Jesse Roberts			100	Smith Cr.
John Roberts				
Elijah Rogers		3		
Moses Robinett				
Sarah Ross		2	200	Spring Cr.
John Rogers		2		
William Rollen		1	200	Spring Cr.

History of Cumberland County

Names of Persons over 21	Blacks	Horses and Cattle	Acres	Streams
James Russell				
Geo. Rogers		2	200	Sinking Cr.
Archibald Ritchey		1		
Mack Renfee	6	4	200	Beaver Cr.
James Ryon		4	200	Beaver Cr.
Thomas Ray		1	100	Mosser Cr.
Matthew Small		2	200	Sinking Cr.
John Slaton	1	6		
William Scott		4		
Geo. Smiley		5	200	Mad. Co., Silver Cr.
Andrew Stephenson		3	2,300	
John Seal		4		
Martin Sims		3	200	Otter Cr.
Peter H. Stockton			200	Otter Cr.
William Smith		1		
Thomas Stone		2	200	
John Sanders		3	200	
John Seeley				
Ezekiel Stone		1		
David Smith		1		
Henry Small		1		
John Small		2		
Thomas Smiley		3	150	Sinking Cr.
Geo. Singleton			200	Beaver Cr.
Henry Small		1		
John Sharp		6		
Azel Skinner		2		
Richard Slaven		1		
Thomas Small		3	100	Sinking Cr.
William Salley		1		
Jesse Stanley		2	200	Beaver Cr.
Samuel Stouts				
William Small		1		
William Sims		3	200	
William Smith		3	200	
Joshua Sexton		1		
Paul Steel		1		
Henry South		4		
George Sexton	1	3	200	Illwill Cr.
John Stockton	1	4	200	Spring Cr.
Robert Stephenson		3		
Michael Speck		1		
Nathaniel Sailsbury	3		200	Cumb. R.
Joseph Smith		1		
Geo. Smith		2	200	Smith Cr.
James Smith		1		

Names of Persons over 21	Blacks	Horses and Cattle	Acres	Streams
Philip Smith				
Joseph Stephenson			200	Sinking Cr.
William Sharp		2	200	
Thomas Stockton Jr.		1	200	Spring Cr.
Thomas Stockton Sr.	4	3	200	Spring Cr.
Nathaniel Stockton		1	100	Spring Cr.
William Thomas		1		
Nicholas Talbott		5	100	Spring Cr.
Aaron Turpin		4	200	Maple Swamp
John Tully		2	200	Smith Cr.
Waddy Thompson			200	Spring Creek
John (?) Twiney		1	200	Indian Cr.
Richard Thurman		1		
John Thurman	17	3	1,800	Cumb. R.
William Ussery		5	600	Otter Cr.
Geo. Upton				
Abraham Vanwinkle		3		
Thomas Virgin		1		
John Vaughn		1		
Robert Wallis			200	Otter Cr.
Isaac Wilton		3		
John Willis		1		
Dorson Wade		3		
Christopher Wiedman		1	150	Kennedy Cr.
William Wade				
Joseph Wade		2		
Geo. Wolfkill	3	8	200	Beaver Cr.
James Walker			200	
Jeremiah Walker		1		
Samuel Wilson		2	200	Beaver Cr.
James Wood			200	Spring Cr.
William Wood		3	200	Spring Cr.
Samuel Wood		3		
James Williams		3		
Joseph Wheeler		1		
Williams Wells		4	200	Near Highway
Henry Willis		2		
William Ware		1		
Isaac West	1	4	200	

Total white males over 21 (boys 27) 350
Total blacks 87
Total horses and cattle (2 stallions) 790

This is a certified copy of District 2, Cumberland County, signed by James Allen, C.G.C.

The part of the county north of Cumberland River is not on file.

The total population of Cumberland County by its first census in 1800 was 3,284. Cumberland at that time included large parts of Clinton, Wayne, Russell, Monroe, and Metcalfe counties. In 1870 it was 7,690; in 1940 it was 11,923.

EARLY MARRIAGES OF CUMBERLAND COUNTY

The fire that destroyed the Cumberland County court house, December 30, 1933, destroyed the marriage records from 1799 to 1882. Prior to the fire Mrs. Nora C. McGee made a copy of the marriages from 1799 to 1817 which will be found below, which is the only existing record. Some of the clerks were poor scribes, hence the spelling was difficult to interpret.

Benjamin Coyle & Nancy Jobe, July 30, 1799
William Logue & Hannah Jobe, August 6, 1799
James Cole & Ann Wood, August 13, 1799
By John Mulkey.

Jeremiah Walker & Sarah Campbell, November ——, 1799
Jonathan Stark & Priscilla Davis
John Dale & Agnes Piris
Robert Pottinger & Fanny Gee
John Sprowel & Elizabeth Irons

I hereby certify that the above marriages have been solemnized within the past twelve months.
By William Ray.

William Owen & Susanna Owen, July 24, 1800
Nathan Potts & Elizabeth Green, September 27, 1800
William Preast & Amy Wallis, September 27, 1800
By Elliott Jones.

William Davis & Polly Davis
Isham Woods & Rojannah Thompson
Fredrick Shores & Margaret Walbert
Thomas Carr & Elizabeth King
Jesse Bland & Nancy Kirkpatrick
Allen M. Wakefield & Betsy Thurman
Matthew Scammehorn & Sallie Gibson

Certified for the year of 1800
By William Ray.

William Bartelson & Margaret Green, November 20, 1800
By Elliott Jones.

Titus Gragg & Charlott Rentfro, March 19, 1801
William Wilkey & Martha Irvin, January 29, 1801
Paul Ingram & Sarah Stogell, January 13, 1800
Peter Bumpts & Hannah Lynn, March 13, 1800
David Brown & Jenny Gordon, February ——, 1800

Nicholas Owens & Mary Myers, February 18, 1800
Robert Irwin & Mary Evans, November 1, 1800
James Walker & Polly Campbell, December 18, 1800
John Jones & Nancy Meck, December 9, 1800
Clement Lee & Susannah Beck, September 19, 1800
By Isaac Denton.

William Murley & Mary Care, June 22, 1800
Hannaniah Lincoln & Lucy Wilson, February 14, 1801
John Martin & Nancy Harris, April 2, 1801
By William Ray.

Joseph Shaw & Sallie Hotlett
By Robert Stockton,
Minister of Barren County.

Robert Hunter & Sally Martin, 1798
Alexander Martin & Nancy Dabney
Lewis Lilliard & Polly Lynn
Mashaiah Sexton & Betsy Burks
James Price & Peggy Ewing
Alec Cox & Betsy Thurman

I here certify the above were united in the holy bonds of matrimony within the past year, this December 5, 1801.
By David Haggard.

Radolen Thompson & Polly Ray, September 17, 1801
William Webb & Jane Willis, November 21, 1801
Lewis Potter & Sarah Wiseman, December 31, 1801
Henry Jarrett & Anna Smith, January 7, 1802
Geo. Criner & Patty Galoway, January 14, 1802
By William Ray.

John Montfort & Esther Fergus, February 18, 1802
By Joseph Bledsoe.

Samuel Evans & Polly Stephenson, March 17, 1801
Samuel Davis & June Sprowl, September 17, 1801
Joseph Smith & Susanna Rider, October 15, 1801
William Smith & Margaret Rider, October 15, 1801
Joseph Philips & Mary Bates, December 17, 1801
By Isaac Denton.

Tobias Moredock & Nancy Nevans, April 1, 1802
Laurance Snap & Fanny Lastly, September 7, 1802
By William Ray.

George Logan & Esther Robinson, September 30, 1802
By Joseph Bledsoe.

Newberry Mann & Mary Blankenship, March 2, 1802
By Joseph Bledsoe.

John Howard & Sallie Ray, September 30, 1802
Francis Wisdom & Susanna Wisdom, October 7, 1802
David Robertson & Elizabeth Ray, November 11, 1802
By William Ray.

Thomas Robertson & Polly Stone, January 28, 1803
Morris Davis & Rebua Davis, January 28, 1803
By David Haggard.

William Parrish & Betsy Chilton, March 6, 1803
Daniel Bashens & Celey Lewis, June 16, 1802
By Joseph Bledsoe.

James Breckenridge & Betsey Crocket, June 7, 1803
By Isaac Denton.

Francis Wisdom & Nancy Hogg, January 16, 1803
Pollard Wisdom & Elizabeth McCarty, April 28, 1803
Johanan Smith & Rebekah Studdart, November 20, 1803
Adam Garmon & Eva Allen, February 3, 1804
By William Ray.

John Mills Wallace & Phoebe Crawford
Chas. Burks & Anna Thurman
John Hunter & Betsy Price
Francis Emerson & Unity H. Thurman
   The above were united in marriage within 1804.
By David Haggard.

Samuel Shepherd & Betsy Ashburne, May 16, 1804
By Rice Haggard.

John Carter & Nancy Williams, December 17, 1804
By Eliott Jones.

William Jackson & Chloe Fugate, November 22, 1804
By Lewis Ellison.

William Allen & Patsey Halsel, October 22, 1804
Right Nash & Sallie Martin, March 28, 1805
By William Ray.

Jonathan Young & Betsy Kinsey, August 29, 1805
Joseph Conn & Jane Smith, August 17, 1805
Abalum Farris & Cally Johnson, October 24, 1805
John Armstrong & Judith Thurman, January 2, 1806
Shadrack Richardson & Elizabeth Garrett, January 2, 1806
Joseph Inks & Polly Ewing, July 26, 1804
By Jeremiah Abell.

James D. Spain of Green County & Margaret Matthews of Cumberland County, September 6, 1807
Thomas White & Pricilla Baxter, January 30, 1806
William Andrews & Polly Kirkpatrick, June 12, 1806

Early Laws of Kentucky 43

John Lough & Polly Hughes, December 23, 1806
John Whetson & Grace Rush, February 15, 1807
James Baxter & Jane Hiestand, May 31, 1804
         By John Mulkey.

Isaac Taylor & Jane Baker, January 22, 1806
Samuel Elliott & Nancy Lynn, May 28, 1806
William Scott & Sallie Scott, January 22, 1806
Benjamin Haggard & Rhoda Baker, March 14, 1806
Andrew Cummins & Polly Johnson, October 18, 1806
Garret Jackson & Betsey Hill, October 12, 1806
John Palmer & Mary Lewis, November 21, 1806
Geo. Robinson & Polly Logan, November 3, 1806
Lemuel Williams & Polly Ritchey, September 4, 1806
Benjamin Bowman & Nancy Minor, November 24, 1806
Marice Carter & Betsey Harris, December 10, 1806
Samuel Ultite & Martha A. Thurman, October 8, 1806
Reubin Alexander & Eliza A. Miller, August 8, 1806
Leonard Garmon & Polly Snowder, February 2, 1806
Absalom Scott & Philis Stamfield, May 21, 1806
Daniel M. Daniel & —— Blakeman, May 21, 1806
Anthony Thornton & Nancy Lee Barrett, November, 1807
         By Lewis Ellison.

Thomas Dunbar & Nancy Whitesides, June 3, 1807
Hudson Blankenship & Elizabeth Karns, October 30, 1807
Edward Nichols & Anna Johnson, December 31, 1807
         By David Wells.

John Miller & Polly Harris, September 16, 1808
Francis Biggs & Ellander Pamley, March 30, 1808
Samuel Laugherty & Sallie Chandler, April 5, 1808
John Chandler & Winnie Littrel, April 5, 1808
William Hall & Sallie Ray, December 15, 1808
James Smith & Nancy Smith, December 16, 1808
         By Lewis Ellison.

Michael Gutsler & Rebekah Johnson, March 10, 1808
Joseph Coffey & Jane Graves, September 29, 1808
Richard Graves & Sallie Thomas, December 7, 1808
Ephraim Pierce & Nancy Blankenship, January 1, 1809
         By David Wells.

Abednego Richardson & Sally Claywell, January 20, 1809
William Murley & Jane Green, March 9, 1809
William Ferrell & Elizabeth McCown, December ——, 1809
John Young & Polly Young, March 16, 1809
John Strong & Betsey Williams, October 13, 1808
Samuel McDowel & Abigal Harrison, March 9, 1809
Lewis Wright & Mahala Denton, March 10, 1809
Robert Owen & Elizabeth Smith, June 15, 1809
         By Isaac Denton.

Joshua Butcher & Sallie Reneau, October, 1804
William Frogg & Polly Merit, October 4, 1804
John Reneau & Betsey Thurman, November ——, 1804
John Stockton & Luctrie Daniel, May 16, 1805
Reason Wright & Mary Ann Lewis, January 23, 1806
Benjamin Wilson & Betsey Conner, February 19, 1805
Hiram Crabtree & Margaret Johnson, May 18, 1806
Hopkins Bond & Mary Husk, September 18, 1806
Matthew Young & Dorcas Carpenter, February 18, 1806
Josiah Brown & Hiley Williams, May 24, 1807
James Guttery & Salley Atchley, January 7, 1808
John Lewis & Matilda Grimes, February ——, 1808
Moses Wooten & Patsey Williams, March 27, 1808
William Reneau & Betsey Green, September ——, 1808
Joseph Brown & Sally Cooksey, January 12, 1809
         By Nicholas Talbott.

James Welch & Jane Flowers, April 25, 1809
George Simpson & Nancy Hinkle, July 19, 1809
         By Sela Pain,
         Circuit Preacher.

Isaac Campbell & Polly Wells, March 9, 1809
John Jameson & Susanna Cape, March 26, 1809
Noel Blankenship & Lavina Blankenship, March 30, 1809
         By David Wells.

John Thurman & Curtsey Williams, May 20, 1810
         By John Travis.

William Parrish & Betsey Chilton, March 6, 1803
         By Joseph Bledsoe.

Robert Owenward & Betsey Smith, June 15, 1809
Michael Stockton & Nancy Smith, August 1, 1809
James Harvey & Gladys Green, February 12, 1811
John Spear & Mary Sprowel, April 3, 1811
Zepheniah Woolsey & Ann Crocket, July 11, 1811
Josiah Gooten & Sarah Farris, August 29, 1811
John Farley & Elizabeth Frogg, August 10, 1809
Stephen Conn & Betsey Ritchey, October 25, 1810
James Hannah & Gladys Green, February 12, 1811
Zepheniah Woolsey & Ann Crouch, August 6, 1811
Simon Gross & Mary Owens, June 4, 1812
         By Isaac Denton.

John Ross & Prudence Winfrey, October 24, 1811
Robert Ewing & Jane Scott, February 28, 1810
—— White & Sarah Greden, March 1, 1813
Daniel Higgin & Polly Graves, August 20, 1815
Fredrick Smith & Betsy Self, March 1, 1811
Thomas Williams & Lydia Graves, July 1, 1810

Jesse Easley & Elizabeth Higginbottom, July 8, 1810
Elijah Melson & Polly Jackman, July 12, 1810
George Helm & Sally Jackman, July 12, 1810
Nebuzarden Coffey & Elizabeth Easley, September 13, 1810
Joseph Grider & Nancy Easley, September 13, 1810
George Logan & Fanny Self, August 1, 1811
Wiley Chancey & Susannah Young, November 21, 1811
Thomas Higginbottom & Sarah Easley, February 18, 1812
Edward Wright & Haveriah Yates, March 22, 1812
Franklin Berry & Decy Roe, July 20, 1812
Guy Lee & Polly Matthias, August —, 1812
Richard Clayton & Barbara Smith, October 1, 1812
William Watkins & Patsy Jamison, October 25, 1812
William Winfrey & Sally Wells, November 1, 1812
Abraham Karns & Nancy Blankenship, February 4, 1813
George Green & Polly Young, August 31, 1813
William Morgan & Nancy Howard, November 16, 1813
Alexander Logan & Malinda Goggin, January 6, 1811
Uriah Robertson & Jane M. Bledsoe, January 23, 1811
James Robertson & Lucretia Bledsoe, November 3, 1814
Lon Matthews & Elenor Appleby, November 10, 1815
James Hendron & Dianna Self, January 5, 1815
Robert Appleby & Polly Flowers, February 14, 1815
Richard York & Rhoda Snow, August 24, 1815
Richard Graves & Cynthia Goggin, September 14, 1815
Alfred Ballou & Eliza Ballou, November 19, 1815
Jubilee Goggin & Sarah Fergus, December 26, 1815
John Campbell & Eliza Flowers, December 28, 1815
Robert Higginbottom & Polly Wilborn, January 9, 1816
John Whitearn & Catherine Wright, January 18, 1816
                                        By David Wells.

John Doss & Lydia Stanfield, December 24, 1812
John Bow & Sally Thurman, February 25, 1813
Lively Johnson & Agnes Thurman, April 17, 1813
Isham Burks, Jr. & Amy Young, July 11, 1813
                                        By John Watson.

Daniel Woolridge & Lucy Thurman, October 4, 1812
Joseph H. Tobin & Sally Rion, October 4, 1812
                                        By John Howe.

James Spears & Penelop Jacks, August 12, 1813
Henry Parker & Betsey Willis, September 23, 1811
John Miller & Rachel Edmons, April 21, 1814
John Wicks & Trecia Adams, September 2, 1814
Jesse Claywell & Hannah Humphries, October 13, 1814
Absalom Pharis & Susannah Glidewell, October 27, 1814
William Smith & Polly Smith, March 16, 1814

John Autry & Polly Gee, August 19, 1815
Abner Engart & Sally Stephens, June 27, 1815
Abraham Spear & Sarah Shuelt, March 30, 1815
William Biggerstaff & Nancy Black, June 22, 1815
John Banning & Patience Spear, November 9, 1815
Thomas Cain & Peggy Claywell, February 16, 1815
Jacob Bow & Eliza Shuelts, April 13, 1815
Daniel Shelby & Peggy Shy, September 21, 1815
Pleasant Austin & Sally Hicks, September 28, 1815
Potter Shelly & Jane Shy, October 12, 1815
Morgan Richardson & Polly Woods, December 28, 1815
Samuel Lynn & Abagyle Smith, July 4, 1816
                              By Sampson Keen.

William Fletcher & Sally Blankenship, July 30, 1811
                              By D. R. Haggard.

Henry Lacy & Susannah Will, August 11, 1811
                              By Rice Haggard.

John Blair & Polly Young, September 25, 1811
                              By John A. Lewis.

Beverly Clayton & Sally Rion, June 28, 1814
James Gilmore & Nancy Wilson, May 30, 1814
Samuel Ritchey & Catherine Williams, December 29, 1814
Samuel Woolridge & Rebecca C. Walthall, January 26, 1815
Moses Stalmp & Amy T. Wiard, October 7, 1815
Barno White & Susan Smith, April 11, 1815
James Anderson & Johny Cazzarth, July 2, 1815
Arthur Kerigan & Sally Bland, May 7, 1815
William Hancock & May Wiles, October 5, 1815
Seth Williams & Cyntha Williams, September 27, 1815
Robert Barton & Sarah Johnson, January 15, 1815
Billy Chandler & Judith Fair, December 5, 1815
John Osborn & Ann Garrett, September 26, 1809
                              By Lewis Ellison.

Samuel Goodson & Betsey Beck, December 25, 1814
William Crouch & Martha Martin, August 15, 1816
James Cole & Nancy Brown, November 23, 1816
Isaac Rayfield & Betsey Stopp, October 8, 1816
James Noland & Sally Drumgoold, April 3, 1816
Peter Belshe & Sally Page, November 10, 1816
James Williams & Lucy Appleby, February 19, 1817
Griffin Fenison & Lydia Owens, March 3, 1817
Silas Beck & Margaret Brents, March 31, 1817
                              By Isaac Denton.

Thomas M. Emerson & W. H. Emerson (Thurman),
John Craig & Isabella Smith,
Rich Green & Betsey Davis,

Gardner Green & Sally Childress, February 14, 1816
Wm. G. Flowers & Tabitha Baker, July 15, 1816
Sandrich Moore & Priscilla Bunch, July 18, 1816
           By Rice Haggard.

Jesse Thurman & M. Smith, May 25, 1815
A. Farbush & M. Baker, November 17, 1815
William W. Lewis & S. A. Galbrath, January 31, 1816
S. G. Cheatham & M. K. Cheatham, July 22, 1816
Bordite C. Pile & Letietia Armstrong, January 2, 1817
           By Samuel Brown.

Thomas Griffin & Sally Humphreys, March 7, 1814
Thomas Barney & Rhoda Griffin, September 22, 1814
William Frogg & Polly Smith, March 24, 1815
Isaac Crouch & Nancy Carguile, August 10, 1815
Solomon Hollett & Peggy Y. Talbott, October 18, 1816
James Raney & Sallie Griffin, January 3, 1816
David Mahon & Mary Fletcher, April 6, 1815
           By W. Robertson.

Michael M. Hall & Susan Alexander, October 31, 1816
           By William Warder.

Matthew Cidwell & Nancy Patman, October 6, 1816
William Mitchell & Rebecca Wallace, March 7, 1816
Equilla Hall & Rhoda Obanion, November 23, 1815
James Page & Sally Roice, August 11, 1816
John Young & Polly Vibad, August 8, 1816
John C. Sconce & Citty Farmer, August 11, 1816
Cornelias Vanover & Sally Bennett, July 25, 1816
William Eldridge & Polly Prewitt, August 27, 1816
Daniel Lough & Polly Martin, October 3, 1815
Nicholas Kingston & Delila Stephens, December 8, 1816
Oliver Matthews & Nancy Savage, December 5, 1816
           By John B. Longan (or Logan).

Dallas Scott & Sally Foster, November 14, 1815
           By P. Lawson.

James Hunter & Winfred Dabney, 1810
William Ward & Polly Cape, 1809
John Jackman & Margaret Williams, 1808
Enos Ray & Agatha Dodson (dau. of Joe D.), 1809
George Hall & Nancy Bowman, 1807
William Bowman & Jane Hall, 1807
John Williams & Sally Hunter, 1808
William Smith & Polly Black, 1808
John Hancock & Tabitha Ballew (dau. of John B.), 1806
John Coe & Nancy Scott (dau. of Jesse S——)

FORMATION OF CUMBERLAND COUNTY

An Act for forming a new county out of the County of Green, approved December 14, 1798:

Be it enacted by the General Assembly of the Commonwealth of Kentucky, That from and after the first of July next, all that part of the County of Green, included in the following bounds to wit: Beginning on the Warren line a west course from Marrow-Bone Springs, thence east until it strikes the dividing ridge between Cumberland and Green rivers, and with the same to the wagon road leading from Colonel William Casey's to Burkesville, at the head of Rennick's Creek, thence eastwardly so as to leave the settlement of William Butler, Jr., in Green County, thence to continue such a course as will just leave the settlement of Greasy Creek in Green County, thence east to the Lincoln line; thence south to the State line and with it to the Warren line; thence with the Warren line to the beginning, shall be distinct county and shall be known by the name of Cumberland.

Cumberland County remained thus until she had to give up a part of her territory to form Wayne County (1800), to wit:

Bounds of Wayne

Beginning at the mouth of Indian Creek on the Cumberland River and running by James Sanduskey's cabin to the road that leads from Capt. Thomas Johnson's to Major Alexander McFarland's on Indian Creek; thence to the top of Poplar Mountains; thence with the same till it intersects the State line; thence east with said line till a line going north would strike Rock Creek on main South Fork of Cumberland River; thence with same to the beginning.

Johnson's *History* claims by the first tax list, taken 1801, the part of Cumberland thus taken was 31,854 acres.

Cumberland remained this size until Monroe was cut off, 1820.

Act Approved January 19, 1820

Be it enacted by the General Assembly of the Commonwealth of Kentucky, That all that part of the counties of Barren and Cumberland included in the following bounds: Beginning on the Tennessee State line on Cumberland River; thence east with said line 4 miles; thence to a point twelve miles from the court house in Burkesville in a direct line to Tompkinsville, including Flemming Jones' residence in the proposed county; thence in a direction to a place where the road from Glasgow to Burkesville crosses the county line, as far as the main branch of Marrowbone Creek; thence to Marrowbone Spring; thence to Skeggs Creek one hundred yards below the house of Col. David Hardin; thence to the Barren River at the most eastern point thereon below the mouth of Hungry Creek; thence up said

River and with the Allen County line to the Tennessee State line; thence with said line to the beginning; shall from and after the first day of April next, constitute a distinct county to be called and known as the county of Monroe, in honor of James Monroe, President of the United States.

(Thirteen Justices held the first court in the county of Monroe at Hiram Putnam's house and swore in a clerk who issued subscription papers for donations for public buildings.)

After Monroe territory was carved off of Cumberland she had to yield up another slice to help form Russell, 1825.

ACT TO FORM RUSSELL COUNTY

Be it enacted by the General Assembly of the Commonwealth of Kentucky, That from and after the first day of April next, all that part of the counties of Adair, Wayne and Cumberland included in the following bounds, to wit: Beginning on the Adair County and Casey County line one mile southeast of William Jones' horizontal measure; thence with a straight line to the east end of Aaron Williams' lane; thence to Zachariah Collins, leaving Collins in the old county; thence to a point on Crocus Creek, one mile below James Duncan's run, so as to leave Henry Antle and Adam Miller in the old county; thence to a point on the Cumberland River one mile above the Rock House; thence to Andrew Smalley's so as to include the same; thence to William Hunter's including the same; thence to Sheeks mill on Beber Creek including same; thence to the mouth of Difficulty; thence across the river and up the same to the mouth of Mill Creek which empties in on the north side of the river, opposite Col. Ewing's of Wayne County; thence to Solomon Turpin's including same; thence to a point on the Pulaski and Wayne line three miles from where the same crosses Wolf Creek; thence with said line crossing Wolf Creek to Adair and Casey county line; thence with same to the beginning, shall be called Russell County, in honor of Gen. William Russell.

Approved December 14, 1825.

(Nine Justices held the first court in Russell County at the home of Jonathan Patterson.)

Cumberland County rested undisturbed now for 10 years when another part was taken to help form Clinton County in 1835.

AN ACT, 1835, TO ESTABLISH CLINTON COUNTY

Be it enacted by the General Assembly of the Commonwealth of Kentucky, That from and after the first day of April, next, all the parts of Cumberland and Wayne counties, within the following bounds, to wit: Beginning at the State line due north from the mouth of Wolf River, and thence a straight line to the plantation of Alexander Smith, including it; thence a straight line to the mouth of Tear Coat

Creek on Cumberland River; thence up said river to the Russell County line; thence with said line to within one half mile of Beaver Creek; up Beaver Creek to the mouth of Otter Creek; thence up Otter Creek so as not to run nearer than within one half mile of said creeks, to Jacob Citt's, leaving him in Wayne; thence to the twelve mile post on the road that leads from Monticello to Stockton Valley; thence to the Poplar Mountains, at Peter H. Stockton's, leaving him in the new county; thence up said mountain to the top; thence with the top of said mountains to the State line; thence with the same to the beginning, shall be erected into one separate county and known as the county of Clinton.

Approved February 20, 1836.

Act to Form Metcalfe from Cumberland, 1860

Be it enacted by the General Assembly of the State of Kentucky, That from and after the first Monday in May, 1860, all that part of Cumberland, Barren, Green, Adair, and Monroe counties included in the following bounds shall be erected into one district and known as the county of Metcalfe, to wit: Beginning one mile west from Dripping Spring meeting house in Barren County; thence a straight line to Lazarus' store; Provided said line will exclude the residences of William Winlock and W. J. Wood. If said line will not exclude said residences, making an angle at said residences, so as to exclude them, and then to Lazarus' store as before named; thence on the same course to the Hart County line; thence with the Hart County line to the Green County line; thence with the Green County line to the junction of the south and east forks of the Little Barren River; thence a straight line to where the Cloverdale and Greensburg roads crosses the Caney Forks Creek; thence a straight line to intersect the Green and Adair County line, near the Pleasant Ridge meeting house; thence a straight line to Hiram Pendleton's (leaving him in Adair County); thence up the East Fork Creek with its meander so as to include the residences of James Estes, Thos. Estes, Wm. Pennick, J. L. Yates, Jane Estes, A. York, J. H. Hamilton, P. T. Ellison, Sebastian Bell, Z. D. Wheat, Herbert Kinnaird, Harrison Kinnaird, J. B. Dixon, Eliza Kinnaird, William Hamilton, Edward Hamilton, and S. W. Marrs; and thence with meander with said creek to its head waters; thence a straight line to the nearest point to intersect the Cumberland County line; thence with the Cumberland line to the head waters of Marrowbone Creek, above Arch Ferguson's; thence a straight line to William Morrison's who resides one half mile above Matthew Amy's (leaving said Morrison in Cumberland County); thence a straight line to the nearest point in Monroe County line; thence with the Monroe County line one mile from the Barren County line; thence a straight line to intersect the Monroe and Barren County line, at a point where a straight line from the beginning will include the residence of P. W. Grinstead, Esq., thence to the beginning.

Another rest period of 16 years after Metcalfe County was taken from Cumberland County quietly slipped by until that portion of the county known as Rock House settlement brought about another controversy. The citizens of Rock House Bottom, having to cross the river twice to get to Burkesville to attend court and other county affairs, ask for an annexation to Russell County, for convenience, and through the efforts of Dr. Godfrey Hunter, who was Representative from Cumberland County at that time, 1876, Cumberland County yielded her last portion of land, leaving her with the present size of 387 square miles. (A Govt. survey made 1940 showed it to contain 313 square miles.)

An Act, 1876

All that portion of Cumberland County known as Rock House Bottom, east of a line running as follows, to wit: Beginning at the Russell line where it crosses the top of the dividing ridge between the Sycamore and Sand Lick creeks; thence running on said ridge to the river at the mouth of Buck Branch; thence with said river up to the Russell line; thence with Russell line to the beginning, be, and the same is hereby attached to Russell County.
Approved February 28, 1876.

CONSTITUTIONS

Kentucky has had four Constitutions to the present. The first one was framed, April 1792. Much dissatisfaction existed, due to its failing to meet the needs of the people in general.

The second was framed in 1799 to go into effect June 1, 1800. It met the needs of the people for a while. The greatest reform was in the elections. It provided that the Governor and Senators be elected by the popular vote of the people. The office of Lieutenant Governor was established and made elective. Most county officers were appointed by the Governor.

Corruption soon found its way into the appointing system. Especially was this true of the Sheriff's office. By the Constitution of 1799 the County Court should recommend two of its senior members for Sheriff. The Governor would appoint one of them and send in his certificate, whereupon he would sell out to an outside man, recommend his appointment, and refuse to accept his own appointment. And as the State paid the salaries, which were good, the Sheriff would hire deputies for a mite and live on the balance. This gave rise to Governor Desha's declaration that he was going to appoint no one who was not on the bench and might pay the deputies, dismiss the principal, and save that money.

The third Constitution was made in 1849 and went into effect 1850. Michael L. Stoner represented Cumberland and Clinton counties in the Convention at Frankfort. The greatest change wrought by this Constitution was that of electing all the county officers by the vote of the people. Taylor County having been organized in 1848, making 100 counties, the election of May, 1851, put 100 County Judges and 12 Circuit Judges into office by the new method.

The Civil War having come and gone it became necessary to remodel the Constitution again, so in 1890 the fourth one was framed and is in force yet. J. A. Brents represented Clinton and Cumberland in this Convention at Frankfort.

The change under this Constitution that most affected the county was that relating to the Sheriff. Prior to this the Sheriff was elected for two years and could succeed himself another two years, but under this new one, his term was changed to four years and he was disallowed to succeed himself.

Under separate headings will be found the changes that took place in Cumberland County during these different periods.

Cumberland County, Ky., Order Book A, Page 1

Be it remembered that at the house of Samuel Burks, Esq., in Cumberland County, Ky., on Tuesday, the second day of July, 1799, agreeable to an Act of the Assembly passed at the December Session, 1798, entitled, An Act for the forming of a new county out of the county of Green. A Commission of peace from His Excellency, James Garrard, Esq., Governor of Kentucky, directed to Isham Burks, Thomas F. Lowery, John Irvin, Joseph Black, David Hutchenson, Alexander McFarland and John Thurman, appointing them Justices of the Peace in and for said County. Absent, David Hutchenson and Alexander McFarland. And thereupon Isham Burks, first mentioned in said Commission, administered the several oaths prescribed by law to John Thurman, John Irvin, Joseph Black, and Thomas F. Lowery, Esqs., and thereupon, John Thurman administered said oaths to Isham Burks, Esq.

Hannaniah Lincoln produced a commission from His Excellency James Garrard, Esq., appointing him Sheriff in and for said county, which was read, who thereupon took the several oaths, prescribed by law, then entered into bond with Samuel Burks, Moses Kirkpatrick, Exachel Williams, John Vandevance and William Caldwell his securities in the penalty of $3,000, conditioned as the law directs; then a court was held for said county.

Present: Ishum Burks, Thomas F. Lowery, John Thurman, John Irvin, Joseph Black.

The building of a Court House was the first order of the July Term of the Cumberland County Court, but it was not let until May, 1800, which specifications will be found a little later in this writing.

July Term, 1799, Samuel Burks was first Tavern Keeper with the following rates fixed by the Court: Ordered that Samuel Burks, with Isham Burks his bondsman, demand and receive these rates and no more:

Lodging 6d.=about 12c.
Breakfast, dinner and supper 1/6=about 36c.
Brandy, ½ pt. 1/6
Hay, pasture and fodder by the day 6d.
Whiskey, ½ pt. 9d.
Beer, per qt. 9d.

July, 1799, Ordered that Samuel Burkes's ear marks be recorded, to wit: crap in left ear, slit and bit in right ear.

At this July Term of the Court 1799, Thomas Lewis and Jesse Bland were appointed first Constables of the county. Lewis was given the territory from the mouth of Marrowbone Creek to the upper end of the county and Bland was given from the mouth of the creek to the lower end of the county. Bear in mind this was before Cumberland County gave up part of its territory to form portions of Russell, Monroe, Clinton, Wayne, and Metcalfe counties.

July Term, Ordered that the Court be held in the house of Samuel Burks until a court house can be built. Ordered further that the Public Square be established as the seat of justice until the court house can be built.

July Term, 1799, Jonathan Smith, Alexander Martin, Robert Young, and Joseph Jones are appointed to view the best and most convenient road to the junction of Green County line in the direction of Greentown.

September Term, 1799, Upon motion of William Ray, he is granted license to celebrate the rites of matrimony in this county after making bond with Moses Kirkpatrick surety.

Isaac Denton granted license to celebrate the rites of matrimony after producing credentials of his being in communion with the Baptist Church and making bond of 500 pounds with William Wood and Hugh Campbell securities.

September Term, 1799, Reported that the road should pass through the lands of Thomas Lowery, Abraham Chaplain, Joseph Jones, James Lynn, Henry Rennicks, James Young, Robert Young, and John E. King to the Green County line.

This was the beginning of Highway 61 that leads from Burkesville to Columbia, which we shall describe later.

November Term, 1799, On motion of John Robertson and John Cape, leave is granted them to keep a ferry on Cumberland River, this county, after having made bond in the penalty of 20 pounds, with George Robertson and John Cape as their securities, and it is ordered that they keep a good and sufficient boat at the said ferry with one good and sufficient hand to take care of the same and that they be allowed for horse and man one shilling and for single man and cattle ——.

December Term, 1799, Ordered that Isham Burks, Thomas Young, Robt. Young, and Joseph Jones being sworn according to law do view out the nearest and best way for a road to be opened from Burkesville to the county line between this and Barren County in a straight direction to Barren Court House together with the conveniences and inconveniences attending the same.

This was the beginning of Highway No. 90, described later.

February 1801, Ordered that Dennis Pottinger survey all the lands from the crossing at Jackson's Ferry, Cumberland River, to Col. Lincoln's, his precinct, on the north side in the bend, from the mouth of Meshack's Creek, including the Gees and Biggerstaffs to John Ingart's Improvement.

1801, Land granted to Samuel McGee, 150 acres.

January Term, 1802, Ordered to sell to the lowest bidder the cutting down and clearing of the balance of timber on the Public Square.

January 1802, Ordered that Thomas Lincoln, on his motion, be appointed Constable of this county, he having taken the necessary oath prescribed by law and entered into bond with approved security conditioned as the law directs.

September 1798 (Green Co. Book), Surveyed for William Ray 90 acres.

1801, A certificate was presented to the court by Sarah Black for beef furnished in George Rogers Clark's Expedition. The same was paid.

Hannaniah Lincoln married Lucy Wilson, 1801. Sold his farm in Cumberland County 1814 and moved to Jackson County, Tennessee.

May and June Term, 1800, Ordered that Samuel Burks and John Thurman or either of them show to the undertakers of the jail and Court House where to lay the foundations of them.

August Term, 1800, The Reverend David Haggard produced satisfactory proof of his being in regular communion with the Society called the Christian Church of which he is a member who thereupon took the oath prescribed by law and entered into bond with Lucy Haggard his surety, conditioned as the law directs, ordered the license be granted him to solemnize the rites of marriage between any persons regularly applying with license as the law directs.

1801, Ordered that Isham Burks, Sheriff, do let out the Stocks and Pillory and whipping post to William Spearman for $5.00 in place of John Thurman who was appointed and refused to serve.

1801, Ordered paid for repairs on the dungeon door of jail.

January Term, 1800, Ordered that William Mullen, John Frances, William Jones, Alexander McFarland, being sworn according to law, do view the best and nearest way for a road to be opened from the Ferry at Burkesville up Bear Creek to the county line in the direction to Stoner's Ferry on Cumberland River and that they report the same to the Court. Moses Beck to survey it.

1799, Isaac Taylor appointed first Clerk of the County by the magistrates.

1799, Alexander Martin appointed and commissioned first Coroner of the County with Isham Burks surety.

January 1801, Hannaniah Lincoln, Sheriff, asked that the county pay his expenses to Bardstown, to "compare the polls for President and Vice-President," a distance of 90 miles at 3 cents per mile.

Also to one day's attendance at polls at the August election for President and Vice-President.

January Term, 1801, License granted to Robt. Smith, Baptist, to marry people.

May 1801, David McGill appointed Surveyor of the County.

1801, Isaac Walker and Thomas Walker both certified as owners of land in the county.

FIRST COURT HOUSE IN CUMBERLAND COUNTY

Cumberland Courts were held in the house of Samuel Burkes until the Court House could be built, which was completed in 1800.

Ordered that the Sheriff do let the Court House of the following dimensions to the lowest bidder, viz.: Length 24 feet, width 20, with good hewed logs with 12 inch face and at least 6 inches thick, wall 15 feet high with a good joint shingled roof put on with pegs, except the laths and one course at bottom, two at top and one course up each end; 12 joists sawed, planed and beaded, of oak or ash 10 by 5 inches. Upper floor to be laid with $1\frac{1}{4}$ inch plank planed on both sides; two good batten doors well nailed; two windows, one on each side, to contain 12 lights 8 x 10 inches, with good facing and shutters to be well nailed; with good iron hinges to both doors and window cases; the under floor to be laid with brick or good broad stone; the house is to be chinked with stone and pointed with lime; a good case of stairs with a good door well nailed; a good stock lock; a small gable window in each end; with a Justice's platform $3\frac{1}{2}$ feet wide, from end to end except the steps at one end; with a rail and banister neat and well done; also the steps from the lower floor to the Justice's Seat to be strong and well made; also a Justice's bench; a lawyer's bar, with the platform elevated 18 inches above the surface of the lower floor, with banisters and rail; a clerk's table three feet square, good seats sufficient to contain the Grand Jury; a sheriff's box; the Justice's platform 4 feet above the lower floor; the same to be done and completed in a good neat, workmanship-manner by the second Tuesday in December next ensuing.

George Sexton was contractor and received about $600 in English money, which was in general use at that time. This building was located east of the present one on River Street and was wrecked by the noted flood of 1826.

A new Court House was built in 1858 on the site of the present building. It was 60 feet square, made of brick with 4 rooms downstairs and the Court Room upstairs.

The Court House Commissioners appointed by the Court were: F. W. Alexander, D. R. Haggard, R. C. Logan, and A. G. Waggener.

M. G. Thompson took the contract for $7,103.00 and the old building.

This building was burned on January 3, 1865, by Gen. H. B. Lyon and his army after the records were taken out. (See Lyon's Raid.)

The third Court House was built in 1867-8. It was on the site of the one before it. It was made of brick. It was 50¾ feet square, with most of the offices downstairs and the big Court Room upstairs. The offices had stoves and the big Court Room was heated by two upright, round stoves.

The contractor to build this structure was James M. Boles. A $5.00 poll tax was levied on each of the 1537 taxpayers then living in Cumberland County to pay for the building. Boles took the contract for $18,000. The building committee were A. G. Waggener, W. J. Pace, Reubin Hicks, James Herriford, and Enoch Coop. Stone Brothers did the masonry work.

This building stood until 1933. At 9:00 p.m. on December 30, of that year, the town was alarmed when they saw the smoke and flames bursting through the windows. This being three years before water works were placed in the town, all that could be done was to hastily summon every man and boy to try to save the records which had never been molested from the birth of the county. Books were stacked and piled in the streets and stores, but on the morrow when the excitement grew less, to the mortification of the officers they found that only a portion of the records of the County Clerk's Office and a very few of the Circuit Clerk's had been saved. The County Judge, Sheriff, and School Superintendent met with the severest blow. It was the time for the newly elected officers to take their seats on the Monday following Saturday night of the fire, and some of the officers entering for the first time met with many difficulties in making the start. Tablets and ledgers, such as could be procured at the stores, served until arrangements could be made for the proper books. Cases in court had to be supplied as best as could, and many suits filed and other valuable papers were lost forever. Worst of all were the sacred ancient records of the county that told of its infancy. These were lost for aye.

The first days of the new year were spent in locating offices for the officials. These were found in the new Parkway Hotel. On January 2, 1934, a called term of the County Court was held in this hotel and an order was entered naming the Building Commission. This consisted of S. A. Cary, County Attorney; S. A. Smith, County Clerk; and the writer, then County Judge. This commission was advised to take all steps necessary for the erecting of a new Court House. Insurance in the amount of $10,000 was collected on the burned building. Every man of means within the county was contacted to locate available money which might be borrowed to finance the new building. This being the dark hours of the panic, most men who had money shuddered at the thought of lending at such a critical time. Cortes E. Eden, a wealthy farmer of the county, was the only one from whom the county could borrow. He lent $2,000 which was paid back the following year.

After a survey of the county was made, other sources had to be sought. Under the laws of the Commonwealth of Kentucky a Corporation was formed as follows:

"Know all men by these presents, That we, the undersigned, do hereby associate ourselves together to form a corporation to be known as the 'Cumberland County Holder's Corporation' which shall have no stock nor profit but to be formed for the general welfare of the county in erecting a new Court House for Cumberland County. The members shall consist of not less than 5 nor more than 9, and if at any time the Corporation be without members then the County Judge shall name not less than 5 nor more than 9; the corporation not to exist longer than 20 years, and the indebtedness which the Corporation may incur not to be more than $50,000."

S. D. Pace, President
C. W. Alexander, Secretary-Treasurer

Tanner Ottley
S. A. Cary
B. M. Jones
Dr. J. E. Bow } Members
W. C. Stearns
Wood Hannah

This Corporation, after the proper rendition of the lower courts and the Court of Appeals, respecting the title of the Court House grounds which had been given by Isham Burks, February 27, 1798, received a deed to the grounds. C. R. Hicks, after being authorized by the court, compiled the deed.

The Holder's Corporation in co-operation with the Building Committee set about again to locate funds to finance the building. Court House Bonds to the amount of $35,000 were issued to Banker Bond Company, Louisville, Kentucky, and through the courtesy and co-operation of Wood Hannah, the representative of that company, the money was obtained.

On March 17, 1934, the Fiscal Court took up the question of how to retire these bonds. An order was spread authorizing 10 cents of the county's 50-cent levy, which was the maximum, and an Emergency Tax of 10 cents be set aside, and to this amount $1.00 of the poll tax be added, all of which would constitute the Court House Fund. This has proven a wise act and one that has not burdened the taxpayers.

Edgar W. Archer, 210 Coleman Building, Louisville, Kentucky, was employed as architect to draw up plans and specifications on blue print of the building; his agreed commission being 4 per cent of the first thirty thousand of the cost of the building and equipment, and 3 per cent of the balance of the cost.

Through this homeless period the county occupied three different court houses. First in the Hotel, all of which cost the county $45 per month. Compatibility was exercised where the law allowed to lessen expenses. The second court house was over Rich T. Thomas's Garage, at the rate of $20 per month; and on March 17, 1934, the Presbyterian brick church building was rented at $10 per month, which was held until November 17, when the new Court House was ordered ready.

It was in this last temporary building that the County Court met to open the bids on the New Court House. Several bids were offered, and they varied as much as eight thousand dollars. Fred Pace of Marrowbone, this county, offered the lowest bid of $34,850. On June 25, Fred was awarded the contract by the Corporation and bound to furnish all the material and labor for the work. The material and manpower were drawn from nearly all parts of the United States east of the Mississippi River. Mr. Dix and Sons of Auburn, Kentucky, did the brick work. The first lick struck on the work was at 11:00 a.m., July 25, by Turner Silcox with a pick, while the thermometer registered 102.

Added to the low bid came the plumbing at $733 and the cost of installing the heating plant $1,497, both of which were done by William McShane of Glasgow, Kentucky. This, plus Pace's bid, totaled $37,080, on which Archer based his commission, which was $1,410. The desks, office chairs, tables, etc., cost $2,126.91; the seating in the Big Room some $3,000; and just enough books to get by with, about $1,300.

This building is rented yearly from the Holder's Corporation, and when bonds and interest on the same are retired then the Court House will be turned over to the county. (The last bond was paid off, 1944.)

Chapter 4

RELIGION

The surroundings of the frontiersmen were not such as to encourage and develop religious feelings among them, with the lurking savage red man on all sides, who had to be conquered by the pioneers; with the greed and the grasping for lands; and with bodily exposures and tortures met with in the forest and the dread of wild beasts and outward foes. But still, deep in their souls, there were the desires of religious fervor.

Our being what we are is due to two influences, that of heredity and that of environment. Each plays its part in the life of every human being, as well as that of the lower animal kingdom. Every living being adjusts itself to its surroundings to a great degree. The fish of the Mammoth Cave need no eyes, the camel of the desert needs a water tank, the water fowls need webbed feet, the wild animals and fowls of the temperate zone need their fur and feather coats in winter and lighter coats in summer.

The hardier settlers of Kentucky who had engaged in dances, duels, and pugilistic games, shed their influence in the surrounding communities. They needed a religious awakening to stir up and develop that deeper subconscience and bring its light and activity to the open.

In 1790 Bishop Asbury came to Kentucky from Virginia and preached at Lexington with great power. One old record says "The house was crowded day and night and many times the house floor was covered with the slain of the Lord and the surrounding woods resounded with the shouts of the converted." The different denominations called meetings for a closer communion with the Lord, and so much enthusiasm seized the church members all over the State that it resulted in an outburst of religion and is known in the history of Kentucky and Tennessee as the Great Revival. It commenced in 1797[*] in Kentucky and reached its zenith in 1805, but its results are felt to this day and perhaps will be to eternity.

One of the greatest "onslaught" of sinners perhaps was at Cane Ridge in Bourbon County, where Barton W. Stone had been made pastor of the Presbyterian church there upon his arrival from North Carolina in 1796. The Cane Ridge meeting was held in August, 1801. One writer says every road leading to Cane Ridge was crowded with wagons and pedestrians from all over the country, some coming from

---

[*]This revival commenced in Logan County in 1797, led by two brothers, John McGee, Methodist, and William McGee, Presbyterian.

100 miles away. As high as 20,000 people attended daily. In one week, 1,143 vehicles were registered. The revival was held in a camp in the woods, and one historian says it took 500 candles and many lamps to light the camp at night. This was not the only meeting, but Collins says its "greatest awakening after this was in the Green and Cumberland River settlements."

One observer says, "The more intelligent people did not endorse the teachings and actions of the participants in this high state of ecstasy, but we find that their continual coming drew them into the experience with the others."

As is true with all new and great experiences of the human family, especially when made up of so many different types of characters, divisions will arise; hence we find at this time a split, on account of different opinions among members, came in the different churches and gave rise to different denominations. Even the Presbyterian congregation divided over this and there resulted the establishment of the Cumberland Presbyterian Church, 1802. Little children who were converted were allowed to preach until exhausted.

Another split in the Presbyterian Church, 1803, led by Barton W. Stone, gave rise to the establishment of the Christian Church. The Baptists and the Methodists also had their troubles at this time.

Under a separate heading will be found a history of the different Protestant churches of Cumberland County from their establishment to the present. In the history of the Christian Church is an authentic Order of the Court dated August, 1800, licensing David Haggard (previous to the Cane Ridge Revival of August, 1801) minister of the Christian Church.

Before taking up each denomination separately we might state what has always been taught as the origin of the different church denominations.

Martin Luther, a German reformer who lived 1483-1546, denounced the Roman Catholic doctrine in 1517, which was the beginning of Protestantism, from which all the modern denominations sprung.

The Baptists trace their existence back to the days of John the Baptist.

John Calvin (1509-64) was the originator of the doctrine upon which the Presbyterian churches are built. He was French.

John Fox (1517-87), an English clergyman, bordered on what we call today, the Holiness doctrine. Following him came George Fox, another Englishman, who originated the Quaker doctrine, and the outcome of all of these was the establishment of the Methodist doctrine by John Wesley (1703-91).

Moses Lard and others became the originators of the Church of Christ (Anti-instrumental).

The Nazarene doctrine, an outgrowth of the Methodist doctrine, was begun at Pilot Point, Texas, by a congregation in 1908.

Religion

The Christian Church was in Cumberland County early (see Mulkey). Just a short history of the Campbells. Thomas Campbell was born in Down County, Ireland (1763-1854), and came to America, 1807. His family including his son Alexander came in 1808, to Pennsylvania. Thomas was a Presbyterian, and Alexander (1788-1866) was a Baptist at first. He landed in the height of the Protestant Reformation in America. He and Barton W. Stone, who was another of the great reformers of Kentucky, united at Cane Ridge, Bourbon County, Kentucky, and put the Christian Church on its real footing. Stone had preceded Campbell, as stated heretofore, and was the first to call the disciples Christians, as Paul at Antioch, 43 A.D.

CHRISTIAN CHURCH IN CUMBERLAND COUNTY

The earliest record of this religious organization in Cumberland County was found in Order Book A, page 46, of the court held in August, 1800, and reads as follows:

"The Reverend David Haggard produced satisfactory proof of his being in regular communion with the society called the Christian Church of which he is a member, who thereupon took the oath prescribed by law and entered into bond with Lucy Haggard his surety, conditioned as the law directs, ordered that license be granted him to solemnize the rites of marriage between persons regularly applying to him with a license as the law directs."

The first building was erected for religious purposes, 1836, on the west side of the street south of the public square, on the same spot where the present Methodist Church now (1941) stands. It was built for a union church. The structure was two stories high, the upper room being used for a school room and also a Masonic Lodge room. The lower was the church room with two doors in the east end, between which stood the pulpit bearing the motto in two-inch brass letters, "GOD IS LOVE." Facing the east were long poplar plank homemade benches.

The organization was affected near the beginning of the nineteenth century with Elim Boles, Elisha Flowers, Laheris Bowman, Dr. Joel Owsley, Sr., acting elders. Some of the early members were: Mary Ann Owsley, Mrs. Nancy Haggard, Rowen Emerson, Dr. Stoner, Mrs. Stoner, Milton King and wife, Oscar Owsley, Granville Bowman, Mrs. Elizabeth Dixon, and W. F. Owsley, Sr. (see Old Mulkey).

Some of the pioneer ministers were: Newton Mulkey, William Sweeney, John Emerson, William P. Clark. Raccoon John Smith preached occasionally from 1828 to the time he died, 1868. This first building crumbled to ruins during the Civil War. The greatest meeting of record in this old building was by Brother Clark, 1848, with 104 additions. For about eight years the congregation worshipped in the school building, which was erected on a hill near where Crawford's store now is.

The local Christian congregation realized that they needed a home of their own, so in 1869 a building was erected on a lot deeded to the trustees by Tom C. Winfrey, for which he received $350. Columbus Stone built the house; Dick Cheek and John Nickelson furnished the lumber. This building stood until September 23, 1915, when it was destroyed in the night by fire. James Hoover was the first to preach in this building. The Lyric Theater was used then until a new building was constructed on the same lot, 1916.

A committee composed of R. T. Hickerson, Nora Dixon McGee, and Mrs. Robert Richardson was selected to devise plans for a new building. Their plans were adopted, and C. W. Alexander was chosen solicitor who soon raised $4,500. A Building Committee composed of C. W. Alexander, Sr., J. E. Coe, C. E. Edens, R. T. Hickerson, and W. E. Miller was chosen, who received bids, the lowest of which was that of R. W. Collins, $5,875. Mr. Collins had for his bondsmen J. R. Keen, C. C. Baker, and Dix McComas. John H. Ritchey was Bible School superintendent and R. T. Hickerson, minister.

This new building stands on the northwest corner of the square and is built entirely of brick with rooms sufficient to accommodate ten Bible classes. It is three stories high. It is heated by two stoves downstairs in the main room which has a seating capacity of about 300.

Here is a list of the ministers who have been employed as nearly correct chronologically as can be ascertained: James Hoover, J. N. Davis, Chalmers McPherson, Robt. M. Giddings, B. S. Tipton, Bro. Reece, J. C. Hall, John S. Beasley, Charley Powell, William Baker, Lawrence Williams, J. E. Wilson, Charles Kingley Marshall, Bro. Dewese, J. E. Lewis, R. A. Stailey, T. S. Buckingham, J. M. Weddle, William Stanley, R. T. Hickerson, W. M. Atherton, Thad. S. Tinsley, and Kirby Smith who is now serving his eighth year, 1943. (Rev. H. Hyatt, 1946.)

Revivals have been held by Benjamine Franklin, Wm. Jarrett, Frank G. Allen, John T. Hawkins, H. W. Elliott, Z. T. Williams, Robert Kirby, J. B. Jones, J. Q. Montgomery, R. T. Mathews, L. O. Newcomer, Isaac T. Reneau, Mark Collins, C. K. Marshall, R. E. Moss, W. C. Montgomery, James Vernon, John L. Brant, Kay Reece, Bro. Shelbourne, W. M. Martin, M. C. Corkle, and Edgar C. Yates.

IRISH BOTTOM

The Irish Bottom congregation was organized at the little school house in 1891 by Bro. Z. T. Williams of Montpelier, Kentucky. Church work had been done here in a small measure since 1829, the little log building accommodating the members. Prior to 1829 and sometimes after that date the Christians of the Irish Bottom settlement worshiped with the congregation at Rock House, organized in 1815 by the Missionary Baptists. Isaac T. Reneau was the first minister of power to preach there who belonged to the Christian order.

The following ministers have either been pastors, or conducted Revivals at the Christian Church in Irish Bottom. The school building, of course, being used until 1904 when the new church house was dedicated, and paid for on that day by its members.

Z. T. Williams, 1891-2
Robert Kirby, 1893
Kirby and Lyons, 1894
William Baker, 1896
Rev. McWhorter, 1897
I. C. Winfrey, 1896-7
Z. T. Williams, 1903
Rev. Stailey, 1903-4
Z. T. Williams, 1904
 (dedicated new church)
T. S. Buckingham, 1904
Z. T. Williams and Schrimpsher, 1905
C. C. Lloyd and Rev. Barger 1905-6
Robt. Kirby and J. W. Weddle, 1907
J. W. Weddle, 1908
Robt. Kirby, 1909
W. L. Smith, 1910-12

J. F. King, 1914-15
J. T. Hickerson, 1916
H. Gordon Bennett, 1918
W. T. May, 1920
Rev. Soliday, 1922-3
M. R. Atherton, 1924-5
T. S. Tinsley, 1927-8
C. C. Lloyd, 1930
J. J. Cole, 1931
H. J. Conover, 1932
J. C. Darnell, 1934-5
Oscar Sutherlan, 1934-5
Revs. Mullins and Killo, 1936-7
J. W. Ball, 1938
E. Lyle Harvey, 1938-9
Edgar C. Yates, 1940-2-3-4
T. H. Starks, 1941
Tom Bledsoe, 1944
Edgar C. Yates, 1945-6

In 1893 Ashley Johnson founded the Kimberlin Heights School in which many of the last ministers were educated.

AMANDAVILLE

Amandaville is another church of the Christian order. The people worshiped there in different places until 1915. In May of that year a new church building was dedicated. The land was given by A. O. Baker. This building is on Crocus Creek, 12 miles from Burkesville.

PAOLI

This church was founded in December, 1834, at the town of Paoli, by Isaac T. Reneau, with him and O. L. Ragland acting elders and F. W. Talbott, deacon. The Wolf River Church four years later dissolved, and the members moved their membership to Paoli. Some of the members in Paoli's first years of work were: William Talbott, Lucian Talbott, Wm. A. Smith, J. J. Smith and wife Katherine, Isaac Rains and Susannah, John and Ruth Smith, G. W. Cole and Sarah, James Caldwell and Margarett, F. W. Talbott (songleader) and Rebeccah, Thomas Wood and family, Berry Reneau, Nelly Wood (daughter of W. M. Wood), Charley B. Yates and wife Emiline (Talbott), Christopher Myers and Elizabeth, Rev. Young and family, Jesse Ewing and John Wells, elders 1830; Martha Dodson. From 1850 to 1860: Malinda Wells, Anderson Wells and Lyda, Susan Wells, Nancy Wells, Leslie Wells, Ellis Crouch and wife Hannah (Wells), John N. Reneau, Tilford Neathery and Nancy. W. F. Harrison and B. F. T. Hancock, elders 1876. Lewis Huddleston member 1877, and Walker Cartwright from Adair, 1882.

Some of the weddings in the church were: Lucia Talbott and Jerry McCoy, 1835; Isaac T. Reneau and Mary G. Wood, 1838; Emiline Talbott and Charles B. Yates, 1839; Nancy Young and James M. Emmerson of Burkesville, 1840.

BAPTISTS IN CUMBERLAND COUNTY

The Baptists claim the honor, which they almost deserve, of being the pioneer church of nearly every new country. William Hickman visited Kentucky in 1776 while it was Fincastle County, Virginia, and preached a few sermons, and in the year 1780 Lewis Craig moved into Kentucky. He established a church in 1781 at Lancaster, Kentucky. Nothing further was done in pioneering Kentucky until after the Treaty of Paris was signed, 1783, when the Baptists, in a constant stream, poured into Kentucky.

The Baptists came to Cumberland County from the State of Virginia. The oldest church in this county is the log house on Casey's Fork of Marrowbone built in 1802. It was used for church and school both from 1818 until 1848 (found elsewhere).

One of the oldest and most noted of these Baptist churches is the Salem Church which dates back to July 9, 1808, when 13 charter members given up by the Casey's Fork Church, this county, to constitute a Baptist Church of Christ at the Salem meeting house, on Rennick Creek, met and drew up articles of fellowship, wherein they agreed "to give themselves up to the Lord and to watch over each other with love."

The members that signed in this organization, July 9, 1808, were: James Carter, James Baker, William Baker, Samuel Carter, Fanny Fletcher, Elizabeth Fletcher, Elizabeth Chalkley, Elizabeth Barrett, Elizabeth Ellison, Salley Cheatham, Polly Christman, Nancy Jewell, and James Jewell.

Isaac Denton and Lewis Ellison were the petitioners and the first preachers. Brother Ellison served as moderator till 1840. Brother Denton served a number of years. James Baker was chosen church clerk and acted in that capacity until 1840.

Sister Hannah Willis was the first member to join after the organization. James Carter and William Baker were the first sent to the association, for which they were paid nine shillings for attendance, 1809.

Religion

The church building was made of brick and occupied the site in the flat from which the Salem school house was recently moved. This church must have been built between 1805 and 1808, for the first Bakers settled on Renox Creek, 1805. This building was washed away in March, 1826, by the highest water on record in this county, which we shall relate later.

With the exception of the years between 1809 and 1822, the church has kept a continuous record to the present, showing what took place at each meeting which was on the second Saturday in each month most of the time.

We find listed among the early members of this church the names of Baker, Radford, Cheatham, Smith, Jones, Fletcher, Waggener, Cheek, Carter, Ferguson, Vaughn, Paull, Flowers, Gains, King, Robinson, Willis, Miller, Williams, Ewing, Newby, Taylor, Anderson, Alexander, Cook, Wood, Howard, Cary, and Ray, whose lineal descendants still are to be found in the same neighborhood.

Many colored people belonged to this church in the days of slavery and worshiped with the whites. They were called Black Members and, of course, bore only one name. The following extract from the church record will show this: "December 13th, 1823, Second Saturday, Salem Church, Cumberland County, Kentucky. Bro. Jesse Ellington is about to move out of the bounds of this church and it is agreed by the church that the clerk furnish his black people, Kit, Mollie and Mary, who are members of this church, with letters of dismissal, to join a sister church more convenient to them." It was against the Kentucky laws to preach to Negroes unless one or more whites were present.

The following extracts will show the rigid discipline by which the pioneer church was ruled:

"December, 1808, meeting to be at Mr. Goggin's the last Saturday and Sunday in this month to enquire into the standing of Sister Ferrell.

"September 13th, 1823, ordered by the church that Brothers Ellison and William Baker see Sister Sallie Cheatham, and that Bro. James Baker see Sister Cary and let them know we are unhappy because of their absence. Meeting October 1823, because of the attending on the preaching of John Mulkey and others of that order and failing to go by what we think is gospel, Sister Sallie Cheatham is no longer a member with us." (John Mulkey was a Christian preacher.)

"Second Saturday in March, 1826, no meeting on account of distress of high water."

"Second Saturday in October, 1826, agreed that the brick of the meeting house be sold on the 4th Saturday in October, 1826, after public notice be given of the same and that the money arising from the same be applied to the building of another meeting house."

"Second Saturday in May, 1827, agreed by the church that Bro. William Smith and James Baker, by subscription, try to raise money to rebuild the meeting house." This second house was built in 1827 on higher ground, where the present one stands.

The third house was built in 1869-70, and dedicated February 26, 1870, by Elder Ballenger Wright. The same one stands today, three miles north of Burkesville, on Highway 61, near the site of the Old American Oil Well.

"August 8, 1829, ordered that Bro. Lewis Ellison and James Baker bear this letter to the association to be held at Seventy-Six church house, Cumberland County, Ky." September 12, 1835, the last association was held at Seventy-Six before that part of Cumberland County merged into Clinton County.

Bro. William Carter stated to the church, at the meeting in September, 1847, that, "Woe is me if I preach not the Gospel," upon which the church granted him the right "to exercise his gift."

The following represent most of the ministers who carried on the work at "Salem Meeting House," as they termed it:

Isaac Denton, 1808
Lewis Ellison, 1808-40
William Carter, 1847-53
Elder Gardener, 1851
Bro. Thomas, 1849-57
B. T. Taylor, 1853-54
M. B. Ferguson, 1855-59
Ballenger Wright, 1860-72
G. A. Coulson, 1872-75
J. J. Porter, 1875-79
J. A. Lay, 1880-82
J. W. Morgan, 1883-84
Ballenger Wright, 1883
W. A. Hopkins, 1884
Matthew Ewing, 1886
Isaac Story, 1886

J. G. Bow
John Will Cheek
Billie Williams
E. H. Brooksher, 1887-89
W. F. Payten, 1890-92
Thomas Lewis, 1894

John S. Cheek, 1894
C. M. Morris, 1895-99
J. L. Adkins, 1900-05
Bro. Blackburn, 1901
W. M. Kuykendall, 1904
J. B. Hunt, 1906
L. L. Blankenship, 1909
James R. Hunt, 1907-09
Z. P. Hamilton, 1911-12
W. T. Dart, 1913-14
J. E. Scott, 1915-19
Bro. Howerton, 1920-21
G. H. Lawrence, 1921-25
W. R. Ivey, 1925-28
Warren W. Payne, 1928-30
R. T. Hadley, 1931-32
C. M. Day, 1934-35
F. M. Masters, 1936-39
H. C. Caviness, 1939-40
Rev. Kelly
Rev. Welch
Rev. W. O. Mers, 1945-46

Mud Camp

Mud Camp Church was organized in 1800 by Rev. Robert Stockton, Rev. John Mulkey, William Bishop, Thomas Shirley, with the following charter members: David Robertson, Sarah Robertson, William Howard, Mary Howard, Robert Smith, Dorcas Smith, Lewis Ellison, Dorcas Wisdom, Robert Galoway, Martha Galoway, Mary Ray, Elizabeth Smith, Sally Best (?). It was moved to Casey's Fork

Religion

in 1818 and united with that church which was two years its junior, while Clear Fork was one year older than Mud Camp.

SEXTON'S FORK

This church was organized in 1876. The land was donated by Isaac Garner to be laid off in two-acre lot. This church is still active.

LAWSON'S BOTTOM

This church was organized in 1879. The land was donated by M. B. Ferguson, and in 1910 the members agreed to change the church to a Union organization, embracing the Methodist, Nazarene, and Christian. Lot for parsonage from J. B. McCoy by L. D. Smith, pastor. The Salem Church members organized a church in Lawson's Bottom about 1825. Meetings were held at Goggin's home, 1808.

MOUNT PISGAH (BOW)

This church was organized in 1885. The land was donated (2 acres) by J. C. Riddle, W. G. Riddle, L. V. Riddle, P. A. Riddle, R. R. Riddle, E. E. Riddle, to J. W. Graham, J. M. Riddle, and James Scott, Trustees. It is an active church yet, and singings of old time songs are held there every year.

BURKESVILLE

This church was organized in 1901. The lot was purchased from W. F. Owsley for $300, by the Trustees, J. E. McMurtrey, Wm. Cheek, and L. Dalton. The building was finished in 1902, and was burned to a hull, November 11, 1941. Rev. J. W. Blackburn was its first pastor and died there 1903. Baptist congregations worshiped at Burkesville in rented buildings as early as 1892. Sold 1946. To Columbia Str. in 1947.

UPPER MARROWBONE

This church was organized in 1913 and is located on Highway 90, three miles above Marrowbone town. The land was purchased from W. D. Cardin and wife, and W. M. Gray and wife by E. L. Carter, J. W. Garmon, and L. A. Garmon for $55.

BRANHAM

This church was organized in 1940. The land was obtained from Rhoda Branham (widow) for $1.00, by W. C. Stearns and H. C. Caviness, Trustees. It is not far from Hegira P. O. Moved to site on surfaced road in 1947.

SULPHUR

This church was organized in 1809 after John Spears had given the land on which the old church was built. This church is still there, but about abandoned. Covered by Dale Hollow Lake, 1945.

Casey's Fork

Casey's Fork Church is an old church. It was set aside as a Baptist Church house in 1802, and used from 1818 until 1848 for church and school. Members from this church went and established the Salem Church on Renox, 1808, which has been described. The old Casey's Fork Baptist Church ceased to function about 1856.

Seventy-Six

The Baptists established a congregation at Seventy-Six in 1808, but the records do not show a deeded lot on which the building was to remain until 1823. Samuel Goodson who owned quite a bit of land there at the time and was owner of the mill after Semple died, sold to Moses Beck, Jacob Holsapple, and J. Ellis, Trustees of the Baptist Church, 4 acres and 4 poles of land for $2.00. This church has never ceased to worship at the same place.

Mount Pleasant

Mount Pleasant was an old Baptist Church on the waters of Illwill Creek. The land for the building was donated by Timothy Vincent to John Garner, James Smith, and John Pierce, Trustees, in 1855. A meeting was held September, 1850. The building was near Green Grove Post Office.

Rock House

The Rock House Church was organized as the "Liberty Baptist Church" in 1815. Joseph Matthews donated the land to Joseph Bledsoe, Geo. Chapman, Thomas Graves, Chas. Thomas, and John Self, Trustees. It was on the road from Rock House to William Jackman's Ferry.

THE METHODISTS IN CUMBERLAND COUNTY

The first appearance of Methodism in Kentucky was through itinerant ministers in 1783, one of the most outstanding of whom was Francis Clark. After the ice was broken by itinerants the State of Virginia sent out two regular preachers in 1786. They were James Haw and Benjamin Ogden. Kentucky at that time constituted one Circuit and they made it all on horseback. At the close of 1787 they could boast of 90 members in this District, and the task was so hard over such a territory the Kentucky District was divided into three at the close of the year 1787—Lexington, Danville, and Cumberland. In 1800 there were five circuits in the state with 1,741 members. In 1840 there were 83 circuits; in 1850, 123; in 1860, 173; in 1870, 213.

The Louisville Conference was instituted in 1846 and at present the state is ruled by two Conferences—Kentucky, which embraces the eastern part of the state, and the Louisville which embraces the western part. Each has 7 districts which do about the same work as the old-style circuits.

The district that contains Cumberland County is known as the Columbia District and includes the counties of Green, Adair, Taylor, Metcalfe, Casey, Russell, Wayne, Clinton, Monroe, and Cumberland, and a part of Barren and Pulaski, with 32 charges and 131 churches. (The whole Louisville division has 201 charges and 547 churches.) The presiding elder of the Columbia District is Brother Henniger. Cumberland County has four charges—Bear Creek, Renox, Peytonsburg, and Burkesville, plus one mission at Burkesville. Within the bounds of Cumberland County there are 20 Methodist churches, besides a few others wherein they own an interest. While the Methodist people were preceded by Baptist, Christian, and Presbyterian in Cumberland, yet today they own quite a few more churches than any of their predecessors.

Below is given a brief history of the different churches now working in the county.

Sugar Grove

The Sugar Grove Church was organized by the Bakers in 1815. Elizabeth, wife of Obadiah Baker, was a woman of deep religious convictions as well as one of superior intelligence. She called together the scattered settlers at a place on the banks of Little Renox Creek and got the men interested to the extent that soon there was work going on in the virgin forest of the little valley near the "sugar camp."

The building was soon up. It was made of yellow poplar trees which grew all around the camp. The building was 40 by 28 feet. This building stood as it was until 1867, when one acre of ground was deeded to Richard C. Bowlin, Chas. English, R. K. Young, Wiley Patterson, and Robt. Englis, Trustees, by Robert K. Young, this being the same lot of the original house of 1815. A new one was put up in 1939.

Rose of Sharon

This church was set up by Michael Craft and his wife Elizabeth Craft donating 4 acres of land, January 24, 1823, to George Richards, Reubin Bryson, James Guthrie, Geo. Guthrie, Benjamin Spear, and John Gentry, Trustees of Methodist Meeting House. A big spring is specified.

Guthrie's Chapel

This church was built in 1880 on land donated to the trustees, Ashford Skipworth, Philip Ellison, and B. L. Marcum, by Albert Guthrie, for whom it was named. It was burned down in 1888, and G. A. Henson solicited subscriptions to erect a new one.

Jones Chapel

This church was organized in 1881. The land was donated by Robert S. Smith and wife and C. J. Jones and wife to the trustees, R. M. Cole, R. S. Smith, and C. J. Jones.

In 1883 a tract of 105 acres of land adjoining the first lot was purchased for $290, from Mrs. F. J. Martin by the trustees, R. S. Smith, J. M. Patterson, G. A. Young, H. C. Norris, and Joe A. Traylor, for a parsonage site.

Spears' Chapel

This church was organized in 1883. Sallie Spears donated the site for the church. The church was to be open to all orthodox preachers when not in use by the M.E.S. (Mormons excepted).

Grider

This church was organized in 1869. The land, 1¼ acres, was donated by C. H. English and wife to H. C. Norris, Geo. A. Young, William E. English, and J. A. Dillon, Trustees. The same house stands today. It was erected under the directions of D. S. Boles, who preached there for three years. Named for first settlers.

Bear Creek

"Aunt" Bidsey Claywell gave land for the first log church, but this church was organized in 1891. The land was obtained from J. R. Keen and wife for $1.00.

The old building stood until 1940, when a new one with modern arrangements took its place. Dedicated July 29, 1941, by I. H. Owens.

Chestnut Grove

This church, located on the headwaters of Sulphur Creek and on the Albany road, was established in 1892. The land was donated by Mary J. Wesmorland.

New Chestnut Grove

This church was organized in 1900. The land was donated by Lucinda Garrett and her husband, J. P. Garrett, to George Jenning, J. M. Ledbetter, M. B. Capps, Trustees.

Goose Creek

This church was organized in 1897. The land was donated to the trustees of the church by George Burchett. It contains two acres.

Wash Bottom

This church was organized in 1886. The land was donated by Norman Allen to A. Cloyd, P. B. Ellison, J. N. Thrasher, Trustees. Jim Eads purchased this site later.

Mt. Union (Hegira)

This church was built in 1880, and a road to the spring in the hollow was given by J. S. E. Thrasher.

Religion

MARROWBONE

This church was organized in 1907. The land was bought from J. B. Harvey for $650 and deeded to J. D. Beck, Wm. Hurt, P. Sandidge, Trustees. It is in the limits of Marrowbone town.

HOWARD'S BOTTOM

This church was organized in 1906. The land was donated by H. C. Parrish and wife to Reubin Hicks, Alex. A. Morrison, and J. F. Radford, Trustees. The old Methodist Church was built at the place in 1830.

SEMINARY

This church was organized in 1922. The land was obtained from Thomas Booher, Sr., Thomas, Jr., Virgil Booher, and is open to all Protestant denominations when not in use by the M.E.S. ($1.00). (See Seminary School.)

BAISE CHAPEL

This church was organized in 1928. The land was donated by A. B. Baise to J. D. Wray, R. S. Glidewell, and Otis Carter, Trustees.

LIBERTY (BEAR CREEK)

This church was organized in 1919. The land was obtained in 1908 from John Rush.

DUTCH CREEK

This church was organized in 1939. The land was obtained from Mrs. Lou Wathall by A. G. Bryant, Amos Fields, and Grady Lewis, Trustees, for $25.00.

BURKESVILLE

The Burkesville Methodist Church was built in 1885 on a lot bought from R. K. Young and wife, by E. O. Grisham, W. S. Guinn, and J. L. Grecian, Trustees, for $150. The old one was torn down and a new brick with a full basement and modern equipment was built in 1940, at a cost of approximately $8,000.

HOLLY GROVE

This church was first organized on West Fork of Crocus, and in — it was moved to its present site near Bakerton. It was called Providence before it was moved.

PLEASANT HILL

This church building is on the ridge east of White's Bottom. The land was donated by J. F. Ellington.

One thing of note about this building is that it is a large structure made of one single poplar tree that grew there.

The walls, floor, ceiling, frame, weatherboarding, benches, and pew coming from this one tree tell the old story of Cumberland's virgin forest.

Some of the ministers who have held revivals at the Methodist churches in Cumberland County or have been pastors at the dates given are:

Samson Keen (1818), John F. Keen (1845-91), D. S. Boles (1869), Anthony Hicks (1824-54), Richard T. Phelps (1830-45), Chas. Smith (1830-81), Rev. Grecian (1885), James Lapsley (presiding elder, 1890), Pleasant Edwards (presiding elder 1891), A. R. Casey (1903), Wm. Phipps (1909-21), O. T. Lee (1921-5), J. C. Clemens (1888-90), Tom J. Winfrey (80's and 90's).

PRESBYTERIAN CHURCH IN CUMBERLAND COUNTY

David Rice was the Presbyterian pioneer of Kentucky. In 1783-4 he made a visit to Kentucky. A petition to Hanover, Virginia, resulted in the establishment of the Transylvania Presbytery, 1786, in Kentucky. Many presbyteries followed this one in Kentucky. The one organized in Logan County is the one that touched the lives of the people of Cumberland County. The Cumberland Presbyterian Church began in 1802 at the Synod at Lexington, Kentucky.

The uninterrupted beginning of the Presbyterian Church in this county seems to have been in July, 1830, when Rev. Caleb Weeden, a pastor from Glasgow, Kentucky, came to Marrowbone, accompanied by Joshua Barton, and preached a few sermons which seemed to be "attended by divine favor." At the close of the sermon an invitation was given to those who desired an interest in the prayers of the Godly people to come forward. To this invitation 12 responded. On the 25th and 26th of this same month Rev. Caleb Weeden came back to Marrowbone and held a revival in which many united with the church, Susan Bailey being the first one to join.

On July 26th we see the members uniting under the following resolution to which they subscribed their names:

"We, whose names are hereunto written, being desirous of the prosperity of religion in our neighborhood and in order to organize ourselves into a better form, and to secure a minister, hereby form ourselves into a society at the Marrowbone Meeting House, on Marrowbone, Cumberland County, Kentucky, within the bounds and under the care of Logan Presbytery of the Cumberland Presbyterian Church, signed, James Daugherty, Jacob Brown, James Haggard, Susan Bailey, Lucy Ann Pace, Clarissa Miller." Many were added from time to time and on April 3, 1831, David Allen and James

Ritchey were elected the first elders, and on May the 7th, T. B. Stockton, Dabney Alexander, and Daniel Williams were elected and ordained by Rev. Caleb Weeden.

Between the years 1831 and 1864 the following elders seemed to have served most of the time: Lemuel Williams, James T. Williams, J. H. Alexander, Thomas J. Cloyd, Sr., W. R. Davis, W. W. Alexander. In 1864 W. R. Davis was elected clerk, which place he held until his death, 1906.

To those who do not know the origin of the Presbyterian church we might add that the first church by that name was founded by John Calvin in Geneva, Switzerland, 1541, and from there to Scotland in 1560 by John Knox. Many of the Puritans of England preferred that form of worship to the Episcopal then in England, and in 1707 it was agreed that the Presbyterian church should be the national church, as state and church in England had to go hand in hand, which is forbidden by the Constitution of the United States. There are different organizations of the Presbyterian church in our country.

BURKESVILLE

The Burkesville Presbyterian Church was built on the land donated by R. M. Alexander to R. M. Cheek, F. C. Baker, and R. M. Alexander, Trustees, in 1886; completed in 1888.

MOUNT HOPE (ARAT)

This was built in 1887 on land obtained from Z. W. Cloyd and wife by W. R. Young, A. L. Cary, H. L. Carter, and Lonus Cloyd, Trustees, for $82.00 from sale of old church.

LOWER DUTCH CREEK

This church was built, 1914, on land obtained from M. V. Felkins by J. K. Buchannan, W. E. Fudge, A. M. Fudge, C. W. Gray, W. E. Davis, and J. F. Norris, Trustees.

CASEY'S FORK (LATER)

In 1881, J. M. Alexander gave 1½ acres of land ($1.00) to the Cumberland Presbyterian congregation there, which was open to all denominations when not occupied by the Presbyterians. (This church was sold to J. F. Garmon, 1895.)

CASEY'S FORK

A Presbyterian church was organized at Casey's Fork in the spring of 1848, by a Bro. William Neal, who was appointed by the Cumberland Presbytery April 10, 1848. Casey's Fork is a tributary of Marrowbone Creek. It flows into Marrowbone Creek a short distance southeast of the village of Marrowbone.

It was here in a log school building used sometimes by the Baptist members of that neighborhood that the Casey's Fork Cumberland Presbyterian Church was organized, which had regular preaching most of the time except when the Civil War upset all churches and schools of the country.

In 1878-9 a new building was erected at the place of the old one. It stood until 1898, when it was moved to Marrowbone village and became the Presbyterian Church U.S.A.

Some of the ministers that preached at the old Casey's Fork church before it was moved to Marrowbone village were: Rev. P. A. Edwards, J. B. Waggener, H. S. Parrish, James Menzick, W. F. Thompson. Afterwards, L. Layman and J. R. Crawford.

As has been related heretofore Casey's Fork was organized in 1802 by the Baptists. A full record of the minutes of that church from 1818 until 1856 is in the Baptist Seminary Library of Louisville. It will be interesting to relate here some of the entries of events which took place at the "Meeting House."

Briefly I give the Rules of Decorum of Casey's Fork:

1. The church shall be opened and closed by prayer.
2. A moderator and clerk shall be chosen by suffrage of church.
3. Only one person shall speak at a time, who must rise.
4. He shall not be interrupted while speaking.
5. He must adhere to the subject and cast no reflections.
6. No one shall leave the church without leave of the church.
7. No one shall rise and speak more than three times.
8. No member shall have liberty to laugh or whisper while in.
9. All members must be addressed as Brother or Sister.
10. The moderator shall not interrupt any member while speaking.
11. The moderator shall have the same privilege to speak.
12. If any member miss two meetings he shall be reproved by church.
13. Eleven o'clock shall be the hour of meeting.
14. Any member breaking any of these rules shall be reproved by the church as she thinks proper.

The third Saturday was selected as meeting days, and often in bad weather the scant crowd gathered at the private homes.

Rev. Lewis Ellison was their first minister, 1818-20
Rev. Carter Warriner, 1820-22
Rev. Vachel Dillingham, 1830-34
Eight years without a minister, 1834-42
Lewis Ellison, 1842-47
J. G. Wright, 1848-49
R. W. Thomas, 1849-55
Sinnett L. Summers (salary $30.75 annually), 1855-56

Thomas Alexander was elected song leader. The clerks were: Thomas Johnson, 1818-23; Thomas Barton, 1824-38; Herbert G. Waggener, 1839-48; Stephe Bowman, 1849-56.

Names of some of the members of this church follow: Peter Gearheart and wife, Ingrim Alexander and wife, Thomas Johnson and wife, Thomas Alexander and wife, Tom Barton (deacon) and daughter Sookey, Geo. King, Anderson Page and wife Fanny, Lewis Ellison, Epharim Williams, Elizabeth Martin, John Portlock, —— Chandler, Wyatt Pace, John Wright and wife Nancy, John Wash, James Turner, William Grey, Elizabeth Nunn, Betsy and Emily Dillingham, James O'Banion and wife Elizabeth, Jackson Hurt, Eva Hurt, John Hurt and wife Margaret, David Cruse, Stephe Bowman and wife Alpha, J. S. Page, Joe N. Shaw and wife Nancy.

Like all other early Baptist churches the letter of the law was applied to members who violated their rules or who they thought violated the teachings of the Bible. Note some of their strict dealings:

Dorcas Collins excommunicated for failing to attend three times (1833).

Brother Reubin (colored) excommunicated for taking a wife with one still living.

Sally Hunter tried for her transgression, but was acquitted by telling she was innocent in "jining" the Methodists.

Obedience Gearhart unfellowshiped for communing with the Presbyterians (1832).

April, 1838, "the church finds William Gray has joined in confederacy with the 'Camulit sistum' and is excluded and the church is no longer accountable for his conduct."

In 1834 a dispute arose between Wm. Gray and Geo. King over a Negro man. Casey's Fork failed to settle the dispute, and the church called on the sister churches to help. Mill Creek sent John Whitson, Ben Rush, Isaac Denton, Rice Maxey, Wm. Oldham, and Wm. Howard. Renox sent Lewis Ellison, James Baker, Isaiah Carter. Glover's Creek sent John Button, James Rush, Martin Harvey, Isaiah Smith, Joe Ferguson. Upon this they both acknowledged being in the wrong, shook hands with each other and with the members, and were restored. (How well did Jesus see fit to send out two's to do his work.)

All of those trials were taken up "after divine worship."

Flat Rock Church

One of the most famous and best known church buildings of Cumberland County was the one located on Dutch Creek, near the Burkesville-Glasgow Road about six miles from the county seat of Burkesville. It was constructed in 1853-4 and known as "Flat Rock Church," named for the massive flat rock near the building over which the Dutch Creek pours its waters and above which can be seen in the summer seasons numerous rainbows.

This building was 52x40 feet, with the eave-drip 16 feet from the ground, all made of yellow poplar, put together with square nails, underpinned with carved stone, 4 windows in each side, two chimneys, yellow poplar shingle roof which lasted till 1888, when H. S. Pace was appointed to have the building re-roofed. He contracted with P. Lloyd to furnish shingles at $2.00 per hundred, 18,000 of which it took. Its two broad doors were of the most beautiful work.

The house was bought by Mrs. Ella Carter Alexander, 1932, after a peaceful, accommodating life of 79 years.

THE CHURCH OF CHRIST

Scarcely was the Christian Church half a century old when a dissension arose among its members as to whether or not instrumental music should be used in connection with worship in the churches. It began to be talked, about 1825, but did not reach the high pitch of dissension until the Civil War. In 1851 a letter was addressed to Alexander Campbell asking him to "commit himself on the question," to which he replied that, "such aids would be as a cowbell in a concert." His later writings eased up on its use.

Its use became an issue as early as 1859 when Dr. L. L. Pinkerton of Midway, Kentucky, placed a melodeon in that church. The controversy grew more bitter as the years came and went. The greatest strife covered the period between 1864 and 1870, when it was debated by J. W. McGarvey, Moses Lard, I. B. Grubbs, and Isaac Errett, all of whom had published articles opposing its use. Moses E. Lard was the most bitter antagonist. In his *Quarterly* of 1864 he wrote, "(1) Let every preacher resolve at once never to enter a meeting house where an organ stands, (2) Let no brother from one church ever unite with a church where an organ is used, (3) Let those brethren opposed to the use of instrumental music in churches first, with kindness, remonstrate, and if the organ is brought in then let them at once, without letter, abandon the church and unite elsewhere."

In spite of the growing opposition the organ and piano have found their way into the many churches. They came mostly through the Sunday Schools of the different churches.

In the last years of the nineteenth century and the first ones of the twentieth century did this strife culminate in the establishment of two different branches of the Christian Church. One of which is the title of this story, "The Church of Christ."

About the year 1899 a minister by the name of Shrigley made a tour through Cumberland and adjoining counties proclaiming the "Anti Doctrine," which found quite a few followers and resulted in the organization of the present Church of Christ in this county, which refrains from using any form of instrumental music in its churches.

BURKESVILLE

This church was organized in the building on the grounds purchased from J. F. Young and wife, 1928, by D. F. Anderson, G. L. Collins, and J. C. Smith, Trustees.

Religion

Midway

This church was built in 1926 on the lands donated by Wm. Riddle to P. V. Irby and C. A. Coop, Trustees, a half acre lot.

Salt Lick Bend

This building was erected by the members of the Church of Christ in 1936 on the lot purchased from Robert Biggerstaff by Lex Collins and Frank Baise. One-third acre.

Christian Chapel

This church was organized in 1891, then a Christian church, at the old church on Sulphur Creek. The land was donated by Katherine Odle to J. W. Watson, J. T. Odle, W. G. Smith, and Burl Willis, Trustees. Later it was moved out on the ridge, where it now stands.

Judio

This church was organized in 1900. Dr. W. K. Richardson gave the lot to the Church of Christ.

Hickory Grove

This church was organized in 1912. The lot was donated by W. M. Smith. The building was almost demolished by the tornado of May, 1933, but is still in use.

Waterview

This is another Church of Christ.

Mud Camp

Like all of the communities of the county, Mud Camp worshiped at the school building until 1919, when Jefferson Gray gave land and Ewing Wilson later gave a piece on which the Mud Camp building was erected. (See Baptist Churches.)

Old Mulkey and Mill Creek Churches

It was in the year 1775 that 13 immigrants left their home in North Carolina and came to what was then Fincastle County, Virginia. (Later Kentucky County, Virginia.)

Philip Mulkey and wife, Stephen Howard and wife, Obadiah Howard and wife, Joseph Breed and wife, Benjamin Breed and wife, Charles Thompson and wife, and Rachel Collins were the 13 pioneers who erected cabins and built a church house, known as Mill Creek Baptist Church, in what is now Monroe County.

This church stood for 25 years, when it was burned down. These settlers built, in 1798, what is known today as Old Mulkey Church, standing in the middle of a twenty-acre woodland near Tompkinsville.

The building is of logs and the structure is in the shape of a cross, so made as to have a corner for each of the twelve apostles.

Philip Mulkey was preaching the Baptist doctrine in the Carolinas, according to his history, in 1756. His son, Jonathan, was a preacher and moved to Tennessee. His son, John, is the founder of Mill Creek Church. John disagreed with the Baptist people and moved his affiliations to the Christian Church in 1809 and preached in Cumberland County, where he organized the Christian congregation that same year, at Burkesville.

CHURCH OF THE NAZARENE

The Nazarene Church of Cumberland County is the most recent religious group to enter the county.

In the year 1908 three holiness denominations of Pilot Point, Texas, united under the name of The Church of the Nazarene. Ministers were sent out to all parts of the United States proclaiming their doctrine, which is very much like that of the Methodist people.

John and Grace Roberts were the first to enter this part of Kentucky, having held a revival at Highway, Clinton County, in the summer of 1908.

The following year they returned to Highway and Bro. Alex M. Ferguson, a citizen of Lawson's Bottom, now of Burkesville, Ky., took his wagon and team and drove John and Grace to the new church building in Irish Bottom, Cumberland County, where a two weeks' revival was conducted with much interest. Sister Grace, the wife of John, led the singing with such indelible force that it still lingers in the hearts of many yet living.

In 1910 they and Ernest Roberts, brother of John, and his wife all came to Lawson's Bottom and held another revival. It was in this meeting that the Rev. L. T. Wells was converted. They held a meeting in the Court House at Burkesville the same year.

There are at present (1946) about 100 followers of the Nazarene belief in Cumberland County, but they do not have a church building within the limits of the county. They have one organization at Lawson's Bottom in the northern part of Cumberland County which worships in the Union building at that place. Much preaching is done in outdoor tents, through the warm months of the year.

L. T. WELLS

Rev. Lewis Tom Wells is at present (1946) a great leader of this religious movement. He is a product of Irish Bottom, Cumberland County. Born November 20, 1887, on a large farm of that place owned by his father, T. B. Wells, he mastered the grades in the little school building of Irish Bottom from which he went to Olivet, Illinois, where he was graduated in 1915.

He has pastored the following churches: Lawson's Bottom; Creelsboro; Richmond, Indiana; Hammond, Indiana; Glendale, Arizona; San Jose, California; Lindsay, California; and Topeka, Kansas.

In 1926 he was elected by the Assembly at Lexington, Kentucky, as State Superintendent of the Nazarene churches of Kentucky together with 23 counties of West Virginia, which position he still occupies in 1947, except that the West Virginia district has been dropped.

The number of churches have climbed from 31 to 112 and the membership grown from 1,300 to approximately 6,000 within the first 14 years of his superintendency. He resided at Science Hill, Pulaski County, Kentucky, until 1942, when he moved to Lexington, Kentucky, during which year he still held his office, and in 1945 was re-elected for the twentieth consecutive year.

UNION CHURCHES

Ferris Fork

In July, 1854, a church was built on "Pharris' Fork" of Marrowbone Creek. The land was given by Josiah Smith and was free for all denominations, and was donated for school purposes as well. Walnut Grove was the name of the church.

Bear Wallow

This church was dedicated to both Baptists and Methodists by L. C. Butler and wife in 1907.

West Fork

This church was organized in 1876, and was built on a lot of one-half acre donated by John Hurt and wife to J. T. Norris, O. G. Willis, and John Hurt, Trustees, and was free to all Christian denominations.

White Hill

This church was built in 1905 on a tract of land donated by Mary Susan Thurman to J. W. Coffey, Riley Wisdom, and Jefferson Page, and was made free for all Christian denominations. The church house stands close to the Cumberland-Adair County line.

Claywell Chapel

This church was built in 1926 on a tract of land donated by John Claywell and was established for all denominations. It is on the Myers Ridge (by which name it is sometimes called), about three and one-half miles north of Highway No. 90, on the Irish Bottom Road. The building was burned from forest fires, April 6, 1942, and built back, 1943.

Sparks Chapel

This is a small church built on Jones' Ridge by Verner Sparks, who donated the land and material for the building in partial "recompense to the Lord for his time wasted in moonshining liquor."

Creelsboro Now in Russell County

The Creelsboro Church was organized and the house was built on a half-acre lot sold to the Trustees of the Creelsboro Church, June 11, 1822, located in the southeast corner of the town and was free for all denominations. It was sold by Thomas Graves and six heirs of Edward Flowers to the Trustees for 5 shillings.

The town was laid out in 1809, and the first proprietors were E. & E. Creel, but it was not surveyed and marked off into streets until April 22-3, 1819. Then the town was laid out by Richard Graves after Isaac Taylor had surveyed and marked 70 one-half acre lots.

UNITED BRETHREN

Smith Grove

This is the only United Brethren church in the county. It was organized and the building erected in 1908. Alex A. Morrison donated the land to J. C. Teel, Joe E. Cross, and Volley S. Smith, Trustees. It is on the ridge between lower Whetstone and Brush creeks.

This church is noted as having the largest church bell in Cumberland County. It weighs about 700 pounds and can be heard five or six miles away.

COLORED CHURCHES

Burkesville Methodist

The Burkesville Colored Methodist Church house was first built in July, 1880, on the same lot on which it stands today. The land was donated to the Trustees by Joe A. S. Miles (colored) and wife. The old house was torn down and a new one built in 1896.

Burkesville Baptist

This church was built in March, 1893, on a lot secured through M. O. Allen for the sum of $55.00 and deeded to the Trustees of the Missionary Baptist Church, Ollie Owsley, Finis Baker, Pete Tobin.

Burkesville Christian

This church was built in 1929 on a lot sold to the Trustees by John Rowe and wife for $50.00.

Religion

LIBERTY BAPTIST

This church was organized in 1892. The land was purchased from Robert Young for $20.00 by John T. Alexander, Simon Grider, William Elliott, Trustees.

NOAH CHAPEL, PRESBYTERIAN

This church was organized in 1889 and a building was constructed on a lot donated by John T. Alexander, to the Trustees of the Cumberland Presbyterian Church (colored). This old log church was abandoned and a new one built about 1933.

BURKESVILLE CHURCH OF GOD

This church was built in 1934 on a lot donated by Aunt Belle Sprowles. Fire destroyed the building in 1940, and the same year it was replaced.

MOUNT MORIAH, METHODIST

This church stands on a prominence between Marrowbone and Waterview.

Chapter 5

EDUCATION

Education in Cumberland County dates from the beginning of the county history, but to a very limited degree.

The first Constitution of Kentucky, 1792, made no provisions for public education in the State. It was the general idea in Cumberland County, as well as in the other counties, that public education was only for the poor, underprivileged children; hence, private schools were the only means by which other children could obtain an education, and this education was open only to those whose parents were able to pay the school tuition.

The schools were taught in private homes; or a few individuals would get together and construct a rude log hut for the traveling pedagogues to teach in. These schools were called "old field" schools, due to the fact that they were located in some old worthless field. The term was measured by the money available for tuition, usually two or three months.

The Legislature, in the latter part of the eighteenth century, attempted to establish in each of the counties of the State, an "Academy" or "Seminary of Learning."

The first move that was made in Cumberland County, of record, is found in Order Book A, page 266, which was entered at the July Term, 1807, and reads as follows: "On motion of Francis Emerson, Esq., James Ghoulson, Esq., and William Smith, Esq., Commissioners are hereby appointed and authorized to contract with whom they conceive competent, to locate six thousand (6,000) acres of land or any less quantity, for the use of a Seminary of Learning, agreeable to the Act of the Assembly, in that case made and provided; and make a report thereof to the County."

The Legislature of 1808 made it mandatory that a "seminary be and is hereby established in each county of Kentucky." The records show that the State donated the 6,000 acres to Cumberland County to be surveyed by the County Court and that the Court should appoint trustees to administer the affairs of the "Seminary of Learning."

Francis Emerson and James W. Taylor were appointed agents to survey the land, which they did, and made their report at the February Term, 1809. The lands were located on the headwaters of Bear Creek, near the site of the present school building that bears that name. Yet no record is available to show whether or not an academy or seminary was ever established in this county, but the records do show that other counties received some of the proceeds from this land. (See Seminary Lands.)

The Legislature made a mistake in delegating to the trustees the power or right to sell these lands for school purposes, as they would bring only a few cents per acre, not producing sufficient sums to erect school buildings, therefore the project was counted a failure in this county.

To make sure Cumberland did get this land we find at the July Term, 1813, on motion of James Fergus, the Court appointed James W. Taylor, Robert S. Ferrell, James Fergus, Jr., to establish the bounds and corners of this land; and John E. King, James Ghoulson, James W. Taylor, Isaac Taylor, and William Cole were appointed trustees of same in 1815. These were not to be free schools.

Under another heading will be found the authentic records of these Seminary Lands donated for educational purposes. Very few people of the county know how our lands were gobbled up by these seminary trustees. The intentions were good in the beginning, but later it turned out to be a scheme of speculation. Of the ten counties that once held most of the land of Cumberland County, only two perhaps reaped a benefit from the sales. The sales were made to private persons for small sums of money which were used with poor judgment; yet the spirit of education was awakened in the hearts of the early settlers.

Religion and education were so closely related in pioneer days that one building served for both. The early deeds found on record in the clerk's office of this county verify this statement. These school and church houses were made of logs cut from the surrounding forests and built on a simple plan. They were heated by large fireplaces which covered one end of the building, and were very poorly lighted and ventilated. Not only were they used for these two purposes, but for all kinds of gatherings and speakings. This is why the "little country schoolhouse" holds such a sacred place in our lives. All denominations worshiped together on church days. The schoolteacher was the source of authority on Sundays as well as on school days. His judgment was final.

It is amusing to see how frightened the people would become at the mention of a school tax. Many records of the county show how liberal they were with their lands in donating lots for school purposes provided the court would exonerate them from future school taxes, which were from two to five cents on the hundred dollars' worth of property. The hatred for England's obnoxious tax laws of Revolutionary days still lingered with them and they had much rather give of their money and other property than be forced to pay taxes no matter how low the rate.

Thus was education cradled in our county and brought up with religious teachings, the two being inseparable. The Bible was the main textbook. Spelling, reading, and ciphering to the "Rule of Three" was the course of study. Webster's Blue Back Speller was issued as early as 1783, and was used by some schools of this county until 1895. The W. H. McGuffey Readers were published, first, second, third, and fourth, in 1836-7 and the fifth and sixth in 1844. They were used in all the schools during the rest of that century. They were revised in 1891 and adopted for five years by the county superintendent. The use of numerous books followed that period, until 1904 when the textbooks were put on a state-wide basis. Change after change has taken place in the textbooks, until now they are selected by a State Textbook Commission and since 1934-5 have become free to all children from grade one to eight.

The adoption of free textbooks has brought the educational opportunities closer to each student. Many children who never had the privilege of having their desks full of books to study before the free law, are now happy to claim them as their own. Drawbacks and disadvantages are met with in all phases of life. It is thought by some that the free book induces the student to become more careless and wasteful, knowing that he will be supplied with another if that one wears out or is changed. And again, the untidy hands that handle the book one year may pass disease to a more careful child the year following. When the father compelled the son to labor for money with which to purchase his books, a higher appreciation for them was usually shown. In former days when one book had to last a student for years and perhaps for life, the mother was careful to see that the book had a nice cloth cover sewed upon it before the boy or girl started to school, and a "thumb card" was swung by a string to the top of the book and when a leaf was turned to a new lesson, the string was moved also, always with caution never to let the thumb fall on the leaf of the book. Under care of this kind little Johnnie's book could be passed on to Mary and used throughout the family. Of course there are students who go through life and never know what it means to be saving with anything. The writer has known boys to gnaw the four corners of their spellers until the book would become perfectly round, and the boy would play with it by rolling it over the floor.

In 1825 the Legislature of Kentucky passed a more liberal act whereby as few as five trustees might get together and organize a school in their immediate neighborhood. In many places in the county this was done as noted elsewhere in this writing, but the present free school system had its beginning in 1836 when Governor James Clark presented to the General Assembly of Kentucky his message urging that some plan be worked out for a free school system in the state. On June 23, 1836, Congress divided the accumulated surplus which had collected in the United States Treasury from the sale of public lands, among the states, and the states among the counties. Kentucky got almost one and one-half million dollars. In 1837 Governor Clark made another appeal to which the Legislature responded by setting aside one million of this for the establishment of a free school system; this was known as the State School Fund.

Education

Upon this foundation was established our school system. Various laws were enacted year after year regulating the tax system and the selection of commissioners and trustees in the county. In 1847 an election was held in the state, by counties, for the levying of 2-cent tax on each hundred dollars' worth of property for school purposes, and Cumberland County turned it down, with 350 for, and 417 against. This was increased to 5 cents in 1855; 20 in 1869; 22½ in 1882; 25 in 1884 with $1.00 poll, and is at present 75 cents with poll.

Many changes have taken place during the life of the county with respect to its administrative authority. Trustees of schools once collected the money, hired the teacher, and made all the teachers' reports to the commissioners. Sometimes there was one and sometimes five trustees. Sometimes there was one commissioner and sometimes five. These commissioners acted as do the superintendent today, only more simply.

In 1830 the county was divided into three districts, from each of which a commissioner was elected annually. In 1837 the state board appointed five for two years; in 1839 the number was reduced to three; in 1850 the county court appointed them for two years; in 1856 the number was reduced to one. In 1861 the county judge and magistrates appointed him; in 1884 the title was changed from commissioner to superintendent, and he was elected by popular vote of the people for two years, which was changed to four years in 1886, and that method held until 1920 when the county board was created with the power to appoint the superintendent for four years, which is still the law.

The salary of the first superintendent was $1.00 per day not to exceed 20 days per year. This was changed to $2.00 per day not to exceed 75 days per year. In 1884 the court of the county fixed his salary, and in 1888 the law gave him from 10 cents to 20 cents for each school child reported in the school census, not to be under $250 nor over $1,500 per annum.

The work of the trustee has always been donated service. Districts were first by number. In 1871 a vote was taken in all the 38 districts in the county to buy a Collins' History; 30 out of 38 refused. Trustees grumbled over the spending of any money.

Early teachers were selected to teach if they had an "English education" and could work to the "Rule of Three," but in 1842 the schools were taken out of the hands of the county and given over to the three commissioners who appointed three examiners to grant certificates* to teachers, who were required to teach three months so the districts could get their part of the State Fund. These examinations were held orally in a private room, "separate and apart." M. O. Allen tells of his first examination for a teacher's certificate. He said he was called on to spell, read, and answer a few questions in history

---

*A certificate of olden days read:
"Miss Elizabeth H. Paull is qualified to teach a Free School in Cumberland County, Aug. 7, 1860."

                                                Joseph S. Bledsoe, Com.

and arithmetic, all orally, to which the examiners replied: "You have passed as a teacher."

Teachers were poorly paid for a long time after the formation of the free schools, 1836. From 1842 to 1869, they were hired with a guarantee of from $12.00 to $30.00 per month for three months of the year. In 1869 the salary changed with a guarantee of from $30.00 to $45.00 per month for five months. The five-month schools continued until 1904, with the exception of the panic year of 1873 when they were for four months. Certain provisions governed the five-month schools: 45 pupils and up gave five months; from 35 to 45 gave four months; and under 35 pupils cut the term to three months. The Act of 1904 increased the term to six months, and the Act of 1922 raised it to seven months where it remained until 1946 when it was changed to eight months.

The old Institutes for the teachers will never be forgotten. They had their beginning in 1867 and lasted until the Legislature passed the Act of 1922 which called for their discontinuance. Teachers who taught before 1922 may sit and tell the younger teachers of that Big Family of Teachers who met together every day for a week, sometimes within the term, sometimes before the term, and discussed teaching problems. This was the teachers' normal school for 55 years. An instructor was hired by the superintendent for around $50.00 and paid for by the $2.00 fee each teacher paid and if there was a surplus from fees it went to the Teachers' Library. Cumberland never had a surplus until 1896. Our library burned in 1933.

At these week-long meetings the timidity was overcome, when each teacher was called on to take the floor and give his views on teaching and school management. Each face became familiar to all before the end of the week, and ties of love were strengthened between teacher and teacher, much like those of brothers and sisters.

Among the instructors that held the Institutes in this county were: McHenry Rhodes, Messrs. Eubanks, Peterman, Noe, and Miss Cora W. Stewand.

While little was required to become a teacher, there was little to be taught. The preparation of lessons was done with a loud hum which merged into outspoken words by all. The lessons were often prepared in book hours by singing them off in a humdrum tune, then there came a period when silence and order must prevail.

The writer having started to school at the age of four, in 1885, well remembers some of the surroundings of that day. Living two miles up West Fork of Indian Creek from the little log house made it very inconvenient to attend on rainy days when the creek road was all water. On one occasion when the creek was about waist deep to us youngsters we all joined hands, there being a dozen of us, and met the rushing tide abreast for two miles, landing in home after dark—soaked and tired out but far from being cold—to the delight of our parents who were relieved to know we were all living.

Education

This little log schoolhouse was 20 feet square, and into it were packed 45 scholars. Schools were five months long; out at Thanksgiving, just far enough into the winter to raise a two-inch blister on each heel with the new brogans.

The building was low and dark, with one door in front and two windows on each side high from the ground. The benches were made of split oak logs, with the bark side turned down, into which four saplings were inserted to support them. The split side made the seat, and the splinters that were not dressed off at the beginning of school were either worn off or very bright and shiny at the close, after five months' squirming on those backless creatures. Anywhere from six to ten boys sat regularly upon the one I did—it was next to death to occupy another if caught. By my side on that bench lay a speller, a reader, and a slate. Much caution had to be exercised to keep the slate lying on the bench, with a wriggling lad on each side and one in front and behind with their feet dangling in the air about eighteen inches from the floor. If the slate should head over onto the floor, a lad of today would think of a T-model taking off. To break one meant 20 cents more from Dad.

A "dunce stool," which was a small round board eight inches in diameter mounted on three legs one yard from the floor, to make the occupant look as conspicuous as possible, stood in the "dunce's corner" of the room, and upon a wooden peg nearby hung a "dunce cap," made of tough cloth and tapering to a point two feet from the bottom that it might fit any head. To laugh at one while sitting "robed and crowned" was a sure forecast of the next occupant.

Spelling classes were numbered 1, 2, 3, and 4. First was the highest. A headmark was given to the one who stood head of the class during the whole lesson. Five- or ten-cent merits were rewarded the one winning the most headmarks at the close of school. Spelling was by syllables, repeating every back syllable with each new one spelled. Writing was on slates. Pencils were mined in the "pencil quarry." One day some of us decided we would find out what chalk was like. When the teacher went to his boarding place for dinner we climbed upon the wall to the top crack in the house and gently removed a little wooden box. It was handed down to the other boys on the floor and they were commanded not to open until the climber had descended. We all examined it thoroughly, even going so far as to taste it. A vigil was kept. Our curiosity satisfied, it was placed back. That was the first we had ever seen. That was the last time a child had a piece in his hands that term.

I shall never forget the morning we all played until worn out before the teacher arrived. About eleven o'clock a pedestrian passing the playground told us he saw our teacher lying up the creek under a cliff drunk. Throbbing of hearts, deep respirations, scratching of heads. "My," some said, "Let's go home." Some said, "I'm afraid to go." An older lad climbed a tree near the schoolhouse and located the cliff. He saw the teacher staggering out and making for the school. Most of the children being small, a dead silence was the order the rest of that day.

During the hours of intermission the children would engage in games of base, bullpen, fox-and-hound, mumblety-peg, or marbles. The noon hours of the last month of school were used by the scholars in dragging poles of wood or old rails to be chopped up by the teacher for the next day's fuel. How vivid on memory's wall is the picture of Dr. J. A. Grider, the writer's old teacher, as he stands in front of the door of the little log house, preparing his school wood for the next day by placing one end of the pole on the ground and the other about one foot from the ground upon a rock, while with those brawny arms of his he raises high above his head a large square limestone rock, of about one hundred and twenty pounds weight which he lets fall edgewise upon the dead pole, and with a quick backward jump, discovers that one more stick is ready for the stove. Useful, useful old teacher. How different today.

In 1903 the Legislature passed an act providing for the consolidation of schools. Due to so many existing barriers in this county it has not met with the approval of the people. When the county has worked out a system of hard-surfaced roads over which school buses can travel, then districts may unite into a fewer number, but in the loops of Cumberland River where bottoms are isolated, the only plan that will work is one like that of the present, let each little kingdom have its own school.

Many changes have been made within the present century which have been an uplift to education and to the schools. In 1908 a law was passed making the county the unit. Buildings, school supplies, and fixtures were placed in the hands of the county board to be paid for with tax money. Back in the nineteenth century all the buildings were kept up by the districts. New districts under this new law may be formed by the superintendent and his board.

An extract from the superintendent's report from this county in 1890 gives 44 school buildings for white pupils valued at $120 each, and 3 buildings for colored pupils at $100 each.

In the county at present there are 48 rural school buildings for white pupils valued at $75,000, and four for colored pupils of about the same value each. The white districts employ 62 teachers and the colored employ one each. In recent years, substitute teachers are selected by the board in case the regular teacher is compelled to be absent for a short time. Previous to this the teacher would leave the school in charge of one of the older students, which usually brought about a bit of misconduct by the other pupils.

The salaries of the teachers have climbed from the first free school to the present year. Under the law which placed the per capita as a basis for teacher's salaries, a scramble was made by the teachers who held first-class certificates, for the large districts having about one hundred children in them. This brought about dissatisfaction. Bribes were used to secure the big schools, and often the third-class schools which could be taught by teachers holding third-class certificates had the greatest number of advanced students in them. In these little districts then the teacher would become much embarrassed when some of the pupils would cause him to "stick up in arithmetic." Teachers who were able to get the schools that had 90 children at the rate of $2.10 per head were thought of as occupying a higher class than the teacher whose district had 35 children in it.

As a contrast to the report of 50 years later, I publish the following:

CUMBERLAND COUNTY, KENTUCKY, 1898

FIVE-MONTH SCHOOLS
T. S. Scott, Superintendent

District No.	Teachers	Salaries
1.	A. A. Huddleston	$307.80
2.	Alice Alexander	127.12
3.	J. W. Baker	123.12
4.	Sam Cary	118.56
5.	Ethel Cloyd	132.24
6.	C. B. Jones	109.44
7.	O. C. Collins	102.60
8.	Addie Jones	143.64
9.	Pearl Alexander	102.60
10.	Guy Davis	102.60
11.	J. T. Huddleston	186.68
12.	Nannie Huddleston	102.60
13.	Carrie Alexander	150.48
14.	Maude Perry	109.44
15.	C. V. Davis	102.60
16.	R. D. Bass	191.52
17.	J. F. Allen	164.16
18.	D. J. Frazier	134.52
19.	Armead Young	196.08
20.	Fayette Simpson	141.36
22.	L. L. Cary	148.20
23.	Irbie Shepherd	102.60
24.	S. D. Rainey	157.32
25.	Minnie Glidewell	186.96
26.	J. E. W. Moore	193.80
27.	Dora Huddleston	228.00
28.	L. S. Rush	168.72
29.	C. F. Glidewell	118.56
30.	Sarah Mullinix	186.96
31.	Cinda Davis	148.20
32.	J. C. Ewing	102.60
33.	E. H. Guthrie	102.60

34.	Bettie Simpson	228.00
35.	W. B. Smith	145.92
36.	Belle King	209.76
37.	J. L. Carver	200.60
38.	S. P. Leveridge	109.44
39.	J. T. Glidewell	114.00
40.	Vinnie Williams	129.96
41.	Sarah Huddleston	129.96
42.	J. I. Ewing	111.72
43.	Florence Mackey	139.08
44.	G. R. Hicks	152.76
45.	Bernice Bow	123.12
46.	C. R. Hicks	164.16

In contrast to the report of 50 years ago:

CUMBERLAND COUNTY SCHOOLS, 1940

Seven-Months Schools
E. E. Garrison, Superintendent

School and Teacher	Salary
Salem, Pearl Black	$514.25
Lewis Creek, Maggie Baker	538.00
Holly Grove, W. B. Smith	510.50
Lawson Bottom, Letha Bledsoe	552.50
Irish Bottom, J. W. Wells	372.50
Elliott, Mrs. Shelly Norris	627.00
West Fork, Robert A. English	469.75
Jones Chapel, Josephine Strange	517.25
Jones Chapel, Nell W. Thomas	506.50
Sugar Grove, Beulah Cash	487.00
Sugar Grove, Olene Huddleston	476.50
Jones Ridge, Shelly Norris	510.50
Morgan, Bertha Williams	625.50
Black Gnat, Mrs. W. T. Anderson	514.50
Leslie, Mrs. Lucy Garrison	514.50
Leslie, Janet Flint	559.50
Ashmole, Nettie J. Sartin	474.00
Leatherwood, Walter Fudge	508.50
Pitman, Mrs. Walter Fudge	508.25
Mud Camp, Della J. Morgan	514.25
Young, Nina Cary	524.00
Allen Chapel, Grady Armstrong	509.00
Moores Chapel, Helen Stockton	552.50
Salt Lick Bend, Madie Appleby	508.25
Judio, Jewell Murley	508.75
Bear Wallow, Mary Welsh Hoots	422.00

Kettle Creek, consolidated with
  Ashlock and Bear Wallow.
Xerxes, Rettie Williams 524.50
Spears, William Wells 622.50
Spears, Ethel Anderson 508.50
Pleasant Hill, Van Anderson............................ 497.00
Poplar Grove, Milland Shepherd.................... 503.00
Gains Hill, Clarence Carter.............................. 516.25
Guthrie's Chapel, Lillie Garner....................... 503.75
Guthrie's Chapel, Mary Newby....................... 626.50
Elm Shade, Willard Garner.............................. 516.00
Slate Hill, Mary E. Flint................................... 487.50
Beech Bottom, Lyle Webb................................ 492.75
Cary, Mrs. Letha Hunter.................................. 551.50
Ashlock, Mrs. Dewey Wells.............................. 530.25
Stony Point, James Stephenson...................... 562.50
Bow, E. E. Shepherd... 350.00
Bow, Mrs. Ray Logan.. 557.75
Chestnut Grove, Ray Logan............................. 619.25
Chestnut Grove, Vela Norris........................... 512.50
Hegira, Mollie W. Scott.................................... 518.50
Hegira, Golda Graham 519.25
Seminary, Will E. Hunt.................................... 511.25
Seminary, Nell Hunter 483.00
Vincent, Clarence Rush 516.50
Vincent, Carl Williams 484.75
Bear Creek, Jim Harry Flint............................ 521.25
Cedar Creek, Claude Rush............................... 576.00
Cedar Creek, Lewis Williams.......................... 475.75
Goose Creek, Ruth H. Thomas........................ 492.50
Howards Bottom, Regina Morgan.................. 536.00
Smith Grove, Susie Radford............................ 507.25
Myers Ridge, Herbert Easter........................... 653.25
Myers Ridge, Mrs. Herbert E. 646.00
Little Renox, Golda Booher............................. 502.50
Cherry Tree Ridge, Roy Welsh........................ 393.25

COLORED SCHOOLS OF THE COUNTY

Bakerton, Bessie Adams $621.50
Beech Grove, Flora D. Allen............................ 615.50
Marrowbone, Eliza Ellington 353.00
Coe, T. E. Coe.. 353.00

The school per capita reached $4.00 in 1912 and ranged from that to $8.00 until 1934, when it went to $11.00. It stood at $11.00 and $12.00 until 1943-4. The $3,000,000 appropriated by Governor Willis raised the per capita to $17.66; and in 1944-5 it climbed to $19.16. The Teachers Retirement System went into effect July 1, 1940. It is a retirement annuity system to compensate old teachers, retiring at the age of 60 or compulsorily at 70 years of age. A small per centum of the acting teachers' salaries together with aid from the State constitute the upkeep.

A survey in 1944 showed 411 teachers receiving annuities in Kentucky. Of this group 63 per cent lived in town, the rest in the country; 46 per cent were in good health; 97 per cent happy, 3 per cent not; 90 per cent church members; 80 per cent owning their homes, some of which were small; 8 per cent pay income tax; and 17 per cent depend on their retirement annuity, which ranged from $100 to $300 annually. Cumberland County started with 2, J. W. Wells and J. E. W. Moore, each receiving a bit over $100 annually. Wells teaching 32 school years; Moore 45. Thirty is the minimum. In 1946 the Kentucky Legislature trebled this annuity.

SCHOOLS OF CUMBERLAND COUNTY

Clear Fork

Many hardships were endured in the early schools of Cumberland County. Most all of the teaching was done in buildings other than school houses—such as mills, barns, cribs, sheds, and often in tents made of skins. There came a period in the county's history while the Seminary spirit was engaging the minds of the people when they saw that good government and a righteous people had to go hand in hand with education. The use of separate houses was soon discovered to be the best way of collecting the children for educational purposes. Houses were built for a long period of time to accommodate both church and school. One of the first of these in the original county was the one at Clear Fork of Spring Creek (now in Clinton County). The land was given to the trustees of the Clear Fork Baptist Church by Jacob Myers, November 25, 1815, three-fourths of an acre in size, "for the purpose of a school." And if title is not good, "said Myers is to give back $6.00 and be exonerated from all damage."

Irish Bottom

This is one of the oldest schools of the county. The land was granted to the Irish Bottom church and school November 16, 1829, by Elisha Embree and Nancy Embree, his wife, for "education and worship." A deed was made for the same lot only larger, May 14, 1888, by J. P. C. Fergus and Nancy, his wife, and "included the lot where the old house is now standing." The new house now standing replaced the old log building in 1888-9 and was paid for by district taxation under the new law of 25 cents and $1.00 poll. The first school taught in the new building was a subscription school, 1889, by P. M. Sewell; and the first free school by Frank Carnes, 1889. Fergus received $25.00 for the lot, seven-tenths of an acre.

Education

BURKESVILLE FEMALE ACADEMY

The school was conducted in a building which occupied about the site where the present New Methodist church stands. The two lots of one-half acre each were purchased from the President and Directors of the Bank of the Commonwealth of Kentucky, by the Trustees of the Burkesville Female Academy, for $75.00. The structure was put up in 1836 and stood till 1895, when it was condemned by T. S. Scott, Superintendent, and sold.

FERRIS FORK OF MARROWBONE

A building known as Walnut Grove was erected prior to 1854 on a tract of land donated by Josiah Smith, a friend to "morality, religion and education." It was used for school and church both. A new building stands there now.

CLAY LICK BOTTOM

In 1856, W. E. Carter and Eliza, his wife, donated a tract of land containing one acre, for school and church, to the Trustees of Clay Lick Bottom School and Church.

HALL CHURCH AND SCHOOL

In 1856, a two-story building was constructed on May's Branch on a one-acre tract of land lying on the east side of said branch where the Hanover Road crosses. It was bought from Reuben, Philip, and James Alexander, and the upper part of the house was to be used alone for "Masonic purposes and the lower for church and school." "If discarded the land should go back to the heirs and the house to the subscribers to the building." This was old Ashmole, near the new school building by that name. The Hanover Road was what is now Noah Hollow Road.

BEECH GROVE

In 1857, a four-acre tract of land was donated to school and all denominations of worship. It lay between the waters of Big and Little Renox creeks, and was given by John Fodge and Polly Fodge.

GOOSE CREEK

In 1858, a tract of one acre was sold to the Trustees of Church and School of Goose Creek, by George Scott and Sally Ann Scott. This was just above the present school.

ELLIOTT SCHOOL

In 1859, one and one-quarter acres of land on Crocus Creek was sold by Robert Elliott and R. G. Cole to the Trustees of Elliott School District. Consideration, $5.00. This was used until 1936, when a new school building was erected on the two-acre tract purchased from Robert Baker and Lucy Baker for the sum of $100 (1935).

Christian College of Burkesville

In 1859, the old Christian College of Burkesville was established by the Christian Church. The building was located on the west side of High Street, about half way down that street. It was made of brick and was in the shape of the letter T. It, like most school buildings of those days, was paid for by public subscription. George Bicksy, a Yale graduate, taught in this building. It was destroyed by fire and a second one was put up. In this one we know of James Hoover and J. U. Biggers having taught.

Clover Creek

In 1874, J. H. Neeley sold, for one dollar, one acre of land from his farm for school purposes, and a house was erected and used until ...., when it failed to be used and reverted to the Neeley farm.

Rock House

In 1874, a tract of land in Rock House Bottom, on which the Liberty Meeting House had been built, was set aside by the Trustees of the Church for school purposes as well as worship. C. S. Jones, F. M. Snow, and Israel Winfrey, Trustees, authorized S. T. Lester, School Trustee, to have school taught in the building.

Caseys Fork Creek

In 1876, James M. Garmon and America Garmon sold for $1.00, one acre of land on Caseys Fork, at the mouth of Wisdom Creek, to the Trustee, for school purposes.

Guthrie's Chapel

Guthrie's Church building was used for worship and school from about 1880 till 1894, when John A. Guthrie sold for $1.00 one-half acre of land to the Trustees of the Common School District for free school purposes.

Caseys Fork

In 1881, a tract of one and one-half acres of land adjoining J. L. Garmon on Caseys Fork was deeded to the Trustees of the Church for $1.00 to be used for school purposes; it "being the same lot on which the new church now stands," said the old papers.

Raft Creek

In 1884, one acre of land was deeded to the School District on Raft Creek waters adjoining the Three Log School House. Said tract was donated by William R. Neeley and Lucy, his wife. In 1884, Elizabeth Webb donated to the Trustees one acre near the head of Raft Creek for school purposes.

Education

LOGAN SCHOOL

In 1888, John A. Logan donated one acre to Trustees of District 48 (not the present 48th District) for school purposes, only.

LEE SCHOOL

In 1883, William Lee and wife donated one acre to the Trustees for school purposes so long as used.

THREE LOG SCHOOL

This is one of the oldest and most noted of all school buildings. It was built in 1832 near what is now Stony Point. The deeds give it (1832) this name because it was erected with only three logs to the side, poplar trees some five feet through hewn flat.

SEMINARY

In 1860, a tract of two acres of land was sold by William Harper of Clinton County to W. L. Wright, W. D. Wright, Davis Riddle, James Summers, and John Vincent, Trustees of the Methodist Church, in the Seminary, to be used for school purposes and worship for all denominations. Consideration, $1.00. First Methodist log house alluded to was built on the Seminary land here in 1807 for church and school, but not an Academy.

HAGGARDS BRANCH

In 1865, one-half acre and five poles of land was bought from D. B. Williams, H. E. Williams, and Victorie Williams, being part of the lands of R. L. Williams, deceased, for school purposes. It was used until ...., when it reverted. It is now (1945) occupied by Boyd Cary.

WASH BOTTOM

The first school building was constructed on a parcel of land donated by T. C. Duerson in 1867 to be used for school and church purposes. This was used until .... when it reverted. A new school building was erected in 1913 for this neighborhood on a tract of one acre of land bought from Robert Armstrong and wife, which took the name of Allen's Chapel. Consideration, $40.00.

SALT LICK BEND

In 1869, a tract of 48 poles was sold by James Humes and Caroline Humes to the Trustees of Salt Lick Bend School, on which a house should be erected for school and church purposes. Consideration, $1.00. This was used until .... In 1884, Joe M. Baise donated one-fourth acre for schools. In 1912, a one-acre tract was purchased from B. F. Coe and Martha Coe for $75.00, and a house was erected the following year; and in 1925 another tract adjacent thereto was purchased from Geo. L. Armstrong for $100. This building is still in use.

Alexander College

The Alexander College that stands today is a great landmark in Cumberland County. In March, 1871, a deed to the Trustees of the "Presbyterian Church and College of Burkesville," was made by Nancy G. Alexander, Wm. F. Alexander, P. P. Alexander, W. G. Hunter, Sue A. Hunter, and others, for three acres and 78 poles, on which the old college was built. The land cost $697.50. This structure was put up in 1870 at a cost of $15,000. It burned down in 1883 and was rebuilt in 1886. It was later transferred to the Trustees of Alexander College. The first building was paid for by contributions from the Presbyterian people scattered over many different states. It was through the tireless efforts of J. P. McMillan that the work was finished. Prof. McMillan was chosen president of the school and served for the first 25 years of its life.

The land and buildings were sold to private persons in 1909, and the spirit having risen to a high pitch for a non-sectarian school, and with determination to overcome all hazards to educate the boys and girls of this and surrounding territories, the people went to work and raised $21,000, and built an up-to-date structure* of brick with two dormitories, all of which were placed on an eminence overlooking the town from the west. A heating plant was installed and through the persistent work of the women of the town and county it was well equipped inside. Prof. Charles R. Payne was chosen president** and all things went well for two years, then the brick began to soften and run down the sides of the building. What now? The spirits which had been running so high educationally commenced to fail. Danger was predicted for the attending students, so the best thing for all seemed to be to dispose of the costly structure as advantageously as we could. So it was auctioned off and bid in by W. E. Miller for about $5,000.

This left Burkesville again as a renter for a short time, but the minds of the hungry people began to swing back to the "rejected stone," the Old Alexander College. So it was repurchased by the Board of Education and a public elementary and high school was started. It has undergone various changes since then. In 1935, through the solicitation of S. M. Young and C. M. McGee of Burkesville, a gift of $10,000 by Joel Cheek of Nashville, Tennessee, who was raised in Cumberland County, was secured with which a new and up-to-date gymnasium and auditorium were built. This has meant as much to the youth as the school building. In 1936, through the efforts of Leon Cook, superintendent of the Burkesville graded and high school, together with those of S. M. Young, chairman of the Town Board of Education, a W.P.A. grant was made and the building was changed into a modern school structure with steam heat and a sanitary water system. The same year the women of the town solicited subscriptions for roll tapestries for the stage, which amounted to over $400.

---

* Three-story with 16 rooms.
** January 5, 1909, first term.

Education

Today Burkesville can boast of one of the best high schools in southern Kentucky, with an attendance each year of about 500 boys and girls. Since the above was written this college was destroyed by fire, May 7, 1947.

A story of how James P. McMillan got to Burkesville in 1871 to take charge of the school in the new Alexander College, shows the ill conveniences of the times. The story is told in his own language:

"The unfraternal steamboat failing to meet me at Burnside, I purchased a frail bark and set sail for Burkesville, about 100 miles down the river. I stopped and stayed all night with a nice family near the stream. On the morrow I was sailing through Fawbush Shoals at a rapid speed when my bark struck an invisible object, upset in deep water, and left me struggling for my life. A few minutes found me safe to the shore, wet, cold, trembling, and robbed of my valise, filled with all the clothes I had and twenty-five of my best sermons, to be seen no more.

"A kindly lady comforted me with a good fire, while her husband took his canoe and took out after mine and brought it back up the river. Being dried, I took off on the voyage again and stayed a second night with a former student. After a Sabbath Day's journey I landed at Burkesville. My joy was marred when I was told soon after my arrival, that they had understood while on my way down to Burkesville I had joined the 'Campbellites.'"

Later principals of Alexander College are: Lewis Clifton, Rev. C. R. Payne, P. L. Hamlet, Rev. R. H. Wade, Leon Cook (10 years), N. J. Anderson (3 years), R. A. Palmore, Jerry Bowman. Grade teachers of long standing are: Nida Miller, Thelma and Beulah Baker, Mrs. Lura Reeder Fudge. William P. Maupin (colored) has served 30 years as janitor.

WESTERN NORMAL

Kentucky has two state normal schools for the convenience of her students who wish to complete their training for teachers. One is located at Richmond, Kentucky, and the other at Bowling Green. Cumberland County is in the Western, or Bowling Green District. Hundreds of students have attended this school since its organization in 1907.

I here quote a statement found in the *Cumberland News* of February 6, 1908:

"The Western Normal, though only one year old has enrolled 1,084 students with the following from Cumberland County: Misses Lee Cheek, Mattie Glidewell; Messrs. Irvin E. Beck, L. L. Cary, U. B. Collins, Roy Helm, and W. M. Gray. We commend these young people as being the first to attend this institution from Cumberland County."

Prior to the year 1876 the young people of Marrowbone had to go to Pleasant Hill or Caseys Fork to school. In the year 1876 a three-months school was opened at Marrowbone to run under the leadership of Cassius Breeding as teacher. Following this was added a two-months subscription school, making the term five months. This subscription school was carried along here as in other villages and towns for many years. Only the ones who were able to pay the tuition could attend. The building had additions as time went on, and so was the term lengthened and the faculty increased to take care of the enrollment. The first high school class was graduated in 1923.

In 1925, Gilliam Norris of that neighborhood, later of Louisville, sponsored a movement for a new high school building; and the following year the school moved into a new brick structure near the highway. Mr. Norris named it Martha Norris Memorial School in honor of his mother. The school was changed to a county high school in 1934. Further conveniences were: a gymnasium in 1937, a free bus in 1938, and a farm shop, 1941.

Edwin and Gilliam Norris of Louisville have helped to promote education in the Marrowbone valley with their contributions.

Poplar Grove No. 27

This school was begun in 1885. The land was sold by J. M. Ledbetter and wife to Trustees for $1.00. It is on the ridge of the head waters of Kettle creek.

Lawsons Bottom No. 8

This building was erected in 1892 on a parcel of land sold to the Board of Trustees by Moses B. Ferguson for $20.00, one acre.

Howards Bottom No. 23

The land on which a schoolhouse "should be caused to be built" was sold to the Trustees, 1894, by Susan M. Smith, for $12.00. An additional lot was added in 1916 by Antha Keen and C. P. Keen for $47.50.

Pleasant Hill No. 26

This school had its beginning in 1894. James Ellington and wife donated the lot of one acre, for "good will and love for education."

Bow No. 36

Bow was deeded to the Trustees for the school, 1897, by W. G. Riddle, and M. E. Riddle, for "love for children." One acre.

Gaines Hill No. 28

The land for this schoolhouse was donated, 1906, by G. A. Henson and Mary E. Henson.

Education

BEAR WALLOW NO. 22

In 1909, one and one-fourth acres of land was sold for $1.00 by John Logan and Mary Logan for school purposes.

KETTLE CREEK NO. 23

Kettle Creek school site was purchased from W. T. Blythe and wife, 1909, and from W. H. Wells and wife. It was abandoned in 1937.

MYERS RIDGE NO. 46

This school was set up in 1909. A four-acre tract of land purchased from Geo. W. Bowen and Mary Bowen for $10.00 constitutes the site. The old school was established in 1865. The land (one acre) was donated by Jordan Easter, Sr.

CEDAR CREEK NO. 42

In 1909, William Glidewell and Hettie Glidewell sold to the Board of Education two acres of land on Bear Creek and near Cedar Creek for school purposes. Price paid, $50.00.

SEMINARY NO. 40

In 1910, two acres of land was purchased from J. A. Pharris and Lizzie Pharris, and house was built which is still in use.

SLATE HILL NO. 31

This school was started in 1910. The site was purchased from M. W. Hood and A. D. J. Hood for $15.00, one acre.

WEST FORK NO. 6

This school was set up in 1910 on a tract of land purchased from the Lacy heirs for $25.00.

LEATHERWOOD NO. 15

In 1910, a tract of one and one-fourth acres of land was sold to the Board of Education for $1.00 by C. L. Faulkner and wife for school. The school operated there until 1933, when a great freshet swept the building away. Then the school was transferred to Hominy Creek and a one-acre tract was bought from Rene Anderson and wife for $75.00, and a new house erected.

CARY NO. 33

The Cary school was set up in 1911 on a tract of land bought from V. T. Cary, Walter Cary, Maude Cary, and Valerie Cary for $1.00. It is on the ridge east of Salt Lick Bend.

LESLIE NO. 13

This school site was purchased from Lewis Stockton and wife, 1912, for $22.50. It contains one-half acre.

Vincent No. 39

The tract on which this house was built was purchased from Rhoda Wolfe in 1912. Its area is one and one-fifth acres and it cost $30.00.

Mud Camp No. 16

In 1911, one acre and 8 poles of ground was purchased from S. H. Smith and wife for $40.00 and a schoolhouse erected thereon.

Beech Bottom No. 32

In 1914, one acre of land was deeded to the Board for school on Sulphur Creek, by J. B. Murphy and Mary Murphy.

Moores Chapel No. 19

In 1914, three-fourths acre of land was deeded to the Board by E. L. Cary and Fanny Cary for school purposes. It is near Leslie on Stockton Ridge. Price, $25.00.

Jones Ridge No. 10

Jones Ridge school site was purchased from Al Jones and Martha Jones in 1914 for $2.50. It is on the ridge between Big Renox and Crocus creeks.

Xerxes No. 24

The deed to this tract was made by A. C. Ranes and wife in 1915 for three-fourths acre. The house was built prior to the time this title was given and sold for $5.00 at the time the present one was erected.

Chestnut Grove No. 37

The title to lot 1 was made by Edward Miller and wife, 1913. It was for two acres. Lot 2 was sold to the Board, 1924, by P. V. Irby and wife for $5.00.

Judio No. 21

The deed to this school was made in 1915, and the consideration was the worth of the old building. Judio is in the southern part of the county. Land, one-half acre.

Ashlock No. 34

The deed to this school was made in 1917 by C. A. Ashlock and Lizzie Ashlock to the Board for $40.00. Amount, one acre.

Hegira No. 38

Two tracts constitute the ground for Hegira; one deeded by H. R. Watson, 1920, for $55.00, and the other by B. E. Garner and M. O. Garner, 1923, for $20.00.

Education

Martha Norris Memorial High School

The Marrowbone High School was constructed in 1925 on a tract of land consisting of four acres deeded to the Trustees by H. G. Davis and wife for $1,000.

Lewis Creek No. 1b

Lewis Creek School was taken from Salem District and lies on Lewis Creek. It was deeded to the Board as a parcel of land for education, 1931. It was a donation.

Pitman No. B

Pitman is a part of Leatherwood. It is on Pitmans Creek, a tributary of Marrowbone. Two deeds cover the district, one of 1933 by J. P. Gray, Mary Gray, Jennie Meers, W. R. Meers, Annie Alexander, E. C. Alexander, W. D. Carden, Jesse Carden, and Alice Carden. One acre. The other deed is by A. O. Sharp, special commissioner, 1934. First tract, $1.00; second, $10.00.

Smith Grove No. 45

This is a new school building erected in 1935-6 on a tract of land purchased from K. C. Smith and Tina Smith, 1934. It is close to the old building. Price paid, $60.00.

Elm Shade No. 30

This school was built about 1912 on a parcel of land deeded by A. W. Sharp to the Board, and in 1935 was exchanged for present Elm Shade land from H. N. Jones. It is on Sulphur Creek.

Jones Chapel No. 7

This school received a deed in 1934 from Sellie Thomas and Etta May Thomas of one acre for $150. The school is on Highway 61, on Big Renox Creek.

COLORED PEOPLE OF CUMBERLAND COUNTY

Cumberland County being one of the counties of Kentucky blessed with rich creek and river bottom lands, naturally attracted the moneyed men of the Eastern states. And as they came in search of more wealth they brought their slaves along with them. If you remember, as we stated before, one of the first five men to see this country was a colored man.

Cumberland County being a granddaughter of the State of Virginia, one would expect the perpetuity of slavery, for it was in that grandmother state that the first twenty Negroes were sold in 1619 to the white settlers. The early settlers usually erected a log cabin in the yard back of their dwelling for the colored man and his family. Sometimes a kitchen connected by a long floorless hall answered for his quarters. As a usual thing the black man was kind, obedient, and faithful. The good old "mammies" will never be forgotten. The happiest hour of the day to the slave man was when the disc of the sun began to touch the western horizon. Then, free from all cares of the past and with no burden of the morrow bothering his mind, he closed the day with a whoop and a song as he rocked to his haven of rest.

In 1799, there were 207 slaves besides a few free Negroes in Cumberland County. Jack Coe brought a number of Negroes to the southern part of the county at the beginning of the nineteenth century. They married Indians and populated all the headwaters of Kettle Creek, including Coe Town and what was later called Zeke Town. This intermarriage produced a fierce race of people who, for a long time afterwards, were guilty of perpetrating crime. This race has made much improvement in the last half century. T. E. Coe, one of the original Coe descendants, has taught the Coe free school of that district for over 45 years and was still teaching in 1945. At this date there were 780 Negroes in the county.

The question of slavery agitated the minds of the white people for more than one hundred years. The members of the first and second Constitutional Conventions labored to make the State of Kentucky free, but all in vain. But little change was made in the third Constitution. In 1808 the U. S. passed an act prohibiting the importation of slaves. In 1833 the State of Kentucky enacted a law prohibiting the sale of slaves in this state, brought for that purpose from another state, but that was repealed in 1849. These laws did not deny the immigrants the right to bring along with them their own slaves, for they were no more than other personal property. They were brought by the early settlers to help subdue the forest.

The institution of slavery was considered by most people as being wrong. Nothing good ever resulted from it. It came near wrecking our nation. The churches of the state took action against it. In 1809 the Baptist members who were opposed to it refused to commune with those who owned slaves and caused a split in that church. Two years later another split came over slavery. Some Methodists declared those who owned slaves were not fit to preach and they divided into North and South branches. Families were divided over the sin of the institution.

Free slaves were the ones set free by the owners on account their religious beliefs or those paid for by the state. Runaways sometimes caused trouble. Laws bound the slave up until his sphere was very limited. He was not allowed to carry a gun, shot, powder, club, or any other weapon. Neither was he allowed to join in an argument with the whites or testify for or against. Penalties for infraction of these laws were from 10 to 39 lashes. If he committed a crime that called for hanging the State paid for him.

Negroes, like horses, sold for their working abilities. When sold, a deed was required, as for land. Prices ranged from $1,500 down. Below are reproduced two deeds.

"This indenture made and entered into this March 14, 1823, by and between James Saufley and Harold Saufley, Parties of the First Part, and James Smith, Party of the Second Part.

"Witnesseth, that said Saufleys have this day sold to James Smith one negro boy named Miles, age 12, and one girl named Fillis, age 13, for $700 each. We guarantee them both to be sensible and healthy.

"James Saufley
"Harold Saufley"

"For and in consideration of the sum of $140, cash in hand this day paid, I have bargained, sold and delivered to Rane Staton, one negro girl, 4 or 5 years old, named Louisa. I do warrant the title to be good and her to be sound and healthy, August 1, 1833.

"Joseph Bledsoe."

BILL OF SALE OF RANE STATON: 1842

One red cow	$ 5.00
One red heifer	3.25
One lot of hogs	6.75
One crib of corn	4.12
One sorrel colt	13.00
Three stands of bees	1.50
One gopher plow	.50
Two bottles of ink	.37
Eight yds. of calico	3.00
Ten first class sheep	10.00
One negro man, 75	11.00

Monroe's administration, 1817-25, was known as "the era of good feeling." Political differences were set aside, the ravages of war had subsided, and the whole country centered its attention on internal improvements. The harsh treatment of masters toward their slaves softened to the degree that many of them began to believe slavery was wrong. Thousands of the people agreed to set their slaves aside if the Government would provide a colony to which they could be shipped. This was done in 1817 by purchasing a strip of land, about 36,000 square miles, on the northwest coast of Africa, from the natives living there. The colony was called Liberia, meaning "liberty," and the capital was called Monrovia. The burden of transportation was met by contribution. This complicated the business, for those who had given their slaves freedom thought that was their part, so it fell to the churches and freewill contributors to raise the money to defray the transportation costs of $36.00 per slave. The panic of 1837 slowed the business, but following that period there were thousands of slaves from the whole country freed and shipped to Liberia. News from the colony which reached the ears of the ones back here in the States was always discouraging and the scheme died before the Civil War. Cumberland County at Burkesville was the "port of embarkation" where steamboats received the few that were shipped from here. In 1823 there were four and in the 40's there were seven others, according to available records.

By the first Government census, 1810, as given by James Fergus, assistant to the Marshal of Kentucky, there were 6,191 people in the county. Of this number there were 922 colored slaves. The population of Burkesville then was 86 whites and 20 Negroes, slaves. From 1809 to 1810 there were born in the county both colors 230 babies and 26 deaths occurred among the population. From the first Monday in August, 1819, to the following August, 1820, there were born 263, died 37. In 1940 there were born in the county 285; died 97, 10 blacks.

Besides the four free slaves who went to Liberia as James Fergus stated, there were 15 free slaves living in Burkesville, all of whom preferred to live either by themselves or with some white family. John M. Emmerson, Isaac Taylor, John Baker, John Alexander, Thomas Cloyd provided them with homes, and some lived in cabins alone. Stepney was in her 116th year and was supported by the county. At this date there were 1,332 slaves in the county.

Burkesville had an auction block near the court house door on which the Negroes were stood for sale. The auctioneer stood by their side, clad in a coat that reached to his knees, a large hat 24 inches in diameter, and with a gavel in his hand. Slaves were graded according to several standards. Men were called "old bucks"; boys, "young bucks"; women were called "old wenches"; girls, "young wenches"; and children, picaninnies.

At to blood, they were blacks, mulattoes, quadroons, and octoroons. Black men usually commanded the highest prices for if one had been bred too "bright" he probably might pass as a Caucasian. "Before auction day," says Uncle Dick Sewell, "an old man was polished and tweezered." His face was greased and rubbed until it showed a patent leather shine, and his head was cleared of all gray hairs, if not too many, by the younger children with tweezers.

Age, working ability, and health were the main requisites for men, while women brought higher prices if endowed with two other characteristics—that of looks and fecundity, especially did these two qualities play a big part during the period from 1833 to 1849, when the laws of Kentucky prohibited the importation of slaves into the state for sale. It was during this period that the African race lost much of its original identity. The scarcity of slaves led men to break the Seventh Commandment, and often they would sell their own children. Records and tradition both relate instances where beautiful mulattoes and quadroons, some from refined white families, were stood upon the auction block before the gazing crowds and exposed to inspection, that the purchasers might see they were symmetrically built. This of course would excite men's carnal nature, and bids would climb to extravagant heights.

There were no laws governing the marriage of Negroes. If they should desire to marry, their master would hold a broomstick about twenty inches from the ground and give the signal. If both jumped it at the same time, their master pronounced them man and wife. If one failed to clear it then the wedding was postponed until another day for that day was ruined by "starting life with a blunder."

The children of "Massa" and "Missus" were required to be addressed with a title. Boys were "Mahs John" or "Mahs James"; girls were "Miss Lucy" or "Miss Mary"; small children were "Little Miss Mary" or "Little Mahs Henry," etc.

North of the Ohio River was free territory including Canada, and cruel masters often lost their slaves who slipped away from them to this territory. Runaways became so numerous that the state established the Patrol System in 1830, and each county was furnished with these "pat-a-rolls," as the Negro called them, whose business was to guard the ferries and apprehend runaways and return them to their owners. If the owners could not be contacted at once the Negro was placed in jail, advertised, and sold for expense at the end of six months.

If the runaway had in his possession a release from bondage given by the County Clerk, witnessed by his owner, then he was turned loose; or if he had a "time permit" to visit some family or go to town he was given freedom until its expiration. On any of the three occasions that he was out from home there was a constant dread of the "patarolls," for even the little slave children were saturated with fear at hearing the Negro song played and sung: "Run, nigger, run, er the pataroll 'll ketch you." A public whipping post stood on the public square at about the entrance of Glasgow Street to the Square. Here the rebellious slave was tied and given from 10 to 39 lashes on a nude back, the stripes of which he carried through life. Disobedient or rebellious slaves were generally sold to the hated "nigger traders" and boated or driven to New Orleans to work in the cotton or cane fields under the most cruel masters. Before leaving town they were chained together with a log chain and branch lines about three feet apart. When night overtook them they were crowded into "nigger pens" which lined the road to the southern states, resembling our line of garages and filling stations. It was scenes like these that led Stephen Foster in 1853 to put into that immortal song the words: "A few more days and the trouble all will end in the field where the sugar cane grows."

Pea Ridge Colony

The Pea Ridge Colony or Zeke Town, heretofore mentioned, started with two colored girls named Betty and Sookey. They came to Cumberland County with John Coe early in 1800. Their mother was a Negro and their father an Indian. They became mothers by a white father soon after their arrival. Betty had two sons named Ezekiel and Rance. Sookey had a son named Riley and a daughter named Patsy. Mr. Coe was kind to them, but Riley was too "bright" for a slave, for the reason that he might pass for a Caucasian. So Mr. Coe put him on the auction block, and he was sold to go "down the river." "Down the river" was a detestable phrase to the colored man's ears, but John Coe was pleased with the $1,600 sale.

Nine months later, one day while John Coe and Zeke were walking down Kettle Creek, Zeke saw tracks in the mud which he recognized as Riley's, and that night Riley came sneaking into the cabin of Zeke after dark. Zeke concealed him for eighteen months, during which time the "patarolls" and his new master scoured the country from Cumberland County to the Gulf States to no avail. Then the man proposed to sell his chances back to Coe for $500. He hesitated at first, but Zeke told Coe to buy him back and he would help him find Riley. The deal was made, and Riley once more became the property of John Coe.

Zeke married Patsy by "jumping the broomstick" held by John Coe, and to them were born 14 children, all of whom moved to Pea Ridge the next year after slaves were freed and started colored Coe Town, which was drenched with blood for nearly 100 years on account of racial strifes. Surrounding the colony lived the Taylors, Shorts, Capps, Pruitts, Longs, and Vaughns, whose young folks would get too much alcohol for their safety and run their horses through the settlement holloing, which would arouse that Indian vengeful spirit in them. Two of Zeke's boys, Old Bill and Calvin Coe, became the leaders of the town. One day Calvin was in his house resting and some of the white lads passed and called out: "Buffalo Bill, from Bunker Hill, never was curbed and never will." He took this as an insult and grabbed his gun and spread the alarm throughout the town, but the white boys left without further disturbance. Strife grew more and more bitter between the whites and the black Coes, and resulted in much bloodshed on both sides. It was whisky on the side of the whites, and ungovernable temper on the other side.

Bill Coe married Mandy Kirkpatrick, who had been the slave in a fine family that taught her to read and write and filled her with a desire to treat others as she would like to be treated. She went to Indiana and became converted to the Holiness doctrine, came back and began to preach salvation to lost souls, and eventually became the Apostle of her race. Thomas E. Coe, grandson of Zeke, absorbed much of her teaching. Coe Town is no longer considered a dangerous country to go through.

After the divisions had arisen in the different churches over slavery, the members decided to leave the slave question to the civil authorities to settle and content themselves with teaching the Negroes to read the Bible. The church-going people always took their slaves with them to church. They were not allowed to have organizations of their own, neither were they permitted to listen to preaching except in the presence of two or more white people.

After the Negro was turned into a citizen of the country by the Fourteenth Amendment to the Constitution of the United States and given the right to vote, 1870, by the Fifteenth, he was still lost in the world and many remained with their masters. Some were turned loose on their own initiative and others were set up to housekeeping by their masters. Having passed through so many generations depending on the judgment of his master, it had become a part of him not to be self-reliant. He still likes to listen to the white man's counsel. He is not prone to hold grudges or ill feelings against those of his own color only for a brief period of time.

This was tested out in 1936, when a certain colored man and woman approached the County Judge with a complaint against one of their color for misconduct. After a few hours of meditation by the plaintiff, he begged for a withdrawal of the warrant. At another time within the same year another man was arrested and tried for a misdemeanor, and a colored jury was impaneled. The jurors were smiling most of the time while the evidence was offered. They went to their room to make a verdict. Two minutes more and the jury-room door flew open and each one came down the aisle wearing a broad smile on his face, and without being asked if they had made a verdict one read in a loud voice: "We, the jury, find the defendant not guilty."

Of the 1,964 farmers in Cumberland County only 66 are colored (1940 census). Most of the colored people live in Burkesville, i.e., it is the most densely settled part of the county. Of 1,092 people in Burkesville, 360 are colored. Of this number about 180 are legal voters, and they are proud of this "balance wheel in elections." It opens the way for that familiar reiteration, "You help me and I'll help you."

Notwithstanding the narrow places through which he has had to go, the colored man of this county has developed into a reasonable citizen. He delights more in public works than private works. His education is far in advance of that of 50 years ago. Singing is one of his greatest delights. Harrison Newby and his children constitute one of the best quartets in Kentucky.

The colored man of this county has never shown an aspiration for political recognition or for public office.

That spirit was quenched during the reign of the Ku Klux Klan, which was started in 1870 by the whites of the Southern states, who banded themselves together and rode at nights around to the colored quarters, hooded and robed in white, for the purpose of intimidating the race and to frighten them beyond political thoughts. Many stayed away from the poles and many were punished and tortured who were falsely accused. This unlawful practice reigned until about 1878, and led to the Klan's punishment of many poor whites for misconduct.

The Negro having been allowed one week at Christmas time to celebrate, always considered it having "real Christmas" to get drunk. This ignorant belief is still practiced by some of both races. (What a shame!)

While it is generally thought by the people living today that Negroes were the only race of people sold into slavery, yet among the settlers of Virginia there were many whites who were bound to other whites for a certain period of time to compensate for favors or for expenses in transporting them to America. These laws were kept in force far into the history of Kentucky, and numerous cases are to be found on record in Cumberland County where fathers would bind their children to some business man as apprentices for long periods. Sometimes they would be bound from the age of two until they became 21. In each case the old law of the state compelled the grantee to teach or have him taught to "read, write, and cipher to the Rule of Three," and, on arriving at the age of 21, his master was required to give him three and one-half pounds (of English money) and a new suit of clothes.

Below is a copy of one of those white "human deeds":

"This indenture made and entered into this May 9, 1804, witnesseth for a good cause, I bind to Richard Harris Melton, my son, John Lewis, for a term of two years. Said John Lewis is to behave himself, obeying reasonable commands and keeping all his master's secrets. The said Melton is to teach him the mystery of the Hatter's Trade and to teach him to read, write, and cipher to the Rule of Three and before he sets him free is to give him three and one-half pounds and a new suit of clothes.

"Thomas Lewis
"John Lewis
"R. H. Melton."

The "mystery" of carding wool, the "mystery" of farming, the "mystery" of pegging shoes, etc., were expressions used in their deeds.

By the school census of 1840 there were 1,268 slaves in Cumberland County valued at about $440,000. At the close of the Civil War which brought an end to slavery, there were 234 slave owners in the county.

COLORED SCHOOLS

Burkesville

Scarcely had the colored race been freed, when their education was planned. Many of their school buildings, like those of the whites, have crumbled to ruin and the places thereof forgotten. The slaves were freed in 1865, and made citizens by the Fourteenth Amendment, July 28, 1868, and on July 29, 1868, George W. Kingsbury sold to the "Freedmen of African Descent" one-fourth acre of land with house on it, 40 by 25 feet, to be used for both school and church. This was used for a number of years and then sold to H. E. Alexander (colored) in 1932. The Trustees paid $660.80 for the lot and building.

Lawsons Bottom

This school was built on a lot sold to the Trustees by W. D. Mays in 1903 and was known as school "B". It was used for school purposes until .... when it was sold to Richard Guffey. Mays received $2.50 for the lot. There is no colored school in Lawsons Bottom now.

Clay Lick Bottom

The school building known as "G", was built in 1897 on a one-half acre lot adjoining the Colored Baptist Church in Clay Lick Bottom, which was bought from Robert Young and Dollie Young for $5.00.

Marrowbone

This school received a deed from Bose Nunn in 1916 for one-half acre of ground in the town of Marrowbone for school purposes. Consideration, $275.

Beech Grove

The Beech Grove lot was purchased from James Herd and Betty Herd, in 1917, for school purposes. It is not far from Waterview. Consideration, $50.00.

Coe

There was an old Coe building on Coe Ridge, which is now abandoned. In 1932 a deed to a parcel of land was secured from T. E. Coe and wife and John Coe, Sr., for school, for $15.00.

New Burkesville School

In 1932, Sid S. Davis sold to the Board of Education two acres of land in south Burkesville, on which a nice school structure was built to accommodate all the colored children of the town. Consideration, $300.

Chapter 6

COUNTY OFFICERS

On the organization of Cumberland County it became necessary that officers be elected at once to administer the affairs of the local government. The first ones were the Justices of the Peace, commissioned by Governor Garrard in July, 1799. They were seven in number, found elsewhere in this volume.

Most of the business was administered by these Commissioners. The Magistrates elected the Clerks. Sometimes the same man occupied two offices at the same time. The Sheriff was commissioned by the Governor. The schools were few and simple and the affairs were administered by Commissioners, which will be treated under the proper heading. There was no county election for county officers through 1850. The first one was in May, 1851. There were no County Judges until 1851. Following will be found a list of the county officers from the beginning to the present. They took their office at the middle of the year, usually following the November election in the beginning.

COUNTY JUDGES

1851-1854, John M. Emmerson
1854-1858, S. H. Boles
1858-1862, James Haggard
1862-1866, Thomas C. Winfrey
1866-1870, M. O. Allen
1870-1874, J. Q. Owsley
1874-1878, Rus. G. Cole
1878-1886, John G. Craddock
1886-1893, T. J. Williams
1894-1897, G. T. Herriford
1898-1901, J. J. Simpson
1902-1909, C. H. Carter
1910-1913, J. M. Collins
1914-1917, C. H. Carter
1918-1921, J. G. Jones & W. E. Miller
   (Jones resigned)
1922-1925, B. L. Simpson
1926-1929, J. G. Jones
1930-1933, B. L. Simpson
1934-1937, J. W. Wells
1938-1941, A. O. Sharp
1942—   , B. R. Norris

JAILERS
Partial List

Henry Cary, 1799
John Miller, 1820
John Brummel, 1824
Adam Saufley, 1839
Tom Boles, 1842
William Eston, 1851
Robert Davidson
W. E. Paull, 1874
S. T. Bow, 1882
T. L. Fletcher, 1886
U. G. MacFarland
William Murley
William Lee

J. W. Norris
H. L. Cummings
W. E. Mayfield
Jas. A. Lee
W. L. Garner
W. H. Higginbotham
W. B. Huddleston
Ernest M. Garner
B. M. Smith
John Perkins (called to Service, 1943; F. T. Norris and Roy Groce finished term to 1945)
Roy Groce, 1945—

DISTRICTING CUMBERLAND COUNTY

By the Constitution of 1850, the county had to be re-districted for convenience at the poles when county officers were first elected. The division was as follows:

No. 1, election precinct at Burkesville
No. 2, election precinct at Robt. Elliott mill
No. 3, election precinct at house of Elisha Lawson
No. 4, election precinct at Miles Williams' house
No. 5, election precinct at Walter Pace store

The four men appointed by the General Assembly to do this work were Fontain Alexander, James H. Gains, James English, and Jubal Goggins.

POLITICAL DIVISIONS

There are eight Magisterial Districts in this county. When the county was organized, 1799, there were seven. A Magistrate is elected every four years to fill office. These eight Magistrates, with the County Judge acting as chairman, constitute the Fiscal Court. This court looks after the affairs of the county relating to the expenditure of the tax money in paying off claims against the county. The Fiscal Court is one of most importance, and should be considered well by each voter when elections are held. Each Magistrate draws $6.00 per day while court is in session.

Following are the districts with the voting precincts in each:

Magisterial District	Voting Precincts
No. 1, Burkesville	North Burkesville (1); Lewis Creek (2); Lower Burk (18); Gaines Hill (3); Bow (19)
No. 2, Cole Camp	Big Renox (4); Cole Camp (5)
No. 3, Whetstone	Smith Grove (7); Whetstone (6)
No. 4, Carver	Carver (8); Chestnut Grove (9)
No. 5, Spear	Spear (10); Coop (11)
No. 6, Cary	Cary (12); Bend (13)
No. 7, Leslie	Leslie (14); Grider (15)
No. 8, Marrowbone	Marrowbone (16); Mud Camp (17); Waterview (20)

Population of Each District

District No. 1, 3,105; No. 2, 1,391; No. 3, 1,045; No. 4, 1,598; No. 5, 1,494; No. 6, 711; No. 7, 1,235; No. 8, 1,344.

Justices of the Peace

The Justices of the Peace filling these offices in 1946 are:
Burkesville, Chester P. Prewitt, on his second term
Cole Camp, L. E. Thomas, on his third term
Whetstone, J. A. Smith, on his first term
Carver, J. A. Capps, on his fourth term
Spear, Hugh Spear, on his second term
Cary, Bert Smith, on his first term
Leslie, A. B. Butler, on his first term
Marrowbone, J. O. Alexander, on his thirty-fifth year.

For 52 years the fiscal affairs of Cumberland County were carried on by the Fiscal Court altogether, there being no County Judge until after 1851. The office of Justice of the Peace has always been one of the most important of the county. In allowing claims and fixing the tax rate and other important businesses of the county it stands head, but, due to the low salary which it pays, often unqualified men are elected to the office. But at times the office has been filled with the best the county could produce.

In a tiresome search through the County Records which escaped the fire of 1933, the writer has assembled the names of most of the members who have constituted the Fiscal Courts of our county. The dates herein accompanying the names do not always tell when they began serving or when the service ended—only a close date to the first of the terms.

On July 2, 1799, the Governor of Kentucky commissioned the seven first Justices of the Peace of this county. From their number a chairman was chosen. They were from the seven different districts of the county, embracing territories now included in the surrounding counties which then belonged to Cumberland County. Many of them served long terms.

Ishum Burks, 1799
Thomas F. Lowery, 1799
John Irvin, 1799, 33 years
Joseph Black, 1799
David Hutchinson, 1799
Alex. McFarland, 1799
John Thurman, 1799
David Wells, 1802-20
William Wood, 1804
Francis Emmerson, 1807
John Gholson, 1807
William Smith, 1807
James Fergus, 1812
Robt. Alexander, 1815
Robt. Galbraith, 1816
Sam Young, 1816
Robt. Ferrell, 1816
James Gee, 1816
William Taylor, 1816
James McMillin, 1816
Abraham Engart, 1816
James Cowen, 1816
Radford Maxey, 1818
William Cole, 1818
John Hillis, 1818
Chas. Dougherty, 1818
Sam Wilborn, 1818
Geo. Swope, 1820
Nicholas Talbot, 1820
William Wood, 1820
Tom Baker, 1821
John Coe, 1821, served 35 years
J. M. Emmerson, 1821
Abner Bryson, 1821
Geo. Bowman, 1821
Christopher Cheatham, 1822
Charles R. Palmer
Vincent Taylor, 1825
Gilbert Rowland, 1825
Anthony Garnett, 1825
Reuben Alexander, 1820-28
J. W. Williams, 1820-28
Robert Crop, 1820-28

W. T. Coop, 1872
A. G. Waggener, 1874
R. G. Cole, 1874
J. E. Coop, 1874
C. I. Alexander, 1874
John Vincent, 1874
Isaac Dick, 1882
G. N. Allen, 1882
M. L. McCoy, 1882
Isum Dicken, 1882
Geo. Perry, 1882
R. M. Philipps, 1890
H. J. Yates, 1890
D. G. L. Allen, 1894
J. D. Sharp, 1894
W. R. King, 1894
D. L. Capps, 1894
Wm. M. Smith, 1898
D. J. Thrasher, 1898
Bal Spears, 1898
John S. Hicks, 1898
Obediah Baker, 1830
E. Shugart, 1832
F. H. Winfrey, 1832
Joel Owsley, 1832
Harold P. Saufley, 1832
Daniel Myers, 1834
M. S. Stoner, 1835
William Spearman, 1840
Washington Watson, 1840
Joseph L. Bledsoe, 1844
Robert Elliott, 1844
Israel Winfrey, 1849
James M. Franklin, 1852
James Baker, 1852
J. J. Cloyd, 1852
Gideon Pharis, 1856
W. H. Spears, 1856
E. L. Miller, 1858
Enos Morgan, 1858
A. D. Robinson, 1865
Reubin Hicks, 1865, 32 years
John E. Coop, 1872

F. E. Baker, 1898
J. O. Alexander, 1898
C. H. Carter, 1898
Bedford Lollar, 1921
U. S. Miller, 1921
J. B. Cox, 1921
H. W. Jones, 1921
E. E. Cole, 1921
W. L. King, 1921
W. H. Higginbotham, 1921
J. T. Huddleston, 1921
J. H. Strange, 1925
B. B. Allen, 1925
J. A. Capps, 1925
T. S. Spencer, 1925
Dennis Armstrong, 1925
J. W. Easter, 1925
G. C. Groce, 1925
Geo. T. Bartley, 1925
J. R. Needham, 1927
W. H. Williams, 1927
U. W. Thrasher, 1927

Ebb Carter, 1927
W. R. Glidewell, 1927
W. H. Jones, 1927
Will Long, 1929
B. R. Norris, 1929
J. C. Myers, 1930
L. E. Thomas, 1930
P. G. Cary, 1930
Chester P. Prewitt, 1933
M. C. Wells, 1933
Hugh Spears, 1933
J. Wes Melton, 1936
J. F. Butler, 1937
Bert Smith, 1937
Jim A. Smith, 1937
W. L. King, 1941
M. R. Cary, 1941
Kenneth Booher, 1941
John L. Smith, 1945
W. G. Hopper, 1945
J. O. Alexander, 1945, 44 years

FIRST CIRCUIT COURT

The Hon. James Garrard, Governor of Kentucky, appointed Allen W. Wakefield first Circuit Judge of the district composed of Cumberland, Green, Barren, and Adair counties. Moses Kirkpatrick and Thomas T. Lowery were appointed by the Governor as his assistants.

The first court was held Monday and Tuesday, February 14 and 15, 1803, with all three Judges present. Francis Emmerson was first Commonwealth's Attorney, with Samuel Brents, who had been practicing in the quarterly sessions in the county, taking the oath to practice in the new Circuit Court with Emmerson.

The Grand Jury was composed of "Twenty stalwart men, with the worthy Joseph Jones foreman."

The first presentment was against John Williams and Osburn Bland for breach of the peace, which was dismissed in the May term. There were thirteen civil cases, eight for debt, three attachments, one trespass, one chancery, and several criminal cases.

The first order of record was: "Ordered that the first Saturday succeeding the second Monday of every month be and the same is appointed the day for taking the rule in the Clerk's Office."

Elections have been held in nearly every month of the year from March on, and fiscal years have started in various months from April on. Old records speak of the fiscal year ending October 10, 1863; June 30, 1876; December 31, 1870, etc. This accounts for two different men being found in the same office within one year. As has been stated before, in the beginning of the county's government compatibility was practiced with several officers. For more than 25 years, Milton King was both County and Circuit Clerk at the same time.

Circuit Judges

Allen Wakefield, 1803
Christopher Tompkins, 1818-24
Ben Monroe, 1824-36
Richard Buckner
Christopher Tompkins, 1837-48
Zachariah Wheat, 1849-55
Thomas E. Bramlett, 1858-62
T. T. Alexander, 1862-9 and 74

Preston H. Leslie, 1872 and 84
James Garnett, 1875
D. R. Carr, 1886-90
Wallace W. Jones, 1890-6
H. C. Baker, 1903-9
J. C. Carter, 1909-45
J. C. Carter, Jr., 1946—

Circuit Clerks

Isaac Taylor, 1798-1803
John E. King, 1803-24
Milt King, 1824-51
Robert C. Logan, 1852-8
E. J. Ellison, 1859-64
J. M. Boles, 1865
John W. Williams, 1869 and 84
W. E. Miller, 1886-97

J. H. Myres, 1898-1903
J. T. Glidewell, 1904-9
J. G. Jones, 1910-15
N. S. Hume, 1916-21
C. H. Carter, 1922-27
Will A. Keen, 1928-33
Mayne Miller, 1934-45
Eunice E. Hicks, 1946—

Commonwealth's Attorneys

Francis Emmerson, 1803
Thomas Thurman, 1811
Thomas E. Bramlett, 1850
E. B. Gaither, 1854
J. H. C. Sandidge, 1862
M. H. Owsley, 1862-74
A. M. Adair, in 1874
D. R. Carr, 1875
S. M. Payton, 1882
J. C. Muncey, 1890

John G. Craddock, 1886
N. H. W. Aaron, 1899
A. A. Huddleston, 1903-27
——— Crabtree, —
W. A. Coffey, 1934
Tanner Ottley
  finished Coffey's term
Chas. Fair
Ray Montgomery
Harold M. Garner, 1946

Clerks of the County Court

Isaac Taylor, 1798-1803
John E. King, 1803-24
Milt King, 1824-51
James Haggard, 1851-8
N. B. Cheatham, 1858-66
L. A. Waggener, 1866-78
N. B. Cheatham, 1878-86
J. J. Simpson, 1886-95
Dr. J. E. Bow, 1895-7 (resigned)

J. M. Collins, 1897-1909
Dr. C. J. Simpson, 1910-13
J. H. Coe, 1914-7
J. W. Collins, 1918-25
S. A. Smith, 1926-42 (died)
Mrs. S. A. Smith, 1943
  until November election
Mrs. Edna Collins, 1944

History of Cumberland County

County Surveyors

Allen W. Wakefield, 1799-1800
John Montfort, 1800-04
Isaac Taylor, 1805-37
John M. Baker, 1837-58
John W. Williams, 1858-60
Z. Norris, 1860-3
John W. Williams, 1864-7
William L. Philpott, 1867-8
Charles Smith, 1868-74
H. D. W. Patten, 1875-8

Samuel Smith, 1879-86
Samuel Rush, 1886-94
W. T. Coop, 1897-1908
J. T. Lloyd, 1908-09
G. R. Hicks, 1910-18
K. B. Kirby, 1918-22
J. G. Jones, 1922-5
G. R. Hicks, 1925-8
W. M. Allen, 1929-33

In the early years of the life of our country when there was much new land for the settlers to get with little effort, the surveyor's office was the most important office of the county, but since these conditions no longer exist the office goes begging; it has been vacant for a number of years.

Sheriffs of Cumberland County

From the beginning of the county until 1851, Sheriffs were appointed by the state Governor. Compatibility was legal and appointments, as well as elections later, came in the middle of the year. Due to the destruction of records by fire, December 30, 1933, a few names of Sheriffs may be lost.

Nathaniel Owens, 1795, while Cumberland was in Green
William Barrett, also under Green County.

Hanniah Lincoln, 1799
John Robinson, 1803-6
William Wood, 1804
Isham Burks, 1801
Nicholas Talbot, 1809-10
James Cowan, 1817
William Cole, 1822
Lemuel Stockton, 1824
Joseph Alexander, 1825-6-9-30
Robt. Alexander, 1827-8
Frank Winfrey, 1832-49-50
Granville Bowman, 1833
Joseph Alexander, 1834
George Swope, 1834
John Coe, 1842-3
Lewis Waggener, 1844-6, 58
A. G. Waggener, 1845-6-7, 58
William Spearman, 1847-8
T. E. Emmerson, 1866
C. T. Cheek, 1867-8-9
A. T. Keen, 1871

R. M. Cheek, 1870-1892
B. B. Vaughn, 1862, 1874
H. M. Alexander, 1875-6
L. T. Bow, 1877-8
I. S. Bow, 1879-80-1-2-6-8
George Herriford, 1882-3
J. R. Keen, 1889-93-5-6-7-8
B. H. Simpson, 1893-4
A. B. Keen, 1898-1901
J. W. Norris, 1902-5
J. G. Jones, 1906-9
W. B. Garmon, 1910-13
W. H. Jones, 1914-7
P. A. Madison, 1918-21
J. A. Lee, 1922-5
P. A. Madison, 1926-9
J. W. Collins, 1930-3
S. D. Pace, 1934-7
Mrs. (S.D.P.) Pearl, 1938-41
J. T. Brown, 1942-5
J. B. Groce, 1945—

County Officers

SHERIFFS OF CLINTON COUNTY

As Clinton County was for 37 years included within the limits of Cumberland County and the two had things in common so long, I feel it not out of place to name the Sheriffs of that county, from first to last. Clinton also had a fire, losing all records made before the Civil War. Dates show when in office, probably not including full terms.

Robert Crop, 1836-8
Rice Maxey, 1840-1
Wm. Davis, 1845
John Wade, 1846
W. F. Harrison, 1847, also 54
Thomas Bristow, 1848-9
Mark Marlow, 1850
Allen Smith, 1853
Allen M. Elder, 1851, 58
J. C. Burchett, 1866
J. A. Morrison, 1867
W. L. Dicken, 1872-3
C. B. Parrigin, 1875-6-7-8
M. J. Perdue, 1879-80
William Davis, 1881-2
G. H. Piercey and
    A. F. Snow, 1883-4

Jesse Cross, 1884-5-6-7
A. B. Parrigin, 1888-9
G. W. Carr, 1891-2
C. L. Shelley, 1894-6
J. J. Grider, 1898-9-1901
W. A. Dickey, 1902-5
P. A. Madison, 1905-8
J. P. Perkins, 1909-12
C. P. Huff, 1914-7
J. H. Cummings, 1918-21
J. W. Felkins, 1922-5
A. H. Boles, 1926-9
W. M. Winningham, 1930-3
Odell Cummings, 1934-7
J. A. Allen, 1938-41
Bruce Sloan, 1942-5
J. B. Smith, 1946–

COUNTY SCHOOL SUPERINTENDENTS

The office of the County Superintendent was filled from the establishment of the county free schools, 1840, up to the year 1884, by from one to five men at a time called Commissioners, as mentioned heretofore. The first report shows three, which was the law at the time.

William Cheek, Joseph Alexander, Harold P. Saufley, 1841
Joseph Alexander, Joseph Bledsoe, 1852-6
Joseph S. Bledsoe, 1856-64
M. O. Allen, 1864-5
John G. Craddock, 1874-8
William Cheek, 1874
J. W. Williams
J. A. Dixon, 1884-9
Jess O. Ewing, 1890-8

T. S. Scott, 1898-1902
R. D. Bass, 1902-9
J. W. Bowman, 1910-13
Cora S. Payne, 1914-21
R. D. Bass, 1922-8
Ewing Wilson, 1928-32

Earl Garrison, 1933-42 (called to Service, April 27, 1942)
Samuel Alexander, 1942–

REPRESENTATIVES

Representatives that served in the Kentucky Legislature from the 38th District which embraces Cumberland County, as given by Emma Guy Cromwell, are as follows:

Samuel Burks, 1800
William Crawford, 1802
Samuel Burks, 1803
John L. Lowery, 1804, 5
John W. Semple, 1806, 7
William Wood, 1808, 9, 10, 11, 12
Samuel Wilson, 1813
James W. Taylor, 1814
James Fergus, 1815
Granville Bowman, 1816
James Gholson, 1817
Samuel Scott, 1818
Lemuel Williams, 1819, 20
Edward King, 1820
Lemuel Williams, 1821, 2

Lemuel Williams, 1824
George Swope and
   Joel Owsley, 1825
George Swope, 1826
William Davenport, 1827
Edward King, 1828
Joel Owsley, 1829
James Baker, 1830, 1
Ambrose Bramlett, 1832
William Cheek, 1833
Francis Winfrey, 1834
Ambrose Bramlett, Cumberland
   and Monroe counties, 1835
Francis H. Winfrey, 1836

Joel Owsley and Hiram S. Emerson, Cumberland and Monroe counties, 1823

CUMBERLAND AND CLINTON COUNTIES

Burr H. Emerson, 1837
Thomas S. Ellison, 1838
James Haggard, 1839-40, 40-41
Thos. E. Bramlett, 1841-42
Francis Winfrey, 1842-43, 43-44
David Haggard
   1844-45, 45-6, 46-7, 47-8
Joseph Bledsoe, 1848-9
John Q. A. King, 1849-50
Joel Owsley, 1850-1
Francis H. Winfrey, 1851-2
J. Q. A. King, 1853-4
Samuel Long, 1855-6
Thos. C. Winfrey, 1857-8
R. M. Alexander, 1859-60
Otha Miller, 1861-2

J. H. Sandidge, 1863-4
D. R. Carr, 1865-6
Martin Miller, 1867-8
P. W. Barron, 1869-70
C. P. Gray, 1871-2
Dr. W. Godfrey Hunter, 1873-4, 75-6
W. T. Dicken, 1877-8
Jacob S. Bruton, 1879-80
Dr. Godfrey Hunter, 1881-2
J. A. Brents, 1883-4
L. T. Bow, 1885-6
Geo. W. Burchett, 1887-8
I. S. Bow, 1889-90
J. A. Perkins, 1892

CUMBERLAND AND ADAIR COUNTIES

T. J. Winfrey, 1894
L. T. Neat, 1896
W. H. Cole, 1898
M. R. Yarberry, 1900
W. C. Keen, 1902

L. C. Nell, 1904
W. H. Cole, 1906
G. L. Perryman, 1908
W. G. Keen, 1910

Walter S. Sinclair, 1912
A. W. Sharp, 1914
L. T. Neat, 1916
Joe Huddleston, 1918

County Officers

CUMBERLAND AND CLINTON COUNTIES

S. G. Smith, 1920
Sam Cary, 1922
W. B. Agee, 1924
C. A. Page, 1926
S. G. Smith, 1928
Caleb A. Page, 1930
Bruce Sloan, 1932

Frank C. Bruton, 1934
Bruce Sloan, 1936
Clarence Rush, 1938
Bruce Sloan, 1940
Dr. W. C. Mann, 1942
T. H. Dyer, 1944
Lyle H. Webb, 1946

SENATORS

The 16th Senatorial District of Kentucky, which includes the County of Cumberland, has had several changes since its formation. At present it contains the following counties as fixed by the 1918 Legislature: Clinton, Cumberland, Monroe, Russell, and Wayne.

At times, Adair and Pulaski have been included. The list below shows the members that have represented this county since its formation and what county furnished each.

(Furnished me by Emma Guy Cromwell, State Librarian)

1808-1813 Edward M. Cullen, Cumberland County
1814-1821 William Wood Cumberland County
1822-1824 Granville Bowman, Cumberland County
1826   William Wood, Cumberland County
1827-1832 Martin Beaty, Wayne County
1833-1836 John M. McHenry, Pulaski County
1837-1840 William Bradshaw, Russell County
1841-1842 John Garth, Wayne County
1843-1844 John Alexander, Cumberland County
1845-1847 F. H. Winfrey, Cumberland County
1848-1849 Shelby Stone, Russell County
1850   John Buster, Russell County
1851-1854 Joseph S. Bledsoe, Cumberland County
1855-1858 William Hagg, Cumberland County
1859-1861 Samuel H. Boles, Cumberland County (Resigned)
1861-1863 Shelby Stone, Russell County
1864-1865 Ben S. Coffey, Adair County
1866-1872 Isaac C. Winfrey, Wayne County
1873-1874 D. R. Haggard, Cumberland County
1875-1876 B. W. S. Huffacre, Wayne County
1877-1880 Joseph Bertram, Wayne County

1881-1883 James Garnett, Adair County
1884-1888 W. F. Neat, Adair County
1889-1892 J. H. Shearer, Wayne County
1894-1896 E. M. Nell, Adair County
1898-1901 W. E. Miller, Cumberland County
1902-1904 J. W. Catron, Clinton County
1906-1908 L. C. Nell, Adair County
1910-1912 E. Bertram, Clinton County
1914-1920 Robert Antle, Russell County
1922-1932 Frank M. White, Monroe County
1934   W. C. Farmer, Clinton County

ONLY WHITE MAN HANGED IN COUNTY

The only white man ever hanged in Cumberland County was Joe Coleman, which occurred on Tuesday, May 25, 1847. He was tried and convicted at the April term of court on April 17, of that year.

He was convicted on circumstantial evidence of killing his wife. His wife went to the woods to get some bark. He immediately went to the woods and took his shoe knife with him. Soon he came carrying her dead in his arms, with the report that he had found her dead. His shoemaker knife was afterwards found with blood on it in the woods. The murder took place in Adair County, and Coleman was granted a change of venue from Adair to Cumberland.

Here are the jurors: Elisha W. Newby, Jack Lollar, Samuel Brooks, Daniel Swift, John Carter, Pleasant Garret, Geo. Smith, John Rush, John Fudge, William L. Radford, Irvin Keeton, and James Glass.

Christopher Tompkins was Judge of this Circuit at that time. The above jury were selected from Cumberland and Clinton counties. Coleman was hanged on the hill south of Burkesville. He was driven to the gallows by Jack Doherty, a colored man, who received $5.00 for the job. Coleman sat upon his coffin which was placed on a two-wheel cart drawn by a yoke of oxen. Coleman played the violin as he went to his doom. Tommie Low beat the drum and Evan Shaw played the fife.

A. G. Waggener tied the knot and the cart was driven from under him. His body was carried back to Adair County.

Many years before this act, a Negro slave called Uncle Pete was hanged near the same spot, for killing a white woman. He lived on Marrowbone, Cumberland County.

Chapter 7

PROFESSIONAL MEN, BANKS AND BANKERS

DOCTORS

Following is a list of the doctors who have practiced in Cumberland County. Some of the dates of their service were not available.

Dr. Joel Owsley, 1790-1869
Dr. David Haggard
Dr. Elisha Embree, 1830
Dr. H. A. Staton, 1821-87
Dr. Stoner, 1848
Drs. F. J. & Wm. Hutchins
Dr. Brown
Dr. Geo. Hutchins, 1840
Dr. Harvey Ryon
Dr. Hiram Bledsoe
Dr. Dan Claywell, 1870
Dr. Ed Alexander
Dr. James Cheek
Dr. Ellison
Dr. T. T. Baker
Dr. S. B. Cheatham
Dr. W. P. Alexander
Dr. J. R. Schooling, 1890
Dr. John Waggener
Dr. R. M. Alexander
Dr. R. L. Richardson
Dr. W. R. Thrasher, 1890
Dr. Bedford Richardson
Dr. Ed Sandidge
Dr. Clarence K. Haggard, 1890
Dr. W. G. Hunter

Dr. Wm. Burchett
Dr. James C. Herriford, 1888
Dr. J. A. Dixon
Dr. Herbert Davis
Dr. John B. Ryon, 1848
Dr. Perry Allen
Dr. Chas. Alexander
Dr. W. C. Keen
Dr. Oscar Keen
Dr. Hutchens
Dr. H. C. Cartwright
Dr. W. S. Taylor, 1904
Dr. J. A. B. Huddleston, 1890
Dr. E. D. Turner
Dr. J. W. Bowman
Dr. Aarons
Dr. J. D. Sharp
Dr. J. G. Talbot
Dr. J. E. Bow
Dr. Fayett Owsley
Dr. J. R. Webb
Dr. Blackerby (County Health)
Dr. Max Blue (County Health)
Dr. Joe Schickel (County Health)
Dr. P. D. Moore (County Health)

DENTISTS

Drs. Caldwell and Shaw, 1888
Dr. W. C. Richardson, 1892-8
Dr. K. M. Hill, 1928—

LAWYERS

Samuel Brents, 1799
Thos. Lowery, 1799
Allen Wakefield, 1799
Thomas Thurman, 1811
— Baker, 1811
William R. Allen, 1829
Zachariah Wheat, 1829
John R. Johnson, 1829
William Jones, 1842
Edgar B. Gaither, 1842
Alfred King, 1842
J. H. C. Sandidge (b. 1830)
J. E. McMertery (first 1880)
M. O. Allen
J. O. Ewing
Samuel B. Emmerson, 1820

Hiram S. Emmerson, 1821
A. A. Huddleston
Allen Sandidge
Preston Sandidge
Wm. Cheek
S. H. Boles & W. K. Botts, 1874
Craddock & Walker, 1874
C. J. Clair
Henry Barron
Tanner Ottley
Chas. R. Hicks
B. L. Simpson
S. A. Cary
Ben M. Jones
Harlin E. Judd
Luke Roberts

BANKS

The first bank chartered in Kentucky was the Bank of Kentucky, in 1806, with Robert Alexander president. It grew out of the Kentucky Insurance Company of 1802, which issued notes (paper money) to shippers of goods or farm products against loss in transit. These paper bills were made "payable to bearer," thereby circulating over a wide range of country as our greenback bills do today.

The Bank of Kentucky established 13 branch banks in different parts of the state. They kept up the practice of the Kentucky Bank, or Insurance Company, with respect to paper money.

The State Legislature chartered 46 branch banks in 1818, which were Independent Banks, with capital ranging from one million down to one hundred thousand dollars. It scattered them all over the state for the purpose of providing for the wishes and needs of the people for more money. They were given the power to issue this paper money up to three times their capital minus their indebtedness. Burkesville, Cumberland County, was one of the small towns that got one of those banks of 1818 with capital of $100,000, with 1,000 shares at $100 each.

With all these 46 banks working almost day and night issuing this paper money, the country was flooded with it, and it seemed for a while that every county in the state was a Utopia. Old debts could be paid. Speculation ran high. Money was on every side and easy to get. Old spinning wheels which had been manufacturing the home garments were set aside, and every individual could easily obtain, with or without money, the gorgeous fabrics with which England was flooding the country. Prices of land went up and farm products were bearing good prices. This spirit ran high as long as the tide of "bills" was flowing from the banks; but alas, the day of redemption soon came, when the banks all asked for pay in specie (gold or silver). This brought about hard times, a drop in values, and on many hands bankruptcy. Notes, many times, were discounted 90 per cent and a general gloom of depression enveloped the country, which was known as the "Panic of 1819." This dark age was charged to the banks, but it should have been checked against the near-sighted legislators.

February, 1820, sounded the death knell to these Independent Banks, and of course the one known as the "Cumberland Bank of Burkesville," ceased to exist, leaving Burkesville with a bit of banking experience only.

An old "bill" on file at the Bank of Cumberland testifies to this bank. Isaac Taylor was cashier and Peter Zimmerman was president. The building was located on the west side of what is now known as Elm Street. It was a two-story dwelling house.

In 1854, Governor Powell vetoed a bill to change the Deposit Bank of Covington, Kentucky, into a savings bank, with branches at Springfield and Burkesville.

Once more the Bank of Louisville was chartered in 1858, for 20 years, and required to establish a branch bank at Burkesville with a capital of $150,000. This bank was established and ran into the late 70's, with F. W. Alexander president, and W. F. Owsley cashier. It operated on the north side of North River Street facing the Public Square, where Marvin Jones now keeps a restaurant.

At the cessation of this bank, Cumberland County was again left for about ten years bankless.

In 1889, the clarion note was struck for a permanent banking system for this county, when J. A. Dixon, H. C. Trigg, and a Mr. Barton got their heads together and organized the Bank of Cumberland.

I here quote a report from the State Banking System which will give its standing in infancy: "Bank of Cumberland, 1890, capital $20,000, surplus $1,518.09, H. C. Trigg, president; J. A. Dixon, cashier."

This bank, up to the writing of this book, has had three presidents. H. C. Trigg, two years; Chas. W. Alexander, forty-four years; C. Wickliff Alexander since 1936. The building of the last bank named was used until 1892, when the new brick building now in use was constructed. The 18,000-pound safe was brought down the river and hauled from the Burkesville landing on a large sled, drawn by ten yoke of oxen.

When President Roosevelt called for all the gold of the United States to be turned in, $8,000 emerged from hiding places in Cumberland County and went on deposit in the Bank of Cumberland. The year 1940 shows $503,000 on deposit in full, $35,000 surplus, and a change in capital stock to $25,000.

The Bank of Cumberland has stood like the Rock of Gibraltar through all the panics of its life. It has always been supervised by men of high business qualities and men with such strict moral and religious convictions that it has grown into an institution which has won the confidence of all who know it.

Cumberland County has another bank at Marrowbone, known as the Bank of Marrowbone. It was established in 1902. Dr. J. A. Dixon helped to organize this bank, and became its first president. Following him were, James I. Alexander, Reubin Norris, J. F. Pace, Mrs. J. F. Pace, and J. F. Pace again.

The cashiers have been Sydney Pace, J. E. Pace, Guy Davis, L. A. Miller, and J. B. Holcomb (Monroe County).

MONEY

In August, 1786, our present money system was worked out. The first money coined in the United States was at the mint of Philadelphia in 1794; but enough of it could not be made to drive out the foreign money until the close of the third decade of the nineteenth century. Pennies were the first denomination of money coined.

Cumberland County being an old county, Burkesville became a center of exchange of goods early, due in part to its location on the river. From what the old records reveal, doubtless Burkesville handled more types of money than any other town within a radius of a hundred miles. While most trading of early times was by barter, it was not all so.

The products bartered were skins, tobacco, corn, wild meat, ginseng, cotton, and alcohol. Fur skins which were easily obtained from animals that infested the canebrakes always found a ready market in any of the European countries. Tobacco was pressed into hogsheads of from 500 to 2,500 pounds, rolled to the river, placed on a flatboat and floated down to New Orleans, where it was sold or exchanged. Ginseng, or "sang," grew in large quantities in the rich hills and hollows of this county. It found a ready sale in the markets of China and Japan. One old record makes the statement that "it often brought its weight in gold or silver."

Liquors were used to pay bills, purchase cows, horses, and even to pay the salary of ministers and buy marriage licenses. One old family record tells of the purchase of "Sambo," a slave, for "ten gallons of whisky and a two-year-old coon dog."

Hogs were fattened mostly on the mast and sold to the Atlantic States. Salt was the first product manufactured in the county, and was the means of bringing many early settlers. It sold at 20 shillings per bushel.

With the above train of products moving to so many different markets, money, though scarce, was of many different makes. Most of this money, regardless of what country it came from, was of gold or silver, yet some other metals were used.

In 1815 a machine was made to cut the silver dollars into eighths, called "bits." This is where we get the phrase, "four bits." They were of such ill shape and so pointed that carrying them was difficult, but it soon led to the introduction of smaller denominations.

In 1837, silver disappeared from circulation and was replaced by "shin plasters," some of which may be seen yet, held only as keepsakes. The greenback paper money we use today was first printed in 1862. This being the time of the Civil War when the Government was shaky, brought about a fluctuation in its value. When first made it sold for 88.3 cents; in 1863 it was worth 79 cents; in 1864, which was the darkest period of the war, it ranged from 67.8 to 38.7; in 1865 it rose from 46.3 to 70.4 From 1865 to 1879 it varied; and in 1879 specie payments were resumed, when gold and greenback became equal in value and this has remained so ever since. The only change was in 1936, when the paper dollars were reduced in size.

No other word in the English language except L-O-V-E spells more than the five letters that spell M-O-N-E-Y. It is of interest to everybody. It spells lands, houses, bank accounts, security, power, influence, travel, luxuries, food, clothing, and a thousand other things to each individual. Behind the screen of life, money holds the joys and tragedies. If permitted to rise between us and God, it becomes "the root of all kinds of evil."

Money is education; it is intelligence; it is flesh; it is blood; it is life itself. Work all day for five dollars, put it into your purse, and you have one day of life in your pocket. Besides this, you have a portion of time, energy, thought, and skill.

Money erects churches, distributes Bibles, spreads the Gospel, saves souls, populates heaven, gladdens the heart of God if used properly. It is an everlasting blessing or an eternal curse. Which is yours?

Chapter 8

NEWSPAPERS AND PRINTING

Paper at first was made from the skins of animals. Then from various plants, barks, and leaves. Egypt, China, and Japan used paper hundreds of years before the Christian Era. China has the honor of having first made and used paper, but Egypt gave it the present name as derived from the "papyrus" plant, which grew there and from the body of which thin strips were riven and glued together to form sheets. About 170 B.C. the Chinese invented paper made from cotton, which did not reach Europe for nearly 1,000 years. It found its way to Spain through Arabia and then to Italy, France, and Germany. About this time linen was compounded with cotton to make a better grade of paper. Up to the time of the Revolution, paper was made by hand processes, and it fell to the lot of a Frenchman to patent a paper-making machine. Today it is made from dozens of different kinds of plants.

Although printing was discovered by the Chinese hundreds of years before Christ, John Gutenberg, a German mechanic, is generally given the honor of fashioning the first movable printing press made of wood in his workshop, about 1440. By this the Bible was printed in Latin, as the first work of printing. From wood he turned to soft and then hard metals. This Bible was printed in 1455, and by 1476 printing presses crossed the Channel into England. The first to be set up in America was in Mexico in 1536, and the first in the United States was at Harvard College, 1638, at its founding.

Many books and thousands of documents had been printed up to this date, but it was not until 1550 that the people conceived the idea of collecting and printing the current happenings of the times and pass it out to the public as a "news paper." The *London Gazette* is the oldest continuously published paper of the world. It started in 1665 and still lives. The first "news paper" in the United States was published in 1704 and known as the *Boston News Letter*, which was more of a pamphlet in style.

In 1786, John Bradford of Lexington, Kentucky, ordered a press from Boston, Massachusetts, but due to transportation handicaps he did not get it until the following year, and his first issue was on August 11, 1787, and the paper was known as the *Lexington Gazette*.

The first paper in Louisville was the *Public Advertiser*, in 1818, a weekly. The present *Courier-Journal* is the outgrowth of the *Focus* of 1826; *Louisville Journal*, 1830; *Louisville Daily Democrat*, 1834; *Louisville Morning Courier*, 1844; the *Courier-Journal*, November 8, 1868, as it stands today (1945).

Coming to Cumberland County we find the first newspaper starting in 1870 at Burkesville and known as the *Cumberland Courier*, edited by Walker and Matthew, two attorneys of Cumberland County. In 1878 it assumed the name of *Burkesville Courier*. From 1880 to 1884 the name was *Burkesville Bulletin*, edited by Alice Matthews.

In 1885 it became *The Herald*.

The Herald was edited by A. E. Nell during the last 80's, until August 28, 1890, when O. L. Winks and J. J. Alexander purchased the press and continued its publication, and on November 1, 1891, Alexander sold out to O. L. Winks, who was an attorney in Burkesville. Winks continued its publication until March 24, 1892, when he sold to J. O. Ewing, ex-superintendent and J. P. Shaw, who had been Burkesville's dentist for several years, having come from Danville, Kentucky, back in the 80's. They ran the paper until 1896, when Tom Scott took charge and edited it the rest of that century. A few issues are lacking along here, but we find in 1903 E. E. and S. C. Strange to be the editors.

The *Cumberland News* was published in 1908, and in 1912 the *Burkesville Banner*, then the press was purchased by S. A. Cary in 1915 and called *Cary's Weekly* until 1920, when W. Tanner Ottley, a Burkesville attorney, bought it and changed the name to *Cumberland News*. He sold out, 1925, to Ira T. Shannon, who edited the paper until his death, 1931, when it fell to his widow, Mrs. Annie (Jones) Shannon, and her children, who changed its name to *Cumberland County News*, which it bears to date (1945). It is issued each week by James Shannon, chief editor (and his wife, Braddie). Two Shannon sisters, Ruth and May, assist in typesetting.

Thousands of improvements have been added to Gutenberg's wooden type to make it what it is today. Like all other metal articles, type was first forged by hand. It was made in this manner until 1838, when David Bruce invented a typecasting machine, which added to the volume of printed matter. The greatest boost to printing was in 1885 when Mergenthaler invented the type-setting machine, the linotype, used today by the larger printing establishments.

The *Cumberland County News* is still set to type by hand and passes through the roller printing press patented in 1818.

Extracts from the *Cumberland Courier* of 1874 read as follow:

"Mail at Columbia each Monday, Wednesday, and Friday. Mail at Celina every Saturday. A. P. Green boat passed Burkesville to-day on way to Nashville (May). Burkesville-Glasgow Stage Line, leaves Burkesville at 6:00 a.m. and arrives at Glasgow each Tuesday, Thursday, and Saturday, 4:40. Leaves Glasgow at 7:00 a.m., arrives at Burkesville at 6:00 p.m. Wednesday, Friday, and Sunday.

"A. J. Phelps, all kinds of merchandise, Burkesville. Emmons & Grissom, mill men. S. H. Boles & W. K. Botts, attorneys. William

Cheek Attorney & School Commissioner. R. Gibson, Poor House keeper. Craddock & Walker, attorneys. Police Judge, Josiah P. Franks. Ben. Rioll, Police.

"Joel Cheek, Jacob S. Bruton of Burkesville, and M. C. Gettings of Judio, authorized to solicit advertisments and subscriptions to the Cumberland Courier. Club rates with the Courier-Journal, $3.25 per year. Little Maud Franks gave the Courier a nice boquet. Mattie Waggener married to James A. Nunn. Baker & Cheatham general merchandise at Bakerton, Ky. Circuit Court 2nd Monday in March and September. Severe drouth in May. John S. Keen preaching at Salem."

Chapter 9

TRANSPORTATION

STEAMBOATS

When we mention steamboating, our minds swing back to days gone by and we wonder who first hitched steam to the wooden vessels that had for centuries been propelled by the hand of men or forced along over the water surfaces by the pressure of wind against sails which were stretched upon the mast poles as propellers.

Robert Fulton is often thought of as the inventor of the steamboat. But this is just another case of usurpation. Another poor man spent his life in trying to carry out his inventive ingenuity, in the person of John Fitch, a Kentucky inventor.

John Fitch constructed more than one boat that proved a success on the Ohio River. He received a patent, 1791. The vessels made about six miles per hour. On account of financial handicap he was forced to abandon his work, after laying his plans before his friends, his Government, and the kings of England, France, and Spain, and receiving no support.

At the time Fitch was working on his boat, two other men who came into Kentucky from Virginia, were trying the same kind of work. One was James Rumsey, the other was Edward West, who made a success of the application of steam to a boat that moved on the water, in 1794, on the Elkhorn River.

After Robert Fulton constructed the *Clermont*, in 1807, which steamed up the Hudson River from New York to Albany and back, great excitement seized the whole United States, and it was not long until the largest streams were shaken by the "Water Monsters." The first one to come down the Ohio River was in 1811. It came to Louisville and on account of the falls there, could proceed no farther. The first one to pass up the Mississippi River was the *Enterprise*, in 1817, and it too had to stop at Louisville on account of the falls in the Ohio.

Immediately, the national Government and the legislatures of the different states began to enact laws for the opening up of the different watercourses that needed it. A private company was organized to construct a canal around the falls at Louisville. In 1829 it was completed and boats could go to New Orleans with the new country's products. Toll was charged at this canal until 1874, when the state assumed control.

The only river that touches Cumberland County is the Cumberland. It answered as an outlet for the agricultural products of all southeastern Kentucky until the ushering in of the first hard surfaced road in 1928. Not only did the Cumberland River answer for Kentucky, but for much of Tennessee as well, before the advent of the railroad, for both exports and imports.

As early as 1836 the state appropriated $40,000 for the improvement of Cumberland River. Snags were removed, shoals were deepened and preparatory work was done for the coming steamboat.

In viewing out the possibilities of the stream for an easier way of transportation than the old flatboat method which had been in use since the birthday of the river, March 17, 1750 (in the knowledge of white man), the first steamboat to pass through Cumberland County was the *Mayflower*, in 1833, as evidenced by an inscription on a large beech tree that stood on the bank of the river about six or seven miles below Burkesville until it was sawed down and brought to the postoffice building in Burkesville, by Mrs. Nora McGee, postmaster there. It is still in a good state of preservation. The inscription reads:

FIRST ST. BOAT
FEB. 2, 1833

Other steamboats that ran the river were, the *General Jackson*, which was the first steamboat to appear on Cumberland River, February, 1818, and stopped at Nashville. In 1820 the *Rifleman, Robertson, James Ross* were running to and from Nashville from below, and in 1823 *The Cumberland, Green, Nashville, Feliciana* were making trips up the river to Carthage and Celina and in 1833 the *Dover* and *Randolph* and *Mayflower* were coming up to Kentucky. From 1845 to the Civil War, the *Tennessee, Jones, Harry Hill* and *America* were passing through this part of Cumberland River occasionally. A list of the boats that passed through this county to Burnside were: *Muckbay, Philips, John Bransford, McDonald, A. Baker, A. P. Green, Odil, Olivette,* about the 60's and 70's. *C. H. Webb, Pearl, Armstrong, Dover, Ella Hughs, Umpire, Dora Cabler, Nashville, Ashland, Shipper's Own, Fountain City, Celina 1 and 2, I. T. Rhea, E. P. Ewall, John Fowler, Jno W. Hart, Bob Dudley, C. M. Pate, Burnside 1, 2, 3, J. N. White, Thomas D. Fite,* were about the 80's and 90's.

Joe Horton Fall, Reubin Dunbar, Cumming, Julia 1, 2, Thomas, Sam Keith, Bedford, Albany, Harley, Clyde, Paul, Crescent, Burnside, Patrol, Burkesville, Celina, and *Rowena* are the boats that filled the period from 1890 to 1927.

Some boats lasted for 15 years, and it is impossible to give the exact period of each boat. Gasoline boats replaced steamboats in the last years of river transportation. These boats were small and slow.

Lower River, by the old map, included the river from Nashville to Burkesville, and was later extended to Whetstone on account of its volume of trade, and the upper line extended from Burnside to Celina, Tennessee. Occasionally, the Nashville boats would make the entire route.

River transportation was often disappointing. Poultry cooped to meet the boat at a certain hour, would often remain on the bank for hours and sometimes through a day and night. The same thing would happen to hogs and other livestock. Corn bags have been known to stay ricked up on the bank for shipment for nearly a week, and if a second river came it would all have to be handled again.

Hogs were fattened during the winter months in order to meet the shipping season on the river, which ordinarily lasted until April. Sometimes a farmer would take the risk with a herd in grass time and venture to drive them through to Glasgow, Burnside, or some other railroad terminal. This took two or three days. After the first day's drive, every puncher had to arm himself with a whip or rod with which to persuade the poor animals to rise to their feet, which had been worn to the blood. After a few surges by the animals, accompanied with a constant squeal, they were ready for another march.

Greater relief seldom came to a man than that to the pilot of the boat when he set his foot upon the pedal of the whistle pipe and sent out on the air that melody of "two longs and two shorts" that bespoke his intention to land.

Much interest was manifested by the youngsters on the shore as they watched the breakers dash against the banks and the massive stage swing around to the landing, covered entirely with rousters ready to hop into the mud at the stern command of the mate. Sometimes it would take hours to unload the cargo, but it had to be done immediately regardless of the weather. Rousters, or roustabouts, were mostly of the colored race, but not always.

If the boat did not happen to burn, get stuck in the chute, or have to tie up on account of high water, the shippers would get returns from their stock or produce in a week or ten days. The Geo. P. Taylor Company and others of Burnside afforded a ready market for produce for a long time. This made the people feel like they had a market in their back yard, compared with that of former days at New Orleans or the Orient.

What a change today. The truck drives up to your barn, loads on the stock after breakfast, rolls off to market, you pocket your check and are back home for dinner. And instead of saddling Old Mary or Old Tobe early Saturday morning that you might have time to get back before night with the next week's groceries, you just walk out to the yard gate and order the day's supplies from the Rolling Store, without even putting your hat on.

The following copy from an old record of the county shows better the contrast.

"Boyd & Zimmerman, Burkesville, Kentucky, March, 1818

"Left Burkesville, Kentucky, March, 1818, with 48 hds. of tobacco, arrived at New Orleans, La., May, 1818. $4.34 per C."

This was a flatboat trip down the river.

The last steamboat to make a trip on the Upper Cumberland was the *Celina* in 1926. It was piloted by Frank Bedford, and Luther McWhorter was captain.

The *Joe Horton Fall* of the lower river made a trip in 1927-9.

The *Albany* was the most powerful boat that ever ran on the Cumberland. It was used to tow barges.

The *Dora Cabbler* and *Juliett*, which ran in the late 70's both had calliopes. They rendered beautiful music.

The *Reubin R. Dunbar* was a boat that forbade drinking or the handling of intoxicants by people traveling, or its officers.

The *Rowena* was said to have the most beautiful harmonizing whistle.

The boat that created the most excitement was the *Thomas D. Fite*. It was a lower river boat. It ran in the early 80's of the nineteenth century. It had a "wild cat whistle" when it passed through this part of the river trip in the night with its "whow, whow, who-whow," many people were awakened from their sleep. Some took their guns down from the rack and stood at the door. Some called the dogs and went out to chase the monster. People who were more or less superstitious made some extra move to try to kill it or appease it in some way or other to save their families and their belongings. It is truthfully reported that a certain neighbor laid a ham on the doorstep that it might eat it and move on. Others rose on the following day and "sure found its tracks in the woods." Some threatened to kill their dogs because they would not trail it. One story is told by some who witnessed a chase. Their dogs struck a trail in the open and followed it to the woods, with the men following hard by their heels with their guns ready to shoot at sight. On through the woods went the dogs until they came to a small opening and passed on. One of the men saw the animal and thought it was reversing its course, and in order to save their own lives they all located it and fired at the same time. They caught their breaths on seeing it fall, and mustered courage to walk up and see what it looked like. At the firing of the guns the dogs had returned to the spot and met the men at the dead animal's side. With all eyes standing on stems and each heart creating within itself an exerting dynamo, they discovered to their sorrow that they had laid low their neighbor's old blue Jennet.

J. E. Morgan, long a pilot of the Upper Cumberland, furnishes the following schedule of old Steamboat Landings in this county:

Winfrey's Landing	0 miles
Winfrey's Ferry	2
Dove Branch	3
Orchard	5.5
Brownwood	6
Lick Branch	7

Albany Landing (Whetstone)	8
Phelps	9
Crocus Creek	11
Dicks	12
Bakerton	13
Renox Creek	16
Scotts Ferry	18
Burkesville	21
Bear Creek	24
Neeleys Ferry	29
Paul Ferry	30.5
Newby	32
Marrowbone	32
Parmley	34
Potters Creek	34
Galloway	35
Philpott	35
Ararat	37
Cloyd Landing	39
Bluff	40
Mud Camp	41
Gettings	46
Judio Creek	50

Some of the captains of the Upper boats were: William Reeves, Frank Reeves, Lewis Ramsey, James Ramsey, T. M. Allen, long captain of the *Odil* in the 80's and 90's. Records show this boat carried more families from Cumberland County to Burnside on their way to Bells, Texas, than all others.

First tide of emigrants from the county went down the river because of the difficulty of travel upstream prior to steam transportation. From Burkesville to Nashville, Tennessee, 236 miles; from Burkesville to Clarksville, 300.9; to Cumberland Island, 427 miles. This is 2.1 miles below Smithland, the beginning.

After the test had been made of all the different watercourses of Kentucky as means of transportation, another way was fast taking the attention of the people. It was that of overland travel. While most of the people were moving inland, commercial roads became a necessity for the removal of the surpluses rapidly accumulating on the farms of the remote settlements.

As has been stated, the two main routes of egress and ingress were by the Ohio River and the Mississippi River. A limited amount of commerce was carried on by way of the Cumberland Gap. It was only a trail until 1794, when it was so widened that wagons and other vehicles could pass over it.

History of Cumberland County

TURNPIKES AND RAILROADS

By 1812 the people were talking "turnpikes," and along with this was the scramble for railroads for more than half a century. The first railroad was built in 1826 in Massachusetts. Four years after that, on October 22, 1830, Governor Metcalfe of Kentucky drove the first spike at Lexington, on the road that would tie that town and Louisville together; and on August 15, 1832, the governor together with 39 of his friends mounted the first train to run in this state, on the one and one-half mile stretch that had been built up to this time. The trains of Kentucky were drawn by horses until 1835, when steam replaced the animal power.

Two great railroads have passed around Cumberland County at a shy distance of about 40 miles each. The L. & N., which was commenced in 1849 and finished November 1, 1859, from Louisville to Nashville, a distance of 185 miles, and which was built by the city of Louisville, a branch of which reaches Glasgow, Kentucky, brought Burkesville within forty miles of the outside world.

The Cincinnati Southern Railroad, which was built by the city of Cincinnati, 1873-81, at a cost of $28,000,000, after a squabble and deadlock in three different sessions of the Kentucky Legislature over the charter, missed Cumberland County at Burnside by 54 dirt miles. In taking the sentiment of the people of this county on the railroad, the election went in favor of issuing bonds for its construction, but it was never carried out, due to the distance of the survey (1852).

In 1825 Governor Desha of Kentucky urged "a speedy move on internal improvements." In 1828 nine new turnpike companies were formed in the state, and Governor Metcalfe called upon the state for aid in the construction of turnpikes in many parts of the state. In spite of Andrew Jackson's anti-doctrine, between 1828 and 1844, 900 miles were built in the state, one of which was the noted L. & N. pike. These pikes charged toll and had a toll gate every few miles, which was only a pole swung across the road and watched by the toll-man. When one wanted through, he would turn the poll or "pike," hence the name "turnpike." These toll gates operated in different parts of the state until near the close of the nineteenth century. Cumberland County had only three miles, account of which is found under a different heading.

The latest chance for a railroad line for Burkesville and Cumberland County was in 1891. Judge T. J. Williams called a special session of his court on March 27, 1891, to test their feeling on the issuing of $100,000 in bonds to construct a railroad from Glasgow, which was already connected with the L. & N., to Burkesville about forty miles east of Glasgow. The Court then consisted of 14 Magistrates as follows: Matthew Ewing, Isaac Dicken, Reubin Hicks, Daniel Wray, F. B. Austin, John Lollar, William Smith, S. W. Young, Thomas Collins, Moses Stewart, D. G. L. Allen, Anderson Garrett, D. L. Capps, and G. W. Coop.

Eight voted in favor of the County Judge calling an election and six voted against. The time set for the election was the following April 30, and if voted on then the Judge was given the power to issue the bonds when the railroad was completed, ranging over a period of 20 years for their maturity with the privilege of paying at any date within this period. It was necessary for at least 25 landholders of the county to sign before the election could be called. The following affixed their names: E. F. Mullinix, W. J. Garner, D. B. Williams, W. H. Potts, G. N. Allen, E. P. Hutchins, R. Young, C. W. Alexander, M. C. Williams, J. J. McGee, A. J. Lewis, J. A. Baker, E. G. Alexander, H. S. Pace, J. W. Norris, B. H. Simpson, D. J. Thrasher, J. M. Bow, W. S. Tobin, C. T. Carter, Sam Smith, William Brake, G. J. Campbell, Pitts Coop, I. S. Bow, William Ellison, A. T. Scott, J. D. Sharp, J. M. Ledbetter.

Great excitement prevailed on both sides, some for, some against. Increase in the value of lands, additional profits figured on the sale of farm products, and the speed in getting products to and from markets were the points emphasized by those who favored the road; while the ones who were against the road hollowed high taxes, with a favored few reaping the profits, especially on the north of Cumberland River while the remote sections of the county would have to pay the same rate of taxation while reaping but little benefit from the road. Many influential men of the county were opposed to the road. It was rumored that Glasgow was working hard against Cumberland County. Glasgow denied it.

The election was held as planned on April 30, with the county turning out 1,523 votes—715 for and 808 against. Sorrow lurked in every heart of those who had worked so hard to bring the county out of the mud.

In the meantime Glasgow had sold her branch road for $150,000, to a number of New York capitalists, and Monroe County had, soon after the defeat in Cumberland, subscribed $75,000 for the road to come through that county. So the people of Cumberland County believed that another trial would bring victory after a few had expressed themselves on being wrong in the first election.

Judge Williams called his Magistrates together again and June 15, 1891, was set for the date of the second election. The petitioners— J. M. Skipworth and Albert Alexander—obtained the following names to the second call: Wix Donelson, J. M. Snow, B. B. Wright, W. L. Jones, John G. Jones, H. C. Rutledge, C. W. Alexander, J. A. Vincent, Francis Abston, J. M. Vincent, D. J. Thrasher, Isaac Garner, W. M. Ooten, J. R. Scott, J. K. Buchanan, Joe H. Pipher, C. J. Clair, G. N. Allen, Lewis Compton, J. G. Huddleston, J. E. Whitley, W. H. Potts, W. A. Wisdom, J. M. Ledbetter, W. F. Felty, James H. Davis, W. M. Bryant, A. W. Bryant, W. F. Needham, J. L. Johnson, E. B. Pace, R. F. Alexander, R. L. Gorman, J. C. Marshall, E. P. Hutchins, Fanny Hutchins, T. L. Bow, Dock Williams, Dora Strange.

While the figures stood at 93 majority in the first election against the railroad, the people were worse disappointed when the count in this second election showed 109 majority stood for the defeat of the road. Thus Cumberland County had her last chance for a railroad snowed under by her own people.

ROADS

The first roads in the county were made by wild animals. They acted pretty much the same way domestic animals do now. Watch your hogs, cattle, and sheep form paths and trails through fields to feed lots, watering places, and salt haunts, and you will observe they go in file rather than abreast. You will also notice they take the way of least resistance. Likewise did the large wild animals of the forest mark out the courses of the first roads of the country. The constant trample of the hoofs of the buffaloes, deer, and wild swine to the streams, springs, and salt licks soon wore off the soil and vegetation, making winding paths down streams and around trees and rocks to their goal. These paths were followed, to a great extent, by the hunters and pioneers; and, once found, they were blazed and used over and over by subsequent travelers. When vehicles came into use, these paths were widened and became the first road system of our county. From this you may determine why our county dirt roads were so crooked. With that same languid spirit we suffered the first graded and surfaced roads to be built on that plan of dodging rocks, mounds, and buildings, which has brought extra trouble and expense later.

Court action was taken immediately after the organization of the county, to open up more convenient roads than those laid out by dumb beasts. Three roads were surveyed in Cumberland County before it was six months old. They were Big Renox, Marrowbone, and Bear Creek (found elsewhere).

Marrowbone or Highway No. 90

The Marrowbone road to the Barren County line followed the bed of the creek most of the way. When it was not in the creek, it was crossing and recrossing. It was kept up by the citizens living along the road, who donated their labor and time six days out of each year. This was in August or September; and fills that were put in today might be washed out tomorrow and remain that way until the "road working season" the following year.

This kind of road and road work was the practice for more than one and a half centuries. Over it were hauled thousands of tons of goods yearly. It was also the chief mail route to Glasgow. Beaumont, once in Cumberland County, was the stage coach station where the teams were taken out, stabled, and fed and replaced by fresh horses for the other 20-mile drive to Glasgow. Usually two days were consumed in making this trip.

During the winter and spring months the clay roads have been known to be worked up so thin and deep that the wagon beds would glide along on top of the mud as the teams jogged onward.

High bidding for mail carriage on roads of this kind was always expected. At one time (1912) J. F. Ross purchased two stages and 12 horses at Monticello to be used on this road to carry the United States mail. He drove them over to Mill Springs and boated them to Burkesville. He tells us he got $1.00 per mile for carrying veterans to Louisville to be examined. In 1924-28 he took the contract for four years on this mail route for $10,000. This being the construction period on this road, the mail was carried on cars, trucks, and tractors.

Large livery stables were kept in Burkesville to supply the stage operators and others who did hauling. We notice an old record makes this statement: "1886-8. Livery stable owned and operated by J. D. Carter, B. C. Baker, J. H. Ritchey, C. W. Alexander, adjoining J. P. Frank's saddle shop on one side and P. M. Sandidge and Company's drug store." This was where the Burkesville Garage now is. During the 1890's E. E. McGee ran a stable in Burkesville.

Also we notice another one, thus: "Livery stable by C. C. Baker, W. H. Shelley, J. F. Ross, and M. F. Snow, 1911-12." This was where the wholesale business of Allen Waggener now operates. Tickets to Louisville via Glasgow & L. & N. cost $5.50.

With the coming of automobiles to this county in 1913, the good road fever hit the county with great force. Through the efforts of M. E. Gabbard, a retired Presbyterian minister, who made a trip to Frankfort to contact Governor A. O. Stanley for convict help to start the road, 45 convicts were furnished the county, and the work was started on the Big Hill, west of the town, 1916. In 1917 the work was begun at the Big Hill and reached to Ferris Fork of Marrowbone. This was done by force account and public subscription along the road and in town. In 1920, it was graveled with gravel obtained from Marrowbone Creek and Cumberland River.

In 1924 S. D. Pace and Company (this was S. D. Pace, J. E. Lewis, A. O. Beck, and T. W. Roberts) took the contract for another seven-mile stretch, two of which were in Cumberland County and five in Metcalfe County, for $110,000. This same year marks the building of a bridge on this road by Ferrell and Wair. In 1926 this seven-mile road was graveled by S. D. Pace and Company for $27,000.

In 1927-8 the gap from Elbow Springs (Barren) to the Metcalfe line was finished. This connected Burkesville up with the outside world by way of Glasgow. One hundred and thirty years had transpired since the formation of the county before the first road was built, so a hilarious celebration was put on at Burkesville, December 5, 1928, with nearly 5,000 people attending from all over Kentucky and much of Tennessee. The occasion lasted all day with a generous lunch furnished by Cumberland County people. Dr. M. E. Gabbard was the first speaker. L. W. McGee, president of the Chamber of Commerce, and Tanner Ottley, Burkesville attorney, also made talks.

W. P. Combs headed the largest delegation from outside towns. He led 500 from Glasgow. Chattanooga and Knoxville also had large delegations. This is now Highway No. 90.

HIGHWAY NO. 61

The next road contract was that from Neeleys Ferry, three miles south of Burkesville, to the Adair County line, on Big Renox, a distance of 15 miles, excluding the town limits of one mile. This was built by Lewis and McComas Company (J. E. Lewis, Dan Lewis, Dix McComas, John McComas, Robert Armstrong, and T. W. Roberts). It was begun in 1927 and finished in 1929, contract price, $265,000. Warden Company put crushed stone on this road in 1932-3, thereby opening another road by way of Columbia to the outside world. Gravel contract price, $33,000.

The same story as told of the Marrowbone road will apply to this one as to the former inconveniences of following the creek bed, with one exception on this road. About 1870 a turnpike company was organized in the county, which constructed three miles of turnpike beginning at the town square and extending to Renox Creek, towards Columbia. It was maintained by toll collected at the gate, which stood where the widow Newby now lives. This road not being self-supporting was given to J. P. McMillan, 1875, and was run until about 1890, when it was abandoned as to toll.

A light coat of black top was put on this road in 1937, and it is known as Highway No. 61. It leads to Columbia, 30 miles distant.

OTHER HIGHWAYS

The third road built in the county was the Burkesville-Albany road, now a part of Highway No. 90, reaching from the west bank of the river up Bear Creek to the Clinton line, a distance of nine miles. It was built by the Cumberland Construction Company in 1931-2. This company consisted of S. D. Pace, T. W. Roberts, Dix and John McComas, Robert Armstrong, Ledman Alexander, James Gray, and Reubin Norris, all of the county. The contract price was $180,000; and in 1932-3 it was graveled by the same company for $30,000, making a through road to Albany, as Smith and Company of Albany had just completed the other nine-mile stretch from the Cumberland line to Albany.

The fourth road in the county was the Leslie road, built in 1934 by the Cumberland Construction Company. It reaches from No. 90 to Leslie, a distance of about three miles, and was built for $28,000. In 1935 it was extended to Ararat for $29,000, and made connection with the W.P.A. road of Wash Bottom built in 1936-7.

The fifth road in the county was that of Clover Creek from Neeleys Ferry to the foot of the hill about two miles, built by the Cumberland Construction Company, for $29,000. In 1937-8 this road was extended to Kettle, about the same distance, by Brantley Company for $48,000. This connected up with the new W.P.A. road built in 1935-7.

The sixth state highway was the three and one-half mile stretch from Page's store on No. 90 towards Irish Bottom, called the Whetstone Spur. This road was started by a W.P.A. grant of $5,000 in 1934, by hands under the supervision of Tip B. Wells. Then, in 1936, the state contracted with the Cumberland Construction Company to build the road 3.35 miles for $29,000. Two years later the Rural Roads Department graveled this road with creek gravel from Bear Creek. The same year, 1936, the W.P.A. commenced at the Russell County line and built three and one-tenth miles in Irish Bottom towards the state road, but it lacked about two miles of connecting, leaving a gap in the middle. When this gap is finished, it will open up one of the most fertile districts of the county. The citizens of Irish Bottom spend about $350 each year on this gap in order to get out.

The part of Highway No. 90 in this county was rebuilt and straightened in 1941. First contract, from Curtis Smith's at the junction of the Leslie road to Marrowbone town limits, was let to Frank Snider from Elizabethtown, for around $239,000. In 1941-2 that part of same road from Free Ferry to the Clinton County line was finished.

The road from Burkesville to Albany and down to Static, Tennessee, a distance of 22.68 miles, was topped with Rock Asphalt Seal during the year 1945. The White Consolidated Company of Chicago did the work for $130,774.60, making it the best road in the county.

Another road built in 1945 was the Smiths Grove road, known as Road No. 11, reaching from the middle of the Irish Bottom road to the Smiths Grove schoolhouse, a distance of six miles. This road was graded and rocked. The money was obtained from three different sources—donations from the citizens along the road, $400; Rural Road Department of the county, $1,000; and $4,500 from the National Government. There is a story connected with this road that deserves notice. At the terminus of the road there lived a Mr. Alex A. Morrison, who owned several hundred acres of virgin timberland. The fine oak growing thereon had been protected by Mr. Morrison during his long life. Many times he had been offered exorbitant prices for it by men who wanted to make staves for barrels. Mr. Morrison, being a hater of liquor, would tell them that he never aimed for his timber to go into whisky barrels at any price. He kept his word, and after his death, when the National Government was in need of all the timber for war purposes that it could get, the heirs sold it to some agents for that kind of lumber as needed. The Government then had to put a hard-surfaced road to the farm before it could be trucked out. So the people living in a radius of six or seven miles today are enjoying the conveniences of a good road as the result of a temperate life of one good man.

In March, 1945, the Bow Schoolhouse road from the Bow Schoolhouse to Kettle on the Pea Ridge Road, a distance of 4.03 miles, all of which traverse a ridge, was contracted for by the Cumberland Construction Company for $19,956.19, and built the same year; that is, graded, drained, and rocked.

In spite of these late roads, Cumberland County is still 85 per cent in the mud. Of the 17 big creeks and the eight expansive farm river bottoms, only two creeks and no bottoms have hard-surfaced roads; notwithstanding that there is where the food mostly originates.

Another gap of Highway No. 90, from one-half mile east of Marrowbone town to Ferris Fork Creek, R. B. Tyler Company, Louisville, Kentucky, contracted to grade, drain, and surface for $179,208.05, 1946.

As this volume goes to press (1947), J. Stephen Watkins, State Highway Commissioner of Roads for Kentucky, has committed himself on two other deserving projects for Cumberland County, which when completed will heal the two worst sores that have been in the way of the progress of a vast territory, not only in this and adjoining counties but throughout southern Kentucky, and have hindered public travel in general. First, is a bridge across Cumberland River at Burkesville, where people have been crossing since 1776 in a ferry boat, and since the ushering in of automobiles they sometimes remain lined on either side for hours at a time waiting their turn. Often the boat gets out of commission and citizens living one or two miles on the opposite side of the river will have to drive more than 100 miles to reach their homes.

The second project is a gap of one and seven-tenths miles in a road known as the Whetstone road, which would open up over 400 square miles of rich bottom and creek lands, out of which during the World War II, one-quarter million dollars worth of livestock were driven through the rains and slush for eight miles to truck chutes; it being a county-seat-to-county-seat road. When Mr. Watkins carries these two projects to completion, his name will go down in history as one of the greatest liberators of humanity. And his picture in this volume is deserved.

CUMBERLAND RIVER

Cumberland River runs through the county from northeast to southwest. It touches the county first at the mouth of Tear Coat Creek and makes eight long bends or loops within the county before its exit into Monroe County. Where the river first strikes the county it forms the boundary of the county with Russell County on the opposite side down to Buck Branch, a distance of a little more than three miles, and then is within the county of Cumberland until it strikes the county of Monroe where another boundary is formed for about six miles.

According to the old "Steamboat Schedule" found elsewhere, Cumberland County has a distance of 50 miles of river, while the

HON. J. STEPHEN WATKINS

Commissioner of Roads
Frankfort, Kentucky

distance in the same direction by air is about one-third as great. Cumberland River, within the county, is from 110 to 150 yards wide, low water mark, which is from five to 25 feet in depth except at the shoals where it often reaches the low of one foot in the dry seasons. The bottom of the river is either gravel or solid rock. The small rock and gravel have been turned over and over until the corners have worn away, making most of it oval in shape. In places this gravel collects in great masses and forms bars or islands. The gravel is very useful for road building and is accessible most years, about seven months of the year. The gravel has a first-class sand mixed with it which make a good concrete filler.

There are five large islands entirely within the county. Beginning at the north are: Spearman, Scotts, Herriford, Carter, and Wilborn. Besides these islands there are 16 shoals in Cumberland's part of the river. Beginning at the north they are: Self, Willis Creek, Spearman, Crocus, Renox, Bakerton, Goose Creek, Neeley, Ellington, Wilborn, Galloway, Double, Cary, Stalcup, Cloyds, Mud Camp.

A recent survey on the river gives the fall throughout the county as 32 feet. The fall in the river from the Tennessee-Kentucky line to Burnside at the head of the river, 92 feet. This much fall does not produce such rapid current unless modified by other forces. The rapidity depends upon the local rainfall. If the rainfall is widely distributed from here to the head of the river then the rise is gradual and the current is moderately swift; but if the rainfall is mostly at the head of the river and not enough here to swell the large creeks that gush out into the river and shoot to the opposite side from their mouths and hold in check the headwaters of the river, then the current assumes a higher velocity, and if it is high enough to cover the river bottoms, much damage results. The worst damage is the washing of soil and tearing of fences. These are called "wild-cat tides."

One of these wild-cat tides occurred on March 25, 1929. Coming this late in the winter, or rainy season, it found the farmers with their bottom lands already turned for the crop, and as it whipped over the banks along the river it carried with it all the upturned soil, and at many places, especially in the bends of the river, holes five or six feet deep were hurled out, and at other places heaps of sand were left scattered here and there, all of which presented a very unsightly appearance. The same rise produces different heights at different places on the river. A record breaker may occur at one point while ten or twenty miles up or down the river may vary a foot or more.

Cumberland River has had many high tides since its discovery. In the history of the river we find tides usually coming by periods; likewise low tides coming by periods. The greatest and highest water that ever came in Cumberland River since white men have known it, as relating to Cumberland County, was that of March, 1826. It was within the first half of the month and was much above any other tide that has come since then. This was the one that floated the courthouse out of Burkesville and swept the brick Renox Church-house away at Salem, three miles north of Burkesville. Beside these, there were many residences up and down the river bottoms which this tide destroyed, one of which was the brick building at Winfreys Ferry on the Irish Bottom side.

The second high tide was that of December 9-10, 1847. This tide by the record was four feet under the 1826 tide, but still was one that heaped the waters high over the river bottoms and the creeks that feed the river. Then there was a big river in 1886.

A third high tide was that of 1918. The crest of this tide reached Cumberland County, January 30, 1918. This rise was the result of both snow and rain. On December 7, 1917, a two-inch snow fell and the earth was not free from snow until January 25, when a heavy two-days' rain fell, melting the 22 snows that had kept the first one hid for nearly two months. These 23 snows had packed down and was 18 inches deep over most of the country. This tide inundated all of lower Burkesville, besides hundreds of homes throughout the Cumberland Valley. Having been a period of moderately high tides, people had ventured down with homes to lower levels, some residents went so far as to say high tides were over with. Some families on this 1918 tide cut holes in the tops of their dwellings for doors to which a skiff was anchored for outings. This 1918 tide was two feet eight inches under the 1847 overflow.

Following the 1918 tide was the one of 1922, some four feet under the 1918, but which wrought much damage due to the zero weather at its crest when it crushed all fences and small timber and froze and smashed the valuable canebreaks with its four inches of ice on the backwaters. Then in 1924 came a large tide of about the same volume.

December 25-28, 1926, a very unusual kind of tide came. On the 20th of December the river was already over the bottoms and had begun to recede. Much corn was still in the fields but not so much damaged by the tide yet. It had been a very wet fall to harvest the crops. Just as the tide started back, there fell a very heavy rain which brought the river back, swelling it four feet above the first rise. Burnside was contacted at once which replied that a 59.5 foot rise was on its way. Every farmer knew his crops were doomed. This was a tide of three weeks' duration. Other rivers of the country being flooded caused the Mississippi to produce a record-breaker in 1927.

At the north end of the county, the river rises for 48 hours after the rain ceases and at the south end about 60 hours. The river has been known to rise as much as 20 feet in one day or night, but falls no more than seven or eight feet. Overflows usually come within the winter or spring months, yet many summer overflows are on record. This is when heavy damage comes, for if corn is inundated sufficiently to cover the buds or ears a total loss may be expected. The diary of Allen W. Grider, of Cumberland County reads: "May 15th, 1896, 40 ft., July 18, 45 ft., Aug. 3d, 57 feet rises." Other summer tides were 1900 and 1928, which were overflows.

Transportation

During the winter of 1937, when Louisville was inundated by the Ohio River with its 11-foot rise beyond all former floods, the Cumberland took on a moderate rise.

January 1, 1942, a 60.5-foot flood was recorded at Burnside, which put it under the big 1929 rise here in the county only 17 inches.

After a downpour of nearly 24 hours of rain January, 1946, an overflow surpassed the big 1918 tide by one inch, as measured on the same gauge, the 10th of the month. This would be classed as the third biggest tide. No doubt the water that it took to make this big river of 1946 was as great in volume as that that made the record-breaker of 1826 heretofore described. The valleys and creeks were covered with gigantic trees then, from two to ten feet in diameter. Billions of cubic feet of space were filled by the bodies of these trees. And the trees retarded the currents, causing the water to spread over more territory. Time has removed this timber, making a vacuum for water.

For comparison of Burnside and Cumberland County, I here note records for Burnside, Kentucky: January, 1822, 73.4 feet; March, 1826, 72.4 feet; March and April, 1886, 61.4 feet; March, 1902, 64.4 feet; January, 1918, 70 feet; December, 1926, 59 feet; July, 1928, 54 feet; March, 1929, 69.4 feet; February, 1939, 65.2 feet; January, 1943, 64 feet; January, 1946, 66 feet.

The National Government has at numerous times attempted to improve the river to benefit man. The first such attempt to improve it has been given in a previous chapter, and the second one was in 1882 when Cumberland County got about $10,000 to rock the shoals. This money was spent on Willis Creek, Neeleys, and Wilborn shoals. Thousands of tons of rock were blasted out and laid in oblique dams in these shallow places to shoot the current to one side and make an all-year-round outlet for boats. This worked well for a few years, and then the dams began to collect around them huge bars, and today they may still be seen just above the surface.

During the first quarter of the twentieth century a lock-and-dam fever ran high, and several were built on the lower river and one on Upper Cumberland; but they all missed Cumberland County more than 60 miles. This work subsided, as a means of navigation, with the advent of good roads, 1941 being the period of defense preparation for the on-coming second World War; an electric dam is much before the public, now, at Wolf Creek, about 20 miles by river from this county. With the building of this dam another big change in the life of Cumberland River will be wrought. This is a power and flood control dam, 238 feet high, one mile long, which creates a lake 102 miles long, and holds the run-off of 5,810 square miles—approximate cost, $55,000,000. Act passed in May, work to start in June, 1941. Called off during the war.

Cumberland River for more than 150 years has been the source of much sport for the people dwelling near it. It has been filled with fish of numerous kinds, the most common being the blue cat, yellow cat, drum, red horse, sucker, bass, salmon, buffalo, perch, eel, trout, and sturgeon. Also the gar and soft-shelled turtle, which are not eaten.

At the close of a hard week's work either on the farm or indoors, no better recreation can be had than to hie off to the river with hook and line, and spend a few hours coaxing the water dwellers to take a nibble. Who is it that would not be thrilled to the end of his fingers and toes, when, silently slipping along a trot-line, he feels just ahead of him a sudden jerk, jerk, and now and then a whirlpool bursts upon the surface, followed by a quivering, trembling pull to the bottom of the stream? Whose hat is it that could remain on the ends of the perpendicular hairs of the head, when, after a few moments of wrestle and worry, a fifteen- or twenty-pound cat is landed safely into the vessel of the fisherman? Who is it that would worry the least if his clothes should get spattered and soiled when he sees, as he balances his fish basket over his boat, a whole school of blue cats from one to two feet in length, floundering and wriggling over one another?

Such is the experience of many, many persons; but alas, it is too often enjoyed by just a few people who make fishing a livelihood and rob the streams of fish in the most drastic manners with a disregard for law.

A minor sport is that of frogging. This is a night sport, and all that is needed is a light boat, a light, and a gig or pole with which the large green-frog is slain as he sits upon the bank a few feet above the water. His white vesture and his guttural "Jug-'o-rum" are his betraying signals. This, like fishing, is not only a sport but a source of good food.

The winter high-tide sport is not so popular as it once was, but is yet indulged in by both men and boys when the wild animals become stranded on small islands and floating objects. Scarcely has the river reached its highest, when an observer can see, running hither and thither, boys and dogs, with a "hie," and "sick-him," echoing and resounding among the hills. Horrible, horrible, to take advantage of these poor stranded creatures.

The writer has labored under a heavy condemnation of conscience ever since the high tide of 1918, when J. Hiram Morgan and myself took off for some fun. We carried our .22 guns along with us and also took our dogs. What we thought would be islands were only hidden lands with stumps and posts rising above the water. Upon the tops of these were crouched rabbits by the scores and occasionally opossums and badgers. As many as three rabbits were often seen on top of one stump or post. We had no use for a gun. I carried in my hand a small hand ax and as the boat sidled up to the place of refuge a tap on the head and the poor animal fell victim to his wicked foe. We had loaded 35 rabbits into our vessel and caused many others to lose their lives struggling in the water, before a realization of the atrociousness of the deed dawned upon us. After that remorseful seizure of conscience, we resolved to be guilty no more of a crime so appalling.

I introduce this story here with the hope that other boys may profit by the mistake we made in taking so many of those precious inheritances of which we would dare to give one—Life.

PEARL SEEKERS

Cumberland River bed is paved with mussels, especially where the bottom is gravel, so numerous are they that one can scarcely step without his foot striking one or more upon its sharp edge. Prior to the year 1929 the banks of the river were dotted here and there with groups of men sitting in boats or skiffs, with their heads bent low as if in the attitude of prayer (but many of them were far from that), holding in one hand a knife and in the other a mussel which had been plucked from the great heap lying before them, diligently seeking their fortune hid away for them in the form of a tiny pearl within some mussel—which would be sure to be opened either "today or tomorrow." But days and months would go by and find them still faithful at their jobs, knowing that "it can't be much longer until Old Cumberland is going to pay me for my labor." Finally, about the time their patience began to grow weak and maybe a few from each group would drop out for a day or two over discouragement, a report would reach their ears that someone of the faithful bunch of this or that place had found a large biscuit pearl that would bring the finder $500 or more (in his estimation). New courage would seize every one that ever cut a mussel before, and he would be so stimulated at the news that another four weeks' burning sun or downpour of torrential rains would not bar him from his job.

Very little was ever accomplished by these hopeful workers, but most every one would declare he was making wages. On a few occasions it is true that rare pearls would sell for $200 and from that down to fifty cents. Several from this county's part of Cumberland River have brought from $50 to $100. Two of the biggest dealers in pearls were Cyrus Campbell of Creelsboro and H. A. Staton of Whetstone, this county. Staton had in his possession at the time of his death, May, 1916, a full quart of different sizes of pearls. They were distributed among his heirs, J. H. Morgan of Crocus being one of the heirs.

The Legislature passed an act at the 1926 session, forbidding this kind of work to go on, and the Game Commission on April 5, 1929, declared the mussel beds closed for a term of five years in Cumberland, Monroe, Wayne, Pulaski, McCreary, Clinton, Bell, Knox, Whitley, Harlan, Russell, and Laurel counties. This put an end to this long distance fortune seeking, and the next thing we knew the boys were trying to exchange their mussel grabs for a hoe or plow, which we think was a wise act.

Chapter 10

WEATHER

The weather is something everybody is concerned about. It is used more than any other subject to introduce conversations. One of the following list of clauses is always heard after a how-do-you-do has been said, and is usually in the form of a question: "It's a fine day"; "Isn't it fine weather?" "What d'u think of this?" "It's somewhat rainy, foggy, cold, snowy, windy, hot," as the case may be.

Repeated complaints sometimes become chronic. Though little good it does, in times of adversity you hear those people saying, "I wish this rain would stop"; "Isn't this awful?" "This is what I expected"; "Everybody will die if this is kept up."

If the wishes of men were granted with respect to weather, a Joseph's coat condition would prevail. One farmer would want rain, another would want sunshine. The same man would want it to rain on his newly set tobacco patch and just across the fence want sunshine and dry weather until he could get over his corn field—and he'd want it to be sure not to rain on the road until the children get to school and back. After all, we might just as well sit mum and take it as it comes, for that is what we have to do finally.

We do read in the Bible where Elijah prayed for it not to rain, and rain was withheld for the space of three years and six months. Science teaches us that when the world was formed natural laws were fixed, and under certain conditions certain things happen. But I am persuaded to believe that when a universal cry goes up in faith to God, "that will He do."

Observations have been made for years by the rural people, and a number of rules accepted by which weather may be predicted. These rules work at times, and at times they fail. Some are good, some sound like superstition. Three of the surest are: (1) If the sun goes down in a bank of clouds on Sunday night, rain will come before the following Wednesday night; (2) if it rains on Monday, look for rain two more days that week; (3) if it clouds up on a heavy frost early, falling weather will be within 24 hours. Lightning in the north at night means rain in 24 hours. A dewless warm morning brings rain within 24 hours. Halo around the sun, falling weather. Roosters crowing on the roost at sunset bring rain in three days.

Almanac forecasts are worth but little. Bill Oliver remarked to the writer once that he could come as close to the weather as the almanacs. He said they could tell a month before it was going to rain, and he could tell a month after it rained. In 1891 the Government established a Weather Bureau, which gives the weather forecasts

Weather

of the country and the weather happenings; and if a man will connect these up with a good knowledge of geography he will be benefited.

The surest instrument by which to tabulate the weather is the thermometer made by Gabriel D. Fahrenheit, a German, a few years before he died, 1740—two hundred years ago. It was a few years before it reached Kentucky but records have been kept ever since the Revolutionary War. Meteorologists have kept records every day for 40 years. No two days have been found the same.

The coldest winter in history was that of 1779-80. Rivers of the eastern states and northern states froze over to a thickness of three feet. Cumberland River from here as far as Nashville, Tennessee, was frozen over thick enough to allow cattle, teams, and people to cross on it from November 15, 1779, to February 15, 1780. This spell greatly reduced the number of wild animals in Kentucky. The very early immigrants related they saw myriads of buffaloes, deer, bears, panthers, wolves, and birds frozen to death.

One of the longest winters was in 1788. The streams were locked with ice from December 26, 1787, to March 18, 1788.

The same day is not the coldest all over Kentucky or even Cumberland County. Weather dips in pools. Some of the extremes are: 1807, 20 degrees below zero; 1818, February, 22 degrees below zero; February, 1823, 20 degrees below zero; January, 1835, 21 degrees below zero; January, 1856, 20 degrees below zero; January, 1857, 20 degrees below zero; January, 1864, 20 degrees below zero.

Later extremes for Cumberland County are: 1895, 15 degrees below zero; February 12, 1899, 20 to 30 degrees below zero; 1936, 10 below zero, many times; January 26, 1940, from 16 to 30 below.

Cumberland County has many creeks and ridges which modify weather conditions. Charlie C. Smith, who had a good thermometer which he hung on his porch post at his home on Bear Creek January 26, 1940, had a reading of 32 degrees below zero.

Droughts do not hurt Cumberland County as do rainy seasons. Some dry years have been: 1805, 1838, 1839, 1845, 1862, 1881, 1913, 1936. It was in 1936 that the western Kentucky people had to dispose of all their cattle unfattened. The U. S. Government purchased the poor cattle, killed and canned them to be given to relief. Cumberland County did not suffer very great losses. The valleys made fair crops of corn and hay, but tobacco was very short. Tobacco commanded a good price, selling from 40 cents to $1.15 per pound.

The only twister to visit this county was at 9:00 p.m. May 9, 1933. It came across Monroe County from Tompkinsville and hit the southern part of the county, at Judio. Mr. Lewis Stewart was selling goods on the road near Judio, and his entire stock was blown away. Some of his goods and papers were found later more than 20 miles from the place. The metal roof of his store was seen wrapped around trees a mile from home. He and his wife and baby occupied a small building near the store house. It was moved across the road and left them unharmed. Bob Spears lived in a large log building a little farther up the path, and it was entirely demolished. Even his hearth rocks were carried many feet up the hill from their beds. Bob suffered a broken neck from which he recovered. The other members of the family escaped unharmed. The path of the cyclone was about 100 yards wide. No timber was left in the path except when it would bound upward. Large oak trees two and three feet in diameter were either twisted off or uprooted. One large oak was observed by the writer. It was about 150 feet high and 30 inches in diameter. When it was uprooted it carried with it tons of earth, and exchanged ends, leaving the top where the stump would have been.

The Cumberland River Valley is overhung with dense fogs during the spring and summer months, which are beneficial to the crops when they are in need of moisture. On hot mornings the farmers like to get out early in their crops and enjoy the cool foggy atmosphere, with the sun obscured until about eight or nine o'clock. These fogs back up the creeks and sometimes spread to the highlands. For a long time these highlanders believed these fogs were unhealthful, but time and experience have proven different. Atmospheric surroundings do work an influence on man and beast. Rigid climates generate energy, physical and mental. Light climates have the opposite effect. Sluggish weather brings sluggish feelings to man and beast. Cumberland County is in latitude North 36-30 and 37-01, and in longitude West 83-12 and 83-35. This puts the county near the divide between the South and North, and if not modified by mountains, streams, and forests the climate would be mild, but a very diversified climate exists.

The temperature as recorded shows a variation from 30 degrees below zero to 105 above. Snowflakes have been seen in every month but July and August. The year 1816 was without a summer; snow fell all around but none in this county, though a light frost was reported on June 12 and August 30 here in the county. Frosts are very rare after the first of May, yet the fruit has been killed within the first half of May, and light frosts are on record for September 20, 21, 23, but without damage. Frost on September 26, 1928, killed everything.

Snows for the winter months are uncertain; as many as 25 and as few as one may fall. They vary in depth from a mere flurry to 24 inches. The winter of 1941 had only one snow and a flurry, the winter of 1918 had 23 different snows. The deepest snows of record were in 1886, averaging 22 inches everywhere over the county. Another deep snow fell in 1892. The next one was that of 1929, which fell on February 20-21 and reached a depth of 18 inches. The above snows were single ones, unlike the 18-inch snow coverage of 1918 which was many together.

The big snow of 1892 was the deepest on record for March. It began Thursday, March 17, and continued until the 18th, making a 22- to 24-inch snow over the entire county. The Burkesville high school dismissed Thursday and Friday. The snow melted rapidly and resulted in a high tide in Cumberland River which was welcomed by the raftsmen.

CHAPTER 11

CREEKS

Cumberland County is bounded on the north by Metcalfe and Adair counties, on the east by Russell and Clinton, on the south by the State of Tennessee (Clay County), on the west by Monroe and Metcalfe. Cumberland River, which winds its way through the county from northeast to southwest, is fed within the county by 17 large creeks, 5 from the north and 12 from the south. Those flowing into the river from the north side beginning at the northeast corner are, Crocus, Big Renox, Lewis, Marrowbone, and Mud Camp.

Those emptying into the river from the south side are, Crow, Big Willis, Upper Whetstone, Lower Whetstone, Brush, Goose, Bear, Raft, Clover, Potters, Galloway, Judio.

Other large creeks which are mostly in Cumberland County are Sulphur, which leaves the county just before it empties into Obey River in Tennessee; Kettle, which leaves the county just before it empties into Cumberland River in Monroe; Illwill, which leaves the county just before it empties into Wolf River in Clinton County.

Besides these, there are numerous branches and about 35 more creeks which are tributaries to the 17 large creeks named above.

MARROWBONE

Marrowbone Creek is the largest creek in the county. In fact, its bottom lands are more extensive than many rivers are. At one time in the life of the county, it took in all of Marrowbone and all of its tributaries, but when Metcalfe County was cut off of Cumberland in 1860, it lost the upper creek and the branches at the head of some of its tributaries. Not very much bottom land was lost, for that far up the creek the bottoms are narrow and more rare.

There are two theories as to how it got its name. The first theory is that when Jane Allen and her children came from Virginia and settled on Allens Creek near where it empties into Marrowbone, some of the older boys provided food by stealing out among the brakes of the big creek and shooting down some bears for food. One of the children would eat nothing of the fresh meat but the spinal cords. Day after day, food was obtained in this way. This child overfed itself one day on this "marrow of the bone" and became very ill. No doctor was in reach, and herbs from the forest were the only remedy. The child recovered, but told the brothers he did not want any more of that "marrowbone meat."

The second theory is that when the explorers and viewers were locating lands for the state of Virginia to grant the soldiers and officers of the Revolutionary War, they became thrilled with excitement at the sight of so many rich bottoms over the country, but the state of ecstasy was reached when the report went back that all were good, but they had at last found the real "marrow of the bone."

This creek and Big Renox were set aside by the state of Virginia as "Districts for the Soldiers and Officers of the Revolutionary War," says the record of 1787-8.

This creek was not settled as early as some other parts of the county. When it was taken up by the first settlers they chanced to be the very best people that Virginia and North Carolina could furnish, and to this day their descendants strive to honor those good old pioneers by following in their footsteps. The Williams people owned the greater part of the Marrowbone valley from Waterview down, the Alexanders from Waterview to Caseys Fork, the Davis, Pace, Nunn, Gearheart, and Norris people from Caseys Fork up the creek. The Allens, Ritcheys, Garmons, and a few others had large grants of land, and their descendants still live close to the same places.

This creek does not rise to the height that some others do, on account of its level broad bottoms and low banks. Twelve feet will catch the height of the largest tides. In the life of the creek there have been many destructive overflows. The one of the greatest magnitude was in 1875. This being in the month of July, the corn and wheat crops were swept away. Other summer tides were: April, 1911; August, 1916; September, 1935. A new concrete bridge spans the creek at Waterview, which was built in 1936-7. It retards the current in a small measure. The highest tide of all was in 1842, and 1891.

Marrowbone Valley in this county is about 15 miles long. "Hill Top" is one of the most picturesque views to be found in the United States. Besides the hundreds of white spots that designate the homes there are two towns, Marrowbone and Waterview.

Marrowbone, which was founded in 1809, is the larger. It was named in honor of the creek which is described elsewhere. Marrowbone has a consolidated and high school and a large school for the colored children. There are also a bank and four stores. S. A. Graves has a general store; there is one run by J. P. Gray and another by J. W. Smith; F. A. Strange runs a large grocery store. Clyde B. Norris operates a garage in the town. Pace and Davis are undertakers. There is a Modern Woodman Chapter, established in 1907, and a Masonic Lodge. In 1936, G. R. Davis, J. P. Gray, and F. A. Chism donated land for a gymnasium for the school. The town has a Methodist Church, a Cumberland Presbyterian and a Presbyterian U.S.A. The well kept cemetery in the edge of town has its lots numbered.

The Garden Club of Marrowbone holds regular meetings about the town. It has adopted the poppy as its flower.

Highway No. 90 which passes through Marrowbone, as described elsewhere in this writing, was improved as an aid to the traffic going to the Wolf Creek Dam, 26 miles northeast, in 1941.

CROCUS CREEK

Crocus Creek occupies the northern part of the county. It flows southwest and empties into the river about ten miles above Burkesville. It has five tributaries from the west and two small ones from the east. Ascending, they are Beech Branch, Pine, West Fork, Cedar, and Harrods Fork on the west, and Collins and Puncheon on the east. This creek is noted for its fertile bottoms. They are fed by the overflows in the creek at times and at other times all this deposit may be swept away. Heavy, quick rains are the ones that do the damage. These big rains may cause a rise of 15 or 20 feet. If they come in the growing season of corn, which is the main crop, much damage results. This seldom happens. On September 4, 1935, a heavy rain hit the western tributaries and swelled Crocus uncommonly large. The Hopewell Baptist Church, which stood on Harrods Fork, was swept away, torn to pieces, and carried into Cumberland River. Crocus shot across the river with such force and volume that it tore out a great gap in the opposite bank of the river up into the field, uprooted all the timber there and turned Cumberland River upstream for 8 miles. Parts of the church building passed Shoestring Bottom up the river, a distance of seven miles.

The early settlers of these creeks are listed elsewhere. Their descendants still live in about the same neighborhoods. The pioneers were an intelligent, venturesome class of farmers, and these qualities are perpetuated. They take pride in their farms and homes.

Crocus has three school buildings and one church building. It has one small village about 12 miles from Burkesville named Amandaville. For years the people have been handicapped by bad roads; the creek being the greatest obstacle.

A new W.P.A. highway has been started up the creek. In 1934, through the solicitation of a committee composed of T. W. Roberts, S. D. Pace, ——, and the writer, contacted the W.P.A. representatives, headed by Thomas Rhea at Russellville, Kentucky, and obtained a grant of $5,000 with which the road up the creek was started. Robert Baker was chosen supervisor. From this the county in cooperation with the W.P.A. has built four miles of hard-surfaced road out of the creek. It was at the instance this committee and at the same time that the Whetstone road was started, as described elsewhere. Both of these roads were worked for the first year with pick and shovel and horse and mule teams furnished by the citizens whom the roads would serve.

Crocus Creek is surrounded by the largest scope of timber to be found in the county. Saw mills, heading mills, and stave mills have been running at times, not far apart, for over one hundred years, and yet there is timber.

The creek received its name through the "viewers for the soldiers of the Revolutionary War," because the Indians then living there so resembled the Crocus tribe. They haunted the region of the "Healing

Waters," later called Sand Lick, where thousands of early settlers paid visits for the healing of all manner of diseases.

The reputation of its healing power spread to all parts of southern Kentucky. Strangers would come and erect cabins for their families to live in while being treated. The stately beech trees standing bear record of many who were cured of rheumatism, scalp diseases, lameness, scrofulous and cutaneous diseases. Robert Blakey said a lodging house was built as early as 1812 by the whites and later by Nathaniel Morgan. Some tree data just disappearing are: R. Tate 1836; T. C. Grider and J. Mack Grider 1867. The bombastic publicity spread through the columns of the daily newspapers of other healing waters at Hot Springs, Arkansas, and other places caused these springs to lose much of their ancient fame. Dr. Godfrey Hunter, who had not been weaned from his native country across the seas, refused to rely on their curative properties, but made a trip to Carlsbad, Germany, to have his rheumatism cured with practically the same waters.

OTHER CREEKS

Big Renox Creek received its name from Col. Henry Rennicks, a Revolutionary officer who was given grants of land to recompense him for his services in the war.

Lewis Creek was first called Lewis' Run Creek for Thomas Lewis, who had large grants on the creek, 1798.

Tear Coat Creek received its name from Daniel Clift's daughter who was sent up the creek to drive the cows up to milk, and after a short time she reached the homeplace on the river bank almost breathless and with but little dress coat left, and just enough breath to tell she had been chased by a grizzly bear.

Whetstone creeks were named for the factory (by hand) that ran in 1799, making grindstones on the lower creek where sandstones were available on the nearby ridges.

Brush Creek was named by the military surveyors of the eighteenth century, because of its obstructions to the surveyors as a result of Indian fires.

Goose Creek was named also back in the 1700's, but history leaves us to suppose as to its connection with geese.

Bear Creek was called such by the early pioneers, who obtained most all of their meat from the animals which were there in abundance. One record says that settlers were forbidden to return to Virginia on summer visits, lest on their arrival back home they should find their crops entirely destroyed by bears.

Sulphur Creek in all the early records was called "Sulphur Lick Creek." This was for the buffalo lick just east of Speartown on the creek.

Kettle Creek was named by the viewers in the latter part of 1700. There were as many as five of them who carried their cooking utensils with them (for full details see following pages).

Creeks

The names applied to other creeks heretofore named were the names of men who figured in early history connected with them.

Some of the tributaries of Marrowbone might be mentioned: Groves Creek (now Dutch) was named by George Groves, 1800, for his father who died in Augusta County, Virginia. Ferris Fork was named for its first settlers. Casey Fork was named for William Casey, who fought the Indian battle, 1790, on Renox Creek and also visited the place that bears his name.

HIGHLANDS

Between the creeks of the county there are high ridges. Some of them are extensive level lands, part of which are of a marshy nature covered with trees. Some are backbone-like. Some are undulating, dotted with clearings. In the narrowest ridges at the head of many of the creeks of the county are gaps. These gaps are nature's great benefactors. People in passing up one of those creeks may easily step through these gaps onto the head of another creek without climbing hills. This makes it very convenient. Only the creeks on the north side of Cumberland River have these gaps. In passing from one to another on the south side you are encountered with two slopes, which are usually very steep.

The price of land being in reach of most anyone on these ridges accounts for the thickly settled communities in much of this territory.

Between the waters of Kettle and Sulphur creeks is Pea Ridge. It is one of the largest ridges in the county. Tradition linked with what records are available account for its name. In early days of that part of the county the pea, found growing wild, was grown for seed. There were ready markets with the farmers on Kettle Creek, Sulphur Creek, and Wolf River. The farmers of those bottoms depended on Pea Ridge for their seed peas, which were sown for hay for horses and cows, the only live stock of the day. In growing this legume so extensively on this ridge, before the realization dawned on the people so engaged, they had let their soil slip away from them. Much of the ridge today is poor. Old fields are neglected, turned out, and growing up in trees and bushes. Here and there are spots devoted to agriculture. Surrounding Speartown is a fairly good farming region. Hay is the principal crop. Some of the country is covered with timber. This is true of the headwaters of the creeks and spurs of the ridge.

Though inhabited by some of the best people in Cumberland County, Pea Ridge for the last hundred years has been accredited with more moonshine stills and criminal acts than any other part of Cumberland County. Two reasons account for this. First, it got started wrong. The early immigrants of that part of the county indulged in the liquor traffic. Crime is the outcome of all liquor indulgences.

Kettle Creek itself was named from the acts of an intoxicated man. It was on this order: a number of prospectors had come to that part of the county and, night overtaking them, they pitched their tent on the banks of the new creek, spread down their bedding, stacked their cooking vessels close to their place of rest, and reclined for the night. One of the men, whose name we failed to find, awoke from a horrible dream of having spent the night with their kettle under his head. The dream was so real to him that he sat up, rubbed his crazed head, and moved to a small peninsula across the creek to spend the remainder of the night. When sleep had come upon him the same dream impressed him, only with greater volume. He arose on the next morning and related his terror to his comrades. After a jovial catechizing by the members of the party, they fell on the name for the camp. Hence, the name of the creek.

Pea Ridge has one village—Speartown. It is surrounded with a good settlement of people. It has a large two-teacher school, one church house, and a store. Payton P. Spears is a progressive farmer of the community.

The village received its name from the people of that name who have lived there ever since Mary Ann Spears took up her large grant of land there in 1802. Several hundred Spears occupy this ridge.

The second reason for the illicit practice that has tortured the minds of the good people of Pea Ridge for the past hundred years is isolation. If there is one germ of evil in a man he seeks isolation to develop it. This handicap is being overcome by the construction of the new highway, 1935-8, which leads entirely through the country of Pea Ridge to the outside world. People are erecting better dwellings, seeing more travelers, and associating with different friends. In the near future there is predicted a remarkable change for Pea Ridge, and we hope the old trees and stumps standing almost within a stone's cast of each other will rot and perish and take with them the memory of the atrocious murders they have been perpetuating.

There are spurs of Pea Ridge that make off to the east and west. Poplar Grove Ridge makes off to the west, and it has many homes on it, but no surfaced highway. Some valuable timber yet remains there.

Guthries Ridge is another long ridge that makes off to the west. It has three churches and three schools at different places. The postoffice of Tanbark is on this ridge. The soil is medium; much is washed away and gone. Timber grows in localities, while wood is in abundance.

Stalcup Ridge also makes off to the west. A new road is now under construction there, leading to Black's Ferry. It was named for the people by that name who were early settlers. This is a good timbered scope of territory, mostly oak timber.

There are other spurs to Pea Ridge going west but not so long and well settled.

Ashlock Ridge is one that occupies the southern part of the county. To reach it you go through Tennessee and bend back into the county. It is a good neighborhood, but poor.

Coe Ridge is a colored community adjoining Kettle Creek, and its soil is of a poor quality. This is an old settlement.

Making off to the east from Pea Ridge there are small ridges that lead to Sulphur Creek. Patches of good land may be found here. On one of these is virgin timber owned at present by A. A. Huddleston. Fine oak and poplar are there.

Between the waters of Sulphur, Bear, and Illwill creeks lies an extensive area of upland. From north to south it is about 12 or 14 miles long. From east to west about 3 to 5 miles wide. It is known as Chestnut Grove Ridge, but is called by other names in different sections. The north end abutting Bear Creek is called Modoc Ridge. To the east it is called Green Grove Ridge, and to the west it is known as Bow Ridge. The Bow Ridge on the north is a tie to Pea Ridge. From this tie to the Tennessee line Sulphur Creek divides Pea Ridge and Chestnut Grove.

This is one of the most thickly settled ridges in the county. Ninety-eight per cent of the population on this ridge are Republican. Office seekers of the county (which is four-fifths Republican) seek to carry with them to this district all of their political caresses. A host of good people live on this ridge. The several churches and schools here are treated under a separate chapter.

The soil is moderately good and produces sufficient food for the people, and in some localities a surplus is raised. Scopes of timber are yet found on branches and hollows. The noted chestnut tree that once graced this ridge is gone. These trees were used for lumber and rails to make fences. They have been known to grow seven feet in diameter and to a great height. What trees were not worked up and used, have been killed by the chestnut blight of 1925. Not one is left living. The nuts were gathered from the burrs and sold at an average of $2.00 per bushel, but brought more by the quart.

A new W.P.A. road connecting with Highway No. 90 at Bear Creek opens up this ridge to the Frogue postoffice, 12 miles, and will soon be finished to the Tennessee line. This road was started at the bridge that spans Bear Creek in the summer of 1936.

East of Salt Lick Bend and in the crook of the river, is a most remarkable ridge called "The Narrows." Connecting to this is Carys Ridge, named for the people who first settled it and whose descendants still own the lands. At one place one may stand upon this ridge and cast a stone almost into the river on both sides, while it is 15 miles around the bend. The people have a school building upon this ridge named also for the inhabitants, Cary. This is a good fruit region.

Myers Ridge is an old settlement, named for the people by that name who came here early. It has one school and one church. A section of it called Seminary Ridge from the Seminary School that tried to function in this county and failed, has one church. The people are of a good class, but poor. A new road leads through the ridge from south to north, leading to Irish Bottom. A few scopes of timber may yet be seen, but most of it has been cut away since the new road was built, 1936.

Connecting with it and making off to the west on the waters of Brush and Goose creeks is Smith Ridge. This ridge has flat woods with a large scope of small trees growing. The soil is fairly good, but somewhat wet in many places. It has one school and one church building. A spur of this ridge is String Ridge, which leads to the west. Many homes are on this ridge. Timber has been the source of income on all these ridges for over 80 years. Most of the work was cross-tie hacking.

Between the waters of Willis Creek and Crow Creek is a ridge some three miles long and two wide. This ridge has no cleared lands. It is in woods some of which is suitable for use, but most of it is too rough for lumber. One high backbone with several deep branch gorges leading off east and west, all covered with trees, make up this ridge.

NORTH OF THE RIVER

The ridges or highlands are not so large as the ones just described south of the river. Beginning at the north end of the county, the first one is the ridge lying between Cumberland River and Crocus Creek. This is one of unbroken forest and reaches from the mouth of Crocus Creek to the Russell County line, and there it continues for over 25 miles to Columbia, Adair County. No homes are on this ridge, only timbered lands, in this county.

The next ridge going west is Jones Ridge. It lies between Crocus Creek and Big Renox. It is mostly cleared land, except in places. Like most ridges it has been cleared a long time, and the neglected places are growing up in bushes. The land is moderately good for corn and hay. It is very fine land for fruit. One school and one church house are in use there. There are no hard-surfaced roads closer than No. 61 on Big Renox. Continuing north from this ridge is Traylor Ridge, a timbered ridge to the Adair County line.

The other ridges between the tributaries of Marrowbone Creek are all wooded territories.

Stockton Ridge is just east of the village of Leslie. Many people live on this ridge. It has a north and south course. J. W. Bull and his descendants have made the ridge famous as a fruit-growing region. Apples, peaches, grapes, and other fruits thrive well. There is one school on this ridge.

WHAT CUMBERLAND COUNTY LOST

Cumberland County lost some curiosities by having to give up some of her territory to help form other counties. On the part sliced from this county in 1876 and annexed to Russell County, she lost the Rock House. Prior to 1801 it was known as "The Great Arch." Some might call it a natural bridge but it differs in many respects from a freak of that class. A small branch runs through it but above is a common high hill covered with forest. This house is about one mile from the Cumberland County line. It is nothing more than a square hole through a river bluff, with one entrance facing the east and one facing the west. The eastern door is 116 feet wide; the western, 100 feet wide. Its length from door to door is 150 feet, with a smooth ceiling 50 feet from the dirt floor at the eastern door. Cumberland River flows by the eastern door and a ten-foot rise puts the river at the front door, but it takes 35 or 40 feet to cause the water to flow through the house and pass on down to the slough to meet the main river again, which has flowed some seven miles around.

When the river is high enough to reach the ceiling much of the stream gurgles through the Rock House, somewhat like the water from a bottle's neck when angled downward, and the gurgle is so powerful that the large timber growing above the ceiling trembles and the turbulent waters that pass through the aperture are converted into huge maelstroms that are dangerous to boatsmen.

Many religious revivals have been held in this Rock House during the dry months of the year. It will hold hundreds of people, and enough loose rocks are there to afford seating for all.

Numerous places elsewhere in the United States not nearly so remarkable as this one have long since been converted into parks, but owing to bad roads in this part of Kentucky this natural curiosity is little known.

Another loss to Cumberland when the territory that formed most of Clinton County was removed in 1835, was the 76 falls. This is a perpendicular precipice of solid limestone over which the headwaters of Indian Creek plunge. In the dry season of the year this creek dwindles to a tiny stream, then before the waters reach the bottom of the 83-foot fall they are changed to a fine mist. In the winter months this mist freezes on the timber below and along the creek banks and forms tons of white ice in thousands of different shapes and contours which present spectacular scenes.

Chapter 12

WILD LIFE

BIRDS

Cumberland County has around 70 different kinds of birds. Some of the most beautiful birds in the world are found here, and among them are many sweet songsters. Most of the song birds are here in the warm months of the year.

The wild turkey, which disappeared about 1900, was the largest and most important bird of all the large types. It and the pheasant, which is also a bird of history in this county, hatched their young in the forest in nests made on the ground, taking four weeks to hatch. The young wanted to stroll as soon as hatched. Usually from six to fifteen eggs were found in the nests at a time.

The quail is here yet. The mother quail makes her nest in June in a depression in the ground out in some grassy place. There she lays around 17 eggs, which are hatched in three weeks. No other bird is more imposed on than this one. Nowadays its struggle for life is increased. Snakes, rats, owls, and hawks are its natural foes, but man with his shotgun and bird hound is its biggest enemy. Farmers, who feed and protect the quail eleven months out of each year, shudder to hear the "bang bang" from the sportsmen during the other month of the so-called open season. Unless landowners unite to curb this onslaught, this beautiful, happy, useful little creature will perish from the earth. Children who find quail nests should be taught to respect the mother birds enough to leave them there and let them hatch; but an old man, many of whom have been seen carrying hats half full of eggs home for dinner, can offer no excuse for his ignorance other than that he has more wild beast in him than man, or that he is too trifling to make a living for his wife and children.

Other food birds are the duck that is to be found on Cumberland River more or less throughout the year and the wild geese seen along the watercourses in limited numbers in the month of November while on their way south.

The robins, since 1922, when the canebrakes nearly all died, have been reduced in number. The wild pigeon, that once obscured the sun, disappeared about 1892. The starling, which is a specie of black mocking bird, has come in great numbers within the last decade.

The Kentucky cardinal is the most beautiful bird that haunts the thickets of Cumberland County. It is perennial. The male is deep red and the female is brown. Unlike the animal kingdom, the males of all birds surpass the females in beauty.

Wild Life

There are dozens of useful birds, too numerous to mention; and there are birds whose usefulness is questionable, such as the crow, blue jay, English sparrow, the last of which was imported from England in 1850 to eat the insects on the rice plant, but, contrary to his calling, took to the grain. Aged citizens of the county tell us it made its appearance here in Cumberland County 35 years later.

Most small birds raise from four to six to the brood. The cooing dove has only two eggs to the sitting, and they are hatched in poorly constructed nests up in trees. The oriole is the most beautiful small bird. The junco comes from the north in November and remains throughout the winter months. Many different migratory birds visit the county from the north in winter and from the south in summer.

The destructive birds are the eagle, owl, and hawk. The last eagle of record was caught in a trap after it had slain a lamb, in 1889.* The hoot owls are plentiful. They rear from two to four in hollow trees. Hawks are of five different species, all harmful to useful birds and domesticated fowls. The chicken hawk has the keenest eyesight of all birds, also is one of the swiftest on wing. They have been known to locate small chickens on the earth from a height of a full mile. Their age is that of man.

The vulture, brown and black, once thought to be a useful and necessary bird, in destroying dead carcasses, is no longer to be regarded as such, but on the contrary now takes its position with other disease germ carriers, especially of cholera and black leg to livestock. They lay speckled eggs, three or four, in some dark cave or bluff, which hatch out white birds. The grown vulture has the most acute smell of all birds, being able to locate dead bodies from a distance of three to four miles.

Birds, like most all other living things, are attracted to localities with food. Since the land has been cleared of much of its rubbish, and weed seeds have deteriorated through repeated mowings, farmers should not covet what few seeds or what little fruit the birds take in exchange for their untiring services in destroying harmful insects.

Generations of people come and go, and with each one is perpetuated the thrill of sporting. With young boys this thrill is experienced by the fall of birds as their first prey, and one time calls for another until they discover that ere long the premises no longer abound with twitter and song. Educate children to love birds and administer to their needs, and home life will be made more cheerful and happy. The topography of the southern part of Old Kentucky has held the flora and fauna in its fullest measure of perfection.

---

* In February, 1891, Mr. John Collins caught an eagle which measured over 6 feet from tip to tip. On January 1, 1891, Mrs. D. L. Thrasher, of Browns Cross Roads, caught in trap one measuring 6 feet 6 inches from tip to tip. This one had killed a goose.

WILD ANIMALS

When Daniel Boone and the Long Hunters roamed over what later became Cumberland County, it was filled with many different kinds of wild animals, many of which have long since become extinct. Buffaloes wintered in the dark, dense canebrakes of the river and creek bottoms. An old record of Cumberland County mentions settlers at "buffalo lick" on Indian Creek in 1800. George Rogers Clark tells us that he and his company killed 14 buffaloes at one time in Kentucky in 1781. Whether or not Clark helped to slay these large animals of this county we fail to find recorded, but he made tours through this county to hunt and visit with his relatives.

We do know that the buffaloes were ruthlessly slain and wasted. Sometimes for their skins, sometimes for their meat, and on one expedition they were killed for their tongues only. The last buffalo was killed in 1790 in Kentucky; last bear in 1898.

Deer were here by the thousands. They were raced and killed 102 years after the last buffalo disappeared from Kentucky. They, like buffaloes, gave birth to single young, mostly. A long time after the deer were all killed horns were often found fastened between trees telling of tragic deaths. Squirrels enjoyed gnawing these horns. Several people yet living remember the taste of venison.

The lynx passed out about 1880; the otter, 1894; the beaver, 1875. The wild cat was here in 1930, and perhaps a few are in the Crocus hills yet (1942). The wild turkey went soon after 1900. The fox is the largest wild animal now living in the county. There are gray and red ones. They live among the creek and river hills. They raise annually from three to five. With gray selling around $2.00 per pelt and red about $8.00, much hunting and trapping goes on. The near future may find them scarce.

The raccoon, so plentiful in 1915, is rarely seen. Trappers that make trapping a livelihood are extinguishing the lower animals. The mink (rearing from three to six per year), in spite of all her cunningness, fails to escape the trapper's snare. The skunk and opossum are the most plentiful lower animals now found in the county. The skunk has from three to six per year. The opossum as many as 16 in one brood. The "possum" is a pouched animal. It carries its young in its pocket until about the size of a mouse and then they are left in a warm bed in some tree or log. It is an exciting scene to watch a mother possum moving over the ground with from 12 to 16 fluffy little fellows clinging to their mother's fur coat, trebling her in size. These pelts sell for about 25 cents, and young boys cannot wait until the first frost falls to make nightly raids on this poor stupid animal, and in this way shamefully butcher them ere the fur has developed. In 1851, James Hurt, Sparks Neeley, Richard Taylor, and Gideon Pharris were allowed $1.00 each for killing wild cats, and Sam Sprowles accounted for three cats at one term.

Wild Life

The gray rabbit, rearing as many as two litters per year with from three to six per litter, is here in abundance and is about the only means of sport to hunters now. The squirrel, red and gray, are here but in limited numbers. The red is about one-third larger than the gray, but fewer in number. They both raise from three to six annually. If there is plenty of mast then they rear two broods per year. The professional hunter in this county picks his time when the landlord is absent or not on duty and does his intruding, thereby slaying the cherished pets. The slaying of timber has destroyed the homes of the squirrels and made them an easy prey.

The lowest kinds of animals in the county are the snakes, frogs, and the two crustacea, turtle and terrapin. Two of the snakes are poisonous, rattlesnake and copperhead. The rattlesnake grows to be five and one-half feet long. It got its name from the horny appendage on the end of its tail. They have been killed with as many as 14 rings to the rattle. Their use is not known. They grow about two or three rings a year. The mother gives birth to broods of seven to twelve per year. They live in the forest.

The copperhead grows to 33 inches. It is named for the color of its head. Its venom is poisonous to man and beast. It haunts the rocky regions of the county. The mother copperhead gives birth to from four to eight per brood. The young measures one-third the length of the mother snake. Unlike the rattlesnake, it sounds no warning before fastening its fangs into its victim.

Garter snakes are more numerous by far than any other kind. They have large broods. Records claim 60 at one time. The writer of this volume witnessed the scene of a garter's nest which was plowed up by Ed Cash in 1921 on the bank of Cumberland River. Under a stump was the mother garter and 47 little baby snakes in one nest. The viper, small green, cow or chicken snake, and the black snake are the other kinds that inhabit Cumberland. A few live in water also.

The black snake is the only kind that lays eggs. They usually deposit about two dozen in their nest in some soft dry soil. The sun hatches them in thirty days. If the mother snake is disturbed while in sight of the eggs, she will swallow them all and move to another place of hiding.

Chapter 13

AGRICULTURE

Cumberland County is a farming county. Its 12 big river bottoms 10 of which are around four miles long and from one-half to three-quarters of a mile wide; and its 17 large creeks with all their tributaries, beside numerous small branches, furnish the county with many acres of good farming land. The ridges that lie between these creeks are not so fertile as the bottoms but they produce fairly good crops of corn. Commercial fertilizers have increased their production during the past 25 years. The ridges are more adapted to wheat and fruit than the bottoms. The main crops raised in the county are corn, tobacco, wheat, hay, potatoes, apples, and peaches.

Of these, corn takes the lead. The Indians grew corn here before white man came. Some of the bottoms were cleared into patches by the Indians. The pioneers were surprised to see so few fields free from timber and stumps in such broad, fertile valleys. About the only clearing done by the Indians in the river bottoms were strips along the river. The banks are higher next to the river and not as susceptible to overflows. The soil is sandy. The Indians liked to go by boats. For these reasons mainly, they cultivated near the streams. Creeks were inhabited and more land was cleared on them than the river. The main reasons were to avoid high waters and be close to good everlasting springs, which were big factors in determining the location of Indians as well as the white pioneers.

Corn has furnished bread for over 90 per cent of the population of Cumberland County throughout its history. The few dotted clearings of the Indians of 1790 have grown into 1,964 farms up to 1940, and the few Indian wigwams of 1790 have climbed to 2,779 separate homes in 1940.

Fifty years ago (1890), 16,233 acres were devoted to corn in the county with a production of 321,886 bushels. In 1940 there were 22,931 acres in corn with a production of 551,910 bushels. Land has been mistreated in this county. Too much corn has been the sin; i.e., too many years in corn and not enough rotation. For the last decade the farmers have begun to see the value of other crops besides corn. Along with corn come hogs. In old steamboat days, corn was shelled, sacked, and shipped to Burnside or Nashville. In truck days it is marketed through livestock. The greatest factor in determining the price of corn is supply and demand. A bumper year it goes cheap, in a lean year it sells high. In steamboat years freight was high and transportation slow and the local market did not keep pace with the city markets, but now a more uniform price governs the corn market.

Agriculture

In 1893 corn sold for 20 cents per bushel; in 1918 it sold for $2.00 per bushel, quite a fluctuation. In steamboat days when all goods were hauled from the landings on the river by teams by the hundreds, corn commanded good prices, as it was almost impossible to have corn shipped in. This market of haulers is now ancient history. Bottom lands yield from 5 to 13 barrels per acre, if rested. Ridge lands about half as much. The old rule for feeding corn was 50-cent corn 5-cent hogs, 60-cent corn 6-cent hogs, etc.

Wheat is not grown so extensively in this county as it once was. The most flourishing period for wheat growing was from about 1880 to 1920. W. F. Owsley brought the first wheat reaper into the county in 1872. Like all new things, it was handed from neighbor to neighbor, and of course this called for more threshing machines, both of which stimulated wheat production. Flour mills sprang up over the country to take care of the wheat crops, and soon everybody had biscuit every day in the year. Then this wheat generation commenced to die out, reapers and binders were allowed to go to ruin, threshers failed to function and were left in the barns, flour mills ceased to pay and were sold out of the county or allowed to crumble and ruin, bread factories sprang up all over the country, and the wheat farmers turned their attention to other things.

I here quote a few figures that will verify the statements which I have just made. In 1890 Cumberland County grew 20,745 bushels of wheat; in 1940 it grew 2,636 bushels of wheat. Loaf bread can be had so quickly after it has been baked that many housewives have forgotten the taste of one of those tall, round, white, fluffy little terrapins that once adorned the breakfast table. At the beginning of World War II there were 17,000 bakeries in the United States, 200 more were added for Army use.

Tobacco is the second great money crop of Cumberland County. Tobacco, like corn, is an American plant. Neither of the two was known before America was discovered, 1492.

Scarcely had the settlers of Cumberland County provided themselves with shelter, when they began to grow tobacco for sale. It was then of the dark type. Many old records of our county now tell of its growth and shipping. The market was at New Orleans, at the mouth of the Mississippi River. Foreign buyers were there to make the purchases. It took about three months to make the trip down the river and back home. Many shipments were lost in transit. Some of those operating the boats never returned after they left Burkesville. Others returned with the claim they were robbed on their way home. All early shipments were by flatboats propelled by man power. Tobacco averaged around $4\frac{3}{4}$ cents per pound. Hogsheads were made by hand from timbers of the forest. Boards were cut five feet long and set on the ends forming a circle 4 or 5 feet in diameter, surrounded with 4 runs of hoops on the outside, which were nailed to each board. A bottom was then placed inside and an extra hoop encircled the interior to hold it in place. Then the prizing came. It was done with a prize pole. The head was then placed inside, another hoop was nailed on to hold it in, and it was ready to roll to the river for shipment.

Tobacco was used as a medium of exchange by the grandmother state of Virginia until after the admission of Kentucky to statehood, 1792; but the first Legislature of Kentucky passed an act, "That all officers' fees, which are now chargeable and receivable in tobacco, shall in the future be charged in money and collected in the currency of the State; and that all fines and forfeitures charged in tobacco may, by suit, be collected in money." This medium was used for a while in this county after this law was passed.

Here are a few authentic reports from some of the tobacco traders of Cumberland County of long ago:

New Orleans, La.,
Nov. 30, 1843.

James Paull & Smith,
Burkesville, Ky.,
Gentlemen:

I herewith enclose to you quotations on the three grades of tobacco for this season, which has been a quiet month:

$2.00 to $2.75 per c. for No. X
3.00 to 3.75 per c. for Gr. S.
4.00 to 4.75 per c. for Gr. Firsts.

Benj. Sutter, Jr.

Have on hand about 300 hhds.

Sale bill of John M. Alexander shows prices of the year 1849:

24 sheep..................................$10.00
Cow and Calf............................ 7.80
50 geese.................................... 5.25
Still 12.62

Louisville became the greatest tobacco market in the world upon the admission of the state, and as soon as transportation from here to there started, all of Cumberland County's tobacco went to that market. Dark tobacco was the crop until the teens of the twentieth century, when burley entered in. Now white burley is raised altogether. It will grow thicker on the ground than dark but will not produce as many pounds, yet the money yield is much better. Anderson Garrett sold first crop of burley, 1889, $125.00.

Since January 1, 1933, the Government has tried to control the price and acreage of tobacco, which has been a help to the growers. Before this was done prices varied as the seasons changed. One year with high prices would stimulate the growers, and the following year all would do their utmost and the result would be a heavy drop. I here quote one instance of this kind that followed a lean year: 1933, J. C. Murphy, of the county, shipped 900 pounds from his farm to

Agriculture

market and awaited his check. Some weeks after his shipment he called at the office and it was there. On opening the letter he found a dun for $4.50 to pay expenses for selling. Some crops sold for ½ cent a pound during that year.

Beginning with the 20's of this century, loose leaf tobacco houses have sprung up in nearly every county seat of the state. In one day farmers may drive to market and back, sometimes bringing their checks home with them. While there are a few in the county whose church affiliations do not admit of tobacco raising, the most of the population of Cumberland grow it. Stripping is rushed in order to get it to market before the Christmas holidays that the landlord may get his tax money and the tenant may have Santa Claus for every child in the family.

Burkesville organized a tobacco company in 1921 and erected a large building on Celina Street. It prospered for about three years, and then ceased to be. The barn was sold to Fred McCoy and turned into other uses.

In 1943 the United States had 42 houses, and Kentucky had 21 of them.

In 1890 there were raised in Cumberland County 256,350 pounds of tobacco. In 1940 the county put out 1,384 acres which yielded 1,278,922 pounds, which averaged $16.40 per hundred.

The 1944 tobacco crop of Kentucky, sold mostly in 1945, averaged the high of $43.93.

Hay is another great crop of the county. It is on the increase, due to two reasons; first, cattle bring better prices than formerly, and then farmers take more pride in the conservation of the soil. Clover and timothy are the two old well established grasses, but of late Lespedeza is grown in great quantities for hay and pasture.

Potatoes are extensively grown in the county, mostly for home consumption. It is another plant of American nativity. It was carried to Ireland, and the people went so wild about it that it was eaten three times a day. The other countries declared the Irish lived on it alone, hence, its name. The sweet potato is grown on the ridges of the county much more than the bottoms. It is a good food.

Apples grow better on the highlands than on the low. So do peaches. When the pioneers first came to Cumberland County, they never forgot to bring their peach stones. This statement is found in various records. Wild fruits were in abundance, but the first things planted were peach stones. The peaches of today are much larger and more delicious than those planted by the pioneers.

Apples are grown more extensively than peaches. Next after the peach orchards came the apple orchards. The soil was fertile and well suited to them. Apples furnished a healthful diet for the settlers, but many of those old hardy Virginians thought brandy was a necessity. For this, as much as for food, were apple orchards planted. A few scraggy old trees may yet be seen standing in the old orchards of the county. A statement reads as follows:

"March, 1842, paid to Geo. W. Scott for trimming 167 apple trees, at the rate of one shilling apiece.

"Rane H. Staton."

This old orchard is gone with the exception of one old scrag. On Lewis Creek, three miles above Burkesville, on the farm of Miss Sally McMurtrey, stands an old apple tree, which was a large tree 80 years ago, and it is still bearing apples. It is a very large tree, measuring about 15 feet in circumference a distance of two feet above the ground. Later trees are not so long to live as those old seedlings. In this age, people have to spray their trees if they bear good fruit. Joseph Melton and John Parrish now own the largest apple orchard in the county. It is on a high ridge on the west side of Big Renox Creek. They spray and care for their trees, and thousands of bushels of apples are sold annually from the orchard. The quality is good. The keeping is like that of the northern fruit. There are other good orchards in the county. The Bull Brothers of Leslie village are fruit growers. Their orchard is on high land. Dix McComas has two large orchards of apples and peaches. Not as many people take interest in fruit growing as should in the county. Many still have that old Daniel Boone spirit, and depend on blackberries which need no attention.

Along with agriculture goes livestock. This county has long been noted for its good horses and mules, but since the automobile has come into use little interest is shown in horses and just enough interest in mules to supply the demand for the farm work. Very seldom does one see teams on the roads now. In 1941 there were 1,241 head of horses and mules in the county. The number was greater than this in 1810.

The cattle industry is on the mend. Thousands of head are grazed every year, some for beef and some for milk. The ox age went out with the nineteenth century. Will Cary, a big farmer in the southern part of the county, still keeps a yoke of large oxen, for "old-times' sake." Ox teams and poplar logs went out together.

Cattle in the county are much improved in quality over that of 20 years ago, Hereford and Aberdeen being the choice breeds. In 1890, 50 years ago, there were 4,892 head of cattle in the county with only one purebred cow and no bulls. In 1940 there were 6,063 head of cattle, with over 300 full stock and hundreds of half and mixed stock close to purebred. The cows from this herd produced 925,002 gallons of milk and 186,456 pounds of butter. All this butter was eaten by the local people, except 7,537 pounds. The milk too was nearly all used by local people. From these figures one may see Cumberland Countians are a milk-consuming people.

The hog industry has long been the leading livestock industry of the county. Fifty years ago hogs were grown in the woods and then were brought out and sold or fattened. The ruthless slaying of timber has annihilated the mast trees. In a way it was better for the farmers.

Agriculture

It has caused them to acquire better breeds of hogs, and take more interest in them. People have learned that instead of letting the hog grow wild for two years and then fattening him, it is better to push him from birth and never let him see his second birthday. In 1940, 13,000 head of hogs were fattened in the county. The hog market is one of uncertainty. It will lift you or bankrupt you quicker than any other business. Modern conveniences in transportation have added ease and profit to this industry. Pinhookers handled most of the hogs of former days. Hogs were bought from $1.00 to $1.25 of the market by them. Then this price came lower and lower until the advent of good roads brought an even break with the pin-man. Today the farmer ships his own hogs and many times takes them in his own pickup.

It might be well enough here to list a few of those old buyers who brought glad tidings to many, many farm boys by relieving them of a week's task of marketing. They were: Wiley Bouldin, Tilden Waggener, Dix McComas, J. C. Murphy, Clayton Snow, Thomas Phelps, Finis Phelps, George Russell, Emanuel Sloan, Berry Buster, Leonard Mann, Dink Mann, John and Charley Campbell, Ed Young, Bob Young, Richard Newby, Dick Baker, Ed Morgan, Bob Richardson, Bert Gorman, G. T. Herriford, Charles Herriford, John Frazier, J. R. Alexander, Gid Alexander, Horace Alexander, Charles Alexander, Sid S. Davis.

Home butchering was practiced by many old-time citizens. The meat was salted and sold locally, sides usually at 10 cents and hams at 12½ cents. For example, Gid Alexander killed 65 hogs in December, averaging about 400 pounds, and put the meat in his smokehouse.

Sheep are raised all over the county. They are raised for their wool and for the lamb marketing. They are the cheapest livers of all livestock, thereby bringing more clear money. The worst drawback to this industry is the sheep-killing dog. In the pauper counties it is difficult to collect the damage on sheep killed by these dogs. As high as 10 or 15 have been killed in one night. Better breeds of sheep have found their way into this county of late. At present there are 2,900 sheep in the county, which produced in 1941, 5,802 pounds. It sells at 43 cents per pound.

Statistics show the following for 1940: Ducks, 181; turkeys, 131; honey, 3,737 pounds; molasses, 9,412 gallons.

Chickens are raised by every homekeeper in the county. The rural people obtain most of their living from them. In 1940 there were 98,000 chickens raised in the county. The housewife looks forward to her eggs and chickens as does the man to his tobacco. The grocery bills are paid with chickens and eggs.

Every industry has its handicaps. Every rose has its thorn. Chickens have their enemies. The chicken hawk is one of the worst enemies of chickens. He comes swooping out of the sky and is gone with a chicken in his talons before the human eye can see. The hoot owl is another enemy, but not so bad as the hawk. His work is done during nights after the chicken is grown. The mink and weasel are foes that make nightly raids and destroy many at a time. Heavy June rains drown hundreds if not sheltered while young. Diseases can be fought with greater success than living enemies. Chicken thieves still exist in a limited number.

The wharf rat is another pullback to the chicken industry. Beside destroying thousands of young chickens in the county, the rat makes great inroads on corn, wheat, and other foods. They are heavy producers of young, as many as 16 have been found in a single nest, and not a runt in the bunch. Observations have been made on the rat here which showed a loss of as many as two ears of corn in one crib per night. This times the number of grown rats on a farm will surprise you. An eye witness tells of 63 rats in one group and 135 in another all being killed on the same farm. This included all sizes.

The chicken or cow snake is another enemy to chickens and birds. Other species of snakes seldom bother the chickens. This chicken snake is a large type of reptile. It measures about 5 or 6 feet in length, four to six inches in circumference when grown, and is covered with white spots scattered over his brown coat. His mouth is from one to one and a half inches wide at a normal position, but it is easy for him to pass through it a three-inch chicken or turkey.

Most chicken diseases may be prevented by feeding at regular times. Their feed should never be spread on the ground. This causes diarrhea and gapes. No medicine has been patented that will cure the gapes. The only safe remedy has been discovered in this country. It is this: take a horse hair as course as possible, about twelve inches long, double it in the middle, twist together, leaving a loop at the end three-fourths inch long and about one-eighth of an inch wide, sit down and place the chickens feet both between your knees, and with your left hand hold his mouth open and with your right hand hold the looped hair with loop just inside of chicken's bill and watch down its throat to see the larynx open, which will happen at each gape, then quickly insert loop into the trachea one or two inches, make five quick twists of the hair and pull out quickly. In the loop will be one or two red worms. Put the chicken down and forget about him.

Cumberland County, as well as its sister counties, has kept abreast with the shifting changes brought about by demands of the times. Many products of former days have ceased to be grown and others have taken their places. The same is true of many by-products.

One of those ancient crops of this county was hemp. Many acres were devoted to its growth. Every farmer who was able to own slaves grew enough of this plant to supply his own needs. An extensive factory located near the river on upper River Street, near the site of the old Williams & Ritchey mill, now in decay, was set up in 1812. It turned out products used by the local people. They were ropes, cordage, cables, calking, and cloth. Ropes and cables were in great

Agriculture

demand. The large cable was used by lumber and raft men. After the trees were cut on the level spots a cable was used to roll the giant logs from the deep hollows. Then the cable was used to anchor the large rafts of logs to the banks of the river.

The principal use to which hemp was put was the making of cloth. This cloth was of a coarse nature. It was used to make shirts, pants, towels, bedticking, sheets, and caps for the slaves. Enough was raised and manufactured in the years 1825-30 to afford a reasonable income to its producers above the local demand. This business went on until the abolition of slavery in 1863, after which its cultivation gave way to other crops. For nearly three-fourths of a century hemp plants were not known, but a demand arose at the outbreak of World War II for rope. We had been importing from the Philippine Islands enough to supply our needs until the capture of those islands by the Japs in 1942. On March 25, 1942, while Wainright was waging his last battle for the islands, the Government, seeing their doom, called on the citizens of the country to restore this ancient crop; so on that date Burkesville held a meeting in which 105 farmers of Cumberland County subscribed their names to an agreement to raise 200 acres to meet this emergency. Seed was all that was wanted from this crop. As a result 2,000 bushels were raised that yielded the growers $8.00 per bushel. The next year another crop was grown, but in November of 1943 the Government agencies called off hemp in Kentucky; the ground and time to be devoted to the growth of food for the war. The reason for this calling in the hemp was that the United States was able to secure the necessary hemp from Central America and jute from the Mediterranean countries, the U-boat menace in those waters having been destroyed, making shipment possible.

Another new crop of the county is soybeans. It was not grown until the beginning of the twentieth century. History of China shows that country grew them 2,838 years before Christ for food and oil. The farmers are now learning their value for hay, legume, and for hogs along with the corn crops.

FARM IMPLEMENTS

Farm implements first used in this county were the same as those used in other places, for there was only the one kind. The distinction between the little farmer and the big one was the number of tools he owned. The wooden moldboard turner was used in this county until about 1830, when the cast plow took its place. A bill of sale of 1823 says, "sold to —— three bar plows." These were wooden turners with strips of old saws or their like fastened on them. Records show that by 1840 the metal turner was in general use, replacing "barshires."

The "scooter" plow was used in the county to cultivate corn and gardens until the Civil War, and some used it until about 1890. Some people follow Pope's advice, "Be not the first by which the new is tried, nor yet the last to lay the old aside." The double-shovel was invented in 1830. Its first work was much criticized. Some said the shovel plow did not leave a deep furrow and corn could not be grown that way. Others said one foot would cover up the weeds and the other foot would instantly uncover them. Others said when you lean your shovel plow one foot is in the air. Of course all this criticism was a result of ignorance.

A lad was usually put to "splitting middles" in the corn row with scooters, his first plowing experience. Those middles were made by daddy or an older hand by running next to the corn with two furrows and leaving the middle some fifteen inches broad. In rows of corn two hundred hills in length, an active lad, in trying to hold the scooter plow on that middle, by the time he would reach the other end of the field, would have at least as many sections of the middle as there were hills in the row.

In 1888, a great excitement was created in the Indian Creek settlement when it was reported that William Neathery had a plow that would plow the corn and split the middles all at the same time. A dozen of the neighbors gathered at his house after dark to look at the "wonder plow." This was the first double-shovel in that neighborhood, the first in the county, 1844.

The corn rows were marked off with the scooter plow four feet apart both ways and three grains of corn were dropped into the cross and covered with the eye-hoe. This was plowed four times just as deep as the plow could run, the last of which was about the time the corn was putting out its tassels and silks. If the season chanced to be rainy and the weeds or grass took hold, then a turning plow was used to cover up the weeds, though the corn was in the roasting-ear stage.

Corn drills were patented in 1853 and reached this county about 1870. The two-row planter came in 1885.

Tractors were first used successfully in 1906; experimentally, 1892. The first to reach this county was about 1908, and there are now in use 100 in the county. They are used to turn, disk, and cultivate. With the scooter one could plow over 2 acres; with the shovel, 4 acres; with the cultivator, 10 acres; and with the tractor, 35 acres, per day.

The greatest industrial awakening in the history of the United States was around 1830. The wooden-tooth harrow was used in this county until about that date when the iron-tooth took its place.

The best harrow for the farmer that thus far has been invented is the disk harrow. It was invented by G. Page in 1847. It is an American invention, but Page got the idea from the Japanese, who had used something like it for centuries. The first one to be used in this county was in 1891 by Marrowbone farmers. Now farming would be almost impossible without the disk.

The horse rake was invented in 1820 and the reaper in 1831 by Cyrus McCormick, of Virginia. The reaper has undergone many

Agriculture

changes from the first to the present. It first consisted of knives and the guard and section blade were not used until 1851. This was on the reaper, and sometimes the reel was removed and the machine was used for mowing hay. The separate mowing machine was not invented until 1865. Before this date, hay was cut with the scythe. The wheat reaper as first used would cut the wheat, and later it would bunch it for tying; but it was not until 1881 that John F. Appleby invented the needle that tied the wheat into bundles. In 1877, Charles Whittington had invented a needle that tied the bundles with wire, but Appleby's attachment tied with twine as it does today.

The first reaper was brought into this county in 1872 by W. F. Owsley, and the first binder in 1885 by Barton Philpott of Washes Bottom in the southern part of the county; first mowing machine by Elam Cheatham of Crocus Creek, 1870.

Virgin soil was soft and loose and wooden turners could plow well. Points were introduced about 1815 by Thomas Wiard; and his son Harry in 1860 patented the Chilled Plow and in 1876 set up his factory at Syracuse, N. Y., where the modern steel beam turner, hillside plow, and sulky plow were made by him. The first manure spreader was made in 1878 with two wheels. In 1895 the sulky plow was used in this county. A common shovel plow was fastened beneath the axle of the two-wheeled sulky and answered for the cultivator. No way of shifting plows was possible, therefore if rows were not on bee-line and the teams kept perfectly straight with the rows you know the result. About all one got from this mode of cultivation was a gay ride. First steel turner was brought in by Joseph H. Beck in 1858.

The wild pigeons which swooped down and picked up grass seed as fast as sown prompted the invention of a seeder that covered the seed as sown, 1859.

While the years of the flail-and-fan for the separation of the small grains from the straw, date back to about 1890, several living in 1945 can still see those flails made of an 8-foot green hickory sapling about two inches in diameter and "withed" two feet from the big end to bend in all directions when the stroke was made down upon the grain straws spread upon the smooth barn floors. Many old square barns made of logs with those tight floors are standing today to tell the story of that hand-threshing period. After the grain was beaten out by hand, the old fan was poured full of the mixed grain and chaff and turned by hand to blow away the trash from the grain.

The "groundhog" thresher lived during this period. It was a horsepower cylinder that did the same work as the flail. Any neighborhood was lucky to have one of those machines to do the threshing for the whole community. Swapping of work was a delight to one and all who had grain to thresh. Lavish meals were prepared for the big day. Sometimes more than one day was required to get through.

The combine that was invented about 1886 was made for the huge farms of the prairie countries of the United States. It was also

172   *History of Cumberland County*

a crude affair, but perfect, drawn by twenty mules and operated by several hands. The header followed this make of machine, and then the present model of combine which is drawn by gas power and threshes all kinds of seeds entered in.

The first combine to reach Cumberland County was in 1939. It was brought into the county by Wallace Roberts, a thriving farmer of Marrowbone Creek. The following five years saw six in the county.

OIL IN CUMBERLAND COUNTY

Three miles north of Burkesville on Highway No. 61 near the Renox Bridge stands a monument. This marks the site of the first oil well in America. It is known all over America as the "Old American Oil Well." This marker was erected in 1934 and was paid for with money appropriated by the Legislature of Kentucky. Frank Bruton, Jr., was serving this county at that session. The face rock is an old millstone once used in one of the oldest mills of the county on Sextons Fork of Illwill Creek. Mrs. Nora McGee has the honor of obtaining this rock and sponsoring the other work.

FIRST AMERICAN OIL WELL, 1829
On Highway 61, Burkesville, Kentucky

Agriculture

This well was drilled in by parties searching for salt water in 1829. I reproduce here a letter, the original of which is in preservation, giving the exact spelling and punctuation of same:

"Mar. 15, 1829

"Mr. Edmon Rogers
Mont Hope
Barren City, Ky.
By Dick

Mr. Rogers

"We have no news Except Cols. Emmerson & Stockton has been boring for salt on Rennox creek Struck a lake of oil The well has been running for the past three days throughing out large quantities of Rock Oil it would spout out at least fifteen feet above the top of the ground as large a stream as a mans Boddy—Perfectly Pure. Cumberland River has been covered from Bank to Bank for three days the River was set on fire I have no doubt but in time it has been running to speke in the bounds of reason that five hundred thousand gallons of oil has run down Cumb. River it is still running but not quite so fast Col. Emmerson has barrelled up twenty barrels of it it burns well in lamp & is good to paint and oil leather & I have no doubt it will be a good medison for man's complaints particularly the Rumatick pains the hole atmospher is perfumed with it it is a complete phenominon I could rite a hole shete and not say half it is late and I am sleepy

"I am yours, etc.
Thomas Ellison"

In 1934, P. J. Keymel leased the land that has on it the Old Well and removed the wooden casing. It was a poplar log twelve inches square and had been hollowed out and soaked with oil and stopped up with a cedar log sealed with flaxseed. Logs were set on top of each other to a depth of 171 feet. They were in a good state of preservation, but when the air struck them they soon crumbled. The well was drilled with an 80-foot teeter pole. This oil was shipped to England down the Mississippi River, and we are told today there are samples of it in the Museum at London. Bottles of the oil were kept in the homes of this, and adjoining counties and used as a panacea for children's ills.

It was in 1854 that the use of oil was discovered in its true sense with respect to light and lubricating properties.

In 1864 the Burkesville Kentucky Oil and Mining Company was organized in this county to "develop oil and minerals in Cumberland and adjoining counties." A few wells were drilled in, covering a wide territory, before this company dissolved.

Brief trials were made after this date up to 1902, when the Cumberland County Oil and Gas Company with the head office at Burkesville was organized to develop oil and gas in this and surrounding counties. A great hit for this period was that of Salt Lick Bend, on the Thomas Graves farm in July, 1902. It shot out over the derrick, caught fire and destroyed much machinery. This well produced for about four years. Others were drilled in the county during this excitement. In 1904 a gusher was struck in Irish Bottom on the J. E. Morgan farm, which spouted into the air and ran down the river for several days, covering its entire surface. Pipe lines were laid to take care of oil, but eventually the flow began to recede and at last the business disappeared from the county.

In 1936-40 another spell of testing was made in the county, in the southern part and around Bear Creek, with small producing wells. In 1921 a refinery was put up on the river bank at Burkesville, but it was soon abandoned.

MILLS

The burr corn and wheat mill dates back close to the beginning of time. The Bible tells of the grinding at the mill. Samson was harnessed and made to grind with the mill 1,120 years before Christ. Mills for grinding have been used almost as long as teeth have been used. The many changes through the years have been in the power to turn them. We gather from history these progressive changes—man, ox, water, wind, steam, oil, gas, and electricity.

Wind and water were the two powers used in all the colonies, and during the first 35 years of the Independence of the United States. Within two years after steam had been harnessed, Lexington and Louisville were operating factories through the use of steam. Most spindles are turned now by gas and electricity.

The early sawmills were of the whipsaw type. The circular saw was not invented until 1777, in England by Samuel Miller.

The pioneers of Cumberland County either brought with them their bread burrs or the tools with which to make them. Stone was plentiful and so was power. Cumberland has long been called the county of creeks. Mills run by water usually held their original places until decay. After steam and gas came into use they changed locations often.

Samson Allen had a mill in operation several years before 1801 on Allens Creek. This is the oldest record of a mill in the county. Robert Ferrill had one in the Stockton Valley in 1799. These were corn mills.

Joshua Sexton and his son, Daniel Sexton, built a dam and mill on Sextons Fork of Illwill Creek in 1799. William Ritchey ran a grist mill on Marrowbone Creek in 1801.

In 1817, Peter Zimmerman had the County Court to condemn a mill site on the farm of Edward Cheatham, on Lewis Creek, where

Agriculture

he ran a mill for some time. George Sexton in 1817 had a site condemned on the northwest side of Big Renox Creek between the junction of the two creeks and the river. The Bakers, who came to the county, built a mill on Big Renox in 1805.

The first sawmill in the county was put up by William Smiley on a tract of land purchased by him from William Ritchey. The mill was set up in June, 1808. Smiley was required to keep the mill and dam in good condition. It was on Marrowbone Creek, adjoining William Ritchey's grist mill.

The only mill in original Cumberland which has lived a continuous life is Seventy-Six. It has had very few millers: 1806-24, John Semple; 1824-40, William Goodson; Abijah Guthrie; John Andrew; Hance Piercey; Rev. J. T. Wells.

William Ball operated a mill at Meshacks Creek, 1811. Fred Appleby built the first grist mill on Willis Creek, 1830.

TIMBER

Two-thirds of this county is still in woods. Ninety different kinds of trees make up this big plant family. The yellow poplar, black walnut, oak, cedar, chestnut, hickory, sugar tree, maple, linn, beech, gum, elm, and sycamore are the most important kinds and the ones that have added so much to the income of the inhabitants of Cumberland County.

With the exception of two tracts in this county, one in the southern part on Sulphur Creek, owned at present by A. A. Huddleston, and the other in the northern part, owned by A. A. Morrison, the forest lands have been cut over time and again since first settled. The greater part of the timber was cut, rafted, and floated down Cumberland River and sold. From the time of the Civil War until the beginning of the twentieth century, Nashville, Tennessee, afforded the best market for this fine timber.

Logs were cut during the fall months and hauled to a point on some creek where the backwater would reach them the following winter or spring, when they were rolled into the water and rafted and dropped down the backwater to where the creek empties into the river. When the receding tide reached its proper height the raft was shoved out into the river on its way to market. Some rafts had as many as five hundred logs in them, but usually a fewer number. The rafts were made by placing the logs in the water side by side, touching each other, across each end of which were placed long slender hickory poles some four or five inches in diameter. A hole was bored through the poles directly over the center of each log, with an inch auger, and into the hole was inserted a raft pin made of seasoned hickory which was driven into the log four inches. A long oar stem about fifty feet long, made of a young poplar tree to which a broad oar blade was attached, was pivoted on each end of the raft and operated by from two to four men under the command of the pilot, to keep the raft in the channel of the stream while it floated on with the current. A 25-foot tide was preferable, and that on a receding tide was the best one to make it easy to keep the raft away from the banks and bluffs, because of the concavity of this kind of tide. Before the iron grab was invented the logmen used wooden pegs driven into the end of the log to which two or three yoke of oxen were hitched to snake the logs out of deep narrow hollows.

Cedar rafts were made on a different style. Cedars were usually left the full length of the growing tree. A few large poles were chosen for the frame of the raft. Two-inch holes were bored through them, into which hickory grubs were slipped from the bottom side and left standing upright about five feet high. When the frame was well tied together by overlapping the frame poles, the rest of the logs were laid upon this frame and made ready for running upon the water. Forty years are required to grow a cedar post.

Many farms were paid for with the timber growing on them. The most reckless way of destroying the virgin timber was the way pioneers butchered it in clearing the lands for cultivation. Trees, one of which would today bring a small fortune, were girdled and left to die, then they were cut down and put into lengths of ten or twelve feet and rolled together and burned, regardless of the kind.

"Log Rollings" were enjoyable occasions. Fifteen or twenty neighbors would gather at a home and donate their time for a day or two in rolling those huge logs into heaps to be burned. "Heaps" were of different sizes but usually of three or four ply. The number of bottom logs will always determine the number of plies, that is, four, three, two, and one make a four-ply heap, and log rollers found this method to be self-feeding when the torch was applied. At different homes in the neighborhood this co-operation would go on for weeks with the wives following to do the cooking for the crew of men. Sometimes the women would spend the evenings in sewing or quilting to make the day profitable.

The crime of carelessness with fire, even down to the present day, annually destroys millions of feet of timber by burning over woodland. One day's fire will destroy what it will take nature one hundred years to replace. "Fighting fires" fifty years ago was a task to face every fall, and sometimes in the spring when the leaves got dry. To control these fires a path at least a yard wide had to be swept across some level place, far in advance of the fire, or several feet from the foot of the ignited hillside, for if allowed to start up the slope the suction would sweep everything before it in a moment's time; while descending would take hours. This was the period in the history of the county when the wooden fence was in use, and if burned much timber was slain to replace the fences so destroyed.

Another great demand for wood up and down the Cumberland Valley was that of the steamboat. Up to 1900 wood was the main fuel. It was cut four feet in length and sold for $1.50 to $2.00 per cord. Thousands of cords of this wood were cut and burned every year and the ones who furnished it prepared it with the least labor possible, so the best trees were cut and only the smooth part of the body of the tree was worked up and the rest left to decay. This accounts for so many bare knobs along Cumberland River. The introduction of the gasoline engine into the county in 1902 provided another means by which timber suffered, for the mills now are moved to the woodlands with little effort. The advent of hard-surfaced roads has caused most of the timber bordering them to be removed.

In going through the woodland now (1945) you will still see mounds where trees have been blown up by the roots, with good sized trees growing on the mounds. You may wonder just when this happened. It was in July, 1891.

In order for the readers of this book to have an idea how our timber left the county in former days, we shall introduce the following records:

During the late summer and fall of 1890, on Marrowbone and Mud Camp creeks, Sam Chism, Joe Gorman, Jim Skinner, Jim Williams, C. T. Gray, Marshall Alexander, Zib Norris, Elihu Norris, have been running 35 teams of oxen from two to six yoke to the team in hauling logs. These logs are poplar, ranging from two to five feet in diameter. They await a tide in the spring to raft and run to Nashville.

Williams and Ritchey, who established their new mill on the river bank at Burkesville in 1889, now have on hand 200,000 feet of poplar and ash lumber for sale, March, 1891.

Orlando Smith and his father, of Big Renox, made 6,000 rails the winter of 1890.

A million shingles have been shipped from Big Renox Creek, from 1888 to 1890; poplar, at $2.00 per thousand, and chestnut at $2.50 per thousand.

Log rollings are the order of the day, 1890.

L. F. Neathery has the honor of running a larger raft of logs cut from the Jim Davis farm in Clinton County than anyone else. They ranged from four to eight feet in diameter, 1893.

Chapter 14

TOWNS OF CUMBERLAND COUNTY

SEVENTY-SIX

Seventy-Six, which is now in Clinton County, was settled by John W. Semple in 1806. He put up a mill to grind corn and also had a cotton factory there, all run by water power. He also had a shop and a large general store. In 1817, the Cumberland County Court vested a part of the lands of Semple in the hands of trustees, who laid out the town of Seventy-Six, consisting of 116 lots around the "Big Indian Creek Falls." Semple's dreams never came true, only a few lots were sold, and in his will of 1824 he willed to Lucy, his wife, 15 lots and one-ninth of the Big Falls. Tradition tells us the town was named from the height of the falls over which Indian Creek plunges, but an authentic record says it was named for the "station number" in the original survey where they had built a shop and lodging quarters. This number was very near the precipice, which measured 83 feet in height, composed of beautiful limestone rock. For nearly 100 years people would go there for meal and flour; and for a long time for woolen goods.

PAOLI

This community was established by the sons and brothers of those who fell at the horrible "massacre of Paoli," September 20, 1777, when 54 of the American Patriots were slain by the British after surrender. On arriving in Cumberland County, 1798, they found settlements on Spring Creek, and on September 20, 1817, Chester County, Pennsylvania, erected a monument in memory of those who had been so cruelly butchered at Paoli, Pennsylvania. In order to perpetuate their memories, it was decided to call the new town Paoli, the same year, and in 1821 it was laid out and governed by trustees, the relatives of the fallen, among whom were: Sam Huff, Sam Scott, William Wood, Michael Gabbart, William Frogg, Nicholas Talbot, William Talbot, John Reneau, and James Cole. The town ceased to thrive when Albany became the county seat of the new county. The Talbots, Woods, Reneaus, and Myers composed the town when the place was named in 1798.

MARTINSBURG

Martinsburg was laid out as a town in 1818 and marked off with streets and 76 lots. It was a center of trade in that part of the County, in the early years, but Burkesville having outstripped it in trade, it never grew into a large town. It went into Monroe County in 1820.

CREELSBORO

Creelsboro was laid out as a town in 1809. The proprietors were E. & E. Creel for whom it was named. Other proprietors at its beginning were: Joseph Bledsoe, James Fergus, Thomas Graves, Richard Graves, Edward Flowers.

Some of the early settlers of the town who still reside there are: Busters, Elliotts, Irvins, Claytons, Bells, Manns, Higginbothams, Leisters, Joneses, McClures, Beards, Millers. The town went into Russell in 1825-6. (See Postoffice.)

BURKESVILLE

What will be said here will only add to what shall be found all through this volume about this town. Burkesville was laid out and marked off first on the plat of land given by Ishum Burkes, February 27, 1798. A Green County record on file calls the place "The Cumberland Crossing," as recorded in June, 1776. Military claims surrounded the place of the town from 1780 until the founding of the town. Burkes and John Thurman were the two first ferrymen of record who were running the ferry when Moses Kirkpatrick, Nathaniel Montgomery, and Nathan Owens surveyed the road in 1795, from Emmerson's Ferry on Green River to Thurman and Burkes' Ferry at Cumberland Crossing. They both campaigned for the name of the town, for they belonged to the "land gentry," but Burkes received a few more votes than Thurman—hence Burkesville was so born.

Ephraim Dicken, grandfather of Leslie Dicken of Marrowbone, built the first warehouse on the west side of the river, 1807.

In 1804 Isaac Taylor and John Montfort surveyed the land consisting of 134 acres up to Thomas Todd Lowery's 638 acres purchased in 1798 for 638 pounds.

Burkesville was incorporated in 1810 with Francis Emmerson sole proprietor from 1807 till his death, 1815. He was absolute monarch of the town during this period, yet James Emmerson, James W. Taylor, and William Cole were acting trustees after 1811.

In January, 1804, John Montfort surveyed a site for the first prison house adjoining Francis Emmerson and the Hatter Shop, including the big spring. The first jail of size was built west of the courthouse in 1829 by two contractors, Granville Bowman and Joseph Alexander, for $1,400. In front of it was the whipping post.

OLD HOTEL, BURKESVILLE

Burkesville's first edifice of renown was the "mansion building" put up of brick by Granville Bowman in 1812. It stood on the same lot that now holds the New Parkway Hotel, but one lot farther south. It was erected for family use, but turned into a hotel. It was occupied until it was condemned in 1891.

Joseph S. Bledsoe, Bowman's son-in-law, was proprietor for most of his life. Susan, his wife, kept every room neatly furnished with fat feather beds, the feathers of which were picked from white geese only. The tables were heaped with Cumberland County's bountiful supply. The waiters were neatly clad colored men always wearing a pleasant smile. "Uncle" Charley Bledsoe living at this writing, was one of those agreeable waiters.

The waiting room was the Town Hall used by County, State, and Nation. Here politicians and traders gathered for business. The registration book showed: Judge Richard Buckner, Judge Christopher Thompkins, Judge Zach Wheat, Gov. P. H. Leslie, Gov. Thomas E. Bramlett, Gov. J. Q. A. King, Judge William Simpson, Judge T. T. Alexander, Senator S. B. Maxey, Gen. W. T. Ward, Hon. Aaron Harding, and George D. Bristow.

It was in this building the noted "Negro traders" of the South met to locate slaves for the auction block. It was in this Town Hall that Lincoln's call was responded to in the forming of Colonel Wolford's First Kentucky Cavalry, and it was also the birthplace of Col. David Haggard's Fifth Kentucky Cavalry.

A little later than this date, we are sorry to say, this Cumberland County cradle of liberty, by force, became the headquarters of the overpowering Rebel Colonel.

Stores of early Burkesville were kept by James and Harold Saufley, 1811; Peter Zimmerman, 1815; John M. Philip and Reuben Alexander, styled "J.P.R.," in 1814.

Chapter 15

POSTOFFICES AND POSTAGE RATES

On the day Kentucky was admitted as a state, the following rates were charged for mailing letters which were classified as single, double, triple, quadruple, etc.—single meaning one sheet, double two, and so on.

Single letters carried under 30 miles, 6 cents; letters up to 60 miles, 8 cents; from 60 to 100 miles, 10 cents; from 100 to 150 miles, 12½ cents; from 150 to 200 miles, 15 cents; 200 to 250, 17 cents; 250 to 350, 20 cents; to 450, 22 cents; and all over 450 miles, 25 cents. If the sheets were doubled or tripled the postage was likewise doubled and tripled. Every package was charged at 24 cents per ounce up to four pounds.

These rates as of June 1, 1792, remained practically the same, with a few minor changes, until 1845, when the rate on letters was changed to 5 cents under 300 miles and 10 cents on single letters over 300 miles. The double and triple law still applied in each case.

Letters, as well as other pieces of mail, were rolled or folded to mail. Envelopes were not invented until 1839, but Cumberland County continued to roll and seal her letters until into the 1850's on account of the cost of early envelopes, which were selling from 5 cents to 10 cents each.

Mail day was a busy, rushing time for the recipients as well as the postmasters, for postage was collected then at the destinations. Quite a bit of checking and bookkeeping were done by the postmasters and their assistants on the arrival of the mail, as to its mileage and classification.

On March 3, 1847, the whole country changed its way of handling mail. The United States Government invented and printed the first stamps. They were in the two denominations—5-cent with Franklin's likeness, and 10-cent with that of Washington, and they paid for the same distances as above. There were 860,380 printed the first year, not so many as are now used in a very small town in one year. In 1855 the rate was reduced to 3 cents on single and 6 cents on double, etc. Another change took place in March, 1863, when the sheet system was done away with, and letters were charged for by the ounce or fraction thereof, at 3 cents. In 1885, the 2-cent stamp was sufficient for letters, which held until 1917 when the 3-cent was again required, until August, 1930, when the 2-cent went into effect continuing until July, 1932, when the three-cent was again required, and has been the minimum ever since.

January 1, 1913, the parcel post law went into effect, the mails carrying parcels weighing to 11 pounds; in 1914 this was raised to

50 pounds. This increased the burden on the country mail carriers, who at that time carried all mail on horseback or in dilapidated buggies. Cumberland County being an isolated county with few hard-surfaced roads, it continues to carry much of its mail on horseback. The parcel post law was the beginning of the end of the country merchants in this county and was a great boost to mail order houses.

BURKESVILLE

Postoffices and Postal Rates of Cumberland County

Burkesville is the oldest postoffice in Cumberland County. It was used as a deposit of mail in 1800 and was called Cumberland Court House or Burkesville, but the first postmaster was appointed by the Government and rendered his first account as of January 1, 1807. This was Christopher Brooks.

The first Government route was from Greensburg, by Adams Court House, Cumberland Court House, and Jackson Court House, to Blackburn's Springs. This was from October 1, 1809, until September 30, 1811, and was known as Route No 193. Burkesville got mail semi-monthly.

The following list of postmasters with the dates of their appointments represent some of the best families of Cumberland County:

Milton King, May 24, 1813
Hiram Emmerson, March 13, 1820
Muhlenbergh Emerson, October 10, 1821
Peter Zimmerman, August 16, 1823
Granville Bowman, March 3, 1828
John M. Alexander, Jr., May 6, 1828
Matthew C. Boles, February 2, 1835
Joseph S. Bledsoe, January 30, 1836
Jesse Ewing, March 5, 1842
Robert Reid, June 16, 1848
Fayette W. Alexander, November 19, 1849
Wakefield W. Samuels, February 24, 1851
James M. Boles, December 10, 1851
John B. Ryan, November 5, 1853
Martin L. Alexander, November 15, 1854
Hiram R. Hays, January 4, 1856
William J. Dixon, February 23, 1859
W. Godfrey Hunter, May 3, 1869
Abner J. Phelps, October 10, 1870
James Bruton, February 20, 1874
Abner J. Phelps, June 1, 1874
Jacob S. Bruton, January 20, 1876
Elias Emmons, January 7, 1879

Willie F. Alexander, January 23, 1883
James L. Grissom, April 13, 1893
John E. Allen, September 7, 1893
Willie F. Alexander, July 29, 1897
William E. Miller, January 15, 1902
Charles W. Alexander, Jr., September 22, 1913
Leonard W. Thrasher (acting), July 30, 1921
Leonard W. Thrasher, September 12, 1922
Sam. A. Cary (acting), September 8, 1932
Nora Dixon McGee (acting), January 1, 1933
Nora Dixon McGee, May 1, 1934

MARROWBONE

Marrowbone was established as a postoffice, January 15, 1829. It is ten miles from Burkesville, located in the beautiful valley of Marrowbone Creek. It got its name from the creek, described elsewhere in this volume. All the postmasters that have served to the present are shown with the dates of their appointment:

Richard Wade, January 15, 1829
Gideon McDaniel, October 18, 1830
Thomas Strange, October 11, 1833
Ingram Nunn, January 12, 1837
Walter J. Pace, March 15, 1842
Orlando C. Pace, January 23, 1878
William Barton, February 13, 1878
James D. Davis, October 9, 1899
James B. Harvey, January 18, 1910
James P. Gray, December 2, 1912—

Peytonsburgh was established on April 28, 1871, with Peyton Parrish as the first postmaster. It was discontinued May 29, 1873, and re-established August 24, 1874, and called Peytonsburg. It got its name from its first postmaster.

Albany Landing, about eight miles from Burkesville, was established May 15, 1876, with Lorenzo J. Chancy as postmaster. It got its name from the county seat of Clinton County, because all the merchandise and articles that went to Albany were deposited here in huge warehouses awaiting the oxen and mule teams to haul them to Albany and other points, to be used and sold. The name of Albany Landing was changed to Whetstone, October 21, 1899, with John S. Gibson postmaster. It got its name from the two creeks that empty into Cumberland River near its location. The creeks (Whetstone) were named because a grindstone or whetstone factory operated there on the lower creek about 1799. Lewis Allen was the last postmaster when it was discontinued 1943.

Hegira was established in Clinton County, not far from its present location, on October 13, 1881, with Rufus C. Lucy as the first postmaster. It was changed into Cumberland County where it now stands, January 16, 1885. It has grown into a small village with two stores, a mill, and a large rural school. J. W. Reeder did business there for a great many years and was succeeded by his son, William Reeder. Cruso Graham operates the other store. The place got its name from the flight of Mohammed from Mecca, July 16, 622 A.D. It is about ten miles from Burkesville.

Dubre postoffice was established July 1, 1937, with Mrs. Delie B. Jeffery postmaster. A number of names were sent off and the one chosen was in honor of the early settlers by that name, many of whom still live in the neighborhood. Dubre is on Marrowbone Creek a short distance from the Metcalfe County line. Florence I. Anderson is the present postmaster.

Modoc. This postoffice was established June 6, 1892, with John G. Jones the first postmaster. It was discontinued, April 28, 1894, and re-established June 19, 1897. This office was again discontinued May 31, 1935, and mail ordered to Bow. J. G. Jones lived there and did business at the place at the time he had the postoffice established. Mr. Jones wanted to name the place Cherry Hill, but the Government would not accept that, and while he and his wife were talking what name might be best for the new office, he stepped out into the yard to cut weeds and said, "About all I do is to mow dock." (For it grew there in abundance.) His wife, being a very alert woman, seized the opportunity and remarked to him, "Maybe we might name the new office 'Modoc.'" They sent it up to Washington, and it was at once accepted.

Amandaville postoffice was established April 11, 1884, with Asa O. Baker as first postmaster. It was called Amanda until June 18, 1884, when it assumed the name Amandaville. It is located on Crocus Creek about 12 miles from Burkesville. It got its name from Amanda Elliott (Miller), who was there at the time of its organization. Baker and Brockman did business for a long time and the office is kept by Mrs. George Brockman, in the same building of its birth.

Bow postoffice was established June 7, 1901, with William Glidewell the first postmaster. The office was discontinued October 15, 1918, and re-established April 23, 1919. It was named for I. S. Bow. It is on Highway No. 90 about three miles from Burkesville going east. A good stock of general merchandise owned by G. I. Davis, who has been there since 1920, is being carried there. Mr. Davis is the present postmaster, having begun in 1926.

Grider postoffice was established on April 6, 1866, with Daniel B. Williams the first postmaster. On December 26, 1884, it was discontinued and mail ordered sent to Burkesville. This remained so until May 13, 1911, when it was re-established with J. W. Jeffers postmaster and moved from the Nelson Hurt place to its present location.

Ararat postoffice was established June 15, 1898, with J. F. Allen postmaster.

Ireland postoffice was established April 18, 1898, and was discontinued about two years later. It was in Irish Bottom and its first postmaster was William Self. This office was re-established August 24, 1920, and named Ribbon, with L. A. Hadley postmaster. Its location was changed from the southern bank of Cumberland River, in this county, to the northern side of the river, in Russell County. From 1900 to 1920 no postoffice was in operation on the eight-mile stretch from Whetstone to Creelsboro, but in 1920 the citizens of Irish Bottom took weekly turns carrying the mail on horseback until the Ribbon office went into effect, which was under L. A. Hadley, until January 31, 1934, when Mrs. Trixie Back was made postmaster who is selling goods at the place now. Its name was chosen from a list sent up by the citizens.

Leslie postoffice was established May 7, 1878, with Silas W. Young as its first postmaster. This office has had only three other postmasters, Elbert P. Hutchins, 1892; William R. Young, 1893; Thomas J. Smith, May 1, 1906; who is still acting (1946).

Cloyds Landing postoffice was established July 10, 1872, with Thomas J. Cloyd the first postmaster. The postmasters that followed were: John M. Hume, 1890; Martin C. Graves, 1915; Herman E. Collins, 1919; Robert D. Bass, Jr., 1922; Henry C. Collins, 1924; George T. Collins, 1938.

Cloyds Landing was named in honor of Capt. John Cloyd, a Cumberland County pioneer from Virginia, who became a thriving farmer on Cumberland River near the postoffice that bears his name.

Kettle postoffice was established July 22, 1881, with John Bridgefarmer as the first postmaster. The following have served as postmasters: Mitchell Ledbetter, 1884; Nannie O. Huddleston, 1893; Ben H. Simpson, 1895; Nannie Huddleston, 1898; Albert Sharp, 1899; Printis M. Bristow, 1900; Jesse L. Bristow, 1901; Mary E. Sharp, 1907; H. J. Gass, 1911. The office was discontinued, 1915, and re-established, 1919. Hulet Gass, 1919; Virgil B. Guthrie, 1920; K. B. Kirby, 1922. It was discontinued, February 29, 1936, and re-established December 3, 1940, with Nora Selma Adams as postmaster.

The office was named for the creek of the same name, which is described elsewhere in this writing. At the time of its establishment it was located on the ridge of the headwaters of the creek. It is about five miles from town, in the southern part of the county on a new W.P.A. road.

WATERVIEW

This postoffice was established March 6, 1888, with Reubin Alexander first postmaster, and since then have served: Edward G. Alexander, 1891; Vinnie V. Williams, 1899; Belle P. Alexander, 1900; Bertha Alexander, 1919 to 1946.

This office is situated on the east bank of Marrowbone Creek, six miles from Burkesville. In front of the little village is a deep, clear section of Marrowbone creek, hence, the name.

BAKERTON

This office was established May 29, 1848, with Miller Alexander postmaster. It was discontinued November 7, 1848, and re-established March 16, 1854. It was discontinued November 9, 1854, and re-established May 15, 1876, with James E. Baker postmaster; it was discontinued July 23, 1877, and was re-established September 15, 1890, with Tom E. Goff postmaster, and is still in operation with Muncy Koomer postmaster. It is about seven miles north of town on a W.P.A. Road. Named for the Baker pioneers of that place.

BLACKS FERRY

This office was established March 18, 1884, with James G. Maxey postmaster. It was discontinued November 4, 1890, and on December 1, 1890, it was re-established with Robert Richardson postmaster. This was switched to Monroe County, and latter it was moved back to Cumberland County. It is the extreme southern office of the county on a dirt road, by the river, 30 miles from town. Named for the first ferryman.

CLAYWELL

This postoffice was established May 10, 1921, with Jepthan W. Vincent postmaster. It is on Smith Ridge surrounded by the waters of Whetstone, Goose, and Brush creeks. It is on a dirt road about six miles from town. It was named for the family of people by that name who once lived there.

CREELSBORO (NOW RUSSELL COUNTY)

Creelsboro postoffice was established as Creelsburgh on January 17, 1828, with Thomas Graves as first postmaster.

On July 21, 1864, the name of the office was changed to Creelsborough, and on August 21, 1893, the name was changed to its present name—Creelsboro.

ALBANY (NOW CLINTON COUNTY)

Albany was first established as Paoli postoffice in Cumberland County, July 25, 1833, with William H. Preston, first postmaster. The name of this office was changed to Albany on September 4, 1837, at which time it was changed into Clinton County. The office was discontinued December 20, 1864, and re-established January 25, 1865.

TOMPKINSVILLE (MONROE COUNTY)

This office was established on January 17, 1819, with Joseph G. Hardin first postmaster.

Postoffices

While much of Monroe County was taken from Cumberland County, in 1820, and the county line was in dispute for a number of years, it was later decided that the present site of Tompkinsville missed Cumberland County about two and a half miles.

EDMONTON (METCALFE COUNTY)

A part of Cumberland County was given to form Metcalfe County, but this office was on the part taken from Barren County.
Edmonton was established in Barren, March 24, 1826, with Everard Clark first postmaster. It was changed into Metcalfe County, July 7, 1857.

DESDA (CLINTON COUNTY)

. This postoffice is just across the line in Clinton County and, as many of the Cumberland County citizens have used it for their office, it seems proper to note its history. Desda was named by Hiram Irvin for his sweetheart. The first office here was Ariadne, established by David G. Orton, 1888, who served till February 18, 1892, when James T. Wells was appointed. The following have served: I. F. Andrew, October 23, 1895 (Established); W. P. Stephenson, October 20, 1897; William H. Hammond, January 4, 1899; I. F. Andrew, April 1, 1902; Charles A. Orton, July 15, 1905; Jennie M. Orton, February 15, 1906; Robert L. Conner, May 6, 1907; W. C. Owens, September 27, 1912-35.

It was discontinued November 15, 1935, and mail ordered sent to Aaron. Desda is not far from the west end of the Wolf Creek Dam and is likely to become a place of note later.

Tanbark postoffice was established November 27, 1920, with Thomas B. Guthrie as postmaster. Mr. Guthrie still sells goods at the place. It is about five miles from Burkesville on a dirt road. It got its name from the business once carried on there of collecting oak bark from the trees that grew there on that ridge, with which to tan leather to make the family shoes.

Mud Camp office was established February 28, 1916, with William M. Hardin postmaster. This office is about seven miles from Burkesville on Mud Camp Creek from which it received its name.

Littrell postoffice was established August 20, 1901, with George T. Roberts postmaster. It is on Pea Ridge, eight miles south of town. It is on a new W.P.A. road. It was named for Miss Willie Littrell, daughter of Mack Littrell of Albany, Kentucky. Her sweetheart named it in her honor.

Frogue postoffice was established November 26, 1904, with John L. Miller postmaster. It was named for merchant Frogue who was selling goods there at that time. It was formerly called Chestnut Grove and has grown into a small village with two stores, a church, and a two-teacher free school. At present William King, of King & Bertram, operates one store and Elmer Biddle operates the other with the postoffice. The place and not the office was called Chestnut Grove. Frogue is about 13 miles from Burkesville.

La See postoffice was established October 9, 1925, with William A. Lacy postmaster. It was named for its first postmaster and was operated by him until his death and is now run by his wife, Mrs. Lacy. It is on West Fork Creek of Crocus, about 10 miles from Burkesville.

Ellington postoffice was established May 20, 1898, with J. T. French postmaster. It was first set up on the ridge near the Pleasant Hill Church and later moved into Whites Bottom, where it is now. It was named for James Ellington, who donated the land for the church house and the site of the first office. It is about six miles from Burkesville, and is operated now by W. Frank Goff, in connection with his store.

Forest Cottage postoffice was established first in Clinton County, May 15, 1876, with Crawford L. Holseapple postmaster. On February 23, 1886, the name was changed to Euclid, but was changed back to Forest Cottage January 31, 1889, which it holds today. It was moved into Cumberland County, 1936, with Edgar Higginbotham postmaster.

Xerxes postoffice was established July 3, 1900, with Young McFarland postmaster. It was discontinued August 31, 1906, and was re-established October 31, 1916, and is still in operation. Up to the latter date Xerxes was in the southern part of the county, later at Brownwood. Xerxes was discontinued July 31, 1942.

Seventy-Six (now Clinton)

This postoffice was established in Cumberland County, April 27, 1830, with James M. Goodson postmaster. It was called Goodson until May 17, 1834, when it was changed to Seventy-Six. It went into Clinton County June 20, 1836, and has functioned there ever since.

Chapter 16

SILENT CITIES

HOWARD BOTTOM

Tabitha A. Young	1829-1863	Reuben Hicks	1812-1909
Louvina Campbell	1830-1907	Margaret Smith Hicks	1833-1924
Caleb Radford	1824-1896	Rev. Charles Smith	1810-1881
Fount Radford	1890-1917	Belle Vincent	1860-1920
Lon Radford	1884-1939	John E. Rowe	1831-1878
Mrs. James Radford	1859-1933	Pauline Rowe	1807-
James Radford	1856-1929	Mrs. G. M. Dillon	1886-1908
Edgar B. Radford	1882-1907	Hershall Baker	1868-1899
Gran J. Campbell	1829-1899	J. A. Baker	1828-1910
Jane F. Parrish	1859-1924	Anna C. Baker	1808-1890
Docia Howard, wife of Clayton Miller	1807-1892	Jasper Baker	1802-1855
		G. M. Baker	1845-1912
Mrs. Tom Edmonson	1889-1925	Kate Williams	1852-1931
W. M. Smith, Co. C. 5th Ky. Cav.		Ellen Williams	1875-1925

WALTHALL

Charles Guthrie	1876-1932	Nancy Thomas Walthall	1825-1911
Minnie May Guthrie	1891-1922		
Sallie E. Scott	1867-1923	A. W. Walthall	1851-1911
William Guthrie	1842-1918	W. A. Walthall	1846-1918
Vie Guthrie	1843-1919	B. P. Walthall	1858-1923
J. B. Smiley	1844-1922	W. H. Walthall	1865-1927
Lewis Smiley	1873-1895	A. S. Walthall	1847-1917

THE SILENT CITIES OF IRISH BOTTOM

	Born	Died
I. F. Andrew	4-23-1850	12-18-1931
D. E. Andrew, wife	9-13-1851	10-19-1918
Israel Winfrey	12-12-1802	4- 9-1894
Martha Winfrey, his wife	5- 5-1805	2-17-1892
Columbus C. Winfrey	1-11-1822	6-30-1893
William F. Winfrey	5-14-1843	7-17-1913
Ray Winfrey, son of A. J. Winfrey	8-15-1895	8-15-1895
William Morgan	3-30-1835	1-27-1892
Malissa Morgan, his wife	11-25-1836	4-25-1927
I. Y. Morgan, their son	1-22-1861	12-19-1935
Emily E. Morgan, wife of I. Y.	10-18-1866	10- 1-1937

History of Cumberland County

	BORN	DIED
Willie Morgan, their son	11-18-1890	3-25-1896
Mattie Wood, wife of J. R. W.	12-22-1865	6-22-1893
J. B. Wood, her son	10- 5-1891	2-22-1895
Sam V. Morgan	11-19-1859	4-14-1905
Sarah Thomas Morgan, wife	11- 7-1857	2-29-1936
Stella Cook	5- 1-1907	9-30-1910
Howard Reneau	4-20-1917	7-17-1917
Fount Morgan	4-11-1884	7-16-1908
Norman C. Andrew	3- 4-1927	7-14-1927
J. Mont Wells	8-13-1881	2- 5-1907
T. B. Wells, Sr.	5-20-1849	3-27-1934
Lou M. Wells, his wife	12-14-1853	3- 2-1926
William J. Self	11-25-1829	9- 4-1898
Mary C. Self, his wife	2-17-1830	10- 5-1896
Robert A. Self, son	7-26-1851	10-24-1900
Mary, wife of Hiram S.	5-11-1861	1-12-1899
Sallie Self, her daughter	5-24-1892	10- 1-1894
Asa Self, her son	8-23-1887	12-18-1892
Chena Self, her daughter	11-26-1882	5- 7-1886
Julia Morgan, wife of J. E. M.	7-30-1868	3-12-1910
Infant of J. D. Irvin	8- 9-1890	8- 9-1890
Ruth Irvin, daughter of J. D. I.	1-21-1896	10- 1-1896
John Davis (drowned)	12-18-1892	7- 6-1900
Micajah S. Hunter	12-18-1806	4-26-1873
Arintha Lawhorn, wife of A. L.	2-25-1845	3- 7-1875
Joseph Lawhorn, her son	10-14-1866	11-11-1866
Martha Lawhorn, her daughter	8-24-1872	2-22-1873
William P. Smith	7-21-1851	7- 9-1935
John H. Smith, his son	4- 9-1895	12-13-1933
William Ross	3- 8-1884	9- 7-1904
Lala Smith, daughter of W. P. S.		3-25-1898
Joseph Smith, son of W. P. S.	4-28-1894	6- 5-1894
Stella M. Ross	5-25-1896	10-15-1896
Esther Jackman	4-18-1853	8-26-1873
C. R., son of R. L. Snow	5-13-1891	7-15-1891
D. Neathery	1- 6-1794	1-31-1873
Sallie, his wife	5- 1-1794	1- 7-1863
Hallie Armstrong, daughter of W. J. A.	1887	1888
Luke, son of W. J. A.	9-28-1874	10-21-1874
Tarleton Carnes, son of F. C.	11-21-1885	3- 1-1886
Minerva Carnes, wife of F. C.	4-29-1857	2- 3-1886
Isa Dora Fergus	11-12-1859	2-18-1887
J. P. C. Fergus	3-22-1825	6-10-1889
Lillian Fergus	4-28-1884	4- 4-1886
J. W. Ballew	1-10-1853	11-23-1931
Lucy Ballew, his wife	7-16-1856	12-23-1916
Haul A. Ballew, his son	1-15-1894	10- 8-1906

Silent Cities

	BORN	DIED
Claude Ballew, son	5- 6-1896	5-17-1898
John Ballew, son	11-29-1885	10- 8-1888
Adell Ballew, daughter	12-19-1882	8-10-1894
Jesse Murphy	1-28-1903	9-27-1907
W. Lawren Allen	3- 8-1849	1-28-1904
D. G. L. Allen	3-27-1853	11- 8-1924
Lizzie Allen, wife	1-29-1856	12-28-1935
Lula Allen, daughter	3-11-1890	12- 1-1905
L. B. Wells	1- 9-1847	7-24-1928
S. M. Wells	7-11-1853	3- 8-1934
William Vining	2-11-1829	7- 7-1866
Jane Vining, wife	3-21-1832	7-17-1869
Elvira Vining, daughter	8- 9-1861	8-27-1864
Hiram A. Staton (Dr.)	10- 3-1821	3-24-1887
Nancy W. Staton, his wife	1- 1-1824	12-27-1902
Tena Staton Morgan, wife W. E. M.	4- 8-1862	4- 9-1892
Hiram A. (Boge) Staton	4-14-1863	5-12-1916
Allen W. Grider	1- 8-1846	2-18-1903
Emma Sewell Grider, wife	3-26-1849	8-10-1904
Nancy Sewell, wife Joe S.	4-11-1820	4-19-1875
Julian Grider	9-10-1872	6- 9-1875
Mamie G. Morgan, wife J. E. M.	1-23-1875	7-17-1899
Annie Wells, daughter J. W. W.	2- 8-1908	6-10-1908
Lottie Wells, daughter J. W. W.	10-24-1909	10-26-1912
Peter M. Sewell	12-21-1846	8- 9-1917
Richard Haden	7-30-1776	2-15-1837
Rachel Haden, wife	12-31-1797	9- 3-1834
Eura Murphy, wife J. C. M.	4-16-1877	2-16-1930
J. C. Murphy	7-31-1874	3-25-1941
Alice Smith	7- 1-1863	2-17-1942

SILENT CITIES OF BURKESVILLE

Thomas J. Williams........1831-1906
Nancy Williams 1829-1904
Nancy (d) Williams......1854-1904
Bryant Keen 1865-1904
Anna P. Owsley 1882-1931
Sallie A. Owsley 1853-1904
Grant Owsley 1890-1935
Dr. J. G. Talbot.............1872-1939
Elenor Talbot 1844-1925
Susan Talbot 1876-1912
Sarah Talbot 1901-1901
William D. Snow 1894-1918
V. C. Pulliam ....   -1928

Mary Pulliam ....   -1925
Flossie Pulliam 1887-1916
J. E. Jones 1867-1936
Myrtle Jones 1898-1921
Ira Shannon 1887-1931
Frank Allen 1912-1913
Roy Baker 1887-1929
Charles L. Baker 1840-1921
Grover Young 1884-1893
Myrtle Young 1875-1897
J. C. Winfrey 1874-1925
J. R. Neeley 1856-1930
Mattie Short 1864-1925

Charles Neeley	1893-1934	A. M. Alexander	1882-1912
Bessie Neeley	1891-1926	Jennie Alexander	1852-1909
Delia Neely	1889-1917	C. W. Alexander, Sr.	1859-1938
I. C. Winfrey	1845-1913	W. B. Alexander	-1858
Millard Winfrey	1849-1925	Mary Ellen Alexander	-1860
Cassie Rich	1866-1929	Victoria Alexander	-1858
Ruby Rich	1897-1916	Ruth Richey	1892-1907
Henry Hale	1856-1910	Fayett Owsley	1889-1919
Ruth Ewing	1908-1910	Laura S. Ritchey	1892-1923
J. O. Ewing	1867-1921	James Ritchey	1897-1900
J. P. Lollar	1856-1908	John H. Ritchey	1858-1925
William Keen	1853-1930	Nannie Ritchey	1861-1902
Mrs. E. Keen	1864-1933	John Ritchey	1883-1886
Rev. J. W. Blackurn	-1903	Mary Stone	1852-1882
Josie McDonald	1845-1896	William Stone	1868-1882
Dr. W. T. Burchett	1873-1897	B. F. Jones	1850-1887
George W. Burchett	1843-1935	R. C. Bouldin	1813-1896
Anna M. Burchett	1844-1930	Emma A. Bouldin	1827-1894
Ed L. Burchett	1875-1918	Mary A. Owsley	1834-1881
Walter Mayfield	1875-1937	W. F. Owsley	1813-1910
A. Mayfield	1875-1918	Gurtie Hunter	1876-1892
A. E. Blankenship	1885-1918	C. M. McGee	1872-1936
Jesse A. Smith	1894-1922	J. A. Dixon	1850-1903
Sam O. Smith	1899-1923	Abner J. Phelps	1818-1885
John H. Coe	1882-1932	Annie M. Phelps	-1888
Nettie Collins	1909-1910	Georgia Alexander	1853-1925
Sam Carter	1856-1928	W. F. Alexander	1848-1918
Margaret Carter	1859-19	J. W. Williams	1827-1888
Owen Parish	1921-1925	Elizabeth Williams	1837-1874
Norman Parrish	1927-1932	Sallie E. Williams	1852-1899
Cecil Rainey	1898-1931	Cora W. Alexander	1885-1924
J. J. Grant	1873-1927	Horace K. Alexander	1854-1920
S. D. Rainey	1869-1925	R. A. Cary	1858-1904
Rhoda Rainey	1877-1934	Mary Collins	1862-1920
Drude Rainey	1908-1932	Malcolm Melton	1923-1924
Ben Rainey	1906-1924	M. H. Melton	1891-1918
F. R. Baker	1867-1934	J. U. Curtis	1863-1927
Infant of E. M. G.	1925-1925	Dotsey Parrish	1922-1927
Genevieve Baker	1926-1929	Stella P. Guinn	1912-1934
Sallie Alexander	1853-1904	R. M. Bass	1846-1927
Sell M. Young	1880-1938	J. H. Wade	1852-1928
D. B. Williams	1837-1895	Ernest Cash	1903-1936
Hattie Williams	1850-1900	Ernest Cash, Jr.	1928-1928
Marshall Williams	1843-1902	W. H. Newby	1861-1915
Ira B. Simpson	1885-1919	Newby infant	-1908
M. O. Allen	1838-1911	James Thomas	1901-1910
M. O. Allen, Jr.	1869-1894	Sallie Garrett	1906-1918
Julia Allen	1842-1927	Robert Keen	1871-1916

Silent Cities

J. A. Melton	1859-1927	Amelia Rowe	1845-1904
Mary Melton	1855-1924	Mary Wesmorland	-1936
S. F. Scott	1851-1916	Hall Easter	-1926
Mrs. Scott	1849-1925	Benny H. Myers	1927-1930
Mrs. J. A. Bow	1840-1893	Joe Spencer	1906-1933
Warren Tobin	1807-1887	Susie Bean	1875-1938
Hettie Tobin	1831-1901	John Ed Bean	1913-1935
William Smith	1849-1926	Helen Firquin	1849-1904
Elva McGee	1868-1938	Josiah P. Franks	1819-1891
Pearl Smith	1880-1925	H. E. Williams	1831-1886
Capt. J. L. Strange	1838-1917	Annie Franks	1887-1888
Mary M. Strange	1847-1940	Joe G. Baker	1874-1911
W. H. Cheek	1852-1934	J. P. Franks	1854-1935
George F. Baker	1838-1891	Etta Frank	-1881
Addie Baker	1845-1902	T. J. Lawhon	1856-1929
J. R. Stinson	1882-1908	Nannie Lawhon	1863-1938
Infant son	-1907	Burdell Franks	-1879
Infant d. of Stinson	-1908	W. E. Fitch	1886-1925
Elva Scott	-1909	Jeramiah Scott	1842-1909
S. T. Waggener	1876-1937	Dora L. Scott	1849-1901
Jennie Waggener	1870-1933	Jesse P. Scott	1898-1922
Lewis A. Waggener	1825-1894	Sellie S. Davidson	1916-1934
Sarah E. Waggener	1834-1898	Fred Easter, Jr.	1930-1933
Pres Sandidge	1881-1934	J. R. Baker	1903-1931
J. H. C. Sandidge	1830-1915	Bertha Glidewell	1879-1930
America Sandidge	1842-1896	Lucile Carter	1929-1929
Allen Bow	1886-1893	Sam T. Irvin	1860-1930
Infant of S. T. Bow	1882-1884	Knoxie Simpson	1910-1931
Bertie Bow	1880-1884	C. R. Hicks	1868-1935
Albert Bow	1894-1899	G. I. Madison	1880-1931
Gordon Bow	1889-1919	Lerrell Smith	1909-1932
S. T. Bow	1853-1895	Grover Collins	1888-1941
Joe B. Firquin	1818-1887	Bertha Collins	1891-1932
Mary Firquin	1820-1891	Florence Street	1896-1935
J. J. McGee	1834-1921	N. S. Hume	1870-1931
Sallie McGee	1839-1917	Mrs. J. W. Capps	1892-1931
J. G. McGee	1860-1894	J. F. Short	1872-1930
W. E. Miller	1858-1934	Tina M. Sharp	1872-
Estelle Miller	1890-1900	John D. Sharp	1854-1928
Godfrey Miller	1891-1897	J. R. Keen	1850-1931
Jennie Miller	1888-1892	Emma Keen	1859-1936
Sallie Barnes	1838-1898	Bessie Bybee	1890-1931
Charles E. Scott	1912-1931	Bernard Bybee	1930-1932
Lorene Scott	-1911	Don Neenham	1925-1934
Lucy Scott	-1915	Charles A. Keen	1932-1934
Maggie R. Scott	1880-1920	Grace Needham	1905-1936
J. B. Young	-	Nettie Bryson	1866-1938
F. W. Bruton	1868-1937	J. T. Bryson	1862-
John C. Rowe	1840-1909	Bedford Hill	1863-

Cora Hill 1875-1936
J. C. Burns 1896-1936
Myrtle Burns 1900-
L. W. McGee 1870-1936
John R. Cloyd 1907-1936
Dan W. Cloyd 1867-1937
Mary J. Cloyd.................1858-1933

J. W. Short 1870-1937
Mary J. Short 1871-1936
Florence Ferguson 1861-1940
Infant of L. S. McCoy.. -1937
Fred Paul McCoy .... -1937
Bobby Williams 1932-1933
Henry Willis 1911-1937

KING CEMETERY, BURKESVILLE

John E. King 1737-1828
Alfred King 1808-1836
Susan King 1829-1833
Susan Alexander 1821-1842
Mary Owsley 1843-1843
Mary Owsley 1823-1847
Mrs. Rice Haggard......... -1862

James Haggard 1811-1882
Ellen Owsley 1847-1847
Dr. Joel Owsley 1790-1869
Mary Ann Owsley.................1795-1874
Richard Harris 1842-1849
Col. D. R. Haggard......... -

SILENT CITIES OF MYERS RIDGE

Dr. J. H. Myers.. 2- 2-1861   6- 4-1930
C. C. Myers 5- 2-1863   8-11-1920
W. H. Myers 9-12-1885   3-25-1890
Tilford Myers 4-12-1887   11- 9-1909
Ben Myers 5-10-1899   4-30-1902
C. H. Myers (Civil War) ....
J. Crit Myers ....
William Surratt (Civil War) ....
J. T. Surratt 11- 8-1882   8-15-1905
James Booher 1-28-1900   11-21-1911
Hazel Booher 5-16-1906   12-13-1906
L. C. Easter 10-31-1855   6-18-1932
Ellen Easter (wife) 1-19-1847   7-15-1932
A. N. Daniels 9-13-1870   11- 8-1913
Arnold Teal 1-20-1924   1-23-1927
J. W. Easter 9-17-1867   2-13-1941

SILENT CITIES OF LAWSON BOTTOM

Jubilee Goggins 1791-1872
Sarah Goggins 1794-1838
Eliza J. Thomas 1819-1877
J. E. Goggins, Jr.................1834-1898
Robert Ferguson 1819-1873
Brooks Ferguson 1856-1875
Joe Fount Morgan.................1884-1917
Richard Newby 1863-1923
Mack Newby 1841-1923

W. B. Newby 1821-1883
Sarah J. Mackey 1867-1887
Rev. R. T. Phelps.................1807-1845
Amarilla Phelps 1797-1845
Joe R. Terry 1792-1877
Bethany E. Terry 1808-1895
Robert G. Phelps.................1829-1904
Mrs. Robt. Phelps (2)..1845-1902
Mrs. Robt. Phelps (1)..1834-1961

Silent Cities 195

Sarah Allen 1830-1876
James A. Mackey 1834-1919
Vienna Macky 1834-1921
Pemelia Allen 1848-1896
Robert Keeton 1863-1927
Ottilla Allen 1849-1917
Elijah A. Bledsoe 1918-1937
Pemelia Coffy 1889-1925
Lula Feuston 1899-1927
Vena Phelps 1873-1902
P. Eve Smith 1904-1907
Lillia M. Rioll 1836-1895
John Will Appleby..........1861-1904
Bertha Ferguson 1859-1941
Robert Wells 1921-
William A. Tweedy 1859-1922
Ralph Garrett 1925-1931
Joe F. Morgan..................1884-1917
Eva Morgan 1889-1907
J. W. Morgan's 3 ch.....1872-1879
Robert Ferguson 1819-1873
Brooks Ferguson 1856-1875

Simon B. Allen 1847-
  (son D.G.L. Sr.)
Gersham Allen 1880-1882
  (son D.G.L. Jr.)
Ottilla Irvin, wife of
  Lewis Irvin 1829-1873
Treir, 4 children
  (died) 1852-1860
Jubilee G. Murphy..........1832-1885
Lee Ann Murphy............1846-1928
Sam H. A. Murphy..........1861-1862
James Perry Murphy.....1866-1896
Dick Murphy 1872-1892
Hiram W. Murphy 1880-1913
His wife Alma 1879-1906
Lillie Murphy 1891-1907
Henry W. Bledsoe 1870-1926
Hiram L. Bledsoe 1907-1929
Robert Appleby 1838-1918
Sallie Appleby 1836-1907
Robert Appleby, Jr..........1882-1905
Drucilla A. Williams.....1830-1862

Chapter 17

WEAPONS OF WAR

It is an interesting story to study the development of firearms. It makes one shudder to think how much time, talent, and money men have wasted on these weapons with which to butcher and slay their fellow man. Though the years of war are far less than those of peace, yet the military budget greatly overbalances that of everything else of our country. War is the result of sin, and no other excuse can be offered than this. The first man that was born on earth was a murderer. Envy and jealousy were the sins that caused Cain to declare war on his brother and slay him. A wooden club was the only weapon used in this first war. Wooden weapons were the only kinds used for hundreds of years after that, for people had to experiment with other materials a long time before they were able to make discriminations. The first war spoken of in the Bible between nations occupied a fourteen-year period beginning in 1918 B.C. No doubt within the long period from creation and perhaps a long time thereafter the simplest of wooden weapons were used in combat.

Wooden weapons tipped with flint, bone, and stone then followed; following this was the period of bronze; then came the iron and steel age, with such weapons as the sword, javelin, spear, dagger, ax, battering-ram, and along with these also went the different armors of metal to protect the body. The bow and arrow was an ancient weapon used by more than one nation. The bow was made of wood or metal. England adopted the long bow, about six feet in length, with the arrow half its length, tipped with metal. The Normans introduced the cross-bow which found its way to other countries. Greece (1000 B.C.) used bronze weapons. The most cherished type of armor was the breastplate, carried in one hand to ward off all the above types of missiles.

Gunpowder (invented by Ger. Schwartz) was first used in 1327 in the army of Edward III, King of England on his invasion of Scotland. The gun was of a heavy, bunglesome make. The first mention of the cannon in history was 1339, but the first time in action was that of the above King's army against France at the great battle of Crecy in 1346. Bows and arrows were the main weapons in this battle, aside from this cannon. In using these first weapons of war, either large or small, it took two to fire them—one to take aim and the other to touch them off with a coal of fire. Following this was the match-lock gun of 1476. This musket was fired with a match, which method saved carrying a coal of fire with you. A match as here noted was a small strip of wood tipped with sulphur surrounded with tinder (fluffy cotton), which was ignited by a spark made by hand with flint and steel. A few years later than this came the wheel-lock gun, which was discharged when a spark fell upon the priming pan of powder just beneath the spring revolving-wheel.

About the year 1625 an improvement over all the former weapons of war was wrought, which later meant so much to America, Kentucky, and even Cumberland County. It was that of the flint-lock gun. It could be shot by one man alone. A hammer placed on the side of the barrel would strike the flint to produce the spark in the priming-pan, while the operator was using both eyes to bead his target. It was this make of weapon that the brave soldiers of the Revolutionary War used to help gain our independence, and also to help win our freedom on the seas in the War of 1812. It was this weapon, mainly, with which the distinguished Kentucky and Tennessee riflemen won the battle of New Orleans. It was this make of gun also that helped subdue the forest from the savage red man, ferocious beasts; and it was through its use that the tables of the early settlers were furnished with meat. The flint-lock musket was the weapon of Napoleon's War (1799-1815). Large bullets and smooth bore were characteristics of all the early weapons.

In 1842 the percussion musket was invented by a Scotchman. This did away with coals and matches. It is better known as the muzzle-loading rifle. This weapon was made, 1851, with a long thick steel barrel with rifles, or grooves, encircling the inner surface of the windage, to throw the projectile in a rotating manner. Into the right side of the rear end of barrel was screwed a cylinder into which was screwed the tube or nipple upon which was placed the percussion-cap. This rifle was loaded by pouring into the muzzle end of the barrel a charger full of powder. Then a jack knife was brought from the pocket with which to cut a piece of domestic about one inch square which was laid over the muzzle, then the bullet was placed upon this "patching," and the ramrod was slipped from its thimbles beneath the barrel, where it always stayed, and with the rod the bullet was pushed down the bore to rest upon the powder. Next the hammer was cocked sufficiently to let the cap slip over the nipple, but before the cap was slipped on, a close inspection was made to see whether or not the powder had found its way down the barrel, out the cylinder and up into the tube. If all of these things had happened then the gun was ready to fire again, but if the weapon was not fired for several days, or if it had been exposed to dampness, the powder would "cake in the tube" and a brass pin was used, another extra utensil that had to be looked after when out on the firing line. The bullets were molded at home from bars of lead which were sold at all country stores, and the powder was carried in a horn from a steer's head. Powder usually cost twenty cents a pound and so did lead. Caps five cents per hundred.

Six years before the invention of the percussion musket or rifle, a patent had been issued for a percussion revolver which was put on the market by Samuel Colts, 1838.

All the firing weapons heretofore listed used bullets or shot which were spherical in form, but in 1851 the elongated projectile found its way into the armies of the world. This kind did not meet with the approval of military authorities until the breech-loading gun made its appearance. Spencer invented the breech gun in 1860, of single shot with a projectile more than half an inch in diameter. This weapon did not become popular, but was the foundation on which future improved ones could be built.

Following the Civil War, Benjamin Hotchkiss, an American inventor, patented the magazine rifle; and in 1882 he made the machine gun, which has become so popular in recent years of military activities. Paul Mauser, a German inventor, put his famous rifle on the market and it became the favorite weapon of the German nation. It was a magazine gun of small bore.

Up to 1892 lead balls were used nearly altogether, with the exception of the very early cannons which used stone, and following that came iron and other metals. During the Civil War scraps of iron or anything that a cannon could swallow was hurled into the armies.

Hundreds of different things were used as weapons of war in World War II. Among the many things were: mines attached to every device that might be picked up; booby traps; barbed wire; liquid fire; poison gas; rocket bombs; robots; potato bugs (dropped on England by Germany); and every make of gun from the tiniest to the big 240 millimeter cannon (a 25.4 millimeter makes one inch).

SHIPS

The ones who read this, as well as many other treatises, may wonder why such things should be related in the history of Cumberland County when it, and also the state of which it is a part, are so distantly removed from the great ocean highways. To some it may seem out of place, but when you think how the first quarter of 1900, with all its speedy ways of travel and communication, has made the world so much smaller and brought even the most distant nation and tribe to our front door, you will see that what affects one affects all; especially is this true in time of war or rebellion.

Not a citizen of Cumberland County has ever lived within its domain but that his ancestral American life began at the embarkation of some old ship. The ships that brought our forefathers and mothers to the American shores were made of wood. They were propelled by hand oars and by cloth sails. The wind was the principal power used, and the speed depended on its behavior, for it served as both friend and foe. About two months were required to make the trip across the ocean. Ships were small—about ten-ton vessels. Freedom and wealth were the two main incentives, yet you will find other reasons for the sailing of those ships.

Wooden vessels made up the navy of the Revolutionary War. Our first foreign war of 1805 was won over the Pirate States of

Africa with a Navy of wooden ships; ending piracy and ransoms. The War of 1812 was fought and won with wooden ships, many of which were constructed from timber cut from the shores at the time. It was at this time that the idea of iron ships began to be talked of, but not until 1830 was the first iron ship launched. This make of ship was ironed by placing strips of iron close together on the wooden hulls.

The Mexican War was fought and won with wooden ships mainly, but a new way of power had come into use since 1807—that of steam boilers connected to two wooden wheels, one on either side. The first wheel steamship crossed the Atlantic in 1819. Then began the use of one wheel at the stern, which was kept up on stream vessels the rest of that century, but the ships fell on the use of a new kind of propeller in 1838. It was the modern screw-propeller invented by John Ericsson that year.

In 1859 the United States began the making of iron ships. By 1861 our Navy had several ships covered with armor or iron hulls made in a sloping manner to ward off the missiles. From ten to fourteen knots was the speed limit. Monitors sprung into use after 1862. They were also made of wrought iron. In 1889 our country woke up to the fact that iron ships were lighter than wooden ones and soon after that it also learned that steel vessels were lighter than iron ones. From that time on our Navy and also ships that are not for military uses have been made of steel, from 4 inches to 18 inches thick, as needed.

The submarine was used as far back as the Revolutionary War, but not until 1875 did John Holland fashion the modern type that has been such a menace to our shipping in the two World Wars. The German U-boat will be remembered by grieving fathers and mothers who had to sacrifice their precious sons in the two wars. The submarine was added to the navies of the United States, Germany, France, Italy, in 1900.

Large warships and passenger ships are made as long as 900 feet, with a tonnage of 35,000 and a speed of 35 knots. The year 1943 saw more ships built than any previous year. It also saw more of our boys and our neighbors' boys sailing and working aboard ships than all previous years. In less than a week a huge passenger ship with some two or three thousand soldiers aboard could reach the European countries.

Soldier boys from Cumberland County rode and worked on every type of ship connected with our marine operations during World War II. This brings the story of ships to our front door.

Battleships constitute the backbone of our Navy. They deal the final blow in battle. They are from 800 to 900 feet long, covered with a 12- to 16-inch armor over the exposed parts. Their double bottom has many apartments, so if one is punctured the others will prevent sinking. They carry huge guns from 11 to 16 inches, besides many smaller guns three to six inches. Their speed ranges around 30 knots (a knot is 804 feet over a mile) per hour and capacity is around

35,000 tons. According to a former ruling of Congress they are named for states.

Cruisers are large and small, determined by the gun caliber and not the size of ship. Heavies carry guns of about 8 and light 5 inches. They are built for speed as high as 40 knots, requiring over 130,000-horsepower engines; armor is from one to five inches thick. Named for cities.

Destroyers are around 300 feet long, lightly built, armored, and carry 6 four- or five-inch guns; and, like other ships, are modernly equipped with anti-aircraft guns. She dashes out ahead and, like a hornet, deposits her torpedo sting. The most fearless men are used on this boat. Usually named for noted men.

Aircraft carriers are a speedy type of ship. They perform what their name suggests—carrying planes. This ship is built 800 or 900 feet long and 90 feet wide, to accommodate some 120 planes. The deck is smooth to furnish take-off and landing space. Beneath the deck are dozens of planes which are brought up to top deck by elevator. This ship is a prize sought by the enemy, for one injury to the take-off deck stops the flight of all on board. Named for battles or events.

Minesweepers, so extensively used in World War II, are used to rid the waters of mines, by towing 1,000 feet of saw-toothed cable some 600 feet in the rear to saw the anchors of mines which then rise to the surface to be exploded by machine guns. Usually named for birds.

Submarines are "lone wolves." They do not co-operate with other parts of the fleet. They are slow-going ships, 10 to 15 knots per hour. They are propelled under water by electric batteries. Merchant ships are their prey. Each carries from four to eight torpedoes. Named for fish.

Mosquitoes are the most speedy ships, going 50 knots per hour. She darts into the enemy's nest, deposits her torpedo, and returns.

Among the other scores of ships are the patrol, repair, cargo, tug, submarine chaser, seaplane tender.

AIRPLANES

For centuries people have dreamed of flying. In fact ever since the Bible told them of the angels. The stories of mythology tell of wings of wax attached to living beings who flew upward until the sun melted the wax wings and they were forced to earth. One writer even drew an imaginary picture of "airships" sailing across the English Channel; they were oval in shape. Sometimes ideas linger in the human mind for several generations with little value or improvement before the proper man arises to shape them into usable realities. In fact, ninety per cent of the inventions and discoveries bring honor to those who perfect some other men's ideas.

The Chinese had crude contrivances back in the thirteenth century that would rise above the earth. The kite gave them the idea. They were balloons filled with hot air. China being a nation of closed doors, their ideas did not reach the outside world unless by visitation.

The French were the first to experiment in aeronautics. In 1782 they made a balloon that would rise when filled with gas. The first ascension was fifteen feet. In the following year one 35 feet in diameter filled with gas rose to a height of 1,500 feet. This was lighter-than-air flying. Then calculating the difference between the weight of the air displaced and that of the balloon they concluded that objects nearly equal to that difference placed in the balloon would rise with it; so a sheep, a rooster, and a duck became the first aerial travelers. A few months of experimenting went on before an individual would risk his life by going up; but in November of that year two Frenchmen climbed on and remained in the air about 30 minutes.

Balloons were spherical shaped until 1852, when they were elongated and called dirigibles. They soon took on small 3-horsepower engines to furnish gas inflation, and later the hand propeller types were exchanged for the steam propeller style. The gas balloons were used in the beginning of the twentieth century; they could make 15 miles per hour.

The next idea of air navigation was suggested by one of God's creatures—the flying bird. Steps in different directions were taken by Europeans to model after this little creature. This being a machine that was heavier-than-air, puzzled the brain as to how to make it rise, move, and make safe landings. In 1891 a German constructed a plane that was called a "glider." It required an elevation from which it could be shoved off into the air, when it would angle rapidly to the level below. He kept improving this model until 1896, when he was killed in one of his own machines.

From this small beginning two boys of Ohio continued the work. They were Orville and Wilbur Wright. The glider engaged their attention for a few years, and they believed it possible to drive this machine by attaching combustion gas engines. Wings were also a perplexing problem. Four types were thought of and tried out—flapping wings, biplanes, triplanes, and monoplanes.

The summer of 1903 found the Wright Brothers busy trying to put their new idea into action. On December 17 of that year a little 200-pound, 25-horsepower engine was connected onto their plane. One of the Wright boys climbed on. A host of people of Kitty Hawk stood watching. What was the result? The motor was started. The plane took off and then rose. The crowd shuddered. A landing was made after a flight of 12 seconds. This was the beginning of aviation. The aviator had superseded the aeronaut.

Improvements continued to be made thereafter, but especially did the work of making planes go by leaps and bounds from 1909, at which time it was tried out for military use. World War I changed the location of warfare from earth to air. Capacity, activity, and speed have been the lines of development. The plane of 1909 made 47 miles per hour; 1913, 125; 1943, 400 on a flight and 700 on a dive. The capacity has grown from the weight of one man to that of 70 tons. Horsepower has climbed from 25 to 8,800. Weight of plane, from 1,000 pounds to 24 tons. Motors, from one to twelve. Length of plane, from 33 feet to 150. Ascent, from 100 feet to 8 miles. Air endurance, from 12 seconds to 420 hours. Sphere, from the place of birth to every spot on the globe. No place on earth is more than 60 hours from the United States.

The two uses of planes in World War I were reconnaissance and attack. In World War II they grew into transports, fighters, rockets, amphibians, divers, freighters, helicopters, mail carriers, etc. Gliders are still used by being towed upward by motor planes to the place of destination and then unhooked to be steered to the place of need. In May, 1918, the first mail was carried between Washington and New York, being Army letters and small packages. The following year the Postoffice Department took over the air mail, and 1920 found letters going across the continent by air; but it was four years before mail planes could make the trip without stop. November 1, 1920, the first commercial and passenger route was established, from Florida to Cuba—130 miles.

Charles Lindbergh, an American lad, flew from New York to Paris, France, a distance of 3,600 miles, in 33½ hours, in May, 1927. The May previous to that, Richard Byrd, another American boy of the United States Navy, circled to the North Pole and back safely in 16 hours. To January, 1944, there had been 50,000 non-stop flights made across the Atlantic Ocean.

The helicopter in years to come will supersede the automobile and truck in transportation of freight and livestock. This plane can rise or lower vertically. This type was invented in 1908 by Igor Sirkorsky, a 19-year-old lad of Russia, who came to the United States and labored on his machine until 1940, before its unsurpassed worth was seen in lowering food and rescuing isolated soldiers.

In September, 1943, the Greyhound Bus Line filed applications for authority to operate 29 helicopter lines covering the Southeastern portion of the United States, for carrying mail and passengers. Route No. 10 of this set-up, beginning at Paducah and swinging southeasterly, will include in its 10 stops the towns of Campbellsville, Columbia, Glasgow, and Bowling Green. So, if it functions, Burkesville will be close to this route.

Airplanes are coming into use in every quarter of the globe, and in the course of a few years they likely will take the place of automobiles. Accidents are no more frequent among planes than cars. In the last World War 22,000 planes had accidents with a loss of 23,000 lives.

The world will become smaller and smaller as the plane lives. The first non-stop flight across the Pacific Ocean took place November 1, 1945, when four big Superfortress 29's with 43 men aboard, flew from north Japan by the way of Alaska to Washington, D. C., a distance of 6,544 miles in 27 hours and 29 minutes, at a cost of nearly 8,000 gallons of gas. Then within the same month an A-26 bomber circumnavigated the globe just north of the Equator in about 97 hours with but few stops.

In the year 1916 the first plane passed over Cumberland County. It was going east at a height of some over two miles. Every eye angled upward regardless of where and what the occupation was. The writer was teaching a country school of some fifty children crowded in a little schoolhouse nestled in the Cumberland Valley hills. When words and threats failed to keep heads from protruding through the windows, the school took a five-minute recess that teacher and all might share alike. All passed the same judgment on it—that it looked very much like a chicken hawk.

In May, 1943, the first ten gliders passed over the county, towed by planes, with the silk cords glittering between them.

It has become very common for planes to take passengers up and over the country for rides.

The first plane to be owned in the county is the little Aeronca owned by Chatten Chowning, a young man of Crocus Creek, who was driven from his home by the Dale Hollow Dam. He purchased it at Bowling Green, January, 1946.

RADIO

Fifty years ago, if someone had told you that some day not far away you would be able to sit in your own home in the mountains of Cumberland County, Kentucky, or even in the rugged valleys of California, and turn a little button, and hear a man breathe on the opposite side of the world, you would have classified that man with the most stupid of visionary dreamers. Little did anyone think that there were thousands of beautiful songs, able sermons, oratorical displays, theatrical performances, baseball games, and the like, passing right by our ears unheard, day and night. Instead of waiting until the last of each week to get the markets on livestock from the little country postoffices through the weekly newspaper, one can now sit in his home, regardless of its isolation, turn a little knob, and count the head, hear the sale, read the price up to the moment, though he may be a totally handicapped illiterate.

Having learned that heat would radiate into the air, a few scientists concluded that electricity would do likewise and that a metal conductor was not essential for this purpose but all that was needed was an instrument that would start and stop these electrical waves. The scientist who brought the "wireless telegraphy" to practical use was William Marconi, an Italian. In 1895-6 he made successful experiments between buildings. In 1899 he succeeded in crossing the English Channel, December 12, 1901, a signal was sent from Newfoundland, and in 1903 a message was sent from America to England, nearly 3,000 miles.

CHAPTER 18

OUR FLAG

AND LONG MAY IT WAVE

The first flags adopted by our forefathers to best bespeak the day were symbolical of their surrounding struggles with the wilderness of a new land. The pine tree, the beaver, rattlesnake, were the insignia so used, each of which carried its distinct significance expressed in their mottoes, respectively, "An Appeal to Heaven"; "Industry"; "Don't Tread on Me."

From the year 1603 until the middle of 1776 the "Grand Union Flag," consisting of 13 stripes alternate red and white, with its upper left corner bearing the crosses of St. George and St. Andrew, signifying the union with the mother country, was the banner used by the 13 colonies. It was under this banner that Washington and his brave Continentals struggled for independence.

Upon the adoption of the Declaration of Independence, July 4, 1776, it became important that an emblem be patterned that would bespeak the semblance of unity at home, whereupon General Washington and a few of his co-workers framed a skeleton flag that retained the 13 stripes but replaced the crosses with a circle of 13 stars in that field of blue and the sketch was handed to Betsy Ross, a seamstress of Philadelphia, Pennsylvania, who took a portion of her own garment together with her husband's red shirt and fashioned them into the first American Flag, which the Continental Congress adopted on June 14, 1777, to be the emblem of the new nation, with its stars from heaven, its red from our mother country, and its white a token of peace and liberty wherever it might fly, all of which has meant so much to the nations of earth.

Under the new nation Congress was given the right to add to Old Glory one stripe and an extra star for each state that should come into the Union. Vermont (1791), Kentucky (1792), brought the stars and stripes to 15 in 1794. It remained thus until 1818, but as states were coming into the Union much faster than at first thought, Congress at once saw how bunglesome and awkward such an emblem would be if this practice was kept up, so it was reduced to the original 13 stripes and an extra star has been added for each new state making the present forty-eight.

Cumberland County was born under the 15-15, and lived its first twenty years under this flag.

CHAPTER 19

CUMBERLAND COUNTY AT WAR

REVOLUTIONARY WAR

It was 15 years after the Revolutionary War before Cumberland County was formed. Few people were here during the war, but it was well enough known that many flocked to this county at the close of the war to receive land grants in pay for their services in the war. A list of them is incomplete, because many of the soldiers died in the county and were buried without markers to commemorate their noble deeds. The land grants were given by the Government for a while after the war closed, but it was not until 1818 that Congress passed the first pension law.

Below is the full list of the ones who received money pensions for service (Cumberland County):

Under Act of March 18, 1818

Lawrence Conner, private, Sept. 14, 1818, Va. Line, $96, age 73
John Monroe, private, June 9, 1818, $96, age 90
James Maccoun, private, Jan. 24, 1824, Va. Line, $96, age 90
William Rowe, private, June 9, 1818, Va. Line, $96, age 78

Act of June 7, 1832, Government Record

John Baker, serg., Apr. 1, 1833, Va. Line, $120, age 83
William Baker, priv., Mar. 3, 1833, Va. Line, $21.66, age 70
Benjamine Brummel, priv., Mar. 3, 1833, Militia, $40, age 70
Francis Barrett, serg., Mar. 26, 1833, Va. Line, $99.16, age 72
William Burchett, priv., Sept. 24, 1833, Va. Troops, $30, age 79
John Burchett, priv., Nov. 15, 1832, Va. Troops, $20, age 73
Charles Carter, priv., Dec. 18, 1832, Va. Line, $20, age 76
William Cheatham, priv., Mar. 8, 1833, Militia, $38.34, age 72
William Cary, priv., Mar. 8, 1833, Militia, $44.99, age 78
John Chapman, priv., May 18, 1833, Militia, $29.43, age 72
Shadrach Claywell, priv., July 8, 1833, Va. Cavl., $70, age 74
John Creasy, priv., June 6, 1834, Militia, $20, age 80
Robert Crocket, priv., Sept. 2, 1833, Va. Militia, $45.53, age
Godfrey Elam, priv., March 8, 1833, Militia, $40, age 71
William Ferguson, priv., Nov. 15, 1833, Va. Line, $60, age 71
Martin Gryder, priv., June 30, 1833, N. C. Line, $60, age 83
Valentine Gryder, priv., Aug. 17, 1833, N. C. Line, $60, age 72

John Gibson, priv., July 10, 1834, N. C. Line, $63.33, age 84
William Goodman, ensign, Nov. 7, 1834, Va. Militia, $240, age 75
Joseph Jewell, lieut., Apr. 12, 1834, N. Y. Militia, $320, age 82
George King, priv., May 13, 1833, Militia, $20, age 85
Morgan Morgan, priv., May 13, 1833, Va. Line, $76.66, age 73
John Miller, priv., May 29, 1833, Md. Militia, $20, age 72
Francis Pierce, priv., Mar. 18, 1833, Va. Line, $20, age 74
Solomon Prewitt, priv., Aug. 9, 1833, Va. Line, $80, age 84
George Richardson, priv., May 6, 1833, Va. Line, $80, age 77
James Radford, priv., Oct. 31, 1833, Va. Line, $50, age 72
Samuel Smith, priv., Apr. 10, 1833, N. C. Militia, $30, age 79
Joseph Sewell, priv., June 17, 1833, S. C. Troops, $60, age 80
John Scott, priv., Aug. 9, 1833, Va. Line, $80, age 73
Moses Webb, in Green's Army, 1777
Joe Rutledge, battles of 1779
Isaac McBee
John Self, priv., Aug. 9, 1833, Militia, $30, age 72
Charles Thurman, priv., Mar. 10, 1832, Va. Line, $80, age 76
James Williams, 2d. priv., Aug. 29, 1833, Militia, $80, age 72
Richard Wade, Sr., priv., Sept. 26, 1833, N. C. Militia, $80, age 82
Thomas Williams, priv., Dec. 27, 1833, Militia, $80, age 79
William Whittacre, priv., July 10, 1834, Militia, $70, age 74

Pension Under the 1828 Act

John Emmerson, lieut., 13 Regiment, Va. Line, Feb. 12, 1829, $320

There were five Revolutionary pensioners living in Cumberland County in 1840 (Collins History).

> Elijah Bledsoe, age 68
> Thomas Brothers, age 62
> Thomas Cash, Sr., age 65
> John Gibson, Sr., age 95
> John Hurt, age 71
> (Error in above ages)

List supplementary to above:

> Henry C. Haggard, King Cem.
> John E. King, King Cem.
> John E. Rowe, Howard Bottom
> Thos. B. Hudson, Wathall Cem.
> Geo. Rose, Crocus Creek
> Columbus Winchester, Brush Creek
> Obediah Baker, Little Renox
> W. E. Goggins, Lawson Bottom
> William Smith   Philip Lawson
> John R. Thurman   Abraham Estes
> Milton King   Dave Bowen

The soldiers of the Revolutionary War who lived in Cumberland County made the following statements in applying for pensions:

Lawrence Conner states that he was born 1752 and was engaged in five major battles, where he got his present wound, and that he has four children now (1820): Esther, age 30; Cornelius, age 18; Jimmie, age 16; and Margaret, age 13.

John (or James) Monroe states in 1820 that he is 80 years old and was born in Amherst County, Va., and his children are: Susan b. 1785; Fanny b. '87; Annie, '89; Lucy, '91; Sally in '93; Mary in '96; Andrew, '99; Henry, 1800; Elizabeth, 1802; John, 1804.

James McCowan states he was born in Rockbridge County, Va., and that he is now (1824) 90 years old.

William Rowe states (1820) that he is 64 years old and married Sally Towler (or Fowler) of Culpeper County, Va., in 1787 and has Sally (1804), Mary Ann (1809), Lou (1811), Hiram (1810), Robert, and Joe.

William Burchett states in 1833 that he was 78 years old and that he was drafted in Lenningburg County, Va.

John Burchett, his brother, was 72 the same year, and states that he came to Cumberland County in 1807.

William Cheatham in 1832 stated he was 69 years old and came from Chesterfield County, Va., to Cumberland County in 1807 (to Ark., 1837).

William Cary states in 1832 that he was born in Chesterfield County, Va., and was 77 years old, that he moved to Clayborn County, Tenn., 1808, and to Cumberland County, 1829.

Shadrach Claywell stated in 1833 that he was 73 years old, born in Worcester County, Md., 1760, and moved to Bedford County, Va., and to Cumberland County in 1806.

John Creasy stated in 1834 that he was born in Cumberland County, Va., and was 80 years old; that he moved to Henry County, Va., and to Cumberland County, Ky.

Robert Crocket stated in 1833 that he was 78, born in Barryville, Va., moved to North Carolina; to Greenville County, Tenn., and to Cumberland County, 1800.

Godfrey Elum says he was born in Chesterfield County, Va.

William Ferguson stated in 1833 that he was 69 years old, born in Amelia County, Va., that he married Juda Wood and came to Cumberland County, 1813.

Martin Gryder stated in 1832 that he was 81, born in Pennsylvania, 1750, enlisted in Burkes and Wilkes County, N. C.; moved to Madison County, Ky., 1778 (must have been 1798), and from there to Cumberland County, Ky.

Valentine Gryder stated in 1832 that he was 70 years old, born in Loudoun County, Va., 1762, enlisted in Burkes County, N. C., as a substitute for his two brothers, Jacob Grider and Cornelius Grider;

and that he married Mary Fugate of Lee County, Va., in 1816, and that he lived in Rock House Bottom, this county.

John Gibson stated in 1834 that he was 83, born in Hanover County, Va., 1750, and enlisted in Surry County, N. C.; made several moves, the last one to Cumberland County, Ky.

William Goodman (or Goodson) in 1833 stated he was 73, born in Fredrick County, Md., 1759, moved to Virginia, Tennessee, and then to Cumberland County.

Joseph Jewell in 1832 said he was 80, born in Huntington County, N. J.; went to Orange County, N .Y., in 1776; to Virginia, 1784; to Cumberland County, 1808. He states his daughter is Sarah C. Lewis.

George King said in 1833 he was 83 years old, born in Northumberland County, Va., 1750, went to Henry County, Va., and to Cumberland County, 1819.

Morgan Morgan stated in 1833 he was 72, born in Lancaster County, Pa., 1860; enlisted in Montgomery County, Va., 1776; went to Wythe County, Va., 1795; and to Cumberland County, Ky., 1802.

John Miller stated in 1833 he was 71 years old, born in Montgomery County, Md., moved to Surry County, N. C., from there to Cumberland County, Ky., 1812; that he married Elenor Garner, of Surry County, who was a daughter of John Garner of the same county, and had three children—Jacob, b. 1798; Martin, 1800; Nancy, 1803.

Francis Pierce stated in 1832 he was 72, born in Carolina County, Va.; enlisted in Albermarle or Orange County, Va.; moved to Wilkes County, N. C.; and from there to Cumberland County in 1801.

Solomon Prewitt said in 1829 he was 79, married Mary ——, and that he served in the Revolutionary War with John Scott and James Radford.

George Richardson stated in 1832 he was 75, born in Bedford County, Va.; moved to Tennessee, 1798; and to Cumberland County, 1802, and that he served with Shadrach Claywell.

James Radford stated in 1833 he was 71, born in Powhatan County, Va., 1762; enlisted from Buckingham County, Va., from which he came to Cumberland County, 1810; that his present second wife, Hannah Wilborn, whom he married, 1830, had one son named Lufus Radford.

Samuel Smith stated in 1832 he was 77, born in Pittsylvania County, Va., and moved to Burke County, N. C., in 1773 and to Cumberland County, Ky., 1802, and that he served with Valentine and Martin Gryder. He further says he married Rachel —— and had at that time, John, Martin, and Nancy (his will shows he had other children).

Samuel Smith (2) states in 1834 he was 74, born in Amherst County, Va., 1760; moved to Russell County, Va., then to Cumberland County in 1804. He married Dorcas —— and reared Polly, Jane, Britain, Fanny, Robert, Samuel, Dorcas, Margaret, Elisha, William. (Sam, Sr., died 1844.)

Cumberland County at War

Joseph Sewell stated in 1832 he was 79, born in Howard County, Md., in 1753; enlisted in Wilkes County, N. C., on April 1, 1775, and in 1785 moved to Carter County, Tenn., and about 30 years later to Cumberland County, Ky.

John Scott stated in 1829 he was 68, served with Solomon Prewitt and Joshua Watson, Watson having married a sister (Nancy Murry) to his wife, Sofa Murry Scott.

Moses Webb stated in 1818 he was in Gen. Green's Army, 1777, with John Emmerson. He further stated he had only one broad-ax, two planes, two chisels, one auger, and one pair of compasses.

Joseph Rutledge stated in 1830 he was 81, from Surry County, N. C.; served, 1779, in N. C. Line in Capt. Spear's company, regiment of Col. Joseph Williams.

Isaac McBee said in 1840 he was 76, born in Halifax County, Va.; enlisted in Green County, N. C.; and came to Cumberland County, 1803.

John Self stated in 1832 he was 70, born in Amelia County, Va., came to Kentucky, 1798, and to Cumberland County in 1809.

Charles Thurman stated in 1820 he was 62, enlisted in Henrico County, Va., 1777; served with John Scott, Philip Lawson, John R. Thurmen, and William Smith.

James Williams stated in 1833 he was 70, born in Sullivan County, Va., came to Cumberland County in 1802, and was soldier in next war, 1812 to 1814. (Went to Arkansas, 1838.)

Richard Wade in 1833 stated he was 81, born in Goochland County, Va., moved to Madison County, Ky., and then to Wayne, 1801.

Thomas Williams said in 1833 he was 79, born in Brunswick County, Va., and came to Cumberland County in 1813.

William Whittacre in 1834 said he was 74, born in Burnsville, N. C., and moved to Cumberland County —.

John Chapman said in 1832 he was 70; he was born in Halifax County, Va., and served under Joshua Powell for three years.

Benjamin Fields said in 1832 he was 76, born in Culpeper County, Va., and married Mildred Slaughter after coming to Kentucky.

Hardin Williams in 1833 stated he was 68, born in South Carolina, came to Cumberland County in 1803, and married Jane Hart.

Joseph Wright in 1832 stated he was 80, born in Fredrick County, Md., then to Tennessee, and Cumberland County, 1812. He said he had two brothers—Joshua and James. (Joseph died in Clinton County, 1843.)

Matthew Amyx was examined by Joel Owsley and Michael L. Stoner, in 1827, for pension, for services in Revolutionary War.

William Cary stated in 1832 he was 77 years old; born in Chesterfield County, Va.; moved to Clayborn County, Tenn., in 1808, and to Cumberland County in 1829.

WAR OF 1812

Only 30 years had elapsed since the British forces surrendered at Yorktown, ending the struggle for peace and freedom from the yoke of British despots, when another war cloud gathered—on the waters this time. England could not fully convince herself that young America was entirely beyond her control. Needing men to assist in her war in Europe she continued to impress our men into her armies while they were peacefully sailing the high seas for the purpose of trade only. This time was for freedom on the seas. Things grew worse and worse, until she began firing upon our ships, whereupon the young U. S. A. declared war on her, June 19, 1812.

Most of the fighting was along the border of the United States and Canada and on the Atlantic Ocean. We established three centers, one at Detroit under Harrison; one at Niagara under Dearborn; and one at Lake Champlain under Hampton. The east and center did little. William Hull took part of Harrison's army and crossed into Canada and, hearing that the British 700 strong under General Brock and Indians 600 strong under Tecumseh were coming, recrossed and prepared to arrest their movements. The Americans stood with lighted matches, but Hull ran up a white flag which gave the British all of Michigan—and a black eye to our soldiers.

The following year a body of soldiers made a stand on the River Raisin, just south of Detroit. General Proctor agreed to protect the wounded American soldiers who fell on the Raisin, but left them in the reach of the savage Indians, who tomahawked and burned the last one, dragging some of them through the streets of Detroit. Most of those brave men were Kentuckians. Five counties of Kentucky were named for some of them.

Oliver H. Perry's victory on Lake Erie, 1814, with his nine ships made from the growing timber on the banks, brought new life to the war. Other naval victories also kindled hope. On Chesapeake Bay the British scoured the coast to Baltimore. At Ft. McHenry, near Baltimore, the engagement lasted all night, but the sentiment of the National Anthem, "The Star-Spangled Banner," written then and there, reveals the truth of this engagement. General Ross at the time was devastating the Capital, which he burned with the early records of our country. This has been a drawback to those interested in research work. The writer of this volume has met with many disappointments along this line.

The treaty of peace was signed in Ghent, Belgium, December 24, 1814. With only ship communications propelled by sails across the expansive Atlantic, the news did not reach America until after a great unnecessary battle at New Orleans was fought and won by our boys—mostly Tennessee and Kentucky "flint-lockers." Seven killed and six wounded bespoke their skill.

In this battle of January 8, 1815, and the Raisin, Cumberland County played her biggest role. An incomplete list of the county's

Cumberland County at War

number will follow. The national debt had soared to $127,000,000, a midget compared to 1945. Freedom of the seas was gained in this war, and has lasted.

Soldiers from Cumberland County, mostly under David McNair (taken from the record):

Samuel Wilson, Lt. Col.
John Ritchie, Major
James McColgan, Major
James Allen, Brig. Gen.
Isaac Tate
William Thompson
Edward King
James W. Taylor
James Ghoulson
Thomas M. Emmerson
John Cape, Lt. Col.
James Campbell, Major
Sam Scott, Major
Gardner Green
John Harvey
Gilbert Rowland
Hays Murphy
Jacob Shults
Benjamin Sims
William Walthall
Josiah Akin
Isaiah Cheatham
Thomas Cary
George Martin
Thomas Minor
Solomon Hollett
James Lollar
John Lewis
John Murry
David Ogden

Sam Rush
William Thurman
Littleberry Thurman
William Tooley
William Wilborn
William Winfrey
Robert Young
James Helm
Richard Hicks
John French
William Eldridge
Edward Wilborn
John Williams
Thomas Ashlock
Israel Bunch
George Craft
William Agee
William Cross
James Cowan
Thomas Logan
John Owen
John Carter
Andrew Cowan
Alfred Ballew
Asa Harper
James Macky
Andrew Smalley
John Pierce
John R. Cumming

CIVIL WAR

Soldiers from Cumberland County, Kentucky, helped to fill the ranks of several branches of the fighting forces of the state, but the 5th Kentucky Cavalry, 3d Regiment Kentucky Volunteer Infantry, 16th Volunteer Infantry, and Home Guards embraced most of the Cumberland boys.

The 5th Kentucky Cavalry was organized at Gallatin, Tennessee, under Col. David R. Haggard of Burkesville, Kentucky, March, 1862, with 789 men, most of whom were from this part of Cumberland

Valley. Losses were reported from this regiment in the following battles and skirmishes: Burkesville, Gallatin, Monroe Cross Roads, North Carolina, Adairville, Millers Grove, and Sweet Water, Georgia.

The 3d Regiment Kentucky Volunteer Infantry was organized at Camp Dick Robinson in October, 1861. Its first line of march was from camp to Lexington, Camp Dick Robinson, Rock Castle, Crab Orchard, Somerset, Wayne County, Pulaski, and on November 19 to Columbia, where sickness and death of many of the soldiers held it there until January 7, 1862, when the able ones marched to the mouth of Renox Creek near Burkesville, Cumberland County. There they camped until January 16, '62, when the 300 men marched to Russell County, trebling their strength, embarked on a steamboat for Nashville, Tennessee. During the four years of war this regiment covered most of Kentucky, Tennessee, and Georgia, engaging in 22 of the heaviest battles of the Civil War.

The 16th Kentucky Volunteer Infantry was organized at Maysville, Kentucky. It wintered in southern Kentucky, 1862. Cumberland County was overrun by guerrillas from Tennessee. At Marrowbone, this county, this regiment engaged the guerrillas. Champ Ferguson was the fiercest guerrilla of this and adjoining counties.

Tom Keeton, Home Guard, bushwhacker, skirmished with the Rebels at Brownwood in Lawsons Bottom. The Rebels were camping on the opposite side of Cumberland River in Irish Bottom, the site of the skirmish. A few soldiers were killed and buried there. Keeton then chased Ferguson up Crocus Creek and out up Puncheon Creek with Ferguson firing at Keeton's men over his shoulder.

John Hunt Morgan camped with a part of his army at Salt Lick Bend where he stripped the country of most of its meat, grain, and vegetables. He also stayed at Pleasant Hill near Whites Bottom, for three weeks. Here the country was also stripped of its products. Tom Skipworth, a citizen of Pleasant Hill who is now (1944) 97 years old and in perfect health physically and mentally, tells us this story about Morgan and how all the school children were scared and how the teacher adjourned school for the duration at his approach. Many two-inch steel balls have been found in these parts of the county, together with ½-inch lead balls then much used.

Company 1 was formed of men in Cumberland County, with Michael H. Owsley, Captain; Jesse M. Carter, first lieutenant, and Anderson T. Keen, second lieutenant. It was formed in July and August, 1861.

A company of cavalry was organized in July, 1861, at Albany, Kentucky, with John A. Brents, captain, John A. Morrison, first lieutenant, and John P. Miller, second lieutenant.

These men were promoted during the struggle, and with Colonel Wolford and many others fought in many engagements to rid this part of Kentucky of the enemy under John Hunt Morgan and the guerrilla, Champ Ferguson. Jesse M. Carter was killed at Columbia and Brents took his place.

General John Hunt Morgan made his first raid in July, 1861. He entered the state through Monroe County, where a battle was fought, and moved on toward Louisville, but turned east through central Kentucky and out by the way of Monticello, Wayne County. In this month of raids he captured 17 towns, dispersed over 1,500 Home Guards with the loss of only 90 men.

Two raids were made in 1863 that touched closer to the life of Cumberland County than the former. In January of that year he made a raid on Columbia and Campbellsville, and on February 12, 1863, two companies of Morgan's cavalrymen encountered Col. Wolford in Burkesville, this county. Morgan was on the south side of the river near the old Ferry, and Wolford was on the Burkesville side of the river. The Federals were defeated with the loss of seven men. On July 2, 1863, the Federals were again defeated at Burkesville, but made their escape to their encampment at Marrowbone, skirmishing on the hill east of Waterview, and with the aid of artillery and fresh men, Morgan was repulsed.

On his fourth trip into Kentucky he found himself followed by strong forces with intentions to get hold of him some way. On September 4, 1864, he was betrayed near Greenville, Tennessee, and surrounded by the cavalry of Alvin C. Gillen, he was killed. Some authorities say he was killed after his capture. Anyhow, the story goes that his body was placed upon a mule and held there while they paraded the town with shouts of joy. It was then turned over to the Confederates who interred it at Richmond, Virginia, and in 1872 it was removed to Lexington, Kentucky.

In 1865, another desperado visited this part of Kentucky, in the person of General Lyons. He burned 28 county seats, or parts of them. On December 23, he burned Campbellsville Court House, and on January 3, 1865, came into the town of Burkesville, robbed all the stores, empressed all the best horses, supplied his men with food from stores and smokehouses. He took the benches of the Court House, split them into kindling, and set fire to the building, after the records were removed, which resulted in its total destruction.

Of the 390 battles and skirmishes fought on Kentucky soil during the Civil War, this county escaped well with these few.

SOLDIERS OF CIVIL WAR

The list of Union Soldiers is complete with the exception of a few who were killed, missing, or disappeared in other ways.

(Arranged in order of the letters of the alphabet)

NAME	CEMETERY
Samuel Anderson	Guthrie
Jesse Anderson	Bow
John N. Anderson	Howards Bottom
Matthew Armstrong	Crocus Creek

NAME	CEMETERY
John Alberson	Dutch Creek
John Alberson	Burkesville
James Anderson	Slate Fork
Frank Abston	Mt. Pleasant
Jesse Anderson	Modoc
J. M. Arms	Hardy
Wilson Anderson	Modoc
T. S. Anderson	Taylor
William Anderson	Watkins
Thomas Ashinhurst	
John W. Asberry	
Shadrick T. Austin	
Tom Anderson	
Columbus Akin	
Ephraim P. Brummitt	Liberty
William Brake	Liberty
A. K. Bruton	Modoc
Jacob S. Bruton	Slate Fork
William W. Burns	Hegira
J. B. Bruton	Rose of Sharon
Isaac W. Bow	Mt. Pleasant
W. A. Barnes	Barnes
John M. Bow	Hardy (Bow)
Milton Branham	Modoc
Henry Branham	Leslie
Henry Blakely	Guthrie
Charles Blythe	Prewitt
Loren Baker	
Fayette Bow	Modoc
Ben F. Branham	Mud Camp
James Ballard	Mud Camp
Joseph B. Brake	White Hill
George Branham	White Hill
William Burchett	Burkesville
George W. Bowen	White Hill
Gabriel Booher	
Christopher Booher	
William J. Biggerstaff	
William S. Blankenship	
Milton Bunch	
J. A. Bowen	
Peter Baker	
Jesse Blankenship	
Henry K. Baker	
James Bow	
John C. Baise (d. at Burkesville)	

NAME	CEMETERY
James Black	
William D. Bradshaw	
Peter Brents	
Michael Booher	
Ephriam J. Boykin	
Loren Brake	
Jacob S. Bow	
James Bolin	
Andrew Bolin	
Charles Ballard	
Henry K. Baker	
Jesse Bryant	Dutch Creek
Thomas Burks	
John C. Bow	
Sam Biggerstaff	
C. W. Baker	
John S. Bryant	
Hance P. Claywell	Smith Grove
John Carter	Burkesville
Jesse M. Carter	Burkesville
G. L. Craft	Rose of Sharon
Milborn Coop	Christian Chapel
George W. Coop	Peytonsburg
Moses B. Capps	Capps
John M. Capps	Capps
Bennett Capps	Capps
Allen Capps	
W. C. Collins	Mud Camp
Thomas Collins	Howards Bottom
Robert J. Cox	Brush Creek
Granville Campbell	
Anderson Claywell	
William H. Carter	
John F. Cash	
Martin Coffey	
Levi Cotton (d. at Burkesville)	
John W. Coffey	
Lewis Capps	
Francis M. Cole	
William S. Cloyd	
Adam Coop	
Elijah W. Claywell	
Milton H. Claywell	
William M. Campbell	
Marion F. Cary	
Everett Cary	
James Capps	

Name	Cemetery
Elzie Carter	
Harrison Cox	
Rufus A. Craft	
Powhatan Crawley	
John N. Cloyd	
Calvin Carter	
— Chancey	
James P. M. Cox	
James Davidson	Prewitt
Anderson Daniels	Bow S. House
Rufus Dishman	Big Renox
John Davidson	Christian Chapel
John W. Daniels	Bow S. House
John M. Davis (d. at Burkesville)	
Alfred Davidson	
James K. Davis	
Elijah Daniels	
William B. Dunn	
Richard Dishman	
George H. Dishman	
Joseph Dooley	
W. M. Ellison	Guthrie
Travis Elmore (d. at Burkesville)	
Allen Elmore (d. at Burkesville)	
Marion Elmore (d. at Burkesville)	
J. R. Elum	Spears
Noah English	
Richard English	
John M. Feuston	
Sam Fitch	
William Farr	Vincent
George Farmer	
James M. Flowers	Frogue
Joseph Ferguson	Bow S. House
Isaac K. Feuston	Lawson Bottom
Mose Ferguson	Crocus
William Garrett	Irby
John Gentles	Rose of Sharon
James W. Graham	Bow S. House
Grady A. Groce	Peytonsburg
George W. Groce	Frogue
John A. Groce	Frogue
Joseph Graves	Littrell

NAME	CEMETERY
William Guthrie	Frogue
J. A. Guthrie	Guthrie
William Garret	Walthall
James C. Gilbert	Brush Creek
Lewis L. Garrett	
Pleasant Garrett	
Harlen Galen	
Ben M. Gilreath (k. at Atlanta)	
Berry Garner	
Joseph Garmon	
Andy Garmon	
Pleas Groce	Frogue
John Gilbert	
John Herd	
Charter Hume, Roy Huddleston	Leslie
Judson Huddleston	Leslie
J. A. B. Huddleston	Poplar Grove
James Hill	Bow S. House
John W. Hoots	Spears Chapel
G. H. Hood	Gain Hill
Daniel Hardy	Hardy
William L. Hoots	Sulphur
T. J. Howard	Howard Bottom
William M. Hurt	Grider
David R. Hadley	Burkesville
William Hunt	Smith Grove
David R. Haggard	Burkesville
William Hunt	Howard Bottom
Reubin Hicks	Howard Bottom
James H. Haggard	
John W. Hay	
Ambrose Holsapple	
Thomas B. Hood	
S. F. Haggard	
Thomas B. Hudson	
James H. Herd	
George W. Hood	
Robert Higginbotham	
James Hill	
William H. Hooten	
Green B. Hooten	
Jacob H. Holt	
Luke Hutcherson	
David Harvey	
John Holman	
Ephraim W. Henniger	

NAME	CEMETERY
John A. Hardasin	
George W. Harris	
Hugh Johnson	Marcum
John W. Johnson	Ferguson
Andrew J. Jones	Ellington
William L. Johnson	
Sherod W. Jarvis	
Fielding Johnson	
James T. Key	
William S. Keen	
William P. Keen	
R. C. Keeton	Whetstone
J. D. Key, Cpl. (d. at Burkesville)	
Alfred D. Kirgie	
Solomon Long	Spears
James F. Lloyd	Brush Creek
Dick Lewis	Myers Ridge
Charles Lewis	Dutch Creek
Charles G. Lawrence	Vincent
James Luttrell	Vincent
Berry Lawson	
Alvin Lewis	
James Long	
James Lawlace	
J. McClain, Capt.	Burkesville
Alvis R. Murphy	Slate Fork
John Melton	Slate Fork
S. C. Monk	Neighbors
Ambrose Melton	Smith Ridge
Joel Moore	Long
Nicholas J. Mercer	Spears
Melvin McIntyre	Pierce Ridge
Jim Miller	Big Renox
James H. McCoy	Willis Creek
Martin McIntyre	
Richard Moore	
John H. Mills	
Lewis C. Martin	
Charles H. Myers	
Martin L. McCoy	
Dudley McClusky	
Randolph Maxey	
William H. Murray	
Charles Mackey	

NAME	CEMETERY
Sam Mackey	
Robert Mackey	
James McComas	
George Murphy	S. L. Bend
James A. Marcum	
A. J. Nelson	
James N. Norris	Modoc
John Neighbors	Rose of Sharon
H. B. Neighbors	Neighbors
G. W. Neighbors	Neighbors
William Napier	Thacker
Nathan Norris	
Crit S. Norris	Sulphur
Benjamin F. Norris	
William (Bill) Norris (d. in Tennessee)	
Baily Owens	Bow
James Owens	
Sandy Odle (farrier)	Christian Chapel
Absalom Pharris (k. at E-town)	
H. B. Prewitt	Prewitt
Michael Pharris	Bow
Van Pharris	
Joe Pipher	
Ephriam D. Prewitt	
James W. Phelps	
James G. Phelps	
John R. Page	
Ben D. Phelps	
Alvin C. Pierce	Pierce Ridge
James Perdue	
Sol Prewitt	
John Prewitt	
Jackson Prewitt	
John Prewitt	Prewitt
Joseph Perkins	Frogue
Elijah Palmore	Mud Camp
A. J. Phelps	
J. R. Pine	
George Rush	Liberty
James C. Rush	Vincent
Samuel Rush	Rush
Joseph F. Riddle	Frogue
J. S. Riddle	Bow S. H.
J. M. Riddle (farrier)	Bow School House

NAME	CEMETERY
Arthur Riddle (k. at Burkesville)	Bow School House
William Raney	Taylor
Joe C. Riddle	Bow School House
James Riley	Riley
George W. Rayborn	Watkins
Benjamin F. Rioll	Burkesville
Thomas A. Rowe	Burkesville
Henry Rogers	Myers Ridge
Henry C. Rogers	Smith Ridge
John C. Rowe	
Ranson Rich (wag)	
Andrew J. Raney	
James A. Raney	
Joseph O. Riddle	
Ben Rush	
F. R. Riddle	
William Rutledge	
Pleas Shy	
Alex Strange	
J. L. Strange, Capt.	Burkesville
Sidney Spencer	Burkesville
C. W. Simpson	Rose of Sharon
W. M. Smith	Smith Ridge
Samuel Smith	Modoc
James L. Stockton	Leslie
Ben. H. Simpson	Hegira
Gentry Smith	Christian Chapel
J. J. Smith	Christian Chapel
Pleas H. Smith (k. in action, Bakerton, 1862)	
William Sevier	
William Smith	
E. B. Smith	
R. F. Smith	
Briton Smith	
Jerry Scott	
James Sams	
William Spears	
Alfred Scott	
Tilman Stinson	
Lewis C. Story	
James M. Smith	
George W. Scarberry	
Jonathan Simpson	
Edward B. Smith (wounded at Burkesville, 1863)	

Cumberland County at War 221

NAME	CEMETERY
James K. Shaw	
Enoch C. Smith	
Richard C. Smith	
(captured by guerrillas and lost)	
Isaac Smith	
John B. Spears	
Granville M. Shepherd	
John Spears	
Ezra Stephenson	Bow
John B. Thurman	Smith Ridge
James W. Taylor	Bow
Eli Thacker	Frogue
John W. Thrasher	Leslie
D. J. Thrasher	Rose of Sharon
Daniel Thacker	Frogue
W. B. Thrasher	Vincent
Martin Thacker	Thacker
Isaac Tallent	Lawson Bottom
Henry Tallent	Lawson Bottom
Daniel Thacker	Howard Bottom
William P. Surratt	Myers Ridge
John W. Tuttle	Burkesville
Lewis Taylor	
Aaron Tallent	
James Taylor (d. at Burkesville)	
Berry Thurman	
Allen D. Thrasher	
Richard A. Thurman	
George H. Tayloy	
Edward Vincent	
James A. Vincent	Modoc
J. W. Vibbert	Leslie
A. J. Vaughn	Guthrie
James W. Vibbert	Mud Camp
Hezekiah E. Vibbert	
John Vibbert (bugler, killed)	
Axum Vaughn	
John B. Vincent	
William I. Vincent	
Richard Watson	Christian Chapel
Daniel Wadkins	Frogue
Matthew Williams	Ferguson
Alexander Williams	Ferguson
Henry Ward	Frogue

NAME	CEMETERY
Nathaniel Williams	Davis
George Wright	Shy
Dick Wilson	Mud Camp
George W. Welch	Smith Ridge
David Willen	
Burl Willis	
William M. Wilborn	
R. W. Wright	
Pleas S. Wright	
William D. Wright	
Joseph N. Wadkins	
John Williams	
George W. Wade	
James Watson	
Tom Williams	
William N. Williams	
James C. York	Spears
Melvin G. York	White Hill
John A. Young	
Joseph Young	

SOLDIERS OF THE CIVIL WAR (COLORED)

Henry Clay Haggard
Samuel Clark
John Jackson
Isaac Huddleston
George Flowers
Sherrod Railey
John Maupin

Jim Ritchey
George Smith
Harold Alexander
Milton Bleadsoe
Obediah Baker
Zeke Coe, Jr.

SOLDIERS WHO MADE GRADES

These soldiers of the Civil War from Cumberland County n grades. Most of them were in the 5th Kentucky Cavalry and the and 21st Infantry.

David R. Haggard, Colonel
James L. Strange, Captain
Jesse M. Carter, Captain
N. H. Owsley, Captain
Anderson T. Keen, Captain
James T. McClain, Captain
Lafayette Dunbar, Captain
William C. Bradshaw, Captain

Daniel R. Gray, Captain
Newton M. Hutchenson, Captain
John R. McClure, Captain
John B. Riggs, Captain
John R. Poindexter, Captain
Isaac S. Bow, Captain
Crawford L. Holseapple, Captain
Daniel W. Claywell, Captain
William P. Sanders, Colonel
John W. Baker, First Lieutenant
William D. Baugh, Second Lieutenant
Langston P. Bryant, First Lieutenant
John Brown, Second Lieutenant
J. M. D. Corrigan, Second Lieutenant
Christopher T. Cheek, Colonel
Allen Keen, Major
Eli C. Keen, First Lieutenant
Granville B. McGee, Second Lieutenant
G. S. Nunn, Second Lieutenant
Michael Owsley, Major
John Q. Owsley, Major
Elijah C. Riddle, Second Lieutenant
J. H. C. Sandidge, Adjutant
Andrew J. Vincent, Second Mate
Edward Vincent, First Lieutenant
Israel C. Winfrey, First Lieutenant
A. V. Winfrey, Surgeon
Marcellus Baugh, Chaplain
F. Q. Walker, Surgeon
F. H. Winfrey, First Lieutenant
Elijah Palmore, Corporal
William Guthrie, Corporal
William L. Hoots, Second Lieutenant
James A. Vincent, First Squadron
Francis Abston, First Squadron
Crit Norris, First Squadron
Granville M. Hogan, First Squadron
A. S. Marcum, First Squadron
James J. Simpson, Corporal
James H. Brown, Corporal
Joe T. Taylor, Corporal
James L. Hogan, Corporal
Franklin Keeton, Corporal
James S. Anderson, First Lieutenant
James C. York, First Squadron
John G. Johnson, Corporal
Richard C. Smith, Corporal
Joseph Graves, Corporal

Thomas A. Gilbert, Corporal
William T. Owsley, Surgeon
James H. Mackey, Regiment
W. H. Carter, Sergeant
H. M. S. Vaughn, Sergeant
Edward M. Johnson, Sergeant
Robert Higginbotham, Sergeant
Benjamin F. Ewing, Corporal
William D. Wright, Corporal
Alvin C. Pierce, Corporal
James Graham, Sergeant
James Sams, Corporal
Andrew J. Jones, Sergeant
John Melton, Corporal
Pleas W. Groce, Sergeant
Tom O. T. Thrasher, Corporal
Bennett Brake, First Squadron
James F. Lloyd, Sergeant
Thomas A. Rowe, Corporal
Ben F. Rioll, Corporal
Milt W. Triplett, Corporal
Robert T. Allen, Corporal
Milton Branham, Corporal
Daniel Bridgefarmer, Corporal
John W. Daniels, Sergeant
William H. Poindexter, Sergeant
James D. Key, Corporal

Lieutenant George W. Burchett's Kentucky National Legion consisted of 14 select soldiers—Lewis F. Hopkins, Sam Mackey, James P. Zimmerman, Newton C. Avery, J. Burchett, Dan E. Huddleston, William Huff, Garland A. Mann, Robert Mackey, Thomas Riley, William Haden Summers, John G. Talbott and William D. Wright.

REUNION OF CIVIL WAR VETERANS

On October 9, 1890, 350 Civil War veterans, besides 2,000 visitors, gathered at Green Grove, Cumberland County, with Captain Isaac S. Bow leader, and organized the Old Soldiers Reunion. Lieutenant Edward Vincent was master of ceremonies.

Captain Bow gave orders to fall into line, march to the grandstand, and be seated; S. P. Hulse offered prayer, after which the Tompkinsville Band played a piece, and Dr. R. M. Alexander was introduced as first speaker, whose eloquence brought tears to many eyes.

Ajt. J. H. C. Sandidge spoke next in behalf of those who had fallen, urging that their noble lives ever be kept in memory by the living.

Hon. O. L. Winks spoke of the Flag, and what its colors typify.

Dr. C. K. Haggard, son of their old Colonel, made a touching speech. F. A. Tabor of Adair County then spoke. Hon. J. S. Bruton gave a touching rehearsal of the hardships they had all shared together.

Other speakers were Prof. A. A. Huddleston, Rev. F. M. Mills of Albany, Rev. R. Watkins of Adair County, Hon. J. C. MacMurtrey. Rev. Watkins had lost both feet, by freezing, in the war.

A call was made for the widows of the fallen, which brought forth a gush of tears. Uncle Pleasant Shy of Hegira, 87, brought his flag which he had carried throughout the Rebellion.

The Regiments represented were: 51st Tennessee Cavalry; 3d, 5th, 6th, 7th, 13th, 15th, 37th Kentucky Cavalry; 2nd, 9th, 12th, 13th, and 37th Tennessee Infantry; and South Cumberland Battalion.

This was made an annual affair for decades to come, or at least until the number of living Civil War veterans dwindled to a few in number. This sacred spot once so dear to this big family of freedom-loving brothers, with the passing of their lives has ceased to be of any attraction to following generations. So goes life.

SPANISH AMERICAN WAR

Soldiers of Cumberland County

Clinton Keen, Howard Bottom
Esco L. Bybee, West Fork
Charles Myers, Myers Ridge
Charles Edd, Burkesville

CHAPTER 20

WORLD WAR I

What affects a nation affects a state and county. I shall give a brief history of this war in order to show how it was our county boys had to go and where they had to go.

At the outbreak of this war in 1914, there was an agreement among certain nations of Europe that bound them to go to one another's assistance in time of need. There was the Triple Alliance, embracing Germany, Austria-Hungary, and Italy which had been binding since 1882. Then there was the Triple Entente, embracing France and Russia of 1895, England going to them in 1900 to make the "triple." An ally in one war may be a foe in the next war. History has proved this over and over. Another thing time has shown is that wars are not of a spontaneous nature but on the contrary are the result of a germ which has been developing for years. This was true of World War I. Decades of prosperity in science, education, commerce, and manufacturing had preceded the crash. Co-operation had lulled the civilized nations into a sense of security. The increase of population and the enormous bulk of manufactured goods demanded an outlet market. Greed began to seize the minds of European leaders. Jealousy took hold of them in the fear of dominating powers. Altruism could be seen to fade in the presence of militarism. Soldiers were called and trained, to be ready if needed. Germany rehearsed the slogan of her heart: "Might Makes Right." Envy, jealousy, and covetousness grew to a bitter end, and all that was needed was a spark to set the passions of the war-mongers on fire.

That spark was set off in the assassination of the Austrian Archduke, Francis Ferdinand, and his wife at a town in Austria-Hungary, June 28, 1914. A peaceful settlement was tried, but without success. Arbitration days were over. Austria-Hungary demanded of Serbia that a jury composed of Austro-Hungarians be allowed to sit in Serbia to bring the assassin to justice. This was denied. Thirty days from the assassination, Austria declared war on Serbia which set the unparalleled orgy ablaze. Ninety per cent of the world became involved. Nineteen nations on the side of the Allies entered the conflict, besides nine other nations which broke diplomatic relations with Germany. Four nations—Germany, Austria-Hungary, Turkey, and Bulgaria—composed the Central Powers.

Nonbelligerent nations suffered, both on sea and in the homelands. The year 1914 ended with the Allies weakly in the lead; 1915 with Germany in the lead; 1916 with the Allies barely in the lead, while the ushering in of the new year 1917 was the gloomiest period of the war. Half a million soldiers for both Germany and France had lost their lives at Verdun; the German U-boats had destroyed 5,000,000 tons of shipping the previous year; airplanes were bombing both London and Berlin, and the food situation was becoming serious.

The United States tried to stay out. German submarines continued to sink our ships. May 7, 1915, the Lusitania, a British liner going from New York to Ireland, was torpedoed with a loss of 1,153—114 of whom were Americans.

The United States severed diplomatic relations with Germany on February 3, 1917. On April 6, 1917, war was declared on Germany, and on December 7 of the same year on Austria-Hungary. American ships made the first move. Several destroyers entered the "War Zone" to co-operate with the Allies, May 4, 1917. May 18, President Wilson signed the Selective Service Act. This was the first time since the Civil War that soldiers were drafted, and much confusion prevailed throughout the country. On June 5, 1917, all men from 21 to 31 registered; and on June 5, 1918 also; then on September 12, 1918, all from 18 to 45—24,234,021.

Just six weeks after the signing of this Act, American soldiers began to land in France (June 26, 1917). By the first of December, 1917, General Pershing had an American Army of 250,000 with him in France. The landing of this big army caused the German leaders to become jittery. Since July of 1917 Russia had had internal troubles, which brought about a separate peace with Germany; and by December 15 Russia was out of the war. This enabled Germany to withdraw her force from the East and place it on the West, to try to arrest the Allied invasion. With her army she brought her big new gun that would shoot 75 miles, with which she intended to demolish Paris.

At Cambria, November 4, 1917, the American boys had entered their first combat with the Germans. They were of the Engineer Corps and had thrown aside their shovels and tools to assist the French in closing a gap in their line, in which they were successful. Following this, the Americans were assigned a sector on the Aisne River. On June 2 the Germans had taken Chateau-Thierry near there. General Pershing asked that his army be tried out against the German force there. On June 3, 1918, the Germans attacked, and by the 13th the Americans had stopped their advance. Here was fought the battle of Belleau Wood, June 11, and by June 30 the German Army was routed with great loss, and retreated. This was the turning point of the war. On July 21 the conquering army took over Chateau-Thierry. This was accomplished by the 1st, 2nd, 3rd, and 26th divisions of Americans.

The first all-American battle took place at Saint Mihiel, which resulted in a great victory for General Pershing's boys, who captured 16,000 prisoners and 450 guns, but with a loss of about 7,000 Americans. At the time of this battle the American Army had swelled to two million men in France. Saint Mihiel was fought October 12,

1918. Along with this battle went the slaughter at Argonne Woods, near the Neuse River. This engagement lasted from September 26 to October 10. The Germans were beaten here and the Americans made a long advance.

While this battle was raging, Bulgaria made an unconditional surrender to the Allies, September 29. The Central Powers had received blows that had crippled them beyond repair. Along with this, the food situation was critical, and the end seemed near. October 31, Turkey surrendered; November 3, Austria made an unconditional surrender; and November 9, Kaiser William of Germany abdicated and fled to Holland. German representatives met General Foch at once and agreed to the drastic terms of the Allies, the gist of which were: "Within two weeks Germany must evacuate all occupied territory, withdraw her troops from her Allies, surrender her warships and other war equipment to the Allies." On November 11 the Armistice was signed, and the conflict ended.

The United States lost 49,000 killed; 204,215 wounded and missing.

The approximate cost of the war was $20 billion. Of this sum about $7 billion covered loans to other countries.

SOLDIERS OF WORLD WAR I FROM CUMBERLAND COUNTY

With Dates of Overseas Service

W. A. Adams—5-18 to 1-1-19
George O. Adams, Private
Jesse R. Akin, Private
Alonzo N. Alexander, Corporal
Percy McGee Alexander, LTMC
Mell O. Allen, Sergeant
W. Homer Allen—9-1-18 to 7-15-19
Charles R. Anderson, Private—4-16-18 to 9-8-19 (Wounded)
George Anderson, Sergeant
Harry Anderson, Private
John Anderson, Private—9-8-18 to 1-29-19
Leslie Anderson, Private
Virgil Anderson, Private—2-27-18 to 6-27-19
Albert J. Arms, Private—5-12-18 to 4-13-19 (Wounded)
Ambrose S. Arms, Private
Carley Ballou, Private—(Killed in action)
Ned Baker, Private
Radford Ballard, Private—6-28-18 to 3-27-19
Morris Beasley, Private—9-3-18 to 4-16-19
Rollin W. Bennett, Private
Will F. Bybee, Corporal—9-9-18 to 6-7-19

Charles Blankinship, Private—9-1-18 to 7-23-19
Henry D. Blankinship, Corporal
Iner Blankinship, Private
Charles Blythe, Private
Harold R. Booher, Private
William Pascal Booher, Private
Rassie Bow, Private—4-18 to 3-31-19 (Wounded)
Harold Branham, Sergeant—9-9-18 to 7-6-19
Hobart Branham, Private
Lucian T. Branham, Cook—3-16-18 to 7-28-19
Willie Branham, Private
Marvin Brewington, Private
Clarence W. Brown, Private—4-12-18 to —
James H. Brown, Private
John S. Brown, Sergeant
Willie Brummett, Private
John Bruton, Machinist—3-16-18 to 5-12-19
Mike Bruton, Private—6-18 to 4-11-19 (Wounded)
William E. Burchett, Private—4-18-18 to 12-17-19 (Wounded)
John C. Burnes, Sergeant—8-26-18 to 6-18-19
Ben. H. Capps, Private—10-11-18 to 5-13-19
Cordell M. Capps, Private
David A. Capps, Private—9-9-18 to 6-1-19
Joe T. Capps, Private
Richard B. Capps, Private—7-18-18 to 7-12-19
Clarence W. Carter, Private—4-9-18 to 2-7-19 (Wounded)
Francis M. Carter, Corporal—5-12-18 to 4-13-19
John W. Carter, Private
Lawrence C. Carter, Private
Charles Cary, Private
Creed A. Cary, Private—5-12-18 to 4-13-19
Harrison M. Cary, Private—9-2-18 to 4-16-19
Lewis Cary, Private
Marion R. Cary, Clerk—9-9-18 to 7-5-19
James S. Cash, Private
John S. Cash, Private—10-5-18 to 3-8-19
Frank A. Chism, Sergeant—10-6-18 to 7-7-19
Clarence W. Chansey, Private—7-26-18 to 5-1-19
Alonzo O. Claywell, Private—5-12-18 to 10-1-18 (Killed)
Fred E. Coe, Wagoner—8-14-17 to 1-14-19
Hershel D. Coe, Wagoner—10-6-18 to 6-28-19
Fayett R. Cole, Corporal—9-8-18 to 8-17-19
Charles F. Coleman, Wagoner—8-28-18 to 9-19-19
Henry C. Collins, Private—8-16-18 to 7-7-19
William L. Collins, Private—8-16-18 to 7-7-19
Gorder Coop, Corporal
Eugene McKinley Coop, Seaman—7-4-18 to 11-11-18
George P. Coop, Private—4-9-18 to 8-17-18 (Killed)

Lucius B. Coop, Private
Walter F. Coop, Seaman—7-7-18 to 11-11-18
Willand L. Coop, Mechanic—8-16-18 to 9-8-19
Elisha T. Cox, Private—4-9-18 to 7-22-19
Jesse F. Crawford, Sergeant
Edwin C. Crawley, Private—7-9-18 to 7-7-19
Leon Curtis, Wagoner—10-6-18 to 7-13-19
William Turner Curtis, Machinist
Shelby Daniels, Private
William J. B. Davidson, Private
Frank Davis, Private— — to 8-6-18 (Wounded)
George I. Davis, Private
William F. Davis, Private—7-9-18 to 7-7-19
Henry Day, Private—(Pneumonia)
William G. Dicken, Private
Harrison Dubree, Private—9-9-18 to 2-15-19
James H. Dulworth, Private—6-4-18 to 3-28-19
Charles Hall Easter, Private—8-14-17 to 2-3-19 (Wounded)
Jesse F. Ellington, Corporal
Virgil Earlee, Private—8-28-18 to 5-29-19
Homer E. Farmer, Private—7-31-18 to 4-15-19
William Felty, Private
Charles E. Ferguson, Private
Lonnie Ferguson, Private—(Pneumonia)
Fred Feuston, Private
Grady B. Fletcher, Private
Jesse M. Fletcher, Private—8-1-18 to 6-18-19
Talbott Fletcher, Private
Bradley L. Flowers, Corporal—5-12-18 to 4-13-19 (Wounded)
Hershel Flowers, Wagoner—8-14-17 to 1-14-19
James D. Flowers, Private
Chalmer D. Gorman, Private
Curtis E. Gorman, Private
Ernest M. Garner, Private
Edward Garrett, Private
Prentis R. Gibbons
William Gilbert, Private—4-9-18 to 4-15-19
Robert Glass, Corporal—4-9-18 to 7-22-19
Jesse Grider, Private—4-9-18 to 7-31-19
Robert Allen Grubbs, Corporal
Thomas A. Grubbs, Sergeant
Guy T. Guinn, Private
Joe Guinn, Private—10-2-18 to 7-5-19
Henry Clay Hale, Private
Benton Hardin, Corporal—9-8-18 to 8-17-19
Lesley V. Herd, Corporal
Aubrey Helm, Private—12-14-17 to 3-13-19
James L. Higginbotham, Corporal
Ed Hill, Private—3-15-18 to 12-7-19

World War I

Chat Hogan, Private—5-18 to 5-20-19
Homer Hollinsworth, Private
Luther G. Holman, Private
Olison C. Hood, Cook—9-6-18 to 5-6-19
Henry T. Hoots, Private
Martley D. Horner, Sergeant—3-16-18 to 8-28-19
William A. Horner, Sergeant—6-14-17 to 7-9-19
Judson Huddleston—(Died in Kentucky)
Roy V. Huddleston, Seaman—(Great Lakes)
William Robert Huddleston, Seaman—11-24-16 to 11-21-20
Hurshel B. Hulse, Private—9-3-18 to 4-16-19
Ruel Humphrey, Private—7-9-18 to 3-5-19
Walter F. Hunley, Wagoner—10-6-18 to 7-8-19
David O. Illyes, Surgeon's Assistant—7-4-18 to 7-8-19
James Fayette Irby, Shipcook—12-10-14 to 11-11-18
Mart Irby, Sergeant
Ras. A. Irby, Private
Henry Jennings, Private
John B. Jennings, Private—8-31-18 to 6-17-19
Chester W. Johnson, Wagoner—8-14-17 to 2-28-19
Edgar Johnson, Private
Charley Jones, Private
Claude Hulse Jones, Private
Floyd Jones, Private—7-31-18 to 6-21-19
Hubert H. Jones, Private—4-16-18 to 6-26-19
James Carl Jones, Private—11-13-18 to 6-4-19
Joe B. Jones, Private—7-22-18 to 7-12-19
Luther Parker Jones, Apprentice Seaman
Marvin B. Jones, Private—10-6-18 to 6-6-19
Charley Keen, Private—6-12-18 to 3-30-19
Dr. Oscar Keen, Medical Corps
George W. Key, Private—9-1-18 to 6-23-19
John G. Key, Private—8-6-18 to 6-12-19
James B. Lackey, Private
Cortis B. Lee, Private
Bob Logston, Private—8-8-18 to 6-19-19 (Wounded)
Ben E. Long, Private—4-9-18 to 3-24-19 (Wounded)
Len A. Long, Private
Willie C. T. Long, Private
Walter Less McComas, Machinist
George McDonald, Corporal—6-10-18 to 6-26-19
Herman McDonald, Private—6-6-18 to 7-5-19
William Lee McDonald, Seaman
Daniel MacIntosh, Private—8-16-18 to 7-19-19
Ben. Melton, Private—2-27-18 to 6-27-19 (Wounded)
James Melton, Private (Wounded overseas)
Shadrack G. Melton, Private
William C. Melton, Private

History of Cumberland County

Mayne A. Miller, Quartermaster Ava.
John W. Morrison, Private—4-9-18 to 7-22-19 (Wounded)
Otha Murray, Private (Killed overseas)
J. Tom Myres, Private, Corporal
Millard T. Netherton, Private
Newman L. Morgan, Private
Scot Nixon, Private—8-16-18 to 7-7-19
George E. Ooten, Private—7-9-18 to 7-7-19
Isaac P. Ooten, Private—7-9-18 to 7-7-19
Grant A. Owsley, Second Lieutenant
Caleb A. Page, Private—7-9-18 to 7-7-19
George D. Parrish, Private—9-9-18 to 2-26-19
Hance Parrish, Corporal—4-9-18 to 7-22-19 (Wounded)
William Hiram Parrish, Private
Howard Philpott, Private
Arthur B. Pierce, Private—3-4-18 to 8-18-19
Ernest Pierce, Apprentice Seaman
Finis Pierce, Private
Hershel Pierce, Apprentice Seaman
Ray Poindexter, Private—9-9-18 to 2-15-19
Joe Poulston, Private
Tom R. Potts, Corporal—2-10-18 to 6-18-19
Paul C. Pryer, Machinist
Otis Radford, Private—5-7-18 to 12-16-18 (Wounded)
Cecil C. Raney, Private
James B. Riddle, Private—4-9-18 to 7-22-19
Porter H. Riddle, Private—4-9-18 to 12-20-18 (Wounded)
William B. Riddle, Private—7-10-18 to 4-8-19
William C. Riley, Private—7-8-18 to 7-7-19
Clura W. Ross, Private—6-21-18 to 4-2-19
James C. Rush, Private—5-12-18 to 9-29-18 (Killed)
Dallas O. Scott, Corporal—4-9-18 to 6-9-19
Eddie B. Scott, Private
George C. Scott, Wagoner—7-14-18 to 6-19-19
Virgil L. Scott, Private
James M. Sewell, Private—9-30-18 to 6-18-19
Otha A. Shoopman, Private—6-15-18 to 10-23-18 (Killed)
Howard B. Short, Private—6-27-18 to 4-2-19
Sullivan Short, Private
Ben L. Skipworth, Second Lieutenant
John Elva Skipworth, Wagoner—4-9-18 to 7-22-19 (Wounded)
Edgar Smith, Private—4-9-18 to 7-22-19 (Wounded)
Ferd C. Smith, Private
Clyde Smith, Private
Cordell Smith, Private—8-6-18 to 5-14-19
Herbert E. Swanson
Dennis E. Smith, Private, Wagoner—10-6-18 to 4-16-19
Elvin R. Smith, Private

World War I

James W. Smith, Private—4-16-18 to 7-26-19
Jesse Smith, Private—6-11-18 to 4-11-19
John H. Smith, Wagoner—6-14-17 to 5-24-19 (Wounded)
Lander C. Smith, Corporal
Lucus E. Smith, Wagoner—7-14-18 to 2-24-19
Samuel O. Smith, Private—1-24-18 to 3-25-19
Travis Smith, Private—4-9-18 to 7-22-19
William A. Smith, Private—4-9-18 to 4-20-19
William F. Smith, Private—7-6-18 to 3-12-19
William R. Smith, Corporal—Missing 11-27-18
William Smith, Private
George Milt Spears, Seaman
Ernest Spears, Corporal—10-7-18 to 2-14-19
Jesse F. Spears, Private—(Pneumonia)
Robert Spears, Private—8-14-18 to 2-14-19
Howard J. Spears, Private
William C. Spears, Private—9-3-18 to 4-14-19
James A. Stailey, Private
William M. Stailey, Corporal—5-12-18 to 9-29-19 (Killed)
James Lanus Stockton, Private, Seaman—(Died)
John G. Talbott, Dr., Medical
Ben W. Taylor, Ensign
Granville M. Taylor, Corporal—7-31-18 to 7-27-19
John Rile Teel, Private—6-28-18 to 6-9-19
Ben Thacker, Private
Brad Thacker, Private—9-9-18 to 2-15-19
James L. Thacker, Private
Porter L. Thompson, Private
Eddie H. Thrasher, Private
Leonard W. Thrasher, Private
Joe C. Traylor, Machinist—10-6-18 to 4-17-19
William Tweedy, Private—2-13-18 to 7-2-19 (Wounded)
Columbus T. Vibbert, Private—4-9-18 to 2-11-19
J. Ben Vibbert, Private
John T. Vibbert, Private—4-9-18 to 7-22-19
Tom B. Vickery, Private—9-30-18 to 6-18-19
Andrew F. Vincent, Private
Jeptha O. Vincent, Private
John Wadkins, Private
Garnet Walker, Private
Finis Wallace, Private—6-27-18 to 4-2-19
Richard E. Ward, Private
Daniel Wadkins, Private—8-6-18 to 6-12-19
Will Wadkins, Corporal—6-10-18 to 3-7-19
William Wadkins, Private
Arnold Wadkins, Private
Dr. J. R. Webb, Medical
Dillard G. Wells, Private

James M. Wells, Private—8-6-18 to 4-2-19 (Wounded)
Walter B. Wells, Private
Murison White, Private—4-9-18 to 10-14-18 (Killed)
Herman Whited, Private—8-16-18 to 9-15-19
James R. Williams, Corporal—4-12-18 to 4-13-19
Verner G. Williams, Wagoner—10-6-18 to 4-16-19
Randolph Wilson, Private
Theora H. Wilson, Private—10-5-18 to 5-20-19
Verner R. Wray, Private—9-15-18 to 6-23-19
Delbert Wright, Private—6-4-18 to 3-28-19
Marvin York, Private—11-15-18 to 7-18-19
Jesse G. York, Private—8-22-18 to 3-24-19
Luther B. Young, Private—9-9-18 to 12-31-18 (Wounded)
John A. Zichgraf, Corporal—8-14-18 to 6-30-19

COLORED

Harry Alexander, Private—9-20-18 to 7-23-19
Samuel H. Alexander, Sergeant
Verner Alexander, Private
Bill Allen, Private—9-8-18 to 6-5-19
John Allen, Cook—8-22-18 to 6-18-19
Luther Allen, Private—9-20-18 to 10-9-18 (Pneumonia)
Tom Tyler Allen, Private—11-12-18 to 7-10-19
Sam Baker, Private
William T. Barksdale, Private—9-20-18 to 7-23-19
David Carter, Private
Gillim Duvall, Private
Horace Duvall, Private—9-20-18 to 7-23-19
Shores H. Duvall, Private—9-20-18 to 7-23-19
Julius Ellington, Private—10-8-18 to 12-18-18
Sam J. Elliott, Private—7-31-18 to 3-11-19
Otha Flowers, Private—10-6-18 to 12-18-18
Ed Grider, Private—8-22-18 to 7-18-19
James Ed Groves, Private—9-8-18 to 3-22-19
Spurgeon Groves, Private, Cook
William T. Groves, Private—10-6-18 to 12-18-18
William Herd, Private—9-1-18 to 6-11-19
Joe Esau Holman, Private
Luther Hunter, Private—9-8-18 to 6-5-19
Fayett Hunter, Private—11-12-18 to 7-10-19
Hershel Hunter, Private—9-8-18 to 6-5-19
William T. Hunter, Private
Lewis King, Private—10-6-18 to 7-19-19
Arthur L. Lawson, Private—8-22-18 to 9-29-19
Walter Maxey, Private—6-30-18 to 6-25-19
Cotton McDowell, Private—6-30-18 to 6-25-19
Sam Newby, Private—9-20-18 to 7-23-19

World War I

Harry Nunn, Private—10-6-18 to 7-19-19
Charles Obanion, Private—9-20-18 to 10-5-18 (Pneumonia)
Clarence Owsley, Private, Corporal—8-22-18 to 7-12-19
William Pace, Private
Dan Parrish, Private—(Disease)
James Price, Private—6-30-18 to 6-20-19
Anderson Riley, Private
Elbert E. Rowe, Private—8-22-18 to 7-18-19
Elmore Rowe, Private—10-6-18 to 7-5-19
John Rowe, Private
Hal Scott, Corporal—8-22-18 to 7-12-19
Stanley Smith, Private—10-26-18 to 7-4-19
Jesse Sprowles, Private—8-22-18 to 2-12-19
T. Richard Sprowles, Private—10-27-18 to 7-4-19
Norman W. Staton, Private—9-8-18 to 6-6-19
Lee Tobin, Private—(Pneumonia)
William S. Tobin, Private
Emmett Turner, Private
William Walthal, Private, Wagoner—8-22-18 to 7-18-19
Joe Williams, Private

LIBERTY LOAN: Chairmen, J. T. McGee (2); C. W. Alexander (3); C. W. McGee. About $270,000 subscribed for the county.

Local Draft Board:

    S. S. Davis, Chairman
    Dr. W. F. Owsley, Medical Examiner
    H. K. Alexander, Secretary
    Miss Jewell Williams, Clerk.

Chapter 21

WORLD WAR II, 1937-1945

The peace officers and reconstruction authorities of the winning nations of World War I failed to bind Germany up in a way that would be a guarantee to world peace for the future. Overconfidence in the promises she made has led to a worse struggle in World War II.

During the twenty years following the first World War Germany made speedy preparations for the day when she would mass her great armies of men, tanks, and planes, and first crush the small helpless countries of Europe, from which she planned to secure soldiers, food, and other military equipment that would enable her to override the stronger nations before they had time to make preparations even to check her, and thereby establish a "New Europe" under Hitler.

On the other side of the world was Japan, being led by the same spirit. Even our own country, though innocent, was selling to Japan millions of tons of junk iron each year which she was shaping into ships, tanks, planes, shells, and other weapons of war that would be turned against our country in the near future. The covetous eyes of the greedy are ever alert for an opportunity when the wild beast may spring from its lair and feast on the prey of its might.

So the atrocious conflict which has merged into a "global war" had its beginning on July 7, 1937, near Peiping, China, when a quarrel took place between a group of Chinese and Japanese men who were working on Marco Polo Bridge, where some blood was shed, which started Japan in an undeclared war on China, which is Japan's usual way of beginning wars. The conflict went on for some four years with losses and gains for both sides.

Adolph Hitler, who had been dictator of Germany since January 30, 1933, was watching every move of the struggle with an eye of greed and a burning desire in his heart for conquest and popularity. Being unable to suppress his anxiety further, he decided to carry the struggle into Europe. He secured the assistance of troops from Hungary and Rumania, and in March, 1939, invaded Czechoslovakia. While this seizure was being carried out, Poland, becoming alarmed, asked England for a mutual assistance agreement with her which was signed in August, 1939.

On September 1, 1939, Hitler's army made a sudden attack on innocent Poland, which country was conquered in less than 30 days and divided up between Germany and Russia. England being so bound up with Poland declared war on Germany at once, and so did Canada and France. While England and France were making preparations for the war, little realizing what a task confronted them, Hitler continued his powerful drive through the countries of Denmark and Norway in the month of April, 1940; and in May pushed on, overriding Holland, Belgium, Luxemburg, and France.

From France he hoped to spring over the English Channel and subdue Britain before she had time to prepare to offer much resistance. So the summer and fall of 1940 looked dark for London, as she was bombed to the ground in many places. England returned the compliment by sending her first all-out airplane raid on Berlin, August 26, 1940. A report came on October 7 that London was receiving her thirtieth consecutive nightly raid, but the belief was that Germany was easing up on Britain and contemplating a move in another direction. So within this month Hitler directed his devastating armies into Rumania, Bulgaria, and Yugoslavia, the last of which afforded Hitler a road by which he might march his army into Greece, which he did, and after a stiff resistance by the brave little Greek country, it was finally forced to yield to the invading German and Bulgarian army. Thus by June, 1941, his work in the Balkans was finished, and feeling so puffed up over these victories, he launched a surprise attack on Russia, June 22 of that year. Here Hitler made his saddest mistake.

While all this was going on, our country was at peace. Some members of Congress were asking that if we were forced into the struggle our boys would not have to cross the seas to foreign soil. Prayers were offered daily to this end. The Chief Executive lent an ear of interest to these pleas, yet on October 16, 1940, all male citizens between the ages of 21 and 35 were required to register for military service if needed. On July 1, 1941, another registration of 21's was made.

Never did a mighty host march with more speed and destruction than did Hitler's army to reach Moscow before winter. Hitler had promised his generals that the capital city would fall before winter. The world thought his dreams would come true; for in October, just four months from the time he launched his Russian drive, he was close enough to Moscow to see the steeples of the high buildings. Hundreds of cities had fallen. Booty untold had been seized. With no respect to humanity, had this army rolled on. A story is told that will illustrate these cruelties: One of the large cities that fell into the hands of Germany was Kiev, the Ukraine capital. It was a proud city of 1,000,000 souls. Thousands were killed. Seventy thousand hid away in cellars, and 100,000 civilians were taken three miles out of town to Yar Ravine, shot, and buried there, together with 25,000 Russian prisoners who had also been shot after capture. Before the Germans left the city they forced 100 Russians to spend the month of August digging up those putrified bodies, carry wood, and burn them all till nothing remained but ashes.

The winter of 1941-2 proved to be the most severe in 40 years, which was a handicap to both sides, but the Russians being used to that kind of weather, forced Hitler to move from Moscow. This counter-offensive kept Hitler on the run until that summer, when his head turned in another direction; this time for the rich oil fields in southeast Russia. With 10,000 tanks and 1,000,000 men the army overran the country with heavy losses on both sides. On August 25, 1942, the siege of Stalingrad, the last iron city before the goal town of Baku, was begun. Another winter, which begins in November in Russia, was endured by both armies. The old year passed with each army contesting by the yard in the city. One month of the new year of 1943 died away with the Germans weakening in the awful slaughter. Dead bodies were heaped up in every street. On February 2, the last remnant of this mighty German Army capitulated. This was at a cost to the Germans of 330,000 killed and wounded, 1,517 tanks, 60,000 trucks, 14,000 guns, 76,000 rifles, 744 planes, 16 generals, and 800 dogs. Russian loss was heavy too. Very few Americans took part in this drive, but the story is introduced here to give an idea of some of the sacrifices made by the Russian people for us. This ended Hitler's dream for the rich oil fields of south Russia. The German Army after this was put on the defensive, yielding town after town as the Russians drove them from their territory with still heavy losses for both sides. Kharkov exchanged hands five times.

When Germany was bringing France to her knees in 1940, Italy thought it an opportune time to "stab France in the back" and share in the pie, so in June of that year Italy declared war on France and England, and in September began an invasion of Egypt for the purpose of wresting it from England. This led Britain to send soldiers, planes, and ships to defend her possessions in Africa. Fighting went on there throughout the year of 1941, with Germany in the lead most of the time. The contest finally settled down between Marshal Rommel with his "Afrika-Kore" of 141,000 men and General Montgomery with his 8th Army.

While war was raging on the three Eastern continents the United States was yet at peace. There had been a minor discord between our country and Japan. First of December, 1941, two Ambassadors of peace flew from Japan to Washington, D. C., to confer with authorities respecting the small differences. They were accorded the greatest of honor by the authorities at the Capital. On December 7, while they were conversing with Cordell Hull, news flew over the radio that bombs were falling on our ships at Pearl Harbor, Hawaiian Islands, 2,300 miles from San Francisco. Japan had begun war on the United States. It was later found that 18 of our ships had been sunk or damaged with 2,343 casualties.

Early the next morning, December 8, 1941, Congress met and in a joint resolution declared war on Japan. On December 11 Germany and Italy declared war on the United States, and on the 13th Hungary and Bulgaria followed them. Every citizen of our country saw at once the predicament into which we had been thrown. All hopes were gone for an adjustment this side of an awful war.

World War II

We had in our possessions a string of islands used as supply stations from our western shore to the Far East. Beginning next to Japan they were: the Philippines, Guam, Wake, and Hawaiian Islands. Naturally, Japan saw fit to seize them first. Guam was seized on the 9th, and the same day the Nipponese began to pour into the Philippine Islands. Due to the submarines infesting the waters of the Pacific, it was hard to rush reinforcements to these outlying possessions. Gen. Douglas MacArthur was in command of the American and Philippine forces in the Philippine Islands. Manila was forced to surrender January 2, 1942, and the Americans took their stand on Bataan Peninsula, which was bravely defended by MacArthur until March 17, when MacArthur left it in charge of General Wainright, who fought off the Japanese until April 9, when Bataan fell to Japan, with a loss of 36,853 Americans made prisoners. General Wainright escaped to the fort of Corregidor in the harbor. Here he held out against the Japs until May 6, when he and 7,000 of his army became prisoners of war. Cumberland County boys were in that group.

On December 16, 1941, Wake Island was under siege, held by 400 Marines, who gallantly defended this atoll island with no assistance from the mother country. The heroism of those 400 Marines before its fall stands out as an act of unsurpassed bravery. After Pearl Harbor the Japanese made few attempts to get control of the fourth link in the chain—the Hawaiians.

Thus you see the United States was laboring under a gloomy sky during the first months of 1942. Britain also was having her troubles in the Far East at the same time. Singapore, at the tip end of the Malay Peninsula, which had been under the British flag for 118 years fell to the Japs, February 16, 1942, with 60,000 British soldiers taken prisoner and much war equipment. The remaining part of the British Army escaped to the East Indies, where fighting went on through the following spring with the Japs gaining control of all the big islands of that archipelago. The British-American forces chose Australia for their base, where the first American contingent of soldiers landed, March 16, 1942, amid cheers and shouts by the Aussies.

It was the following April 18 that Jimmy Doolittle took off from a ship 800 miles from Tokyo with 16 planes with 80 men on them to give Tokyo her first bombing. After bombing that capital city, Doolittle flew towards China, but was forced down. One man was killed, 2 were missing, 5 landed in Siberia, 8 fell into Japan's hands, and 64 wandered back to safety. Some of the 8 were killed by Japanese officers later.

After the capture of our island possessions above noted, Japan threatened continental America by landing 20,000 soldiers on Kiska Island, one of the Aleutian group that stretches from Alaska to within 2,000 miles of Tokyo, June 7; and on Attu Island June 12. This forced us to send an army of our boys to that cold country. About 2,000 Americans encountered that large Japanese force for one year, lacking one week, with a loss of 342 and a Japanese loss of 1,500 before its recapture. After this, most of the heavy fighting went on in the Solomon Islands, beginning on Guadalcanal Island August 7, 1942, and lasting for 180 days before its capture. Both sides suffered casualties.

October was the gloomiest month of that year in the Solomons. Our entire loss in casualties was 3,776, while the Japanese loss was much heavier, during the six months' fighting. Up to this date, Guadalcanal was the scene of the greatest loss of life, though scattered over one-half year's time.

The year 1942 was filled with registration days. February 16th for those up to 45; April 27th from 45 to 64; June 30th, 18 to 20; in December those who were 18 to 19, with the two dates in 1940 and '41 made six dates in all. From these registrations Uncle Sam hoped to secure an army of 10,000,000 men.

By the end of the first five months of the war we had eight expeditionary forces scattered over the face of the globe. Uniforms were made to suit the many different climates, from the sultry jungles of equatorial Borneo to the seventy-below-zero winds of Alaska; from the parching deserts of the African Sahara to the bleak shores of Iceland. Many boys from the County of Kentucky to which I ascribe this volume were in every one of these forces, together with a great number who were sailing the two great oceans, afloat and submerged, and those who were piercing the blue dome of the heavens.

January 26, 1942, the first big convoy of soldiers stepped ashore in Ireland without the loss of a man; March 16, the first in Australia; May 18, the first large one in Iceland; November 8, the first one in North Africa; July 10, 1943, the first big army in Sicily; September 8, on Continental Europe in Italy.

The first American army landed on the Solomon Islands, August 7, 1942; the first on the Gilbert Islands, November 22, 1943; and others followed.

Between the dates of the first landings of all these armies and the capture of the places or the extermination of the enemy from them, America continued to furnish men, ships, and planes to all the places until the work was completed.

I shall here treat each one separately in the order named herein.

IRELAND

This place together with England served only as a concentration camp for soldiers to be trained for further duty elsewhere against the enemies.

Australia, like Ireland in Europe, was used as a base in the Pacific warfare.

Iceland was also used for that purpose and as a mediator between the European enemy countries and our own America.

NORTH AFRICA

North Africa was quite different from the above. It furnished battlegrounds for the Army, Navy, and Air Forces for six months, lacking one day. As far back as June, 1942, American airmen and service troops were helping General Montgomery's 8th Army in Egypt push the Nazis from that country. Those were dark days for Britain. Tobruk, near the Egyptian border, surrendered to the Germans, June 21, with some 25,000 British soldiers. This meant Egypt for the Nazis. The other countries lying west of Egypt were Libya (to Italy), Tripoli (to Italy), Tunisia (to France), Algeria (to France), Morocco (to France).

The fact that the Nazis and the Italians were then fighting together made it easier for them to go through Libya. Rommel received blows in Egypt that brought a retreat through Libya. The first English victory was October 24, 1942. From this date on, the German army under Rommel was on the retreat westwardly most of the time. By November 4, 1942, he was in full retreat pursued by General Montgomery's men. Tripoli was taken by the Allies.

On November 7-8, 1942, our first United States Army landed in North Africa, convoyed from England 1,200 miles away. There were 850 boat loads of men, numbering around 150,000, with the best of equipment. The landing was made on the coast of Algeria, at Oran. No sooner had they stepped ashore than they met the French army. A land battle and a Naval battle at Casablanca lasted four days, in which our loss was 1,910 casualties, 860 of whom were killed. This was our first encounter with the enemy, with an army. General Eisenhower commanded the troops. Cumberland County had a larger number in this landing than any other up to this date, sixteen United States ships sank. At the end of the four days' battle France began to ask for terms, in accordance with which she agreed to surrender to the conquering army, both Algeria and Morocco.

Rommel was still fleeing westwardly through Tripoli, headed for Bizerte in Tunisia, where he planned to annihilate both Allied armies. The Allied Army took Tripoli, January 22, 1943. All went fairly well with us except at Faid Pass where our army was forced back 35 miles by the Germans. General Montgomery was pushing from the east, Americans under General Patton from the south, and Anderson from the west. The Rommel Line was broken April 7, and General Montgomery and General Patton met, capturing 6,000 Nazis. Rommel slipped away to Italy leaving General Arnim in command. On May 7 the Americans took Bizerte, a very strong fort, and General Montgomery and his men took Tunis in Tunisia. This ended the African drive of 1,500 miles from Egypt. A mighty army of Germans was destroyed, and Africa freed of Nazis. There were 266,600 taken prisoner, 30,000 killed, 26,400 wounded, 6,000 planes and 185 ships lost for the enemy; while the Allies lost in the Tunisian battle 2,184 killed, 9,437 wounded, 6,937 missing, 1,500 planes. Italy lost her

African possessions. This practically freed the Mediterranean Sea of the submarine terror, so the next move was across the sea to Italy. In the last-named battle Cumberland County lost several boys.

ITALY

Before Italy could be invaded there were three small islands and three large ones in the Mediterranean to be taken. The three small ones were taken by bombing until surrender; but the first large island of Sicily, two miles from the "toe" of Italy, was captured by General Patton's army after battling for 38 days. Two thousand shiploads of soldiers were moved onto it July 10, 1943; and after a continuous march to the north end it surrendered August 17, with 140,000 German prisoners taken.

Most of the Germans escaped across the strait to Italy. Besides the prisoners, they lost 1,691 planes. Our loss was 1,455 killed, 5,213 wounded, 1,756 missing, and 274 planes.

British and Canadians were the first to land on the toe of Italy, September 3, 1943, under General Montgomery, who began the invasion up the eastern coast. General Mark Clark landed an American army on the west shore south of Naples. This was a part of General Eisenhower's host known as the American 5th Army. From September 8 to 15, a bloody battle was waged at Salerno, close to Naples. Here the enemy was beaten with big loss. Our loss here was 511 killed, 5,428 wounded, 2,368 missing.

On July 25, Mussolini, Prime Minister of Italy, resigned. On September 8, Italy unconditionally surrendered to the Allies. This was a blow to Germany. After that day Italy became a co-worker with the Allies. One of the first moves made by the new ally was to take Corsica Island, one of the three large ones, from the Nazis. Mile after mile were the Germans pushed up Italy. Naples fell September 30. Over mountains, through valleys went both armies, losing and gaining ground. On October 13, Italy turned her back by declaring war on Germany. Thus the first enemy country fell out of the war. November 10, 1943, Rommel took 165,000 soldiers and barbed wire enough to form a "winter line" 75 miles south of Rome, across Italy. Here he hoped to hold the two great armies through the winter. On the 30th of this month General Montgomery broke the line, and on December 2, General Clark broke the west end, and again sent the Nazis on the go north towards Rome.

The new year of 1944 opened with bitter fighting in Italy in and around Vittora throughout the month of January.

On January 22, General Alexander landed his army of 50,000 Americans and British soldiers in Italy at Anzio beachhead, 22 miles south of Rome. Bitter opposition was met with, and casualties soared here until its capture, May 23. Its fall was partly attributed to the 82nd Airborne Division, which landed January 31; the 3rd Infantry also played a big part.

World War II 243

During this period, General Mark Clark's Army was hammering the Germans at Cassino, Italy, 50 miles farther south. It fell to the Americans, May 18, and on May 25 the two armies met after routing the Germans 255,000 strong. Twelve days later the two armies marched into the ancient city of Rome amid great rejoicing by its inhabitants, the German Army fleeing north. The total campaign in Italy had cost us, up to the capture of Rome, about 65,000 casualties.

The next strong point was Florence, in northern Italy. The Allies took it August 21, after fighting their way up to it. Then the Gothic Line was formed to keep the Allies out of the Po River Basin. This line was broken September 4, but fierce resistance continued throughout November and December of 1944. Snows and mud hampered all movements. For the Italian campaign American casualties neared the 100,000 mark.

The Gilbert Islands are a group of atolls lying just north of the Equator in mid Pacific. The Japanese had a strong base on these islands, and, like other islands, they were in the way on our road to Tokyo. The American Air Force bombed those islands long before the Army was landed there.

The strongest Japanese base was on Tarawa while there were bases on Makin and Abemama islands also of the Gilbert Group. On November 22, 1943, the American Army landed on Tarawa, assisted by the Navy and Air Forces. Some of the ships hung on a coral reef just before reaching the harbor, which made them an easy prey for the Japs on shore. From November 22 to 26 a fierce battle took place here before the capture of the island. The other two were taken with smaller loss to our side. Within 76 hours we lost 3,772 killed and wounded, 1,026 of them killed on Tarawa alone, and 66 on the other two. This was the worst loss in lives thus far in the war—lacking 4 of equaling Solomons' six months' fighting. Japan lost 5,700 men and 46 planes, with the Gilbert bases.

December 15, 1943, the Americans landed an Army on the west end of New Britain Island at Arawe with loss of many, and on the last day of the year Cape Gloucester, a strong Jap base on the same island, was taken.

On December 24 a flock of 3,000 planes flew from England to Berlin and other places in Germany and wrought havoc to the places visited. Two days later Britain sank the German 13-inch plated war ship, *Scharnhorst*, with a loss of 1,461 aboard, leaving Germany with but two large ships. Thus the old year went out with the American and British morale at high tide. Eighteen of Germany's 31 war cities were in ruin from Allied bombs.

REVIEW OF TWO YEARS OF WAR

The year 1942 marked the shift from peacetime manufacturing to that of war. When the Japs destroyed 350 airplanes at Pearl Harbor we were left with but a few hundred military planes at our command. The year 1943 was a year of output. During '42 the United States finished 47,873 military planes, and in '43, 85,946. On the second anniversary of Pearl Harbor the 150,000th plane was rolled out of the factory. As high as 8,300 planes were completed in one month. Improvements on planes as to capacity and speed were marvelous.

In World War I our Air Force was hardly 200,000; in 1943 it was 2,800,000. In the first war the United States had only 80 tanks, in '43 we sometimes turned out 2,500 per month. At Pearl Harbor date we had 344 warships; December, '43, 917. Some 150,000 different factories were running almost day and night turning out war equipment. One tank cost $90,000, and one Springfield rifle, $60.00.

With an Army and Navy of 10,410,000 at the close of 1943 to be equipped, our national debt soared from $112 billion to $170 billion in one year. In World War I, we borrowed military equipment from other nations, in this war our Lend-Lease agreement, from its first start March 11, 1941, to December, 1943, amounted to some over $18 billion.

The year 1943 closed for the Allies with little accomplished. Russia had pushed the German armies 850 miles toward Germany. The United States had a large army fighting from the toe of Italy (within 75 miles of Rome), and a very large force of men and equipment in England ready for a Western Invasion. We also had all of North Africa from which we were able to fly and bomb the enemy Balkans. Seven raids had been made on Bulgaria and two on Greece. Our casualties to December 31, 1943, were approximately 140,000; of these 35,000 were dead men, and the rest about equally divided among wounded, missing, and prisoners. Our overseas force was given out as 3,800,000 men scattered over the earth, on about 15 vital points. The end of 1943 found five enemy nations fighting 44 Allies. Four enemy countries over the Atlantic; one across the Pacific.

Little had been accomplished on the Pacific side. The bases herein mentioned being a mere fringe held by us as compared with what we had given up to the Japs in 1942. The Pacific is so full of islands between the United States and Japan, most of which were held by the Nipponese Government, that our road to Tokyo was a slow, dangerous highway of water from 5,000 to 10,000 miles wide. Hawaii, the only Pacific base left us by Japan, is nearly 2,400 miles away, and Wake Island is still that much farther west, and another stretch of water about equal to both of these westwardly is to be met with before Tokyo is reached. It was within this last great expanse of water that Japan grew into an empire in the beginning of our participation in the war. Besides the Philippines, Wake, and Guam, which belonged to the United States, Japan took from Britain, Hongkong, Malay, Burma; and from Holland, Borneo, Sumatra, Java, Celebes; and from France, Indo-China. To these she added about one-third of China mainland. Going East of these, she had in her possession many groups of small islands dotting thousands of square miles of the Pacific—all of which were strongly fortified. So 1943 ended with her in full control of nine-tenths of this ill-gotten Empire.

It was on December 1, 1943, that the four-day conference at Teheran, Persia, with President Roosevelt of the United States, Winston Churchill of England, and Joe Stalin of Russia in attendance, ended; wherein they agreed to mass their forces on Germany first, and then on Japan. Hence, the war was slow on the Pacific side of the world. This was the sixth such meeting outside of the United States.

At the close of 1943 Germany still controlled four-fifths of her conquered territory in Europe, all of which was held by German soldiers and the best of war machinery. Her aim was to crush the Allied armies ere they reached the borders of the German nation. She had 40 divisions in France, 25 in Italy, 18 in Bulgaria, 7 in Norway, 7 in Finland, and 197 in Russia. Besides these she had about 5,000,000 other armed men.

During the first two years of the war we had knocked out 18 of the 31 cities of Germany where war materials were worked up. The U-boat menace had been cut 60 per cent in the Atlantic.

James Doolittle, from his base in North Africa, according to a Government report, had downed and destroyed on the ground, in 1943, 5,572 enemy planes, while the United States Air Force from England downed 4,100 German fighter planes over Europe. Our losses were 819 for Doolittle and 1,150 for the 8th Air Force of Britain for the same period. Berlin alone was bombed 100 times, while London since the first of the war had been bombed 693 times, mostly in 1940-1. About 200,000 tons of explosives were dropped over Europe by our boys within these two years.

Within this period of two years, the United States furnished to the Allies 28,000 planes—21,000 by Lend-Lease.

The year 1944 in the Pacific started by the landing, January 30, of 50,000 United States troops in the Marshall Islands, some 700 miles north of the Gilberts and 2,300 miles of Tokyo. At Roi we lost several lives, and during the time of the capture of the 32 islands, ending August 23, we lost 286 killed, 1,148 wounded, 82 missing. Japs dead were 8,122.

Caroline Islands, 2,000 miles from Tokyo, were visited by two reconnaissance planes, February 4th and bombed on the 16th, and later taken over by our Navy landing on Truk Island, the strongest fortified one of the group. Forty Jap ships were destroyed here.

Marianas or Ladrone Islands were the next step towards Japan. They are 1,480 miles from Tokyo. Guam is one of this group. On February 22 our first bombing began on these islands. A softening-up usually precedes an invasion. June 18 the landing was effected on Saipan. Strong opposition was met here. The Japanese fleet appeared for the first time in these waters. Constant fighting occurred on Saipan until it was taken July 8. Tinnian Island was then captured, and on July 21 Guam was invaded, and taken August 9. The battles on these three islands go down in history as among the hardest, most costly victories. Our loss in lives was the heaviest to date: 3,049 killed; 13,054 wounded. Jap loss: 26,277 killed; 2,069 prisoners. A Superfortress Airplane base was established on Saipan, from which we took off to bomb Tokyo.

September 8-11 much fighting took place in and around the waters of the Philippines. Our planes were based on aircraft carriers. Nearly 200 Jap ships and over 500 planes were destroyed during this period.

Palau archipelago just south of the Philippines was invaded September 14. Peleliu was the island of this group where we suffered severest loss. The Japs lost over 9,000. Softening up was continued until the Philippine invasion.

Leyte was next. On October 16, 600 American ships from the recently captured islands, carrying over a million soldiers, steered for Leyte, a center island of the Philippines. On October 19, Suluan, a small island, was taken, and the following day the American Army went ashore at three different points on Leyte, 53 miles farther west. Heavy Jap opposition was met in which we lost four LC's and some small boats. Our casualties were light. Fifty-seven Jap ships and 89 planes were lost. Survivors of Singapore and Bataan, both English and American were there. For two months heavy toll was paid. About 35,000 Jap troops slipped in at Ormoc town, which was taken December 11. Ten other attempts were made to land reinforcements to Yamashita, but all were sunk. On October 25 the big island of Samar, north of Leyte, was taken.

December 25 was a sad day to the Jap Army on Leyte. It suffered its greatest defeat thus far in the war, with over 114,000 killed; 493 prisoners; 2,748 planes; 41 transports; 27 warships. We also paid a heavy debt in the loss of 2,623 killed; 8,422 wounded; 172 missing. General MacArthur had previously moved his headquarters to Leyte.

Mindoro, 600 ocean miles and 228 air miles north of Leyte, was invaded December 15 by landing 15,000 men on it, meeting little opposition at first. This put us in 155 miles of Manila, capital of the Philippines, and much closer to Tokyo.

The last three months of 1944 found our Superfortress B-29's raiding Tokyo almost daily from our Saipan base. The first raid was on June 15, 1944. This B-29 is our largest plane to date. It is 141 feet long, manned by four 2,200-horsepower engines, consuming 8,000 gallons of gas from Saipan to Tokyo, loaded with forty 500-pound bombs and 12 men, and going at an altitude of six miles, with possible speed of 400 miles.

With the year 1944 came stronger talk of the western invasion of Europe. Incessant bombings continued night and day in preparation of the invasion. January 11, 1,500 American planes heading for Berlin surprisingly met 1,000 German planes in the air 400 miles before reaching their intended target. The greatest air battle to date followed, in which we lost 605 men, 65 planes, an $18,000,000 loss. The Germans lost 152 planes, and their war plants were smashed.

On January 14, Hitler brought out his boasted "secret weapon." It was a pilotless plane controlled by radio to its target, where it exploded and wrought havoc to lives and property. During the first two months of its work this robot bomb destroyed or damaged one million homes in England and killed over 10,000 people. It was at this time that Hitler fell to making anti-aircraft guns to stop the heavy Allied drives.

Hitler built a "Western Wall" along the shore of Normandy, France, to prevent the invasion of France. Incessant bombing of this wall and of the roads between it and Berlin went on the first half of 1944, and thousands of soldiers and tons of equipment were being taken to six ports of southern England.

On Tuesday morning, June 6, 1944, at 5:00 a.m., the greatest armada that ever assembled at one place covered the waters that wash the shores of Normandy, France. The fleet consisted of 4,000 large ships and thousands of smaller vessels. The United States had 1,000 large ones and myriads of smaller ones. Every type of ship was there; 11,000 planes flew across three minutes in advance to soften up the job. At 6:30 the first foot-soldier stepped ashore, and at the same time the 82nd Airborne Division with about 20,000 men dropped behind the German Army. About one-quarter million men (and women) were in this noted crew. News flashed over the air to every known spot of earth that the Invasion was on. It is said that all of the 3,073 counties of the 48 states of the Union were represented that day, and England with her big family of possessions was also represented there.

Gloom overshadowed the lives of untold millions at home. Congregations assembled at their local places of worship to petition God for safe guidance; lips that had never uttered prayerful words before trembled at the outburst of their troubled hearts; past joys were superseded by the deepest anxiety. Some prayers were answered, some came too late, for the enemy had already swept into eternity the souls of many a mother's pride and joy. Their remains were seen floating on the ocean's bosom. Hundreds were carried down with their sinking vessels. Many left only their fading footprints as their last mark of bravery before their final fall on the Norman shore.

Seven American and eight British ships were lost on D-Day landing. The brave men, living and dead, gave to Freedom a foothold. Passing years may obscure their names and forms but their noble deeds shall live forever. It was left for the survivors to complete the unfinished task ahead. The number taking part in the invasion is given as 124,000.

No halt was made, but a forward move was ordered. The British and Canadians under General Montgomery headed for Caen, a strong German-held fort, under Rommel the German war horse of

North Africa. British and Canadian troops captured it on July 9. The Americans under Gen. Omer Bradley captured Bayeux June 7, for their first town. The Americans then headed for Cherbourg City at the tip end of Cherbourg Peninsula, which fell June 26 with 20,000 German prisoners, bringing the total to 70,000 to date, while our casualties were 24,000.

The next strong German position was at Saint Lo, France, which, after heavy encounters, fell to the Americans July 18. The going then became easier, as the Germans were in retreat toward Paris, Capital of France. The pressure was so strong that the Germans turned northeast, leaving Paris to the south. Upon this, General Eisenhower ordered its capture left to the French Army, who took it August 23, on agreement of evacuation by the enemy. Scarcely had the Germans made their exit, when they turned upon the waiting French. A cry went up for American assistance. Part of Bradley's Army flew to the rescue, and on August 25 Paris was liberated from a three-years' Nazi rule. It took longer then to suppress the jubilant French of the city than it had taken to conquer the town.

General Patton's Army crossed the Seine River 35 miles north of Paris August 20 and pursued the fleeing Germans up the Marne Valley, finding themselves at Chateau-Thierry, August 28, on the spot where their fathers had stopped the German advance and saved Paris 26 years ago. August 29 the American Army crossed the Aisne River at Soissons and the Marne at Chalons, still in pursuit. During the first week in September our army seized the Argonne Woods, Saint Mihiel, and Verdun, battle grounds of World War I, and then entered Belgium with light opposition.

At this time the Americans had three large armies, ranging from north to south, the Second, First, and Third, covering a 60-mile front, marching toward the "Fatherland."

On August 15, at 7:30 a.m., a Fourth Front was opened as a surprise to the enemy, on the South coast of France. A 125-mile strip, including Marseille and Toulon, was supported by 800 warships and 14,000 planes and a big number of parachutists. First day's casualties were light, but at the end of five days they had soared to 1,221 killed and 1,751 wounded.

On August 23 Marseille and Toulon fell, with 20,000 prisoners. Then came the task of clearing the Rhone Valley north to the south end of the Siegfried Line near Nancy, France, which they reached and united with the Third Army, September 7. This made four big armies of nearly 3,000,000 men, all headed for the Siegfried Line which Hitler had constructed of concrete pyramids, dragon-toothed, besides every other conceivable obstruction to hold the invaders out. This line reached from Switzerland on the south to Kleve city, 460 miles north. General Patch commanded this 7th Army from the Mediterranean. A strip of German territory between this line and the Rhine River was 40 miles wide except at the northern and southern

World War II 249

ends where it almost came to a point. It was here that the enemy hoped to crush the Allies before they reached the "Sacred Rhine." It was here that each of the four armies tried to be first to enter the German homeland. On September 10 the First Army fired twenty 55mm. shells, from a distance of 10.5 miles, into Germany. It took 59 seconds to go. The same day General Hodge and his army took Luxembourg City, and the following day the Americans were stepping on German soil near Aachen. Rotgen was our first German town captured. While these moves were being dealt, the British were closing in on LeHavre Port, that we might have a place of landing material; and on September 20 Brest fell to us. Belgium and Holland, like France and Italy, were happy to be rid of the Nazi rule.

Our next move was to cross the Rhine at the north and come down behind the fortified enemy places. Right here let us state, as was later learned, the Allies were a little too optimistic. September 17 the first attempt was made by dropping about 12,000 paratroopers into Holland near Arnhem, in the Rhine Delta, and the same day dropping glider troops of the 82nd Airborne Division, as at Sicily, Italy, and Normandy, near Nijmegen. They were instructed to hold the bridge spanning the Rhine until troops could be rushed to them, whereupon all would fall in and march into the heart of the Reich. I might say here that paratroopers take only what they carry on their backs; airbornes take other equipment, such as jeeps, etc. Eight days of grim fighting ensued; 15,000 Germans were slain. The bridge was lost. The awaited support failed to arrive. Only about 1,800 of this brave crew returned.

Aachen City was put under siege October 9, there General Hodge's First Army met constant slaughter until October 20 when the remaining 10,000 Germans surrendered. Our loss the first five days was 5,000 killed; 14,000 wounded. Aachen is 40 miles from the Rhine.

It was at this time (October 15) that the Ninth Army joined the First after marching from fallen Brest, across France, Belgium, and Holland. This made seven armies on the West front: First and Ninth American at the north; Third and Seventh American at the south; First French, extreme south; First British and Canadian, extreme north.

The 40-mile strip of German territory previously referred to was set with many natural barriers before reaching the Rhine. There were seven rivers to cross and several strongly fortified cities to be taken. The rich Lorraine valley lay to the south and the prized Saar Basin to its north. The Saar Basin in peacetime had furnished Germany with 13,000,000 tons of coal, 2,000,000 tons of steel and iron each, annually, hence its importance in wartime.

November found General Patton's Army taking the city of Nancy, France, and Metz with its 22 German forts; also Strasbourg, two miles west of the Rhine, with its 14 forts. Other strongly fortified cities of the Saar Basin were taken, and siege to Saarbrucken, the capital, was begun in this month. At the north, British and Canadian armies had taken Antwerp, on the Rhine Delta, which brought our supply port from 400 miles to within 75 miles of our front.

The First and Ninth fought their way through the Hurtgen Forest and moved onto Duren, Germany, on the Roer River, 20 miles from Cologne, the strongest city on the west banks of the Rhine. Heavy loss was met in this drive. The first week of December, 1944, found the Seventh American and the French First reaching the Rhine at the south end of the Siegfried Line. Things were going well now with five big armies inside Germany. All seven armies were killing an average of 9,000 Germans daily with only one-third that loss for us. Another time the Allies became too optimistic. Dark days were just ahead. Russia had withdrawn her forces mainly from Poland to Hungary; Britain was moving troops into Athens, Greece, to quell a civil disturbance in the political arena there. Factories in our homeland were arranging to shift from wartime to peacetime manufacturing, and the President denied there ever was an "Atlantic Charter."

In the face of all this, the Nazis seized the opportunity to break down our invading forces by smashing through our line at the north, held by the First and Ninth armies.

On December 16 news spread over the world that this had happened. The millions of homes in America were suddenly wrapped in stupendous grief much greater than that of D-Day because so many more loved ones were engaged. German reports were greatly exaggerated, yet every father and mother had the feeling that their sons were among the number of casualties.

An official report stated that it was on Saturday, December 16, at 5:50 a.m., that Marshal von Runstedt with nearly 200,000 selected German soldiers opened the heavy artillery barrage on the 106th Infantry Division of the United States First Army, which was at the time spread along Schnee Eifel Ridge two by ten miles long near the city of St. Vith, Belgium, astride the Siegfried Line.

The 422nd and 423d regiments of this 106th Division suffered the greatest loss. They had dwindled to less than 300 and these went over to the 424th which was trying to hold St. Vith, but after suffering 416 killed; 1,246 wounded; over 7,000 missing, they had to withdraw. Our army had lost here in one day and night all it had conquered in one month.

The 101st Airborne Division and others were surrounded at Bastogne, Belgium, and fought for several days with meager equipment. On the 18th, the call came for help but, due to bad weather, this was almost impossible. Over 10,000 American casualties at Bastogne were suffered in a very short time. On December 19, the Government called on General George Patton of the Third Army of the south to take the job of arresting the march of Von Runstedt's armies in Belgium and Luxembourg. Patton delighted in mobile warfare, so we find him headed for Bastogne, slaying as he goes, and on December 27 he reached the surrounded spot, to find 200 demolished tanks and heaps of dead Germans. On the same day the German armies had advanced 20 miles into Belgium.

On the high speed of these German movements, Hitler, who had been in seclusion for five months, burst forth with his usual declaration that German victory was surely coming. In this breakthrough the names Stavelot, Oumont, and Malmedy became sacred spots, especially the last-named place, where 130 captured American soldiers were compelled to stand with both hands up while the German machine gun was turned on them.

Day after day the enemy pushed forward towards the Meuse River. On December 25 the Germans got within three miles of the river where we determined to make a last stand to check the invaders; this was about 60 miles of westward march for the enemy. It was there at Sells and Ciny that they were turned back. In four days the enemy was 12 miles from the Meuse River and we were on the offensive. Though the task was hard, we continued to push them out of Belgium and Luxembourg until January 23 of the next year when we got back to St. Vith, where the break-through started. In December alone our casualty list ran to 74,788—10,419 killed; 43,554 wounded; 20,815 missing. Our total from Pearl Harbor to the end of 1944 was some over 721,000. British Empire were 1,044,000 while Russia was 20,000,000. These last figures covered the period from September, 1939, to December, 1944, for Britain and Russia.

The fruit of these sacrifices mostly came in 1944 by the fall of the following: Rome to Allies, June 4; Paris, France, to Allies, August 23; Bucharest, Rumania, to Russia, September 1; Helsinki, Finland, to Russia, September 4; Brussels, Belgium, to Allies, September 4; Tallinn, Estonia, to Russia, September 22; Luxembourg, Luxembourg, to Allies, September 10; Kaunas, Lithuania, to Russia, October 10; Sofia, Bulgaria, to Russia; Riga, Latvia, to Russia, October 13; Athens, Greece, to Allies, October 14; Belgrade, Yugoslavia, to Russia, October 20. With these capitals went their countries, and with the countries their influence and assistance went from the Nazis to the Allies.

The last two weeks of 1944 were the darkest period of the war. Despair seemed to be a very close neighbor. To deepen the gloom, all the draft boards were authorized to reclassify boys from 18 to 26 years old, putting them in 1-A, that a call might be made at once for 900,000 to fill the ranks of those who went down in that December disaster. A check-up showed that the war was costing the country $3,000 per second; that the debt had soared to $232 billion; that 100,000 wounded had been flown back to England for treatment.

Our plane loss for the three years of war was 13,491. During this time 1,202,159 tons of bombs had been dropped on the enemy and 1,566,329 sorties had been made; the enemy lost by these 29,316 planes. Our output in planes for 1944 was 96,369; and ships, 1,677.

The year of 1945 was ushered in with the war cloud hanging low over the Allies. Before the month of January had passed by, the sky had appeared in large spots over the European and Pacific centers of military operations.

Russia, who had been lying dormant on her northern fronts, but who had been centering her attention in Hungary, resolved to "end the war" by launching an all-out drive on Germany, through Poland. Collecting five great armies of over 3,000,000 men, Russia started the winter offensive 120 miles south of Warsaw, capital of Poland, and 60 miles from the German border, on January 12, 1945. This sweep was over 800 miles long, reaching from Hungary to the Baltic Sea. After five days' conflict, the capital city of Warsaw fell, January 16.

Two other strong points and large cities, Lodz and Krakow Poland, fell January 19. On that same day the First Ukraine Army reached the border of Silesia, the eastern province of the "Father Land," just where Germany invaded Poland, September 1, 1939, to start World War II. Simultaneously the Third White Russian Army crossed from Lithuania into East Prussia, three years and seven months from the time Germany started her invasion of Russia. East Prussia is a German province which is separated from main Germany by a few miles of Poland's territory.

During this period of warfare, Russia had fought German armies all the way to Stalingrad and back to the starting point—some 2,400 miles, with losses and horrors untold—having freed her homeland of the enemy besides bringing liberty to all the German satellite countries except one.

On January 21, 1945, the Russians captured Tannenberg, East Prussia, the place where Von Hindenburg defeated the Russians in World War I. This day also saw the surrender of Hungary to the Russians, with agreement to restore stolen territory to Czechoslovakia and Yugoslavia and to pay to Russia $200,000,000.

By January 27 the Russian armies had overrun Silesia, reached Breslau, crossed the Oder River; and had killed 295,000 Germans, taken 86,000 prisoners, destroyed 590 planes, 2,137 tanks, 25,000 trucks, and conquered East Prussia. All this caused Hitler to emerge from his hiding place and take command in person, and draw troops from Norway and the West Front to check the Russian avalanche.

On January 31, the sound of cannon could be heard and the glare of lights from the discharge of Russian guns could be seen only 45 miles from Berlin. Russia all the while was using American weapons and tanks. Thus far she proved to be a real ally. Terrific blizzards accompanied by deep snows, the worst in 70 years, hampered military activities, bringing hardships and suffering.

The setback of December, 1944, called for a closer co-operation among the Allies. So the "Big Three"—Roosevelt, Churchill, and Stalin—met at Yalta, Crimean town in south Russia, February 4-11, to lay plans for future activities. The two most important agreements were: first, to strike Germany from four sides; second, to occupy Germany soon after her downfall.

The British and Canadians started their offensive at Nijmeger, Holland, and marched to Kleve, which fell February 12, 1945. At the same time the Americans were pouring down bombs from the sky on Cologne on the west bank of the Rhine River 20 miles away where the Germans had threatened a stiff stand. The American First and Ninth armies reached Cologne on March 4, and on the 6th she surrendered after having endured the 167th bombing, totaling 50,000 tons of explosives.

During February, 1945, 100,000 sorties were made over Germany, and a check-up from D-Day to March 1 showed 955,000 prisoners had been captured on the Western Front alone.

On March 2 an all-out offensive by all the Allies began, and on the same day William Simpson's Ninth Army reached the Rhine at Meuse, a west-bank suburb of Dusseldorf, Germany, at the junction of the Ruhr and Rhine rivers. In 24 hours Meuse fell, and 19 American boys crossed over the Dusseldorf bridge and back 15 minutes before it was bombed into the Rhine River, 1,180 feet wide and 50 feet deep at the place.

On March 7 General Patton reached the Rhine at Coblenz; the Russian Army reached the Baltic Sea; a second Russian Army was within 25 miles of Berlin; and General Hodge's First Army crossed the Rhine at Remagen on the Ludendorff bridge, 30 miles south of Cologne, which three daring engineers dashed across, cut the wires which the Germans had attached to blow it up if necessary, and saved the bridge over which 150,000 Americans crossed before it collapsed, March 17, with the 200 engineers working on it.

By March 22 all Allied armies reached the Rhine from the West Front. That day Patton crossed at Mainz on assault boats, and the British and Canadians crossed at the north, while General Patch's Seventh Army crossed on boats four days later, making a force altogether of 1,250,000 headed for Berlin.

Our casualties mounted rapidly every day, while the Germans were surrendering by the thousands. March ended with our armies from 40 to 150 miles beyond the Rhine, with many large cities overrun while the Russians were in possession of Danzig, free city of the Baltic Sea, with other Russian armies invading Austria.

A vast stretch of territory between the Rhine and the Elbe rivers, holding Germany's lifeblood, spread before the Allied armies. Essen, where the great Krupp iron works of military Germany operated, fell to the First and Ninth American armies in early April, with 316,930 prisoners; and other strong points soon fell.

The Elbe River, 57 miles west of Berlin, was the point at which the West armies were to halt until the Russians reached Berlin, as agreed at the Yalta Convention. So the United States Ninth Army reached the Elbe at Magdeburg, April 11, 1945. Part of the army crossed the Elbe, but was driven back the next day. It was here the news reached them of the death of President Roosevelt on that same day, April 12, 1945.

On April 13 Vienna, capital of Austria, fell to Russia, making the 18th capital since the first of the war, 10 of which had fallen to Russia. That left five more to go with the downfall of the German Empire.

April 14 Patton's Third Army cut Germany into two parts, thereby checking the flow of German soldiers from the north to Bavaria in the southern part of Germany, where Hitler hoped to mass his entire strength for a stand among the impregnable mountains. Four days later found Patton racing into Czechoslovakia to meet the oncoming Russians.

On April 20 the First Ukraine and the First White Russian armies with their 20,000 tanks, and 2,500,000 soldiers reached the suburbs of Berlin. Stiff resistance was met for a few days, but on May 2, 1945, at 3:00 p.m., the proud Imperial City had to yield to the mighty force. The city had been bombed by the American Air Forces 301 times, laying three-fourths of it in ruins. This was the first time Berlin had had to kneel to its conquerors in 185 years, during which time it had grown to an area of 341 square miles.

Part of the Russian Ukraine Army had pushed on to Torgau on the Elbe River 58 miles from Berlin where they met the American boys for the first time, at 4:40 p.m., April 25, 1945, where great rejoicing from both sides was manifested. The two armies had traveled 5,900 miles to meet each other—the Americans 3,900 by water and 700 by continental land, while the Russians had battled 1,400 miles from Stalingrad to their meeting place on the Elbe. This 25th day of April marked other events of note. It was the day on which the last bomb was dropped on Europe by the 8th Air Force, totaling 2,453,593 tons, during the War, 1,000,000 of which were British and the rest American, at a loss of 15,165 U. S. planes; 12,550 British; 40,823 German. It also was the meeting day of 46 peace-loving nations in San Francisco, whose purpose was to set up a World Peace Charter for the future world.

The Fifth Army had been hung up in Italy for six months, until April 21 when it burst out of the Apenine Mountains into the Po River valley, where it captured Bologne and other points. This Italian campaign of 20 months had cost the American Fifth Army 21,577 killed; 77,248 wounded; 10,338 missing. Uncounted thousands of Nazis had been killed and nearly 100,000 were held prisoner by the Fifth Army, besides those slaughtered and captured by the Allied Italian Army, which captured Mussolini. He, and 17 other gangsters, were executed April 28 by their own people, one of those killed being Mussolini's sweetheart who with Mussolini was hanged by the feet for public inspection near Milan city. So perished the once proud Premier whose steps in life had been—beggar, teacher, radical, fascist, traitor. General Patch's Seventh Army, after fighting its way up through France, Germany, and Austria, halted ten miles inside Italy.

On April 29, 1945 all German forces in Italy and west Austria unconditionally surrendered to Gen. Mark Clark, the American com-

World War II

mander in Italy, and to General Alexander, the British commander, to take effect May 2, which was signed near Naples, Italy. Thus ended the Italian struggle. Dozens of German generals were surrendering. Hitler disappeared; his death by suicide was reported. Forty-seven of the 78 prison camps in Germany had been captured by this date, so the end of the European struggle seemed near.

On May 5 Hitler's Berchtesgaden in south Germany was taken with all of Hitler's wealth, but he was not there. On his disappearance, April 30, he had appointed Doenitz to take his place, who on May 7, 1945, seeing the doom of his boasted Empire, ordered all the German soldiers on land, sea, and in air to surrender unconditionally. The hour was Monday, May 7, 1945, at 2:41 a.m. The treaty was drawn up and signed in a little red brick schoolhouse near Rheims, France, where General Eisenhower had made his headquarters. Sixteen sat at the table. Four nations signed four copies in four minutes —Walter B. Smith for the United States, and Gustaf Jodl for Germany. Thus ended the worst struggle the world has ever known. Five million of the enemy had been put out of action by the Western Allies at the hands of 4,000,000 American and 1,000,000 British soldiers, while the Russians had brought up their side with more than three times as great a loss.

With a graveyard 2,100 miles long from Normandy to Stalingrad, and one over 2,500 miles long from North Africa to the Alps, and the unfinished task of subduing the other enemy beyond the expansive Pacific waters haunting the minds of the ones both at home and abroad, no outburst of rejoicing was thought appropriate, yet down in the souls of every living being was breathed a prayer of thanksgiving either silent or spoken.

Germany was crushed. Now came the task of redeployment. Each soldier of the 4,000,000 then in Europe naturally would think he was the one to get to go home. Besides the soldiers there were 3,000,000 small arms; 11,000 artillery pieces; 350,000 automatic pieces; 62,000 combat vehicles, and 371,000 other vehicles to be moved.

Northern ports of France and Belgium were selected as places of embarkation. In the United States 22 different places were designated as places of arrival for future arrangement. Camp Atterbury, Indiana, was the place selected for Indiana, Tennessee, and Kentucky. Here the Army boys were either discharged or shipped to the Jap side of the world. May 12 was R-Day, and from that day back soldiers were placed on a point system to determine their future status. These points, determined by length of service, months overseas, active service, and dependent children, were set up as a standard of discharge; first, at 85 points for disharge, but later it was lowered.

Our casualties from D-Day to V-E Day in Europe were 514,534. Of this number, 89,477 were killed; 367,180 wounded; and 57,877, missing. This was four times as great as World War I (259,735). Of the missing, many were later found in prison camps.

Germany was divided into quarters among the four big nations, which were to keep armies of occupation there until she was rebuilt. General Eisenhower controlled the part allotted to the United States.

The International Date Line, which practically follows the 180th Meridian from north to south, confuses many readers as to days of the week. It is a place where the days begin and end. If it were not so and a plane should fly around the earth as fast as the sun goes, then you could start at noon—say, Sunday at noon—and go west and you would have Sunday noon all your life if you kept it up. A soldier standing on the prow and a soldier standing on the stern of a ship midway the line would have Saturday on the east end and Sunday on the west. News of battles fought in the Pacific area may be heard 24 hours before they happen.

On January 8 (CWT), 1945, the welcoming news flashed over the radio world that General Douglas MacArthur, with 800 ships loaded with soldiers and material, had landed on Luzon Island, at Lingayen Gulf, 120 miles north of Manila, at the same spot the Japs began landing troops December 10, 1941, which resulted in our downfall in the Philippine Islands. This was on Tuesday, January 9, but we heard it on Monday, January 8, our time. Planes from the enemy caused some damage to our convoy ships. It was General Kruger's Sixth Army from Leyte that took the lead here. General MacArthur had said when the Japs routed him from the Philippines in 1942 that he "would return." He did.

The march toward Manila was begun in earnest. Day by day, the army forged forward, with light opposition. On January 24, 1945, General MacArthur captured Clark Field Air Base, a very strong base 49 miles north of Manila. Nine miles farther south, resistance was met. A second army was landed on Luzon west coast north end of Bataan Peninsula, January 29, and also one 41 miles south of Manila.

The most electrifying news thus far from the Philippines was that of January 30, when Col. Henry A. Mucci with his 6th Regiment Battalion stormed a prison camp 60 miles north of Manila, burst open the doors, killed the 200 Jap guards, grabbed the 510 emaciated prisoners, placed them on carts, on animals, on backs of men, and hurried them to the American quarters. Of the number, 486 were Americans. They had secretly constructed a radio in prison which kept them posted on the war and knew MacArthur was coming closer each day. They had endured over two years of incessant suffering from toil, mistreatment, and malnutrition. The many thousands of brave captives of Bataan and Corregidor had dwindled to this number. Most of the crew could stand up, some could walk, but one died of overjoy at the approach of the Yanks. All were immediately sent home to their people.

The north half of Manila was soon captured and on February 8, our army crossed the Pasig River, which divides the city into two parts. Here the Japs were sheltered behind the Old Spanish Wall. Severe fighting here brought the city back into the hands of the American people, February 24, 1945.

February 21 Bataan was captured, after 18 days of bombing. It took Japan 93 days to take it in 1942.

Corregidor was invaded February 19, and fell eight days later. Other small islands of the Philippines were captured during these days. On March 9, 1945, Mindanao, second in size of the Philippine group, was invaded and soon taken. March 18 the large island of Panay was invaded and Iloilo, its capital was taken; and along with these were the islands of Negros and Cebu, bringing the number of Philippine islands recaptured to date to 30. All this time Jap homeland cities were being brought low by our B-29's.

Within this February Turkey, Egypt, Chile, Peru, Paraguay, Ecuador, Uruguay, and Venezuela declared war on Germany and Japan. Later on, Argentina declared war on Japan.

On February 18, 800 ships loaded with soldiers from our newly captured bases in the Pacific stormed into the harbor of Iwo Jima, one of the Volcano Islands, 750 miles from Tokyo, and put ashore 30,000 Marines under Maj. Gen. Harry Schmidt. The island had been bombed 74 times by our planes before the invasion. It was found to be about eight miles square made up of caves and Jap pillboxes inhabited by 20,000 Jap soldiers. It proved to be the toughest nut to crack thus far in the Pacific War. The shore was sandy, but a short way back a steep bluff rose 560 feet high. This bluff had to be overcome before reaching the Jap nest. Climbing in the face of machine guns was the task to be performed. Five days of heavy loss to our brave boys brought them to the summit of this bluff, where they planted Old Glory and showed the world that few things are impossible for Americans when led by the Red, White, and Blue. Bitter fighting continued until March 16, when the island was officially announced captured after an American sacrifice of 4,189 killed, 15,308 wounded, and 441 missing. During this time the Japs killed were 21,000 and 80 prisoners. Capture of Iwo Jima brought our air base in reach of Tokyo at an easier flight.

On Easter Sunday, April 1, 1945, 1,400 ships took part in the landing of 100,000 troops of soldiers and Marines on Okinawa Island, one of the center islands of the Ryukyu Archipelago stretching from Japan to Formosa Island. Simon B. Buckner had charge of this group, known as the Tenth Army. He was a son of Kentucky's Governor by the same name. Okinawa was 10 by 65 miles in area and only 325 miles from the mainland of Japan. Like all other Pacific islands of that quarter Okinawa is rough and rocky.

The Japanese people had been misinformed as to the way they would be treated by the Americans if captured. Many times when the Japs saw they were cornered they would commit suicide rather than surrender; so, as the American Army approached the landing many Jap citizens on Okinawa tore off strips of their own garments, stuffed them down their throats, and strangled to death.

The conflict on Okinawa through April, May, and June was the worst of the Pacific warfare. Our casualty list ran high, and so did the Japs'. The island had over 80,000 Jap soldiers to be conquered or killed. May 4 they tried to land reinforcements, but the Americans shot down 150 plane loads of them into the sea. On May 29 the Americans captured Naha, the capital of the island. Right here our whole casualty list in both theaters of war reached the million mark. The Jap suicide plane in which a Jap would seal himself and his bomb, and take off for our ships proved to be the worst foe our ships had to contend with.

On June 21, 1945, Okinawa fell. The American loss to its fall was great. There were 9,602 killed; 25,514 wounded; two generals—Buckner, who was killed in action two days before victory, and Easley before him. Our other losses were 30 ships sunk and 223 damaged. The Jap loss was far above the number that covered the island on its D-Day. The island proved to be a valuable base for planes and ships the rest of the war. Ie Jima, small island just west of Okinawa, was captured by our men. On it Ernie Pyle lost his life, making the thirtieth reporter to die. The Okinawa battle lasted 82 days.

Fighting continued on the Philippines with loss to both sides until July 4, 1945, when General MacArthur declared them free after nearly three years in Jap hands. Nearly half a million Japs had been annihilated there. Our loss was some 48,000.

Through July and part of August unceasing bombings hit the homeland of Japan, the B-29 playing the biggest part. Japan planned to bomb our home country with her paper balloons, 230 of which struck our country, with little damage. One reached Kentucky. On Germany we had tried the 2-ton Blockbuster, 4-ton Factorybuster, 6-ton Earthquake, 11-ton Volcano, last of which was over 25 feet long and nearly four feet in diameter and used first March 14, 1945; but there came a bomb of a new make that we had been working on for years which, when tried on Japan, brought her to her knees in 48 hours.

This new bomb was the Atomic Bomb, which compared to the 11-ton Volcano, weighed only 400 pounds but was two thousand times as strong—stronger than 20,000 tons of TNT. The first one tried on the enemy was on August 6, 1945, at the city of Hiroshima, on the west coast of Honshu Island not far from Tokyo. It was let from a plane and exploded some 1,500 feet in air above the city. Pen cannot describe its horror. Sixty per cent of the city was wiped off the map. For six miles square there was not anything left. Everything was pulverized. The explosion could be heard 250 miles away. Houses ten miles distant were wrecked, and people jarred from their feet. The world was awed. The minds of the Japanese war lords were seized with consternation. Then in order to clinch its effect,

World War II

a second A-bomb was dropped on the city of Nagasaki, just south of the first city, August 9. This was more than Japan could stand. Over 100,000 dead and 180,000 wounded were toll of the two A-bomb shots.

On top of this destruction, Russia, in conformity with an agreement reached at the Potsdam Convention by Truman and Stalin, declared war on Japan one second past midnight, August 9, and on the same day started the march of her army down into Manchuria and Korea, both countries of Asia controlled by Japan. One month's fighting here cost Russia 8,219 killed and 22,264 wounded in her brief war.

A truce, on August 10 to 12, was asked by Japan until peace terms could be studied, the main issue being to give up the ill-gotten territories but spare their ruler. On the 13th light fighting began again, but Hirohito, their Mikado, whom the Japanese people consider their God (being the 124th direct descendant of their Sun Goddess), yielded to the terms of the Potsdam Convention which was unconditional surrender, accepted August 14, 1945. Thus ended World War II, which had drenched the world in blood.

Unlike the surrender of Germany, the victory was celebrated with shouting and singing, the ringing of bells and the firing of guns. The tired nerve-wracked soldiers all poured from their souls an avalanche of praise and thanksgiving while tears of joy flowed down their cheeks. The God of righteousness had triumphed over evil. This was VJ-Day.

Humanitarian teams and supplies were dropped at the many prison camps in Japan, Manchuria, Philippines, Formosa, and other places where soldiers of every theater of war were found. Some were in fairly good condition, but most of them were in poor health, some skin and bones. The living, though weak, broke their monotony into pandemonium. Food, medicine, and clothing were rushed to them until their removal. General Wainwright, the hero of Bataan, was rescued in Manchuria. Four of the eight men taken prisoners from Doolittle's early flight over Japan were still alive.

Plans were next made to draw up a treaty and occupy Tokyo and Japan. The first to land were airborne troops, who went ashore, August 25, 18 miles south of Tokyo. Our fleet had been detained on account of a raging typhoon and did not reach the bay until the 26th. At 9 a.m. of the 28th the first Americans landed in Japan from Flying Fortresses. Tuesday, August 30 General MacArthur landed at Yokohama surrounded by soldiers.

It had been planned to sign the treaty on the ship, Missouri. This was done by General MacArthur, September 2, 1945. In short, this put Japan back where she was when Perry caused her closed doors to open to the world by a treaty with the United States in 1854, to which Japan always claimed she owed her prosperity and growth.

The work of the B-29's can never be correctly calculated. They flew 32,612 missions in 100,000,000 miles, with a loss of 437 B-29's and 3,000 airmen.

With the 169,421 tons of bombs dropped from them 59 cities were destroyed; 1,400 Jap planes; and out of 382 combat ships she had only 55 remaining. Air bombing killed 260,000 Japs and wounded 420,000 more. This still left about 7,000,000 Japs to surrender. Japan, like Germany in this war was occupied for a while after the war ceased.

Our total casualties on both sides of the world at the close of the war were about 1,072,000; of this sum there were 260,000 killed; 652,000 wounded; 44,000 missing, and 123,000 taken prisoners, many of whom had been counted as missing but were rescued later. Of the wounded in the United States, 16,000 lost one or all limbs.

In round figures this war cost the United States $320 billion ($40 billion of which was Lend-Lease); Russia, $192 billion; Britain $120 billion, and the big enemy countries, Germany $273 billion, Italy $94 billion, and Japan $56 billion. This runs into the trillions. If a man should count $250 to the minute, using 24 hours per day and never stopping, it would take him over 7,600 years to count this money.

Cumberland County from July 1, 1941, to January 1, 1946, bought $1,062,588.55 in War Bonds and Victory Bonds. This was several thousand beyond the quota. C. W. Alexander, Jr., was chairman, assisted by Mrs. Daisy Pace and Kyle Norris during the eight war bond campaigns to raise this sum.

Cumberland County lost 37 in this war, and the six counties which were once a part of this county lost: Adair 45, Wayne 40, Monroe 36, Russell 30, Clinton 24, Metcalfe 17.

DONATIONS AND HELPS IN WORLD WAR II FROM CUMBERLAND COUNTY

Beginning with the first quota of January, 1942, this chapter of the Red Cross, with Mrs. Annie Shannon as chairman, made and shipped to the Armed Forces in the various quarters of the world the following articles made or provided by the chapter: During 1942-4, 104 turtleneck sweaters, 137 Army sleeveless sweaters, 111 Army helmets, 29 Navy scarfs, 3 Navy helmets, 43 Army mufflers, 45 pairs of Army wristlets, 6 pairs Navy wristlets, 37 Navy sleeveless sweaters; 1,264 kit bags filled.

BLOOD DONATIONS

With Mrs. Nora D. McGee as chairman, three groups of donors in 1944 (one in January, 1945) motored to different places in Kentucky to give blood plasma. The four groups gave 214 pints.

World War II

SOLDIERS OF WORLD WAR II FROM CUMBERLAND COUNTY

In Order of Letters of Alphabet
Abbreviations

Overseas Listings Are Incomplete

Ovs.—Overseas
Ovs.P.—Overseas, Pacific
N.—Navy
Col.—Colored
D.D.—Disability, Discharged
W.—Wounded

Sub.—Submarine
N.C.G.—Navy Coast Guard
K.—Killed
Ovs.A.—Overseas, Atlantic
Disc.—Disability, Discharged
Appr.—Apprentice

A

Denton L. Armstrong
George Ross Adams
Archie Van Ashlock
John Frank Alexander
James Edward Anderson
 (Car wreck, W.)
William McKinley Abner
George Sam Anderson (Ovs.)
Bedford William Anderson
Albert Richard Alexander
Cpl. Van Anderson
Stanley Rich Arms
Guy Herbert Anderson
Elmer Lloyd Adams
Keith Kermit Alexander
Cecil Thomas Anderson
Elmer Holland Anderson
 (W. in Action)
Waller Beck Alexander
Cluman K. Alexander
William Ralph Anderson
Charles Howard Allen
James Willard Allen
Marcus Aaron Allen (Ovs.P.)
Roger Alexander (Ovs.)
Lloyd Adams
Russell L. Anderson (N.)
Lt. Alonza D. Alexander (Ovs.P.)
Jesse C. Alexander (N.)
James H. Alexander (Col.)
Gleman Alexander

2nd Lt. Eldon Allen
Taylor R. Anderson (Ger. Pris.)
James I. Alexander (Col.)
Edward Alexander
Alonza Millard Alexander (N.)
Lonas C. Aaron
Kyle Harding Anderson
Kenneth Anderson
William D. Arms
Hall E. Anderson
Elva G. Anderson (D.D.)
Prof. N. J. Anderson (N.)
Ralph K. Anderson
Elron Alexander
Horace Lewis Alexander
Leon Allen
Buster Allen
Robert B. Armstrong
James Roy Alexander (Col., N.)
Roy H. Anderson
B. D. Anderson
Maurice Marvin Abney
Clyde O. Anderson
Lee O. Anderson
Walter Clay Anderson
Johnie Anderson
James L. Alexander
Dan Finies Anderson
Jesse H. Aaron
Herbert Talbot Anderson
Bill Anderson

B

Wendell Lee Booher (Ovs.)
Elvis Cary Baker
William Horace Baker
Sterling Prentis Bow (Ovs.)
Charles Everet Booher
Ervin Fred Brake
John Milton Burbridge (Ovs.)
Thomas Corbin Branham
Herbert Holland Baker
Cpl. James Eston Brake
Jesse Edwin Bow
Donald Walker Baker
Owen Russell Burbridge
Jesse Raymon Brown (Ovs., W.)
Elvin Earl Baker
Kent Baise
Orville V. Branham
Malcom Edward Branham
Kyril Bruton
Ezra Bailey (Ovs.P.)
James Martin Bowen
Cloyd Denver Brewington
Charles Raymon Brown
John Edward Brake (Ovs.)
Willard Brewster (Ovs.)
Leslie Clifford Bow (Ovs.)
John Ben Brown
Paul Leonard Brewington (Ovs.)
Henry Otis Barger
Jesse James Booher
Robert Paul Brake
James Everett Booher
Allen C. Beck
William Hall Blythe
Jesse Fayette Brummitt
William Brance Baise (Ovs.)
Robert Paul Baker (Col. Ovs.)
Newman D. Bryant (Ovs.)
James Grant Butler
John William Brake
John H. Baker (N.)
James Edwin Bradshaw
Lloyd Brown (N.)
Charles F. Brake
Silas L. Bean
William A. Burns
Clyde M. Brown

Lonas H. Bow
Heron Beckham
James W. Baker (Ovs.)
Cpl. Ernest Brake
James Baise (N.)
Kelsay Brown
Luther Brown (N.)
Cpl. Malcolm H. Booher
Sgt. George Baker
Erim Ballard
Henry Ballard
Frank C. Bruton
Clyde C. Branham
John W. Bull (N.)
Reid Bryant (N.)
Howard Clarence Brown
Leman A. B. Booher
Raymon D. Baker
Shelly Branham (N.)
Clarence Branham
Ray Booher
Roy Booher
Paul Martin Booher
Porter Floyd Brown
Everett Burchett
William F. Butler (N.)
James L. Bean
Melvin Booher
Reid Booher (N.)
Rufus Berge
J. G. Booher
Bernice B. Bowlin
Dudley G. Branham
William T. Buchannan
Lewis A. Brown (N.)
William Blythe
William P. Brown
Lyle S. Brewington
Edward C. Bryant (N.)
Raymon Darwin Baker
Dennis Brown
David I. Baker
James Cleveland Brown
Charles Glendon Bryant
Lenis Lawrence Branham
J. E. Brown

World War II

C

Charles Clyde Capshaw
Barnie Ray Cloyd
Willard Raymon Compton
Fred Drew Cooksey
George Alford Conner
Willie Bart Cyphers
Clarence Robert Carter
Benton Allen Claywell (Ovs.)
Daniel Cary
Jack Creasy
Geo. Barlow Cyphers (Ovs.)
Herriford Millard Cooksey
Sam Leslie Collins (Ovs.)
Malcolm Nelson Conrad
Hall Riddle Capps (Ovs.P.)
Everet Wilson Cary
Ruel Hiram Cash
Otis Ray Coop
Leslie Bow Carter
Cpl. Fred O. Coop (Ovs.P.)
Herman Edwin Crawley (D.D.)
Austin Ezra Cary (Ovs.)
Warren Dixon Conner (Col.)
Charles Bruce Cheatham
Jack Coe
John Dempsey Coomer, Jr.
Hershell Alva Cary
Charles Menville Cary
James Emery Carter
Edward Lloyd Coomer
Colonel Elmer Capps
Capt. William Fowler Cary
Sgt. Jesse Martin Capps (cook)
Robert N. Cooksey
Harvey K. Crawley (N.)
Robert M. Cole (N.)
William Crawford (Ovs.)
Ralph Cary (Ovs.)
Loland Ewell Cross (D.D.)
John Sam Cary (N.)
Roy H. Carter
Hollin C. Carter (N.)
Sgt. Thomas E. Cheatham (Ovs.)
Taylor Capps (Ovs.)
Richard Capps
John B. Cary (Ovs.)
James M. Carter (Ovs.)

Radford Cary
Charles Thomas Cooley
Fred D. Cooksey
Sgt. James M. Collins (Ovs.)
James R. Coop
Robert Cary (Col., N.)
Lester F. Carter (Ovs.P.)
Fred Henry Cloyd
Curt Otha Coats (Col.)
Tyler Cary (Col.)
Irlin M. Cloyd
Edward L. Coomer
Raymon L. Cary (Sub.)
Ruel H. Capps
Ilus E. Cash
Homer A. Cooksey
Everett V. Coop
Ike Cashaw (N.)
James B. Cross
George C. Coomer (N., C. G.)
Raymon D. Carter (N.)
Orlyn J. Claywell
William Gilbert Cary
Van B. B. Coe
Jesse F. Capps
Ester Ford Coe (Col., N.)
Leonard Lee Collins (N.)
Floyd Cox
R. G. Coop
James Comer Cary (Ovs.)
Roy H. Carter
Charles W. Crawford
Delbert Charles
Brance C. Capps
Cecil E. Capps
Troy W. Carter
Joseph D. Coffey
Carval Howard Capps
Elzie Collins
Wayman D. Coop
James C. Cummings
Roy Cloyd
John D. Coomer
James Earl Chapel
George Willie Curtis
Donald Conatser
William Lloyd Capps

D

Paul Allen Davis (Ovs.)
Cecil Daniel
Jeff Cranville Dyer (Ovs.)
Fred D. Dicken
James Roy Daniel (Ovs.)
Millard Goebel Davis
John B. Doris
Glenn Ruel Dyer
Herbert Daniel
Hayden Richard Davis (D.D.)
James Daniel
Leslie A. Dicken
Russell Milt Daniel
Elver Ray Davis (D.D.)
Robert Hymen Davis
Martin L. Dyer
Oscar Capshaw Daniel
  (Ovs., W.)

John Willard Dyer
Aaron Davis (Marine)
James L. Davidson
William Kenneth Dishman
Lillard Davidson (Ovs., W.)
Charles D. Davis
Hubert Donaldson
R. L. Daniels
Clarence B. Dicken
Ray R. Dyer (N., D.D.)
Joe D. Duvall (Col., N.)
Roy H. Dicken (N.)
Buddy W. Daniels
Jesse Buford Daniel
Herman Allen Daniel
William T. Day
Paul E. Dishman
Benton Glenn Dishman

E

Alex Robert Easter (D.D.)
Tyler J. Elliott (Col.)
Keith Allen Easter
William S. Elliott (Col.)

Sam H. Edmonson (Ovs.H.D.)
Lewis H. Easter (Ovs.P.)
Ira Edens
Bryant Garth Eden

F

Kent Richard Felty
Lona Roscoe Ferguson
Julius E. Fletcher
William Hershell Flowers
Van Preston Firkin
Mike Allen Flowers (D.D.)
Orestus Flowers (Ovs.P.)
James Ervin Firkin
Millard Stanford Fletcher
Rollin C. Fudge
Milton Fletcher
Melvin J. Firkin (Ovs.)
Erbie Farlee
Charles W. Fletcher
Oscar R. Farlee (N.)
Jesse P. Flowers (N.)
Ira B. Fletcher
James Flowers (D.D.)

Robert Firkin
James Firkin
Sgt. Norris Frazier
James Fudge (D.D.)
Sgt. J. H. Flint
Grant Ferguson
Andrew P. Ferguson
James Fletcher
Joe P. Fudge
Hubert M. Farris (Col.)
Ray Fletcher
Welby Flowers
Amey V. Fletcher
Rufus Froedge (N.)
John H. Flowers (Ovs.)
Wade Fletcher
Lewis Flowers
Willie V. Flowers

World War II

Robert R. Fletcher
Dallas L. Fletcher (N.)
Raymon Fletcher (N.)
Harvey Marshall Flowers (N.)
Melvin H. Farris
James Richard Farr
Edd W. Ferguson

Cecil Odell Ferguson
John C. Finley
Arny N. Fletcher
Fred Felty
Willie Roscoe Finley
Alton B. Fletcher

G

Rollen Earl Graves
Clura Odell Groce
Clarence Albert Groce
Ralph Branford Guthrie
John William Gordon
Stanley C. Gilbert
Ernest Ever Guffey
Richard H. Guffey (D.D.)
James Verner Garner
Henry Wesley Garret
James Hunley Garmon (Ovs.K.)
Miley Lee Garner
Lefur R. Gilbert
Daniel Webster Guinn
Sherman Dennis Glass
Sgt. Leslie Paul Garner
Ruel Sherman Glidewell
Waymon Clydell Glidewell
Denzel Floyd Garner
Wayman Hall Garner
Charles Hardin Grider
Mitchell Everet Groce
  (Ovs.H.D.)
Leonard Oldham Graham (Ovs.)
Jesse James Gibson
William Jones Glidewell
Melvin Hall Garner
Ralph Vernon Groce
James Norris Gray
Sgt. Morris Wayne Guthrie
  (Ovs. A. & P.)
Joe Fred Guinn
Edsell Graves (N.)
W. C. Garrett (D.D.)
Lester B. Garner (N.)
Albert K. Glidewell (Ovs.)
William M. Glass
Malcolm Graves

George E. Garmon
John L. Glidewell (N., Ovs.P.)
Kenneth Garmon (Ovs.)
James Edward Grubbs (N., Ovs.)
Willard C. Garner
Hershell Groce
Lewis Glidewell
Robert E. Groce
Paul K. Gibson
Marshall Groce
Norman W. Groce (Ovs.)
Roy A. Glidewell (Smn.P.)
John Wesley Graves (Col.)
James Logan Guffy
Cpl. Ralph Garmon
Ralph O. Guthrie
William E. Grider
Charles Geralds
Charles Grider
Emmine E. Garrett
James E. Goodhue
William Howess Guffy
Orlan F. Guthery
Albert W. Gibson (Marine)
Boo O. Groce
Millard B. Groce
Denzil Garmon (Ovs.)
Johnie Garmon
Kenneth Glidewell (D.D.)
Henry H. Garner (D.D.)
Hubert B. Goodhue
Ernest W. Guinn
Marcus K. Garrett
Floyd W. Garmon
Manson Groce (N.)
Tyler Glenn Gray
Jesse L. Glidewell
Harvey Gibson

James Groce
Hubert Groce
Clay F. Goff
Carl L. Graham
Russell K. Gilbert
Welby E. Groce
James E. Grider
Wilbur Jones Gibson
Robert A. Gibson
Kenneth Gray
Alex Gray

Columbus W. Gilbert
Lester Garmon
Roy Howard Garner
Eddie Hays Garrett
James Ed Groce
James H. Graham
Lem H. D. Graves
Charles F. Glidewell
James Sanford Groce
Homer Vernon Grider

H

Norman Robert Higginbotham
Riley Edward Harris
Sanford Humphrey
Guy Winford Hunley (Ovs.)
Howard Hardin
Sgt. Cecil L. Henson
Thomas Hausley
Clarence Carl Hausley
James Humphrey
Sgt. George Eugene Humphrey (Ovs.)
Lee Warren Hausley
Haskell Odell Hay
James Burrel Huddleston
Fred Herman Holman
Jim Lee Humphrey
Alton Levie Hoots (Ovs.)
William Paul Huddleston
James Robert Hurt
Charles Ray Hardin
James Lyle Hardin
Nathan Esau Holman (Col.)
Marshell Therman Hopper
James Claud Humphrey
James Huff
Wash Hunter Huddleston (N.)
Joseph Menford Humble
Ralph Clifton Hollinsworth
Ottley Kyle Hunter
Jesse Paul Humley
William M. Hulse (Ovs.)
Delmus Willard Hume (N., P.)
Herbert Lyle Higginbotham
Buel Hickey

Jesse Edward Hoffman
Claud Thomas Hunter
Calvin C. Humphrey (N.)
Emmitt H. Huff (N.)
Coolidge Humphry
John F. Holman
Ralph H. Hurt
Dave Hardin
Cpl. Haynes Huddleston
Murry F. Humes
Sambel Ellis Humbles (N.)
Raymon P. Hoots
Hoy Willard Holman
Roy C. Hogan (Ovs., Missing)
Luther George Humes (Ovs.)
Conrad R. Higginbotham
Benton Hurt (Ovs.)
Robert C. Hoffman (Sub.)
Johnie Hughs
Lt. Twyman John Hicks (Ovs.)
Cecil Higginbotham
Paul H. Haden (D.D.)
William Paul Huddleston
Ray Helm
Edwin R. Higginbotham (N.)
Roy O. Hardin (N.)
Ralph M. Hunter (N.)
William L. Hoots (Ovs.)
Virgil M. Hughes
Alfred Hughes
Riley E. Harris (Ovs.)
Bernal Alexander Hurt
Ray Hopper
Ray W. Huddleston

World War II

Cleadus C. Holman
Dudley Hendricks
William Hildrith Hurt
Orvill Huff
Jesse Talbot Hardin

Allen Everett Hoots
Sam Fount Hunter
Hildrith W. Hurt
Neely W. Hay

J

William Haze Jennings
Stf. Sgt. John Will Jones (Ovs.)
Raymon Fayette Jarvis
Rollin L. Jesse
Oris Simpson Jones
Farris Goebel Jones
Cecil Randolph Johnson
William Ray Johnson (Ovs.)
Travis Fred Jones
Guy Johnson
Reid Jennings (Marine)
Hugh Russell Jones
Marvin Johnson
Holland Johnson (W.,
   Discharged 7-16-43)
John R. Johnson
Homer D. Johnson (Ovs.)

Elvin Jarvis
Sgt. Sidney Johnson
Ted W. Johnson
John Paul Jones
Will Ed Johnson
Jack A. Jones (N.)
John M. Johnson
John H. Johnson (N.)
Joe Jones (Ovs.)
Homer Allen Johnson (N.)
Willie Jones (Ovs.)
Paul Jennings (Ovs.)
James C. Jones
Ruel P. Jones
Nicholas F. Jones
William R. Johnson
John Hubert Johnson

K

John Ray Kidwell
Raymon Hade Kidwell
Carl Kidwell
Russell Clifton Keeton
William Barlow Killman
Raymon Paul Key (N., Appr.)
2nd Lt. Earl Kirby
Lt. Jack Kendall
Jesse H. King
Jesse E. Kernell
Henry Thomas Killman
Sgt. James Keen (D.D.)

Stanley Edward Key
G. C. Kelley
Lester L. Key
Hall E. Keeton
Domer C. Kerr
Damon P. King
Harold L. Key
Howard King
Deman Dutch Key
Otha Preston Key
Lloyd Dean Keeton

L

Buford Grant Long
William Daniel Logan (Ovs.)
William Kent Lawson
Boyce Clifton Lawson (Col.)
James Martin Logan (Ovs.P.)
George Wesley Lacy

Clarence Kyle Lewis
Fred James Lynder
Granville Webster Lynder
Paul Logan
Gayron Beatrice Lee
Clura Hunter Long

Waval Grant Lee
Hildrith Reed Lawson
James Harold Lore (Ovs.)
Esmond F. Lewis
Wendell H. Lewis
William K. Logan
Edward C. Lee
Fred E. Lewis (N.)
Cpl. Millard Lewis
Fred Morrison Lollar (Ovs.)
Fred Linder (Ovs.)
James Russell Lollar (D.D.)
John Lee

Leo C. Long (Ovs.)
Lesley Fred Long
George Edison Lacy (Ovs.)
Clyde H. Lacy
Cordell O. Long (N.)
Melvin Lackey
Thomas Edward Lawhon
William R. Logan
Marvin M. Long
James Paul Lewis
Will Ed Lee
Hoy R. Long

M

Ted Madison (from Ill.) (Air C.)
John K. Madison
Jim Alfred Morrison
Herbert Elzie Melton
Marvin McIntyre
Bill Moore (Ovs.)
Ryman Melton (Ovs.P.)
Ewell Jackson Morgan
Vernor Morrison
Richard Cordell McClusky
Sam Clayton Murphy (Ovs.)
William Aubrey Morrison
Ray Elva Melton
Dallas Richard Morrison
Arthur Corbet Means
Hiram Abell Morgan
James Thomas McClusky
George Edwin Murley
Cpl. John Hall Moon (Ovs.)
Ray Melton
Mitchell Moore (Ovs.)
Sam Edwin Mullinix
Reed Ewell Mackey
Letha Haskell Melton
Harley B. McCoy
Malcolm T. Miller (Ovs.P.)
Tim Hamilton McElhany
Allen French Mullinix (D.D.)
Lonas William Melton
Herman Floyd Melton
Hershall B. Moon
Oscar Lee Moore (Col.)

Roy Morrison Melton (N.)
James Robert Myers
Eddy Fred Melton
Russel Hill Melton (Ovs.)
Walter Leslie McComas
Lt. Philip Dixon McGee
Edwin Robert Murphy (N.)
Everett L. Moon
Paul McComas
Hollie D. Miller
Keith McComas (Marine)
Albert Melton
Robert McDonald (Ovs.)
Grover Moore
Sgt. Jesse Mee
Denver Glen Moore (Col.)
Raymen Oliver Mullinix (N.)
Arthur Garfield Moore (Col.)
George Millard Melton
Rosco H. Melton
Paul E. McCoy (N.)
John F. Melton
Raymon Murray
Carlos McDonald
Jesse R. Melton (N.)
William H. Maupin (Col., N.)
John Tom Myers (N.)
Willard Corbet Myers
Herman Dewey McCoy
Rayman Moseby
William P. Moore (N.)
Rufus McCormack

James G. McCoy
J. H. Melton
William M. Melton
Thomas A. Miller
Guy Duard Morgan
Clifton Melton
James A. Melton

Jesse Melton (N.)
William Martin Melton
Tillman Melton
Vernon Money
Tom Burr Melton
Audie C. Moore
Mayford Melton

N

Denzil Allen Norris
Nathan Isaac Norris
James Russel Norris
Robert Norris
Cpl. Denver Talmage Norris
Willard Mathus Neal
Reditus Taylor Norris
Otis Lawrence Nation
Sgt. John Albert Neeley
Raymon Howard Norris
Ralph Norris
Leslie Harold Norris
Garnet Johnson Nance (N.)
Robert Wyley Needham
William Fred Neeley
Charles R. Norris
William R. Norris
Dannie R. Norris
Sgt. Gene Newby (Ovs.P.)
J. A. Neeley

Walter K. Norris
Leslie Norris
Lt. John S. Newby
Elbert Lee Norris (Ovs.)
William Frank Newby (Col., N.)
Willard H. Norris
James J. Needham (N.)
Granville C. Nation
Cecil D. Nance
Elwood Norris (Ovs.)
Miles Allen Norris
Ester Ford Newby (Col.)
Edward Glee Norris
John E. Netherton
Charlis Norris
Campbell A. Neal
William Elwood Norris
Richard Newby
Eldon Nance
Edward Luther Norris

O

Guston Ewell Oliver
Fred Nelson Oliver
Elbert Allen Orton
Hunter Owsley
Jerry Peyton Ooten (D.D.)
Willie Ooten
Russell L. Ooten

Chester A. Ooten
William Oscar Owsley (Col.)
Capt. John W. Ottley
Kenneth Ooten
Floyd A. Ooten
Elva Glenn Orton

P

Fletcher Hurshel Prewitt
Malcolm Woodrow Propes
Willie Pharris
Clifton Odine Pharris
Cpl. Taylor Clayton Parrish
  (Ovs.)
Carl Taylor Pitcock

Thurman Lee Pike
Orville Kenneth Pitcock (Ovs.)
Earl Russel Prewitt (Ovs.)
William Lesley Page
John Arnold Poindexter
James Howard Prewitt
Cpl. Ivan Preston Propes

Barney Parrish
Watson Parrish
Bernie M. Pharis (N.)
Jesse E. Pharis
John C. Perkins (N.)
L. E. Powell (N.)
Virgil E. Pelston (N.)
Hollin Price (N.)
Lonas E. Page (N.)
2nd Lt. Stanley C. Pace (Ovs.)
Ruel Perkins (Chaplain)
James H. Pitcock (Ovs., W.)
George T. Perkins
Russell A. Pierce

John Jackson Philpott (N.)
Earl C. Poindexter
Lt. K. C. Phillips (Marine, Ovs.)
Cpl. Ralph Patterson
Virgil H. Pierce
Marus Holland Pierce (N.)
Howard Phillips (Ovs.)
Ollie G. Prewitt
James C. Prewitt (K. Ovs.)
Jesse Philpott
Sam R. Poulston
Nolan K. Petty
John H. Prewitt
Tom Ray Potts

R

William Anderson Riley
Tech. Sgt. James Walter Reeder (Ovs.)
Oscar Benton Rigsby
Frank Alexander Riddle
Harvey Paul Riddle (Ovs.)
Hershell Clarence Riley
Tom Edson Riley
Edward Allen Rose
Ewell Riddle
Elmore Junior Rowe
James Wilbur Radford
Newell Hayden Riddle (Ovs.)
Orvis Clinton Riley
Walter Leslie Riley
William Hall Riddle (D.D.)
Lyle Long Radford
Pfc. Zola Earl Rowe
Sam Redus Rowe
Claud Earl Riddle
Otis C. Rigsby
Roy Rains
Thomas R. Riddle
John William Rainey
Arthur Radford
Stf. Sgt. Ewing Rush
L. H. Rush (N.)
Welby Riddle
William F. Riddle
Richard Radford
Eddy Richardson
James E. Reeder

Charles Richardson
Earl B. Riley
Frank Radford
Leslie M. Riddle (Ovs.)
James W. Riddle (Ovs.)
Frank Riddle (Ovs.)
Hershell Riley
Harley Riddle (Ovs.)
James C. Rowe
George H. Roach (N.)
Tom Rush (Col. N.)
Wendell F. Radford (N.)
James A. Rose (N.)
Thurman Roach (N.)
Lewis Riddle (N.)
Robert R. Radford (N.)
Wix Rush
Hershell N. Radford
M. Sgt. Jesse C. Riddle (Ovs.)
William Riley
Leonard Riley
Elware Reliford
Leo Riddle
Thomas E. Radford
Henry N. Riley
Ralph H. Rowe
Eugene Rowe (N.)
James W. Riddle
Calvin Arthur Radford
Ewing Seph Riddle
Ilus Graham Riddle
Walter Douglas Riley

S

Osbie Edward Scott
Clarence Clyde Scott
Cecil G. Scott
Edward Mars Spears
Charles Albert Smith (N.)
Winton Edward Simpson
Hill Alexander Smith
Eula Fred Spears
Robert Alexander Scott
Ralph Sartin
James Preston Shepherd
James Arnold Stephenson
Henry Clay Stephens
Newell Sanders Stephens
Joe Leonard Smith
William Edward Sevier
John Barlow Spears
Mitchell Odell Spears
Herbert Nell Smith
Pvt. Waymon Willard Simpson
Lt. James Morris Stewart
   (Ovs., K.)
Frank Holland Sevier
Herbert Lee Short
Hanvy Sherrell
Granville Stoner Sewell
Norris Glendale Shaw
William Martin Sewell
John Morrison Shaw
Charles Edward Shaw
Eddy Haze Spear
Walter Vince Spear
Demus William Stalcup
Ralph Wesley Spears (D.D.)
Jerry Staily
Willard Hyman Smith
Cary Branston Scott
Donald Alexander Street
Clarence Brown Stearns (Ovs.)
Robert Garner Simpson
Cordis Holland Smith (Ovs.)
Robert Lee Sharp
Millard Clinton Sharp
James A. Smith
William Talbot Simpson
Edward C. Scott

Troy Evert Spears
Joseph Schickel
Thomas Smith
Tilman Powell Strange
Volley Bryant Smith (Ovs.)
Joseph Ralph Shannon
Houston Faye Short
Lawrence Russell Shepherd
Julius Middleton Stephenson
Clarence Sanders (N.)
Foree Smith (N.)
Millard Short
Wendell Ray Stone (D.D.)
Delmer Spears
William R. Scott
George W. Sherrel (D.D.)
Walter R. Spears
Grady C. Spears
Willie C. Stone (N., D.D.)
Etchel E. Skipworth (Ovs.)
Keith Strange (Ovs.)
John Paul Stearns (Ovs.)
Kenneth M. Spears
Rankin Sharp
Sgt. Newman Sprowles (Col.)
Leslie M. Smith (D.D.)
Prentis B. Smith
Russell K. Scott (Ovs.)
Ivo M. Skipworth
James A. Smith
Albert E. Simpson
Virgil E. Shaw (Ovs.)
Perry Scott (Ovs.)
Sgt. Denny Sewell (Ovs.)
Willie Smith (Ovs., W.)
2nd Lt. Paul T. Smith
Maj. J. W. Smith
Sgt. Melvin Sparks
Paul E. Stockton (Ovs.)
Eular F. Spears
Miley B. Spears
Stanford R. Sprowles (Col., N.)
Otis Sharp
Sgt. H. Clifton Smith
Kelley R. Spears
Earl R. Smith

Hill A. Smith
Granville Stoner Sewell
James Dullis Shaw
Tyler Sampson (Col.)
Sgt. Corbett Street
Wilkie E. Smith (Ovs.)
James S. Spears
Clarence A. Stinson
William T. Stephens
James G. Scott
Roy H. Sewell
Richard C. Surratt
Hascal Scott
Finis P. Smith
Travis P. Spears
Sgt. Dennis Sewell (N., Ovs.)
James W. Smith (N.)
Joseph W. Stephenson (N.)
Charley R. Shoopman (N.)
Carmon C. Scott (N.)
Warren C. Sells (Ovs., W.)
Travis L. Smith (N.)
Leo J. Simpson
Amon Sevier
Otis Skipworth (D.D.)
Alvis W. Sewell
Paul Edward Sewell
Jonathan E. Stapp (N.)
William C. Stailey (N.)
Fowler R. Smith
Lewis C. Smith
William H. Smith
Hubert R. Smith
Henry C. Stephens (K.)
Roy W. Stephens
Senous B. Scott
Andrew W. Smith (Col., N.)
Travis Scott
Gene Sharp (N.)
Woodrow B. Smith (N.)
Roy L. Spears (N.)
William Delmus Scott

Troy Stanley Scott
Luther Austin Spears
Clint Skipworth (N.)
Charles W. Smith (N.)
Joe E. Smith (N.)
Charles C. Smith (N.)
Henry A. Smith
James Welby Scott
Jerry Stailey (Ovs.)
Berchie L. Scott
Henry K. Stephens
Carval H. Scott
Menvil K. Spears
Arval B. Spears
Reuben P. Spears
Wallace R. Sparks
Fred D. Sharp
Ula O. Spears
Russell Sheley (N.)
Willie D. Spear
Zilbert T. Shaw
Paul A. Strange
William H. Smith
Millard L. Sewell
Orlan T. Scott
Terry Humble Scott
Clarence Denzil Smith
Clifford E. Smith
Shelby A. Scott
Chester Raymon Smith
Mayford Noel Spears
Roy Stephenson (N.)
Fowler R. Smith
Stanley R. Spears
William Madison Spears
James Joseph Spears
Robert Sam Shoopman
Jesse Ray Scott
William J. Spears
Charles Elmer Spears
Tal Lee Smith
J. E. Short

T

Raymon Noble Thrasher
Joe Parker Traylor
Horace Cheek Turner
Lyle Newt Taylor

Charles Troy Teel
Otis Taylor Turner
George Edward Turner
James Douglas Thrasher

Homer J. Thomas (Ovs.)
Holland P. Thrasher (N.)
Martin Thrasher
Odie M. Thacker
Ira Benton Thrasher
John Sam Thurman
Wendell Hall Lewis (N.)
Edward Thrasher (N.)
William Tweedy (N.)
Robert Tweedy
Sgt. Paul Berton Taylor
James M. Thrasher (W.)
Sellie B. Thomas
Capt. Roger Tuggle (Ovs.P.)
Fred B. Tuggle
George Thomas Tweedy (N.)
Maj. Tommie Terrill
Sgt. Eubert Taylor
Dennis C. Thomas (N.)
Kenneth Thomas (Ovs., W.)
Joe Paul Thurman (N.)

Joe McKinley Thrasher
Arnold V. Taylor
Baker Thrasher
James C. Thomas
Verner Thacker
Sam B. Thrasher
Howard Thurman
Clarence Tobin (Col., N.)
F. W. Tobin (Col., N.)
Preston O. Thurman (N.)
Bud Robert Thurman
Lovell Taylor
Prentice Thrasher
Adrion L. Teal
Curtis Tweedy
Ruel C. Tweedy
Phelemon G. Thompson
Chester P. Tweedy
James T. Tweedy
Reubin Roy Teel
J. Walter Thurman

V

Harvey Vernon Vibbert
John Robert Vickry
Hall Clark Vibbert
Martin Vickry Vincent
Homer A. Vibbert
Linder M. Vincent
Ewing D. Vibbert
James C. Vincent

Sgt. Thomas Ray Vibbert (Ovs.)
Thomas L. Vincent
Charles H. Vickery
William C. Vibbert
James O. Vibbert
Clarence R. Vibbert
Paul McKinley Vincent

W

Earl Wynn Watson
Manuel Harold Wesmorland
Jim Zelma Watson
Kenford Francis Watson
Robert Willis
Pfc. James Iva Williams
William Henry Wesmorland
James Lee Wallace
Martin Oscar Wells (Ovs.)
Elmore Wilborn
Sam Lewis White
Carl Leon Williams (Ovs.)
Curtis Williams

Cander Williams (Col.)
Ralph Kinnard Williams (Col.)
Howard Pleas Williams
Prentis D. Wray
Pvt. James Lloyd Williams (Ovs.)
Charles Austin Wallace
Herman Lewis Ward
Keith George Wallace (Ovs.)
Simpson Wilborn (Col.)
Prentis Hall Wright (K. in Fr.)
Kenneth Claud Williams
Casey Kyle Watson
Tom Clifton White

Iva Leslie Winchester
Clyde Eston Wright
Esmond Wilbur
Kenneth Clark Williams
Reid Raney Watson
Capt. Frank Curtis Williams (Ovs.)
Edward Johnson Williams (N.)
Lewis Pershing Williams
Lester F. Williams
William E. Wells
Chester Gardner Wyatt
Kelsey Williams (N.)
Jesse A. Wray (N., D.D.)
Paul D. Williams
Charles M. Watson (N.)
John H. Walthall
James L. Willians
Robert White
Lawrence White
James H. Williams (N.)
Charles M. Watson (N.)
Sgt. William W. Ward.
Ralph Walthall

Tech. Sgt. Joseph Wm. Wells
Cpl. James Allen Wells (Ovs.)
Preston Whitley
Morris Williams (N.)
Harold Elvin Wright
Lt. Lyle Webb (Ovs.)
Robert G. Wilborn (K. crash, S. C.)
Marshall C. Webb
John A. Wray
William Williams
Felix Watkins
Malcolm Wells (Ovs.)
Harvey Woolsey
Oliver Watkins
Gordon W. Walker
Cecil A. Wray
Perry A. Watson (Ovs.)
Clavin L. Wray
James C. Watkins
James Alexander Wilson
Will Ed Williams
Almond Robert White
James Ellison Wright

Y

Wilmuth L. Young
Willie H. Young
Emmit Clyde Young
Allen Owsley Young (Ovs.)
Carl B. Young (Ovs.)
Ernest W. York

Wm. Paul Yarbarough (Ovs. P.)
Sellie Y. York
James H. Young
Maurice Young (N.)
Wendell D. Young
Fred York

CASUALTIES, CUMBERLAND COUNTY SOLDIERS

Hall Melton died on the way to Louisville to be examined.

Charles C. Capshaw was killed in a wreck in Louisiana.

Sgt. Ted Johnson at the end of three years' service was killed in a wreck at Los Angeles, Calif., March 12, 1943.

Sgt. James C. Prewitt was killed in a battle in North Africa, March 31, 1943.

Eular Spears, wounded in North Africa, March 22, 1943.

James H. Pitcock, wounded in action in North Africa, April 23, 1943.

Grant Ferguson, wounded in North Africa, May 6, 1943.

Willie Willis, wounded in Tunisia, Africa.

Raymon (Punch) Brown, wounded in Africa.

World War II

Sgt. Marshall Groce, wounded in crash of bomber in Idaho, April 24, 1943.

Warren C. Sell, wounded.

Lillard Davidson, wounded in Italy.

Sullivan Wolfe, son of Albert and Sarah (Pace) Wolfe, formerly of Marrowbone, Cumberland County, killed in Marshall Islands, February 4, 1944.

Kenneth Thomas, killed in action in Italy, January 26, 1944.

1st Lieut. Larry Pace, son of Schooling Pace, of Bowling Green, who was reared in Cumberland County, educated at Marrowbone and State Teachers College, Bowling Green, earning his wings at Randolph Field, Texas, was killed in Tunisia, being shot down by the enemy, December 4, 1942.

James Morris Stewart, son of Rev. J. T. Stewart, of Marrowbone, graduated as pilot and was sent to Hawaii, then to the States. September 4, 1942, he flew his Flying Fortress from Massachusetts to England, and October 9, made his first flight from there to France. His plane was crippled, but he succeeded in landing back in England; then one month later, being one of the formation hit by an anti-aircraft gun, fell into the sea and was lost.

Sellie B. Thomas, wounded in France, October 10, 1944, and December 23, 1944, in Luxembourg.

Ralph V. Norris, killed in action in France, September 27, 1944.

Senious B. Scott, killed in Germany, September 30, 1944.

Troy C. Teal, killed in France, September 22, 1944.

Edward Riddle, wounded in Italy.

John B. Cary, wounded in France, September 27, 1944.

Lewis B. Aaron, wounded in Germany, September 15, 1944; second, March 3, 1945.

Rollen Jesse, captured at Bataan, liberated in 1945.

Chester A. Ooten, wounded in France, September 22, 1944.

Haskell Scott, wounded in Germany, September 11, 1944.

James A. Smith, reported missing in France, September 8, 1944; was later located in German prison.

Verner R. Thacker, missing in France, September 8, 1944, later found in German prison.

Roy Booher, reared in Cumberland County, went from California and was killed in Belgium, September 12, 1944.

Ray G. Booher, his twin brother, was wounded January 15, 1945, fourth time.

Robert Norris, wounded in France, September 10, 1944.

Boo O. Groce, wounded in Belgium, September 2, 1944.

Gillium Coop, wounded on sinking ship.

James E. Goodhue, wounded in France, October, 1944.

Ruel P. Janes, killed in France, October 7, 1944.

Finis P. Smith, wounded in Germany, October 5, 1944.

Henry Clay Stephens, killed in plane collision in Italy, May 30, 1944.

Prentis Hall Wright, killed in western invasion in France, June 7, 1944.

John Will Jones, reported killed in Normandy, France, June 9, 1944, later reported lost on a torpedoed ship.

Willie E. Smith, wounded in France, June 15, 1944; second, in Belgium, December 24, 1944.

Clifton R. Keeton, wounded in Italy, July 15, 1944.

Ervin F. Brake, killed in France, July 7, 1944.

Hubert Daniels, wounded in France, July 11, 1944, and died the following August 29.

Morris Guthrie, wounded in France, June 14, 1944.

Elmo Wilborn, wounded in France, July 7, 1944.

Eula F. Spears, wounded in France, July 18, 1944.

Paul W. Glass, wounded on Saipan Island in the Pacific, July 9, 1944.

Oscar C. Daniels, wounded in France, July 21, 1944.

Stanley C. Pace, shot down on his 39th mission over Germany, August 3, 1944, when he received wounds from burns. He was taken prisoner and held until liberation day came to him, May 13, 1945.

Holland Johnson, wounded in action in North Africa, April 1, 1943.

Loland Cross, wounded September 20, 1944, in Germany, and October 31, following.

Tech. Sgt. Walter Reeder was drowned and was buried in Iran, Teheran, November 15, 1944. He had been flight engineer at the following places: England, North Africa, South America, Iran, Egypt, Russia, Persia, Greenland, Iceland, Ireland, Arabia.

William Elwood Norris, wounded in France, November 17, 1944.

Earl W. Watson, wounded in Leyte Island, October 25, 1944.

Cpl. James H. Garmon, killed in France, July 15, 1944, by shell.

Charles W. Fletcher, missing in France, November 13, 1944; later German prisoner.

Austin E. Cary, wounded in France, November 21, 1944.

Fred N. Oliver, wounded in France, November 27, 1944.

James Firkin, wounded in France, December 2, 1944.

James C. Jones, wounded in France, in a jeep accident, September 10, 1944.

Willard Norris, wounded in Leyte Island, November 15, 1944.

Lonnie Ward, wounded in Germany, November 29, 1944.

Jesse C. Kernell, missing in Germany, November 27, 1944 (died).

Irlin M. Cloyd, wounded in France, December 4, 1944.

Murry F. Humes, wounded in Germany, December 10, 1944.

Luther G. Humes, killed in Germany, December 9, 1944.

John B. Spears, wounded in Leyte, November 30, 1944.

Otis Nation, wounded in Germany, December 4, 1944.

Kenneth Williams, wounded in Germany, December 19, 1944.
James Daniels, killed in Leyte, December 12, 1944.
Dudley Hendricks, wounded in Germany, December 17, 1944.
Chester Holman, wounded in Belgium, December 24, 1944.
Raymon L. Cary, lost on submarine, November 25, 1944, in Bonin Islands.
Fletcher H. Prewitt, wounded in France, July 31, 1944.
James Baker, wounded in France.
Malcolm Wells, wounded in France, August 15, 1944.
Delmer C. Spears, reported missing in France, August 13, 1944; was found in German prison.
Charles Richardson, seriously wounded in France, August 8, 1944; died nine days later.
Jesse King, wounded in France, August 18, 1944, and December 4, 1944.
Walter R. Spears, wounded in France, August 27, 1944, and September 11, 1944.
Cecil O. Daniel, wounded in Germany, October 12, 1944.
James E. Bradshaw, wounded in Germany, October 7, 1944.
Buford G. Long, missing in Holland, October 29, 1944; later liberated from German Prison.
Leonard O. Graham, reported missing in Italy, October 26, 1944, but back on duty later.
Millard G. Davidson, wounded in Germany, October 29, 1944.
John B. Cary, wounded in France, September 27 and October 26, 1944.
Everett Wilson Cary, killed in Germany, October 19, 1944.
Rufus Berge, killed in France, September 13, 1944.
Charles B. Norris, wounded in Italy, October 19, 1944.
Winton B. Simpson, wounded in Leyte, Philippine Islands, October 21, 1944.
Willie E. Ooten, wounded in Germany, October 25, 1944.
Clarence A. Stimpson, wounded in Germany, October 1, 1944.
Paul A. Davidson, killed in France, November 12, 1944.
Sam B. Edmonson, wounded in France, November 13, 1944.
Staff. Sgt. Charles Smith of Cave City, formerly of this county, reported missing in Germany.
Carson Spears of Glasgow, formerly of this county, and son of Z. D. Spears, missing November 8, 1944, in Germany. Later found to be a prisoner.
Marvin M. Long, wounded in Leyte, Philippines, October 31, 1944.
Stanley Fayette Dalton, son of Sue Pace Dalton, of Aberdeen, Miss., formerly of Cumberland County, killed in the Philippine Islands.
Milton S. Fletcher, reported seriously wounded in France, November 4, 1944.
Lloyd Bean, wounded.

Joseph M. Humble, wounded in Luxembourg, October 24, December 24, 1944.

Capt. Joseph Schickel, wounded on Leyte Island, December 25, 1944.

Raymon D. Carter, S. 1-c, wounded.

Clyde M. Brown, missing in Germany, December 21, 1944. Liberated from German Prison, April 2, 1945.

Ivin P. Propes, missing in Germany, December 21, 1944. Later, German prisoner, liberated April 2, 1945.

Joel Cummings, killed in Leyte, December 3, 1944.

William L. Hoots, prisoner in Germany, November 26, 1944.

Robert A. Scott, wounded in Luxembourg, January 3, 1945.

William Ralph Anderson, wounded in Germany, December 4, 1944.

James M. Bowen, missing in Germany, January 7, 1945.

Buddy W. Daniels, missing in South Pacific, November 11, 1943.

Stanley E. Key, missing in France, January 20, 1945; prisoner, released.

Kenneth Williams, wounded in Belgium, January 9, 1945.

Herman M. Booher, wounded in France, February 4, 1945.

Ralph Garmon, wounded in Leyte, December 10, 1944.

Stanley R. Arms, wounded in France.

Ray Helm, killed in France, February 4, 1945.

Barney Parrish, killed in action in France, January 24, 1945.

Allen C. Beck, wounded in France, February 7, 1945.

James Paul Lewis, wounded in Germany, February 25, 1945.

Jack Dixon McComas, wounded in Germany, February 28, 1945.

Willie P. Brown, wounded in Germany, November 26, 1944.

William R. Logan, wounded in Italy, March 9, 1945.

Kenneth M. Spears, wounded.

William E. Grider, wounded.

Fred Dicken, wounded in Germany, March 6 and also 31, 1945.

James Douglas Thrasher, AOM 2-c, killed in plane crash in the Pacific, April 2, 1945.

Claude C. Smith, wounded in Germany, April 3, 1945.

Wilmuth Young, wounded in Germany, March 31, 1945.

Benton Cary, wounded in Germany, February 22, 1945.

Clay Cary, wounded in Philippines.

Lonas Ferguson, wounded (by his own gun).

Thomas L. Lawhon, wounded in Germany, February, 1945.

Archie M. Lee, wounded in Germany, April 8, 1945.

Paul Ray Potts, killed in Luzon, Philippines, April 5, 1945.

Fred Felty, killed in Germany, 1945.

Lester F. Williams, killed in Indo-China, April 28, 1945, on B-25 at Saigon.

Raymon Lafayette Cary, lost with crew on the Scamp, in the Pacific.

Kenfort Francis Watson, wounded in Germany, April 28, 1945.

Hall E. Keeton, died February 20, 1945, of wounds received February 19, in Germany.

Lyle C. Brockman, wounded in Germany, and taken prisoner.

Otis C. Rigsby, killed in jeep accident, in California, June 4, 1945; had been overseas.

Jesse M. Capps, killed in action, with Navy, May 27, 1945.

James L. Alexander, wounded in Saipan, June 17, 1944.

David I. Baker, killed in Germany, June 2, 1945, in a jeep accident.

John Willard Dyer, wounded in Germany, April 29, 1945.

Albert W. Gibson, wounded in Okinawa, June 21, 1945.

Van Blythe, wounded in Pacific, February 9, 1945.

Mitchell O. Spears died in Jap prison, July 23, 1942.

Henry Ballard, wounded in Germany, April 5, 1945.

Raymon D. Fletcher, wounded in Iwo Jima, March 10, 1945.

Glenn Dishman, wounded in Germany, 1945.

Fred F. Irby, Jap prisoner, December 7, 1941; liberated, 1945.

Roger Tuggle, Jap prisoner three years. Died on Jap ship, being moved, January 11, 1945.

CHAPTER 22

OUTSTANDING CHARACTERS

Cumberland County has produced many men of prominence, and the county has been blessed with the presence of many other great men who were born elsewhere but came here to live and work. The men who entwine themselves with public business are not always the best characters to be found in a country. Some of the very best people a country produces are those who never enter public life, but content themselves with their little homes, with their families, schools, churches, environments of nature, and a happy association with a few surrounding neighbors with whom they can mingle and plan for the betterment of their little kingdom. This home and community spirit is the foundation of happiness and sound government.

Cumberland County is made up of this kind of people. While this chapter is headed "Outstanding Characters" we do not want to lose sight of this class of citizen. The good old pioneer hospitality is on the decline, but enough of it remains to bind us into one big family of brothers and sisters. Take a journey into a distant part of the country where all are strangers who pass you by unnoticed, and get the feeling. Then meet with one face familiar to you and get that feeling. How different. How soothing. It is then that you begin to appreciate the sight of those faces and the exchanging of views with the ones, you, like Thomas Gray, had classed as "born to blush unseen and waste their sweetness on the desert air." It is then that the home ties grip tighter around your heart. It is then that the shackles of that desire to wander are shaken off and the ever-lingering picture of home and loved ones prompts you to carry into execution the words of the Prodigal Son, who, in the sweetest of all stories, said to himself, "I will arise and go to my father."

While we are proud of the class of noble people just described, there are ones who have made great sacrifices in life to make their country better. It may be from a religious standpoint, or financial, or from the view of public improvement, that they deserve publicity. Space will not allow here the names of all the great characters who have brought about improvement in the County of Cumberland. Under different chapters will be found the accomplishments of many different men in their special work.

If it is true that Abraham Lincoln was born in Cumberland County, then he becomes the outstanding character of Cumberland's sons. We believe Lincoln was born in this county, but Larue has been given the honor. Thomas Lincoln was the name of the father

Outstanding Characters 281

of Abraham, and there were only two Thomas Lincolns living at the time of Abraham's birth in 1809. History tells us one of them lived in Fayette County, Kentucky, and was an uncle of Abraham's father. He was a wealthy man, but allowed himself to become addicted to strong drink and lost all his substance.

The other Thomas, who we think was the father of the "Rail Splitter," lived in Cumberland County a number of years and was here at the time Abraham was born. Thomas Lincoln served two terms as constable of Cumberland County, 1802-4. In the Clerk's office is his bond of $500, with Moses Kirkpatrick and Jesse Gee sureties, bound to James Garrard, Governor of Kentucky, which was made January 12, 1802, and bears the exact signature of Thomas Lincoln, father of Abraham.

Surveyor Book A, page 396, tells of a plot of land, 100 acres, surveyed for Thomas Lincoln, lying in Cumberland County and leading from Moses Kirkpatrick's toward the Marrowbone Springs, on the north side of Cumberland River. This was granted by the county in 1801, but not delivered to him until 1815. Page 309, Book B, shows another tract of 98 acres lying on the north side of the river surveyed for him. Both are attested by Isaac Taylor, Clerk of the county. This Thomas was in the county till after the birth of Abraham. Every school child knows the story of "Honest Abe." He worked his way from poverty to the highest office the country can offer. His life has been next to that of the Good Shepherd to the youth of Kentucky.

Another great character of old, who came to this county at the age of 11, was Raccoon John Smith. He was born October 15, 1784, in North Carolina (later lived in Tennessee). George Smith, his father, came to Virginia, 1735, and married Rebecca Bowen, an Irish woman, and to this German-Irish union were born 13 children, 8 boys and 5 girls. John was the ninth child. He went to the three-month school in North Carolina. George left his family, except Joe and John, in the Powell Valley, 1795, and with three horses and three cows they bent their way toward the Kentucky wilderness. The father and two sons settled in the Curve of the Poplar Mountains, called Stockton Valley (named for Thomas Stockton), built a cabin, and spent the winter there. They cleared a garden and made preparations for the family in the spring. This was in the territory that became Cumberland County in 1798. In the spring the father sent John to Dix River Mill to get seed corn to plant out the little crop. He made the 100-mile ride safely. When the crop was out and ready for work, the father left it in the care of the two little boys and went to the Powell Valley to get the rest of the family. Late summer found them happily united.

In the summer of 1799 Robert Ferrell, a teacher from Virginia, set up a mill and school combined. John Smith, then 15, was a pupil under Ferrell. Bible and history were the two branches taught. Smith mastered the Bible and became a Baptist minister soon after his baptism by Isaac Denton, who had gone from Burkesville in 1799 and established a little church on Clear Fork Creek then in Cumberland County. Smith preached the Baptist doctrine until 1828, when he became affiliated with the Christian Church and remained until his death, 1868. He held meetings in Burkesville and other parts of the county. His remains rest in Lexington.

Something in Nature, it seems, influences living beings to the extent that they acquire the same dispositions or personalities. A neighborhood that furnishes a genius will also produce another and another. Of course occasionally one may spring up like a flower in a desert. Along this same line of thought are cases of young couples who become so agreeable that sooner or later marriage results. Back in the line of ancestry have the personality traits been transmitted, for maybe four or five generations, that cause the harmonizing intimacy which really is from the same ancestors of which they may be ignorant. The writer has observed this by the study of genealogies. For example, far removed from their native state two came in contact with each other. Their words, tones of voice, line of conversation, seem to harmonize. Their interest grew in each other. They married. Later, to their surprise, records proved to them that their great-grandmothers were sisters.

Back to my line of thought—I am persuaded that the topography, climate, and soil fertility play a part in the development of character as well as body. The strongest characters of our country have been formed in the rugged hills, where striving against hardships developed energy of both body and mind, thereby laying the foundation for future encounters.

In the rugged hills and hollows within a radius of ten miles were born some of the greatest characters of the United States, from the standpoint of religion, education, and statesmanship. With the ones I have thus far given, I might here name some of the other great men.

Rev. Isaac T. Reneau, born in Cumberland County near the Tennessee line, will be given under "Reneaus." Another was Timothy Frogg, who was a great divine of the Methodist Church, born and grew up near the same neighborhood. Rev. Sewells will be found under "Sewells."

United States Senators Cullom of Illinois and Maxey of Texas spent their childhood days in this neighborhood also. Just over the Cumberland line in Tennessee was born Governor Benton McMillan of Tennessee, and later the renowned Cordell Hull, Secretary of State under F. D. Roosevelt. At the Three Forks of the Wolf River, which is now in the same place, as then, Isaac T. Reneau tells us of teaching a school and boarding at the home of John M. Clemens, who was the father of Samuel L. Clemens, called "Mark Twain," who became the greatest humorist of the world. He was conceived there in that log cabin but was born five months later at Florida,

Missouri, 1835. John M. married Jane Lampton of Columbia, Kentucky, born 1803, died at Keokuk, Iowa, 1890.

Of the 55 governors furnished other states by Kentucky, this County has furnished two, and in all Cumberland County has given birth to three governors. Thomas E. Bramlett, who was governor during the Civil War, was born in Cumberland County, January 3, 1817, and died January 12, 1875.

Preston H. Leslie was born in Cumberland County, March 8, 1819, and died February 8, 1907. He was governor of Kentucky, 1871-5, and governor of Montana, 1887. He was the first governor of Kentucky to receive colored votes.

Both of these governors were born in that part of Cumberland that merged into Clinton, 1835.

Governor Norris was the third man from Cumberland County to become governor. Edwin L. Norris was born on Marrowbone Creek August 16, 1865, and went to Montana, where he became Governor of that state, 1908-12. He died there in 1924.

On the waters of Renox Creek within a few miles of each other were born five Circuit Judges of Kentucky. H. C. Baker, whose paternal grandfather was the pioneer William Baker who came to Cumberland County in 1805, and whose maternal grandfather was Joseph Alexander who came to the county in 1824 after his marriage to Nancy Bouldin, granddaughter of Thomas Bouldin of Virginia. H. C. Baker was born 1841, and his life was spent with public affairs. He began the practice of law in Columbia in 1863, served in the Legislature 1873-4, and on the bench for Adair, Russell, Metcalfe, Casey, Cumberland, and Monroe counties, 1904-9, as Circuit Judge.

William Wallace Jones was another of those five Judges. Born 1855, in the county, his father, Levi Jones, who was of Welsh descent, was born in Cumberland County, 1835. W. W. Jones moved to Casey and then to Adair County. He was admitted to the bar in 1877 and served the 29th Judical District, 1892-1903.

Another of those men of public affairs who resided out of the county but who wielded his scepter over Cumberland County was Judge Rollin Hurt of Columbia. He was a grandson of William Hurt (1757-1842), who served through the Revolutionary War and went through the suffering of Valley Forge. In 1782 he was captured by the Indians and taken to Canada, where he was held for five years. He then came to Bourbon County, and in 1794 to Adair. William first married Elizabeth White and second Elizabeth Murray. To the last union were born 13 children. One was named Young, who became the father of Rollin, who has served as Judge of the Third Appellate District, which covers Cumberland County. Much of his work has been in this county.

Besides the outstanding men heretofore referred to, nearly all other types of humanity can be found in this county that can be found in any other part of the United States, in the Caucasian and

Ethiopian races. In fact, the races of men bear similar resemblances the world over.

The two qualities that elevate man above brute animals are, first, his desire for possessions above that which he is able to eat; the second is that sense of immortality. While we look around us each day and see men and women holding both of these qualities in low repute, we are prone to conclude that something is still lacking in the human family today.

Man is either a benefactor or a malefactor. There is no middle ground, neither is there such a thing as a blank. Paul said, "No one lives to himself, and no one dies to himself." His trail of life leaves its influence along the way for good or bad. Man's aim greatly determines his outcome. There is only one aim that is always certain —aim at nothing, nothing is accomplished.

The majority of our people believe and show by their lives that there is a life beyond this one which they long to attain. Others believe the same way, but their lives do not testify to their belief. Procrastination is their besetting foe. A few infidels have lived and died within our county; a few still live within its domain.

On approaching a citizen once I asked if he could furnish me with a good outline of his Family Tree. He replied that he had always been a little fearful in giving his Family Tree too great a shake lest a dead limb hit him in the head. Many things enter into the shaping of humanity, both seen and unseen. Natural barriers breed provincialism. People on one side of Cumberland River may do the same things differently to those on the other side. Good roads have their influence; mud roads have theirs. Cars and trucks wrought a change for good and bad; so will planes.

The two World Wars have been instrumental in shedding the worst influence on morality. Nightly shows have their enticing powers which, generally speaking, are obstructions to morality and enmity to frugality. Ancestry cannot be credited or blamed for all the good or bad traits in people, yet it does play a very big part. In a genealogical research one finds the same characteristics prevailing in the progeny to a limited degree.

For illustration, in the pioneer days of this county a certain man and woman cohabited and reared a family of illegitimates. The fifth generation of this family still finds some in this family extremely amorous, practicing coquetry, polyandry and nearing the brink of turpitude. Occasionally a member may attain the zenith in decorum.

More often than not we find farmers, lawyers, doctors, mechanics, teachers, merchants, postmasters, lumbermen, fishermen, hunters, traders, bankers, and ministers treading the trail of their progenitors.

The second big factor in molding man is environment. This is, one's surroundings. Surely if a stalk can make a black frog green, enlightened man should not forever remain a chameleon. It is here that environment wields its influence on man. It often takes generations to banish the bad and graft the good. Some men are like tea, the sooner they are steeped in hot water the quicker the good will appear.

Among the many characteristics revealed in men we have one that is outstanding in more men in the county than any one other. It is veracity. While this is a virtue that is dominant, we also have a number yet who have a reputation for mendacity.

There is the generous man. He is usually loved by all. He is beneficent. He is credulous, and many soon learn this. The mendicant is about the first to find him, and every ill luck or misfortune is laid at his feet and at the same time he is covered up with fallacious words so often used in his mendicity. Mendacity usually precedes mendicity.

Cumberland County has many provident families. Their every act is profitable. With the limited opportunities that come round, they are ever on the alert to seize them on the wing. They are frugal. Sometimes one carries his frugality to where he is in danger of becoming parsimonious. In the utmost extreme we also have a few misers. Should the last two types live to see the prodigality of some of their children their anger would approach malice.

Then we have the sanctimonious man. You cannot judge him from looks or talk, but by association or through business transactions.

There is the chronic penitent who renews his vows to God every time a revival comes round, and yet no one outside his family ever sees him in the wrong. There are those who believe it impossible to live above daily sin, whom you will find, after a day of the purest living, imploring God at the close of the day to forgive their sin. Along with these you will see those who believe it is possible to live above sinning daily, and from their acts we have no right to dispute their word; and also you may meet with a few whose lives contradict their religious egotism.

From a physical standpoint we have midgets, very little larger than Tom Thumb; pudgy people of both sexes; corpulent people of both sexes, traced to ancestry and not "stall-feeding"; tall, thin people, whose physique also is an ancestral inheritance. A rare number of ambidextrous men are here.

The highest art among females, old, young, fat, or lean, is "Cosmesis." In this age of the world with every showcase full to overflowing with cosmetics to alter any coloring or facial appearance, the fair sex has little trouble in transforming themselves into what they're not. This art accompanies intellectuality and the tawdry alike.

The obstinate man is found in most neighborhoods. He seeks to dethrone every idea of which he is not the instigator. He is not lenient. He is not open to convictions, thereby barring himself from improvement. He will not own his mistakes. Anything you propose, suggest, or hope for is heaped with rebuff or with mention of the difficulties it will produce. He does not have opinions, but opinions have him.

The raconteur is a man of ready wit. His hobby is telling anecdotes, and his mind is chock full. His delight is to produce laughter. Rarely serious. On street corners and at political gatherings are his coveted spots. A constant curb is required to prevent his drifting to obscenity.

Charlatans are not so numerous as in former days. Their business is suicidal. The medical field formerly held most of this type of person.

The malingerer is a character found most numerously among tenants on Saturdays, or among church congregations on pay-day, or on farms when Old Sol presses the 100 mark.

The negrophobist has softened down to annihilation and has been replaced by the negrophile of modern times.

The neoterist is the man that gains the attention of more different people than any other being. He is generally popular for the time being. His way of hypnotizing his listeners prompts them to action; he secures his pelf and is gone, leaving his work to praise or condemn. In the literal realm you would think him a pantoglot.

Lastly, we have some that are always cross-eyed and some that are always cross-grained. Then there are the pugnacious who have never read with interest Ephesians 4:26; and the inebriate who has his doubt of Proverbs 20:1; the imbecile; pusillanimous twaddler; thus seemingly Cumberland County has been the rendezvous for every type of person with the exception of the nincompoop.

CHAPTER 23

THE 120 COUNTIES OF KENTUCKY
(1940 Census)

COUNTY SEAT, ORIGIN, AREA, POPULATION

ADAIR, *Columbia*

Adair County was formed, 1801. Named in honor of John Adair, Kentucky Commander at New Orleans, Governor of Kentucky, U. S. Senator, and Member of Congress. Carved from Green. Area, 393 square miles. Population, 18,566.

ALLEN, *Scottsville*

Allen County was organized, 1815, from parts of Warren and Barren. Named in honor of John Allen, a distinguished lawyer, who lost his life at the battle of the Raisin, 1813, while leading his Kentucky men. Area, 364 square miles. Population, 15,496.

ANDERSON, *Lawrenceburg*

Anderson County was established, 1827, from Franklin, Mercer, and Washington, and was named in honor of Richard C. Anderson, Louisville, who served as a member of Congress, diplomat to Columbia, South America, and represented the United States at Panama, 1826, where he died. He was a brother of Robert Anderson. Area, 206 square miles. Population, 8,936.

BALLARD, *Wickliffe*

Ballard County was formed, 1842, from parts of Hickman and McCracken counties and was named in honor of Capt. Bland Ballard, who came to Kentucky in 1779 and fought along with George Rogers Clark. Area, 259 square miles. Population, 9,485.

BARREN, *Glasgow*

Barren County was formed in 1798, from Warren and Green counties, and got its name from the "barrens" or the timberless tracts of land in its territory, made so by the annual burnings of the gigantic grasslands in Indian days. Area, 486 square miles. Population, 27,559.

BATH, *Owingsville*

Bath County was formed in 1811 from Montgomery County. It owes its name to the great number of mineral springs where people once went—and still do go—to obtain medicinal, mineral waters. Area, 297 square miles. Population, 11,451.

BELL, *Pineville*

Bell County was organized in 1867. It was first called Josh Bell for a silver-tongued lawyer of Danville, but was given the name Bell by the Legislature, 1873. It was carved from Knox and Harlan counties. Area, 370 square miles. Population, 43,812.

BOONE, *Burlington*

Boone County was formed in 1798 from Campbell County and was named in honor of the fearless Indian fighter and Kentucky pioneer, Daniel Boone. Area, 252 square miles. Population, 10,819.

BOURBON, *Paris*

Bourbon County was formed in 1785, taken from Fayette County. It was named in honor of the Bourbon family, who occupied the French throne and gave their sympathy and assistance in the War for Independence. Area, 300 square miles. Population, 17,932.

BOYD, *Catlettsburg*

Boyd County was formed in 1860 from parts of Greenup, Carter, and Lawrence counties. Named in honor of Hon. Lynn Boyd, Lieutenant Governor and Speaker of House of Representatives in Congress. Area, 159 square miles. Population, 45,937.

BOYLE, *Danville*

Boyle County was formed in 1842 from parts of Lincoln, Mercer, and Casey. It was named in honor of Chief Justice John Boyle of the Court of Appeals. Area, 181 square miles. Population, 17,075.

BRACKEN, *Brooksville*

Bracken County was organized in 1796 from Mason and Campbell counties and was named in honor of William Bracken, who was first settler of the county, and who was killed by an Indian at the place of settlement. Area, 206 square miles. Population, 9,389.

BREATHITT, *Jackson*

Breathitt County was formed in 1839 from parts of Clay, Perry, and Estill counties. It was named for Governor John Breathitt, who died in office in 1834, at Frankfort. Area, 486 square miles. Population, 23,944.

BRECKINRIDGE, *Hardinsburg*

Breckinridge County was created in 1799 from Hardin County and was named for Hon. John Breckinridge, Attorney General in President Jefferson's Cabinet. Area, 566 square miles. Population, 17,744.

BULLITT, *Shepherdsville*

Bullitt County was formed in 1796 from parts of Jefferson and Nelson counties and was named for one of its first settlers, Lieutenant Governor Bullitt. Area, 300 square miles. Population, 9,576.

Counties of Kentucky

BUTLER, Morgantown

Butler County was carved from Logan and Ohio counties, 1810, and named for General Butler of Revolutionary fame. Area, 443 square miles. Population, 14,368.

CALDWELL, Princeton

Caldwell County was formed from a part of Livingston County, in 1809, and was named for Gen. John Caldwell, who moved from Virginia, 1781, and served as State Senator, 1793, and Lieutenant Governor, 1804. Area, 357 square miles. Population, 14,499.

CALLOWAY, Murray

Calloway County was carved from Hickman County in 1822, and was named in honor of Col. Richard Calloway. Area, 407 square miles. Population, 19,041.

CAMPBELL, Alexandria

Campbell County was formed in 1794 from Mason, Scott, and Harrison counties. It was named for Col. John Campbell, one of the early settlers and largest landowners of the time. Area, 151 square miles. Population, 71,918.

CARLISLE, Bardwell

Carlisle County was formed in 1886 from part of Ballard County and named for John G. Carlisle, Speaker of the House of Representatives in Congress. Area, 196 square miles. Population, 7,650.

CARROLL, Carrollton

Carroll County was formed in 1838 from part of Gallatin County and named for the renowned patriot, Charles Carroll, signer of the Declaration of Independence. Area, 131 square miles. Population, 8,637.

CARTER, Grayson

Carter County was formed in 1838 from Greenup and Lawrence counties and named for Col. William Carter, Senator for four years. (Early settlers claim it was named for a Carter family, who made salt there as the first settlers.) Area, 402 square miles. Population, 25,545.

CASEY, Liberty

Casey County was formed in 1806 from part of Lincoln County and was named for Col. William Casey, an early pioneer and an Indian fighter of that part of Kentucky. Area, 435 square miles. Population, 19,962.

CHRISTIAN, Hopkinsville

Christian County was formed from a part of Logan County in 1796 and was named for Col. William Christian, a noted Indian fighter, who fought the Indians out of Kentucky, 1786, but got killed in the battle. Area, 726 square miles. Population, 36,129.

CLARK, *Winchester*

Clark County was formed in 1792 from Fayette and Bourbon counties and named for George Rogers Clark, Kentucky's second great pioneer and general of Revolutionary fame. Area, 259 square miles. Population, 17,988.

CLAY, *Manchester*

Clay County was formed in 1806 from Madison, Knox, and Floyd counties and named for Gen. Green Clay, one of its early pioneers. Area, 475 square miles. Population, 23,903.

CLINTON, *Albany*

Clinton County was formed in 1835-6 from parts of Wayne and Cumberland counties and named in honor of Gov. De Witt Clinton of New York, who had just soared to prominence the world over, 1825, by opening up the western part of America with a ship canal from Albany, New York to Lake Erie. Area, 206 square miles. Population, 10,279.

CRITTENDEN, *Marion*

Crittenden County was formed in 1842 and named in honor of Hon. John J. Crittenden, U. S. Senator, who fought in the battle of Thames; Governor in 1848; Attorney General in Fillmore's Cabinet. Area, 365 square miles. Population, 12,115.

CUMBERLAND, *Burkesville*

Cumberland County was formed in 1798 from Green County and named for Cumberland River, which got its name from the Cumberland Mountains, which were named by Thomas Walker in honor of the Duke of Cumberland, England. Area, 313 square miles. Population, 11,923.

DAVIESS, *Owensboro*

Daviess County was organized in 1815 from part of Ohio County, and named in honor of Col. Joseph Hamilton Daviess, who was an able lawyer of Danville, Kentucky, and who fell at the Battle of Tippecanoe, 1811, while commanding his men. Area, 466 square miles. Population, 52,338.

EDMONSON, *Brownsville*

Edmonson County was organized in 1825 from parts of Warren, Hart, and Grayson counties, and named in honor of Capt. John Edmonson, who came to Kentucky in 1790. In the War of 1812 he fought with his Kentucky Riflemen and was killed in the battle of the Raisin, 1813. Area, 304 square miles. Population, 11,344.

Counties of Kentucky

ELLIOTT, Sandy Hook

Elliott County was formed in 1869 from parts of Morgan, Carter, and Lawrence counties, and named in honor of John M. Elliott, a member of the Confederate Congress, from Kentucky, and Judge of the Court of Appeals, who was shot on the streets of Frankfort, 1879, while Judge. Area, 240 square miles. Population, 8,714.

ESTILL, Irvine

Estill County was formed in 1808 from parts of Madison and Clark counties and named in honor of Capt. James Estill, who engaged the Wyandot Indians at Mount Sterling, 1782, in a bloody battle, in which he lost his life. Area, 362 square miles. Population, 17,978.

FAYETTE, Lexington

Fayette County was taken from Kentucky County in 1780, and was one of the three first formed by the Virginia Legislature in Kentucky Territory. It was named for the Hon. Marquis de La Fayette, the noble Frenchman who left his home and came to help us in the struggle for freedom, 1777. Area, 280 square miles. Population, 78,899.

FLEMING, Flemingsburg

Fleming County was formed in 1798 from part of Mason County and named for Col. John Fleming, an early pioneer. Area, 350 square miles. Population, 13,327.

FLOYD, Prestonsburg

Floyd County was formed in 1799 out of parts of Fleming, Montgomery, and Mason counties. Named in honor of Col. John Floyd, first Colonel of Militia of Jefferson County; wounded in Indian battle near Shelbyville; Judge of Kentucky District 1783; ambushed by Indians, 1783. He had refused a huge bribe by the British, 1779, and title of Duke if he would betray his men. He refused. Area, 402 square miles. Population, 52,986.

FRANKLIN, Frankfort

Franklin County was formed in 1794 from Woodford, Mercer, and Shelby counties and named in honor of Benjamin Franklin. The two-million-dollar marble Capitol Building, built with money collected from injuries of the Confederate Army, is located here. Area, 211 square miles. Population, 23,308.

FULTON, Hickman

Fulton County was formed in 1845 from a part of Hickman County and named for Robert Fulton, the inventor of the steamboat, 1807. It was here that the heaviest earthquake occurred in the United States in 1811 that reversed the current of the Mississippi River and formed Reel Foot Lake, 2 miles wide by 17 miles long. Area, 205 square miles. Population, 15,415.

History of Cumberland County

GALLATIN, Warsaw

Gallatin County was formed in 1798 from parts of Shelby and Franklin counties and named in honor of Albert Gallatin, a Swiss who served in many offices and diplomatic capacities. Area, 100 square miles. Population, 4,307.

GARRARD, Lancaster

Garrard County was formed in 1796 from Mercer, Madison, and Lincoln counties and named for James Garrard, Revolutionary War officer, and second Governor of Kentucky. Area, 234 square miles. Population, 11,907.

GRANT, Williamstown

Grant County was formed in 1820 from a part of Pendleton County and named for Col. John Grant and his brother Samuel Grant, who moved there from North Carolina 1780; Samuel being killed there, 1794. Area, 250 square miles. Population, 9,876.

GRAVES, Mayfield

Graves County was formed in 1823 from Hickman County and named for Maj. Benjamin Graves, who was killed at the head of his men at the River Raisin, 1813.

GRAYSON, Leitchfield

Grayson County was formed in 1810 from parts of Ohio and Hardin counties and named for Col. William Grayson of Virginia. Area, 514 square miles. Population, 17,562.

GREEN, Greensburg

Green County was formed in 1792 from parts of Lincoln and Nelson counties and named for Gen. Nathaniel Green of Revolutionary fame. It was originally a large county but parts of Cumberland, Adair, Pulaski, Hart, Barren, and Metcalfe counties have been taken from it. Area, 282 square miles. Population, 12,323.

GREENUP, Greenup

Greenup County was formed in 1803 from Mason County and named for Christopher Greenup, a Revolutionary War officer and third Governor of Kentucky. Area, 350 square miles. Population, 24,915.

HANCOCK, Hawesville

Hancock County was formed in 1829 from Breckinridge, Daviess, and Ohio counties and named for John Hancock, President of the Continental Congress. Area, 187 square miles. Population, 6,807.

HARDIN, Elizabethtown

Hardin County was formed in 1792 from Nelson County and named for Col. John Hardin, an Indian fighter of 1790. Area, 616 square miles. Population, 28,108.

HARLAN, *Harlan*

Harlan County was formed in 1819 from parts of Floyd and Knox counties and named for Major Silas Harlan, who was one of the 70 brave Kentuckians killed at Blue Lick, who followed the reckless McGary across the Licking River into an Indian net, 1782. Area, 465 square miles. Population, 75,275.

HARRISON, *Cynthiana*

Harrison County was formed in 1793 from parts of Scott and Bourbon counties and named for Col. Benjamin Harrison, an early resident of Bourbon County and its first sheriff; also member of the first Constitution Convention. Area, 308 square miles. Population, 15,124.

HART, *Munfordville*

Hart County was formed in 1819 from Green and Hardin counties and named for Capt. Nathaniel Hart, an officer of the Revolutionary War and a distinguished Kentucky pioneer. Area, 425 square miles. Population, 17,239.

HENDERSON, *Henderson*

Henderson County was formed in 1798 from a part of Christian County and named for Col. Richard Henderson, a Virginian who met 1,200 Indians at Sycamore Shoals and made a treaty in which the Cherokees agreed to relinquish all rights to the vast tract of land between the Ohio, Kentucky, and Cumberland rivers to the company called Transylvania, headed by Henderson, 1775. Area, 440 square miles. Population, 27,025.

HENRY, *New Castle*

Henry County was formed in 1798 from part of Shelby County and named in honor of Hon. Patrick Henry, Virginia Governor and Kentucky's most noble son. Area, 289 square miles. Population, 12,270.

HICKMAN, *Clinton*

Hickman County was formed in 1821 from Caldwell and Livingston counties and named for Capt. Pascal Hickman, a noted officer, who was killed at the battle of the Raisin, 1813. He was a native of Franklin County, Kentucky. Area, 248 square miles. Population, 9,142.

HOPKINS, *Madisonville*

Hopkins County was formed in 1807 from Henderson County, as a result of an act of the General Assembly of December 29, 1806. It was named for Gen. Stephen Hopkins of the Revolution. Area, 555 square miles. Population, 37,782.

JACKSON, McKee

Jackson County was formed in 1858 from chips off Madison, Estill, Laurel, Owsley, Clay, and Rockcastle counties, and named in honor of Andrew Jackson, great Indian fighter and seventh President of the United States. Area, 337 square miles. Population, 16,339.

JEFFERSON, Louisville

Jefferson County was formed in 1780 from Kentucky County, Virginia, and named for Thomas Jefferson, who was the greatest statesman of that day. He had just become the father of the Declaration of Independence, later third President. Area, 375 square miles. Population, 385,392.

JESSAMINE, Nicholasville

Jessamine County was formed in 1798, taken from Fayette; was named from Jessamine Creek, which was named by a Mr. Douglas, a pioneer, in honor of his daughter, Jessamine, who was tomahawked unaware by a skulking Indian there. Area, 177 square miles. Population, 12,174.

JOHNSON, Paintsville

Johnson County was formed in 1843 from parts of Floyd, Lawrence, and Morgan counties. It was named in honor of Col. Richard M. Johnson, Congress Member and a gallant fighter, who with his brave Kentuckians, nearly 3,000 strong, withstood the terrific fire of the British and Indians in the battle of the Thames, near Detroit, in Canada, 1813, in which Johnson sat in his saddle and commanded his men for hours. He slew the Indian Chief, Tecumseh, after which the Indians fled, and this campaign put an end to the war in the Northwest. "Remember the Raisin" rang throughout the battle. Area, 264 square miles. Population, 25,771.

KENTON, Independence

Kenton County was formed in 1840 from Campbell County and named for Simon Kenton, the big hearted pioneer of Kentucky, who fought the Indians at Boonesboro and saved Boones life, and who joined Clark at the "Falls" for his conquest of the Northwest Territory, 1778-9.

KNOTT, Hindman

Knott County was formed in 1884 from parts of Floyd, Letcher, Perry, and Breathitt counties and was named for Governor Proctor Knott of Kentucky, who was then serving his first year as Governor. Area, 356 square miles. Population, 20,007.

KNOX, Barbourville

Knox County was formed in 1799 from part of Lincoln County and named in honor of Major General Henry Knox, of Revolutionary fame, and a close friend of George Washington. Area, 373 square miles. Population, 31,029.

LARUE, *Hodgenville*

Larue County was formed in 1843 from part of Hardin County and took its name from the first pioneers of that place—the Larue family. The Lincoln farm is close to the county seat. Area, 260 square miles. Population, 9,622.

LAUREL, *London*

Laurel County was formed in 1825 from parts of Rockcastle, Clay, Knox, and Whitley counties and received its name from the Laurel River, whose banks were lined with the flower by that name. Area, 448 square miles. Population, 25,640.

LAWRENCE, *Louisa*

Lawrence County was formed in 1821 from parts of Greenup and Floyd counties and received its name from the gallant Captain Lawrence, who was on the Chesapeake ship off Boston Harbor with his feeble crew which attacked the British *Shannon*, 1813, in which Lawrence was mortally wounded, but bade his men: "Don't give up the ship." Battle was lost, but his last words have meant much. Area, 425 square miles. Population, 17,275.

LEE, *Beattyville*

Lee County was formed in 1869-70 from parts of Breathitt, Owsley, Estill, and Wolfe and named for Gen. Robert E. Lee, the most powerful commander of the Confederate States. Area, 210 square miles. Population, 10,857.

LESLIE, *Hyden*

Leslie County was formed in 1878 from parts of Clay, Perry, and Harlan and named for Preston H. Leslie, who had served as Kentucky Governor, 1872-5, from Clinton County, and was at that time Governor of Montana. Area, 412 square miles. Population, 14,979.

LETCHER, *Whitesburg*

Letcher County was formed in 1842 from parts of Perry and Harlan counties and named for Robert P. Letcher, ten years in Congress and Governor of Kentucky at that time. Area, 339 square miles. Population, 40,583.

LEWIS, *Vanceburg*

Lewis County was formed in 1806 from Mason County and named for Meriwether Lewis of the famous Lewis and Clark Expedition, which explored the Louisiana Purchase 1803-6. Area, 485 square miles. Population, 15,686.

LINCOLN, Stanford

Lincoln County was formed in 1780, as another of the three counties formed from Kentucky County before it became a state. It was named for Gen. Benjamin Lincoln of Revolutionary fame. Area, 340 square miles. Population, 19,859.

LIVINGSTON, Smithland

Livingston County was carved from Christian County in 1798 and named for Robert R. Livingston, one of the five who drafted the Declaration of Independence, and also was with Monroe, who negotiated the treaty with France, which resulted in the purchase of Louisiana 1803, which gave us 13 states. Area, 318 square miles. Population, 9,127.

LOGAN, Russellville

Logan County was organized soon after the admission of Kentucky, as a state, 1792, from Lincoln County and named for Gen. Benjamin Logan, a pioneer and a companion of Boone. Area, 563 square miles. Population, 23,345.

LYON, Eddyville

Lyon County was formed in 1854 from a part of Caldwell County and named for Col. Crittenden Lyon, who came to Kentucky in 1801 with his father, who founded Eddyville. Area, 262 square miles. Population, 9,067.

MADISON, Richmond

Madison County was formed in 1785 by the Virginia Legislature from Lincoln County territory and named for James Madison, afterwards President. Area, 446 square miles. Population, 28,541.

MAGOFFIN, Salyersville

Magoffin County was formed in 1860 from parts of Morgan, Floyd, and Johnson, and was named for Beriah Magoffin, Kentucky Governor during the Civil War, who resigned because of his sympathy with the South. Area, 303 square miles. Population, 17,490.

MARION, Lebanon

Marion County was formed in 1834 from part of Washington County and named in honor of Francis Marion, called the "Swamp Fox," who made it hazardous for the British in the Revolutionary War. Area, 343 square miles. Population, 16,913.

MARSHALL, Benton

Marshall County was formed in 1842 from part of Calloway County and named for John Marshall, Chief Justice of the Supreme Court for many years. Area, 336 square miles. Population, 16,602.

MARTIN, Inez

Martin County was formed in 1870 from parts of Pike, Floyd, Johnson and Lawrence counties and named for John P. Martin, a great statesman of Eastern Kentucky. Area, 231 square miles. Population, 10,970.

MASON, Maysville

Mason County was formed in 1788 as one of the nine formed from the Kentucky District. It was taken from Bourbon County and named for Hon. George Mason, a distinguished statesman of Revolutionary days. Area, 239 square miles. Population, 19,066.

McCRACKEN, Paducah

McCracken County was formed in 1824 from part of Hickman County and named for Capt. Virgil McCracken, a gallant fighter who lost his life in the battle of the River Raisin, 1813.

McCREARY, Whitley City

McCreary County was formed in 1912 from parts of Wayne, Pulaski, and Whitley counties and named for Governor J. B. McCreary who was Governor at that time. Area, 441 square miles. Population, 16,452.

McLEAN, Calhoun

McLean County was formed in 1853-4 from parts of Ohio, Daviess, and Muhlenberg counties and named for Alney McLean, noted Circuit Judge of Muhlenberg County. Area, 257 square miles. Population, 11,446.

MEADE, Brandenburg

Meade County was formed in 1823 from Breckinridge and Hardin counties and named for Capt. James W. Meade. Area, 308 square miles. Population, 8,827.

MENIFEE, Frenchburg

Menifee County was formed in 1869 and was named for Richard Menifee, a political analyst of the panic days following the 1837 crisis. It was carved from Bath, Montgomery, Powell, Wolfe, and Morgan. Area, 210 square miles. Population, 5,691.

MERCER, Harrodsburg

Mercer County was formed in 1785 from Lincoln County and named for Gen. Hugh Mercer, killed at battle of Princeton, 1777. Area, 256 square miles. Population, 14,629.

METCALFE, Edmonton

Metcalfe County was formed in 1860 from parts of Barren, Monroe, Cumberland, Adair, and Green counties. It got its name from

Thomas Metcalfe, the tenth Governor of Kentucky, who was afterwards appointed by Governor Owsley to fill out J. J. Crittenden's term in the United States Senate, 1848. Area, 296 square miles. Population, 10,853.

MONROE, *Tompkinsville*

Monroe County was formed in 1820 from parts of Cumberland and Barren counties and named for President James Monroe, fifth President, and the county seat was named for his Vice-President, D. D. Tompkins. Area, 334 square miles. Population, 14,070.

MONTGOMERY, *Mt. Sterling*

Montgomery County was formed in 1796 from a part of Clark County and was named in honor of Gen. Richard Montgomery, who lost his life in the battle before Quebec, in a blinding snowstorm in 1775, which city we lost to the British. Area, 204 square miles. Population, 12,280.

MORGAN, *West Liberty*

Morgan County was formed in 1822 from parts of Floyd and Bath counties and named for Gen. Daniel Morgan, who won the battle of Cowpens, 1781, where he left 600 slain British on the field with a loss of 80 Continentals, and a complete rout of Tarleton. Area, 369 square miles. Population, 16,827.

MUHLENBERG, *Greenville*

Muhlenberg County was formed in 1798 from parts of Logan and Christian counties and named for Gen. Peter Muhlenberg. Area, 482 square miles. Population, 37,554.

NELSON, *Bardstown*

Nelson County was formed in 1784 from Jefferson County and named for Governor Nelson of Virginia. Area, 438 square miles. Population, 18,004.

NICHOLAS, *Carlisle*

Nicholas County was formed in 1799 from parts of Bourbon and Mason counties and named for Hon. George Nicholas, captain in the Revolutionary War. Area, 204 square miles. Population, 8,619.

OHIO, *Hartford*

Ohio County was formed in 1798 from Hardin County and named for the Ohio River which bathes the northern boundary of Kentucky for 720 miles. Area, 596 square miles. Population, 24,421.

OLDHAM, *La Grange*

Oldham County was formed in 1823 from parts of Shelby, Henry, and Jefferson counties and named for Col. William Oldham, who came to Kentucky, 1779, and took his regiment to help St. Clair drive the Shawnee, Wyandot, Delaware, and Miami Indians beyond Kentucky, 1791. Near the Wabash River, in a furious battle, he was one of the 70 officers who lost their lives, to the savage Indian chiefs. Area, 184 square miles. Population, 10,716.

OWEN, *Owenton*

Owen County was formed in 1819 from parts of Franklin, Scott, and Gallatin counties and named for Col. Abraham Owen, who was Aid-de-camp to Gen. Harrison at the battle of Tippecanoe, 1811, where he lost his life. Area, 351 square miles. Population, 10,942.

OWSLEY, *Booneville*

Owsley County was formed in 1843 from Clay, Estill, and Breathitt counties and named for William Owsley, who had just ended his term as Governor of Kentucky. Area, 197 square miles. Population, 8,960.

PENDLETON, *Falmouth*

Pendleton County was formed in 1798 by the Legislature, but not organized until 1800. It was carved from Bracken and Campbell counties and named for the distinguished orator and jurist of Virginia, Edmund Pendleton. Area, 279 square miles. Population, 10,392.

PERRY, *Hazard*

Perry County was formed in 1820 from Clay and Floyd counties and named in honor of Oliver Hazard Perry, who had built on Lake Erie, a fleet of nine ships in the spring of 1813, which destroyed the British fleet in September of that year. Part of Perry's wooden ships were made from growing timber on the bank of the lake. A noble victory it was, after which Perry wrote to General Harrison: "We have met the enemy and they are ours." Area, 343 square miles. Population, 47,828.

PIKE, *Pikeville*

Pike County was formed in 1821 from Floyd County and named for Gen. Zebulon M. Pike, who went to explore the source of the Mississippi River, in 1805, and discovered the high peak in central Colorado in 1806 that bears his name. In 1813 he engaged in an assault against the British at York on the northern coast of Lake Ontario, where he lost his life.

POWELL, *Stanton*

Powell County was formed in 1852 from Montgomery, Estill, and Clark counties and named for Governor Lazarus W. Powell of Kentucky, 1851. Area, 173 square miles. Population, 7,677.

PULASKI, Somerset

Pulaski County was formed as one of the 13 of 1798. It was taken from parts of Lincoln and Green counties and named for the honored Count Pulaski, the noble Polander who came to America to help gain her independence. He lost his life in action at Savannah, Georgia, 1779. Area, 676 square miles. Population, 39,863.

ROBERTSON, Mt. Olivet

Robertson County was formed in 1867 from parts of Bracken, Nicholas, Fleming, Mason, and Harrison counties and was named for Judge George Robertson, an able lawyer and patriot of the trying days of 1864, who was elected Judge of the Court of Appeals that year. Area, 101 square miles. Population, 3,419.

ROCKCASTLE, Mt. Vernon

Rockcastle County was formed in 1809-10 from parts of Lincoln, Pulaski, Madison, and Knox counties and was named for the river of the same name. The river was named for a large, natural rock castle on the Laurel County side, two miles northeast of Livingston. Area, 312 square miles. Population, 17,165.

ROWAN, Morehead

Rowan County was formed in 1856 from parts of Fleming and Morgan counties and named for Judge John Rowan, an able Senator and jurist, who was entangled with the troubles that grew out of Kentucky's two Supreme Courts of 1825, the Old Court and the New Court. Area, 290 square miles. Population, 12,733.

RUSSELL, Jamestown

Russell County was formed in 1825 from parts of Wayne, Cumberland, and Adair counties and named for Col. William Russell, an able lawyer and an Indian fighter of the pioneer days of that territory. Area, 282 square miles. Population, 13,615.

SCOTT, Georgetown

Scott County was formed in 1792 from part of Woodford County and named for Gen. Charles Scott, a commander of the Revolutionary War. He was an Indian fighter of 1791, and destroyed the Wabash Tribe before St. Clair's defeat. He was later elected Governor of Kentucky, 1808. Area, 284 square miles. Population, 14,314.

SHELBY, Shelbyville

Shelby County was formed in 1792 from part of Jefferson County and named for Isaac Shelby, commander at Point Pleasant; King's Mountain, 1780; helped frame the first Kentucky Constitution; was first and fifth Governor of Kentucky; Commissioner who purchased the eight counties of the state lying next to the Mississippi River from the Chickasaw Indians, 1818. Area, 384 square miles. Population, 17,750.

SIMPSON, *Franklin*

Simpson County was formed in 1819 from parts of Logan, Warren, and Allen counties and was named for Capt. John Simpson, who fell in action at the battle of the Raisin, 1813. Area, 239 square miles. Population, 11,753.

SPENCER, *Taylorsville*

Spencer County was formed in 1824 from parts of Nelson, Shelby, and Bullitt counties and was named for Capt. Spear Spencer, who commanded his men while lying wounded on the ground at the battle of Tippecanoe, 1811, where death soon followed. Area, 193 square miles. Population, 6,758.

TAYLOR, *Campbellsville*

Taylor County was formed in 1848 from a part of Green County and was named for Gen. Zachary Taylor who, with the exception of the first nine months, spent his life in Kentucky. He fought in the Mexican war, driving the Mexicans out of the state of Texas, 1846; capturing Monterey the same year; defeating 20,000 Mexicans at Buena Vista, 1847, winning the title of "Old Rough and Ready"; was elected President 1849, and died the following year. Area, 284 square miles. Population, 13,556.

TODD, *Elkton*

Todd County was formed in 1819 from parts of Logan and Christian counties and named for Capt. John Todd, who was one of the pioneers of 1773 who came into Kentucky to locate bounty lands for the Virginia soldiers. When Virginia divided the state into three counties, John Todd was made Colonel in command of Fayette County Militia. He was one of the 70 officers killed at the Indian battle of Blue Lick, 1782. Area, 377 square miles. Population, 14,234.

TRIGG, *Cadiz*

Trigg County was formed in 1820 from parts of Christian and Caldwell counties and named for Col. James Trigg who was another of the officers who fell at the battle of the Blue Lick, 1782. Area, 466 square miles. Population, 12,784.

TRIMBLE, *Bedford*

Trimble County was formed in 1836 from Oldham, Henry, and Gallatin counties and was named for Robert Trimble, Judge of the Supreme Court. Area, 146 square miles. Population, 5,601.

UNION, *Morganfield*

Union County was formed in 1811 from Henderson County and named in honor of the United States, according to one theory; the other is that its name tells of the unanimous feeling for its formation. Area, 343 square miles. Population, 17,411.

WARREN, *Bowling Green*

Warren County was formed in 1796 from Logan County and named for Gen. Joseph Warren, who was among the last to leave Bunker Hill at the end of the third charge when the American ammunition became exhausted at the moment of victory. He was buried on the spot where he fell. Area, 546 square miles. Population, 36,631.

WASHINGTON, *Springfield*

Washington County was formed in 1792 from Nelson County and named in honor of George Washington, it being the first land named for the first President after the admission of Kentucky. Area, 317 square miles. Population, 12,965.

WAYNE, *Monticello*

Wayne County was formed in 1800 from Pulaski and Cumberland counties and named for Gen. Anthony Wayne, called "Mad Anthony," who marched his army against the border Indians north of Cincinnati, in 1794 and drove them from the Northwest Territory for good, thus ending a 40-year Indian struggle for Kentucky. Area, 485 square miles. Population, 17,204.

WEBSTER, *Dixon*

Webster County was formed in 1860 from parts of Hopkins, Union, and Henderson counties and was named for Daniel Webster, the great American statesman and jurist, whose name stands at the top of the list of American orators. Area, 339 square miles. Population, 19,198.

WHITLEY, *Williamsburg*

Whitley County was formed in 1818 from part of Knox County and named for Col. William Whitley, the brave leader in the battle of the Thames, 86 miles northeast of Detroit, Michigan, where he lost his life. It is claimed by some authorities that Whitley was the slayer of Tecumseh here instead of Johnson. Area, 460 square miles. Population, 33,190.

WOLFE, *Campton*

Wolfe County was formed from Morgan, Owsley, Breathitt, and Powell counties in 1860 and was named for Nathaniel Wolfe, who served in the State Senate and House of Representatives, being in the Senate at the time the county was formed. Area, 227 square miles. Population 9,997.

WOODFORD, *Versailles*

Woodford County was formed in 1788 from part of Fayette County, while Kentucky was still a part of Virginia. It got its name from Gen. William Woodford, a Revolutionary officer. Area, 193 square miles. Population, 11,847.

CHAPTER 24

MISCELLANY

RUBBER

Rubber was known to the barbarians centuries ago. It is procured from the rubber tree, which grows in the tropical countries, such as the West Indies, East Indies, Central America, and the extreme southern part of the United States. In its natural form it is white juice beneath the bark—not sap. When Columbus discovered Haiti, one of the West Indies, 1492, he found the little Indian boys playing with crude rubber balls. They had developed crude bottles and shoes also from rubber.

White settlers learned that a medium sized rubber tree would supply about 12 pounds of rubber. This was obtained by cutting down the tree and extracting its whole store at once. But after experimenting they learned that they had been "killing the goose that laid the golden egg," so thereafter the rubber was obtained by tapping the trees while standing.

Centuries elapsed, with the rubber trees growing in all the hot regions of earth, before man's attention was called to any use to which the "sticky stuff" could be applied. As those regions are visited by torrential downpours of rain each year, it was discovered by the Spaniards of Mexico in 1615 that by rubbing this gum over their coats and hats that they were made impenetrable to water. During the next one hundred and fifty years little experimenting followed, until Priestly, an English scientist, in 1770 discovered that it would erase pencil marks. After this discovery, each business man carried a little piece of this "rubber" in his pocket to erase mistakes—hence its name. Before this it was called gum or "caoutchouc."

Another half century rolled by with all the civilized nations experimenting, believing that something yet could be wrought. So in 1820, another scientist converted rubber into elastic threads called "gumbo." Three years later this gumbo was woven into cloth scraps and used as garters, gallowses, and in different webbings.

About 1840 an American while experimenting with the "sticky stuff" accidentally dropped a few drops onto a red-hot stove and to his dismay and good fortune discovered what we call "vulcanized rubber." This marked an epoch in the rubber industry. Thus Charles Goodyear became the rubber champion of the world. Four years later he received his patent. South America, the natural cradle of rubber, was experimenting with it, so in 1852 Brazil shipped to a company in Boston, Massachusetts, 500 pairs of rubber shoes. They were made by running the rubber on a coat of wool which had been shaped to the human foot. These were to be worn as overshoes and sold for $4.00 and $5.00 a pair.

Coats that men could wear were made in 1875, and by 1880 Charles McIntosh of Scotland had created such excitement with his coat that it found ready markets in all the civilized countries of the Eastern and Western hemispheres. The first make of these coats were far from perfection.

In wearing these first coats a horseman had to be very careful not to let his coat slip between him and his saddle while riding, or else dismounting would be difficult. The coats thus made would stick together if not hung up carefully. Really they would catch bugs and flies.

In 1845, Robert W. Thompson, an Englishman, patented the rubber-tired buggy. This tire consisted of a roll of rubber about an inch in diameter, (which later had a small wire running through its center for the full length) and it was glued to the concave wooden rim of the wheels. This caused a smooth glide over the poorly constructed roads, and only the members of the most prosperous and dignified families were seen perched in this type of vehicle.

The dawn of the twentieth century almost wrought miracles in the rubber industry. The coming of the automobile then stimulated the industry far beyond all other forces combined.

The scarcity of rubber over the world suggested the idea of pneumatic tires; so in the year 1847 American scientists began to experiment, but it was not until 1880 that Dunlop brought the pneumatic tire into use, and since 1888 it has been in constant demand.

Three-fourths of all the rubber of the world is consumed by the United States annually. Severing of trade relations between our country and Japan in World War II, which country furnishes ninety per cent of the raw rubber of the world, threatened a rubber panic, but the developing of new districts in South America helped relieve the shortage.

The first "rubbers" to reach Cumberland County were the tiny tips on lead pencils. Combs came next, especially the old-time tucking combs, some of which are known to be over 100 years old, and were used by the ladies who had never dreamed of bobbed hair. Goodyear supplied the world with hundreds of rubber articles before his death in 1860.

The first rubber shoes to reach this county were the ones, 1875, worn by W. Godfrey Hunter in his race for Representative that year. They were more of an overshoe. His opponents called him "Gum Shoe Hunter." Then in the late 1880's G. B. McGee and Brother sold them.

Horace K. Alexander in 1885 brought the first rubber-tired buggy to Cumberland County. For the next 25 years these easy-going vehicles were common means of travel among the moneyed men, which brought the smell of rubber to several homes. The coming of the automobile with the twentieth century has poured more rubber into the county than all the other quarter-million uses to which it is now put. Rubber boots were brought into the county, and farmers found them to be the things long wished for in times of sloppy weather around the premises. Coats, umbrellas, gloves, water bottles, are some of the common home uses of rubber.

Synthetic rubber made of grain and petroleum is coming into production and will grow into more usefulness.

ELECTRICITY

Electricity is thought by some to be a recent discovery, yet its existence was known in medieval days. Until it was harnessed about one-half century ago, it was of little importance to man. It was not until the second quarter of the nineteenth century that electricity was lassoed sufficiently to be a servant to man, though Europe and America both had produced men who gave their lives and fortunes in trying to discover what it was and where it came from. Benjamin Franklin belongs to the American group who revealed some of its hidden mysteries.

The first great pioneer of the electrical world was Samuel F. B. Morris of Massachusetts. He had spent his time and means to the despondent bend in the road, when Congress stepped in and lent a helping hand to him, which gave to the world its first 30 miles of electric telegraph, 1844. Two years after that an American who had been studying and working in England on an electric light secured a patent from the English Government, 1846, named for him—Starr's Light. This was 20 years after the first use of kerosene as an illuminant; 24 years after the first use of gas as an illuminant, and 12 before Cyrus W. Field tied England and America together with his electric cable, over which the Queen of England and President Polk exchanged messages.

At the Philadelphia Centennial in 1876 Alexander Graham Bell demonstrated to the world the first telephone. At that same time two electric lights were put on exhibition at the fair with little effect. But one year after Starr's light "shed its weak glow," a little boy was born in Ohio, whose life revolutionized the world in the electric field. He was Thomas A. Edison. At the age of 16 we find him completely wrapped up in the study of electricity.

In 1878 the world was astonished to learn that a machine had been made that could talk and sing, as men talk and sing. Only those who saw and heard believed. Like Thomas of old, the "thrust of fingers" made believers. This machine was the phonograph.

Among the more than two thousand inventions by Mr. Edison, the most outstanding one is the incandescent light and its accessories. He worked from 1878 to 1882 on the bulb before it was perfected. The bulb would go for a while then perish. He tried many different fibers to maintain the glow inside but all failed; finally he fell on a metal called "tungsten" which, when placed in the light, would endure a heat of 6,150 degrees Fahrenheit. This rewarded him for all his troubles. Thus it has come to all our homes.

Electricity was hard to keep in store, and Edison believed it possible to construct a machine that would generate electricity. His fruit along this line was the modern dynamo; but before he could put it into operation there were 375 accessories to it that had to be thought out and patented.

When he had his dynamo ready for testing, he placed 400 bulbs in that many different places in New York City, and on September 5, 1882, the current was turned on, and all the people of the city experienced a new day, reminding them of the story of creation when "darkness was upon the face of the deep" before God spoke his all-powerful word, "Let there be light," and there was Light.

City after city and town after town began to tear down their old kerosene lamp poles and replace them with electric lamp bulbs. The new dawn spread from east to west and from north to south.

The first light to be offered to the public was the arc light. This light was used on steamboats and in apartments in the 1880's, as superseding the pine knots and kerosene lights, but too flickering for street lights. It was used first in Kentucky at Louisville in stores, 1883. First incandescent light in that city was on the Tower at Fourth and Water streets in the year 1890.

In Cumberland County

Electricity for local use had its beginning in Cumberland County in 1913. The plant was established on River Street, with a D. C. current. In 1926, Less McComas took over the plant, which operated in the Burkesville Garage, and on January 28, 1929, new units were added by him, making an A. C. current. A well equipped dynamo was put into action by him and operated until the summer of 1940, when the Public Utility Company was dissolved and superseded by the R.E.A.

At the time of the dissolution of this company it was furnishing electricity to Burkesville, Marrowbone, Tompkinsville, Waterview, Summershade, and Edmonton.

AUTOMOBILES

The word "auto" means "self acting." When we think of the automobile, the word "Ford" is suggested to us next. Some people think by this that Henry Ford was the originator of the vehicle, because the millions of cars turned out from his factories have found their way to the remotest sections of our country, the sales of which have made him close to a billionaire.

In checking closely the development of self-going vehicles, we find inventors in England having them to move by the power of steam sixty-four years before Mr. Ford began to manufacture them, and in the same country electric autos were made that would go twenty years prior to Mr. Ford's first car. The English government failed to see the fortunes to be realized from this kind of wagon as shown by her stringent laws passed, 1861 to 1896, which forbade speeding over four miles per hour. This drove the business from that country to this. In 1894-5, France gave prizes to the fastest speeders. Fifteen miles won the prize on many races. The first auto in Chicago, 1895, ran seven miles per hour.

While France was contesting these races, an American inventor was constructing his combustion car. This was George B. Seldon, who received his patent for a gas engine motor car in 1895. In 1896, Ford began to turn out cars as the head manager of a certain company. An organization was effected, known as the Association of Auto Manufacturers, whose intention was to monopolize the business while in its cradle. This monopoly required a royalty from all manufacturers of cars—or else quit the business. In 1904, Ford placed it in the courts and seven years' expensive litigation ensued, with Ford and his company winning. This decision brought the auto business to our own country, which has revolutionized every other business both in war and peace times.

At the beginning of World War I the United States had 4,000,-000 automobiles; at the beginning of War II, 27,000,000. On the corresponding dates, Cumberland County had 180 and 869. The automobile has been the means of bringing good roads, and has added thousands of other comforts to the traveling people.

FENCES

Primitive man was confronted with two perplexing problems—one was how to prevent wild beasts from destroying his food and crops, and the other was how to curb the roving disposition of his domestic animals and fowls. Hence, the invention of some kind of fence was the only solution.

The utilization of natural products was the first resort. Where rocks were available they were used to make the fence, some were fitted together, and where they were boulder shaped then they were piled up into heaps four or five feet high around the fields and gardens.

Then came the wooden fence. With the timber cut from the clearings, rails were made which were about ten feet long and were placed in a zigzag line, consuming about five feet of land. There were three different styles of rail fences with posts that preceded the iron fence.

Iron fencing, like other inventions and discoveries, was begun in a simple and crude manner. The iron fence is an American invention. Samuel Freeman in 1859 made the first smooth wire fence in Iowa, but it proved of such little value that in 1861 his son twisted "stickers" on it which was "very effective"! This was the first wire fence, but neither of the two men applied for patent. In the years 1867-8 five patents were granted to that many different men for "thorny fence wire." There were 24 different makes of barbed wire in the United States, and most of them found their way to Cumberland County, pieces of which may still be seen; but the one with which we are now familiar was invented in 1874 when five miles of it were made in America. From this date until 1883 thousands of miles of this fence were made and used as the only iron fence, at which latter date the modern woven wire fence was first made. Two reasons prompted its invention, one was the continued lawsuits against the manufacturers of the barbed wire fences for having made and sold to the people a fence that was "cruel and inhuman," and the other was the waste of land by wooden fences.

The first woven wire was put up by stretching the smooth wires on the posts and then twisting the stays by hand at a proper distance, with a little tool made for that purpose. But soon it was woven by machinery.

In Cumberland County timber was abundant and wooden fences were about all one could see until about 1885 when a barbed-wire fever struck this county and lasted till 1906, when woven wire replaced it and has held the farms and fields apart ever since.

Old chestnut, poplar, oak, walnut, and cedar rails, which are known to be from 60 to 80 years old, can be seen yet in use in the county.

Barbed wire fences made of large size wire put up in the early 90's of the last century, though rusty, are still in service in some parts of the county. The life of woven wire is about 40 years.

SUPERSTITIONS

After more than two thousand years have rolled by since the days of apparition, there are yet to be found in this county, and I suppose the same is true in other counties, communities where the people still believe in haunts and witches. These people are also inconvincible but that things must be done when the "sign is right." Superstition is very difficult to breed out of people, because that ancestral story was related with such force and seriousness that it has found an indelible lodging from generation to generation. The death of a progenitor only strengthens the belief in the progeny.

Some fragments of superstition are listed here which many people take seriously:

A baby will have the disposition of the one carrying it on its first outing. Corn must be planted when the moon is dark, else tall stalks and no ears will result. Beans must be planted in "the sign," else the blossoms will all fall off. Calves must be weaned in "the sign," else they will bawl their lives away. If forced to turn back on a trip, make cross in the middle of the road and spit in it, else bad luck follows. If a hen crows, cut her head off immediately or there will be a death in the family at once. If forced to abandon your sweeping before completed, do not pass the broom to another, let him pick it up, or bad luck follows. Do not suffer another to use a pin you have used, else bad luck will come to both. Do not own 13 of anything, it is very unlucky. Do not move a broom to another house with you. Very serious consequences to one who kills a cat. If a person is drowned, spread his shirt on the bosom of the stream and watch it go to him and sink. If the moon is tilted, the water is out and drought is ahead—people who argue this and witness its failure still contend it never fails. If it is storming while you eat, chew on the right side or there is danger from thunder. Evergreens set out by you bring sure death to you if permitted to grow large enough to shade your grave.

Two persons should never sweep the same room at the same time. An unmarried lady should never step over a broom if she aims to get a husband later. (Seems that the broom is an unlucky utensil.) Sneeze before breakfast, you hear of a death before the week ends. A dog sleeping on his back with paws drawn in is a sign of death, and his tail tells the direction of the one to die. A dog sitting in the open, howling, is only making music unless under your window, then listen for news of someone dying. A clock striking odd when it should be even is sign of death. Drop a dishrag, someone is coming; drop a spoon the guest will be young; drop a fork, a man; drop a knife your visitor will be a woman.

Hogs with weeds in their mouth are a sign of cold weather. Don't watch a loved one through the window until he goes out of sight; if you do, he'll never return. If a baby says "daddy" first, Junior will follow. Hair combed after dark brings sorrow. Don't mend your dress while on, for the stitches will tell the number of lies to be told on you.

One day the County Judge of this county delayed court on account of the tardiness of one of the Magistrates. Just before noon he came in, all drabbled and fatigued. Being asked the cause of his tardiness, he replied, "Ten miles is a long way to walk." When asked if he could not have caught a ride in a car, he said: "I started in one, but two miles from home a black cat ran across the road, and I'm in no more cars today."

A few more omens are: Don't refuse the request of a widow, it is bad luck. Dreams occurring in a strange bed become true if told before breakfast. Accumulations of husbands and wives will be meager until their wedding clothes are worn out. New babies, to be fortunate, should be wrapped in old or borrowed clothes. Children weaned while fruit trees are in bloom have gray hair early. Sing before breakfast, cry before supper. Itching stomachs foretell good news.

OUR MONTHS

The history of our months is a long and complicated story if traced from the beginning. Not a month in the Bible has the name of our present month. Before Christ there were only ten months in the year as used by the Roman Calendar. About the time of the birth of Christ the calendar was reformed. The year had previously started with March. The last four months of our calendar still retain their original names as taken from Roman numerals. Some months derived their names from paganism.

JANUARY derived its name from Janus, the Latin god of beginnings, which had two faces, one looking backward, the other forward. January first had 30 days. Julius Caesar gave it 31.

FEBRUARY was named from Latin Februa, feast of purification, held on February 15. It once had 30 days.

MARCH. This was the first month of the year until Julius Caesar put it third. Named from Mars.

APRIL. This month got its name from a Latin word meaning "to open," referring to the buds and flowers.

MAY. This month was named from the Roman Goddess of Spring, Maia. It was dedicated to the old men.

JUNE. This month was named from a Latin word, *junius*. June has had at different times 26, 30, 29, and 30 days.

JULY. This month was called "Quintillis," meaning "five," until Julius Caesar honored himself by naming it for himself because his birthday fell in it. At the same time he stole one day from February to make it 31.

AUGUST. This month was first called "Sextillis," meaning "six." Augustus Caesar strove to be equal to Julius, so he honored himself by calling the month "August," and he also stole one day from February.

SEPTEMBER, named from the Latin word, *Septem*, meaning "seven." Before the reform it was the seventh month, but the Caesars placed January and February before it, which accounts for the names of the remaining three months—*Octo* (8); *Novem* (9); *Decem* (10), before the change.

OCTOBER has 31 days.

NOVEMBER has had 31, 29, 31, and 30 days.

DECEMBER has had 29 and 31 days.

Miscellany

ORIGIN OF DAYS OF NOTE

Valentine

Named for Saint Valentine, a Roman saint, killed February 14, 306 A.D. The day was celebrated annually by old and young. The youngsters got to writing the names of the girls attending and shuffling them to be drawn by the young men who were obligated, or required, to claim the girl drawn as his "valentine" for one year. From this grew the custom of writing love letters and love cards on this day.

St. Patrick

Saint Patrick, an Irish saint, was born March 17, 396 A.D. He was a great church saint, having founded 360 churches during his life and with his own hands baptized over 12,000 converts. It is an Irish day.

All Fools' Day

All Fools' Day dates from the Middle Ages. It began by holding ludicrous feasts where everyone attending was supposed to prank with each other. Children kept the custom going. A few ignorant ones have not yet learned the difference between a "merry trick," which all were then allowed to play, and an injury to property.

May Day

This is a continuation of the old custom of crowning a girl "Queen" on the first of May.

Mother's Day

Mother's Day was first suggested by Miss Annie Jarvis, of Pennsylvania, and in 1914 the President set aside the second Sunday in May to show honor to the mothers of our land, a red flower for the living, a white one for the mother gone.

Memorial Day

Decoration Day originated in the Southern states soon after the Civil War by the scattering of flowers on a few soldiers' graves. April 26 was first observed, but now it has been set for May 30. It is a day when people visit the last resting places of their loved ones, as well as soldiers, and decorate them with flowers.

Flag Day

June 14 is Flag Day, commemorating the birthday of the Stars and Stripes, as adopted by Congress June 14, 1777.

Independence Day

July 4 tells of the birthday of our country, July 4, 1776.

Labor Day

This day dates back to 1882 in sections of the United States, but in Kentucky to 1902. It is observed on the first Monday in September.

Columbus Day

October 12 is Columbus Day, commemorating the day on which Columbus discovered America in 1492.

Halloween

This means "holy even." To understand this day you will have to step up one day from Halloween Day of October 31. In remote times there were so many saints for which a day was set aside that the Christian nations decided to fix one day for All Saints. So November 1 was fixed in the year 835 to show honor to all saints. The superstitious people believed that on the evening previous to this day of November 1 all saints, good and bad, were walking up and down the earth in spirit. Hence the dusk of October 31, a spooky time.

Armistice Day

The First World War closed on November 11, 1918. This was a day of great rejoicing to all the world, when sons living could return home. Bells were rung in this county and guns were fired by nearly all people.

Thanksgiving

The Pilgrim Fathers met in the little church at Plymouth, Massachusetts, in 1621 to give thanks to God for the first crop of food raised on American soil. Different days have been used, usually in November. In 1864 Lincoln suggested the last Thursday in November and this has been generally followed.

Christmas Day

December 25 is the greatest day of all, celebrating Christ's birthday.

Easter

Easter is a movable day. It shifts from March 22 to April 25. It commemorates the resurrection of Jesus from the grave. In the year 325 Constantine called the Council of Nice in Asia Minor to settle a number of church controversies. Easter was one of them. It was fixed to fall on the first Sunday after the first full moon occuring on or after March 21.

Other Days

Good Friday is the day of the crucifixion, observed on the Friday preceding Easter. Lent is the last 40 days before Easter. Palm Sunday is the last Sunday before Easter, the day on which Jesus rode into Jerusalem. The other church days are based on Easter.

WHAT IS HOME?

What is home? It is a place of rest; a place of refuge; a place of love; a place of joy; a place where the birds sing the sweetest, the fruit grows the fondest, the air floats the purest, the heart feels the freest, and love reigns supremest. Its influence is stronger than death. Home is the child's paradise. It is all the world to him, he knows no other. After his first two years of unrelenting sovereignty he becomes the sacred tie that binds the hearts of father and mother into one—the mediator of purest love and divine guidance.

Ask the frosted, wayworn traveler, whose shoulders are bent with years and whose brow is deeply furrowed with care, what home is, and he will tell you it is the greenest spot in memory, an oasis in the desert of life, and the nucleus around which the fondest recollections cling with all the tenacity of youth's first love; a place that touches every chord of the soul and twangs with its angelic fingers the harp of life eternal.

A few years ago twenty thousand people gathered in the great City of New York to hear Jennie Lind sing. The sublimest songs were handed her from all the great song writers of the world in hope of winning. With a brief glance she gently folded them, placed them by her side and then with an elevated look, began in deepest emotion to pour out "Home, Sweet Home." The audience could not stand it. A shout of applause drowned the music. A gush of tears burst forth from the eyes of twenty thousand people like the falling rain.

John Howard Payne, the author, triumphed over all other great song writers of the known world. Why so great a reputation from so simple a song? Because, next to God and Heaven, the heart vibrates to that sweet sacred theme—"Home."

Home is the place where character is formed. It is a place where God should dwell. Deaf to the calls of future life, we are all trained in the home to meet the responsibilities ahead. Duties may call us to distant lands, disappointments may upset our yearnings, pitfalls may obstruct our pathway, and misfortunes may blight our ambitions, but at the close of each day we can quietly retire to that place called home and have our courage renewed.

All time past has proved that the home of our childhood holds the most sacred spot in the human heart. Even the lower animals cherish a place called home. No school boy or girl can ever read, "How dear to my heart are the scenes of my childhood," and fail to feel its sublimity; for it will again cause us to be borne on the wings of our imagination to that place made sacred by a father's smile, a mother's love, and the happy association of brothers and sisters. When we have come down near the close, the intervening years will have failed to dim the coloring with which memory adorned those joyous hours of youthful innocence.

GOVERNORS OF KENTUCKY

Isaac Shelby	1792-1796
James Garrard	1796-1804
Christopher Greenup	1804-1808
Charles Scott	1808-1812
Isaac Shelby	1812-1816
George Madison	1816
Gabriel Slaughter	1816-1820
John Adair	1820-1824
Joseph Desha	1824-1828
Thomas Metcalfe	1828-1832
John Breathitt	1832-1834
James T. Morehead	1834-1836
James Clark	1836
Charles A. Wickliffe	1836-1840
Robert P. Letcher	1840-1844
William Owsley	1844-1848
John J. Crittenden	1848-1850
John L. Helm	1850-1851
Lazarus Powell	1851-1855
Charles S. Morehead	1855-1859
Beriah Magoffin (Resigned)	1859-1862
James F. Robinson (Acting)	1862-1863
Thomas E. Bramlett	1863-1867
John L. Helm	1867
John W. Stephenson	1867-1871
Preston H. Leslie	1871-1875
James B. McCreary	1875-1879
Luke P. Blackburn	1879-1883
J. Proctor Knott	1883-1887
Simon B. Buckner	1887-1891
John Young Brown	1891-1895
William O. Bradley	1895-1899
William S. Taylor (41 days)	1899-1900
William Goebel (4 days)	1900
J. C. W. Beckham	1900-1907
Augustus E. Wilson	1907-1911
James B. McCreary	1911-1915
A. O. Stanley	1915-1919
James D. Black	1919
Edwin P. Morrow	1919-1923
William J. Fields	1923-1926
Flem D. Samson	1927-1931
Ruby Laffoon	1931-1935
Albert B. Chandler	1935-1939
Keen Johnson	1940-1943
Simeon Willis	1944-1947

Miscellany

48 STATES AND NUMBER OF COUNTIES IN EACH

States	Counties	States	Counties
Alabama	67	Nebraska	93
Arizona	14	Nevada	17
Arkansas	75	New Hampshire	10
California	58	New Jersey	21
Colorado	63	New Mexico	31
Connecticut	8	New York	62
Delaware	3	North Carolina	100
Florida	67	North Dakota	53
Georgia	159	Ohio	88
Idaho	44	Oklahoma	77
Illinois	102	Oregon	36
Indiana	92	Pennsylvania	67
Iowa	99	Rhode Island	5
Kansas	105	South Carolina	46
Kentucky	120	South Dakota	69
Louisiana	64	Tennessee	95
Maine	16	Texas	254
Maryland	24	Utah	29
Massachusetts	14	Vermont	14
Michigan	83	Virginia	100
Minnesota	87	Washington	39
Mississippi	82	West Virginia	55
Missouri	115	Wisconsin	71
Montana	56	Wyoming	24

COUNTIES OF ENGLAND

Beginning at the North

Northumberland	Northampton	Thames
Cumberland	Rutland	Hereford
Chester or Cheshire	Warwick	Buckingham
Westmorland	Gloucester	Sussex
Durham	Huntingdon	Hampshire
Lancaster	Monmouth	Berkshire
Yorkshire	Worcester	Bedford
Derby	Somerset	Devon
Salop or Shropshire	Middlesex ⎫ London	Oxford
Denbigh	Essex ⎬ is in	Wilts
Flint	Surrey ⎬ these	Montgomery
Nottingham	Kent ⎭ four	Cambridge
Lincoln	Suffolk	Stafford
Leicester		Dorset

POTPOURRI

Mammoth Cave was discovered in 1799.

Milton King brought the first blooded horses to Cumberland County, 1818. He came through Cumberland Gap.

First free schools of record taught in the county by Reuben Hicks at Bow in 1849. J. G. Bow taught at Bow, 1869, 65 days for $65.

Teacher's library first at Burkesville, 1896.

First tan yard at Burkesville, Kentucky, on sight of Burkesville Garage, 1845-61, by Harold Sauffley. A Mr. Tutt also operated one on Celina Street.

Hemp rope factory in Burkesville, 1812.

Locust year, 1940; full time, May 25 to June 25. Every seventeen years.

Second Great Revival swept Kentucky, 1826-9. Also this county.

Hopkinsville Insane Asylum for this district established 1848.

First Governor to get Negro votes was Preston Leslie, Cumberland County, in 1871.

In 1850 Kentucky had 982,405 whites; 200,000 blacks.

During one month in 1864, Cumberland County was forced to sell all her hogs to the Government at a loss of $5.00 per head.

In 1875-85 hog cholera completely barred shipment to market.

On August 7, 1869, occurred a total eclipse of the sun, covering this county. Chickens went to roost at middle of the afternoon.

In 1940 there were 2,779 dwellings in the county; 154 unoccupied.

Jenny Etter distributed 50 orphans over this county in 1932, from the Orphans' Home, Louisville.

In August, 1940, Mr. Russak and Mr. and Mrs. Cleveland of Washington, D. C., brought first song recording machine to the county.

May 9, 1939, a large crowd from this county went to Columbia, Kentucky, to see Robert Wadlow, the tallest man in the world. Height, 8 feet 10.3 inches; weight 491 pounds; age, 21 years; shoes, No. 39, cost $85.00. He died July 15, 1940.

Verner Hurt brought the first rubber shoes to Irish Bottom in 1916. Being used to leather ones, he almost leveled his arch the first time he kicked his cow, so says he.

First wagon road from Virginia to this state in 1794.

In 1899, February 12, the Government thermometer at Marrowbone, Kentucky, registered 30 below zero.

Kentucky has had eight capitols; four temporary, four permanent: 1792, log, Lexington; 1793, frame, Frankfort; 1794, frame; 1814, rented wooden house; 1816, two-story brick; 1825, Methodist Church House; 1829, Old Capitol, brick; 1909, new one.

Coal discovered in Kentucky, 1805. First salt, 1778.

Aside from human life, the biggest loss resulting from the kick of a cow was that of 1871, when Mrs. O'Leary's cow kicked over her lantern, causing a loss of $200,000,000 in Chicago.

Miscellany 317

The first telephone in this county was stretched from Albany to Burkesville in 1884. Much excitement and many exaggerated yarns were told about it. One youngster paid a visit to the line and reported to the other lads of the time that every bird that alighted upon the wire while in use, was instantly killed by the "lightning." A crowd collected to go and see this contrivance so cruel to the fledgy family, but were warned by older people not to get too close to it. A search proved the falsity of the report, but yet no one dared touch the "thing." In 1891, the wire, posts, and boxes were torn down and sold for $22.00.

Cumberland County Fair Association, 1906. Cost of ground $644.

Capt. J. T. McLain buried on top of Big Hill. (Was in Civil War.) Said that was close enough to heaven.

In 1940 there were 285 babies born in Cumberland County—275 white, 10 Negro. The same year 97 people died in the county; 22 from heart trouble; 11 from Tuberculosis; balance from various diseases. There were nine doctors and 57 midwives. In 1944 death and war calls reduced the number of doctors to three.

The three wholesale houses—Joe N. Booher, Allen Waggener, and Gillan Baker—sold $313,000 worth of goods in 1940.

Bean Short, Civil War guerrilla, was killed at Blacks Ferry. He killed Marion Cary and Willie Stockton in the county.

Government report places the prospect of oil in Cumberland County above that of any other small center in the United States, 1882.

An Italian invented the piano, 1711.

Three "war babies" were born per minute in 1942 in the United States.

Lincoln pennies first put in circulation in 1909, one century after his birth.

Save your calendars for 28 years and find the days of the year and week coinciding.

From 1910 to 1940, 22 people were drowned in Cumberland County and eight killed in car wrecks.

In 1890 the 7th Judicial District covered Adair, Barren, Clinton, Cumberland, Green, Hart, Metcalfe, Monroe counties, D. R. Carr, Judge.

S. A. Healy contracted to build Wolf Creek Dam, six miles from Cumberland County, July 8, 1941; bid, $15,803,890. Shut down, 1942; resumed, March, 1946, by Wright and Jones Co., of Georgia; $18,395,-934.50. Appropriations were made later.

In 1835 cholera swept Kentucky; 47 died at Greensburg. In and around Cumberland County it appeared in 1832, 1849, 1855, 1866, and 1873. In 1853, three-fourths of the population of Glasgow died.

Back of 1840, bar-share and wooden moldboard turners were used.

"America" was the anthem of United States until 1931, when Congress made the "Star-Spangled Banner" the national anthem.

In 1935 airplane views began. By 1943 every man in Cumberland County had the picture view of his farm.

One extreme usually follows another; 1881 drouth, 1883-4 floods; 1885 drouth, etc.

The Muscle Shoals Dam in Alabama, which wields its influence over this county is on the Tennessee River, begun 1917. It is 4,152 feet long; 98 feet high.

Moses Ferguson, old-time dentist of Lawson Bottom, got his forceps from General Zollicoffer's wife, who was visiting her relatives in Lawson Bottom at the close of the Civil War; they are now in the hands of A. M. Ferguson, Burkesville, Kentucky.

First through truck line from Burkesville to Louisville was begun by Paul A. Davis, 1936; run later by his brother, Hall (Babe).

Writing materials were first stone, then wax, bark, and paper. Writing instruments were stencils in ancient times; quills to 1803; steel attached to small bottles for reservoir; thin steel unslit 1820; modern steel pens then came into use, first in 1830; fountain pens, 1878. Old Cumberland County records were penned with the feather quill first quarter century and many records show the size of the bottle fountain. Typewriter was invented, 1867; used in Cumberland County first by J. O. Ewing, 1895.

In 1827 the first friction match was invented by John Walker, an English druggist. Made of chlorate of potash, sugar, and gum arabic. Sandpaper had to be kept, through which the match was drawn quickly for ignition. In 1831 the old yellowhead, which many of us remember, was made by Charles Sauria. This match could be ignited from side or tip. This was the first make to reach Cumberland County. They sold for 25 cents per dozen at first. Research shows first sold by W. F. Owsley, Burkesville, 1844; Lewis T. Warriner, Creelsboro, 1841. A number of lads gathered at an old gate in Wells' Bottom one summer day in 1852 and paid a small fee to see one "struck to fire." In 1906 the safety match was agreed upon by an international convention in Switzerland. Prior to World War II, the United States alone used 480 billion annually. The necessity of explosives during the war reduced the number. A sale of 1858 shows matches selling at 80 cents per box at two different sales.

The first houses of Cumberland County were made of logs covered with grass. None of these are standing today. Next came a brick wave, which covered a period from 1805 to 1830. Many of these are still standing, and others still mark the places of their existence. Two on Little Renox have dates and are in good condition as homes, bearing date 1814. The John E. King home, north of Burkesville, owned now by the Cheeks, has date on chimney, 1822. Along with this brick wave went the hewed log house, many of which are still standing in the county. They were put together with wooden pegs and square nails. The wrought nail was in use here for a short time, for the heading machine was made in 1810, which cut nails from sheets of iron and headed them at the rate of 100 per minute. Wooden buildings were held together with these until the wire nail came into the county in 1892. Ten miles of wire lasts only one hour in making wire nails. The firm of Eston & Janes brought the first wire nails, February, 1892.

Bourbon Stock Yards, Louisville, Kentucky, which means so much to Cumberland County's livestock shippers, was established in 1834.

In 1830 John Dougherty, of Marrowbone, jugged 4 gallons of honey to be kept until he married. He died a bachelor, so it was divided among his nieces and nephews. Mrs. Jesse Coe, of Burkesville, one of his nieces, still has her quart, 1945, and it is as sweet as in John's day.

Wiley F. Boulden, of Burkesville, Kentucky, is in possession of a letter dated June 22, 1838, written in England by Mary Harding to her father in America telling of the "deplorable condition of the times but that business is improving at present due to the preparation for the Coronation of our Queen Victoria, June 28th, when a public dinner will be given free at every home." She says that one-third of the people in the pottery business are starving to death and that the winter has been very severe. She further says: "A division among the Methodists has taken place but that each branch has large congregations; that Abraham Drugart has left Land's End with a young girl for America, leaving his wife and 7 children, but in good circumstances; also that John Harding still drinks as much as ever."

In 1924 the Legislature added the Bible to the school requirements, that it be read each morning in all free schools. Ninety per cent of the teachers belonged to some church. Three revisions of the Bible have been made; King James, 1611; American Revision, 1881-1901; Standard Revision of the Scriptures by 40 Protestant denominations, 1937-45.

Motion pictures have taken the day. The idea started in 1833, with a cylinder toy with a dancing girl inside. Through this slit in the side of the cylinder the pictures of the girl were viewed as it turned. In 1872 an Englishman placed 24 cameras side by side with a tiny string attached to each and tied across a race track. A galloping horse broke the strings one by one, and so snaps were made in many positions. In 1882 a Frenchman made rapid pictures on a celluloid strip which gave the idea a boost. In 1893 Thomas Edison made his "peep-hole" machine which only one person at a time could see.

The shingle machine was first used in Cumberland County in 1876. After that date for 20 years shingles were extensively used, until metal roofing came. T. W. Nunn advertised, August 7, 1890, in the *Herald*, chestnut shingles $2.50 and poplar $2.00 per thousand at Big Renox mill.

The Howe sewing machine was invented in 1843-6 by Elias Howe, but was bought first in this county by "Reuben Alexander and others" in 1858. For thirty years following this date two or more neighbors would buy machines and take turns in using them.

First stenographer in Cumberland County was Katherine Jones from Beaver Dam, Kentucky. There are two now (1945), Ben M. Jones and Mrs. Jewell (Lawhon) Lemley, who has done court work for one-fourth century.

George Westinghouse invented the air brake for trains, 1869.

In 1824 Samuel Elliott of Cumberland County was paid $60.00 by the Fiscal Court, for making two trips to Frankfort with two horses and buggy.

The first phonograph ever played in Cumberland County was one demonstrated at the printing office by Prof. Frank Eddy, of Birmingham, Alabama, February, 1892. It was that make that had to be heard by placing tubes in your ears. The first ones that listened told the others, "It was plumb audible, just like somebody." A few citizens had gone to the Columbia Fair and heard two that were put on exhibition, August 21, 1890, but most all that were told of it were doubting Thomases. So many gathered at the office that Winks thought of resigning. C. M. McGee is said to be the first purchaser in the county.

How long do turtles live? One was caught at Waterview in the summer of 1891 that had the names of two men with dates cut on its back, the dates showing that it had been cut 37 years before.

Al H. Briggs built a Government gauge on the Cumberland River at Burkesville in December, 1891, and was employed by the Government to make reports on tides. The gauge is gone but records are still available. He was an undertaker at the time. Coffins were sold from $1.50 to $50.00. Now they come as high as $700.

Gasoline cook stoves were first used in Burkesville, February, 1890.

The Brass Band of the 80's and first 90's was composed of Dr. C. K. Haggard, Will Simpson, Elva and Jacob McGee, Robert Eston, Finis Bruton, Luther Grissom, Al H. Briggs, Godfrey Hunter, and W. G. Simpson.

Alexander and Davis will pay 2½ cents for fat cattle, February, 1891.

The 1946 Legislature passed an act authorizing the establishment of six Tuberculosis hospitals. The Sixth District embraces Cumberland County and the hospital is to be located at Glasgow. The 17 counties in this district are Barren, Butler, Edmonson, Hart, Green, Taylor, Casey, Adair, Russell, Metcalfe, Logan, Warren, Simpson, Allen, Monroe, Cumberland, Clinton.

CHAPTER 25

THE ORIGIN OF NAMES

(In orders of letters of the alphabet)

Adam, inspired by the Lord, was the first and greatest lexicographer. The book of Genesis tells us that after God had "formed every living creature he brought them to Adam to see what he would call them; and whatever Adam called them that should be the name thereof." So every animal, great and small, was named; and if we were able to turn back the pages of time to that day and ask him why certain things were so named, like dog, cattle, sheep, rat, snake, fish, etc., he would tell us that every name bore a meaning of identification.

Primitive personal names originated with the creation of man. Surnames did not. For thousands of years after man was made the dominating animal of earth, was he designated by a given name only, and this name always carried with it a meaning. The Old Bible and New Testament will both bear out this statement. For example: Eve, "taken from man"; Moses, "drawn out of water"; Abraham, "father of many"; Joseph, "increase"; Jesus, "Savior of men."

Sometimes it occurred that the name which was applied in babyhood or youth failed to typify the true characteristics of manhood or womanhood. This is found in the case of Jezebel, the wife of Ahab —two of the worst characters the world ever had (up to Hitler). Jezebel, meaning "chaste," has been a by-word for "meanness" for thousands of years.

With the passing centuries, the increasing of human families and the complexity of civilized societies necessitates more specific designations. Most of the surnames, or sire names, fall into the six categories as follows: Localities; Patronymics; Occupation; Offices; Personal Characteristics; and Animals, Birds, and Fishes.

Cumberland County has surnames strung from Creation on down. God named the first man Adam, which means "red earth." Will Adams represents that name here. Under the Family Trees in this volume will be found details of names.

Following the Old Bible period came the New Testament period, which lasted for 100 years. During this period men were either designated by their place of residence or some personal characteristic. Down to the year of 1000 A.D. bodily or mental features gave rise to family designations. Here are examples of this kind:

Constantine the Great (306-37 A.D.), the first Christian emperor of Rome.

Charles the Simple of France (922).

Alfred the Great of England (871).

Louis the Fat of France (1100).

Richard the Lion-hearted of England.

It appears proper here to give a brief history of our Mother Country, England, which will give to all who read this book an idea as to where you and your name came from.

The British Isles were discovered by Caesar, 55 B.C. He found the island to be inhabited by a wild race of people, Celts later called Britons in the south, and Picts and Scots in the north. The Romans were holding control of the Isles at the birth of Christ and did so until 448 A.D., when they withdrew to protect their own country. Upon their withdrawal an army of Angles from north France and Saxons from north Germany moved across the channel to assist the Britons in expelling the Scots and Picts from Briton to their homeland in Caledonia (now Scotland). Having done this, the Anglo-Saxons coveted the rich lands of Briton and made war on the Britons, driving them into Wales, Cornwall, and Britanny, where their descendants yet remain.

The Anglo-Saxons immediately divided Britain into seven small kingdoms—Kent, Sussex, Wessex, Essex, East Anglia, Mercia, and Northumberland. Pope Gregory of Rome, commissioned the Benedictine Monk, Augustine, to go and preach to the pagan Anglo-Saxons. Under his preaching as Archbishop, on Christmas day, 597 A.D., 10,000 Anglo-Saxons were baptized; following this, they tore down their idols and accepted the religion of the Crucified Savior. Then in 827 A.D., the Seven Kingdoms were united under the name of Angle-land or England. Thus you see our Mother Country was born in the atmosphere of the Holy Cross. This same year Egbert was made king.

During the reign of the five kings that followed Egbert, the Danes from Norway and Denmark continued to make inroads on England. Alfred the Great, who was the last of these five kings (871-901), drove the Danes from England and divided the country into counties, called shires. In each shire he instituted a place of learning, for example in Oxford County, Oxford University, the greatest institution of the kind on earth.

The Danes left on the British Isles several family names which have been passed on to our county, for example, Hare, Harris, Fair, Farris, Guthrie, Guffy, Norris, etc.

After Alfred the Great died (901), the Danes succeeded in getting control of England, which they kept for 24 years (1017-41). During a part of this period Harold the Harefoot (named for swiftness of foot) ruled. Then Edward the Confessor restored the Saxon throne, continuing for 25 years.

Up to this time surnames were unknown on the British Isles except as heretofore stated, but on the European Continent they had begun to take root among the Normans, 60,000 of whom landed on the southern shores of England, led by their leader, Duke William the Conqueror (as directed by his father, King Robert the Magnificent of Normandy, France) in the year 1066 A.D.

Soon after the landing of the Normans, war was made on the natives, in which their king was slain and Duke William the Conqueror was King of England for 21 years. This changed the fate of future England.

Within the two centuries following the Norman Conquest most of our surnames were substantiated. The names that were not carried over the Channel by the Normans soon originated in the British Isles. William the Conqueror while king introduced "Serfdom," by taking the lands from the Saxons and dividing them among his favorite Normans, and making serfs or slaves of the peasants. Here is where a great per cent of our present names originated. Places which had already been named by the Saxons generally retained their names.

Bear in mind that many of our familiar names of today have undergone orthographic changes.

PATRONYMICS: This falls under four subheads all of which are taken from that of the father.

(a) Saxon form, John the son of William, became John Williams, Wilson, Willis, Williamson, etc.; Robert the son of Richard became Robert Richardson, Richson, etc.; likewise Davis, Davidson; Thomas, Thompson, Tompkins; Andrew, Anderson; Simpson; Watson, etc.

(b) Norman form, James fils (son of Hugh became James Fitzhugh, and so came all the names with "Fitz."

(c) Gallic form, "Mac" meaning son, as in McKinley, McCoy, McGee, McComas, etc.

(d) Irish form, John the son of Banion became John O'Banion; likewise O'Bryan, O'Neal, etc.

To these the Welsh modified the already endorsed name and made separate family heads to harmonize with their way of spelling, to wit: John ap (child of) Rice became John Price; Robert ap Helps, became Robert Phelps; Harris, Pharis; Howell, Powell, etc.

LOCALITIES: This gave rise to more names than any other source or derivation and was popular in Normandy before the crossing of the Channel. Some of these are: Hill, Barnes, York, Stone, Cane, Meadows, Wells, Hall, Herfors, Radford, Acre, Berry, Cross, Potts, Wood, West, Crawford, Upchurch, Appleby, Scott, Dale, Lee, Brooks, Ford, Heath, Marsh, Moore, Cole, Claywell, Scotts, Garret.

OCCUPATIONS: During the reign of Edward the Confessor heretofore related (1041-66), England enjoyed 25 years of peace and prosperity. The names, most of which originated during this period, show the trend of prosperity. Following is a list of some of them: Miller, Taylor Baker, Waggener, Smith, Carter, Mason, Shepherd, Webster, Curry, Skinner, Bishop, Chaplin, Hunter, Coffey, Gardner, Farmer, Cook, Coop, Wheeler, Wright, Melton, Chapman, Shearer, Cumming, Goff, Garner, Hooper, Page, Ross, Goodhue.

PERSONAL CHARACTERISTICS: John the Small became John Small; Little Black-haired William became William Black, and blond-headed Robert, Robert White. Others of this class are, Long, Short, Wise, Good, Armstrong, Kinkead, Brown, Green, Beard, Hardy, Smiley, Clement, Savage, Gray, Means, Rich, Poor, Swift, Golden, Goodman, Capps, Hood, Curtis, Abston, Paull, Stern, Cheek, Booher.

OFFICES: King, Prince, Duke, Barron, Earl, Knight, Marshall, Summoner or Summers, Burgess, Baily, Bishop, Priest, Clerk or Clark, Squires, Foster, Staton, Stewart.

ANIMALS: Wolf, Bulle, Fox, Lyon, Doe, Hare, Leveret or Leveridge.

BIRDS: Byrd, Hawkins, Martin, Crane, Drake, Cox.

FISH: Salmon, Herring, Crabb, Haddock, Ray, etc.

Thus the names which are so familiar to each of us today had their birth. There are many others which space will not permit publishing, but a few more primitive names are: Fergus (its patronym Ferguson) is a Saxon word meaning "manly strength." Pierce, "hotspur," in battle; Jones, a "dove"; Phillips, "lover of horses"; Stephen, "a crown"; Tom, and its forms, "a twin"; Richard, "powerful"; Vincent, "conquering"; Oliver, "an olive"; Lewis, "defender of man"; Moore, "dark complexion"; Anderson, "manly"; Richardson, etc., "powerful."

About the time of the First Crusade (1096), a custom arose in western Europe for knights to depict certain devices on their shields for identification. This was the origin of "coats-of-arms." In England the king then permitted a device to be worn by each head of family and to be passed down to descendants of the male sex upon sufficient proof. These were means of tracing lineal descendants for centuries.

Poor penmen operating clerk's offices have caused many people to lose trace of their kinsmen on account of wrong spelling.

On the other hand people whose names are spelled alike may not have the same ancestry. For example: 5 Johns from five different families unrelated, under the law, all became Johnsons and reared families of Johnsons, all of them no kin. One family of Coles, to the writer's knowledge, changed their name to "Cowl."

WHERE DID YOU COME FROM?

We read of all the people of ancient time going up to their home city to be enrolled for taxation and other purposes. Jesus was born on one occasion of that kind.

When the Normans landed on the shore of Britain, 1066, William the Conqueror robbed natives of all their land and gave it to the men of his army. From then on for centuries the name of every living person was recorded in a book called "Domesday Book." This book is in the Tower of London to this day. The people became so thickly settled, as I have heretofore related, that the necessity of surnames had to be met.

From 1086 to 1400, roughly speaking, we got most of the surnames that had not already been adopted, and many that had been used were so twisted and carved through the different languages and dialects that they almost lost their identity. Besides the sources which I have referred to, I find in the Domesday Book, Patent Rolls, Hundred Rolls, Pipe Rolls, Charter Rolls, and Court Records of London, at the expense of quite a bit of money and time in laboring to establish the proper origin of the surnames of most of the present families of Cumberland County, that dress, actions, nicknames, pageant costume, and even punning gave rise to thousands of family names. Other sources of research to which I have given much time and labor are ancient and medieval history and the Old and New Bibles.

I have tried to get the origin of the name together with the dates which will show when most of these surnames originated.

The six personal names carried over by the Normans that became bases for dozens of surnames in England I here name in order of their popularity and from all of which the early English inhabitants molded surnames among the hundreds: John, William, Thomas, Robert, Richard, and Hugh.

The following will perhaps be of interest to those whose curiosity has been along this line. Names are arranged in order of letters of the alphabet.

Aaron. This is a Hebrew name of 1491 B.C., means "Mountainous or lofty."

Adam. This is a Hebrew name, oldest on earth; means "red earth."

Allen. This name came from west Asia (see Family Tree), means "harmony."

Andrew. This is a Greek name meaning "courageous or manly."

Anderson. This is a patronym of Andrew, like most names with "son" as a suffix, and bears the same meaning as Andrew.

Abston. This is an English name, meaning "the Abbot's son," as used in the pageants of the 13th century.

Abney. This is an English name, meaning "a waiter at the sanctuary or church."

Akin. This is of English origin of residence and means "oak at the edge."

Ashlock. This is of English origin, meaning "contented by the lake," as used in year of 1256.

Armstrong. This name came from England and meant "stout with the arms," as used in 1202.

Arms. This is an English name no doubt of some arm characteristic.

Alexander. This is a Greek name, meaning "helper of men" (see Family Tree).

Baker. This name is of English origin and belongs to the occupation group, used first as Bakewell, meaning "good cook" (see Family Tree).

Bertram. This name is Norse, meaning "a raven" and German, "fair."

Ballou. This name is Anglo-Saxon, meaning "by the blue."

Burchett. This name is Anglo-Saxon, meaning "a refuge," as of 1200 A.D.

Bailey. This name is Anglo-Saxon and means "outer fortification" or "magistrate."

Byers. This name is a Somerset name of location, meaning "woods."

Brent. This is an English name of place, meaning "brow of a hill."

Barton. This is an English name, meaning "barley town."

Buris. This is of English origin of place, meaning "bower house."

Bloyd. This is a Welsh name, meaning "blood."

Bean. This is a Scottish name of place, meaning "a bean plot," as found at Benedale in Scotland.

Biggerstaff. This is a Lincolnshire name, first at Bickersteth, in a parish, in 1176 A.D. It was a place of landing.

Brewington. This is an English name, meaning "a broth maker."

Bow. This is of Anglo-Saxon origin, meaning "arch"; atte Bow, 1202.

Bishop. This is an English name of title.

Bowman. This is a Middlesex name used as an officer, taken from "borough-reeve," that is, "sheriff" (bow-man), 1202 A.D.

Blakely or Blakeman. This is a Middlesex name, "pale."

Bowen. This is a Welsh name taken from Owen (ab-Owen), son of Owen, meaning "son of one well bred."

Bryce. This is another of Welsh origin (ab-Rice).

Blythe. This is a Welsh name, meaning "a wolf cub." Likely a trait.

Blair. This is a name belonging to Scotland and is a place name, meaning "plane dweller."

Bulle. This is of French origin and connected with the sport of the bull. First as John le Bulle.

Bass. This an English origin place name, meaning "at the base of a hill." First, Robert atte Bass.

Bruton. This is a Somerset name and belongs to the big class of resident names. First, John le Brutun or Bruten, 1273 A.D.

Butler. This is a Middlesex name of occupation, meaning "a button-maker for the King," as of 1202 A.D.

Bryson. This is a French name of place, John de Bryanzun, 1199 A.D.

Black. This is an English name belonging to the pageant period, which got its name from the color of the robe, 1273 A.D.

Brown. This name came from the pageant period also, from the costume and the sword which he carried, as it corresponded to his dress. First, John Brownswerd (brown sword).

Brewster. This is an English name applied to female brewers of 1273 A.D.

Burns. This is of French origin and means "at the burn-house."

Brake. This an English name of residence, "atte Brake."

Brockman. This is an English name, meaning "Badger-man," 1205 A.D., likely reared or killed them.

Booher. This name is of Dutch origin, spelled Boor; and in England as used today means "a rustic peasant," 1216 A.D.

Bristow. This name belongs to the place names, "at Bristol."

Barger. This is from French, Bargery, meaning "a sheepfold."

Beck. This is an English name of occupation from Beake, "maker of metal prows," William le Beke, 1205 A.D.

Brummitt. This name is of English origin of place, meaning "in the broom-field."

Branham. This is an English name, meaning "maker of flaming swords."

Burbridge. This is an English place name, "at the town bridge."

Baise. This is an English name of occupation, meaning "a maker of coarse bony cloth."

Ballard. This name is of English origin, meaning "bright, ball-headed man."

Boulden. This is a French name of royal dynasty; also English, 1202.

Bryant. This is a French name of place, "at Brienne."

Berge. This is German name, meaning, "urban" or "bell-ringer."

Bledsoe. This name belongs to a royal family of Europe.

Blankenship. This name is Norse and means "a cow-shelter."

Bradshaw. This is English, brad (broad), shaw (woods).

Burke is an Irish name, meaning "a freeman, citizen." The name came from Burgh, or de Burgh as it was called in Normandy before William the Conqueror came to England, 1066 A.D. They remained in England until 1171, when they went with Earl Strongbow in an army to Ireland, the result of which placed Ireland under English rule forever.

Carr. This name is Norse, of residence, and means "a fen."

Cox. This name is of English origin, meaning "boat," first, attecock.

Capshaw. This is of English origin, "hesitant in speech," or "cap maker of the hills."

Craft. This is of German origin, meaning "skilled," 1273.

Campbell. This is a Scottish name, meaning "wrymouth."

Cumming. This is of French origin, of place; Nord "at Cumines" (see Family Tree).

Cowan. This is a Gallic name, McGowen, "son of the smith"; in England the "Mc" was dropped.

Cross. This name is English and means "residing at the cross," likely at the cross roads. First, Robert le Cross, 1216 A.D.

Carter. This name was used in France as a trade name and was the same after it reached England. First, Philip la Chartrar or Cartar.

Capps. This is an English pageant name, adopted from the head costume as used in 1273 A.D.

Collins. This is an English name, meaning "char-coal burner of the hills," as in 1273 A.D.

Conrad. This name came down from Germany from a royal dynasty of 911, and means "able counsel."

Coomer. This name is English and came from "new-comer," 1202; first, John le comer, that is, newly moved.

Curtis. This is an English name, meaning "courteous about the house." First, Robert le Curtese, 1203 A.D.

Cook. This is an English name of Surrey County, meaning "cook" and spelled "Robert le Kue" (the cook).

Claywell. This is an English name of place, living at the claywell, John ad claywell, as of 1310 A.D.

Cheek. This name came from France, first, as a nickname, bajoue, meaning "fat or baggy-cheek." In England it was "Cheek."

Cash. This name is of English origin, cache, meaning "catcher," as of 1202 A.D.

Cain. This is a Hebrew name of old, meaning "possession."

Cyphers. This is an old name of Rome, meaning "admirer of the fair sex."

Crawford. This is a Scottish name of place, at Crafer or Crayford; in north Scotland as proprietor of lands.

Cheatham. This name centered in north England as named.

Chism. This name started in Greece as Schism, 1054 B.C., and by the time it reached England had changed to Chiswell, then to Chism. It is a local name of place.

Chowning. This is a Welsh name; first, Shone, from John, then the Cornish name changed to Chown with "ing" added, meaning "favored by Jehovah."

Coleman. This is an English name of residence; first, Cholmondeley, spelled Ceolmund, meaning "on the lea of Colmund," as named from Irish Bishop Colman of the 7th century.

Origin of Names 329

Carver. This is an English name, meaning "skilled in craftsmanship."
Compton. This is a French name, meaning "with a companion."
Conner. This is an English name, meaning "a ship pilot."
Cooksey. This is a patronymic name, meaning "the cook's son" or "the boy cook."
Crawley. This is an English name, meaning "a pen for sheep, fish, etc."
Cole. This is an Irish name derived from the Irish Bishop Coleman, as a variant.
Coffey. This name dates to Old French, means "place in the cave to eat," called "caffy."
Cloyd. This is Welsh name, meaning "very free eater." From Wales to Scotland, then to Ireland, then to America as Scotch-Irish.
Coop. This is English, a confusion of "cape," a garment.
Cape. This is an English name, as a garment (or cape).

Day. This is an Old German name of place, at Daymond, meaning "a farm worker."
Dale or Dowel. This name is English and means "waste land."
Dillon. This is an English name of place, "a swamp field."
Denton. This is an English name of place, "in the hollow."
Dubree. This is an English name of place, at Deubire or Dewsburg, 1202.
Daugherty. This is an Old French name of fame, "de hautree."
Daniel. This is a Bible name of Hebrew, meaning "God is judge," 600 B.C.
Dishman. This name is of English origin and was used to distinguish a man as "one dishmaker or ditcher," 1285.
Dyer. This is one of England's occupation names and used to classify the man as "a colorer of goods."
Dare. A variant of Dyer as above named.
Dicken. This falls into the class of pet names so prevalent in England and comes from "Dickie."
Davis. This goes back to the Bible hero, David, in the Hebrew language, born 1084 B.C., meaning "beloved."
Donaldson. This is a patronym of Donald, meaning "world-wielder."
Duvall. This is Welsh, meaning "from the black valley."
Dodson. This is Old French, taken from "Dottin," a place name.
Denny. This is English, meaning "Dane bye," from Denbigh.

Embree or Emery. This name is of Old German use, and means "work." When it reached France it meant "work in a quarry."
Edmonson. This name reaches back to the year 1000 and belongs to a royal dynasty of England. It carries "happiness" with it in the base word, and "son" is an offspring of Edmund.

Evans. This a Welsh word which is a corruption of "heaven," meaning "abode of the blessed," 1199 A.D.

Edwards. This is of a royal family of England of Anglo-Saxon fame. The Welsh put the "s" to the singular, about 901 A.D.

Easter. This is a Devonshire name of place, "atte Eastway," i.e., "living at the East-Way." First, 1199 A.D.

Ewing. This name is Greco-Latin, meaning "well born."

Eden. This name began with the Hebrews, meaning "pleasantness."

Eubanks. This name is an Anglo-Saxon place name, meaning "by the bank of the mourning or yew tree."

Everett. This is another of the Old French names of place, i.e., "at Eberhard."

Elliott. This name is Anglo-Saxon, meaning "purity."

Ellington. This is English, meaning "draper of the town."

Flatt. This is a Yorkshire name of place, de Flatt (at the flat country).

Franklin. This name is from the Old French and means "French land."

Fletcher. This name originated in Northumberland, England, and means "arrow-maker."

Floyd. This name is Welsh and means "flood," likely "under high water."

Field. This is an Essex name, meaning "an out-dweller."

Fergus. This is an Anglo-Saxon name, meaning "dear choice or manly strength." Dates from 448 A.D.

Ferguson. This is a patronym of Fergus with the same meaning.

Finley. This is a highland name of England, meaning "fair hero."

Fowler. This a Shropshire name, meaning "killer of fowls," as named in German first, 918 A.D.

Fennel. This is an English name, "of plant and blossom," 1202.

Flower. This is a name belonging to the pageant period of England, to distinguish by costume. First, 1199 A.D.

Feuston. This name is of English origin derived from Fusheir, meaning "maker of wooden saddle frames," 1285 A.D.

Frazier. This name came from Old French, first, Frasel, and when it reached Scotland it was Frazer; it meant "peace," 1199.

Fudge. This name belongs to the Angevin Dynasty of French origin.

Ferrell. This is an English name (Furrel), meaning "a shield or scabbard maker."

Felty. This name belongs to the place names of England (Feltous) and means "at the field-house."

Firkin. This is an English name, meaning "operator of fire-kiln," i.e., brick burner.

Farlee. This is of English origin, meaning "less hair."

Flint. This originated in Flanders and coming into the English thinning of names and the play on the five vowels, became a diminutive of Flinder, 1275 A.D.

Farr. This is English and means "hairy."

Gilbert. This name belongs to the Anglo-Saxon days and means "hostage," or one held in derision for pledge.

Griffin or Griffith. A Welsh name, meaning "comic character," as used in 1199 A.D.

Gentry. This is a London term adopted as a family name and means "high rank," usually rich landowners.

Goodhugh. This is a name very popular in England and means "good servant," as of 1199 A.D.

Goodman. This is an English name, meaning "good master," as of 1310.

Glidewell. This is an English name as it now stands and was derived from kite fliers, as "gledewell," in 1202 A.D.

Guinn. This name belongs to the Welsh language and means "white, fair," as originally used (Gwyn) in 1202 A.D.

Goff. This name is Cornish and means "a crimper or ruffler," as applied to that occupation.

Gibbons. This name is Old French and means "held as a pledge."

Garret. This name originated in Old French times and meant "at the watchtower," spelled "garete." In Suffolk it meant "garthwood" to make dams, as in 1202 A.D.

Green. This name is English and is a place name, "atte-green," living by the green, 1273 A.D.

Geoffrey or Jeffries. This name belongs to Germany, means "joyful."

Gorman. This name is Norse (Garnon) and was applied to the men who wore both beard and mustache. About the year 1000 A.D. Gorm founded Denmark (Gorm, the hairy old).

Garner. This name belongs to the occupation group, dating back to 1058 B.C., and was popular in England, meaning "a gatherer of grain."

Grider. This name is Old French or Dutch and means "a guide"; First, John la Guyer, as in 1199 A.D.

Grey. This name belongs to the pageant period of England as a costume color.

Guthrie. This name is Norse. In the Danish, Guthrum; it changed to Guthrie in England, meaning "a dragon or serpent," 900 A.D.

Groce. This name found first in Germany as Gross or Gros. It is an occupation name, and in France (Gros-smith) meant "maker of silk fabric."

Glass. This is a Scottish name applied to makers of glass.

Gibson. This is a patronymic name taken from Gib, meaning "son of one held for a pledge." It belongs to Old French.

Graves. This is of French origin and means "serious"; Richard le Grave.

Grubbs. This name started from a street of the same name in London and means "poor writer."

Gerald. This is of German origin, following Geri, the knight-errant, about 1000 A.D.

Graham. This is a Cumberland place name, Grahame (grey home), 1216, perhaps in the unpainted house.

Humphrey. This is an Anglo-Saxon name, meaning "a giant."

Helm. This name is Teutonic, derived from "helmet," and in English meant "to direct" or guide.

Herd. This is an Anglo-Saxon name, meaning "a guard."

Hogan or Hammond. An Old German place name, as hagun-mund "at the mountain."

Haynes. This name is Old German and means "enclosure or hedge."

Hardy. This name is Welsh and means "residing on hard ground."

Huff. This is Anglo-Saxon from hough, a "hill."

Holman. This is a French name, meaning "holy man."

Hunt or Hunter. This name belongs to England and was applied to "houndkeeper of the king," as per 1202 A.D.

Harris. This name is Anglo-Saxon, derived from "Henry," and means "rich lord," 1202 A.D.

Hurt. This name is English taken from "hart," a deer; first, John le Hert, 1273 A.D.

Hare. This name is Danish, named for the hare, as Harold the Harefoot, denoting "swiftness."

Henson. This is patronymic Danish, as Harrison, meaning "obedient," as used in 1273 A.D.

Hugh or Hughs. This is of French origin, meaning "a servant," as of 900 A.D.

Higginbotham. This is a name of mixed dialects covering French-German origin; but the Anglo-Saxon from which our present name came was Hygeborthe, meaning "servant with courageous mind."

Howard. This name comes through French (Huard); Old German (Hugihart); then Anglo-Saxon as of the British Isles came down to Howard, meaning "strong man of the hot hills."

Hood. This name is the outgrowth of the pageant period and originated in Middlesex.

Hicks. This is a name derived from Richard; used in Saxony, meaning "powerful."

Hopper. This name came from a character in the games of Northumberland, 1256 A.D.

Harvey. This is an English name, meaning "gathering in."

Huddleston. This name belongs to England, taken from Hubble-stan, meaning "rule of stone, or the limit."

Origin of Names

Hunley. This name came from central Asia, as derived from "Hun," the barbaric tribe of Tartary who overran all of east Europe about 375 A.D.

Hendricks. This name belongs to the Dutch and is a derivative of Henry, which means "rich lord."

Hardin. This is a name of place, meaning "on firm ground"; Gilbert del Harde, 1202 A.D.

Hoots. This is a derivative of Hugh, meaning "servant."

Hulse. This name belongs to Germany and England too. It was derived from Hugh, which means "high or lofty." First, as Hullins, then in Germany "Huss," the name of the great reformer who was burned alive for preaching against the Pope, 1415 A.D.

Humble. This name is a place name from Humboldt, Germany.

Hume is another derivative of Hugh, meaning "high or lofty."

Hickey. This name is Anglo-Saxon, derived from Richard, "powerful."

Haggard. This name belongs to Scotland, meaning "hollow-eyed."

Hoffman. German from "hof," meaning "courtier," man of the court.

Hayden. This is Anglo-Saxon and means "enclosure or line."

Hill. This is an English name of place, atte Hill.

Hadley. This is Anglo-Saxon, from Hadwig, "in battle."

Irwin. This name was spelled with I, E, U, and O, as the first letter, but means the same. It is a diminutive of the Anglo-Saxon name, Eoforwine, which means "ever win." The same with either "v" or "w."

Irby. This name belongs to Germany as a place name, from Eber or Eberlin; in England, Irber or Irby.

Jewell. This name is of Old French origin, meaning "an ornament."

Jones. This name has met with several orthographic variations through the different languages. First, it was an offspring of Jonah, 840 B.C.; then a variant of John; and in the Welsh, where its home belongs, it was Jvones; then the English, Jones. Through all this, it held its meaning, "a dove."

Jennings. This name is Norse and means "the iron-man."

Judd. This is a variant of Jordan, which is first mentioned in Genesis 13:10, 1918 B.C., and 180 times in the Old Bible, 15 in the New Testament. It belongs to Essex and means, "going with speed."

Jarvis. This is a French name of place, "living at Jervoux."

Jesse. This name, dating to the father of David, 1312 B.C., means "a gift," as used in the Hebrew.

Johnson. This name in the Hebrew was Johanna, 562 B.C.; then it became John, still in the Hebrew. Next a patronym was the result in England, which was Johnson, England's number one name in popularity. Every John's son became Johnson, hence so many.

Through this evolution it retained its meaning, "The grace of the Lord." John furnished names for over 20 languages—Jan in Dutch; Juan in Spanish; Ivan in Russian; Gomez in Portugese; Shane in Irish.

Janes. This, a confused name from Jacob, means "beguiling."

Kerr. This is a Norse name of old and means "a fen or swamp."

Kidwell. This is a Welsh name of place, first used as at Cadwal, then the Somerset name was Kiddell and English, Kidwell, 1202.

Kimble or Keymel. This name belongs to a province of Thorpe, France, applied to its inhabitants.

Karnes. This name is Scottish of place, first, "at Cairns."

Key. This is an English name of place belonging to Surrey County, England; but the name really is Manx, "at the Quay."

Kirby. This is Scottish name of place, as first used, "Kirkby Shaw," meaning "Church by the Woods."

Keeton. This name is Cornish and is a place name of 1199 A.D.; means "the place of the wildcats or visited by wildcats."

King. This is an official name, dating to 1918 B.C.

Kernell. This name is an English name of place, a variant of Knoll, William atte K-nell or Knoll.

Kelly. This a Cornish name of place, meaning "a grove."

Keen. This name came from Ireland; first spelled Coaine, and means "a conductor or attender at funerals."

Lee. This name originated in the Norse language, and is a place name, as confused with the name found, "living on lea."

Lloyd. This name is Welsh. It is ab-loyd, meaning "blood" or "gray."

Long. This is a Scottish name from "Lang" used in common dialect meaning "length."

Lowe. This name is Irish resident name, named for the family that lived by the lake—John at Lough (lake), 1273 A.D.

Lawson. This name is of English origin and is patronymic, meaning "son-of-the-hills."

Lewis, Louis. This is a French name reaching back to 814 A.D., and means "defender of people or gentle manners."

Lawhon. This is a name originating in Old English by combining two words (law, "hill," and horn, "corner"), hence, "corner of the hills," 1119 A.D., making it residential.

Lemily. This is a place name of England, meaning "a scaly coast," likely shelly rock, as per 1310 A.D.

Lackey. This name is from France and means "without land."

Lacy. This is a Scottish variant of lassie, a young girl.

Linder. This name is French from landri, "owners of land" and belongs to that punning of vowels.

Lollar. This name belongs to an English dynasty called Lollards. They were strict followers of John Wickliffe, the great Eng-

Origin of Names

lish Reformer, about 1400. Most of them were killed for their opposition to the Pope. Martin Luther continued this belief and received the honor, 1517.

Logan. This name was derived from McLagen, hence is a Gaelic name, meaning "a hollow, or surrounded by rising ground," making it a place name. McLagan was a clan affiliated with the clan of Robertson. It merges into a common name, lagoon.

Mann. This is an Anglo-Saxon name, meaning "hero."

Meadows. This is an English name of residence, meaning "meadhouse" or "house of the mower."

Malone. This is an English name, meaning "servant of John."

Murphy. This an Irish name, meaning "a leprous eruption," 1158.

Morgan. This is a Welsh name, meaning "a marine or sea-white."

McKinley. This is a Scottish name, meaning "son of Kinley."

Morrison. This is an Irish name, meaning "Mary's son, or holy."

McFarland. This name is a far-reacher of Hebrew, Bartholomew; and later a Gaelic name from Parlanee, meaning "given of God."

McComas. This name is Gaelic and means "son of Saint Thomas," as used 700 A.D.

McDonald. This is a Gaelic name and means "son of world wielder."

McDowel. This is a Gaelic name, meaning "son of Dane, the dark stranger."

McIntyre. This name came from the Gaelic tongue and means "son of the carpenter."

McClellan. This is a Gaelic name and means "son of Saint Gillon's servant."

McMillan. This is a Gaelic name, meaning "son of bald-head servant."

McWhorter. This is a Gaelic name, meaning "son of a courtier."

McGee. This is a Gaelic name, but Magee is Irish, and means "son of the energetic."

Mackey. This is a variant of Maccabees of Judea, 165 to 135 B.C., and in Gaul it was McKay, then on reaching Ireland it became Mackey, meaning "son of Kaa, the embalmer."

Myers. This name is German and Old French. Meyer is the German spelling; Myer the French. It is from the word "mire," meaning "doctor." First, "atte mire," i.e., "at the doctor's," a place name.

Muse. This is an English place name, "atte Meuse" in Yorkshire, 1199 A.D.

Miller. This name is English and is not found until about 1300, and meant at the time "an official in charge of the King's mill." Yet the name Muller is in Old French, which some authorities believe was its predecessor, and meant "maker of women's goods."

McCoy. This is an Irish name and first found as John MacQuoi, which is "survival of Saint Hugh."

Melton. This is an Irish name, meaning "maker of crude cloth."

McCluskey. This name is Norse, with the Gaelic prefix, and means, "son of cauldron of the gods."

Means. This name is English taken from "means well."

Murley or Murray. This name reaches back to ancient times and was an occupation, i.e., worker in "murra" (porcelain).

Moon. This must have been some characteristic of the moon.

Mullinix. This name is Anglo-French and was derived from garment or worker in "ghostly women garments," likely for shows.

Marshall. This is an English occupation name, told by the following extract of old: "One wyllinge to serve a lorde or mastyre in every thynge."

McCool. This *is* English name, meaning "son of the cook."

Mee. This is English, taken from mead, a meadow, William Smee.

Monroe. Mon (one), roe (red), "one red mountain," French.

Maxey. This is from a Roman dynasty of 300 A.D.

Mosby. This is a variant of Moses of the Hebrews.

Montfort. This is a French name of royalty.

Nation. This name is of English origin, came from incarnation, meaning "to clothe with flesh."

Neal. This is a Norse name (Norse Neil), meaning "victorious over his people," as derived from Nicholas.

Needham. This is an English name with feminine origin, "knead-dame, or dough-worker."

Noaks. This is an English name of place, meaning "atten oaks."

Newby. This is an Anglo-Saxon name as taken from Newbon, meaning "the farmer in the good, or new building."

Norris. This name is Danish as applied to the Scandinavians of the 8th century, meaning "man of the north."

Neeley. This is a medieval English name derived from an occupation, needler, meaning "the tailor-man."

Nance. This name belongs to France as a place name, came from Nains, meaning "pasture."

Netherton or Nethery. This is an English name, meaning "below the town."

Nunn. This *is* a name from the female religious resolutes.

Officer. This a Nottingham name of occupation as used in 1202 A.D., meaning "making embroidery for the King."

Owen. This is an English name, meaning "well descended."

Oliver. This name originated in Sweden, hence belongs to the Norse language. First as Olufer, who was the first king to embrace Christianity and teach his subjects so; 993.

Ottley. This is an Anglo-Saxon name of place, first Ottway, or "living at Ottwig."

Owsley. This is a local or place name of England," at Ouse on the lea."

Orton. This of French origin and is confused with Horton, the combined meaning of which is "the swarthy gardener."

Ooten. This is Anglo-Saxon, Oozen, "at the muddy place."

Parrish. This is a French name applied to certain districts in France and means "equal clergy."

Phillips. This name reaches back to the Greeks of old, and means "lover of horses."

Philpott. This is a variation of Philip and means "little Philip."

Pierce. This is Welsh and as first used meant "hotspur in battle, in piercing armies or hedges." In England the name was applied to the "man living at the piers," 1273 A.D.

Poulson. This a confusion of Paul, means "God sent."

Perry. In trying to trace the origin of this name I found more than one origin. (1) "A diminutive of Peter"; (2) as local, "at the pear tree"; (3) local, "atte pier," this being Welsh from Parry.

Patton. This is English from Patrick, "a nobleman."

Pennycuff. This name originated within the pageant period of England and meant "his doublet."

Pharis. This name is Welsh, derived from Harris, ap Harris, meaning "head of a family." The name Phares is different, with the Hebrew meaning, "a breach," Genesis 38.

Page. This name is English and means "waiting on a superior."

Pruitt. This a French name, meaning "doughty (strong) Preux."

Poindexter. This is of French origin, meaning "square-fisted user of right hand only," 1275.

Patterson. This name is a confusion of Peter, meaning "son of Petrus, a rock."

Pace. This name in Anglo-Saxon was Paach or Pake, as John Pake, ushering into the English, means "relating to Easter."

Propes. This name came from Wales, ap-ropes, or "the maker of ropes." One authority says "hangsman-ropes." 1202 A.D.

Pitcock. This is an English name, meaning "boat-pit."

Perkins. This is an English name of place, at Purkase, and means "pursuit," as of 1273 A.D.

Powell. This is Anglo-Saxon, derived from Paul, meaning in the Greek "ask for."

Petty. This name came from Anglo-Saxon, Pytte, and in the Kentish was Petty, meaning "by the holes in the ground."

Payne. This name belongs to the Passion Play of 1273, as then applied meant "painer or tormentor"; John le poine.

Palmore. This is Old English, meaning "a wooer."

Russell. This is a Middlesex name, meaning "horse painters, i.e., on flags," 1202 A.D.

Rabon. This name is Norse and means "a raven."

Ryan. This name belongs to Somerset, England, "a channel."

Rowe or Roe. This is a Staffordshire name (in Irish, Reo), and means "in a nook or corner."

Reed, Reid. This name is English and means "counsel."

Roberts. This name is Welsh (by adding "s" to father's name) and means, "famous in counsel." From Robert, Anglo-Saxon, meaning "bright, shining." Adding "son" makes patronyms.

Ritchie. This is a Scottish pet name, meaning "abundance."

Ray, Wray. This name is of Old French origin as spelled Ray and means "a king." Rea, Rhea belong here. In Northumberland the name is Wray, meaning "the man with the striped coat from the corner." Presumably a fisherman.

Rioll. This is a French name of place, "at Rioll."

Rutledge. This name originated in Cumberland County, England, home of the people of that name, means "the Duke's fiddler."

Richards. This is an Anglo-Saxon name, meaning "powerful." The Welsh put the "s" to Richard.

Richardson. This is a patronym, meaning "son with power."

Reneau. This a French name, meaning "advice or adviser."

Rains. This is a Durham County name (Rayns), meaning "a strip of land or boundary," 1202.

Ross. This is an English name, meaning "worker in timber, especially bark."

Riley. This is an English name of place, "Atte Ryle."

Rigsby. This is a French name, a variant of Richard, meaning powerful.

Riddle. This is an English name of place, "atte Riddie, a small stream."

Rainey. This name is French, Raine, meaning "a frog," Robert le Rane.

Rush. This name is English as applied to a signalman by the "rushway," and means "safety first."

Roach. This name is a variant of Roe, meaning "red."

Smith. This name had its beginning with "smeethe," meaning "a level place," as an Anglo-Saxon term. Then it fell to mean any operator or craftsman. The first use was Sykelsmith of the plains, i.e., farmer, "Simon de la Smethe." All farmers were "Smeths," hence the large number today. 1205 A.D. Silversmiths date from time of Christ, but surnames do not.

Sherrill, Shearel. This name is English, and means "a gap or division land."

Stockton. This is an English name and means "a stumpy clearing," making it a place name.

Skipworth. This is an English name and means "sheep valuer."

Stewart. This is a Scottish name, meaning "an officer."

Stone. This is an Anglo-Saxon name of place, meaning "from Stoneheard," 1216 A.D.

Stephens. This name dates to the year 33 A.D. as a "man full of faith and the Holy Ghost," and means "crowned." It has come down through the royal families from Greece.

Stephenson is a patronym of Stephen.

Staily. This is a Cheshire name, meaning "a bridge."

Sharp. This is a place name of England, in Lancanshire County, the home of this family, atte Sharples, 1273 A.D.

Shaw. This is an English name, meaning "shoemaker of the woods."

Sells. This family name came from England as a place name, meaning "shop," John atte selde, 1294 A.D.

Stearns. This name is English and means "difficult in compromising."

Stalcup. This is an English name and means "to conceal," as used by early Britons for the name of a horse or other domestic animal which was placed in front of the man while slipping on his prey, that he might "stalk-up."

Schickles. This is a Kent name of place, Robert atte Stycles.

Spencer. This is an English name, meaning "connected with a store room."

Sewell. This is an English name, "sew-well for the mayster" (master).

Simpson. This name is a variant of Simeon, 1751 B.C., and Simon later; but in the English it became a patronymic variant, but still carrying its Hebrew meaning, "an attentive listener." One authority says it is from Bishop Sampson of Cornwall, this I doubt.

Sartin. This is English and means "tailor in the cleared land."

Sevier. This name is English and means "inflexible."

Short. This is an English name and means "low of stature."

Street. This is English and means "city surveyor."

Strange. This name is Scottish and means "a new-comer."

Shannon. This name came from Ireland, Shannah, and means "a story writer."

Shepherd. This name came to us from the Hebrews, as first used 1706 B.C., meaning "a keeper of sheep," at Goshen.

Saunders. This name belongs to England and means "flavoring."

Sprowles. This name is English and means "untrue cavalry-riders."

Sparks. This name came up from Germany and means "self-denial."

Stinson. This is a patronymic variant of Simeon.

Surratt. This is an English name of place. Surr or Sirr was a sovereign title, "living ad Surr."

Shoopman. This is a Dutch name meaning "shopman."

Stapp. This is English from step, "a speedy walker."

Shelly. This is an English name confusion of "shilling," an English coin.

Staton, This is a Middle English word of place, meaning "a landing place."

Thacker. This is an English name, meaning "a good thatcher," i.e., "a grass carpenter."

Terrell. This is an Anglo-French name of place, "at Thurweall."

Thomas. This is a Hebrew name, dating to 31 A.D. as one of the 12 Apostles; then in disguise it came to England as third name in popularity. It means "a twin."

Tobin. This is a Hebrew name, meaning "goodness of the Lord."

Teel. This is an English name of place, meaning "by the large common pasture."

Talbot. This is a Dutch name; bot means boat, "tall boat."

Tweedy. This is a Yorkshire name of place, "on the Tweed River."

Tuggle. This is an English name of personal characteristic, "tugwell," then meant to wrestle.

Thurman. This name originated in Norway, as Thorman, i.e., "cauldron of the God of Thunder." From there it was carried to France into Anglo-Saxon and in England, Thurman. Thor was the God of Thunder; we get Thursday from the word.

Thrasher. This is from Hebrew, Thresher, 1800 B.C., meaning "separator of grain."

Taylor. This name is tailor, "maker of garments."

Traylor. Confusion of the above.

Turner. This name is English, meaning "to change or turn, not as ground, but paper, money, or cattle," as of 1202 A.D.

Tret. This name is a diminutive of tread, meaning "to walk well"; as of 1273 A.D.

Tidro. This is an Irish name, meaning "red people."

Vickery. This is an Anglo-Saxon name as applied to a type of fiefs or controllers of land by serfdom.

Vincent. This name came from the Latins, meaning "conquering."

Vaughn. This is a Welsh name, meaning "small."

Vibbert. This is a Devon name, meaning "food."

Wilborn. This is an Anglo-Saxon name, meaning "castle for refuge."

Walthall. This is an Anglo-Saxon name, meaning "thief of slaughter."

Witham. This is an English name of place in Northumberland, "in the hollow."

Wisdom. This is from an estate in Devonshire which gave the name to its inhabitants—Wisdom.

Webb. This is Franco-German and means "weaver on the farm."

Williams. This name was not in England before the Conquest, but on the Continent was personal. The Welsh put on the "s" to make a surname, for their love of pedigree. Its spelling there was Quilliam. It was second in popularity in England and means "defender of many."

Wallace. This is Welsh and means "foreigner."

Wolf. This is an Anglo-Saxon name form Wulf or Ulf, meaning "saint," 1100.

Wells. This is Anglo-Saxon. In Normandy it was Vaux; in England de Wells, and is a place name, "John atte Well."

Willis. This is a name of place of English origin, first "John in the Wylis" (willows).

Winfrey. This is an Anglo-Saxon name, meaning "a friend of peace," 1273.

Watson. This is an English name, meaning "son of the man by the pool," 1216 A.D.

Wray. See "Ray."

Wyatt. This is a Suffolkshire name, meaning "a painter," 1273.

White. This is another English costume designation. In Gallic it was Bain; in Scottish it was Whyte, 1273.

Whitehead. This is an English nickname meaning "sheep."

Whitney, Whitley. This is an English name as a variant of Whitlock, meaning "white lake," as a place name, 1173.

Wright. This is an English name of occupation, meaning "skill."

Watkins. This is an Anglo-Saxon name, meaning "water-meadow, or King of the water," 1202.

Waggener. This is a Norfolk name as it stands. In Germany it meant "wag-head." In England it retained its meaning, but meant signalizing, as "Waggespere"—Walter Waggespere, 1176.

Walker. This name is of English origin and means "forest-ranger." Crompton says: "And these be walkers assigned by the King for a certain space to look into." This was a daily task, hence the name.

Wesmorland. This is English, from the inhabitants of Westmoreland County, England, about 900 A.D.

Ward. This name was adopted as "minor in care of a guardian."

Winchester. This name is a locality name of England.

Wilson. This is a patronym of William, England's number two name, meaning "defending many."

CHAPTER 26

PIONEER GENEALOGIES

ALEXANDER

The first of the name of Alexander was Alexander the Great, born 356 B.C. He was King of Macedonia, a great warrior, who conquered the known world before his death at 32. The name is Greek and means "a helper of men." The name heads three Emperors of Russia, three Kings of Scotland, and six Popes of Rome.

The Alexanders that populated Cumberland County had their beginning in Scotland. Due to religious persecutions in Scotland many of them fled to Ireland prior to 1740. There were seven brothers who left for Ireland not far from the above time. From there they crossed the waters to America and settled in Pennsylvania. They then came down the Shenandoah Valley to Virginia and North Carolina. Attached to the Mecklenburg Resolutions, which was the forerunner of the Declaration of Independence, are the names of five Alexanders. Frankfort records 13 names as soldiers of the Revolution from Virginia.

John Alexander, born in Scotland in 1741 (by a reliable record), heads the family of Cumberland County. John married Lucy Martin. They were from Henry and Pittsylvania counties, Virginia. This same record gives the names of eleven children: Thomas, Martin, Ingrim, Robert, Reuben, Joseph, Philip, Sally, Obedience, Elizabeth, and Susan. Most of them were born and several married before their parents came to Cumberland County. They arrived in 1805 and opened up a settlement on Marrowbone Creek, on the same farm now owned by Will Ed Davis. Lucy died in 1815, he in 1830, and both lie at rest on the place of settlement. The seven boys all came to the county, Joseph being the last one to come, 1824. Five of them settled on Marrowbone and two on Big and Little Renox creeks.

The Alexanders have furnished some of the very best families of the country. They have been law-abiding citizens and always interested in the welfare of their community from a social, educational, and religious standpoint. Very seldom do you find one arraigned in the criminal courts. Farming, mercantile business, banking, and teaching are their hobbies. The first bank in Kentucky was established by Robert Alexander.

I shall state briefly the genealogical status of these children.

Reuben. One of the seven sons of John, the settler, was Reuben. He married Eliza A. Miller in 1806. To them were born nine children: (1) Louisa, who became the wife of John P. Monroe; (2) Mary A., who married A. Hays, no issue; (3) Sarah, who married Tom Duerson, and reared two, John and Salina who married James Skinner; (4) William, who married Eliza Ellington and reared a family; (5) Charles Fountain, who married Malinda Lucas and had three girls and two boys in Metcalfe County; (6) Millard, who went to Missouri; (7) Reuben H.; (8) Carolina, who married a Strange; (9) John Edward (1811-64), married first, Elizabeth Strange of Marrowbone, 1845. She lived less than one year and he then married Elizabeth McDaniel of Warren County. To them eight children:

Emma M. who married Nathan Chism and left for the West about 1880, whose eight children are in Oklahoma; Melvin who married Carrie Preston of Warren County and reared three, Edward and Preston who are owners of the Alexander Motor Company, Owensboro, Kentucky, and Mrs. Emma Harvey of Glasgow, Kentucky; Edward; Gideon who married Belle Paull, daughter of William Edward Paull, and reared five children, Lelia who married Ritchey Young (see Allens); Maurice who married Mary Lawhon and had a family; Frankie who married Ed Eberhard of Alliance, Ohio; Ledman (see Pace); Lucy who married Dick Lawhon and reared a family on Marrowbone.

S. E. (of John E.) moved to Kansas, 1882, where he married Laura Vaudiver and reared 10 children around Sumner County, Kansas; Reuben (of John E.) married Jennie Wade of Marrowbone and moved to Kansas, 1895, with one son, Frank at Wellington, Kansas. Irenus M. (of J. E.) married Emma Williams and went to Kansas, where they had Clifton, Russell, and Ruth. John Otis (of John E.) married Bertha Needham and has spent his life near Waterview on Marrowbone, where he has served his district as Justice of the Peace for 44 years. He reared three children—Samuel, Frank E., and Agnas all of whom live near Waterview. Samuel is at present (1946) Superintendent of Schools.

Joseph Alexander (1780-1859) waited until 1824 before he came to Big Renox, Cumberland County. He married Ann Bouldin, a daughter of Joseph Bouldin, 1807, who was son of Maj. Thomas Bouldin of Charlotte County, Virginia. To this union were born four— Anna Clark, Fayette W., Sarah, and Hugh. Hugh died in infancy, Sarah Martin married Eleazer Clay Baker, 1831 (see Bakers, of William). Anna Clark married Joseph Baker (see Bakers).

Fayette Wood Alexander (born 1811) married Nancy Gertrude King, 1840, daughter of Milton and granddaughter of John E. King, both long Clerks of the County. To F. W. were born ten children —Preston, Charles Wyckliffe, Mary E., William F., Susan (wife of Dr. Hutchins); Sally (see Owsley); Horace K.; Victoria; Nancy A. (see Ritcheys).

Preston of this group died in the West. Mary E. and Victoria died young. William F. Alexander married Georgia Phelps, daughter of Capt. Abner Phelps (1818-85) and Anna Hooker, his wife, who had come to Cumberland County from New York in the interest of oil and who set up a large store in 1870 and served as postmaster at Burkesville, 1870-74. To W. F. and Georgia were born three—Lillian, 1873; Lalla; Addie Hooker. Lalla married Jacob McGee; no issue. They were leaders in church and benevolent work of the county. He was cashier of Bank of Cumberland. She possessed that kindhearted personality that made her a lovable character. Hooker married Dr. H. B. Simpson and moved to Greensboro, where she was very much like her sister in service.

Charles Wyckliffe spent most of his life in Burkesville, where he operated the bank and carried on other needed activities.

C. W., Jr., took up his father's work in 1936 as president of the Cumberland Bank. He married Mary Keen; no issue.

Settler Joseph secondly married Sarah Bouldin, cousin to his first wife, and daughter of Richard Bouldin, in 1818. To them were born seven—Richard B.; Milton J.; Judge Tom Tyler; Martha B.; Margaret; Joseph H. M.; and Dr. Robert M. Dr. Robert M. married Ellen B. Alexander, daughter of John M., Jr., who was a son of Thomas, Sr. (see Thurman). To them were born ten children—John J.; Hortense C.; Lavell M.; Robert A.; Mary C.; five died. These children served in many official capacities as noted elsewhere, under "Outstanding Men."

Robert, the Settler, married Mary Ann Miller, daughter of Dabney Miller of Henrico County, Virginia. Their farm lay in "The Bowling Green" of that county. He came to Cumberland County and purchased part of the farm taken up by James Coleman, 1796.

Settler Thomas Alexander was married twice. First he married Polly —— and had ten children—Frances, Robert, Edward, Bonapart, Peter, Thomas, Harriet, John, and Walthall, Waller. He secondly married Nancy, and reared Nancy who married John Pace; Philip and Susan (Gearheart); John M., Jr.; Greenwood.

Philip, the Settler, married Susan Bouldin, sister to Joseph's wife, Eliza, and came to Little Renox Creek. They reared John B., Paull, Hillery, Sarah, and James Bouldin.

Ingrim Alexander, the Settler, married Elizabeth Nunn in 1800 and located on Marrowbone. He came from Henry County, like the others. His children—John; Sally, wife of Richard Wade; Philip; Nancy; Reuben; James.

Settler Martin Alexander married Winnie Davis in Henry County in 1798 and came to this county with the others. He left many descendants on Marrowbone in the Davises, Grubbs, Allens, etc.

Obedience (called Biddy) (of John) married Peter Gearhart and reared—John, Margaret, Susan, Thomas, Lucy Ann, Joseph, Sarah (Dudley), Peter, Jr. Peter, Sr., was a leader in his church at Casey Fork and a merchant of power in the 1830's.

For more concerning the Alexanders see "Outstanding Men" of the county. We note from old records that J. Martin gave $1,500 to his Presbyterian Church on Casey Fork in 1885. Also that —— Alexander gave $500 to the college if it would bear his name. Right here we might state that too much stress has always been laid on characters of this caliber. While those people were able to contribute to such causes of their means there have always been others that gave their time and talent in other ways to good causes, to whom little publicity has been given. May praised be their good name. James R. Alexander spent his life in the Bowling Green school, where he had world recognition as a mathematician.

ALLENS

This family of people originated in Western Asia. A tribe bore the name. They migrated to south Russia in 410; from there to south Sweden; here they lost their warlike habits and became fishermen; then they merged with Anglo-Saxons who moved to Britain in 449. Records then have them populating Ireland and Scotland.

In 1737 James Allen, a Scotch-Irish immigrant, settled in Virginia and reared a family. One of his sons, named Robert (1747-1788), married Jane Turk, a daughter of Tom Turk. Jane (1749-1846) and Robert married in 1767, and to this union were born eleven children, Robert, Samson, John, William, Nathan, George, and David. The four daughters were Peggy, Jenny, Elizabeth, and Hannah. These are the children according to his will probated in Augusta County, Virginia. Soon after the death of her husband (who had fought through the Revolutionary War), she and her eleven children came to Cumberland County and settled on a branch of Marrowbone Creek, which was named in her honor—Allens Creek. The children lived with her a while in the new settlement and then scattered over different parts of the country. Robert and Samson owned land in 1796.

Samson

Samson remained on Allens Creek, where he ran a mill for many years before he married Jane Ritchey in 1801. He had five sons and five daughters. The sons were James D., William, Robert, Albert, and Alfred. The daughters were Mariah, Charlotte, Elizabeth, 1819, Betty, and Sally.

James D. married Julia Ann Waggener and had two sons, Albert and William, and two daughters, Alice and Mrs. James Baker.

William (of Samson), born 1809, died 1860. He married Sally Ann Baker, daughter of Obediah Baker. Sally was born 1820, died 1849. They had four children—M. O. Allen (1838-1911), James, Betty, and America.

M. O. (of William) married Julia Williams (1843-1927). They became the parents of Jane (Alexander), John E., W. M., M. O., Jr., Nettie (Ewing), Frankie, and Frank.

Robert (of Samson) married Amanda Turk, had Arch, Adaline, and Eliza, and went to Illinois.

Albert and Alfred (of Samson), no record.

Mariah (of Samson) married Ajournel Baker. Charlotte married George Craft. Elizabeth married Eli J. Patterson. Betty married Moses Hemlet. Sally married Bob Gilmer.

Betty (of William) married Ingram of Monticello. Four children.

James (of William) went west.

America (of William) married J. H. C. Sandidge, attorney of Burkesville. They left seven boys and one girl.

M. O. Allen (of William) spent most of his life in public. He was school superintendent, and county judge when the third court house and the present jail were built, 1866-70. He practiced law until his death, with the style, Allen & Ewing (J. O. Ewing).

William M. (of M. O.) is living at present and has a family of five boys and five girls. He is a public-spirited man, having been surveyor of the county for a number of years. His children, Grace, Mable, James, Nell, Will, John, Preston, Christine, Bobby, and Betty.

Elizabeth

Betsey (of Jane Allen) married Joseph Doherty and raised seven sons and two daughters. Joe was a blacksmith and a good mechanic. He settled near the mouth of Allens Creek, where Mrs. George Young now lives. At that time the whole bottoms were full of wild animals, such as deer, bears, and wild turkeys on which the settlers feasted. The canebrakes were thick and tall. Joe and his boys cleared away the brakes and planted the land in corn, tobacco, cotton, and wheat. He supplied the farmers with plows, hoes, scythes, and even made rifle guns and sold them. The father and his sons drilled a salt well near the house, 900 feet deep, but did not find sufficient quantities to pay. Think of drilling 900 feet with a sweep pole. Richey Young, one of the Allen descendants who lives at the old place, has in his possession one of the old salt kettles used 150 years ago. He also has one of Samson Allen's burr stones from the Samson Allen mill of 1791.

It was here in 1820 that Rev. William Harris and Caleb Weeden began their camp meetings which lasted for ten years before the church was erected. Ritchey Young tells us a few years ago he was excavating where the old church stood and five feet under the ground he struck the top of a large cedar post that was put there in 1830. He also found three large stone marbles by the post. These little reminders should make us thankful for those old pioneers that subdued the forests for you and me, and broke the way into the religious surroundings we enjoy today. This branch of the Allen family is scattered far and wide.

George (Will 1858)

George Allen (of Jane) went from Allens Creek to Leslie to live. He married Parmelia Chrisman and raised Norman, Robert, Lewis, James G., Martha, Mary Jane, and Gervis C.

Robert (of George) married Miss Stockton and went to Mississippi. Lewis married Nunn and left.

Martha married Miltwood Alexander and left.
Norman married a Turk. James married Jane Smith and left.
Mary Jane married George Arnold. Had one son, George Lewis in Missouri.

NATHAN

Nathan (of Jane), twin brother to William, married Sarah Gleaves of Virginia and moved to Allens Creek where he lived until 1835 when he sold out and went to Warren County. He reared five sons and three daughters. Most of them married and reared families outside of Cumberland County.

Elizabeth, the eldest daughter, married Lewis Waggener and lived and died at Burkesville, this county.

ROBERT

Robert (of Jane) married Nancy Cloyd and moved from Marrowbone Creek to Wash Bottom near Carys Ferry, where Will Cary now lives.

Their children were Polly, Jane, Rhoda, Samson, Peggy.
Jane married John Scott. Rhoda married John Hutchins.
Peggy married Harrison Cary.
Samson married Margaret Clemmons.
Polly married Billy Young and had one son, Allen Young.
Allen Young married Susan Wilcox and had Frank, Walker, Willie, John, Albert, and Louisa.
Walker, William, and Albert left. John died and Louisa married William Allen and went to Oklahoma.

Frank married Fanny Depp and reared one boy—Charley D. Young. Charles D. has never married. He has accumulated quite a bit of wealth in and around Burkesville, being the owner of more than 50 lots and buildings in the town, besides a lumber yard and the large hardware store known as the "Building Supply Establishment." C. D. has the honor of erecting many business places which add to the beauty of Burkesville and will be monuments to his memory. He is now past 50 but one of the busiest men in Cumberland County.

Hannah (of Jane) married Tom Gearhart and had Polly, Betsy, Sally, Harriet, Peggy, Bob.

Peggy (of Jane) married Jim Fergus, 1802. They had one daughter, Jenny, who married Lewis Warriner in 1824. Jenny lived 1805-42.

BAKERS

A will of Thomas Baker of Chesterfield County, Virginia, dated 1774, and one of his wife, Sarah, of 1778, mention nine children: Martin, Thomas, William, John, James, Ann (Stinson), Sarah (wife of Anthony Hancock), Jane (wife of —— Morsette), Barbara (Gordon).

John Baker, Sr. (of Thomas and Sarah), married in the above county of Virginia and reared ten children there, whose names were: Martin, Thomas, James, John, William, Ann, Judith, Mary,

Sarah, and Elizabeth. All these children except Ann married in Virginia before coming to Cumberland County. A brief history of them are here given, the five sons all coming in 1805, John being 55 years old and William 41, according to their Revolutionary War records.

Martin Baker, first son of John, Sr., and Sarah, married Sarah Young and to them were born seven children (will 1806): Barbara, Hannah, Rhoda, Ann Young, Mercy, Obediah, and John W. Baker. For this John W. Baker see Cheek Tree, and for the daughters see the various trees. Obediah Baker married Elizabeth Bowman. Obediah Baker was a mechanic and carpenter of note. Two brick buildings yet standing and in good repair testify to his workmanship. One is near the gap on Allens Creek owned by Caleb Day, with date 1814; the other is on Little Renox Creek owned by Charley Keen. Elizabeth was a woman of religious conviction and keen mentality. She organized a congregation near her home and set the men to working on a church building, 1815, which resulted in the establishment of Sugar Grove Church. To Obediah and Elizabeth were born: John M., A. L., Elizabeth (Cheatham), Sarah (Carter), Polly (Jones), Jane (Hutchinson), Sally Ann (Allen). Among the descendants of Obediah and Elizabeth were, M. O. Allen, Circuit Judge Wallace W. Jones, Judge W. P. Sandidge of the 7th Judicial District, and Prescott Sandidge, attorney and Commissioner of the Court of Appeals, Kentucky.

John, Thomas, William, and James came on carts and packhorses in 1805 and stopped in "First Night Hollow" on Big Renox Creek. John was a very conscientious man, and having studied the new Declaration of Independence in its teachings that "all men are created equal" resolved to carry it into practice, so before he migrated to Cumberland County he decided to liberate his 12 slaves on Christmas Day before their 21st birthday. On Christmas Day, 1790, he set free, Bob, Dan, Grace, Ann, and Barbara. Then Tom in 1793, Sally in 1796, Betty and Patsy in 1802, and the other three he brought along to assist in the clearing and planting of a mill for grinding, all of these went free, 1811. John had married Elizabeth Cobb in Chesterfield County and to them were born three children: James, Benjamin, and Elizabeth Cobb Baker, born in 1806. For her descendants see Cheek Tree.

William Baker, the third brother who came to the county in 1805, was the father of Eleazer Clay Baker who married Sarah Martin Alexander, 1831, and whose son Hershell Clay Baker (see chapter on Outstanding Men), married Dolly Lysle and became the parents of Tyler, Lysle, Sallie, Alexander, Nettie, Mamie, and H. C., Jr. Most of these families lived around Columbia, Kentucky.

James Baker, the other pioneer brother who came in 1805, became the progenitor of the Bakerton Bakers. His sons, James, Jr., and Joseph, married Alexanders. James married Sally Alexander in 1822 and Joseph married Ann Clark Alexander, daughter of Joseph and Nancy (Bouldin) Alexander. Their children were Alex Baker, James, Clay, Alice, Fayette, Tyler, Kate who married Candor Williams, Sarah Ann (1832-94) married Owen Cheatham and had Sally E. Cheatham (1852-99), married John Wesley Williams (1827-88), and to them were born a son Hooker and daughter Hattie M. Williams who married Kent Sandidge and reared Kent, Jr., Wesley, and Clay Sandidge.

Judith Baker, daughter of John, Sr., and sister to the five pioneer brothers, married Wilson Cary in Virginia, 1793, and followed her brothers to Cumberland County, settling in the southern part of the county, and became the progenitors of the whole Cary family. Mary, her sister married — Hopper and left descendants in the county; Sarah Baker married Archelaus Chalkley and also left offspring; Elizabeth married Thomas Gregory and left descendants; one daughter Margaret married Newby Hancock, 1812.

Thomas Baker, born 1784, brother of the other boys, married Ann Elliott and to them—Ann P., who married Peter Sublett in Virginia; Martha who married Mr. Ryan of Texas; Phoebe who married Richard Cheatham, Pike County, Ill.; Thomas who went to Oregon, 1835; Samuel who married Judith Robertson; Solomon who married Jane Paxton, who was a relative to Mark Twain, and to them was born Dr. Thomas E. who was the father of Richard, Asa, Finis, and Mrs. George Brockman; James (of Thomas) married Nancy Robison, second a Grisby; Matthew (1805) married Susan Baker, then Julia Dice.

Solomon's second wife was Nancy Elliott. He was born in 1803, died 1861. This Thomas, like his brothers, fought in the Revolutionary War. His offspring still live around Crocus, where they first settled and were a thriving class of people.

BLEDSOES

This family reaches far into the history of the European countries. They are of Saxon origin, being named from a royal line. In that country the name was Bluchers, in Italy Bledicines, in England it was Bletchers, and in America Bledsoes.

Part of the family went to Wales and part to Scotland. The oldest record of the Cumberland County Bledsoes starts with Aaron Bledsoe coming from Wales and settling at Spotsylvania, Virginia, about 1600. His son, William, married a Virginia girl and reared Abraham, Moses, Joseph (born 1732), and John.

Abraham was the leader of the nine Long Hunters (noted elsewhere in this volume) who led the way to Kentucky, 1770.

Joseph and his brother John married sisters—daughters of Hiram Miller, who lived neighbors to them at their place of settlement. John went to Tennessee and became the progenitor of the Tennessee Bledsoes. A county of that state bears the name.

Joseph married Betty Miller November 3, 1759, and reared a family of nine children. He obtained a land grant of 2,000 acres in Lincoln County, Kentucky, on the Kentucky River near Lancaster, Garrard County. He assigned the tract to his brother, Moses, September 30, 1781. The original transfer is in preservation in the county, written on sheepskin. Joseph then came to Cumberland County and settled, 1798, in Rock House Bottom, near the place explored by his brother Abraham.

The following is a brief history of the nine children of Joseph and Betty Miller Bledsoe:

William (4-22-1761); Moses (3-19-1763); Margaret Jane (3-10-1765); Joseph (10-12-1766); Benjamin (7-15-1768); Betty (Peggy) (10-9-1769); Elijah (10-10-1771); Abraham (4-22-1774); Jesse (5-20-1776). To Joseph's second wife (Miss Bates) was born one son—John.

The following data have been collected for each of children of Joseph and Betty Miller.

1. William (of Joseph and Betty M.) married first a Miss Craig of Powell Valley, Tennessee, and had one son—Joseph. William then married Patience Owsley, aunt of Governor Owsley of Kentucky. To this last union were born seven children: Moses, Aaron, Willis, Scott, William, Mrs. Wilmot, and Mrs. Robertson. They lived at Lancaster, Kentucky, and William was buried by his mother, Betty Miller, near Lancaster.

2. Moses Bledsoe (of Joseph and Betty M.) was a very noted Baptist preacher in his day. He married a Miss Jamerson and reared two daughters—Virginia and Mrs. Smart of Mt. Sterling, Kentucky. Virginia married Hon. Albert G. Harrison of Boonville, Missouri. Harrison served as Congressman from Missouri for some 20 years. Harrisonville, Missouri, was named in his honor. Both are buried at Pleasant Hill, Missouri.

3. Margaret Jane Bledsoe (of Joseph and Betty M.) married Thomas Chilton, formerly of Elizabethtown, Kentucky, and who lived at Creelsboro, Kentucky, and owned large tracts of land in and around Creelsboro and Rock House Bottom. He was also a great Baptist preacher of his day. To them were born—Thomas, Jr., Lyssus, Mynor, Mrs. Dr. Ray, and Mrs. William D. Parrish. These children went south.

4. Joseph Bledsoe (1766-1837), (of Joseph and Betty M.), married Agnas Hickman (1781-1836) in 1797. She was a daughter of David Hickman and his wife Clara McClanehan of Paris, Kentucky. David's mother was Hannah Lewis of Virginia and a line of those noted Lewises one of whom married a sister to George Washington. To Joseph and Agnas Hickman were born 15 children.

(1). Hiram Miller Bledsoe (1798-1876) of Joseph and Agnas H. Bledsoe, married Susan Hughes of Paris, Kentucky, and moved to Lexington, Missouri, where they died. Their children were: William H., John, Mrs. Agnas Ingles, Hiram Miller, Joseph, Mrs. Cara Eddy, and Robert.

(2). William H. (1800-29) of Joseph and Agnas Hickman, married Elizabeth Embree and had the following four children: Harriett, who married Richard Howard (see Howards); Mary, who married Dr. James Cheek (see Cheeks); Nancy, who was married to Dr. Hiram Staton (see Statons); and William Bledsoe.

(3). Thomas Chilton Bledsoe (1802), of Joseph and Agnas Hickman, was married to Frances Wilson of Bourbon County, Kentucky, and went to Lexington, Missouri. Their children: Mrs. Mary Elly, Iowa; Mrs. Margaret Cromell; Hiram M.; Joseph; John, and Thomas Bledsoe.

(4). Betty Baylor (1804-25), of Joseph and Agnas Hickman, married Peter Montfort of Cumberland County. No children.

(5). Joseph Scott Bledsoe (1806), married Susan E. Bowman of Burkesville, Cumberland County, Kentucky. Their four children: Granville; Hiram Miller, who was a lawyer of Burkesville; William E., who married Mary Bryan and had two daughters, Emma Blackford, Wilmore, Kentucky, and Agnas McGee of Burkesville, Kentucky; and Agnas, of Joseph and Susan, married William Owsley of Burkesville, Kentucky. Left one son (1852), W. F. Owsley.

(6). Clara Ann (1808-66), of Joseph and Agnas Hickman, married James G. Chrisman, 1827. They lived and died at Raleigh, Mississippi. Their children, Joseph B. (1828); John T. (1830); Pinckney Dryden (1832); Margaret Jane (1834); Mary Ann (1836); Agnas C. (1838); Julia (1840); Henry Clay (1843); Albert (1846); Hiram (1848); Rosa (1850). This Chrisman family lived at Blum, Texas.

(7). Matilda Hord (1810-44), married to Dr. P. W. Dryden, 1827, of Hopkinsville, Kentucky. They had the following children: Sarah who married Andrew J. Wyatt; Susan who married Augusta L. Johnson and reared a family of teachers and lawyers at Ft. Worth, Texas; Matilda who married a bishop; and Agnas Dryden.

(8). David Hickman Bledsoe (1812-43), of Joseph and Agnas H., married Georgia Ann Powell and died in Arkansas without issue.

(9). Margaret Jane (1814), of Joseph and Agnas H., married Thomas R. Hughes, 1832, and had one son, Joseph T. Hughes. Joseph T. married and left three children, Reed Allen, Leona, and Hickman. Margaret died at Lexington, Kentucky.

(10). Nancy H. (1816-88), of Joseph and Agnas H., married William M. Campbell, 1837. Their children: William; Hickman; Joseph; Mrs. Mary Agnas McAndrew; John H.; Mrs. Maggie J. Bryan, Wilmore, Kentucky; James H.; and Nanny Lewis Harvey. Most of this family stayed around Lexington, Kentucky.

(11). Mary Agnas Bledsoe (1817), of Joseph and Agnas H., married Henry F. Samuels, 1834, and lived at Hot Springs County, Arkansas. Their children: David B. Samuels, Dr. D. A. Luther, all of whom lived in Arkansas. Mrs. Mary A. Samuels married the second time (1853) to Mr. Harris and had two children, Alonzo and Mrs. Elenor Jones.

(12). Moses (1819), of Joseph and Agnas, died young.

(13). Susan Bledsoe, born 1822, died 1827.

(14). John Shelby Bledsoe (1823-1901) married Louisa Sharp, 1845, at Hopkinsville, Kentucky. Their children were: Henry Bledsoe, Mrs. Clara Bailey. Louisa was a niece of N. L. Rice, the famous debater of Alexander Campbell.

(15). Vesta Patience Bledsoe (1827-63), of Joseph and Agnas H., was the last of this big family of Bledsoes. She married James T. Stephenson and reared the following family: William Henry, 1850; Mary Kate (1851-53); Corene (1853-54); Hiram (1854-88); Robert A. (1856-80); Walton (1858-1901); Albert; and John. This family lived at Little Rock, Arkansas.

Joseph and his wife Agnas Hickman lived in Cumberland County from 1800 to 1831, when he sold his farm in Rock House Bottom and started in wagons for Columbia, Missouri, in the fall of the year. Winter overtaking them near Hopkinsville, Christian County, Kentucky, Joseph bought a farm nine miles from town and lived and died there.

5. Benjamin Bledsoe (of Joseph and Betty Miller) married ––– Jennings, both of whom lived in Cumberland County. Their children were Jennings Bledsoe, William, Jesse, Mrs. Roberson, and Mrs. Embree.

Jesse (of Ben) kept the United States Hotel of Louisville in the early 60's. Two of Jesse's children were Cicero, who was editor of a Nashville paper, and Betty, who married a Mr. Bushfield of Nashville, Tennessee.

6. Betty (Peggy) Bledsoe (of Joseph and Betty Miller) married a Mr. Baylor of Paris, Kentucky, and went to Texas to live. Their children were George and Betty Baylor.

7. Elijah Bledsoe (of Joseph and Betty Miller) married Judith (Juda) Jamason and to them were born: George Chilton, Willis, John, Tom Walker, Juda, Margaret, Lucy, Frances, William H. H., Elijah Powell Monroe, and Dock.

George C. married Nanny Sloan, sister to Emanuel, and to them; Elijah, a teacher; Susie, who married A. V. Ross whose offspring in Rosses and Reeders live in Rock House Bottom; Viola, who married Berry Self and left; John, who reared his family on Crocus Creek; Willis, who married Bessie Campbell and reared family at Creelsboro. Rev. Tom is one son.

Willis married twice. His first children were Mollie, Lel, and Walter. His second wife was Sarah Acre and children: Charles, Lena, and Delia.

John married three times. His first three girls were Belle, Laura, Fanny. Belle (my mother) see Wells; Laura married Joe Buck Winfrey of Columbia; Fanny married Min Calhoun and left. The next set of children was Rev. Elijah (went to Texas, no issue); Wilmuth; Kots; Ceola.

Tom Walker married Polly Winfrey, of Frank, and reared Elijah, whose son, Tom, became a millionaire in Chicago; Frank, who married Emily Irvin; Lucy, who married Milton Spencer who was born to Sidney and father of Millard; Ellen, who married Sid Spencer;

Maggie, who married Billie Johnson, who was the father of all the Johnsons of Rock House and Creelsboro.

Juda married Billie Warriner. No issue. Margaret married Roe Morrison and had one son who married Mandy Denny.

Lucy (of Elijah, Sr.), married Humphrey Cooffey; Frances married Frank Ross, no issue; Elijah Powell Monroe married Emma McGlassen and reared Ona, 1868; W. H., 1870; Ella, 1873; Mattie S., 1875; John G., 1877; Odell, 1880; Ray, 1881; Berry, 1883; Owen, 1885; Ida, 1888; Major, 1898.

8. Abraham Bledsoe (of Joseph and Betty Miller) married and moved to Tennessee.

9. Jesse Bledsoe (of Joseph and Betty Miller) married and lived at Lexington, Kentucky. He was United States Senator from Kentucky, and an able judge. He was sent to Texas to write the Constitution of that state and died there. His children were John, Mrs. Bodley, Mrs. Brown, and Mrs. Ralph.

Gov. Grant Brown of Missouri was a grandson of Jesse Bledsoe. Jesse adjourned court at Lexington, 1830, to pay tribute to John Bradford, Kentucky's first editor of *Gazette*, who died 1830.

Joseph Bledsoe's first wife (Betty Miller) died and he married a Miss Bates of Creelsboro, Kentucky, and had one son, John. Joseph then died, and his Bates wife married a Mr. Chapman of Cumberland County.

BOOHERS

The Boohers of Cumberland County came from Germany to North Carolina and settled in the Western part which became Tennessee, 1796. Christopher Booher married daughter of Thomas Wood (see Woods and Reneaus), the great-grandfather of the many Boohers now living in this county, headed the list of settlers that stopped in Tennessee on Eagle Creek and lived and died there, rearing a large family. John Booher, one of his sons, married Sallie Booher while in Tennessee, and to them were born seven children: Margaret, Emiline, Mary, Dave, Jim, Tom, and Jake.

After the birth of the fourth child, John brought his family to Clinton County and settled on a farm near the village of Highway. Here the fifth child was born, after which he moved his family to Cumberland County, where he spent the rest of his life.

Margaret died, never having married.

Emiline married Jefferson Cox, and they had two children, Boles Cox and Albert.

Mary married George Bowen, and to them were born a family.

Dave married Mattie Williams and reared three children.

Jim (1850) married Mary Talbot, daughter of Milton Talbot and granddaughter of Nicholas, the Settler, and reared 15 children: Ida who married George Riddle, father of W. Wash; Laura who married

G. K. Steans (as given); Willie who was drowned, 1891; Robert who married Emma Dicken and went to California; Mrs. Winnie Appleby who reared family on Little Renox; Sam who married Connie Sparks and reared family on Little Renox; Eliza who married Cyrus McCoy and reared three—one of whom, James F., is a minister of California; Joe N. who married Bertha Myers and reared family in the county, Joe heads a large wholesale firm in Burkesville; Jim Ed who married Ada Myers, sister to Bertha, and reared 13 children, part of whom are connected with the business of this county and part in California; Julia who married Winborn Capps and went to Oklahoma; Eunice who married Otha Cheatham and reared family in the county; Mrs. Caleb Day who reared family on Little Renox; Charles who married Louvina Young and has family in California; Eula who married Owen Cheatham and has family; Barny, who married Lala Norris, died in California, 1946.

Tom married Julia Williams and reared three children, who are the citizens of Myers Ridge.

Jake Booher got killed.

BOULDINS

The Bouldins of this county were originally from England. Col. Thomas Bouldin married Nancy Clark in Pennsylvania, in 1731. They went to Virginia in 1744, where they reared a family who became prominent in the affairs of their country. Their children were Wood, Joseph, and Richard.

Colonel Thomas was sheriff of Charlotte County, Virginia, captain and lieutenant colonel in the Intercolonial Wars.

His son Wood became Major in the Revolutionary War.

The grandchildren of Colonel Thomas were, Thomas Tyler, James, and Louis C. Thomas Tyler was Senator of Virginia and fell dead on the floor while speaking.

Many of the descendants of Colonel Thomas married into the prominent families of Cumberland County, as found under other families.

Richard Clark Bouldin came to Cumberland County in 1834 and married Emma Dickens, who had come to Burkesville in 1827 with her parents. Emma was a cousin to Charles Dickens, the noted English novelist.

To R. C. and Emma were born Mattie, Jane, R. C., Jr., Henry, Robert, Clara, and Wylie. Mattie married Joe Perry and went to Greensburg; Jane married James Hartnitt; Clara married Sam Elliott; Wylie married Bernice Allen, great-granddaughter of Jane Allen, and to them was born Emma, who married Dr. L. E. Coop.

Wylie has been one of the largest traders in livestock of this and adjoining counties which business he kept up until the trucks and radios did away with pinhooking in the county.

BOW FAMILY

The name Bow is Anglo-Saxon, derived from a place of residence, meaning "arch," i.e., the one living at the Arch, "Henry atte Bow"; unlike Bowman which is an occupation name.

The Bows came from Virginia. The first one of record in Cumberland County was Jesse Bow, who came in 1800. He located on the waters of Raft Creek and moved to Bear Creek, 1802. He married Minerva Story, and to them were born five sons and five daughters: Isaac, Abagail, Fayette, Dal, Stephe, Laura, Albert ——. Isaac was captain in the Civil War and leader of the G.A.R. He was elected sheriff of the county several terms. He married Philipina Scott, and to them were born Mary, Nettie, Dr. James E. who was County Clerk and a faithful doctor all his life; John, Minnie, Ella M., and Mrs. Simpson. Mary married Rev. Tom Hulse; Laura married B. Jones; Hettie, Rev. Lewis Piercey; Ellen (of Capt. Isaac) married W. B. Huddleston and reared a family in the county.

Abagail (of Jesse, Sr.), married Capt. James A. Vincent (see Millers).

Fayette married Belle Taylor and had Ollie, Bernice, Stanley and Huey.

Dal married a Sells and reared Jesse, Ann, Laura, John, Fereby (see J. G. Jones).

Stephe married Julia Williams and reared Gordon, Tyler, Jessie.

Laura (of Jesse, Sr.), married John Williams (see Williams).

Albert married Martha Guthrie, reared Fayette, Ellen, Stephe, Bob, Oscar.

Stephe (of Albert) married Ellen Rush.

BRAKE FAMILY

William Brake, from North Carolina, took up land on the waters of Illwill Creek. His will shows he had four sons in 1829. They were: Bennett, Levi, John, and Jacob.

Bennett married Milley ——.

Levi married Nancy ——.

Jacob married Happy Riddle and reared a family (see Cumming).

John married Ona Bow and reared four children—Ben, Jane, Sally, and William L.

Ben died single.

Sally married James Samuels and went to Missouri.

Jane married Rev. James Guthrie of Rose of Sharon and died without issue.

William L. married Lucy Williams and reared six—Jennie, Edith, Eva, Cora, William V., Fred, and Bessie.

Jennie married Marshall Williams and reared Ruth, who married Luther Bowen and reared a family on Bear Creek; Roxie, who married Bill Shelly and reared family.

Edith (of William and Lucy) married Elam Riddle and went to Missouri.

Eva (of William and Lucy) married William Rush and reared four—Myrtle, who married Horace Carter, a thriving farmer of Bear Creek; Claud, who married ——, and is one of Cumberland's best teachers; Clarence, who married a daughter of Bob Armstrong and is another of our best teachers. He also served as Representative from Cumberland County.

Clayton (of Eva and William) single.

Cora (of William and Lucy) married James Manus and went to Missouri.

William V. first married Ellen Smith, daughter of Samuel S., and to them were born Anna, Ernest, Irvin, Alta, Eston, and Edward.

Ernest is one of our best teachers; Irvin was killed in World War II; Alta married Leslie Sewell of Bear Creek.

William V. secondly married Jewell Pharis and reared Dorothy, Norma, Edith, and Joyce.

Fred Brake (of William and Lucy) married Mollie Smith (d. of Sam) and reared Leslie, Charles, Roy, John, Carr, Robert, Paul, and Lucy. All these children made good citizens and business people of the county.

Bessie (of William and Lucy) married William Tuggle and reared Roger who died in a Jap prison, Fred, and Reba.

THE BURCHETT FAMILY

John Henry, a son of Patrick Henry, the great orator of Revolutionary fame, moved to Kentucky in the neighborhood of Danville the latter part of the eighteenth century. While living there a child was born to him and his wife. They called the little girl Elizabeth. Its mother died, leaving the little child to the care of her father, so he took her back to his folks in Virginia. John Wade, the child's uncle, who had settled on a large farm at what later became Cartwright, Cumberland County, made a trip to Virginia and brought the little girl back to his home at Cartwright and raised her to womanhood. Elizabeth was born in 1798, died 1875.

Icil Burchett and his brother, Solomon, came to Cumberland County to live. Solomon settled on the waters of Indian Creek, where his descendants are to be found today. Icil stopped on a farm at Cartwright, and in 1818 he and Elizabeth Henry were married. They made this community their home and raised a large family of six boys and four girls. Their names are Cooper, Granville, Richard, Polly Ann, Emiline, William, Frank, Calvin, Marintha, Amelia. Icil was born 1796, died 1862.

Cooper was never married and was bushwhacked at home by the guerrillas in the first half of the Civil War.

Granville had one son and moved to Oregon to live.

Richard had three sons, Albert, Bee, and Foxey whose descendants remain in the same locality. Richard was also bushwhacked near home.

Frank married Nancy Jane Warriner (sister to I. L. Warriner) and raised two girls, Cyntha (Piercey) and Maggie (Neathery). He was bushwhacked.

William went to Missouri and stayed.

Marintha married a Mr. Garner and went to Illinois.

Amelia married John Elder. Lucinda married Henry Perdue. Polly Ann married Arthur Reeves, whose descendants are scattered over much of this country. Calvin (1823-1869) married Polly Branham (1824-1888), in 1841, to which union were born 7, George W., Tom, Bill, Frank, Icil, Caroline, Mary Ellen.

Tom Burchett married Nellie Murphy of Cumberland County, and his brother Frank married Victoria, her sister, both reared families in Clinton County.

Bill married Cyntha Neathery and reared a family in Clinton County.

Icil (of Calvin)

Caroline (of Calvin)

Mary Ellen (of Calvin) married Elijah Ferguson and to them were born Calvin, Bill, Molly, Tom, George, Jim, Bob, Laura, Icil, Frank, and Eula.

George W. Burchett (1843-1935) married Annie Lynn and raised the following children: Nettie (Bryson), 1866; Sadie (Williams), 1868; Della (Brown), 1870; Dr. William, 1872; Ed, 1876; Georgia, 1879. George W. Burchett enlisted in the Union Army, 1861, and was in the battles of Mill Springs, Fort Henry, Perryville, Nashville, Knoxville, Waitsboro, Corinth, and many others.

He knew Abraham Lincoln personally, and was one of the 24 men chosen to act as pall-bearers at Chicago and guard the body as it lay in state there. At Springfield, Illinois, he escorted the body from the station to the cemetery. He said the body of Lincoln was drawn by 12 black horses led by 12 Negroes, all of whom were six feet in height, typifying Lincoln's own height. Uncle George, as everybody called him, lived north of Burkesville one mile, where his grandson, Chester Bryson, now lives, until his death, April 4, 1935. He was 92 years old and could mount a horse quite easily. He was always called on to make the first address at patriotic gatherings. His activities in war will be found on another page of this volume.

Two Burchett brothers of Virginia, William and John, took part in the Revolutionary War, after which they both came to Cumberland County to live. Just what kin they were to the pioneer, Icil, we failed to find.

This John from Virginia (1759-1833), settled near the home of the above Burchetts. He was married twice. First wife was a Bartlett and to them were born four children: William, Bartlett, Hannah, who married Tom Stailey; Ailsey, who married Jacob Agee who was the father of James, who was the father of Joseph and Pleasant Agee, whose children live in Clinton County.

Second wife was Sally ——, and to them were born Isham, Patsy, Sally (who married Lewis Brown and lived at Glasgow), John, Peter, Alley (who married Wilson Jones, whose offspring live in Clinton County).

CARTWRIGHT FAMILY

This family does not belong among the pioneers of Cumberland County, but on account of the role it has played down through the history of the county it is worthy of recognition. The name belongs to the list derived from occupation. Many of the name have become prominent in the past.

Samuel C. came from the Carolinas to Tennessee about 1795; from there the family moved to Adair County, Kentucky, in 1798. Samuel's son, Joseph, married Mary White of Adair County and to them were born eight children—White, Nathan, John, Manson W. Hulda, Lucy, Frances, and Sally.

Manson W., 1803, of this group of children figured mainly in the history of Cumberland County. He married Katherine Yeiser of Adair County in 1847. To them were born four sons and three daughters—Walker F., Adam Y., Henderson, Thomas, Lucy M., Susan, and Cora H. The four sons all became doctors.

Dr. Walker F. married Mary Long of Clinton County and to them were born four daughters—Ethie, Nina, Leeta, and Mary.

Dr. Henderson Cartwright married Sallie Breeding and reared two children—Stella and Manson W., Jr. Dr. Henderson was a practicing physician at Burkesville for many years.

Lucy M. married Tilford B. Wells of Cumberland County and to them were born four sons and two daughters—Lewis Tom, Chester W., Tilford B., Jr., Manson C., Cora, and Fanny Kate.

Lewis T. married Jessie Ferguson of Burkesville and became a noted evangelist of the Nazarene Church (see Nazarene Churches).

C. W. married Era Bledsoe and reared three children—Oscar, Anna Kate, and Marvin.

T. B., Jr., married Wonnie Mackey and reared two daughters—Robbie G. and Hazel.

Manson married Fanny Allen. No children.

Cora married Harold A. Ferguson and reared two sons and three daughters.

Fanny K. married Joe R. Winfrey. No issue.

All these children, like their father, have become thriving farmers of our county, with the exception of the Rev. L. T. Wells, who is spending his life in the ministry.

CARY FAMILY

This is a name that dates back to 590 B.C. It falls into that class applied to bodily features. It, like most of names, has undergone many orthographic changes, as Kary, Carey, Kara, and Cary. With all these it retained its meaning down to the discovery of Britain. It means "bald, or with little hair." The Karys came from Asia to Russia and to Germany, England, and to America. Their landing seems to have been in Virginia, for all their line reaches back through that state. Wilson and Henry came first.

They came from Chesterfield County, Virginia, to Cumberland County in 1797. Two brothers came and took up land "on Cumberland River." Wilson married Juda Baker, sister to the five pioneer Bakers, and to them were born nine children. Henry married Elizabeth Hooper. I have found but little about his family.

Wilson had five sons that spread the name—Archibald, Robert, Abner, Harrison, and George. One daughter married Mr. Herd. "Archie" married Evelyn Kirkpatrick who had come from Culpeper County, Virginia, and to them were born Lafayette, Turner, Preston, and Moses. Fayette married Sarah Barron and reared Will G., Ella, Ed, Anna, Charles B., and Frank W. Turner (of Archie) married Ellen Barron, sister to Sarah, and to them three—Albert, Bessie (wife of Bob Goff), and William Walker, all of this county. Preston (of Archie) married Mary Stewart and to them were born Perry G. who served as Justice of Peace several years, and Lizzie who married D. Murley who lost his life while riding his horse over the Big Hill, by being struck by a car. He left a family. Moses (of Archie) married Cassie Philpot and reared a family in Texas.

Robert (of Wilson) married Jane Cloyd and reared Archie, Everett, Abner, Ferdinand, John, Elizabeth, and Ara. Archie left no issue; Everett married a Buford and left three; Abner married a French and left Ottley who died without issue; Mrs. Judge B. L. Simpson who became the mother of four—Regina who married James Keen, Jr., who is first deputy sheriff; Mary who married Russell Marshall, a Government employee; Winton who married Randolph Smith who is the only druggist in Burkesville; the son moved out of the county. The three girls have families here.

Ferd (of Wilson's Robert) married a French and reared four—Creed A. who is a highway officer of Cumberland and has a family in town; Maud who married Wilkie Collins and has a family in Illinois; Sada who married Marvin Rowe and has a family in town; Lovie who married Joe Anderson, with the firm of Curtis & McComas, as clerk.

Abner Cary (of Wilson) born January 26, 1798, married Mary King Williams, and they had the following children: Mary Wilson, who died young; Tobitah, who married Tommie Graves; Alexander C., born January 25, 1842; Virginia, who married James Cloyd; Amanda, born May 3, 1835; Lucenia, who married James Murphy; Cyrus W., born September 1, 1844; John C., who married Dora Collins, born

July 7, 1848, and died May 8, 1923; Nancy, who married Amos Starr, Barren County.

S. A. Cary (of John C.), and Lura Logan Cary had five children as follows: Eula Cary Rogers, living in Chicago; Thelma Cary Stephens, in Louisville; Malcolm Cary, now in the northwest; John Sam Cary, an attorney for the Veterans Administration in Louisville; and June Cary Rogers, living in Bellevue, Kentucky.

John (of Wilson's Robert) went to Illinois. Ara, his brother, married Artemeus Akin and reared four; Elizabeth, their sister, married Teen Akin and had five.

George (of Settler Wilson) moved away. Harrison (of Wilson) married Jane (Peggy) Allen, granddaughter of Jane Allen, the Settler, and to them were born Robert and George. This Robert married and reared Matthew, Miles, Mrs. Vege Cloyd, John, James, and George Matthew of this family married Alice Scott and reared William, Emmett, Jesse, Miles, Nannie, and Eddie. They lived in Cumberland County.

John C. Cary (of Abner) and Dora Collins Cary had the following children, now all living (1946): Leslie L. was born January 16, 1874, married Lula Gray and had five children—Leslie Lee, Jr., died in 1945; Lee Gray, living in Glasgow; Maydell Cary Downey; Stanley Cary and Conrad Cary, living in Louisville; and Eunice (1876), who married John Skinner. She is a noted speaker.

S. A. Cary was the youngest son of John C. and Dora Collins.

CHEEK FAMILY

The Cheeks came from England to America. They originated in France. Cheek is a nickname, Bajoue, meaning "fat or baggy cheek or jaw."

A direct line of our Cheeks began with William Cheek, born in London, 1728, and married a Miss Lindal, to whom three sons were born—Henry, Thomas, and John. His second wife was a Miss Ross, to whom was born one son—Nicholas.

Henry (of William, Sr.), born 1769 died 1838, married Jenny Hancock (1778-1850) in 1797, and to them 13 children were born, two in Virginia and eleven in Adair County, Kentucky. His second wife was Mary Emmerson of Burkesville, with three children.

Thomas (1798) and William (1799) were the two born in Virginia. In 1800 Henry and his wife and two sons came to Adair and built a fine house (1812) about four miles from Columbia on the old Greensburg Road, where his other eleven children were born respectively, from 1802 to 1824: Henry, Elizabeth, Permelia, James H., Nancy, George, Silas, Aaron, Levi, John L., and Mary Jane.

Thomas Cheek (of Henry and Jenny) married Sally Patterson Robertson and they became the parents of two sons—Thomas E. Cheek and Samuel B. The two sons were left orphans early in life and were reared by their grandfather, S. B. Robertson of Adair County. He was a noted Presbyterian minister, and their offspring became outstanding educators connected with Centre College, Danville, Kentucky, and also with the School for the Deaf, at the same place.

William, the second son of Henry and Jenny, spent most of his life in Burkesville, where he served as Representative, sheriff, and school commissioner, besides filling other public offices. He was a shrewd lawyer. In 1835 he married Mrs. Elizabeth C. Baker (1806-71), daughter of John Baker, Jr., and Elizabeth (Cobb) Baker. She had been married to John W. Baker, son of her uncle, Martin Baker, to whom were born three: Sally I, Hetty Ann, and John Walton.

To William and Elizabeth were born five children—Mary (dec.); Richard Menifee (1839); Christopher Tompkins (1842); James (1844); William, Jr. (1849). The four sons were left fatherless in 1852, and Elizabeth reared them to manhood.

R. M. Cheek received his education in the old academy at Columbia. He served in the Confederate Army against his brother, C. T. Cheek, and half-brothers in the Federal Army. He was twice elected sheriff of the county, sold goods, farmed, and was elder in the old Presbyterian congregation for 35 years. He left the county in 1906 together with his wife, Betty Jane Patterson Cheek, and only child, Menifee Reed Cheek, and located on a large farm near Nashville, Tennessee.

C. T. of this family married Anna V. Leslie, daughter of Gov. P. H. Leslie, and reared a family. C. T. served as sheriff.

James (of William and E. C.), (1844-1909), married Mary Elizabeth Alexander, daughter of John Henry Alexander, and reared a family.

William, Jr. (of William and E. C.), married Mollie Baker, daughter of James and Jane Waggener Baker, and went to Idaho.

Dr. James H. Cheek (of Henry and Jenny), 1809-85, married Mary A. Bledsoe, 1823-98, daughter of William and his wife Elizabeth Embree Bledsoe. To them were born Elizabeth (1850); Joel Owsley (1852); Hiram Miller (1855); Thomas, William, and John (the last one buried in Burkesville).

Elizabeth (of Dr. J. H.) married John Nicholson.

Joel Owsley Cheek (of Dr. J. H.), 1852-1935, married Minnie Ritchey of Burkesville and reared a large family at Nashville, Tennessee, where he became very wealthy in connection with the coffee business. His donation to Cumberland County has been related under Education. Minnie Ritchey was a daughter of James Howe and Helen M. Owsley Ritchey of Burkesville.

John Lindal Cheek (born 1821) was the progenitor of the Cumberland County Cheeks now living here. He married Mary S. Donely in 1850 and to them were born Mary Jane, Will Henry, James Oscar, John Simon, Stockton Donely.

Will Henry married Maggie McMurtrey and lived and died north of town.

J. O. (1855) married Mary Lula Ewing, daughter of Matthew Ewing and reared Mary Henretta, Kate, Lee, John Will, Jessie, Minnie S., Jamie, Lizzie, and Ewing.

Mary Henretta married Richard Newby and reared a family in the county. Kate married Charley Strange and reared a family in the county. Lee married Jesse Cole and reared a family here.

Lizzie married Charles Rutledge and had a family. Minnie and Jamie taught in the county many years.

John Simon (of J. L.), 1863-1906, married Minnie Lee Wells and his being a great Baptist evangelist accounts for the many different birthplaces of his five children.

John Frank, born at Madisonville, Kentucky, is (1946) in church work in Chattanooga, Tennessee. Major Oswald (1889) served as missionary to China and now is district missionary over ten counties, at Waco, Texas. Oscar Henry was a Lieutenant Colonel in World War II from El Paso, Texas. Lawrence is in wholesale business at Memphis, Tennessee. Minnie Wells Cheek, now Mrs. John Josey, is young people's director, Amarillo, Texas.

CLAYWELL FAMILY

Shadrach Claywell was the pioneer Claywell. He came in 1799 from Virginia. He was a private in the Revolutionary War, fighting with the Virginia Cavalry. Born in 1759, he died in 1838 in this county. His nine children were: Solomon, Sarah (Richardson); Jesse, who married Hannah Humphry, 1814, and reared family; Peggy, who married Thomas Cain on Bear Creek, 1815, and had a family, most of whom left; John, who died at New Orleans, 1837, of yellow fever while on a trip to take tobacco, and who sent his will back to his wife and three small children; Job; William; and Patsy, who married a Glidewell on Bear Creek; and Shadrach, Jr., who married Amelia Rush and reared John Anderson, Jack, and Micajah.

John Anderson married Sally Appleby and became the Progenitor of all the Claywells left here. His children were Tom, Ed, Belle, Eliza, Frances, Lou, John, Jack, Robert, and Daniel.

Ed is the father of all the Myers Ridge Claywells, John, Joe Lee, etc. Daniel and Robert are the fathers of the Howard Bottom and Smith Ridge Claywells. The progeny of Shadrach's children are given in other families in this writing. Four of them served in the Civil War. Dr. Daniel W. was one of the three orphans—born 1836, went to Texas 1880.

COE FAMILY

This is one of the many families which took their names from occupations. It came from the name "Coo," and we find many families in England in the 15th century and back, bearing that name. There were John Coo, Robert Coo, Benjamin Coo, etc. The name was applied to "cooks," as we term them today. As time went on it, like all other words, underwent changes in orthography, and later became "Coe." Some authorities claim the name came from the English bird by that name and for their proof cite the fact that the family coat-of-arms had engraved on it the form of this bird. It was true that the insigne was a coe bird, but a little reasoning will undermine this belief; in England, a name had first to be established for a family before the coat-of-arms was fixed in conformity thereto. Then this bird was agreed upon because it bore the name "coe."

During the years of 1620 to 1643 especially, was there great persecution in England and Scotland because of different religious beliefs, when the Presbyterian Church was trying to supplant the Episcopal Church. This was the day of the Pilgrims and Puritans. So much dissatisfaction existed that more than 25,000 emigrants left England for the New England states in America. At the outbreak of the Revolutionary War, nine-tenths of the New England population were descendants of these.

A ship with 83 emigrants embarked on April 3, 1634, from England for America. Among this number was a Robert Coe and family of the Puritan group. He had three small children—John, 8; Robert, 7; Benjamin, 5; and Annie, his wife. They landed at Boston, Massachusetts. He was among the number that migrated to Connecticut, and stopped at Wetherfield, from which place he and a Rev. Richard Denton, disagreeing with the church officials, moved to Long Island, where he built a church at Hempstead. When Long Island became Yorkshire County of New York he was elected sheriff of that county, 1669-71. Robert was born in England, 1596, and died in America, 1689. From him came most of the Coes of this country.

They drifted farther south, and his grandson (?) Isaiah Coe (1760-1834), who lived and died in North Carolina, was the paternal branch from which the Cumberland County Coes originated. Isaiah's son, John Coe (1784-1854), moved to Jackson County, Tennessee, in 1809, and two years later to Cumberland County, Kentucky, settling on Kettle Creek in the southern part of the county. John brought with him several slaves, who married into the Indian tribes of Kentucky. John was sheriff of the county for two years and Justice of the Peace 35 years. One of his sons, Jesse, married Caroline Murley and to them were born Elizabeth, Isaiah, Milton, John J., Margaret, Nancy, Ben F., Jesse T., and Bud. Bud (Isaiah M.) took smallpox at Rock Island, Illinois, in a prison camp, during the Civil War and died in nine days, aged 30. Bud married Martha W. Smith and reared Nancy Jane, Frances, and Elizabeth. Nancy J. married George Ashlock and reared 12 children.

Elizabeth Coe married Will Garner of Illwill Creek and to them were born Jesse, John, and Fanny. Their descendants live in the county.

Milton (of Jesse and Caroline) married Mary Berry in 1861, and to them were born Coleby (1862); Jesse E. (1864); Martha; and Willie.

Jesse of this family married Elizabeth Daugherty and to them were born Hershall, Fred, Lucy, and Willie. Hershall married Annie Herd. Fred married a Miss Flemmings; he was deputy sheriff 1942-5, under J. T. Brown. Lucy married Robert Baker of Crocus Creek. Willie married George Crossfield.

Coleby (of Milton and Mary B.) married Sur Townsend and reared Milton Julius, Mary, and Eva.

Martha and Willie (of Milton) died young.

Margaret Coe (of Jesse and Caroline) married Luford Short and to them were born Matilda, Cassie, and Wheeler. Matilda married Tommy Killman of this county and reared a family. Cassie married James Rich of Glasgow, Kentucky. Wheeler married Jane Mullinix of this county.

Nancy Coe (of Jesse and Caroline) married Martin Lee McCoy who came from North Carolina and served in the Civil War. To them were born Lou (dec.); Jesse, John, Jim, and Maggie.

Jesse McCoy married Miss Dishman and reared a family in Salt Lick Bend. He taught school for nearly half century in Cumberland County.

John McCoy married Addie Spears and reared a family in the Bend.

James McCoy married Annie Cloyd (daughter of Dan Cloyd) and reared a family.

Maggie McCoy married Nive Hume and to them were born three daughters: Carrie, Glee, and Winnie. Carrie and Glee were lifelong teachers, having taught most of their time in the Burkesville High School. They also taught music. Winnie married and moved away.

COLLINS FAMILY

The Collins people are English-Irish. The name originated in England as an occupation designation about 1273 and means, "charcoal-burners of the hills."

The people came to Virginia early in the 1600's and moved to the southern part of the state. John Collins (1750-1841) married Dorcas Carroll in Virginia and came to Cumberland County and settled on Mud Camp Creek, near its mouth, in 1809. To him and Dorcas were born three children: Rebecca, William Carroll, and Nancy.

Rebecca married a Mr. Shaw.

Nancy married a Mr. O'Banion.

W. C. married Amanda Phemister and to them were born nine children: John M., Bill, Polly, Bob, Dora, Susan, Delia, James, and Sam.

John M. (1849-1944) married Elizabeth Herd (1845-1903) and to them were born eight children: Orlando C., Wilkie, Franklin, Ida,

Mattie, Ova, Dora, J. Walter. John M. moved from Mud Camp Creek to Burkesville in 1897. He was elected County Court Clerk in 1898 and served three four-year terms in succession. He was Judge 1910-13, and Master Commissioner several years.

Bill married Serena Baise and reared 12 children in Salt Lick Bend, 11 of whom were sons: George, Albert, Forest, Ulysses, Lex, Herman, Reece, Grover, who lived in the county.

Polly (of W. C.) married James Herd and reared a family. Bob married Cora Murphy and went to California. Dora married J. C. Cary and reared Samuel A., who is an attorney and was County Attorney; and Mrs. Eunice Skinner, a public-spirited woman.

Susan (of W. C.) married Sam Hunter and reared a family; Delia (of W. C.) married Samuel (Shady) Anderson and reared a family on Marrowbone Creek. He is now (1947) 99 years of age with full possession of his faculties. James (of W. C.) married Angie Hunter of Marrowbone Creek; Sam (of W. C.) married Anna Stockton and left descendants in the county.

Orlando (of J. M.) married and went to California where he died, 1943; Wilkie (of J. M.) married Maud Cary and left; Ida (of J. M.) married H. E. Thurman and reared a family; Mattie (of J. M.) married Prof. G. Hoffman and reared a family in the county; the other children of Judge J. M. Collins were Ova, Dora, Franklin, and Walter who has been D. C., 1900-18; Clerk, 1918-25; sheriff, 1930-33; D. C. again (see Jones).

Nancy Collins of another family came in 1799 and married a full-blooded Indian of Indian Creek. Her offspring still live around Willis Creek.

CUMMING FAMILY

This name originated in Nord, France, where the family known as Comines owned most of the land and a city by that name. The orthography has been, Cumyn, Comyn, Cuminese, Cumming. Robert Comyn went over with William the Conqueror, 1066 A.D., and was a friend to William, who sent him with 700 soldiers to reduce the Scottish provinces. About 1133 his nephew became Chancellor of Scotland, and by 1250 the Comyns filled the offices of Earls. About 1306 Robert Bruce of Scotland caused nearly all the Comyns to be killed, but enough were left to continue the name. Philip de Comines, a historian, is a branch of this family.

Just when the first of this line landed in America I do not know; but as to the branch that came to this county and southern Kentucky, it was about 1760 when William Cumming, a stocking weaver, came from Scotland and landed in North Carolina. On his way over he met an Irish girl, to whom he was married soon after landing. Her name was Anna Sedwick Robinson; to them eight were born, four of whom were William; Betty (Dotson), whose daughter, Anna, married a Winnum, who owned the Ritter Hotel of Bowling Green, Kentucky;

Mary (Strange); and John Robinson Cumming, born 1794, the youngest of the eight, who married twice. While single he served in the War of 1812. His first wife was Martha B. Land, to whom were born Jane, 1828; William E., 1830, who married Clarinda Lawhon and died in the Civil War; and John R., Jr., 1832, married Martha Lawhon, 1858, and to them six boys and one girl. Oceola Franklin was the first, 1859. He became the father of Odell Cumming, who has been Clerk and sheriff of Clinton County. Second was James, who was also sheriff of Clinton; Big Bill; Lon; Oscar; and the girl married Sherman Vincent.

John R., Sr., secondly married Martha Copeland Baily, to whom were born 12: Ben F. (to Arkansas); James H., 1837, who married a Lawhon and had seven—Ellen married Pleas Huff; Myrtie married Sam Lawrence. Mary Cummin (of J. R., Sr.), 1839, married Nash Glidewell and had a large family; the Rev. R. H. Glidewell is a grandson. Eliza (of J. R., Sr.), married Rockey Holt and went to Tennessee; Harriett (of J. R., Sr.) married Pleas Garner, had three; Anna S., 1847, married Bill Lawhon and had Alice, who married Luther Garner, who was jailer of Cumberland County. Henry Lafayette (1858) married Winnie Katherine Craft, daughter of John and Sally Brake Craft and to them were born seven: James, who married Dora Bruton; Berta Leri, who married E. L. (Capt.) Daniel and reared a family in Cumberland County, one of whom (Kathryn) is a teacher; Alfred A., who married Minnie Norris. Sinda E. (of Fayette) married James H. Garner; Minnie Lee married Millard Lawrence; Lola B. married Bill Gibson; and Vestal Ann married John Robert Cross, veteran of World War I.

These last children are offspring of Michael and Elizabeth Cristie Craft, the founders of the Rose of Sharon Methodist Church of 1820.

John R. Sr., was captured by the Rebels and when he made known to them he was a Mason, they carried him back home.

DAVISES

There seems to have been three families of Davises who came to Cumberland County at its beginning. Just what relationship they bore is unknown. John came to the headwaters of Indian Creek in 1798. From him sprang the people by that name who populate Clinton County yet.

Five brothers came to Kettle Creek settlement at the same time, and their descendants may yet be found.

Two brothers, John and William, came from East Tennessee and purchased land on Marrowbone Creek—John at the mouth of Ferris Fork and William on Hominy, a tributary of Marrowbone.

John married Kittie Alexander, daughter of Robert Alexander, and to them were born Mary, John Dabney, W. R., James H., Miller, and Doc.

Doc got killed at work; Mary married Talbot Elliott; J. Dabney married Mollie Smith; W. R. married Sophia Alexander; James married Bettie Anderson; Miller married Maggie Smith, Russell County. Several of these families left Cumberland County.

W. R. and Sophia had Lauretta, Cornelia, Kate, Will Ed. Lauretta married Dr. Joe Schooling; Cornelia married W. E. Alexander (no issue); Kate married Mr. Smith (both dead); Will Ed married Addie Garmon and raised Rene, Nellie (Grubbs), and J. Clarence.

Miller and Maggie had Dr. Herbert, Will, Clyde, Verna. Dr. H. G. married Ethel Hamilton and had Mary and Elizabeth; Dr. H. G. is in Community Hospital, Glasgow. Will died; Clyde married Eva Depp and had two—Depp and James; Verna married and left.

James (of John) has children scattered. John Dabney and Mollie had Lenora, Walter, Rebecca.

William (who first came) married Patsey Harvey. To them were born Joe, John, Lucy, Sallie, Elender, James, Sam, Wilse, Nathan, George H., and William H.

Joe (of William) married Mary Ann Wade and reared a family.

John (of William) married Minerva Beck and had, James, Nannie, Elihu, Luther, Bob G. (he married Sallie Skinner, had three).

Lucy (of William) married Tom Frazier.

Sallie (of William) married James D. Beck. They reared Virginia, James, Sam, Mollie, Lula. This Lula married Enos Norris and had Clifton and Kyle. Clifton Norris is now garageman at Marrowbone and Kyle is assistant cashier at the Bank of Cumberland.

Elender (of William) married Jefferson Gray.

James B. (of William) married Martha Garmon, had Willie and Eva.

Three, Sam, Wilse, and Nathan, all died young.

George H. (of William) married Sarah A. Beck and to them were born one girl, Daisie. This Daisie married James E. Pace, who reared two children—Fred J. Pace and Georgia Pace.

William Harvey (of William) married Susan Garmon and reared Mollie, Anna, Wilson, Bertie, Lena, Elihu.

Martha (of William) married Albert Gray and reared Sam, James P., Mollie.

This line of Davises living in Cumberland County, who are mostly at Marrowbone, constitute one of the strong factors in the business network of the country.

G. Robert, grandson of the original William, is now, 1943, 72 years old and is very active. He is still the active member of the firm of Davis & Pace, Funeral Directors, which he has headed for 46 years. Also a seller of farm implements, a progressive farmer, and public-spirited citizen.

J. P. Gray, also of this family, runs a large general store of merchandise at Marrowbone town.

J. Fred Pace, of this family, who is president of the J. F. Pace Construction Company, is an active public-spirited man. He is a man of vision. When only 33 years old he made the venture of building the new court house at Burkesville, as contractor. In the late Wolf River Dam project, which is the largest project of the kind east of the Mississippi River, Fred has been one of the strongest advocates in bringing about its possibility, having spent many days in Washington with the President and Congress.

Many of the other members of this family are prosperous farmers of this county.

A later family of Davises came from Tennessee in 1890. This family is headed by Sid S. Davis, who is a son of George Davis of Clay County, Tennessee, who was son of John Davis of the same county. Sid has been Police Judge of Burkesville for 24 years. Sid S. Davis came in 1890 and married Lucinda Rainey and they became the parents of five children: Alta, Anna, Dora, Paul, and Hall.

Alta married Barton Philpott and lives in Warren County.

Anna married —— Petty.

Dora married —— Dunham and lives in Metcalfe County.

Paul married Stella Bow, daughter of Dr. Bow, and at present is proprietor of the Burkesville Garage on the west side of town. He owns half interest in the big garage.

Hall Davis married Miss Huddleston and at present is proprietor of the Burkesville Transfer Company.

DIXON FAMILY

William J. Dixon (1798-1869) was born near Lexington, Kentucky, moved to North Carolina, then to Jackson County, Tennessee, and last to Burkesville, 1857. Most of his life was spent in the mercantile business, having operated a store at Center Point, Monroe County, at Red Boiling Springs, and one at Burkesville, Kentucky. He also operated the postoffice at Burkesville, 1859-69, serving as postmaster.

He was married first to Nancy —— (1802-43) in 1817, this issue I failed to find. His second wife was Elizabeth Neely (1815-1900), who was one of the charter members of the Christian Church of Burkesville, and with which church the succeeding generations of the Neelys and Dixons have been affiliated.

To W. J. and Elizabeth were born Margaret K. (1844); Nancy Jane (1846); Amanda F. (1847); Dr. James A. (1850); Elizabeth Saloma (1854); Fayette (1860).

Dr. James A. received his early education in the public schools of Cumberland County, after which he spent the years of 1866-67 and '78 in Kentucky University, then finishing his M.D. degree in the University of Louisville, where he was classmate of Benton Macmillan of Tennessee and Champ Clark of Missouri. He practiced medicine until 1889, when he organized the Bank of Cumberland, of which he was cashier until his death, 1903. He was also the organizer of banks at Albany and Marrowbone, Kentucky.

Dr. Dixon married Ella Nora Walker of Columbia and to them four sons and four daughters were born—Mary, Nora, Elsie, Annie, Stanley, Ashley, Paul, and James.

Mary, of this group, married Karl E. Rapp of Glasgow and reared two sons—James A. D. and Karl E.

Nora married Curtis M. McGee and had one son, Philip D., 1911.

Elsie married Alanson Trigg of Glasgow and to them were born Charlotte Walker (1910), Eleanor Dixon (1912); infant; Alanson McElroy (1923); Rice Carter Ballard (1925).

Annie married Wendell M. Fry and moved West.

The family of Dr. Dixon have been valiant leaders in the social and cultural life of the communities where they have made their homes, having been pioneers in organizing and supporting music clubs, women's clubs, parent teacher's groups, and various church activities. Mrs. Trigg has served as organist at the Christian Church of Glasgow since 1909, and Mrs. Nora McGee the church at Burkesville since 1901. Mrs. McGee is following in the steps of her grandfather in acting as postmaster of the Burkesville postoffice.

FARMER FAMILY

This family originally came from Ireland to Chesterfield County, Virginia. Two brothers came first to Virginia. Joe went from there to Tennessee. Benjamin Franklin, the other brother, came from there to Turkey Neck Bend, Cumberland County, where he acquired a large tract of land on which he worked his slaves. He was married four times. In all he became the father of 24 children. We find the names of only three of this big family: Katherine (Kitty); William (1), William (2).

Katherine Farmer was married to John C. Sconce (1816), son of William Sconce and Elizabeth Calhoun Sconce, who had previously come from North Carolina and Tennessee and settled on a farm on Kettle Creek, this county. William's two other children were Ben F. and Elizabeth. Elizabeth married J. Hiram Dodson and went to Texas; and Ben F. went also.

To John C. Sconce and Katherine Farmer were born John Calhoun and Katherine Virginia. Katherine V. left Cumberland County with her family about 1857 at the age of 20 and married Edward Jasper Wyatt of Panola County, Texas. Her grandson, Dillard H. Wyatt, married Gladys Brice, daughter of Judge C. R. Brice of the Supreme Court of Roswell, New Mexico, where they lived, 1945.

John C. and Katherine Farmer had one other son and three daughters.

William Two became the progenitor of the Farmers of Cumberland and Clinton counties. He married Rebecca Bell and reared eight children: Kitty Ann, Sarah, Betty, Jane, John, Joe, James S., and Ben. F.

Kitty Ann married her cousin, John C. Sconce, Jr., and left Kettle Creek for the West about 1857.

Sarah married James "Turner" Smith of Shipley, where their descendants yet live.

Betty married a Mr. Murry.

John and Joe both joined the Confederate Army and lost their lives in the Rebellion between the States.

James S. went to Missouri.

Ben F. married first Sally Norris and reared three children—Elizabeth (1853), John, and William.

Ben F. married second, Mary Story and reared five children—Mary, D. Haggard, James E., Sarah, Flora. Mary married Marion Irby whose descendants still live in Cumberland County; D. Haggard married Permelia Simpson, daughter of Charley Simpson, and reared eight children in Texas; Flora married John Simpson, son of Ben Simpson, and went to Texas.

Sarah Farmer (of Ben F. and Mary) married Jasper Lawrence and became the parents of two sons—Dr. Marshall and Cordell. Cordell served as Judge of Russell County, 1933-7. Dr. Marshall taught school a while and then educated himself for physician and surgeon. He constructed a huge hospital at Jamestown, Kentucky, where he is at present (1945) sole owner and operator. At the early age of twelve years he was noted as a mathematician—embarrassing the older classmates and often his teacher with the remarkable endowment he possessed in the solution of the hard nuts to crack in Ray's Higher Arithmetic.

James E. Farmer (of Ben F. and Mary) married Laura Grisham and reared five sons and one daughter—W. C., Wilbur, Homer, Bessie, Beverly H., Ben. All are living except Bessie, and Homer who was gassed in World War I and died. James E. and Laura were both teachers and both are living now (1945) above 80 years of age. Mrs. Farmer still teaches music.

W. C. Farmer married Elva Rush, daughter of George Rush, this county; to them were born four children—Welby, Bessie, Marie, and Harlan. W. C. taught school several years in the rural districts of Cumberland and Clinton counties and also taught vocal music, in which he is a genius. He has served as Senator of the 16th Senatorial District of Kentucky comprising the counties of Cumberland, Clinton, Wayne, Monroe, and Russell, since 1934. He is a full-fledged Republican, and with his two daughters and youngest son and their stringed instruments and a few of the deepest religious hymns of the day, he so hypnotizes his listeners that the spell follows them to the polls on election day.

In supplement to the above history of William Sconce, I may add that Mrs. Judge Brice has discovered that William Sconce and Margaret Murley, a widow, married 1782 in Virginia, and that John

C. and Margaret were both living in 1790, with John about two years old, that Elizabeth could have been his second wife in Cumberland County.

The line of Dotsons connected with the Farmers are: Robert, who married Betty Smith and had Hiram and Stockton. The latter married Polly (Mary) Lollar and reared Lewis (1857), who married Sarah Gray. His daughter Cora married Wallace Page, whose daughter Ruth married D. L. Hays of the D. G. Hays Grocery Co., Leitchfield, Kentucky.

FERGUS FAMILY

The Fergus family is among the pioneers of Cumberland County. They originated in Scotland. The name means, "manly strength." James Fergus, Sr., headed the family that came to Cumberland County. He was born in Pennsylvania, 1756, died in Irish Bottom, 1839. He moved to South Carolina, where he married Sarah Robinson, 1783, daughter of the noted John Robinson who came to this county, as well as to Green, as a surveyor and explorer from 1776 to the end of that century. James Fergus came with his father-in-law, John Robinson, in 1800. In October of that year Robinson purchased of Robert Johnson, a Military Grant of 1,000 acres in Irish Bottom for $1,000, lying from "Willis Creek to Military Line on the north," nearly half of the bottom.

To James Fergus and Sarah were born eight children, all in South Carolina except the last one; Esther Fergus (1784-1872); John (1785-1842); George (1787-96); James, Jr. (1790-1832); Martha (1792); Sarah (1794-1838); Rachel (1797); Nancy Fisher (1800).

James filed claim for 200 acres on Little Willis Creek in 1800, but did not get it approved until 1805. While living on his claim his wife died, 1801, and the following year he married Peggy Allen, daughter of Jane and Robert Allen. Peggy lived until 1822. To them only one child was born—Jenny (1805-42), who married Lewis Warriner in 1824. James Fergus's third wife was Susana Looney, daughter of James Willians of Indian Creek.

Esther Fergus (of James and Sarah) married John Montfort, who came to the county with Robinson and was elected County Surveyor and died in office, 1804. To them was born only one child—Peter Montfort who also served in official capacities in the county. Esther then married Rane Staton in 1816, and for their progeny see Staton Tree.

For the descendants of Sarah Fergus (of James and Sarah) see Goggins Tree.

James Fergus, Jr., married Minerva Embree, daughter of Elisha and Nancy Embree, in 1818 and to them were born five children Albert (1819-61), who married Fanny Ross, daughter of William M. Ross, in 1840; Francis Marion (1821-84), who married Mildred Norvell of Arkansas in 1858; Louisa (1823-89), who married S. M. Keeton of Tennessee, 1843; John P. C. Fergus (1825-89), who married Nancy M. Guinn in 1856. She died in Adair in 1903. To J. P. C. were born three, Isadora, Minerva Embree, and Francis Marion.

Minerva Embree (1857-86) married Frank P. Carnes in 1877, a 22-year-old teacher of Cumberland County who spent several years teaching in the county. To them were born three.

Francis Marion (of J. P. C.) married Leona Coffey of Livingston, Tennessee. To Francis Marion (1861-1903) and Leona (1863-1938) were born four—Emma L.; John R.; Nannie; and Maud. All but Maud died young. Maud married Edward H. Beeson of Arkansas in 1907, and moved to Ft. Worth, Texas, where they were in 1946. To them was born only one daughter—Frances Marion (Frankie), who is a leading teacher of the West. She married Dr. Eugene N. Smith of Texas, to whom one daughter was born.

James Fergus, Sr., and his son James were leading men of their day. They helped lay out the towns of Burkesville and Creelsboro, in which they served as trustees later, and James, Sr., was assistant marshal of this district in which he enumerated the first and second census made by the Government, 1810-1820. He served in many offices, among which was Representative, 1815. His work is noted elsewhere in this book.

Martha Fergus (1792-1831) married Robert Reid who served the county officially.

Rachel (1797-1834) married William Hayden, reared family.

Nancy Fisher married James Young of Barren County, 1818.

Albert (of James, Jr.) married Fanny Ross, daughter of William Martin Ross, and reared five children—Betty, Martin VanBuren, Minerva, Nancy, and Julia.

Betty never married.

Martin VanBuren married Margaret Blair of Alabama and reared five children who live in Temple, Texas, as follows: Fanny, who married Lon Brooks and have Kathleen, Clyde, Mary E.; Mamie, who married Ernest T. Brooks and have Meryle, Aubrey, Maurice, Frances; Marvin V., the youngest child, married Anna Carlton, one of Texas' best teachers, and to them were born three—Max V., Dan M., Guinn C. Marvin is owner of a large bit of Texas land besides the Fergus Motor Company establishment of Temple.

Minerva (of Albert) married John Pedigo of Russell County, Kentucky, and went to Texas. They had four children.

Nancy married Bill Pedigo and reared five in Texas.

Julia (of Albert) married Ben Ross and lives in New Mexico (1946). They have four children.

GOFF FAMILY

Goff is a Cornish name, meaning "a crimper of ruffles." The family came from England to Virginia in Colonial days, and from there John Goff came to Pike County, Kentucky, and from there to Pulaski, where he died and his widow, Salina, came to Cumberland County at the beginning of the nineteenth century. She reared four children—Polly (Middleton), Salina (Roberts), Malina (Griffith), and Hance. She died in 1834.

Hance purchased a farm from Lewis Warriner in Rock House Bottom in 1851, where he married Lyda Winfrey, to whom were born T. Crit, John, Clinton Hance (Bud), Savina, and Fanny.

T. Crit married Mattie Neathery, daughter of Robert Neathery, and reared Hance, Bob, Jim, Tom, Dallas, John, and George.

Of Crit's family, Hance married a Miss Richardson; Bob married Bessie Cary of Judio, where they lived; Jim married Virginia Hunn and reared a family at Columbia, Kentucky; Tom went to Kansas; Dallas married a Miss Parmley and lives in the county; John married Pearl Ross and moved to Detroit.

Clinton Hance (Bud) married Nanny Walthall and to them were born Frank, who reared a family at Ellington, where he sold goods; Lydia, who married a Compton in the county; Lewis, who reared his family at Ellington; and Nanny, who married Otis Phillips —all of Ellington, Kentucky.

Savina (of Hance, Sr.) married Dr. A. V. Winfrey; and Fanny, her sister, married Dr. Almarine Hoy of Adair County.

Hance, Sr., kept hotel at Albany during the Civil War and was drowned at Creelsboro, Russell County, while rafting.

GOGGINS

This name has disappeared from our county rolls, but because there are so many descendants here it deserves notice.

They came along with the Roberts (Robersons), who came to Irish and Lawson bottoms as early as 1784.

William Goggins (1760-1833), married Drusilla Robertson in South Carolina and to them eleven children were born, part of them before they came to Cumberland County, 1799, and the rest in this county.

He acquired large tracts of land in Lawson Bottom, north and south of Brownwood Landing. He built the "mansion brick," now in decay on C. W. Wells' farm. A ferry was established, known as John Robertson and John Cape Ferry, in 1799, which name it held until 1808 when it became Goggins Ferry, then in January, 1891, when Reese Morgan sold to John Wood he gave it the name of Brownwood.

The children of William and Drusilla were Cyntha, Jubilee (Jubal), Polly, Malinda, Green Berry, Milton, Matilda, Eliza Jane, Harry, Lucy, Lizzie.

Cyntha married Richard Graves, (1815), son of Capt. Thomas C. Graves of Revolutionary fame and who helped lay out Creelsboro, Kentucky, where his descendants, in the Winfreys, Bledsoes, Busters, Irvins, Selfs, Claytons, still live.

Cyntha's son, Joseph A. Graves, married Fereby Thurman and to them were born Joseph, Jr., and Thomas C. This Thomas C. Graves married Perlina Cary and they became the parents of nine children, most of whom lived in Salt Lick Bend.

Joseph (of Thomas C.) married Lillie Murphy, daughter of Lorenzo D. Murphy (to follow), and reared a family in the Bend.

Jubilee (Jubal) (of William and Drusilla) married Sarah Fergus, 1815, and to them were born six children: Emily G. 1816; Eliza Jane, 1819; William H., 1825; Artilla R. D., 1829; Sarah Ann, 1830; Jubilee, Jr., 1834.

Emily G. (of Jube and Sarah) married Lorenzo D. Murphy and reared James, Belle, George, Lay and Clay, Lillie.

Eliza Jane (of Jube and Sarah) married twice. First to D. G. L. Allen, Sr., and they became the parents of Simon (dec.); Lawren, 1849, and D. G. L., Jr. (1853). Senior died five months before Jr. was born, and Jubilee, Jr., went to Texas and brought the mother and two little boys to his father, who reared them to manhood (see Allens).

Eliza Jane next married John L. Thomas, Jr., (being his third wife). J. L. was born 1812, died 1863, and to them one daughter, Sarah Artilla, 1857. She married Sam V. Morgan and reared three—Lela, who first married Mont Wells and reared Kenneth, a teacher; Fount; and Mary. Fount died. Mary married Finis Phelps and reared a family at Columbia, Kentucky. Lela secondly married Elmo Reneau and they had one son.

This John L. Thomas was a son of John L., Sr., who owned large tracts of land in Irish Bottom. Senior married Hettie Crawford, daughter of John Crawford who owned most of half of the upper end of Irish Bottom. All the Crawfords went to Missouri about 1832, where John L., Sr., died in 1833.

William H. (of Jubal and Sarah) married Martha E. Snow, daughter of Samuel Snow, in 1853, and his descendants are around Alpine, Tennessee. William was bushwhacked in the Civil War.

Artilla R. D. (of Jube and Sarah) married Lewis Irvin and reared a family in Lawson Bottom, several of whom died young.

Sarah Ann (of Jube and Sarah) married Frank Irvin and reared Allen, Mary, Benjamin, Edward, George, Emily, and Hiram.

Jubilee, Jr., never married.

Polly (of William and Drucilla) no record.

Malinda (of William and Drucilla) married Alexander Logan, 1811, and reared James, George, Thomas, William, David, and Daniel. Daniel's descendants still inhabit Cumberland County in the M. A. Logans (Sweetie) and Marvin, all of the south end of county.

No data on some of the children of William, Sr. Matilda married Guy Self and her descendants are many. Lucy (of William and Drucilla) married Mr. Clayton and reared a family.

Lizzie married Charley Gill and left:

Eliza Jane (of William and Drucilla), 1804-62, married Alexander

Murphy (1793-1862). in 1819 and to them were born 14 children. James W. (1821); Lucy Ann (1824); Cyntha G. (1826); Mary C. (1828); Drucilla L. (1830); Jubal G. (1832); Pleasant (1834); Eliza Jane and Louis 1837); Donald (1838); Victoria (1841); Milton B. and D. C. (1845); Green (1847). Both sets of twins died.

James W. Murphy married Elizabeth ——.

Drucilla L. Murphy (of Alex and Eliza Jane) married Shadrach (Page) Williams and to them were born Josephine, Pleasant, and Capatilla. Pleasant married Ruth Carter and died without issue; Capatilla married George Williams (cousin) and reared Pearl (Cash), Luther and Lula, and Fayette.

Josephine married Samuel Smith (as his second wife), who was a big farmer of Bear Creek and to them were born nine children:

Peyton Smith, who is one of Cumberland's progressive farmers and druggists.

Ida, who married Richard Piercey of Wayne County and moved to a big farm near Nashville, Tennessee.

Ellen, who married W. V. Brake, merchant of Bear Creek and they became the parents of a number of business citizens.

Beulah, who married William Newby and reared a family of noble citizens (one daughter).

Mollie, who married Fred T. Brake, and they also reared a large family of business boys and one daughter.

Georgia, who married Erby E. Shepherd, a lifelong teacher, who reared a family of business boys and girls.

Charley C., who brought up a family of useful children on Bear Creek.

James, moved to Campbellsville, where he became a leading druggist.

Jubal G. Murphy (of Alex and Eliza Jane) married Lee Ann Snow, daughter of Samuel Snow, and they became the parents of 10 children.

Samuel Murphy, 1861 (died).

Rachel (1864-1931), who married Israel Guinn and reared a family in Missouri.

Perry J. (1866-1896), who died.

John R., who married Maud Bell and reared a large family in Rock House Bottom.

Dick (1872), died 1920.

J. Clayton, who married Eura Ballou and reared a large family of sons and daughters in Irish Bottom.

Ottilla who married Bill Glidewell and reared a family at Bakerton, Kentucky.

Hiram (1880), who first married Alma Tweedy and second Leota Perkins of Albany, leaving one son.

Melvina (1882), died.

Reubin (1884), who married a Baker.

Pleasant Murphy (of Alex and Eliza Jane) reared a family in the county.

Victoria (of Alex and Eliza Jane) married Lemuel Ferguson, who reared Alex M., Lou, Inis, Lorene, Ottilla, Sarah, and Mack.

Alex M. married Bertha Matthews and reared Harold, Cortez, Lillith, Gordon, Jessie, Bonnie—all of whom reared families in the county except Lillith who never married. Jessie became the wife of Rev. L. T. Wells of Lexington.

Lou Ferguson married John Will Appleby and went to Oklahoma.

Inis, who married Granville Morgan, reared a family—one son, Dr. Ed is a leading physician of Louisville.

Lorene went to Texas.

Ottilla married James Martin Riddle and went to Texas.

Mack married Nancy Morgan and left.

Green Murphy of Alex and Eliza Jane married Victora Ferrell and has a family scattered.

GORMAN FAMILY

For the origin of the name see Surnames.

The Gormans came to Cumberland County in 1801. There were eight who came together, settled together, and lived on Caseys Fork as neighbors. They took up 1,800 acres of land. Most of them must have been brothers, undoubtedly all were of the same family. They were: Adam, Jr., Isaac, Jacob, David, James, John T., John M., and William.

Jacob married and reared Lewis, who married Sarah Smith and had three—Fayette, Edgar, Mollie. Fayette married Julia Waggener and had three—L. E., J. L., and Lucia. L. E. married Wilma Frazier and had three—one of whom is teacher of manual arts in Cumberland, Maryland; J. L. lives at Marrowbone; Lucia married an Emberton. Mollie married Crit Cole and reared family on Crocus. Jacob's son Lewis operated tan yard on Marrowbone for that country.

John Gorman married Ann Norris and reared Leonard, Rhodes, Henderson, Malinda, David, Nancy (Rowe), John, Jacob, Isaac, Elizabeth (Norris), Sally.

Adam Gorman married Eve Allen, 1804, and to them Andy J., James M., and Elizabeth who married E. C. Davis. From Adam came Sam, Ed, and that family. Sam boasted that his genealogy could be traced to Adam and Eve. The Gormans are a working, contented, plain, good-blooded people.

GRIDERS

The Grider family were an honest, plain group of people. They boast of fewer criminals than any other family of people, and court records very nearly bear out this statement.

They are of German-Dutch descent. The name originated in Old French, 1199, from the word "guier," proof, Johnle guier, meaning, "one who guides." I find nine different forms of spelling the name. Some people are ignorant enough to believe the present way of spelling their family name denies kinship with those whose names are spelled otherwise. One German authority classes it as an occupation name—Kreider, the dresser of Morocco leather.

During the first half of the eighteenth century Germany, Holland, and France were drenched with wars and persecutions. In 1745 Holland families were expelled from that country. It was then that the Griders came to the land of freedom along with their other Mennonite, or Anabaptist, friends, from 1700 to 1748.

Hans Jacob Greiter came from Wurtenburg Grand Duchy, Germany, and sailed up Chesapeake Bay and the Susquehanna River to Chester County, near Lancaster, Pennsylvania, in 1716. The oldest will we find on record is that of Michael Grittor written in High Dutch and "cannot be recorded" 1739. He willed to his four sons—John Jacob, Martin, Peter, and Daniel—his fortune, and "give my wife such maintenance as to enable her to give a piece of bread to the poor."

Checking closely all records of Pennsylvania, Virginia, and North Carolina, and linking them with the available records of Cumberland County, Michael's Martin was the progenitor of the Griders of southern Kentucky. The will of 1758 made by Martin Grider is a different Martin.

Martin (of Michael) moved to southwestern Pennsylvania, lived there a while and then crossed into Virginia. He had six sons of whom we find record, Martin, Jr. (1750-1838); Fredrick Cornelius; Jacob; John (1761); Valentine (1762).

The father of these sons moved to Loudoun County, Virginia, where Valentine states he was born, 1762. The older ones must have been born in Pennsylvania before they moved. In those days people were on the go. The father of the sons purchased lands in Augusta County, Virginia, 1773, and had surveyed for him and Andrew Greer 4,000 acres of land in that county at the time. An inventory made in 1776 in Fredrick County, Virginia, of the estate of Martin Grider is witnessed by Stephe Meir. The will of his father in 1739 was witnessed by Hans (John) Meir. This is good evidence of the same people. This is the last we hear of this Martin.

Martin II and his brothers Valentine and Fredrick all moved to Burke County, North Carolina, soon after the death of their father. In applying for pensions after coming to Cumberland County, Kentucky, Valentine states he enlisted as a substitute for his two brothers —Jacob and Cornelius. He married Mary Fugate of Lee County, Virginia.

Valentine did not come to the county until 1816. At that time he had 11 children, one set of male twins aged 26 years. His family scattered over Russell and other counties.

Fredrick Grider (called Fed) had two wives, one of which died before he moved to Burke County, North Carolina. By this wife he had 12 children, and by the second 10. All of these children who were old enough came to Cumberland County. Some of them died.

It was a custom back there, if a child in the family died, the following child born would be given its name, that "little So and So" might return. This occurred twice in this big family. This paragraph of information is copied from a record kept by James Grider, son of Fredrick, born 1806.

The first set were: John, Fredrick, William, Joseph, Joshua, Martin, Nancy, Dollie, Betsy, Mollie, Geneva, Barbara.

The second set were: Rachel, Cornelius, James (1), James (2), Jacob, Mintie (1) and Mintie (2), Samuel, Allen, Polly.

FIRST SET: John came in 1798 and located on Indian Creek, which was then in Cumberland. Nearly all the first set came about 1800. Joshua located at the mouth of Indian Creek, where his son, Cain, reared a family.

Joseph sold his farm on Indian Creek, 1806, and then moved to Creelsboro, in Cumberland County. Joseph married Nancy Easley at Creelsboro in 1810. He was born 1786, died 1871. Nancy, born 1786, died 1858. To them were born six children—John E. (1812-92); William E. (1814-95); Jane (1817-   ), married 1833; Thomas (1822-97); Joseph M. (1825-52); Allen H. (1829-75).

John E. married Eliza B. Holt, sister to Berry Holt, 1833, and to them 11 children were born: Mary, Joseph, Berry, William, Laura, Nancy, Virgil, Lizzie, Belle, Ellen, Tiny.

Mary of this group married Virgil Morrison and had Joseph. She next married Luther Hancock (brother to Rev. Tug) and reared family in Missouri.

Joe married Sarah Wood, and had three.

Virgil, Berry, and William died.

Laura married Rowe Beeler and reared five.

Nancy married W. F. Winfrey (see Winfrey).

Lizzie married Allen Perryman and reared Asa, Charles, and Nanny, who married Charles Campbell, Jr., and reared family at Creelsboro. The boys also had families there.

Belle married Ed Hadley, and had four.

Ellen married Walter Wright and moved to Texas.

Tiny married Capt. Asa Wells, who was County Clerk at Jamestown, Kentucky. They had no issue.

William E. (of Joseph and Nancy) left one son.

Jane married in 1833. No record.

Thomas (of Joseph and Nancy) married Lettie Lester, sister to Milton and Sam Lester, and to them were born Allen W., Dr. Cullwell and Mack, twins.

Allen W. married Emma Sewell, of Joe Sewell, and reared three —Mamie, Alma, and Bonnie. Mamie married John E. Morgan, had one (Newman). Alma married Luther D. Potts and reared a large family in Irish Bottom. Bonnie married the writer of this book and reared six (see Wells).

Dr. Cullwell married Ellen Clayton and reared family of two— Lettie and Maude. Lettie married Luther Blankenship and went

West. Maude married Lewis Campbell, of Ed C., and they live at Danville. Mack, the other twin, married Amanda Coffey and went to Canada.

Joseph M., no record.

Allen H. (of J. and N.) married Margaret Lester, sister to Lettie, and had four: Bramlett, who married a Campbell, sister to Ed, and reared a family in Russell County; Lennie, who married Tilda Back and had three girls and two boys; Fulton, who married Malinda Blankenship and had five boys on Crocus Creek; Exona, who married John Will Smith and reared three sons and one daughter at Creelsboro.

Dollie (of Fred) married Robert Neathery and left many descendants.

Betsy married Stephe Guthrie in 1804 and to them were born Abijah Guthrie (1806-65), Dempsey.

Abijah married Patsey (Martha) Williams, daughter of John Williams and Sally Hunter Williams (1811-1848). To them were born nine children—Sally (1830); Elizabeth (1832); Stephe (1833); Harriett (1835); John (1838); Mary Ann (1840); William (1842); Maria L. (1845); James N. (1847).

Abijah's first wife died, 1848, and he married Nancy Zimmerman and reared V. McNight, Millard Fillmore, Amanda J. This last group lived in Clinton County.

William (of Abijah) married Vienna Snow (of Samuel) and reared a large family at Burkesville, Kentucky. Cumberland and Adair have many of his descendants.

James N. married Antha Warriner Clayton and reared his family at Ida, Kentucky. Dr. W. J. is of this group.

Martin Grider (of Fred), of the first group of 12, married before coming to Cumberland County. He settled on Lester Creek now in Russell County. He was an extensive landowner. He is listed as selling one farm to Thomas Spencer there in 1810, at which time the census of Cumberland County lists him as having four children —one son under 10, two girls over 16.

His son, Martin, Jr., married Docia Winfrey, daughter of Israel, Sr., and to them were born Fanny (1825-1904), who married Cyrus Wells (1825-77), see Wells; Israel; Sally, who married Washington A. Riddle and reared Sarah Jane, wife of R. M. Mackey (see Mackey and Wells); Frances, who married Dr. Ed Higginbotham (see Higginbotham); Surrilda, who married Robert Guinn and had Alexander, Jack, and all the Willis Creek Guinns; James M., no issue; Docia, who married Alex. Wells and had one girl, Sally, who married Joe Lee Claywell and reared a family on Willis Creek.

SECOND SET (of Old Fed)

Rachel (of Fed) married James Neathery and to them were born William, Tilford, Clinton, Killis, Hannah, and Lizzie.

William married Adaline Grider, cousin, and to them were born Bill, Israel, Alray, Rachel, and Burnett. Their descendants are many.

Tilford married Nancy Ellis and left descendants.

Clinton married Jane Allen, daughter of Jasper Allen, and they have many offspring in Cumberland and Clinton counties.

Killis married Jane Hopkins and left descendants.

Hannah married Micajah Hunter and reared a family, most of whom live in Texas.

Lizzie married Wallace Davis.

Cornelius (of Old Fed) married and reared Allen, Mintie, Mary, Diana, and Stant.

Allen married Isabel Hunter (of Jordan); Mintie married Joel Hunter (of Jordan), and both reared large families at Seventy-Six, Kentucky. Mary married a Cooksey.

Diana married Billie Thomas and reared a family on Indian Creek —Albert, Cullwell, Noble, Ratio, Ernestine. All of these children and their large families remained around Indian Creek. Their offspring are numerous.

Albert and Noble were vocal music teachers. Ruel, son of Noble, headed the 76-Radio Quartette of Renfro Valley.

Stant married a Neathery and went to Texas.

James (2) was born on the way to Cumberland County near Pall Mall, Tennessee, 1806. He married Anna Hunter (1809), and to them were born Frances (1830); Surilda (1832); Hulda (1836); Allen (1842); Exona (1844); Fedrick William (1849); and Hiram.

Frances (of James 2) married John Balou and reared five—Jim, Hiram, Eva, Ona, Shelby. This Hiram is a prominent physician of Russell County, Kentucky.

Jim married Lucy Nortrip and reared family in Irish Bottom.

Eva married Lee Cook and reared family on Indian Creek.

Exona married Dr. W. C. Keen of Burkesville and had four— Dr. Oscar, who became a leading physician of the United States and Central America; William S., who is an attorney in California; Sally, who became the wife of Prescott Sandidge, another leading lawyer and judge of Kentucky; Mary D., who became the wife of C. W. Alexander, Jr., who succeeded his father as president of the Bank of Cumberland, 1936; Shelby, no record.

Hiram (of James 2) married Alice McFarland and was the father of Rev. Tom Fed, Baptist Minister of Glasgow, Kentucky. Surilda (of James 2) married a Kelly.

Matilda (of James 2) married Albert Coffy and left.

Hulda (of James 2) married Jasper Allen and reared Tom, Charley H., William, Pearl. All these children made the best of citizens of Cumberland and adjoining counties.

Exona (of James 2) married I. L. Warriner (see Warriners).

Fed W. (of James 2) married and reared a family at the old settlement on Indian Creek. His son, Dr. J. A. Grider, moved to Central America where he died. His son, Dr. J. A., Jr., was an Army physician in the Philippines in World War II. He lives at Bowling Green. Ann Ellen and Emma Anderson live near the old settlement. The younger boys left.

James G. 2 lost his first wife and second married Frances McFall, 1866. To them were born three—James Samuel, who married Sally Wells, sister to the writer, and reared a family at Albany, Kentucky. He was a thriving farmer and a leader in the Baptist Church.

George, who left; and Sarah, who married Jim Jacob Grider and left four girls. He was an old-time itinerant peddler with a pack on his back.

Jacob Grider (of Old Fed), of the second set of 10, married in Cumberland County. He married Kate Smith and to them were born seven—Ebenezer, Smith, Jim Jacob, Rachel, Adeline, Margarett, Lucy.

Ebenezer married Amelia Sturgison and reared John Jacob, Jarome, Benton, Ellen, and Ada. These children were reared near Albany. John J. was elected sheriff of Clinton County, 1898.

Rev. Smith Grider married Anna Eliza Pierce, daughter of Lewis and granddaughter of Francis, the Revolutionary veteran of Cumberland County. To them were born two—George and Mary, who married Jim Elijah Ferguson and had family in Clinton County.

Rachel married Perry Gamlin and reared family.

Adeline has been given.

Margarett (deaf) married Joshua Hudson (deaf) and to them a large family of boys and one daughter, Lucy, who married Johnnie Reeder of Rock House Bottom, whose children and grandchildren (of Elmer and Luther Reeder) populate the Bottom.

Lewis (of Joshua) reared a bunch of natural musicians. Of all the progeny of Joshua and Margarett not one yet has been deaf.

Lucy (of Jacob) married James Davis and reared Thomas, Jacob, with many offspring.

HICKS FAMILY

Anthony Hicks lived in Powhatan County, Virginia, on a plantation before and after the Revolutionary War. He married Cynthia Maxey of the same county. They raised some of their family in Virginia before migrating to Kentucky. On July 31, 1812, was born a son whom they named Reuben. When he was three years old Anthony and family moved into Lincoln County, Kentucky, where they stayed till 1822, when they all moved on Goose Creek, Cumberland County, Kentucky. Here Anthony lived until 1854, when he took a part of his family and went to Missouri, where he died about 1870.

His son, Reuben, remained on Goose Creek and in Howards Bottom and married Margaret Smith, who was born in Cumberland County, 1833. To this union 11 children were born: Susan Jane, married C. T. Jennings; W. A., died 1881; Martha A., married W. T. Coop; Frank (single); Cintha, (1859-1942), married Alex A. Morrison; George Richard, married a Coop; Ardenia, married J. W. Melton,

Oklahoma; John E. (single); Charles R. (single); Daniel H. (drowned, 1896); Timothy F., married Fanny Lee.

Reuben adopted teaching as his life's profession, though he served in many public capacities during his long life of 96 years. He was a clergyman of the Methodist Episcopal Church, South, Justice of the Peace 32 years, a member of the building committee that erected the Court House, 1867-8, and one of the five that voted for Abraham Lincoln in his first campaign for presidency, in Cumberland County. He has the distinction of having taught the first free school class organized in this county, 1849, and when he retired from the profession he had taught in 72 different schools of the county.

The Hicks family are a shrewd people with high intellectual ability. Their official career will be found elsewhere herein.

Charles R. Hicks of this family, born October 31, 1868, and died June 6, 1935, was a man of great ability. He was admitted to the bar, 1902, after retiring from his teaching career of 11 years. He served as County Attorney 1905-9; 1918-21; 1922-5. He, like all of his family, was a Methodist. In matters of law he chose the right side and always had his lessons well prepared. His views in law matters were clear and dreaded by opposing attorneys. His last great work, which will ever shine out for him, was his co-operative work with the writer of this book in preparing a legal procedure for holding a Local Option election to rid Cumberland County of the operating saloons, 1935.

HIGGINBOTHAMS

This family came from Virginia to Cumberland County in 1800. The Virginia "Headright Law" brought more immigrants to this county than all other agencies combined. It usually required from two to seven years to clear a title through this law. This accounts for the pre-emigration from the mother state before the settler's rights were recorded, as shown in the preceding chapters.

Oglesberry Higginbotham led the way to Cumberland County and became the progenitor of all that name throughout this part of the country. He married Elizabeth Miller of Virginia and became the father of three children, all of Virginia. They were Elizabeth, Thomas, and Robert. The whole family came to this county and within five years, or 1805, began farming on their headright grant of 200 acres on Millers Creek above Creelsboro, now Russell County. Elizabeth and Thomas both married Easleys of that immediate neighborhood and left descendants.

Robert (1789-1855) married Mary (Polly) Wilborn (1800-1863) in 1816, and three years later secured his land grant of 100 acres on Butler's Creek, this county, and reared a family of 12 children, from 1817 to 1843, listed here according to birth: Moses, who lived and died at Creelsboro; Eliza Jane, who married John Miller and reared a family at Lily Dale, Tennessee; John W. (dec.); James D., who went to Illinois; Anderson, who reared his family in Crittenden County, Kentucky; Robert (1829-91); Nancy went to Nebraska; Samuel to Illinois; Mary E. (dec.); Lafayette to Illinois; Charles and Granville, both of whom reared families near Paducah, Kentucky.

Robert, of the 12 children, married Martha Holsapple (1832-1910) and to them were born eight children—ranging according to births from 1852 to 1864: Joseph L., Mary O., Edward L., Dr. William L., James L., Crawford L., Robert L., Thomas L.

Readers of this family record, like myself, may wonder why so many L's to these names. The writer having asked Robert Lincoln, of this group of children, living at 82 and full of wit, if they all had the same name, received in a joking manner the reply that they did not have the same name but that "L" meant "laziness" for all.

Joseph L. reared his family in Texas; Mary O. (dec.); William L. became a Dr. and reared a family in Texas, and Crawford also went to Texas. James L. died.

Robert L. married a Miss Stephenson of Albany and reared a family there. He spent his life in the mercantile business of which he made a success. His son, Robert, operates a large garage now.

Dr. Edward L. married Frances Riddle and reared eight children. He was the leading artist of southern Kentucky for half a century. His work was mostly local and can be seen in many thrifty homes.

His children were: Robert Alex, who taught writing, being a natural penman, like his father, which talent belongs to all of the Higginbotham name. He was one of the 6,000 who perished in the Galveston flood, September 8, 1900. Hampton was bushwhacked in Tennessee; Myrtie lived in Tennessee; Sallie married an Easter and went to Oklahoma; James married Beulah Myers and reared a family in the county; Daniel married Addie Neathery and reared his family in the county; W. Haden married Annie Russell and reared one daughter, Ruth, who is clerk in the Citizens Bank, Albany; Hayden W. served as magistrate, jailer, and first deputy sheriff, 1934-42.

Thomas L., the last of the 12 children, married Ida Ewing and reared 13 children: Oscar, Edgar O., Maggie M., Helen H., Mariba, Joseph, Fred, Virginia, Harvey, Lena, Mary, Stanley, and Jesse.

Other descendants of this family live in Russell County; Billie, having spent his life as merchant at Creelsboro, where his family were reared.

HOLSAPPLE

Jacob was the pioneer of this family. He came from Virginia and settled at Seventy-Six. He was one of the founders of the church by that name, 1808. His son, William, reared Martha (Higginbotham); Virginia (Lawhon); Crecia (Bryson, Speck); Crawford L., who reared a large family most of whom made teachers in Clinton and Cumberland counties; and Louisa, who married Clinton Morrison and reared Alex A., whose children now live in the county.

HUNTER FAMILY

See Surnames.

The Hunters came from Franklin County, Virginia, to Kentucky. William, Moses, Jacob, and John came to Fayette County, 1783, and through Bourbon County to Cumberland County, about 1802.

John had married Sarah Price in Franklin County, Virginia, August 17, 1786. Sarah was an heir to Abraham Price, who founded Judio Bottom, 1787. John became the source of all the Hunters of Marrowbone and south Cumberland, besides many more influential families of the county. His children (1822) were John, Jr., Sam, Joe, Sutton, Charity, Mary (Biggerstaff), David, and Fanny.

William Hunter stopped on Indian Creek. He became the progenitor of all that branch of Hunters. His children were John, Sam, Peter, Joe, Sutton, Micajah.

Anna, the daughter of Peter, was the grandmother of the Griders.

Jordan, the son of Peter, was the father of John, Micajah, William, Sutton, Parker, Sam, James, Solomon, Joel, Isabel (wife of Shelby Hopkins), Mary Jane, Exona.

Micajah (of William) married Nancy and had John, Jane, Shores, Exona, Harriet, William P., Mary. Many of this family left.

JONES FAMILY

The Jones people are so extensive in number that it is an undertaking next to impossible to give a true connection of the different families. Some may wonder why such families as Jones, Smith, and Brown are so numerous. I give an explanation here, briefly.

Jones had an early start from Jonah, in the Hebrew, 840 years B.C. From this name came Jonadab, Jonas, Jonan, etc., and the popular John, in the New Testament. It found its way into over twenty different languages but did not become a surname until after the Conquest, 1066. So many Johns made this a number one name in England. Wales is the home of the Jones family. There it was Jvones. In 1880 a census alphabetically arranged in Wales showed out of 200 names in the J column, 169 were Jones. Through all the different spellings it has held its original meaning, "a dove."

The springboard of the Joneses who came here was the island of Angeby, Wales. They were not the earliest families to come, but many came later. Virginia and all the Atlantic States received some of the family, but our ancestors came by the way of Virginia and North Carolina. Joshua Jones came from Virginia in 1794 and settled in what became Cumberland County, on Spring Creek. Here he took up two tracts of land, one of 1,000 acres on which he established a bloomery. His promises were so certain that the Legislature granted him other tracts of land reaching "not over six miles from said bloomery, to be laid off and paid for not later than December, 1805, $30.00 per c.A."

In the first tax list of Cumberland County in 1799 there were 12 Jones families who settled close to the lands of Joshua. William, John, and Joseph moved to Burkesville during the same year. Joseph Jones was a public man of his day. He took up land on Big Renox Creek where his family was reared. His son, Charles S., married Harriett Waggener, daughter of A. G. Waggener, and reared a family of seven—J. W., William E., Blanton, Mary, Henry, Marvin (dec.), Lockey.

William E. is a leading attorney of Glasgow, Kentucky.

Blanton married Laura Bow and reared his family in the county. His children were Mary, Grace, Ruth, Morrison, Alma, Rena, Hines, Russell, Ruel, and Malcolm. Their father was an elder in the Methodist Church and brought his children up in a religious atmosphere. They were natural musicians. Morrison and Ruth taught for several years. Malcolm joined the Farmer Quartet over the radio. Russell was educated for the ministry. One of the girls married Rev. Wade, another Methodist minister.

The Joneses of Jones Ridge are distant relatives of the original Joe.

Two nephews of Joshua Jones, Jonathan and William Levi, left Pennsylvania about 1796. Jonathan came to Cumberland County and reared his family on Spring Creek where his offspring still reside.

William Levi stopped a while in Virginia and then came to Overton County, Tennessee, just over the line of his relatives, then came to Cumberland County. He married Amily Maclamore before he came to this county. To them were born Henry, Nicholas, Jack, Mary, Elizabeth, Sally, and Nancy.

Henry (1827) married Sarah Livingston and reared Judge J. G. Jones, who spent most of his life in public office in the county, acting as sheriff, surveyor, County Judge two terms, and many minor offices. He was a man of limited education but of sound judgment and business ability. His official activities are found elsewhere. To Henry were born four other sons and six daughters all of whom reared families in the county.

Judge Jones married Lela Bow, daughter of Dal L. Bow, and reared a family in the county. His son, William H., was elected sheriff of the county, his daughter Edna Collins is (1946) County Court Clerk, and his affinitive nephew, J. B. Groce, the present sheriff. Edna, who married J. Walter Collins, reared Paul, Lela, Noxie, and James. Paul is deputy clerk.

Other children of William Levi follow:

Nicholas married Amanda Davidson, daughter of Pleas Davidson, and had four daughters and one son.

Jack married Julia Spears and reared his family on Sulphur Creek in this county; H. N. Jones of Sulphur is a son of Jack. He has a family in the county.

Mary Jones married Ransom Rich and reared five sons and three daughters: William Levi Rich, Katherine, John, Tom, Radford, Jack,

Jim, Mary. Jack Rich married Belle Kelly and went to Ft. Smith, Arkansas; Jim married Cassie Short and moved to Glasgow, where his family is; Tom reared his family at Leslie, this county.

Elizabeth Jones (of W. L.) married Reuben Johnson and went West.

Sally (of W. L.) married a Nipp and left.

Nancy (of W. L.) married Abijah Riddle and went to New Mexico.

Simeon Jones headed another family of Cumberland County. He was the father of Dr. Tom Jones. They lived in Rock House Bottom, where the family was reared. Dr's. son, Ruel, was another boy of the same place that reached near to becoming a millionaire by inventing a device to imprint on soap the name of a company in letters that penetrated the cake and could not be washed off. Dr. J. Tom Jones was one of those old-time dentists that walked over the country, or rode horseback, to do work. Scarcely an old person in Cumberland County or Russell wore teeth made by any other. He is in line with the pioneer Lester. His mother was Sarah I., daughter of James and Amanda Lester. Daniel Lester, the pioneer, descended from the noted English Leisters of Leister County, England. With state-wide reputation is another descendant of Daniel in the person of Kirby Lester, dentist Jamestown, Kentucky.

KEEN FAMILY

The Keen family are of Scotch-Irish descent. They came from Virginia to Cumberland County early. Samson Keen was the pioneer of this family. He was a minister of the Methodist Church and one of the first preachers of Cumberland County. He married Elizabeth Frazier, who was born in Virginia also. To them were born John F. Keen.

John F. (1821-92) followed the steps of his father in becoming a clergyman. He was a farmer and a Mason. John F. married Louisa Neathery (1832-95) of Clinton County, and to them were born 11 children—Ellen, Dr. William C., Lucetta, Burletta, Helen, Dr. Tom W., Bryant A., Robert S., Travis, Louisa, and Sarah (see Self).

Ellen, of this group, married Littleton Balou and reared a family; Dr. William C. (1853-30) received his education in the county and attended the School of Medicine, Louisville, graduated at the University at Nashville, Tennessee, 1880, and spent the balance of his life practicing his profession—except two years in the Legislature. He married Exonia Ballou (see Griders). Burletta married Alvin Cawley; Helen married Martin Smith of Clinton; Dr. Tom died; A. Bryant was sheriff of the county, and was killed in a tornado.

Tramble Keen headed another family, some relation. His son, William, was the progenitor of the other Keens. His son, J. R. Keen, was sheriff year after year. His offspring are—Charles, now deputy sheriff; Samuel, who is an electrician; James, Jr., who is supervisor of the rural road system of the county.

KING FAMILY

Two branches of Kings came to Cumberland County, both from Virginia. They were Scotch-Irish. John Edward King came from Virginia to Kentucky, 1783. He was born in 1757 died, and was buried on his farm in this county, 1828. He came to Jefferson County first and was granted 10,000 acres of land that year for services in the Revolutionary War. He then went to Fayette County, and was granted several hundred more acres in that county. In 1793 he came to Cumberland County to live. From 1793 to 1801 he obtained 3,500 acres here. He settled just north of Burkesville and built a house that is still standing. He was the second Clerk of Cumberland County. While he was on his Fayette farm he married Sally Clifton, to whom were born five— William, who went to Arkansas; Valentine, who went to Louisiana; Rev. Alfred, who lived here and went to Texas, 1859; Milton (1799-1872), who served the longest term as Clerk (see Officers). Milton married Susan Wiles, 1815, and to them were born ten—Sally, who married Josiah Harris, merchant of Adair County; Nancy G. (see Alexanders); Sofa, who married Almarine Alexander; John Q. A., who was Lieutenant Governor, 1863; Ellen, who married W. F. Owsley; Mary Ann, wife of Clinton Alex; Josephine, second wife of Almarine Alexander; Susan, who married Lewis Sweet of New York; and Milton, Jr., an attorney in Missouri.

The other King was Elijah, who came to the headwaters of Sulphur Creek in 1798, where he took up 200 acres of land. His descendants are around the same locality. His daughter, Elizabeth, married Thomas Carr in 1800, and from them came the Carrs of Clinton County by his two grandsons—Thomas and George, the latter of which was Sheriff of Clinton County, 1891.

LOLLAR FAMILY

The Lollards were an English Dynasty about 1400, who sprang up in England. They were strict followers of John Wyckliffe, the great English Reformer (1324-84), who advanced the doctrine in opposition to the Pope. Martin Luther continued this belief and got the honor, 1517. Most of the Lollards were killed for their belief, but from this sprang the name of the family that still continues. The Lollars came to America in the seventeenth century. They have always held to their original practice. Education and religion follows the family.

The Cumberland County record of Lollars began in 1799, when Jacob took up 230 acres on the Cumberland River and Reuben took up 400 acres on the middle fork of Kettle Creek. They have hung around Jacob's place of settlement. There was a brother James also. Bob Lollar of Albany was an offspring of this family. He was a working educator. His grandchildren live there.

MACKEY FAMILY

The Mackeys came from Ireland. The name is a variant of Maccabees, who lived in Judea 165-35 B.C. The Irish give its origin as Gallic, as most Macks are, meaning "son of Kay."

They came from Virginia to Knox County. There James purchased 50 acres of land on the river and left his son, Alex, there while he came to Cumberland County, 1820, and took up 300 acres of land on the waters of Willis Creek 1823. His son, Alex, followed him and married Dorcas Smith (of Samuel the Revolutionary veteran), and to them were born nine—James A., Samuel, Robert, George, Charles, John, Tom, Polly, and Prep.

James A. (1834-1919) married Vienna Talbot (1834-1921) granddaughter of Nicholas, and to them were born John, J. R., Sam, Vienna, R. M., Mary. This John married Docia Phillips and went to Texas. James R. married Douglas Smith and to them were born Willie Pearl, who married Claude Phelps; Alex, who married Sally Appleby and has family in the county; and Hugh, who became Nazarene minister and married Della Blair and has a family.

Samuel (of Alex and Dorcas) married and reared a family in Clinton County. Hunter is of this group.

Robert M. (of J. A.), see Grider and Wells families.

Robert (of Alex) went to Texas; George (of Alex) married Mariba Ewing and reared a family of teachers, of whom A. B. was the most outstanding.

A. B. Mackey, of this group organized the Trevecca College, Nashville, Tennessee, of which he has been president since 1936. Under him it has grown to be the greatest Seminary of Learning of the South, belonging to the Nazarenes.

Charles and Tom (of Alex) both married Tuggles and went to Texas.

Polly (of Alex) married George Howard and reared a family in Clinton County.

(See Civil War soldiers).

McGEE FAMILY

James Curtis McGee was born in Pennsylvania and moved to Harper's Ferry, Virginia, and from there to Nashville, Tennessee, where he married Miss Jones and came to Cumberland County and purchased a farm west of the Big Hill, where his family were reared. On a trip down the Mississippi River to New Orleans with a load of tobacco, he contracted cholera and died. Foul play was suspected.

His widow managed the farm and cared for the children, G. B., James, and J. J.

G. B. first married a Miss Travis. She died without children. He then married Ellen Martin and they had three children—Jacob, Robert, and Mary Jane, who married Henry Lawhon and reared seven—Thomas J., Ammer, Julia, Ella, Trudy, Nannie, and Ida. Already told of these.

J. J. McGee (of J. C.), 1834-1921, became the progenitor of the Cumberland County McGees. He married Sally Baker (1839-1917). Sally was a Williams and married George F. Baker and had two children—B. C. Baker and Nannie, the wife of T. J. Lawhon. J. J. had also been married to Nannie Johnson and was the father of James, Mary, and three infants. This James married Mollie Mitchell of Georgia and reared Anna Lee and Chancy O., the husband of Emily Chew.

To J. J. and Sally Williams Baker were born seven—Elva, Leslie, Curtis M., Hattie, Charles, Effie, Jacob. Elva married Agnas Bledsoe and reared three boys in Florida. Leslie married Lea King Baker and reared three girls at Burkesville; Curtis (see Dixon); Hattie married R. L. Gowdy and moved to Campbellsville; Charles married Carrie Duerson and reared two—James and Lucile, the wife of Attorney Ben M. Jones; Effie married Attorney W. T. Ottley and had one son, John; Jacob T. married Lala Alexander, no issue. The McGees were merchants from James Curtis, Sr., to 1936.

MILLER FAMILIES

There were four Miller families who came to Cumberland County in pioneer days. The Millers are English.

John K. Miller settled on Mud Camp Creek and died there in 1810. His progeny still live there.

Jehu Miller (1784-1846) married Emily Willis in Virginia and soon came to the county. They reared three children—Elzik, Britania (1810), and Clinton W. (1822). Britania married Rev. James H. Haggard (1809-72), a Christian preacher, but they died without issue. Clinton married Martha Ann Davis (1827-78), daughter of Warren Davis, of Virginia. Clinton was a good carpenter and helped build many of Burkesville's best houses. He was the father of 17 children, many of whom scattered from home. William E. (1858-1934) was the only one who spent his life at Burkesville. He taught school, was Circuit Clerk, 1886-97, postmaster 1902-13, and was chosen to fill out the term of County Judge J. G. Jones, who resigned, 1920. He married Minerva Vincent, daughter of James A. Vincent, and to them 11 children were born, five of whom died in infancy. The others were Noxie, who married a Dr. Miller of Michigan and left; Mayne who taught and was elected Circuit Clerk in 1933 and again in 1939. He married Thelma Dishman. Rev. Benton, who is a Christian minister, and also his brother, Kingsley, is a noted minister. Nida, the daughter, has spent most of her life in teaching school at the Burkesville High School. Kasey is another son.

Jacob Miller settled on Crocus Creek in 1798. He left many descendants through the Parrishes, Howards, and others.

MORGANS

The name Morgan means "mariner," as identified in Britain. It originated in Wales, where the Morgans lived, and in that country meant "sea white." Both meanings had reference to the sea. There was a county in Wales called Gla Morganshire. King Arthur's sister was Fata Morganna. Medieval history gives them as a fearless type of people, who very much enjoyed surmounting obstacles; one of their delights was buccaneering the Spanish high seas and selling their booty to their mother country—England—and Wales. In war they were fearless and venturesome. They came from Wales to America about 1600.

There were two families which settled in Cumberland County, one of which has been related in the Five Families; the other was headed by Morgan Morgan. Why so named we do not know. He was born in Lancaster County, Pennsylvania, 1760, died in Cumberland County, 1851. From Lancaster he went to Montgomery County, 1776, where he enlisted as a private; to Wythe County, 1795, and from there to Cumberland, 1800. His father was Daniel Morgan who also went through the Revolutionary War. Morgan Morgan second married Lucy —— and to them were born Enos, John Parker, and Reece. He took up 200 acres on Crocus near mouth of Sand Lick, 1801.

John P. (died 1851) married Lucy Keeton and to them were born five: Abner (1827) who married a Simpson and became a Baptist minister; Enos (1829), who married —— and was the father of Reece, who reared a family in Lawson Bottom; Lucy Ann (1830), who married Tom Back, whose descendants are on Rock House Creek.

Samuel (1832), the fourth child (see Winfreys).

William (of J. P.) (1835) was married to Malissa Winfrey in 1858 by the Rev. James Haggard, the Christian minister who had preached at the log school house in Irish Bottom (see Allens, Goggins, Winfreys).

Morgan Morgan was of the family of Nathaniel, who was the father of Big Ed, Proctor, Joe Sam, Levi, and Granville. Ed married first Tena Staton and reared Joe Hiram; second Lizzie Parrish and reared Bob and Myrtie.

Joe Sam moved to Texas, where he became a noted educator.

MYERS

The Myers Family is of German descent. Jacob Myers, who married Lydia Hindenburg, came from Germany before the Revolutionary War to Virginia, where he made a short stay and then came to Lincoln County, Kentucky, in 1782, from which he established a transportation line for passengers and mail to Pittsburgh, Pennsylvania. He operated this line until 1791, after which he began experimenting with iron. His little furnace was one of the first ones of the kind in Kentucky and proved to be of much benefit to the iron industry later. Jacob developed the industry to where he was able to make pots, pans, and other cooking utensils for the pioneers. Jacob and his two sons drifted farther south in 1800 and took up land on the Wolf River in Cumberland County. Christopher married Elizabeth Wood, daughter of Hon. William Wood, and took a grant of 400 acres there in 1801 where he stayed and farmed until 1823, when he sold out and moved close to the present site of Albany. Jacob's other son Daniel, also took up land below Albany on Spring Creek and in 1815 deeded to William Wood, Benjamin Campbell, and Robert Cross, Trustees of the Baptist Church there, one acre of land to be used for church purposes. He later sold 2 acres and Jacob ¾ acre, making a 3¾-acre lot.

Jacob's only daughter, Mary, married Nicholas Owens in 1800.

Christopher's son, Harrison, later came to Myers Ridge and purchased land. He married Agnas Wood and reared five boys and one girl—John W., Dr. J. H., Charley, Silas, Leo, and Belzora.

Dr. J. H. Myers married —— and had Ada, Bertha, Ida, Crit, Tom, Beulah, Fanny, and Robert.

Rev. John Myers brother of Harrison left a large family of children at the same place.

Dr. J. H. lived on Whetstone Creek near the old settlement. He promised the people if they would elect him Circuit Court Clerk he would use the money he got for his services to make of himself a practicing physician, and never turn any of them down when a call was made. The office was secured by him and he fulfilled his promises. For a quarter of a century before his death in 1930 he rode on horseback day and night, through rain, mud, snow, and backwaters to help the sick and suffering.

Tom Myers (of Dr. J. H.) has served three terms as Tax Commissioner of Cumberland County, 1922-29; 1938-41. He was elected again in 1945 without opposition.

NEATHERY

The widow Margaret Neathery was the mother of the four boys and two girls. The Neatherys came to Cumberland County with the Hunters and Griders about 1806. There were four brothers—Samuel, Robert, Daniel, and James. All of them settled on or around Indian Creek.

By these four brothers came all the Neatherys and their descendants. Daniel had a large family, most of whom were girls. For them see Norris, Smith, Hicks, Winfrey, Orton, Grider, Keen. Someone has said there was a Neathery for every good man or woman.

Samuel did not come until about 1812. At the census of Cumberland County, 1820, he and his wife were under 45, with seven children, three males under 10; one, 10-16; one, 16-26; one female under 10; one, 10-16.

Robert by the census of 1810 was under 26 with one boy under 10; in 1820, had six children. He sold his farm on Indian Creek, 1815, to Charles McGill and moved. He married Dollie Grider (see Grider).

James Neathery (see Grider).

Daniel (1794-1873) married Sally — and reared a family.

NEEDHAM FAMILY

The Needhams of Cumberland County came from North Carolina to this county about the time of the Civil War. They had come from England to North Carolina. The name is English, derived from occupational femininity (knead-dame), meaning "dough worker."

John Needham was born in Surry County, North Carolina, early in 1800 and reared a family there, which he brought to Cumberland County and settled on Groves Creek (now Dutch Creek). One of his sons, Frank, came with him while some did not come here. Frank was the father of Rommie, Sr., Caleb, and Bertha who married Esq. J. O. Alexander, who is the father of Samuel Alexander, present superintendent of schools, this county, 1946.

John's children went to school with the children of the Siamese Twins in the little house on Ararat River in Surry County near the town of Airy, where the twins are buried. Eng and Chang were the names of the twins; in the Siamese this meant "right" and "left." They were born in Burma, 1811; came to America, 1829; died, 1874. They assumed the name of Bunker, their master in the show. They married sisters, Adelaide and Sally Yates, to whom were born large families —none of whom were of malformation. Eng and Chang were grown together at the lower breast bone by a strong, large, ligament and had to walk a little angling to each other. They had nice homes and would take weekly turns at these homes, which their wives kept. Chang died in bed which woke Eng, who died a few hours later. The Needhams cherish their school days for this privilege.

NEWBY FAMILY

Newby is an Anglo-Saxon word, meaning "the farmer in the good building." Taken from the original word "neubon."

The first Newbys came from north England to America around 1700. Virginia does not list them among the first pioneers of that state. Henry and his wife, Mary, were the first ones to come to America. They had seven children and all landed near the mouth of Rappahannock River in what is now Lancaster County. Their children were: Robert, James, John, Ozwald, Edward, William, and Levi.

Henry became involved in a lot of suits in Lancaster County which were kept up by some of his sons after his death.

Henry Newby vs. Robert Wells, ordered dismissed by the court, 1727.

Henry Newby vs. John Pollard, continued from November Court, 1736.

Henry Newby vs. John Cornelius, found 200 pounds of tobacco and four shillings in favor of plaintiff, August, 1741.

James Newby vs. Jonas Parrish, 700 pounds of tobacco in favor of plaintiff.

Ozwald Newby vs. William Redford, found 13-7-9 for plaintiff, 1757.

Henry died in November, 1741, and his wife in 1762. After this some of the children moved on west 100 miles to Chesterfield County, Virginia, while the rest remained at the old home place. They all married and reared families. One branch went south, one north, and the third branch came to Cumberland County.

William (of Henry, Sr.) married Amy —— and reared seven children: William, Elijah, Elisha, John, Sarah, Jane, and Dina. William (of Henry, Sr.), had "considerable property in Virginia."

William married Martha Adkins; Elijah married Judith Farmer; John married Martha Ferguson; two of the girls married Clarks.

Elisha W. Newby of this group of children married Judith —— and reared four, according to his will probated in Chesterfield County, 1826. He left Sam, William, Martin, and Anna, all of whom married in Virginia before coming to Cumberland County. Anna married John Baugh and reared a family. William got 120 acres; others equal lands.

Martin is the progenitor of all the Newbys of this county. He married Anna P. Bowman, daughter of Pleasant Bowman, September 19, 1810, and to them were born five children—Edward, Lucy, Wilson B., Elizabeth, and Elisha W., Jr.

Edward sold out and left. Elizabeth married James Paull, 1828 (see Paulls).

Wilson B. married Cassie Phelps, daughter of Rev. R. T. Phelps, and to them were born Richard, Branch, and Ellis (two died).

Richard married Henretta Cheek and to them were born Henry, Paul, Eugene, all citizens of this county.

Elisha W., Jr., married Mary Jane Paull, daughter of John Paull and Polly Morgan Paull, and reared five—William, Robert, Ellen, Mrs. Joe B. Alexander, and one other.

William, of this group, married Beulah Smith, daughter of Samuel Smith, and reared four: Mary, a teacher of the county and town; Roy, Paul, and John business men of Burkesville.

Robert married an English woman (no issue).

Ellen married Houston Eden, who became the father of Cortez and Herbert H. Eden, two thriving farmers of the county.

NORRIS

The Norris families that settled Marrowbone were: Clayborn, William Waller, Zebulon, and William A. They were of the same ancestry.

William Waller married Sally Ann Beck in Virginia and reared William W., Jr. Senior died in the county, 1836. His son married Martha Ann Nunn, who was 18 years old, in 1858. To them were born three—Gillium, 1859; Edwin Lee, 1865; Reuben 1874.

Gillium married Emma Sanders of Louisville, 1928. They had no children. He accumulated great wealth and honored his mother by giving to the Marrowbone Valley $10,000 to erect a high school building in her name, which has meant so much to that community and shall mean much for years to come. Was part owner of Belknap Company.

Edwin Lee moved to Montana, where he became Governor. He died there in 1924. He married Betty Wilkins of Bowling Green. No issue.

Reuben married Bertha L. Beck of Wayne County. He remained on Marrowbone Creek, where he was a leading citizen. No issue to them. It is claimed that this branch is descended from William Waller of Virginia, who came to Bourbon County, 1783.

William A. Norris came with the Marrowbone Davises. He married Lucy Creasy and they had three—Samuel, Sally, and Fanny.

Samuel married Jane Pace and reared Enos whose two sons—Kyle and Clifton—have families in the county. Kyle is head of the Farmers Exchange of Burkesville and Clifton of the Marrowbone Garage (see Davis).

Sally married John Harvey and they have a family in Metcalfe County.

Fanny married a Frazier and reared a family.

Zebulon Norris was one of the first to settle the county. He served as Deputy Clerk several years. He married Elizabeth —— and reared seven, all before 1823 at his death. Sally married Willie Smith; Elizabeth married Reuben Beck and had a family; Jane married Abraham Dick and had a family; Anna married John Gorman (see Gorman); Lucy; John H.; and William.

Clayborn Norris lived near Richmond, Virginia. He came to Cumberland County early and reared two boys in the county, Richard and Robert.

Richard married a Binns and lived near Leslie in this county, where he reared four children—Henry Clay, John J., James M., and Becky Jane. The daughter died.

Henry Clay married Sallie Neathery, sister to Robert Neathery, and reared four: Alfred D., who reared a family in Iowa; Edward P., who married Myrtie Baker and moved to Chattanooga, Tennessee; Fanny Norris, who married John Jones of Monroe County and reared

Marvin, who has kept a restaurant in Burkesville for 12 years; James M., Jr., who moved to California.

John J. (of Richard) married a Miss Blackborn and reared two sons in Texas. His second wife was Sophia Shibley, to them were born several children out West.

James M. (of Richard) married Mary J. Taylor and reared (according to will of 1862) three boys—Creed Taylor, John F., and William H. Creed T. married Sallie Pennington and reared Mary (dec.), Clarence H., Tom, Carl, Jackie, Alice (who married William Turner), Lola (who also married a Turner), and Frank, who moved to Barren County. John F. married Amelia Sanders of Logan County and reared William E., Vinnie L., and Charles D.

Robert Norris (of Clayborn) married Hannah Akin and reared Clay, Angie, William W., Sam, Lewis, and Martha. William W. reared Carlos, member of the board of education for many years.

A William Norris settled on the waters of Illwill near the present site of Hegira. He became the progenitor of the Norris family that still inhabits that region. He married Elizabeth and reared William, Jr., Carter, and Nathan. William, Jr., married Mary A. Simpson (b. 1837), daughter of William D. Simpson, and reared a family. One of his sons, John W., married Priscilla Ray and reared a large family at Hegira. Judge B. R. Norris is of this group. He and his brothers—Albert, Leonard and —— constitute the Norris Quartette of Cumberland County. Nathan also reared a family at Hegira. His wife was Perlina Allen, daughter of William Allen. He next married Betsy Gilreath and from them came the Little Renox Norrises—Ross, Brad, George, etc.

OLIVER FAMILY

The name Oliver in Latin meant "an olive," but it became a surname in Sweden in 993 A.D., hence is a Norse name. King Olufer of Sweden was the first subject in his country to embrace Christianity and teach his followers so, and as the name moved south and west its orthography merged into the present form. From England they came to America early; and from Virginia they came to Kentucky at the close of the Revolutionary War.

In 1780 John and Thomas came to Lincoln County, on the Cumberland River, and in 1784 took up land and lived to rear families. Richard W. F. Oliver, a son or grandson of John, came down Cumberland River on a coal barge as a hand and stopped at Creelsboro in the 30's, where he married Betsy Ballou and moved to Clinton County, lived there a while, then in 1858 took up 100 acres of land on Salt Lick Creek, where his family was reared. Betsy was a daughter of Cleve Ballou. Richard's two sons, John and Gustus, reared families in Clinton and Cumberland counties. G. C. Oliver, a son of the latter, is chairman of the Cumberland County Triple A Organization.

OWSLEY FAMILY

The Owsley family dates from the Normans in England. The name belongs to that class of names derived from a place of settlement. Records show the people settled on the "Lea" of the Ouse River in England, hence, "Ouse-lea" people. Most names have, through the ages, changed their orthography. The Rev. John Owsley (1635-1714) heads the branch that came to Cumberland County. Rev. John lived in Leicester County, England, and reared a family. One of his sons, Thomas (1663-1700), set sail for America in 1679 but was seized and held by Algerian pirates until a ransom of one English pound 11 shillings and 3 pence were paid, after which he came to Jamaica Island of the West Indies. In 1694 he left his home on that island and went to Stafford County, Virginia, where he was granted 1,000 acres of land. He served as Clerk of Stafford County. At his death he had only one son, Thomas (2). This Thomas married Ann West and reared eight children— five sons and three daughters, to whom he left an estate at his death valued at 12,000 English pounds. John, of these eight children, moved to Tennessee, and then to Georgia, and left descendants over the South. Thomas (3), another of these eight children, married Mary Middleton in 1746 and up to 1773 reared 12 children in Virginia. This big family finally all came to Crab Orchard, Kentucky. Four of this family (and descendants) are woven into the human fabric of Cumberland County. They were Ann B. (1747); William (1749); Anthony (1757); Patience (1772).

Ann B. married Thomas Chilton, whose son, Thomas, became a noted Baptist preacher and a real estate dealer of Cumberland County.

Anthony, whose son, Bryan Young Owsley, became the first Circuit Clerk of Russell County (1827).

Patience married William Bledsoe (of Joseph Bledsoe) and reared seven children. Albert, a grandson of Patience, became a noted writer and politician along about the time of the Civil War.

William Owsley married Katherine Boulden and they became the parents of 11 children: Samuel, Nudigate, William, Dr. Joel, Maj. Jonathan, Margaret, Mary Pearl, Patience, Chloe, and an infant.

Of these eleven children, William became the sixteenth Governor of Kentucky, Representative in Congress, Senator, and Judge of the Court of Appeals of Kentucky.

The Cumberland County Owsleys of today are the offspring of Dr. Joel Owsley, one of the eleven above. He was born in 1790 and died in 1869. His remains rest in the King Cemetery. He married Mary Ann Lewis of Burkesville, in 1812, one year after his arrival in Cumberland County. Dr. Joel was one of the first doctors in this county and was also one of the first ministers of the Christian Church of the county. To Dr. Joel and Mary Ann was born a son—William Francis, 1813. He became one of the first merchants of Burkesville and accumulated quite a bit of wealth. He continued in the mercantile business until 1858, when he helped establish a branch Bank of the Louisville Bank in which he was cashier until into the 70's. He married Mary Agnes Bledsoe, daughter of Joseph Scott Bledsoe, and to this union was born one son, William Francis, Jr. (1852). W. F., Jr., has been one of the leading men of Cumberland County in the rearing of Thoroughbred horses, with which he seldom lost a prize at the different county fairs. He is a strong Christian believer in his grandfather's way of seeing the Bible. At this writing he is past ninety-five and still cultivates his flower garden each year with its hundreds of varieties, most of which he contributes to funeral and burial purposes. One daughter, Mrs. H. H. Grant of Louisville.

William Francis, Jr., married Sallie A. Alexander and to them were born five: Susan, who married Dr. J. G. Talbot, to which union were born Jack, Alexander, William; Mary Agnes, who married Dr. R. C. Richardson; Grant, who died single; Helen who married Sellie M. Young, who spent most of his life as cashier in the Bank of Cumberland; they have one son, Owsley Young, now a soldier in World War II; Dr. William Fayette Owsley, who married Anna Pearl Owings of Lexington.

PACE FAMILY

The name Pace is Anglo-Saxon. The first record we find as John Pake, and the name is often spelled Paach. Its meaning is "connected with Easter." After reaching England, where the people by that name emigrated from, it assumed its present orthography about the year 1273.

Just when the first Pace crossed the Atlantic I have failed to find, but one Richard Pace lived in Virginia at an early date. In Henry County, Virginia, the home of the Paces, there lived two (perhaps more) brothers, Joel and John, the former an officer in the Revolutionary War, and the latter a captain in the same war.

Joel married Mary East in Virginia and moved to Woodford County, Kentucky, and from there to Mount Vernon, Illinois, where his 12 children were reared, the descendants of whom have aspired to many high state and county offices.

Captain John Pace (1751-1825) lived and died in Henry County, Virginia. He first married Elizabeth Nunn and to them were born 10 children from 1773 to 1790, respectively: William Ingrim, Lucy, Thomas, Susannah, Oney, Elizabeth, Sally, John Martin, Jr., Polly, and Milly. John M., Sr., next married Mrs. Polly Stone and to them were born five from 1808 to 1816: James, Green, Jerman, Lucinda, and Matilda.

According to the records only three of those 15 children came to Cumberland County—John (1787-1829); William Ingrim (1773-1843); there must be a discrepancy in the third brother's record, both in name and date, for Langston must have been a younger brother of John, Sr. He was born in 1770 and died in 1846 in this county. Or Langston could have been a second name.

William I. Pace became the progenitor of most of the Cumberland County Paces. He married Sally Nunn (1779-1859) in 1796 and they became the parents of 14 children, most of whom lived near Summer Shade, a short distance west of the county line. The children were: Elizabeth (1799); Nancy G. (1800); Thomas Nunn (1801); Millie (1803); Sanford Raney (1805); John Jefferson (1807); Ingrim Alexander (1809); Dr. William H. (1811); Eliza G. (1812); Sally (1814); Walter Jackson (1816); Lucinda S. (1818); Joe W. (1820); James Marion (1822).

Of this big family Elizabeth married Joseph Clark and produced descendants into the Bybee, Bowles, Greers, and Sartin families, from her five children.

Thomas Nunn married Docia Williams and reared 7 (seen later).
Nancy G. married Sam Clark.
Millie M. married Abner Harvey and reared five children.
Sanford Raney married Meekness Nunnelly and had six children.
John Jefferson married and reared six children.
Ingrim A. died young.

Dr. William Henry married Lucinda Hart and left two in Missouri.

Eliza G. married Whitefield Button and reared three in Illinois.
Sally I. married Jesse Gee and left one daughter.

Walter Jackson married Sally Ritchey and reared three children. One married W. W. Alexander and one Dan B. Williams. His second wife was Julia Ritchey, sister to first wife, and by the second marriage seven were born. (Julia 1827-1915).

Lucinda Sharp married Joe Glazebrook and reared eleven children.

Joe Washington married Harriett Whitlow and reared six.

Thomas Nunn Pace's family, through Henry S., one of his sons, left more descendants in Cumberland County than any other of the children. Henry married Mary T. Barton and to them 12 children were born, namely:

Stanley D. grew up to be one of Marrowbone's most influential men. He was sheriff of the county 1934-7, and belonged to the Cumberland Construction Company, which built many highways in Kentucky. He married Pearl Carter, daughter of the renowned J. C. Carter, 36 years Circuit Judge, and to them were born Stanley, Patty Nell, and Mollie. Mrs. S. D. Pace was also sheriff of this county four years and is at present (1946) chairman of the Republican Party in this district. S. D. Pace lost his life in a wreck.

James E. (of Henry and Mary) married Miss Daisy Davis of Marrowbone and reared two—Fred and Georgia. Mrs. Daisy is president of the Marrowbone Bank and her son, Fred, is sole manager of Pace Construction Company. Besides roads he has been contractor of Burkesville Court House, and the Tuberculosis Hospital of Glasgow, Kentucky. He married Alcie Kinslow, of Bowling Green, and has two girls. Mrs. Fred Pace is a public-spirited woman.

Georgia (of J. E. and D.) married Ledman W. Alexander, who is a member of the Cumberland Construction Company and proprietor of Alexander Company store in Burkesville.

Sidney (of Henry S.) married Bessie Duerson and has one daughter.

Schooling (of H. S.) married Leta Pace and reared three boys and three girls. He moved to Bowling Green, Kentucky.

Nettie (of H. S.) married Taylor Neal and had one daughter at Auburn, Kentucky.

Sue married James Dalton, who moved to Mississippi, where they reared three sons and three daughters.

Kate, Mary, Mabel, and Walter Tom died without issue.

Beulah (of H. S.) married Benton Allen and moved to California, where they reared two sons.

Patty was Caleb Needham's first wife and died without issue.

Langston Pace (1770-1846) lived and died in Cumberland County. He married Millie Nunn and reared William I.; Permelia; Polly; John M.; Elizabeth; Susannah; Sally; Thomas, and Mrs. Hutchins.

William I., of this family, married Sally Vawter (b. 1812) of Marrowbone and moved to McDonough County, Illinois, where he reared a family of eight children. He headed a company of soldiers who went to help arrest the Mormon leader, Jobe Smith, in 1844, at Nauvoo, Illinois.

Polly married John W. Williams, School Commissioner, and reared a family.

John M. Pace married Phereby Williams, daughter of Ephraim and Sally Williams, and reared a family.

Elizabeth married H. S. Martin and reared a family.

Susannah married a Mr. Barton.

Sally married a Mr. Bryant.

PAGE, RADFORD, MAXEY, HICKS

The Pages, Radfords, Hicks, and Maxeys all came together. They came from Powhatan and Buckingham counties, Virginia, to Cumberland County, through the Lincoln County route. (For meaning see Proper Names).

PAGE

Robert Page came to Lincoln County in 1784, where he was granted 250 acres by the Virginia Legislature. Disposing of this, he moved on to Indian Creek, Cumberland County, in 1799, where he was granted 200 acres by the Kentucky Legislature. While here one of his sons, William, married and remained for life. It was he who Gov. P. H. Leslie, in his autobiography, said gave him the first silver money he had ever seen in his life, for gathering "Uncle Billie's crop of corn on his sled by horse power." The amount was $3.00. Robert then followed on to Skaggs Creek, where William Radford and William Maxey had been since 1791. I suppose he died here for he left three sons here, Anderson, John S., and Wesley. Anderson married Frances (Fanny) and lived on Mud Camp. Wesley married a Miss Dicken and moved to East Cumberland County, around Whetstone. Wesley's son, Robert, married Nancy Radford, sister to Caleb Radford and to them six were born: Alvis, who went to Missouri; Lonis to Oklahoma; Mattie, who married Crawford Higginbotham and went to Texas; Robert, who married Lizzie Surratt and reared 13 in Texas and Oklahoma, one of whom, (Ira) became wealthy in the oil fields of Oklahoma. Lillie, a daughter of Robert and Lizzie, remained in Cumberland County, married John Claywell and had 13 children. John Page, son of Wesley married Susan Maxey, daughter of Randolph and Arnilda Campbell Maxey, and reared Vela, who married Ed Gibson, and reared three teachers—Mildrid, Alene, and Lucile. To John and Susan were born: Walter and Caleb C., who live in the county. Walter is a farmer. Caleb is a teacher, ex-Representative, and merchant.

RADFORD and HICKS

William and James Radford were the two first in the county. William took up 2,000 acres of land on Skaggs Creek in 1791. He married and reared four sons—Thomas and William Laten (1793-1875). Tom married Annie Maxey, daughter of Caleb Maxey, and reared Caleb who married Betsy Carter, daughter of Jacob Carter, and became the father of Jacob M.; George T.; James G.; William F.; Sally, who married William Bybee and had a family; Martha, who married James Smiley and reared a family; Amelia, and Thomas Radford. (For Nancy of Thomas, Sr., see Pages.)

William Laten married Jane Hicks, sister to Reuben Hicks, and reared Elizabeth, 1829; Anna, who married Ben Young; William A. (1831); Reuben D. (1836); Charles (1839); Mary (McCombs); John (1846); Zachariah (1849). They went to Missouri in 1853, and Zachariah's grandson is (1946) with the Treasury Department in Washington, D. C.

The descendants of Caleb Radford are many near the old place on Brush Creek near Bakerton, Kentucky. Raymond and Lufus were two other sons William, Sr., must have left.

James Radford, Sr., brother to William, Sr., did not come to Cumberland County until 1810. He had been married before, but he married second Hannah Wilborn in Cumberland County, at the age of 68, and had one son, Lufus, who married the widow Alexander, with no issue.

MAXEY

The Maxeys date back to 300 A.D. They were connected with the Royal dynasties of Italy, Germany, and France.

William Maxey came to the county with William Radford, 1791.

Pioneer Genealogies 401

He located on Skaggs Creek also. They came through Lincoln County also. There were five brothers—Ephraim, Radford, Rice, William, and Caleb. They went to the lower end of Cumberland County, and then Caleb came to Brush Creek in 1804. Here he had a grant of 150 acres in 1805.

They reared families, but left only descendants. Radford was in the public offices of the county and so was Rice. Rice was an attorney at Burkesville, and after Clinton County was cut off, 1836, he moved to that county, where he was elected sheriff 1840-41 and Clerk the rest of the 40's.

Caleb Maxey married Sally Lewis and reared six children—Charles; Betty (Young); Anna (Radford); Tobitha (Pendleton); Mary (Amacks); Randolph, and Sally (Gilbert). These families, except those of Sally Gilbert whose descendants live on Brush Creek, and those given under the Radfords migrated to other states. Betty, who married the father of B. M. Young, left through B. M. a nice family of children in and around Highway, Clinton County. Armead and Laura, of B. M., taught in Cumberland back in the 90's.

Samuel Bell Maxey went from the county to Texas, where he climbed to U. S. Senator for the Lone Star State.

PARRISH

The Parishes came from France to America. The name means "an equal clergy or district." Our Parishes came from Henry County, Virginia, to Cumberland County about 1810, and settled in Howards Bottom. There was a William D. Parrish, who came earlier to Adair and owned land in Cumberland, where he spent part of his time (see Fergus).

John, Sr., was the settler. He married Mary Perlina Stockton and reared John, Jr., Hiram, Peyton, Sally, and Tarpley. John, Jr., married Permelia Howard, daughter of James Howard, the pioneer, and had two—Clayton and Imogene.

Peyton was a merchant and postmaster, for whom the office was named Peytonsburg.

Clayton married Jane Flowers and reared John, George, V. F. (Bush), Jack, and that group of children on Crocus Creek, most of whom made farmers. Bush kept hotel in Burkesville most of his life.

Hiram (of John, Sr.) married Elizabeth Gains and reared Sally, who was the wife of C. M. Dillon; Mary H. (wife of William Slemmons); James W., who married Mary Alexander and reared Hiram, Horace, and James, all in Cumberland County. Elizabeth (of Hiram and Elizabeth) married Big Ed Morgan and reared Robert and Mirtie.

The third Parrish in the county was Billie, who came from West Virginia about 1825. He married Elizabeth Smith, daughter of Briton Smith, and they became the parents of Sim John, George, Bob, Dal, Ivan, and Jo Ann.

PIERCE

Francis Pierce (see Surnames) was born in Carolina County, Virginia, 1760; enlisted in Albermarle County, Virginia, 1779. He states that at the age of ten he and family moved to Orange County, Virginia. After two years of service in the Revolutionary War as a private, he moved to Wilkes County, North Carolina, one year after marriage, and to Cumberland County in 1801, and settled on the headwaters of Smith Creek. He had a grant of 200 acres, 1807, in this valley, "on no stream." The census of Cumberland County for 1810 gives Francis and wife both living, over 45, and the parents of eight children: one son, 16 to 26; two, 10 to 16; two, under 10; and one girl, 10 to 16; two, under 10.

The names of the children we failed to find, except Lewis Pierce, 1808-90, who married Rachel (1818-98) and reared, Francis; David C.; Elizabeth, who married J. S. Parmley and reared a family; Ann E. (see Griders); Susan, who married William Guthrie; Martha, who married Hiram Cook and had a family; Sarah, who married Jerry Tuggle and reared a family; Rebecca who married L. B. Tabor. Nearly all of these children lived in the part of Cumberland that made Clinton County.

Mr. J. A. Browning, who is secretary-treasurer of the firm of Cayce-Yost Co., Hopkinsville, Kentucky, is a direct descendant of Francis by his son, John Pierce.

A John Pierce, who came from Clinton County to Cumberland early in 1800, married Sarah Tompkins of Tennessee and reared Sam, Alvin C., Joe, Malinda, Polly, Nancy, Sally. John M. was lost in the War of 1812. His son, Alvin C., served through the Civil War and married Martha Jane Rowe, and to them was born Elzie Garfield, who has a family of good citizens on Pierce Ridge, Cumberland County.

RAYS

The Rays came early and in large families. All the pioneers left off the "W" in their names. There were Tom, William, Joel, John, and Joseph. They were Baptists, and still are. They were natural vocal musicians, and still are. William settled on Mud Camp, Joseph on Marrowbone, and the other boys in what is now Clinton County. William was a minister. He is the progenitor of the present Cumberland County Wrays. William, Thomas, Joseph in 1810 had seven children to the family, from one to sixteen years old. They are church folk to the present. Daniel, the grandson of Settler William, taught singing schools during his life and his sons and grandsons continue the work. At Bow Schoolhouse Church they hold the only annual Foot-Washing in the County.

RENEAUS

The Reneaus came from France. Like other names, this has undergone spelling changes in passing through different languages. The "eau" belongs to French and is found as Renault, Renauldt, Renaudt, and modified to its present form; while among the early settlers of Pennsylvania, North Carolina, South Carolina, Virginia, and in Cumberland County on its early pages it was spelled Reno. John, himself, spelled his name Reno when he was married here.

They were among the good Huguenots who were driven from France prior to 1700. King Henry IV of France issued his Edict in 1598 which gave to all protestant organizations rights and freedom of conscience equal to the Catholics. Harmony prevailed in a large degree until 1685, when King Louis XIV revoked the Edict and ordered all protestant children to be taken from their parents and instructed in the Catholic faith, and the disobedient parents who failed to yield were to be punished with death; whereupon, he declared an embargo to prevent their escape from France. Notwithstanding, the Huguenots saw their doom, and over half a million escaped to Holland, Germany, England, Switzerland, and America, bringing with them their property and habits of industry. This was a worse blow to France than the previous wars. The early Renos were Amish adherents.

Learning of the "brotherly love" community of Pennsylvania, which was talked of at the time, Huguenots from Germany and the other countries came in great numbers to it and later moved with the tide to Virginia and the Carolinas. Isaac, Sr., 1712, was in Pennsylvania.

Among the first ones to land were (Memorials of Huguenots of America) Claude 1749, Isaac 1751, Peter and Francis 1752, and William and Joseph in 1764. Isaac was the progenitor of the Tennessee and Kentucky branch. George, Lewis, and Charles (progeny of the above) served in the militia at the time of the Paoli Massacre, 1777. Isaac is listed as a German pioneer of Chester County, Pennsylvania, having crossed in the ship *Patience*. All the above were in Allegheny County 1790.

Three of Isaac's grandchildren, John, William, and Aaron, came to Cumberland County and settled on the waters of Wolf River in 1800. John took up 400 acres of land in the county, 1801, and in 1804 he married Betsy (Elizabeth) Thurman and reared a family. Four of his sons lived here and reared families. They were Isaac T. (1805-85), William, Berry, and Joseph. Census, 1820, lists seven children of John.

Isaac T. was the eldest child. His brilliant intellect led him to the study of medicine under Dr. Jourdan in Overton County, Tennessee, which he abandoned later and entered the teaching profession. He taught school at Clear Fork in 1830-1, which five years later became Clinton County. He became very much interested in the work of the Wolf River Baptist Church. This was during the Reformation

Period in Kentucky, and he was led to disagree with the Baptists on several issues and united with the Church of Christ, or Christian Church, in which he became one of the most noted preachers of his day, especially in Cumberland, Clinton, Adair, and Russell counties and throughout Tennessee. He organized churches at Paoli, Albany, Rock House, Irish Bottom, etc.

Rev. Isaac T. married Mary G. Wood, daughter of Thomas Wood, who was brother of Hon. William Wood, an early statesman of Cumberland County.

To Isaac T. and Mary were born nine:

Margarett; Tom W. (to Oklahoma); John M., who was County Surveyor for several years. He married a Mullins and reared a family in Clinton County.

Mariba, who married John Depp and had a family at Glasgow.

Barton (deceased).

Mary R., who married William Beard, the son of Wakefield Beard, who was the son of John Beard, the pioneer of Cumberland. Mary and William reared a family in Clinton County several of whom made teachers. William, Jr., was County Clerk of Clinton, having made the race on his hands, his feet and legs being infant in size.

Joseph W. married Ira Smith, sister of Rev. W. L. Smith, and reared family in Barren County.

Isaac, Jr., lived in Nebraska, near Lincoln.

R. J. Shannon married Kate Sheffield and reared two sons and three daughters. One son, Isaac Oren, is druggist at Albany. He married Hadus Neathery and reared a family. His eldest son, Ned, is following in the steps of his great-grandfather, Isaac T., in serving the ministry of the Christian Church.

Berry Reneau (of John and Elizabeth) reared his family in Clinton County. His grandson, Carvin, has been Superintendent of Schools, Clinton, for several terms.

Descendants of the above pioneer Reneaus are Gen. Jesse L. Reno, who was killed in the battle of Antietam, Maryland, while assisting General Lee, 1862. Another man of note is Hon. Claude T. Reno, Attorney General of Pennsylvania, 1946. Reno, Nevada, was named for Gen. Jesse L.

RITCHEYS

The Ritchey family came from Washington County, Maryland, to Virginia and to Cumberland County. John, father of William owned 48 slaves at his death. The Ritchey family was one of the pioneers, but few of them are left here now. Some of their descendants still remain. They were a noble class of people.

William Ritchey, as noted elsewhere, took up a great quantity of land on Marrowbone and its tributaries. He was the father of William, James, John, and Sam, Jane (Allen), Polly (Williams), Betsy (Conn). Elizabeth (wife of William) died 1819.

James (of William) had William, James, and Julia.

Pioneer Genealogies

William (of James) married Miss Harris and went to Mississippi.

James (of James) married Miss Owsley and moved to Burkesville, where he reared several boys and girls.

Julia married Joe Henry Alexander and reared W. W., Henry, Sam, Charley, Mary (married John Q. Owsley), Sophia (married W. R. Davis), Larissa (married Fayette Beck), Betty (married James Cheek).

John Ritchey (of William, Sr.) married Jane Allen (of Robert and Jane) and settled opposite the mouth of Allens Creek.

Sam (of William, Sr.) married Kathrine Williams, sister of Lemuel Williams, and settled the farm opposite Waterview where Alexander Allen now lives.

William Ritchey, Jr., settled the farm on which Waterview is located. Later known as the Joe Henry Alexander farm.

William Ritchey, Sr., also had four daughters. Esther married Daniel Smiley. Eunice married John Hillis. They came with William, Sr., in November, 1800, and settled on Marrowbone.

To John Hillis and Eunice were born William R., Elizabeth, James, Peggy, Sally, Esther, Polly, Fanny, Sam W., Julian, Milton.

SCOTT FAMILY

Absalom Scott (1776 –) was one of the first Scotts that came to Cumberland County. We find him living in the bottom that bears his name prior to 1804. He married Philipina Stanfield in 1806 and to them were born 11 children: Maranda, George, John, James, William, Alvy, Valentine, Robert, Thomas, Anna, and Nancy.

Maranda married William Claywell, son of Shadrach Claywell.

George married Sally Ann Hayden and reared one daughter, Melvina, who married Pleasant Murphy, and took their family to St. Clair County, Missouri, in 1885.

John Scott married Jane Hayden and reared Absalom, John Richard, Sidney, Philipina, and James D.

Absalom Scott (of John and Jane) married Justany Bow, sister to Judge J. G. Jones' wife. They reared 13 children around Whitewright, Texas.

John Richard (of John and Jane) married Martha Ann Huff and reared three children—Willie, Laura, and Minnie. Minnie married Charley Guthrie, son of William Guthrie, and to them was born one son, Charles, Jr.

Sidney (of John and Jane) married a Miss Anderson and went to Mississippi.

Philipina (of John and Jane) married Capt. Isaac Bow, who was sheriff of Cumberland County many years (see Bows).

Valentine Scott (of Absalom, Sr.) married (1849) Mary Motley, the widow of James Paull, deceased 1847, and to them were born Laura, who married a Mr. Gracey, daughter Mrs. T. P. Smith, Clarksville, Tennessee, Frank, Thomas, Sally, Mollie, and W. L. of Nashville.

Thomas Scott (of Absalom) married a Miss Graves of Creelsboro and reared a family.

Anna Scott (of Absalom) married Lewis Parmley, this county, and reared one son, Fillmore.

Fillmore Parmley married a Miss Walthall and reared three girls, Millard, Gertrude, and Zelma. Zelma married Holland E. Thrasher and reared a family in Whites Bottom; Gertie married Herbert Eden; Millard married Dallas Goff.

Nancy Scott (of Absalom) married William Walthall and reared Wellie, Absalom, Bob, Albert, Clay, William, Jr., and Anna.

Another family of Scotts are descendants of Robert Scott, who first married Mary Hopper and reared three boys; secondly married Polly Hughes and to them were born Stephe, Thomas, and Lewis. Stephe's son, Charles M., has been a faithful church worker with the Methodists. He married first, Maggie Hogan and reared a family. Secondly, a Mrs. Riddle whose children have been educated for teachers and ministers.

SELF

The Selfs came from Amelia County, Virginia, to Kentucky, 1789. In 1809, John came with his family to Cumberland County and settled in the northern part of the county. He was born in Amelia County in 1762, served in the Revolutionary War, after which he married. He brought his large family with him—Robert, Fanny, Diana, Guy, Elizabeth, and others. Most of the children married their neighbors, as is usually the case. Elizabeth married Fredrick Smith, 1811; Diana married James Hendron; Fanny married George Logan, 1811; Guy married Matilda Goggins and had one—William J. (b. 1829), who married Mary (Polly) Guinn, of James Guinn, and to them Berry, James, Hiram, Sally, Julia, Alice, William. The boys all left, but the girls reared families here. Sally married Benjamin Irvin and reared a large family, then went to Oklahoma. Julia married Dr. Tom Keen, secondly J. E. Morgan, with no issue. Alice married James D. Irvin of Creelsboro and had Kenneth and Anna Kate. J. D. was a great blessing to the rich and poor alike, serving them through his mercantile business for half a century, underselling all other merchants of the country, thereby building up an enormous business.

SEWELL FAMILY

The name Sewell is of English origin and is derived from a skilled occupation around the dignitaries of England, meaning "sew well for my Mayster." I do not doubt this, for it has followed down to the present. In observing the needlework of the present Sewell offspring, there is none better.

They came from England to Pennsylvania in the 1600's, and from there to North Carolina, and to Tennessee about 1750. Joseph and

Abraham were in North Carolina before the Revolutionary War, and in Tennessee, 1785. Joseph seems to be the progenitor of the Kentucky Sewells. He was in Carter County, Tennessee, when it was organized, 1796. His son Stephe, married in Carter County and reared 14 children—eight sons and seven daughters. Seven of the boys lived to be grown—four of whom made preachers. They are, Joseph P., Jonathan, Isaac, Jesse Lee, William B., Elisha G., Caleb. He bragged that all had Bible names but one.

Elisha G. was one of the outstanding evangelists of his day, and so were Jesse and Caleb. They pioneered Tennessee and Kentucky during the Reform period of Kentucky. A North Carolina statement made in 1795 was, "with little of this world's goods." Still we learn that after they all came from Carter County to Overton County, Tennessee, and Cumberland County, Kentucky, in 1815, they bought farms on Wolf River, in Kentucky and Tennessee. Religion and some line of education were their hobbies. They were all Baptist. They built the Baptist Church on Wolf River, and the record of that church says, "Stephe gave two-plus acres as his part." Stephe was deacon and his brother, William B., was clerk. While things were going so well, William B. married a member of the Christian Church, and one Sunday he partook of the Lord's Supper with her, for which he was excluded, and Jesse agreed that it was all right, whereupon the church brought him to trial for false preaching, and he asked them what that was, and the charge recorded in the church book reads, "For faith, repentance and baptism for the remission of sin." Here the Baptists lost four ministers, and the Christian Church gained four.

Joseph Sewell came to Clinton County about 1840, operated the hotel at Albany which Judge Smith now owns, until 1853, when he sold out and moved to Sewell Mountain near Albany, where the noted Chalybeate Springs furnished a resort for the afflicted for half a century. He married Nancy Philpott Staten and reared a family (see Statens and Grider).

Stephe's William, by his son Edward Sewell, became the progenitor of the Marrowbone Sewells—Thurston, Willian Thomas—both of whom are business men of Waterview, Kentucky.

William D., of William B., one of those boys, through Hice Sewell became the progenitor of the Bear Creek Sewells, and John F., his brother, also furnished several citizens on Bear Creek. The Carvers, Flowers, Bows, and a lot more are descendants of this branch.

SIMPSON FAMILY

The Simpson family is another one of Irish descent. William was born in Cumberland County, 1801. His parents had come to Cumberland as pioneers. He died in 1887. One of his sons, J. J. Simpson, was born in the county, 1845. He enlisted as a boy soldier and fought throughout the Civil War. At the close of the war, J. J. married Justina Marcum (1849-1941) and settled down on his farm until 1882, when he was elected Tax Commissioner, 1886 Clerk and 1898 Judge for the county, serving in all, 19 years. Nine children were born to this couple: Elizabeth, Edna, W. B., G. B., B. L., Cora, Bernice, Otis, and Marvin.

The two who have figured in the history of this county are Cora and B. L.

B. L. was born in 1878. He taught school in the county nine years, after which he studied law. He was elected and served as County Judge, 1922-5 and 1930-33, and as County Attorney for three terms of four years each.

Other children of William, Sr., are Charles W., Benjamin H., Jane, and Mary A. All reared families in the county then some left. Mary A. married William Norris (see Norris); William, Sr., married Elizabeth Cook (see Farmers).

Cora (of J. J. and Justina) spent most of her life in connection with educational matters. She attended the Alexander College, Burkesville; Western States Normal, Bowling Green; University of Valparaiso, Indiana, with A.B. degree 1905; teacher in Lindsey-Wilson, Columbia, Kentucky; Free school teacher this county, and Superintendent of Schools, 1914-21, in Cumberland.

In 1906 she and Charles R. Payne of Barren County were married, to which union only one child was born, Justina, May 29, 1908. Bro. Payne had formerly married Dora Huddleston, daughter of Dr. J. B. Huddleston, a physician of the county. To his first wife were born twin girls, Dora and Dimple. Dora died at 12 and Dimple made a teacher. Since Bro. Payne died, Mrs. Cora Payne has lived on her farm in the southern part of the county on Sulphur Creek for a number of years. The farm was submerged by Dale Hollow Lake.

During Mrs. Payne's two terms of School Superintendency the county school fairs passed from the old way to the new, it being the period of time when the decorated wagons with their tasseled teams of horses and mules had to give way to the oncoming of the automobile. Many fond memories light up the faces of the ones yet living who sat upon those beautifully decorated wagons when they think of that jubilant crowd of over one hundred happy boys and girls seated upon that cushion of hay, and pouring forth every ounce of energy in song out among the hills that would reverberate with such power that the listeners would find their hair rising heavenward and their hearts throbbing a little beneath their chins. We were one big family then with all things in common.

A Jesse Simpson owned land in Wells Bottom early in 1800.

Also a Joseph Simpson lived in the north part of Cumberland County. His will of 1825 shows his wife Anna and children—Samuel, Thomas, John, Elizabeth (who married a Mr. Elliott), Anna (who married a Mr. Hunter), and Jones Simpson. Anna left a son, Josiah Hunter.

This group of Simpsons moved to Seventy-Six where they still live.

SKIPWORTH

Ashford Skipworth, the pioneer of that family, came to Cumberland County early in 1800 and settled on Potters Creek below White Bottom. He married Fanny Scott, daughter of James Scott, and reared seven children—Milton, Allen, Martin, Tom J., Joe, Bessie, who married G. H. Hood, Nancy, who married Thomas Williams and went to Missouri.

Tom J., of this group, married Della Scott, daughter of Solomon Scott, and reared four—John, of Bowling Green, and three daughters. "Uncle Tom" is (1946) 99 years old, living in his father's old house, is quick and active, often walks to Burkesville and back, a distance of seven miles. He shoots a rifle and reads without glasses. The Skipworths came from Ireland to Virginia.

SMITHS

This family is too numerous to try to single them out into individual groups. For origin see Surnames.

There seems to have been at least six families of Smiths who came to Cumberland County. See Revolutionary Soldiers. Two Samuels were in this group.

First Samuel married Rachel and came to Rock House Creek in 1802. There he reared his family of nine—Nancy, Jane, John, Barbara, Martin, Fred, Samuel, William, and Joseph.

Nancy married Tom Spencer, no issue; Jane married A. Clayton; Barbara married Richard Clayton; Fred married Betty Self; Sam married Fanny Self and reared Bob, Emily, Betsy, Rachel, Lettie, Sally, Tobitha, Miranda, Sam, and John. Bob of this last group married Mary Grider and reared Clay, John Will, L. C. (Brud), Rebecca, Sarah, and Tally. John Will of this family married Exona Grider and reared Bob, Beula, Carlos. The two first live at Creelsboro. Carlos lost his life on a boat. L. C. (Brud) married Bertha Huddleston and resides at Mill Springs. He was a successful teacher in the 90's. Many of this Samuel family went West.

Second Samuel was also born in Virginia. He married Dorcas —— and to them were born Polly, Jane, Britain, Robert, Sam, Dorcas, Margaret, Elisha, William, and Fanny. Britain's two sons—Mack and Enoch—became the progenitors of most of the Whetstone Smiths by Volley S. and John L.

William Smith was the progenitor of the Bear Creek Smiths. He married Mary (Polly) Black, in 1808, and to them were born Rev. Charley (1810-81), Mary (1812-89), George (d. 1847), William K.

Mary married Silas Wells and they became the parents of 15 children (see Wells).

George married Nancy Williams and became the father of two boys and three girls (see Williams Tree).

William K. married Cyntha Neathery and reared a large family near Bakerton, Kentucky. He reared John, Sim, Charles, William, Anderson, Ed., Susan, Margaret, Frank, Sofia, and Cyntha.

John (of W. K.) married Polly Ann Neathery and had two— William P. and Cyntha Ann. W. P. married Alice Ross and had a family in Irish Bottom. Cyntha Ann married Murray Stearns, whose son Granville K. became the father of W. C., who has been mayor of Burkesville several years; James, a thriving farmer; John Paul, another business man of Burkesville; Alma (Keen); Beulah (Smith); and Imogene. (For further descendants see McCoys).

John secondly married Malissa Murphy and reared Fraley, Joe, Sim, Dal, Tom, Angenoma, Eva. Fraley married Nannie Belle Melton, of Rev. Ambrose Melton, and reared Silas A., who served as County Clerk for several terms; John Ed, the barber; Amy, the wife of Caleb Page; Bonnie; Charles; Pauline; Christine.

Sim (of W. K.) married Mary E. Miller and went to Texas; Charles married a Smith; William (of W. K.) married Susan Black and had seven: Kate, who married Asa Wells and had Mont, Mattie, Gertie, Ella, Ezra; Bettie, who married Pete Baker, father of Cube, etc.; Sarah, who married Bud Williams and left; Judson, who married Lela Glidewell; Addie, who married John Wood; and Antha, the wife of Clint Keen; for Douglas (of William), see Mackey.

Anderson (of W. K.) married a Hunt and they became the parents of Jim F., whose children are Elvin, Lucus, and B. P. (Brud). For Margaret (of W. K.), see Hicks. Frank (of W. K.) married Vicie Brooks and had Mary, the wife of Mat Glidewell, who reared 11 children.

The original William K. Smith met a somnambulant death from a steamboat, 1862.

Another William Smith of Marrowbone was sworn in to be a government agent, in compliance with the law of the times, to inspect hemp, tobacco, and flour at Marrowbone, in 1808, which was the birth years of the town. From this grew the firm of William J. whose son Tom J. Smith of Leslie, this county, has grown to be the wealthiest merchant of Cumberland County.

STATON FAMILY

Rane Staton headed the family of that name which settled in Cumberland County. He was born in Virginia, 1768 and died in Cumberland County in 1843. He was of Scotch-Irish descent. His record shows that he was a boat pilot on the James River and that he was a Master Mason many years before his departure from Albemarle County for Irish Bottom, this county, in 1812.

He married Esther Fergus Montfort (1784-1872) in 1816. Esther had previously (1802) married John Montfort, who was County Surveyor when he died in 1804. Rane was a financier of his day. To Esther and Rane were born four children—Nancy (1820), Dr. Hiram (1821-87), William, and James A.

Dr. Hiram married Nancy Bledsoe (1824-1902), and to them were born eight children: William Alfred, James Curley, Joe R., Dick, Hiram (Boge), Esther, Tena, and Lizzie.

William Alfred (of Dr. H.) married a Miss Likes of Texas and reared Luther, Alice, Eula, and Hiram A.

James Curley (of Dr. H.) married Fanny Nelson of Oklahoma City and reared Cora, Edith, Nell, Alice, and Albert.

Joe R. married Maggie Turner of Udall, Kansas. No children.

Dick Staton married Louvina Potts and reared Hiram. His second wife was a Virginian.

Hiram A. (of Dr. H.), called "Boge," never married.

Esther (of Dr. H.) married Dr. Alex Jackman of Creelsboro.

Lizzie (of Dr. H.) died young.

Tena (of Dr. H.) married Ed Morgan, and to them were born Joe Hiram, who married Cora Bryson.

William Staton (of Rane and Esther) married first, Betty Ann Graves and had four children—Martha Jane Pink, Paulina Susan Jane, John Raney, and Tom.

Martha Jane P. married Will Hunter and had Alex H., Tom, Cage, Archie, and one daughter.

Paulina Susan married William Vining and had two children.

John Raney married Polly Shear of Wayne County.

Tom died young.

James A. (of Rane and Esther) married Fanny Winfrey, only child of Billy and Sally (Wells) Winfrey, and to them were born James, Jr., Lucy, Alsipia, and a number of infants.

James, Jr. (of James, Sr.) married Parthina Irvin of Creelsboro, and to them were born 16 children: Eva, Della, Cora, Sadia, William C., Charles, James A., Laura, Thomasine, Roy, John, Herbert and Hobart (twins), Lula, and twin infants.

Lucy (of James, Sr.) married Elzie Smith, a lieutenant in the Federal Army who lost his life at the hands of Champ Ferguson at the battle of Kentucky Salt Works. To Elzie and Lucy were born two sons—Ferdinand and Hiram Smith. Ferd died at 18, and Hiram married a Miss Duise and to them were born seven children: William, James, Hobart, Sally, Ellen, Eula, and Alice.

Alsipia (of James and Fanny) married John Murphy and went to Texas.

Nancy (of Rane and Esther) first married J. H. Philpott and left one son, Rane. He got killed. She married second Joe P. Sewell (1805-76), and to them were born eight children, all of whom died young except, Nannie, Emma, Julia, and Peter Montfort. Nannie never married. Emma married Allen W. Grider, and to them were born four children: Alma, Mamie, Julian, and Bonnie. Peter M. married Sarah (Potts) Grider and had one son; and his second wife was Fanny Williams with one son, Ovid.

Julia (of Joe and Nancy) married Dr. Green Moore of Lincoln County and to them were born five girls—Hettie, Sally, Emma, Margie, and Georgia.

A family article on the Statons claim that Staten Island, New York, was settled by and named in honor of the family, but New York history of old says that the island was first seen on September 2, 1609, by Henry Hudson, the Dutch explorer, and called "Statten Eylandt" for the States General of Holland.

STRANGE FAMILY

This name means just what it says. In Gaul it was "estrangia," meaning "a newcomer." By the coat-of-arms having the same insignia, the lion, as used by all of the name there seems to have been one progenitor originally.

William the Conqueror, 1066, carried the family to England and gave them a colony in Salop or Shropshire County where some remained, but the majority migrated to Scotland. During the reign of King Stephen of England, 1135-54, the remnant left in Salop aspired to political heights. It was then that more than a dozen families came back to England and Wales.

It was not until 1610 that 14 Strange families sought refuge from religious persecution, and John (leaving off their "de" and "le") landed at Portsmouth, Rhode Island, and James in 1619, at Jamestown, Virginia, where he became a rich landlord. One branch called themselves Alloway Stranges, named from Robert Burns's home in Scotland. They retained the "A" for identification for centuries, in all their given names.

William, of the 1619 group, after five years returned to Scotland, married, and in 1635 he and his wife and son, Edmund, together with his brother, Robert Alloway, came to stay. From this Edmund Alloway, two generations populated Virginia and North Carolina and Archelaus Strange of the third generation, born 1780-1852, married Elizabeth Coffey of Wilkes County, North Carolina, and moved to Cumberland County, Kentucky, and settled on Crocus Creek, now Adair County, 1799.

Archelaus and Elizabeth reared 11 children, Clayborn A., William A., Abraham A., Lewis A., Archelaus A., Levi A., Larkin A., Winston A., Elizabeth A., Polly A., and Ellen—all born from 1804-25.

Clayborn married Sallie Walkup.

William married Demoise Davis.

Abraham married Elizabeth Morrison.

Lewis married Jane Biggs.

Archie married Celia Miller.

Levi married Elizabeth Robertson.

Larkin married Mary Simpson.

Winston married Margaret Meadows.

Elizabeth married a Mr. Walkup.
Polly married John L. Thomas, Jr.
Ellen died young.
Many of the above left the county, but some did not.

To Archelaus and Celia Miller were born eight children: Capt. J. Logan, who served through the Civil War. He married a Toomey and reared a family in the county. Elmore was editor of the *Cumberland News*.

The other children were Dr. Archelaus, Shelby W., Commodore, Amanda, Eliza, Bettie, and Vera.

Dr. Archie lived at the mouth of Wolf River a while and then moved West.

Shelby W. first married Mary Byrd and reared Walter and Charley on Big Renox. Second, he married Rosaline Grant and reared eight. Of the eight, Prof. Finis A. Strange is the only one that spent his life in the county. He taught the Marrowbone school for several years, and then engaged in the grocery business at Marrowbone.

Commodore (of Archelaus and Celia) married Laura Gorman (daughter of Andy G.) and reared Isaac H., Archie, Walter, James, and nine daughters all of whom live in Texas.

William Levi and Elizabeth Robinson (married in 1841) reared eight: VanBuren who married Sarah E. Williams (1873); George A.; Houston, who married Sarah A. Blair; Callie, who married W. L. Blair; Dora, who married S. H. Royce; Frank, who married Fanny Bowman; Sarah E., who married Joe Rice; William Levi, who married Kate Hundley and reared Clarence and Darrell. Clarence married Viola Guthrie, granddaughter of William Guthrie; and Darrell married Kizzie Baker, daughter of William Finis Baker, all of Crocus.

It was this pioneer group of Stranges that built the old Republican Church House of logs that served the public until October 22, 1890, when it was burned down, while Mollie Morgan was teaching school. Another was built later. In the old log house is recorded the names of some of the preachers, Isaac T. Reneau, Caleb Sewell, Andrew P. Davis, and William Simpson.

TALBOT

The Talbots came from Virginia. They first settled in Pennsylvania. There were two courses taken by them to Kentucky, one was south, the other north. William stopped around Lexington where he became a big trader, especially in slaves. The Danville Talbots are the same.

Nicholas Talbot stopped in Cumberland County in 1798, though he was here in 1795. He took up 200 acres of land on Spring Creek, where he reared his family. He married Jane Bates, daughter of William Bates of Washington County, Virginia. William died there in 1825. To Nicholas and Jane were born William H., Dorcas, who married James Denton and reared a family here; Sally K., who married

Daniel Myers; Polly K., who married James Cole and reared family in Clinton County, whose lineal descendants through Samuel Cole, whose sons, J. O. and John, made teachers; Peggy Talbot, who married Solomon Hollett; Lurcia, who married Jerry B. McCoy 1835, whose descendants are in business in Burkesville now (1947) in the persons of Jim F., who is a noted livestock dealer, and Leon, who heads an extensive hardware establishment; Fred McCoy is the owner and operator of a garage. Louis, Permelia, and Jean C. were the other children of Nicholas. From these came the Smiths (Bert's family); and also all the Mackeys of Clinton and Cumberland counties. Nicholas was sheriff of Cumberland County, 1809-10, and J. P. when he died, 1820. His line yet lives at Paoli. They were noted singers.

The next family that came to this county was not a pioneer family. It was headed by Dr. John G. Talbot, who came from Danville, Kentucky, in 1897. He was the third generation of Talbots born at Danville after they came there from Virginia.

Dr. Talbot was the fifth child of eleven children of his family. He was born in 1872, attended the free schools, and at the end of 1897 graduated from the Hospital College of Medicine, Louisville, Kentucky, immediately after which he came to Burkesville, where he remained the rest of his life with the exception of about three months spent as captain in the Medical Corps in World War I, 1918.

In 1900, Dr. Talbot married Susan Owsley, daughter of W. F. Owsley, Jr. To this union were born five children: Sarah, who died in infancy; "Jack" G., 1902; Alexander, 1905; William O., 1907; Susan.

Dr. Talbot was faithful at his work and a devoted church worker, always standing for the betterment of conditions for both church and state. He led a temperate life, and when called on to lead in prayer at church he never forgot to ask God's guiding hand to lead our country out of the mire of drunkenness. His affiliation was with the Presbyterian Church, but he attended all.

In his medical practice he never hesitated to attend.the poor as well as the rich.

THURMANS

While the Thurman family has not aspired to many political or educational heights in our county they have composed a link in the chain of business, especially farming. Many noted and influential men became connected with the pioneer Thurman family both by blood and marriage.

There seems to be at least four different families who came from Virginia to Cumberland County to live: John, William, Nathan, Charles.

John (called "Rich John") was the first Thurman to stop in the county. He and Ishum Burks were operating the ferry where North River Street joins the river, in 1795 (Green County Record). He had nine Headright Grants in the county on Bear, Illwill, Otter, and Rennicks creeks, of 200 acres each, besides many more by purchase. Most of his lands were taken in Green County before it became Cumberland. He and Ishum Burks both offered their surnames to the community for a town. Burks received the most votes, so the town was located on his side of the river and assumed his name. John was one of the first Justices of the Peace. His official record will be found elsewhere in this writing. He married Avey —— and reared John R. and Thomas. In 1811 he gave his son, Thomas, 3,000 acres of land on Bear Creek. Thomas lived there a while, and in 1818 moved to Knox County, Tennessee. John, Sr., died 1835. Thomas was Commonwealth's Attorney, 1811.

John R. married and reared five: Mrs. Creed Haskin, Mrs. Sam White, Mrs. Thomas M. Emmerson, Alsey Zimmerson, all of whom headed leading families. John R. died about 1833 (will).

Thomas, the attorney, bought 752 acres of land on the Wolf River, 1808. His daughter, Elizabeth Thurman, married, 1804, John Reneau of Cumberland County, and reared a family of three boys (see Reneau).

Charles Thurman (1756-1836) served in the Revolutionary War under Capt. Elisha White, Capt. John Davenport, and in Capt. John Flemming's company, in Col. George Gibson's regiment in the Virginia Continental Line, and under Washington to Little York. He was in nearly all the battles on to Yorktown and Cornwallis's defeat. He served along with Moses Webb, John Scott, Philip Lawson, Milton King, William Smith, John R. Thurman. He states he was in poor circumstances in 1820 in Cumberland County with two small children.

Nathan Thurman of Hanover County, Virginia, came to the county soon after the death of Andrew Ronalds, in 1798. He and William Smith purchased the "Bottom above mouth of Marrowbone" in 1804, for which they had bargained in 1796. Nathan married and reared seven children in Virginia—William, Alcy, Lucy, Winfred, Martha, Susan, Littleberry. All came to the county.

William (of Nathan) married Mary Ann —— and had Lucy, Katherine, Littleberry, and Sally. This Littleberry served in the war of 1812-14 and was one that witnessed the fall of General Packenham at New Orleans, January 8, 1815.

Alcy (of Nathan) married Nathan Smith and reared four— Harriett, Betsy, Susan, and Frances.

Lucy (of Nathan) married Daniel Wooleridge of Todd County, 1812, and reared a family there.

Winfred (of Nathan) married Willis H. Alexander and reared a family in the county.

Martha (of Nathan) married John M. Alexander, Jr., and reared a family in the county (see Alexanders).

Susan (of Nathan) married Haze Murphy in Virginia and moved to the south end of the county, where he reared his family.

Littleberry (of Nathan) married Permelia Branch Bowman,

daughter of Pleasant Bowman, and reared two children—Edward (1817-63) and Miranda.

Miranda married Marley P. Walthall, and they became the parents of William Archie. Littleberry willed his fortune of 15 Negroes and his fortune in lands on Bear Creek to Archie. Like many others of easy sailings, Archie sold and lived until his last cent was gone and wound up a pauper.

Edward (of Littleberry) married Mary (Polly) —— and became the progenitor of most of the Thurmans now in the county. His children were: Thomas R. (1844), who married Ermon Rogers and they became the parents of five. This is H. E. (Babe) Thurman's family. Belle, who married a Mr. Harrison of Glasgow and reared a family. John B., who married Bettie Thrasher, most of whose descendants are dead.

Pleasant, no record.

Turn Ann who reared a family in the county.

Mickey Ann who had only one daughter, Mollie Belle, who married James Thrasher, and they became the parents of Leonard W., our city clerk.

Sarah F. (of Edward) married George Cox and reared a family in the county.

Nathan Thurman was the second Ferryman at Neeleys Ferry— John Journey having been the first, 1804.

TRAYLORS

George A. Traylor was the pioneer Traylor of Cumberland County. He came in the 90's of the eighteenth century and took up land on Big Renox Creek. Some of the land is still in the Traylor family. George married Nancy Gates in Virginia, and they raised Joe A., Milt, Bill, Nancy, Martha, and Sallie, in this county.

Joe A. married Mary Turk and to them were born eight sons and five daughters. Four of the boys that raised families in this county were Noah, Joe, Jr., Pate, and Charley.

Pate (of Joe A.) married Eliza Cloyd and reared Joe, Bill, Zada, and Jane. Joe married Bessie Lollar, has two children; they live in Texas. Bill married Myrtie Sharp and lives in Texas. Zada married R. T. Thomas and has four boys; they live in Burkesville. Jane married Earl Williams and has one girl.

Milt (of George A.) married —— and had Jim Milt.

Jim Milt married Fanny Harvey and reared Melvin, Malan, George, and two girls.

Melvin Traylor (of Jim Milt) married a Yearby of Texas and has two, Melvin, Jr., and Nancy. Nancy married Robert Snowder and fell off a New York hotel, April 13, 1943, and died.

This Melvin of Jim Milt moved to Chicago, where he became rich.

The Pioneer Geo. A. Traylor built a grist mill on Renox about one year after his arrival.

WARRINER FAMILY

This is another family whose name originated from occupation. Its orthography has also changed. In ancient Europe a street seller or traveling peddler had days in which he would offer his "wares" for sale. We would call it "merchandise" today. His business was so outstanding that he became known as the "waren" man or Warner. This is the spelling of families of that name yet, while the people who settled in this county use the title of this story. A close study of the occupation of people reveals an almost unbroken chain through the ages along that line.

David Warriner came from Virginia at an early date. His son, James, was a young man at the close of the Revolutionary War. James married Annie Pollard of Virginia, and to them were born five sons and two daughters, all in Virginia. The sons were James, Iverson L., William, Jacob, and Carter; the daughters were Elizabeth and Mary.

James, Sr., and his sons, James, Iverson L., Carter, and Jacob, came to Kentucky. Jacob married Nancy —— and reared one daughter. They moved to Adair County about 1810, and later to Casey County. Carter in 1820 lived in Cumberland County with a family of five sons and three daughters. He pastored Casey Fork Baptist Church, 1819.

Iverson L. married Sally Bledsoe, and to them were born 12 children: Lewis T.; Nancy (wife of Kenyon Brown); Martha (Bybee); James P.; Joseph S.; William; Ganaway; Washington; Hiram; Cagan; Benjamin; Lettie.

I. L. purchased a farm in Rock House Bottom 1815, where the present Christian Church now stands and here reared his large family. He died in 1838 and was buried on the farm. His son, Lewis T., who was selling goods at the time of his father's death was the first merchant of that bottom; and the other son, Joseph S., was the first merchant in Irish Bottom who sold goods on the bank of the river where Orchard Landing now is (named for his large orchard).

Joseph Warriner (1813-65) married Margaret Neathery (1818-1901), and to them were born two sons and two daughters: Iverson L., Jr.; Jasper; Mattie, wife of Tom Marcum of Clinton County; and Nancy, wife of Frank Burchett. Joseph was a Baptist preacher and farmer. He moved from Cumberland County about 1857 and located at Seventy-Six, Clinton County, where he was buried. His son, Iverson (1841-1919), engaged in the goods business at that place in 1865 and sold until his death, 1919. During this period he accumulated a fortune of $120,000. Besides his farm and stock of general merchandise at Seventy-Six, he held stock in the Cumberland Grocery Company at Burnside, Kentucky, and was the organizer of the Citizens Bank of Albany and two telephone companies; one known as the Albany-Burkesville Company and the other the Albany-Albany Landing Company. These last ones went under the style of I. L. Warriner

& Son (J. A. Warriner). Iverson married Exona Grider and reared Maggie, James A., Lewis, and Exie.

Maggie first married John Andrew, and to them was born one daughter, Laura, who married a Mr. Frogge; second she married John Hurt, and to them was born one daughter, Verlie, who married a Mr. Pedigo.

Lewis died single.

Exona married Walter McKay and reared a family.

James A. Warriner (1871-1943) married Pearl Meadows, and to them were born six children—Margery (1900), James L., Mary Pearl, Eva M., Ed P., Anna Maude.

Margery married Leo M. Sewell, a thriving business man and mortician of Albany, Kentucky.

Mary Pearl married A. H. Kidd and moved to Atlanta, Georgia.

Anna Maude married Glenn Eversole and lives at London, Kentucky.

Ed P. married Josephine Dempsey of Virginia and they are the parents of three—Katherine, E. P., Jr., and Iverson Lewis.

Ed P. is (1946) a thriving business man of Albany, share-owner of the Citizens Bank; automobile dealer, and owner of the Log Palace Inn in north Albany, where he has done a thriving business, since 1934.

WEBB FAMILY

This family name reaches back to German-French origin and means "weavers on the farm." As far back as I have studied the name it has been connected with medical practice. The Webbs landed in Pennsylvania and from there came through Virginia to Kentucky. Dr. William Webb graduated under the renowned Dr. Ben Rush of Philadelphia. His family came to Garrard County, Kentucky, where his son Richard reared a family of doctors. William, a descendant of this group, came to Cumberland County and he had a son, John Richard, who made of himself a doctor. He spent his life in the county. His son, Lysle, was elected to the Legislature, 1945.

WELLS FAMILY

The name Wells dates back to the year 794 A.D., in the district of Normandy. There it was spelled Vaux. Robert and Jocelyn Wells crossed the Channel with William the Conqueror. The name is residential, "John atte well." The name was spelled Well, Welles, de Wells, Wellys, etc. On the English side of the Channel they collected in a group and it was given the name of Wells County. Jocelyn's descendants became prominent; Hugo Wells was Bishop of Wells County and Lord Chancellor of England. Two names appear on the Magna Charta of England. In running seven generations through the English history we see seven Roberts, eight

Williams', six Johns, seven Thomases, many of whom had recognition in nobility and land gentry.

Hugh and Thomas came to America in 1635, lived in Boston, where their families were reared then moved to Connecticut, where Thomas served as governor 1655-8. Their children, John, Joseph, William James, Thomas, George, Robert, and Nathaniel head different families in Massachusetts and Connecticut, 1635-69. James moved into Maryland, 1693, and his James into Pennsylvania and Ohio, where he left many descendants, going as far as Missouri and Texas. Henry settled in Pennsylvania 1685, John 1690, Edward 1693 and reared large families.

A Thomas Wells who came in the Virginia Company, 1620, and settled in Virginia, whose descendants were William, John, Richard, Edmund, Edward, George, Thomas, Jonathan, Joe, Robert, Henry, Alexander, constitutes the link up to the Revolutionary War.

While the Wells people have always been opposed to war, we find these serving as officers: Lt. Benjamin, Lt. Col. David, Lt. Henry, Col. Jonathan, Capt. Roger, Capt. Hugh, Capt. Samuel, Lt. Bayze, Capt. Chester, Col. Levi, Ensign Stephen, Capt. Joshua, three Capt. Thomases, and two Lt. Jameses, all in the Revolutionary War.

The history of the Wells family of Cumberland County begins with David Wells, who was born in Virginia, 1764, and married Kittie White (b. 1768) of the same state in 1788. To them were born 12 children, five in Virginia and seven after their arrival in Cumberland County: Polly, 1789; Sally, 1791; Jesse, 1793; Joel, 1794; Rebecca, 1796; Solomon, 1798; Isaac, 1800; John, 1803; David, Jr., 1805; Minerva, 1807; Levi, 1810; Hiram, 1813.

David Wells came to Cumberland County in 1798 and settled in Elliotts Bottom, where he lived in a thatched cabin until May, 1802, when he obtained a large land grant in the same bottom, which changed its name to Wells Bottom, which name it has ever since borne.

David's brother, William, also came to the county, 1798.

Of David's children we shall speak briefly. Records of some cannot be traced.

Polly married Isaac Campbell of Cumberland County in 1809, and they became the parents of five sons and five daughters: Sydney, John, Hiram, Robert, and William; Sally, Emily, Mary, Eurania, and Eliza. Sydney of this family married Eliza Rowe and became the grandfather of most of the Campbells now living around Creelsboro and also of Judge Roy Helm, Aubrie, and Effie.

Sally Wells (of David) married William Winfrey, 1812, and had one daughter, Fanny. She married James Staton, whose descendants are scattered over Cumberland and Clinton counties.

Solomon Wells heads the largest group of offspring of the David family now inhabiting this part of Kentucky. Solomon married first Permelia Kelly, and to them were born Tom, Cyrus, Washington, Nancy, Tilda, Joel, and Louisa (John and Agnas died young).

Tom married Kitty Vigles, and had two—Frank and Ellen. Frank married Julia Clayton and has family in Bell Plains, Kansas.

Cyrus married Fanny Grider and to them were born Susan (Triplet); Docia (McCoy); Elizabeth (Allen); Lewis B. (single); Tilford (who married Lou Cartwright); Martin (single).

Washington (of Solomon) married first Clarinda Bybee, and to them were born Alex and Asa. He married second Martha A. Bell, and to them were born William A., Marion, Eliza, Virginia, Henry, and George. The descendants of Washington are many.

Nancy (of Solomon) married James Vigles, and to them were born Taylor, James, Rosa, and Mary.

Tilda (of Solomon) married a Mr. Back and to them, Clemmie.

Joel (of Solomon) married and reared his family in Nashville, Tennessee.

Louisa (of Solomon) married Asa F. Andrew and reared Tilda, Sherman, Cyrus, Etta, Lum, Dan, Jim, Lula, Shelby.

Solomon married second, Rhoda Vigles (1811-91), and to them were born William, Allen, and Henry. William (father of the writer) married Virginia Belle Bledsoe, and to them were born Susie, 1862; Bettie, 1864; Rev. J. T., 1866; Sallie, 1868; Ella, 1871; John, 1873; Mattie, 1875; Esther, 1877; Joseph W., 1881; Iman, 1883. Allen (of Solomon) remained single.

Henry married Adline Bell and to them were born Alfred, Will Frank, Ada, Della, Dillon, Frethise, Don, Lizzie. All had families.

Solomon is honored as the first white child born in what Cumberland gave up to make Clinton County (born July 29, 1798).

John Wells (of David) married Malinda Winfrey (1805-87), and to them eight living children were born: Nancy, who married James Selby, 1842; Anderson, who married Lydia Story, 1840; Polly, who married James Rector, 1858; Hannah, who married John Andrew, 1865; Susan, who married Ellis Crouch, 1850; Asa, who married Lucinda Davidson, 1856; Albert, who married Emily McElroy, 1880; Sarah, who married Milton Andrew, 1859. These children scattered over Kentucky and Tennessee.

Lewis Andrew (of Hannah) lives at Seventy-Six, where his father ran the mill during the Civil War. Polly's descendants live close, in name of Chotes and others. Susan's live in Tennessee.

Levi Wells (of David) moved to Washington County, Illinois, where David gave him a farm. Many of David's children have been lost trace of but the author is working on a fuller history of the Wells family to be edited after 1947.

William Wells, brother of David, first settled on headwaters of Illwill and then moved to Willis Bottom on Obey River in the edge of Tennessee. The Cumberland census of 1810 gives him with a family of five sons and four daughters ranging from one year up. Silas Wells (1810), one of the youngest, remained on Wolf River and married Mary Smith to whom were born 15 children, from 1830-51. Six died young. The rest reared families in Cumberland and

Barren counties and the West. Mathias (1832) married Mary Dotson and had a family, and his son, Rev. Robert Wells, married Ruth Blythe and became the father of J. M., William E., D. G., John, all of whom are business men and teachers of the county. Rev. Robert had five daughters, most of whom died. Martha, of this group, married Ossie Coffey and reared Christine.

Robert Wells' sister, Minerva, married J. E. W. Moore, who has taught in Cumberland County for 45 years. Another married Arthur Taylor.

WILBORN

Thomas and Sam were the two first Wilborns to pioneer Cumberland County; Thomas in the southern part and Sam in the northern part of the county. The children of Thomas were: Robert, John, Edward, Thomas, Jr., William, and Polly (Mary). By William came the Wilborns of Clinton County. For Mary's progeny see Higginbothams.

WILLIAMS

Of Marrowbone

The Williams people of Cumberland County represent several families with the connection in doubt. The name came from Normandy, France, and became England's second name in popularity. In Welsh it was Quilliams. They added the "s" to William which became a surname. It means "defender of many."

The Marrowbone branch was headed by Garrod (Garrot) Williams (1755-1827), who came from Lynchburg, Virginia, to the mouth of Marrowbone Creek in 1799. He had lived here since 1795 while patenting lands north of Burkesville, but had not settled. He married in Virginia and became the father of four children before making this county his home. They were Osborn (1775-1854), Pegrim, Lemuel, and Katherine.

Osborn married Sally Wade, 1797, just before coming to the county. To them were born 11 children as follows: Sally (1798-1846); Daniel (1799-1854); John O. (1801); Betty (1803); Docia (1805); J. Ballenger (1806); King David (1810); Polly (1811); Virginia (1814); Robert L. (1817); George W. (1820-34).

Sally married ——.

Daniel married Jane Daugherty and reared five sons and one daughter: Joseph, John, Albert, James, Turk, and Mary, who married John Ellington.

John O. (of Daniel) married Lou Walthall and lived west of the Big Hill, where he reared six sons and three daughters, as follows: J. W.; Daniel B.; J. O., Jr.; Marshall; Milton; and Henry; Amanda, who married Josiah Franks and reared J. P., Will, Maud, and Lula; Julia, who married M. O. Allen; Victoria, who married Thomas Cloyd, Sr., and reared a family in the county.

Docia, married Tom Pace (see Pace).

Betty married Milt Smiley, son of Daniel Smiley.

J. Ballenger married ——.

Polly married Wash Nunn and reared a family.

Virginia married ——.

Robert L. married and reared a family near Leslie, this county.

King David married Nancy —— (born 1812) and reared seven: Mary Frances (1833); Martha Ann (1835); Robert D. (1837); Sarah Jane (1840); Caleb (1844); Dudley (1848); Cander (1851).

Mary Frances (of King David) married Richard Breeding of Adair County, and to them were born three girls—Nancy, Lula, and Allie. Nancy, of these three girls, married Dr. George T. Simpson and reared Lydia; H. C.; Dr. Ira, dentist of Burkesville; Fred; and Dr. Richard of Greensburg.

Martha Ann (of King David) married a Turk; Sarah, a Bradshaw; Caleb, a Breeding, second a Cole; Dudley, a Slemmons; Cander, a Baker.

Lemuel Williams (of Garrot) married Polly Ritchie, daughter of William Ritchie, Sr. (1806), and died without issue. His political career found elsewhere.

Katherine (of Garrot) married Sam Ritchie, brother to Polly.

Garrot Williams was a mechanic and a noted builder of his day. The brick house on the Milt Smiley place with date 1822 yet testifies to his workmanship. His grandson, Addis Williams, is the leading mechanic of this age, having sponsored bridges, garages, and other structures of note.

A will of Garrod, 1824, tells of his second wife's children: Louisa Ann, Garrot, Pegrim, James C., Susana, Alfred C., Benjamin M. His second wife was named Winfred.

OF GOOSE CREEK

Caleb Williams was the progenitor of this branch of the Williams family. He married Lucy Jones and they became the parents of seven children—Jacob, Frank, Tom J., William, Shadrach, Amelia, and Susan.

Jacob married Mary Ann —— and went to Craighead County, Arkansas, where his descendants live.

Frank married Adeline Green, and to them were born eight— Finis, George, Hiram, Tyler, James, William, Granville, and Caleb.

Finis H. married Novella Murphy, daughter of James Jackson Murphy, and they reared a family of good citizens: Clyde, who was sheriff of Taylor County; Curtis; Muerson; Ed; Paul; Tyler, who is a Methodist minister; and Clara, who married Tom Morrison, another Methodist minister.

George (of Frank and Adeline) married a Williams and had three.

Hiram married a Carter and left the county.

Tyler married a Miss Scott and had one child.

James married a Scott and reared four.

William married a Carter and had one.

Granville married a Williams and reared eight.

Caleb married a Booher and died without children.

Tom J. Williams (of Caleb and Lucy) was County Judge, 1889-93. He married Nancy Long and they had 11 children: Martha Ann (1850); Shadrach (1852); Nancy Jane (1854); Lizzie (1857); Caleb (1859); T. J., Jr. (1861); James A. (1866); Long (1868); David (1873); Mary (1871); Bob (1875).

Judge Williams was ever ready to work for the best interests of his community, town, and country. He urged the building of the Railroad noted elsewhere, and the record shows his interest in the churches. In February, 1892, he refused to grant license to drug stores to sell liquors. He donated the first organ to the Methodist Church in Burkesville.

Martha Ann (1850), daughter of Judge Williams, married Sam Smith as his first wife, and to them were born two, Finis F. and Nancy. F. F., who is a leading farmer of Bear Creek, reared a family, and Nancy who married George Smith of Big Renox and had two boys and three girls.

Shadrach Williams of Caleb and Lucy Jones, see Goggins for line of first wife.

William Williams (of Caleb and Lucy Jones) married Emily Pharis and they became the parents of eight children: Sherrod, who went to Texas; John, who married Laura Bow and reared Claude, Jenny (Bristow), and Ralph; Claude, who went to Illinois; and Julia, who married Stephe Bow and reared a family in the county; Lucy, who married William Brake and left many descendants (see Brakes).

Another Williams who never lived in the county, but whose descendants are here now, was Rev. Z. T. Williams. He was one of the greatest divines of all ages. He is credited with the establishment of a great number of Christian churches. His musical voice attracted great crowds of people. His lineage is this: Aaron Williams, born in Wales, came to Virginia; his son Drewy Williams married Martha Guinn and moved to Rockingham County, North Carolina, where a son, Aaron, was born, 1773, who married Lucy Wall of Virginia, after which they came to Adair County, Kentucky, in 1808. To this last couple was born Preston G., who married Prudence Taylor, daughter of Zachariah Taylor and Nancy (Montgomery) his wife. To this union was born the Rev. Z. T. Williams, who married Clemmie Wheat and reared Luther, Rev. Lawrence, Loran, Lillie, Joe, and Sally, the last of whom married the Rev. Kirby Smith, whose two daughters live in this county.

WILSONS

The Wilsons are not of the Cumberland Pioneer families, yet they deserve some publicity because of their even, calm citizenship.

John Wilson of Virginia, who moved to Meshack Creek in Monroe County, Kentucky, about 1830, was the grandfather of all the Wilsons of this county. His son, Charles, was about six years old when they came to Monroe, and he grew up and married Nancy Ann Vawter and came to Cumberland County. To them were born Joseph, Quintilla, Newton, George, John T., Wolford, and Nancy Ellen.

Joseph and Quintilla died young.

Newton married Sarah Clemmons and reared one son, Melvin, who married Cara White and had four children—Effie, Charley, Harley, and James.

Effie is now (1945) one of the teachers in the Marrowbone High School, where she has taught for a number of years.

George (of John) married a Miss Smith. They became the parents of two children, Ewing and Enos.

Ewing is one of the older teachers of this county and has served as School Superintendent four years. He married Miss Palmore; they have no children.

The pioneer Wilsons have been lost sight of. Hannaniah Lincoln, first sheriff of the county married Lucy Wilson, 1801.

WINFREY FAMILY

The Winfreys that played a part in the early history of Cumberland County came from Virginia.

Israel Winfrey, Sr., of Culpeper County, Virginia, married Frances Holley of Tucker County, Virginia (now West Virginia). To them were born three sons and three daughters, all in Virginia, Billie (1790); Betsey; Susan; Francis H. (1798); Israel (1802); and Docia. In 1804 Israel and Frances and the children turned their faces toward Kentucky. Israel, Jr., being only two years old, rode in his mother's lap; she came all the way muleback. Israel, Sr., located in Rock House Bottom. In December, 1805, he purchased 270 acres of rich bottom land in the Rock House Bottom, opposite the mouth of Tear Coat Creek, from Thomas Chilton of Adair County, who had large grants of land in Cumberland County.

Billie married Sallie Wells, second daughter of Pioneer David Wells of Cumberland County, in 1812, and in 1813 David sold Billie 75 acres of land in Wells Bottom, this county, where he lived and died. One daughter was born to this union. Her name was Fanny, and she became the wife of James Staton, brother of Dr. Hiram Staten. Billie's second wife was Lucy Vigles.

Betsey married Martin Ross, son of George W. Ross, Sr. To them were born G. W., Jr., Frank, and Id. From this union came most all the Rosses of this part of Kentucky.

Susan married a Mr. McGlasson, and no record is available of this family.

Docia married Martin Grider, Jr.

Frank H. married Kittie Graves, daughter of the noted Capt. Thomas Graves who had previously come from Virginia and settled where the town of Creelsboro now is, then in Cumberland County. Frank H. lived until his death (1855) at his father's old home in the brick building which was torn down about 1893. While here, Frank served Cumberland County in many official capacities, Justice of the Peace, sheriff, Representative, and Senator, and was an influential man in his day.

To Francis and Kittie were born 10 children: Polly, Matilda, Israel Clinton, Thomas C., Fanny, Susan, F. Richard, Belle, and Joseph and Kitty (both of whom died young).

Polly married Tom Walker M. Bledsoe, and to them were born Elijah (whose son, Tom, became a millionaire); Frank, who married Emily Irvin; Maggie (wife of Billie Johnson); Ellen (wife of Sidney Spencer); Lucy (wife of Milt Spencer, and father of Millard Spencer); Lydia, who died.

Matilda married George W. Ross, son of Martin, and to them were born William Henry, Americus Vespucia, and Gran. Her second husband was Jordan Judd, and to them was born one son, named Stanley.

Israel Clinton (of Francis) married a Miss Harrison.

Thomas C. was educated at the old Christian College at Burkesville, where he practiced law many years. He represented Cumberland and Clinton in the Legislature, 1857-8, and was Major in the 5th Kentucky Cavalry under Col. David Haggard the first part of the Civil War. He married Virginia Saufley, and to them were born Millard, Frank, Joe Buck, and Tom T.

Fanny (of F. H.) became the wife of George W. Barger; Belle, the wife of Dr. L. G. Hays.

F. Richard (Dick) married Izora Saufley, sister of Virginia, and to them were born Mike C., of Columbia, and Iva Jane who died young. F. R. received his education at Burkesville High School, where he was attending when the Civil War broke out. He enlisted in Co. C of the 12th Kentucky Infantry, on the side of the Union and was promoted to First Lieutenant, 1863. He was mustered out in 1865 and began the study of law at Burkesville, under his brother, T. C., and graduated at the Law University at Louisville, 1867. He served as County Attorney of Adair, 1868-74.

Israel, Jr., married Martha (Patsey) Winfrey, daughter of Philip Winfrey of Adair County, Kentucky. Philip and his two brothers, Henry and John, had come from Pennsylvania and settled on Green River. Henry went from there to Missouri, where he reared a family.

Twelve children were born to Israel and Patsey from the year 1822 to 1847, both inclusive. According to ages they were: C. Columbus, Safrona, Martha A., Fanny, Dr. A. V., Mary Jane, Malissa, Philip, Docia, William F., Israel Clinton, Susan.

Columbus was married four times and died without issue.

Safrona was never married.

Martha A. married Robert Neathery and raised seven children: Mary Susan (wife of Sam Morgan); Sarah Elizabeth (wife of David Orton); Philip; Cull; Israel; Billie; Mattie (wife of T. Crit Goff).

Fanny married Billie Andrew and had three boys—I. F., H. Gran, William. Fanny married a second time and had one daughter.

Dr. A. V. married Savina Goff and reared seven children—John, Billie, Frank, Shores, Jenny, Minnie, Mollie.

Mary Jane married Shelby Guinn and reared seven children—Israel, Lillith, Will H., Joe, Leona, Mary Belle, Bob.

Malissa married William Morgan and reared seven children—Sam V.; Israel Yank; Mattie (wife of John Wood); Shores; John E.; Fount; and Nannie (wife of Tom B. Phelps).

Philip married Fanny Barger and had nine children—Mike, Ella May, Lander E., Lizzie, Shores, Sarah V., Ida, Virgil, and Mattie.

Docia married Bob Wilborn and had six children—Ras, Lura, Eugene, Emmett, Don, and Monta.

William F. married Nannie Belle Grider and had three—Alex J., Ira, and Eliza. The last two died young—A. J. married Ada Phelps and had five, Ray (died), H. D., Joseph R., William Robert, and Eliza. The last two made teachers. Robert is a college graduate and at present is teaching at Marion, Kentucky. He married Lera Cary.

Israel Clinton (of Israel, Jr.) married Mildred Winfrey, daughter of Hamilton, who was a son of Sims, who was a son of Philip Winfrey, of Adair County. To them were born seven children—Logan C., Cora, Curt, Robert, Irvin, Ethel, and Ed. Robert, of this group, enlisted in the Spanish-American War and died in the Philippine Islands.

Logan C. taught in the common schools of Cumberland County for five years, and then took up the practice of law at Albany, 1896. He is at present one of the leading attorneys at Columbia, Kentucky, where he has been located for some time. He married Wonnie Hurt of Albany, and they have one daughter, Lucile, who married Clyde Miller.

Susan (of Israel, Jr.) married Benton Stewart, and to them were born four children—Cret, Palo, Nettie, and Barlow. Cret married Benjamin V. Morgan and moved to Texas, where they reared eight children. Palo never married. Nettie married James Martin Riddle (second wife) and moved to Texas. No issue. Barlow married Lula Norton and reared four children in Texas.

An early Virginia record seems to place William Winfrey as the progenitor of the Kentucky family. He came to Fayette County in 1784 and was a rich landowner there. He is listed as the father of Israel, Sr., Philip, Henry, John, and James. James settled in Warren and Christian counties; Henry stopped in Lincoln County, 1799; John in Adair County with his brother, Philip, in 1799.

John Winfrey (1774-1841), brother of the above Philip of Green River settlement, married Hannah —— (1779-1857), and to them were born two daughters of whom we have record—Jane Patience and Malinda.

Jane P. married John Ross, 1811.

Malinda (b. 1805), married John Wells (b. 1803), son of David Wells, and to them were born Albert, Asa, Anderson, Hannah, Sarah, and Polly (see Wells).

THE FIVE FAMILIES

Five families came to Cumberland County along together—the Bowman, Waggener, Norris, Paull, and Newby families.

John Paull, John Waggener, and Clayborn Norris were brothers-in-law. They came from Chesterfield County, Virginia, about 1799. All but John Waggener settled in the present limits of Cumberland County. He stopped just over into the edge of the present bounds of Adair. The three brothers-in-law had married daughters of John Morgan (sisters to William Morgan, who married Nancy Howard in 1813). Each will be treated under separate heads.

John Paull was related to the first great Naval Commander who made the *Bonhomme Richard,* famous in the Revolutionary War. His name was John Paull, but he added Jones to his surname and went by the assumed name, John Paull Jones, thereafter.

Our John Paull was born in 1777, died 1843. He married Polly Morgan and to them James Paull was born in 1805. James married Elizabeth Newby in Potters Bottom, where they all lived, 1828. To them four children were born—John M. (1829); Sarah (1831); James O. (1833); William A. (1835). His wife, Elizabeth Newby, died in 1838, and James married Mary Mottley, a 15-year-old granddaughter of Pleasant Bowman, in 1842. They had one child—Mary H., who died while teaching school in Burkesville, 1863. James died in 1847 and his wife, Mary Mottley Paull, married Valentine Scott, 1849 (see Scotts).

To John, Sr., and Polly Morgan were born six other children: Mary Jane, who married Elisha W. Newby, Jr. (see Newbys); William Ed, who married Frances ——; Robert B., who married Mary S——; Lucy, who married James Franklin; Eliza, who married Tarleton S. Taylor; and Henry Paull. (See Alexanders.)

John Waggener. This name has been misrepresented as to meaning. Some think it was a maker of wagons. This is not true. The name preceded the vehicle itself. It is a Norfolk of 1176 A.D. word, used for anyone who trudged along with a load. It originated on military fields. First on record was Walter Waggespere, i.e., he that bore the spears.

Original John came from Chesterfield, Virginia, 1799, along with Reuben, while a brother, Richard, went to Warren County. John married Anna Morgan, daughter of John Morgan, of Chesterfield

County, Virginia. He settled in Adair, not far from the Cumberland line. His son, A. G., married a Locky, born in 1803 died 1891. A. G. was much in public office. His son, Lewis, married Elizabeth Allen, of Nathan Allen, and reared 11 children—John; Mattie, (married James Nunn); Alverda (married George Wagner); James; Lizzie (married Dillard Smith); Julia (married Fayette Gorman); Nannie (married Judd, Neb.); Ella (married Tom Dueese); Ora (married Millard Davis); Tildon (married Susie Baker); Jenny died.

For A. G.'s other children see Jones, Garnetts, etc. Elizabeth Garnett married James Waggener; Sarah married John; Mary married Tom W.; Harriett married Charles Jones.

A. G.'s brother, Herbert G., had one daughter, Martha Jane, who married Joe Morgan of Adair County.

Bowman. There were four—Pleasant, Stephe, Ben, and William —who came to the county. Pleasant had seven children: Granville, Frances, Anna, Permelia, Mickey, Wilson, and Lenoras.

For the progeny of this family see Bledsoe, Scott, Bow, Thurman, Owsley, Newby.

William married after he came to the county. He married Jane Hall, and his sister Nancy married George Hall, both in 1807. This family lived on Mud Camp Creek. He had a son, Osiris, whose descendants were the Hon. J. W. Bowman, who became a doctor and School Superintendent in this county.

William's great-grandson, Jerry Bowman, became principal of the Burkesville High School, 1946.

EXTERRITORIAL FAMILIES
Alphabetically Arranged

We give the names of some families who were once within the county and wielded influence but have gone, some leaving descendants.

CLAYTONS. This family came early. Several brothers settled on Rock House Creek and above. Poindexter left more of the name. He married a Miss Bybee and was the father of Alexander, who married Malinda Snow, of Samuel, and to them were born Sam (deceased); Julia (see Wells); Ellen (see Grider); Perry O.; Adolphus A., who married Minnie Holt (of Berry H.) and reared family at Creelsboro; James, who married Maggie Jones (of Dr. Tom) and reared a large family at Columbia.

CONNER. The Conners came from Virginia to Cumberland County. Two brothers, Lawrence and Alexander, came to West Fork of Indian Creek, 1802. Lawrence was born in Virginia, 1753, and went through the Revolutionary War. He married about 1788 and had one daughter, 12, and an infant baby named Cornelius when he settled. James and Margarett were born later. Cornelius, this infant son in 1820, bought a large farm on West Fork at public auction. This became the home of the Conners to this writing, 1947. Cornelius took up 4,000 acres of land adjoining this farm, 1836. Mrs. Granville Smith of Albany is a descendant.

EMBREE. The Embrees were among the strongest pioneers of Cumberland County. They were an energetic people from Culpeper County, Virginia, who belonged to that German-Dutch group. In French it got to be Amrey, Emrey, Imrey, and in Italian it was Amerigo—the name of our country. The word originally meant "work," especially in rock.

John Embree married Frances Burris in Culpeper County, and to them were born eight children, all of whom pioneered this county, 1805. They were middle-aged at their coming; names, John, Elisha, Moses, Sally, Julia, Joseph, Joshua, Elijah. (No record of John.)

Elisha (of John and Frances) married Nancy Wilhoit in Culpeper County, 1801, and became the father of ten children:

Minerva (1802), for her progeny, see Fergus Family.
Frances, who married a Mr. McDaniel, and went to Illinois.
Margarett, who married a Mr. Graves, of Creelsboro, Kentucky.
Elizabeth, see Bledsoes, Statons, Cheeks, and Howards.
Sarah, who married a Mr. Daugherty and left.
Julia, who married a Mr. Winfrey of Green River.
Nancy, no record.
Andrew Jackson, who became a doctor, and moved to Christian County, Kentucky.
Elisha, Jr., who moved to Texas about 1852, where he reared his family, of whom Elisha III lived at Belton, Texas, while Elisha IV lives at Houston, Texas.
John Wilhoit, the tenth child of Elisha and Nancy, followed his brother to Texas and left many descendants, one of whom is Mrs. William Creswell, 133 Woodlane Drive, San Antonio; and one is Mrs. N. A. Sayre, Beverly Hill Drive, Cincinnati, Ohio. All these have been thriving people. Their Kentucky home was on the old Murphy farm in Irish Bottom where their cemetery has almost disappeared, and the house of old Elisha, Sr., is yet standing, having been weatherboarded and built to.

Moses Embree (of John and Frances) sold his 438-acre farm in Irish Bottom and moved to Pine Bluff, Arkansas, where his descendants yet live, 1946.

Joseph (of John and Frances) married Millie Burris and left.
Sally and Julia both married McRoberts and left.
Joshua (of John and Frances), 1770-1813, married Elizabeth Edmonson, Culpeper County, and bought part of Ghoulston Stapp's military grant above Rock House, which he sold to Welcome Martin,

1811. He moved to Gibson County, Indiana, and died there, leaving a fortune for his six children and widow. All the children remained there but Coleby, who came back to Cumberland County and reared four children. Joshua's fifth son, Elisha, married Elenor Robb and became an outstanding politician, being elected to the Indiana Legislature and Senate, Circuit Judge, and Congressman, 1847-9.

Joshua's widow then married again and came to Rock House Bottom to live, and she died there.

The EMMERSON family, so prominent in the early history, have gone. Francis Emmerson was first Commonwealth's Attorney, 1799, and sole proprietor of Burkesville, 1809-15, when he died. He left an estate of $15,000 and 24 slaves to his children. John M. and Katherine, wife of Dr. Michael Stoner. Hiram and Samuel were lawyers in 1820, and Burr, Representative, 1837. If they were his sons it was by a first marriage. Wash left for Louisville, 1855. John M. was the first County Judge.

HOWARDS were here early, but nearly all migrated to other states. James Howard came from Henry County, Virginia, and married Annie King, and to them were born ten children: Parthenia, Docia, James, Jr., Polly, Martha, George, Richard, Permelia, Julian, and Wilson. (See Howard Bottom.)

Richard Harris Howard (of James and Anna King) was born in Howards Bottom 1814, died 1876. He and his wife, Harriett F. Bledsoe Howard, lie at rest in the yard of the old Methodist Church in the Bottom, in which they were married, December 8, 1840. Harriett, born 1822, died 1865. They reared eight children:

Crittenden J., 1841-67.

William B. (1845-71) married Sally Carter; children, Hattie and James.

Armead Howard (1847) married Dallas Carter; children, Weller, Crit, Judson, Elmo, Beulah, and Joe.

Hiram H. (1850) was murdered in the Klondike.

Joseph (1852), single.

John P. (1855) married Winnie Norris; children, Roy, Charles, Harriett, John P., Jr.

Richard Hiram (1857) married Annie Blair; children, Ruth, Armead, Hiram.

Charley (1862) married Florence T. Carnes and reared four— Rassie, Charles H., William C., Dorothy Florence.

These children lived at Moody, Texas, where their descendants still live.

Permelia Howard (of James), see Parrish family.

William Howard was another family living on Mud Camp. Stephe and Obediah were the pioneers of Old Mulkey, the latter of which was the great-grandfather of Dr. C. C. Howard, who has almost wrought miracles as a surgeon at the Community Hospital, Glasgow, Kentucky.

NANCE. This family came in 1798 and is on the first records as landowners. James came from Halifax County, Virginia, to this county. Roy is a descendant yet living on Marrowbone.

SAUFLEYS. This family has left descendants found elsewhere. Harold, who married Jane George of Virginia, daughter of William George, and his brother, James, were lawyers in the early history of the 1800's.

SNOW. The Snows came from North Carolina, following the Griders, but the name has disappeared from our rolls, leaving their progeny in Cumberland and adjoining counties. Archelaus seems to have been the progenitor, but records do not list him in this county. His son, William, came early in 1800 to Indian Creek, where part of his family lived.

Three sons, William, John, and Nash, settled near here, while one branch went to Livingston County and one stayed in Rowan County. Nash went to Casey County and settled on Carpenters Creek, about 1820; John went to Barren County, then Cumberland; William's son, Samuel (1799-1877), married Rachel Briley for his second wife. To both of his wives were born 18 children: O. H. Perry, 1820; Dorinda, 1821; Adaline, 1822; A. J., 1823; Eli, 1825; F. G., 1827; F. M., 1829; J. N., 1832; Jane, 1833; McDonald, 1834; Martha, 1835; Malinda, 1837; W. W., 1839; Permelia, 1841; Via, 1843; Lee Ann, 1846; Ottie, 1848; A. C., 1852. (See Grider, Bledsoe, Goggins.)

WOOD. William and Thomas Wood, who figure so much in the early history of Cumberland County, have left descendants by other names only.

William (1773-1851) married Nellie —— and reared a family in the county. He owned the land Albany is standing on. He served the county officially. His daughter, Elizabeth, married Christopher Myers. His other offspring are scattered.

Thomas Wood, his brother (1779-1834), married Mary Bayler 1777-1863) in 1802 and reared Jonathan, 1803; Reuben, 1805; Anna H., 1806; William L., 1808; Margarett, 1810; Mary G., 1816; Mariba, 1820. His descendants are in Clinton County (see Reneaus).

www.ingramcontent.com/pod-product-compliance
Lightning Source LLC
Chambersburg PA
CBHW020635300426
44112CB00007B/127